BERTOLT BRECHT
COLLECTED PLAYS

Volume 9

BERTOLT

Bertolt Brecht: Plays, Poetry, & Prose

Edited by

Ralph Manheim and John Willett

Wolfgang Sauerlander, Associate Editor

BRECHT

COLLECTED PLAYS

VOLUME 9

ADAPTATIONS

The Tutor

Coriolanus

The Trial of Joan of Arc
at Rouen, 1431

Don Juan

Trumpets and Drums

VINTAGE BOOKS, *A Division of Random House, New York*

Library of Congress Cataloging in Publication Data

Brecht, Bertolt, 1898–1956.   Collected plays.

(His Plays, poetry, and prose)
    I. Willett, John, ed. II. Manheim, Ralph, 1907–   ed.
PT2603.R397A29 1971   832'.9'12   71–113718
ISBN 0-394-71819-4 (v. 9)

Printed and bound by American Book—Stratford Press, New York

Vintage Books Edition, February 1973

Contents

TRUMPETS AND DRUMS

Texts by Brecht

Introduction

Rebuilding the repertoire, 1950–1956

1

In 1924 Lion Feuchtwanger published a poem on "Adaptations" which must stem from his collaboration on *Edward the Second* and could almost be a parody of Brecht:

> I, for instance, sometimes write
> Adaptations. Or some people prefer the phrase
> "Based on," and this is how it is: I use
> Old material to make a new play, then
> Put under the title
> The name of a dead writer who is extremely
> Famous and quite unknown, and before
> The name of the dead writer I put the little word "After."
> Then one group will write that I am
> Very respectful and others that I am nothing of the sort, and all
> The dead writer's failures
> Will be ascribed
> To me and all my successes
> To the dead writer who is extremely
> Famous and quite unknown, and of whom
> Nobody knows whether he himself
> Was the writer or maybe the
> Adaptor.

For Brecht himself was an inveterate adaptor, well aware that in this he resembled Shakespeare and Molière and others of the classics whom he pillaged for his own ends. Even before he and Feuchtwanger started on Marlowe he had been working on Grabbe's *Hannibal*, which he hoped to see staged at the Grosses Schauspielhaus in Berlin, and Selma Lagerlöf's novel *Gösta Berling*, which he was forced to abandon in favor of the authorized adaptor. This sort of work was of course in some measure encouraged by the appointment of dramaturgs in most German theaters, whose recognized duties included the adaptation and improvement of the scheduled plays; and Brecht's only regular jobs in the theater before the Second World War were as a dramaturg between 1922 and 1925. Many of his "own" plays started life as adaptations—*The Threepenny Opera* and *The Roundheads and the Peakheads*, for instance—even if they were not labeled as such; and then there were the adaptations proper, like the Sophocles-Hölderlin *Antigone* (which must have been fresh in his mind when he returned to Berlin in 1949), as well as a whole group of less known adaptations and projects which have not been published in his collected works.

These last included Molière's *Tartuffe* (a very early scheme), radio versions of *Macbeth* and *Hamlet* (broadcast by Berlin radio in 1927 and 1931 respectively, though unfortunately the scripts and recordings seem to have disappeared), Ferdinand Bruckner's translation of *La Dame aux Camélias* (for the Deutsches Theater production of 1924), the Brod-Reimann dramatization of *Schweyk* (for Piscator, who had recruited Brecht to his "dramaturgical collective" in 1927), Haywood's *A Woman Killed with Kindness* (a wartime project), finally Webster's *The Duchess of Malfi* (1943–46), that strange bilingual undertaking whose text we hope to include in another volume of the present edition. By the time of his return to Germany, he had something like fourteen or fifteen assorted adaptations behind him, representing every possible degree of interference with the original texts, ranging from *Der Jasager*, which is largely unaltered translation from Arthur Waley, to works like *The Roundheads* in which the original is hardly noticeable except to the informed. There was little consistency about the attribution of these plays, which sometimes (as in these last two cases) did little to suggest that Brecht owed anything to the earlier author, while at others omitting Brecht's name entirely (as with *La Dame aux Camélias* and *The Duchess of Malfi*). This was in line with Brecht's whole concept of collaborative work and the unimportance of artistic "originality," which was something that led him into trouble more than once. For he always seems to have found it easiest to create by sharpening his imagination against some previous work of art, either adapting and transforming it or (as in such cases as *Baal* and *The Days of the Commune*) arguing and contradicting till in the end he produced what he termed a "counter-play." Nor was it only the work of other authors which he used for this purpose, but also finished and unfinished plays of his own.

None the less the five adaptations in the present volume are essentially different from the rest. Like them they vary widely in their relationships with their respective originals, and the exact logic of their attribution to Brecht is often difficult to grasp; thus *The Tutor* alone appeared over his name during his lifetime, while he seems to have been less closely involved with *Don Juan* than with Hauptmann's *Biberpelz* and *Roter Hahn*, whose adaptation, unlike our five, is not included in the German collected works; not to mention Erwin Strittmatter's *Katzgraben*, a contemporary East German play on which he worked even more intensively, though he never wished his name to appear on it in any form. But the whole situation from which they arose was a new one, since they were written for his own company, the Berliner Ensemble, with the help of the collaborators whom he gathered round him there, and with a view to the Ensemble's particular needs and possibilities and to its long-term objectives. For if one of the company's functions was the performance of the plays which Brecht had written in exile, it was equally part of its job to restore the standards of the entire German theater after the Nazi interlude and the immediate postwar disorganization. And this would not be possible without the establishment of a well-conceived classical repertoire: something for which Brecht had never been so responsible before.

The origins of the Berliner Ensemble still have to be properly studied, but it seems that Brecht must have had some enterprise of the sort in mind at least a year before he finally left the United States in October 1947. Acting on the tentative promise that he might be able to use the Theater am Schiffbauerdamm (scene of the original production of *The Threepenny Opera* two decades earlier) he agreed during the rehearsals of the Berlin *Mother Courage* in December 1948 to start by forming a new ensemble under the wing of the Deutsches Theater. A few days before the play opened this scheme was provisionally approved by the East Berlin municipal and party authorities, and by February he and Helene Weigel were deep in plans. Among these, besides productions of his own *Galileo* and *Schweyk* (for which he hoped to get Fritz Kortner and Peter Lorre respectively), were plays by Gorki, Lorca and O'Casey, Büchner's *Danton's Death*, and Nordahl Grieg's play about the Paris Commune, *The Defeat*, which he hoped Piscator might come back from America to stage. The company was finally set on its feet in June, *Puntila* being scheduled as the first production, with Gorki's *Vassa Shelesnova* to follow, the title part in each to be played by the same actor as had performed it at the Zurich Schauspielhaus, the source of several of Brecht's recruits. It was formally constituted by the Ministry of Popular Education that September, and opened with *Puntila* at the Deutsches Theater two months later. For the time being it had no theater of its own.

Between November 1949 and Brecht's death nearly seven years later the Ensemble staged twenty productions, of which four (plus *Mother Courage*, which was taken into its repertory) were of existing plays by Brecht. About half the remainder involved him relatively little: two Chinese plays put on by his younger assistants, Kleist's *The Broken Jug* staged by Therese Giehse (January 1952), and the three Russian plays: *Vassa Shelesnova*, which he got Berthold Viertel to direct, Pogodin's *Kremlin Chimes* (March 1952) and Ostrovsky's *The Ward* (December 1955). He had a hand in Synge's *The Playboy of the Western World* (May 1956), whose typescript is described as an "adaptation with Brecht and after Brecht," as also in Becher's *Winterschlacht*, which he found himself, against his original intention, having to direct. The plays that really concerned him however were the Hauptmann double bill, the new East German play *Katzgraben*, Goethe's *Urfaust* (or short early version of *Faust*) and the five adaptations which we publish here. There was certainly an element of accident in their selection, as is bound to be the case in so chancy a business as the theater. But, leaving aside *Katzgraben* for the moment, they do seem to represent Brecht's view of a classical repertoire for the modern German theater, such as would open the eyes of the audience and stimulate the kind of writing, acting, and direction which he urgently felt it to need.

2

There is an unpublished note of Brecht's which defines the "Historic Line of the Epic Theater" as running "from the Elizabethan drama via Lenz, Schiller (early works), Goethe *(Götz* and both parts of *Faust),* Grabbe, Büchner. It is a very strong line, easily followed." Though this probably dates from the 1930's, it is a good guide to his approach, and it can be supplemented by another passage of about the same time *(GW Schriften zur Literatur und Kunst,* p. 364), which carries the line on thus:

> The German theatrical realists—Lenz, the young Schiller, Büchner, the Kleist of *Michael Kohlhaas* (for various reasons this novella may be considered as a work of dramatic literature), the young Hauptmann, the Wedekind of *Spring's Awakening*— are furthermore realists in that their plays are tragedies. The tragedy of the bourgeoisie gives way to that of the proletariat (Hauptmann's *The Weavers*). The unfinished bourgeois revolution casts its shadow.

This is very much the genealogy of Brecht's proposed repertory, which did indeed begin with Lenz, that pivotal figure who at once points forward to Brecht himself and backwards to the Elizabethans. (See his note on "The choice of play," p. 361.) Outside Germany Lenz is now scarcely known except to specialists, but it is relevant that he was a parson's son from East Prussia, where he was born in 1751, studied at Königsberg University during Kant's time there, and then became tutor to two young aristocrats. From this experience, which took him to Strassburg where he met Goethe, stemmed his two best-known plays, *The Tutor* (1774) and *The Soldiers* (1776). Confused as these were, so that even then *The Tutor* could only be performed with cuts (and that infrequently), they were unmistakeable works of genius, whose anonymous author was sometimes thought to be Goethe himself. Unfortunately his personality was already disturbed, and from the age of twenty-six onwards he was being treated as a schizophrenic (by Lavater among others), one episode from this period of his life serving as theme for the unfinished prose work which Büchner named after him. Thereafter he seems to have earned a precarious living teaching in Russia, where he was found dead in a Moscow street in May 1792.

Like Büchner, Lenz was rediscovered shortly before the First World War, Ernst Lewy's edition (which Brecht used for his adaptation) being published in Berlin in 1909 and Franz Blei's in Munich the same year. Yet there seem to have been no significant productions of his plays during Brecht's first Berlin period, and the first signs of Brecht's own awakening interest in him date from the later 1930's. It was then that Brecht wrote the sonnet (in the collected *Poems*) contrasting *The Tutor* with Beaumarchais' *Figaro*. "This standard work of German bourgeois realism," he wrote a little later, in one of his "Notes on a Realistic Way of Writing,"

> is a tragedy when contrasted with its French opposite number. You can almost hear the Frenchman's laughter at the German teacher whose venture into sexual relations with his noble pupil, far from furthering his career, forces him to castrate himself in order to remain in service. This laughter on the Frenchman's part and this wild protest on the German's both originate in a revolutionary realist attitude.

It is not clear whether he at the same time read Lenz's theoretical notes, but if he had he would have come across such "epic" anticipations as the passage quoted by Max Spalter in his *Brecht's Tradition*:

> Our practice is to have a series of actions which succeed one another like thunderclaps, each scene reinforcing the next and all of them coalescing in the character of the hero.

Formally as well as thematically he could not help finding such a writer congenial, and from then on he must clearly have had the play in mind, even though it apparently did not figure in his initial plans for the Ensemble. What suddenly turned him to it in December 1949 was the realization that the Party authorities were opposed to *The Days of the Commune*, the "counter-play" which had emerged from his work on Grieg's *The Defeat* and which was to have been the company's third production. Thereupon he set to work, using such younger collaborators as Egon Monk and Benno Besson as well as Ruth Berlau and the designer Caspar Neher who had been involved in the Chur *Antigone* (see Volume 8), and by the end of the month had *The Tutor* roughly in its present form. Rehearsals started on February 14; the première was on April 15. The "Modellbuch" which he began compiling (and for which most of our notes was written) was for some reason never published, but on all the evidence it must have been one of the finest and subtlest productions the Ensemble ever did.

The two Hauptmann plays, which followed as the fifth production nearly a year later (Brecht's own *Mother*, itself an adaptation of an adaptation from Gorki, having been the fourth), are not part of the recognized corpus of Brecht's work; the idea of making a single play of them seems to have been Therese Giehse's. Among the new young collaborators who now made their appearance were Claus Hubalek and Peter Palitzsch, while Monk took over the direction after Berthold Viertel had given it up. The première took place at the end of March 1951, only a few days after the official preview of *Lucullus* at the State Opera, which sparked off the first serious East German controversy about Brecht and his work. After that he turned to the Elizabethans, whom he had not touched since America, but whose reassimilation into the repertoire the production of *The Tutor* had been designed to help. Early in April he was trying his hand at translating *Troilus and Cressida*, for which one of his collaborators had prepared a scheme. Then in May he chose instead to adapt *Coriolanus*, as being "probably the only Shakespeare play of anything like contemporary relevance which we could anything like cast." According to Palitzsch, who with Manfred Wekwerth and Käthe Rülicke-Weiler was among his assistants on this long-drawn-out project, this referred in the first place to the availability of Ernst Busch, one of Brecht's preferred prewar actors who had joined the Ensemble shortly before the *Mother* production.

Coriolanus was not a new play to Brecht, for twenty-six years earlier his ally Erich Engel had staged it for the Deutsches Theater when he himself was one of the dramaturgs there, with costumes and sets by Neher and Fritz Kortner playing the title part. This was the same team as had been responsible for the Berlin production of *In the Jungle*, and already there seems to have been a foretaste of the Brechtian approach to the play. Thus the hero, so critics reported, was deflated, the tone lowered, the Roman Forum presented as a kind of boxing ring, the war scenes made unenticing, with gray and pallid soldiers in fierce combat. It was no longer the "tragedy of pride" but the story of a second-rate, excitable, intensely ambitious man, only his mother, played by Agnes Straub, remaining a queenly figure, which perhaps accounts for Brecht's resentment of her (he refused to take her great speeches in Act Five seriously, contending that Shakespeare had purposely made them unconvincing). To Brecht, writing in 1926, Engel's particular achievement was that "he gave us Coriolanus' story in such a way that each scene stood on its own, only its upshot contributing to the whole. By contrast with the dramatic theater, where everything rushes headlong towards a catastrophe, here the sum total stood unmoving in every scene." In other words, by setting out the story step by step, the production was a contribution to the "epic theater" whose prophet Brecht then was. And a year or two later in a dialogue called "Conversation about the Classics" he was referring to it as his own last attempt to come to terms with them, which suggests the degree of his involvement at the time.

Brecht seems to have worked concentratedly on the new adaptation during November and December 1951, and Caspar Neher's (unrealized) sketches for the set are dated the same year. The all-important first scene, subject of the long dialogue which he wrote four years later, was ready, very much in its present form, in time to be printed in the volume *Theaterarbeit* which was put together under his supervision during the summer holidays and appeared in 1952 as an illustrated record of the company's productions up to and including the Hauptmann double bill. He worked further at the play during the 1952 summer holiday at his new country house at Buckow, and again that December, after which the whole project seems to have been very largely laid aside. It was of course completed after his death, eventually reaching the stage in 1964 in a somewhat more adapted form. But whether he himself would have continued along these lines is more doubtful. Even in December 1952, looking at the changes which he had introduced in Shakespeare's text, he reflected that the play could be left unaltered if the audience's historical sense were only rather more developed. A subsequent note, dated July 18, 1955, and not included in the German collected works, says:

> . . . I once more make an analysis of the first act of *Coriolanus*, and wonder if it would be possible to stage it without additions (made by me two years ago), or with very few, just by skilful production.

That this could in fact be done was shown in 1971, when Wekwerth and Joachim Tenschert, the two directors of the Berliner Ensemble production, staged the play for the National Theatre in London. For they used Shakespeare's text, yet managed to convey what was essential in Brecht's interpretation of the play, save only Coriolanus' changed motive for abandoning the advance on Rome.

The Ensemble presented no further new productions in 1951, both *Lucullus* and the didactic *Report from Herrnburg* being staged outside its framework, while 1952 began with three straight plays, the Kleist, the Pogodin, and Goethe's *Urfaust*. The third of these was important to Brecht both for his own involvement in Egon Monk's production and as a further step in the building of a classical repertoire. In November *The Trial of Joan of Arc* followed, with the same leading actress, Käthe Reichel, directed this time by Besson (his first important job). The adaptation in this case does not seem to have been specially demanding, though the choice of Anna Seghers' radio play had a double significance, first in that it was Brecht's third go at the Joan of Arc story (which had already helped to inspire *St. Joan of the Stockyards* and *Simone Machard*, both at that time still unperformed), and secondly because its author was an old acquaintance and, after Brecht himself, probably the next most gifted of the prewar Communist writers to have chosen to settle in East Germany. *Don Juan*, which followed in March 1954, after Brecht's long preoccupation with the rewriting and production of *Katzgraben*, evidently involved him even less. It was in its way a minor landmark, however, since this rarely performed play was the opening production in the Ensemble's own theater, the long-promised Theater am Schiffbauerdamm.

In *Trumpets and Drums*, the last of our five adaptations, Brecht may well have had something like *The Threepenny Opera* in mind, based this time on Farquhar rather than on Gay. Judging by the amount of relevant material in the Brecht Archive, which is as great as that for some of his own major late plays, he put as much into this adaptation as into any that he did apart from *Katzgraben*. Once again, *The Recruiting Officer*, from which it derived, was not an accepted part of the German repertoire, so that Brecht had a free hand to deal with the original as he wished. Its appeal to him as a satire at once on the army and on class justice is self-evident, and many apparently Brechtian features of the resulting play come in fact from it, for instance the mercenary self-interest of the main characters. Even the song on which Brecht based his finale—

> Our prentice Tom may now refuse
> To wipe his scoundrel master's shoes;
> For now he's free to sing and play—
> Over the hills and far away,
> Over the hills (etc.).
>
> We all shall lead more happy lives
> By getting rid of brats and wives,
> That scold and bawl both night and day—
> Over the hills and far away,
> Over the hills (etc.).

—is like an anticipation of the ballad-singer's song in the first version of *Galileo*.

The main work of adaptation, it seems, was done in the spring of 1955, shortly before Brecht went to Moscow to receive his Stalin Peace Prize. It was intended as a blow against West German rearmament, so he told his friend Bernhard Reich on that occasion, but might prove a somewhat two-edged weapon in view of the East German measures to raise a People's Army. He half-expected, in fact, to be informed that the play was "unconstructive" and asked to postpone its production. At what point the element of anti-imperialist satire was introduced is not clear—the script originally followed Farquhar in setting the story in the early eighteenth century—but in the event all seems to have gone as planned, and Besson's very brilliant production on September 19 was the first première of Brecht's final season.

Once again this inspired the National Theatre, this time under William Gaskill's direction, to reinterpret the original work, somewhat in Brecht's sense. Like the subsequent careers of Brecht's young collaborators (who have become the foremost directors in East and West Germany today) this is an indication of the force of his example even after his death.

3

But all this has to be seen against the background of the time, which in two important ways favored Brecht rather less than posterity has done. For in those days his view of his country's past was largely dominated by what, following Heine and Marx, he termed the "German Misère" ("the sorry state of Germany" in the Prologue, p. 3 below): in other words the lasting division of Germany, aggravated by the ravages of the Thirty Years' War, which caused its development to lag decades behind that of France and England, right through the political and industrial revolutions of the late eighteenth and early nineteenth centuries up to the establishment of the Empire, and in Brecht's view warped many aspects of German life even after that. Not only was this highly critical approach to German history reflected in the gray pessimism of *Mother Courage*, as he and Helene Weigel presented it, but it also dictated their attitude to the classical heritage. Thus *The Tutor*, for him, was no period piece but a wonderful parable of the national Misère, even as it had persisted in the German educational system right up to his own day. Far from outwitting an outmoded aristocracy as Figaro had done, Lenz's tutor castrated himself rather than remain unacceptable in their eyes; and similarly German teachers ever after had tended to lick the boots of those in authority. Accordingly Brecht's adaptation not only heightened the tragedy of Läuffer's self-mutilation and underlined his anxieties about his job; it also went on to ridicule those features of the German Enlightenment which Lenz and many liberal Germans after him had seen as more "positive" factors, in this case by making a semi-educated hypocrite of the privy councillor and showing how the philosophy of Kant (something not spe-

cifically referred to in Lenz's play) could be squared with middle-class self-interest.

Something of the same sharpness was brought into the adaptation of the two Hauptmann plays. "We decided," wrote Brecht
in a letter to Berthold Viertel,

> to trust Hauptmann entirely as far as his powers of observa-
> tion were concerned (i.e., we explored the meaning of every
> tiny detail and preserved it wherever possible) but to have
> less faith in his knowledge of historic essentials. We there-
> fore had to provide visible evidence of the workers' move-
> ment (social-democracy) which he had almost entirely
> overlooked.

Accordingly they replaced Hauptmann's retired policeman
Rauchhaupt by a class-conscious unemployed metal-worker,
thus undermining the authority of the liberal-minded Dr.
Fleischer, who in the original stood for the author's point of
view, much as the privy councillor had done in the Lenz. *Urfaust* too, though not an adaptation, was staged in the same
unflattering light, as further evidence of the Misère—Brecht
was not an unqualified admirer of Goethe, and felt that the
figure of Faust had its comic aspects—and when Hanns Eisler
the composer thereafter wrote the libretto for his proposed
Faust opera it was with Brecht's advice and largely in accordance with his interpretation.

To the party ideologists in East Germany this critical approach to the nation itself and its "national cultural heritage"
was unwelcome for more than one reason. To begin with, in the
prevailing doctrinal terms (as borrowed from the vocabulary of
Soviet Socialist Realism) it was unduly "negative," lacking in
"positive" (i.e. exemplary) figures and in optimistic conclusions.
More practically, like *Mother Courage* itself, it involved gray and
depressing settings which were far too like the actual ambience
of postwar Berlin to help raise the spirits of the audience in the
way traditionally expected of the theater. Of course it was in
utter contrast with all the attitudes that had prevailed under
Hitler, but these had by now become too deeply engrained to
be painlessly flouted, and in Brecht's own eyes the cultural and
critical decline which they had led to was part of the main

problem. At the heart of the matter, however, was Brecht's sceptical, harshly unsentimental view of so many traditions, ideas, and figures that the Germans, including some leading German Communists, had long cherished; in short, he was subversive. Hence the attacks on *The Tutor* which provoked him to the statement on p. 362, and hence also the much stronger criticisms of *Urfaust* and also of Eisler's libretto, which prompted the party paper *Neues Deutschland* to write that the Ensemble was "being led in a wrong direction by the methods and principles applied in the adaptation of the classics by Bertolt Brecht." Faced with an official demand for a more reverent approach, most other East German theaters, according to Egon Monk,

> accepted the establishment view and adopted a more correct attitude to the classics than the Ensemble; that is to say, they went out of their way to perform them with just the same kind of spineless solemnity as had been displayed by the Prussian state theaters in Hitler's day.

This was what Brecht, in an essay prompted by the bad reception of *Urfaust*, called "Inhibition by classical status" (it is translated in *Brecht on Theatre*, pp. 272–73). Instead he reminded his readers of "the classics' original freshness, the element of surprise (in terms of their period), of newness, of productive stimulus that is the hallmark of such works."

But this essay was not published till 1954, by which time the East German cultural administration had been transformed and Brecht's own position was in many ways much stronger. Even then he was unable to overcome the other main obstacle to his aims in this period, which was the difficulty he found in writing on any contemporary theme, or making direct references to the life of the society actually around him. Admittedly when originally planning the Berliner Ensemble he had thought of carrying out his old intention of writing a play about Rosa Luxemburg, and he seems to have done some inconclusive work on this in 1952; he also sketched out an anti-war revue to be called *Der Wagen des Ares*, which would have been a modern satire in a classical setting. The most interesting of these projects, however, was a play to be called *Büsching* (after a character in *Fatzer*, the very important unfinished play of the 1920's which was one of its models) based on a series of interviews with an East German Stakhanovite worker called Hans Garbe. This occupied him in the summer of 1951, then he discussed it again with Hanns Eisler in October 1953, when they decided that it must cover the East German riots of June 17 that year; there is also an eleven-scene scheme dating from November 1954. But in the event his only completed work of topical relevance (and that in some measure oblique) was the sequence of "Buckow Elegies" which he wrote at his country house in the summer of 1953. Anything that he had to say in the theater about the East German situation, for better or worse, went into his work on Strittmatter's *Katzgraben*, a play which he staged in much the same unrelieved grayness as *Mother Courage*.

In a sense, perhaps, this failure also entered into the adaptations. As he wrote to Gottfried von Einem on January 7, 1951, "Trying to build up a new theater has deprived me of the time needed to write for it." But part of his work for the Ensemble was just that process of collaborative adaptation to which the texts in the present volume are due. This was not only designed to provide the company with plays, for the training of the younger dramaturgs and assistant directors was certainly part of the object; and very well worthwhile it has proved to be. At the same time it is obvious that the company itself, its potentialities and its demands, ought also to have been inspiring him to create one or two new works. Even to a lifelong adaptor such as Brecht, adaptation of the kind demonstrated here can only be the next best thing. There were excellent reasons for rebuilding the repertoire, given the situation that Brecht found on his return. It was a less excellent substitute for the writing of his own plays.

THE EDITORS

The Tutor

by Jakob Michael Reinhold Lenz

Adaptation

Collaborators: R. Berlau, B. Nesson, E. Monk, C. Neher

Translators: Ralph Manheim and Wolfgang Sauerlander

CHARACTERS*

HASTY, a tutor
PASTOR HASTY, his father
PRIVY COUNCILLOR VON BERG
FRITZ, his son
MAJOR VON BERG
MRS. VON BERG, his wife
GUSSIE, their daughter
LEOPOLD, their son
THE VON BERGS' MAID
WENCESLAS, a village
    schoolmaster

LISA, his ward
COUNT VERMOUTH
SQUINT and BUTTRESS, students
MRS. BLITZ, a landlady
MISS SWANDOWN
CAROLINE SQUINT
MISS COTTON
MISS MILLER
MISS GOSLING

*See note, p. 330.

Prologue

In which the tutor introduces himself to the audience.

Ladies and gentlemen, the play you're about to see
Was written in the eighteenth century.
A household tutor is the part I play
Ancestor of our teachers of today.
I'm still a servant of the nobility
Teaching their offspring for a meager fee
A little manners, the Bible more fully
And how to sneer and sham and bully.
I myself, though I've had a higher education
Am and remain of humble station.
Of course the times have been changing of late
The middle class is rising in the state.
Unless I read the portents wrong
I'll be serving it before too long.
Adept at toeing any line
I'm sure that I will suit it fine.
With all their trimming, clipping, drilling
Those nobles made me only too willing
To teach what suits the ruling class—
A habit that will never pass.
But what I really do, you'll see
Is spell out the sorry state of Germany.

ACT ONE

1

Insterburg in Prussia. Outside Privy Councillor von Berg's ornamental garden.

Privy councillor. Major.

MAJOR   Things aren't doing too well at the farm, William. No horses to be had, not for love nor money. Zounds! The country still hasn't recovered from the war—seven years of it.— There comes that starveling again, I can't take a step without running into him.
(Hasty passes, bowing and scraping four times. His greetings are not acknowledged)

HASTY   Oafs! The devil take you!

PRIVY COUNCILLOR   Who's that lickspittle?

MAJOR   They tell me his name is Hasty, a pastor's son. My wife asked him to call, she needs a tutor for Leopold; I suppose he'll do as well as anyone.

PRIVY COUNCILLOR   I remember that name. His father's been pestering me to do something for him. He wanted a position at the town school. But he's not trained for it. His father's purse gave out before his finals. What is he to teach your son?

MAJOR   Drum a little knowledge and good manners into him, so he can grow up to be a soldier like me.

PRIVY COUNCILLOR   He may be good enough for that, Frederick.
(He enters the garden, preceding the major, and stops in front of a plant) Farra communis, the common fern, oldest plant on earth.—But tell me, brother, about this Hasty, do you know

what sort of man you'll be taking into your house? What about his ethical maturity? My own inquiries have not been too thorough. I haven't looked into his past.

MAJOR   All I know is that he's not overcharging. And what with the war and the high cost of living . . .

PRIVY COUNCILLOR   I wouldn't want anything cheap. That's why I'm sending my boy Fritz to the university in Halle.

MAJOR   'Sblood! Enough about that lout. We were talking about your fern here.

PRIVY COUNCILLOR   The fern whose remote ancestor, the horsetail, can be traced back to the ice age . . .

2

Gussie's room.

Gussie. Fritz von Berg.

GUSSIE   Fritz! How far is Halle?

FRITZ   Three hundred miles or three miles—as you like. If I can't stay here, Gussie, and you're unattainable in any case, what difference is there between three miles and three hundred?

GUSSIE   And you'll be in Halle and . . .

FRITZ   With you heart and soul! But you won't write to me and I shall cease to exist.

GUSSIE   Then you think it won't be a separation when you get into the coach, not a real separation?

FRITZ   We'll always be together in spirit. Take this, Gussie! (*He gives her Klopstock's Odes*)

GUSSIE   Klopstock! (*Reads*)

"The drunken joy of the long wept-for,
Almost too blissful hour
Which tells the lover that he is loved!"

FRITZ *(continues)*

"And now two beauteous souls, ennobled, feel
Wholly, for the first time wholly, the fullness of their being!"

Oh!—But Uncle will marry you off to that ungodly Count
Vermouth long before I take my degree. My three years at the
university will be a long time in your life!

GUSSIE   Three years or thirty, as you like.—I hear my father
and my uncle in the hall. Let's go out into the garden.

FRITZ   No, they're gone. But I'll come back. Wait, Gussie, read
just this: "Hermann and Thusnelda." The return of the
Cheruscan.

GUSSIE   *(reads)*

"Ah, there he comes, covered with sweat, with
Roman blood and the dust of battles. Never was
Hermann so beautiful! Never did such flames
Flash from his eyes.

Come, I tremble with desire, hand me the eagle
And thy blood-drenched sword! Come, breathe here and rest
In my embrace
From the too terrible battle."

Wait, let's go out to the summer-house.

FRITZ   No, no, Papa's outside. Go on reading.

GUSSIE   *(reads)*

"Rest here that I may wipe the sweat from thy brow
And from thy cheek the blood. Thy cheek's on fire!
Hermann, Hermann, never before
Has Thusnelda loved thee so!"

Oh, Fritz!

"Not even when first in the shade of the oak thou
Seizedst me impetuously in thy tawny arms!

Fleeing I stayed and saw upon thee
The mark of immortality."

FRITZ   Gussie . . .

GUSSIE   Would you—no, I mustn't ask you.

FRITZ   Ask for my life, for my last drop of blood.

GUSSIE   We were going to swear an oath together.

FRITZ   Yes, let us. Magnificent. Let us kneel down here beside the bed. You raise your finger like this and I raise mine.—Tell me now, what shall I swear to you?

GUSSIE   That you'll always fly to the arms of your Gussie at holiday time and come back from the university in three years and make Gussie your wife, no matter what your father says.

FRITZ   And what will you promise in return, my angelic . . . *(Kisses her)*

GUSSIE   I swear that I will never, never marry anyone but you, not even if the Tsar of Russia himself should come and ask me.

FRITZ   I swear a thousand oaths—

(The privy councillor comes in: both jump up with loud screams)

PRIVY COUNCILLOR   Make a clean breast of it. What have you two been up to? For shame, I thought I had a sensible son. You want to study law, and you can't even teach yourself how to behave? Come here, both of you. I choose to see no wrong. If you like to be with your cousin, Fritz, I have no objection, but now it's off to Halle with you to become a beacon to humanity. To make yourself worthy of her. And to learn the meaning of true freedom. Which distinguishes man from the animals. Stallions and mares have to do it, but human beings are free not to. Understand, son? *(Fritz nods shamefacedly)* Consequently I want you to take leave of each other at once, without constraint, pursuant to your better judgment, voluntarily. No letters to be exchanged, except unsealed. Promise? *(Fritz and Gussie nod)* Thoughts are free, but writing will be censored. Now, say good-bye in my presence—and refrain of your own free will from doing anything that cannot be done in the presence of witnesses. *(Fritz makes a bow to Gussie, she curtsies to Fritz)* Yes, children, reason is a hard taskmaster.

3

Mrs. von Berg's parlor.

Mrs. von Berg at the spinet, Hasty stands beside her in a deferential attitude, Leopold stands catching flies.

MRS. VON BERG   I've spoken to your father; he suggested a salary of three hundred ducats and we've settled on a hundred and fifty. In return I must ask you, Mr.—what was the name?—Mr. Hasty, to keep yourself in clean clothes and not to disgrace our house. As to your daily schedule, you will take your chocolate at seven with the young master and see to it that he eats properly; his health is delicate. School from eight to twelve. Afternoon: a walk in the public park and be sure never to let go of his hand, he's a very spirited boy. From six until dinner time you may sit by the bay window and pursue your own studies. In the evenings I shall expect you to entertain our guests. I trust you've got a tongue in your head. I expect you to show good taste and to be honorable as well. The last tutor had to be dismissed for stuffing his pockets with pears.—Do you skate? Could you teach Leopold?—And are you proficient in dancing?

HASTY   I hope your ladyship will be pleased with me. In Leipzig I never missed a ball, I must have had at least five dancing masters.

MRS. VON BERG   Indeed? Won't you show me? A figure from the minuet. Make me a *compliment*. Don't be nervous, Mr. . . . Hasty. Don't be nervous! My son hates books as it is; if his tutor turns out to be a simpleton, that will be the end of him. Just to give me an idea.—Well, well, not bad. Now, if you please, a *pas*.—You'll do. You'll get into the spirit once you've attended one of our soirées . . . Are you a musician?

HASTY   I play the violin and I can get by on the spinet.

MRS. VON BERG Splendid! I've always had to sing for the dear children when they wanted to dance. That will be a great improvement.

HASTY Your ladyship, you overwhelm me. Is there any virtuoso in the whole world who would dare match his instrument against your ladyship's voice?

MRS. VON BERG Ha, ha, ha, you haven't even heard me yet . . . . Wait, do you know this minuet? *(She sings)*

HASTY Ah . . . Ah . . . You must forgive my enthusiasm. *(Kisses her hand)*

MRS. VON BERG I happen to be enrhumée, I'm sure I sound like a crow. Vous parlez français, sans doute?

HASTY Un peu, madame.

MRS. VON BERG Avez-vous déjà fait votre tour de France?

HASTY Non, madame . . . Oui, madame . . .

MRS. VON BERG Vous devez donc savoir, qu'en France on ne baise pas les mains, mon cher . . .

MAID *(enters)* Count Vermouth.

MRS. VON BERG One of my daughter's suitors . . .
(Count Vermouth enters. After a few silent bows he sits down on the sofa)

COUNT VERMOUTH Has your ladyship seen the new dancing master who just arrived from Dresden? A marchese from Florence, by the name of . . . In all my travels I have only seen two who might have been compared to him.

MRS. VON BERG Only two? You do arouse my curiosity. I know what exquisite taste Count Vermouth has.

HASTY Pintinello . . . , isn't it? I saw him dance at the theater in Leipzig. With no great distinction . . .

COUNT VERMOUTH He dances—on ne peut pas mieux.—As I was saying, your ladyship, in Petersburg I saw Beluzzi, who may have been better. But this one has a nimbleness in his feet, there's something so free, so divinely negligent about his stance, his arms, his turns—

HASTY Last time he appeared at Koch's Theater, they booed him.

MRS. VON BERG Be advised, my friend, that domestics do not intervene in conversations between persons of quality. Go to your room. Who asked your opinion?

(Hasty goes toward the door)

COUNT VERMOUTH   The new tutor, I presume?

MRS. VON BERG   Fresh from the university.—Off with you! Don't you hear you're being talked about? All the less reason to stand there listening.

(Hasty goes out. Mrs. von Berg and Count Vermouth take their chocolate)

MRS. VON BERG   It's intolerable that one can no longer get the right kind of person for one's money. Think of it. Five hundred ducats a year! Isn't it dreadful?

COUNT VERMOUTH   As I was saying, this Pintinello dances like a god. My passion for the dance has cost me some thirty thousand ducats, but I'd gladly pay twice as much if . . . *(He sighs)* How is Mademoiselle Gussie?

MRS. VON BERG   So, so, la la. She's been looking a bit pale these last few days.

4

At the skating rink.

Miss Cotton, Miss Gosling, and Miss Miller, skating. To one side Hasty is giving Leopold a skating lesson.

MISS MILLER   I love listening to Pastor Detzer. Those passages in his sermons.

MISS COTTON   About sinning in secret!

MISS MILLER   He's a thunderer, but only by allusion. *(Imitating him)* "You think no one sees it, no one is present, it can never come to light. But I say unto you, the devil lies in wait for those that eat of the fruit in secret."

MISS GOSLING   There's the new one. He's doing figure eights!

(Hasty skates past)

MISS MILLER   You mean him? He's the new tutor at Major Berg's. Don't stare!

MISS COTTON   He's wondering whether to greet us.

MISS GOSLING   He's a fine, upstanding fellow.

MISS MILLER   So they say.

MISS COTTON   Who says? Don't be oracular, Miller.

MISS MILLER   All right, go over to him, let him greet you. I say no more.

MISS GOSLING   Shall we skate past him or . . .

MISS COTTON   I'm for it. (*They skate past Hasty*)

MISS GOSLING   (*nose in the air*)   Methinks there's a whiff of snow in the air.

MISS COTTON   (*bursts out laughing*)   Why not ask your tutor when it's going to thaw?

MISS MILLER   That's enough now. Don't be childish. I don't want him to join us. Before long he'll be as notorious as a yellow dog.

MISS COTTON   How so?

MISS MILLER   Last Sunday he tried to make up to that Beck girl. But she didn't let him, and she's not choosy, far from it, the hussy! (*They whisper together*)

MISS GOSLING   But what is he to do if no decent girl will go near him?

MISS COTTON   If one of us were seen with him, everyone would know it wasn't just for fun.

MISS MILLER   When you go with Hans next door, no one says a word. He may be a whoremaster, but he's not a stranger. But a stranger—why on earth would you want to go with him? Just drinking a cup of chocolate with somebody like that would ruin your reputation in Insterburg for the rest of your life.

MISS COTTON   Here he comes.

(*Hasty, without Leopold, has followed them and now doffs his hat. They stand stiffly without acknowledging his salutation*)

MISS MILLER   There. Now he knows where he stands.

MISS COTTON   'Tis a pity. There aren't many like him in these parts.

(*Hasty has angrily skated back to Leopold who pulls him to the ground by his clumsiness. The young ladies laugh*)

5

Hasty's Room.

Hasty, writing "agricola" on the blackboard. Leopold at his desk.

LEOPOLD *(reads, with incorrect stress)* —cola.

HASTY *(loathingly correcting the stress)* Agricola.

(The major walks in)

THE MAJOR *(reads, with wrong stress)* Agricola. That's fine, that's the way I like it. Busy, busy—and if the rascal doesn't get it, Mr. Hasty, just hit him on the head with the book till he forgets how to get up. Look at him now—making faces again. So touchy when your father speaks to you. I'll make a man of you yet, if I have to whip you till your guts split open, you little sneak! And you, sir, keep after him. I demand it. This essay about the Hero-King that I've been reading is rather sloppy, I should say. The list of his enemies is incomplete. He defied not only the Saxons, the Austrians, the French, and the Russians, he also addressed the British in no uncertain terms. If you leave them out, it's not clear that he was on the brink of disaster—and then the glory doesn't come through.

HASTY I beg your pardon, major. I am at fault. I didn't paint the picture black enough.

MAJOR Are you pulling my leg? Or shielding this little sneak? —Let's see if he knows his Cornelio. Back straight, boy! Chin up! *(He straightens him)* Egad, get your head out of your shoulders or I'll break every bone in your body.

HASTY Beg your pardon, major, but he hardly knows any Latin.

MAJOR What? Has the little rascal forgotten it all? The last tutor told me his Latin was perfect, perfect . . . I'll beat the stuffing out of you *(boxes him on the ear)*—and now you're doubled up again like a question mark. He simply never listens—go away, out of my sight, leave the room! I'll teach you to shake a leg. Out, I say! (*He stamps his foot, Leopold goes out. The major sits down on Leopold's chair. To Hasty*) Sit down, Mr. Hasty. I wanted a word with you, that's why I sent the boy away. Sit down, all the way! Egad, you'll break the chair if you keep teetering on the edge . . . A chair is for sitting on. Don't you even know that after all your travels?—Now, listen. I regard you as a clean-cut, decent young man, God-fearing and obedient. Otherwise I wouldn't do what I'm doing for you. I promised you a hundred and forty ducats, did I not?

HASTY   A hundred and fifty, major.

MAJOR   A hundred and forty.

HASTY   But with your gracious permission, major, her ladyship promised me a hundred and fifty ducats.

MAJOR   Pshaw! What do women know? A hundred and forty ducats, that would come to three—let's see now—three times a hundred and forty, how much is that?

HASTY   Four hundred and twenty.

MAJOR   Are you sure? Really, as much as that? Very well, to round it out, I'm setting your salary at four hundred Prussian thalers. Egad, that's more than I get from my land. Four hundred thalers.

HASTY   But a hundred and fifty ducats equal exactly four hundred and fifty thalers, and those were the terms I agreed to.

MAJOR   Four hundred thalers, monsieur. In good conscience you really can't ask for more. Your predecessor was as happy as a lark with two hundred and fifty. And, upon my soul, he was a learned man. You have a long way to go before you can hold a candle to him. I'm only doing this out of friendship for your father, and for your own sake too, of course, if you work hard.—Now, listen: I have a daughter. She knows her Christianity inside out, but you see she's coming up for communion soon, and you know what our pastors are like, so I want you to do a bit of Christianity with her every morning.

HASTY   Yes, major.

MAJOR   I'm paying you four hundred, and that includes religion for my daughter. An hour every morning; you'll go to her room.

HASTY   Yes, major.

MAJOR   Properly dressed, if you please; not like the young swine we once had here who insisted on coming to table in his dressing-gown. None of that, eh? Do we understand each other?

HASTY   Major, would it be too bold of me to make a most humble request—in connection with your last proposition and in view of the fact that it's difficult for me to meet people and make friends in Insterburg and that living in a big city has become almost a habit with me, because city people are not so standoffish toward strangers . . .

MAJOR   Come to the point!

HASTY   If once every three months, no more, I might be granted the use of a horse to ride to Königsberg for two or three days? . . .

MAJOR   Hm. That might be considered.

HASTY   (jumps up and makes several bows) Oh, most gracious major—

MAJOR   Anyhow it can't be until spring. It's an impossible ride in this winter weather.—Can you draw too?

HASTY   A little, your worship.—May I show you a few things?

MAJOR   (inspecting them) Charming, charming!—Very nice. This one's quite good. You shall teach my daughter drawing too. My resources don't allow me to keep a whole battalion of sinfully expensive tutors on my payroll. But see here, Mr. Hasty, for heaven's sake, don't be hard on her. The little girl is different from the boy. She's my only solace. And she's been rather droopy lately, if you know what I mean. I see the child wasting away, losing her health, her beauty, and so on, and there's nothing I can do about it. It breaks my heart.— I'm telling you this because I want you to be gentle with her.

ACT TWO

6

Halle in Saxony.

Fritz von Berg, Squint in shirtsleeves, sitting at the table. Buttress lying on the bed, Mrs. Blitz.

BUTTRESS Three months in Halle and I still haven't spoken to a girl!

FRITZ After all we have certain ties back home.

SQUINT You've got a girl there?

BUTTRESS Hic Rhodus, hic salta! The gentleman from Insterburg seems to be forgetting his physiology. A man doesn't go to bed with a girl because he loves her, he loves her because he wants to go to bed. You just wait till March!

SQUINT You must be getting the glooms without a girl. Why not move in with us, that will cheer you up. What's the sense in staying with that pastor? That's no place for you.

FRITZ How much do you pay here?

SQUINT We pay—what do we pay, Buttress?

BUTTRESS Nothing.

SQUINT Honest to goodness, brother, I don't know. Mrs. Blitz writes it all down, the rent, the coffee, the tobacco, whatever we ask for. We pay the bill once a year when our allowance comes.

FRITZ Do you owe her much right now?

SQUINT We paid up last week.

BUTTRESS His allowance is due.

SQUINT It will all be yours when it comes. If it ever does, Brother Buttress!

FRITZ   You help each other out? That's very decent of you.

SQUINT   We go halves. I couldn't afford it myself. This time they've cleaned me out. I had to fork over my whole allowance, didn't I, Buttress? And my coat that I hocked last July is still at the pawnshop. Heaven knows when I'll be able to redeem it.

FRITZ   How do you manage in the meantime?

SQUINT   Me?—I'm sick. This morning I received an invitation from Councillor Hamster's wife, and I went straight to bed.

FRITZ   But how can you sit home all the time, in this lovely winter weather?

BUTTRESS   Why not? He reads his favorite philosopher, Immanuel Kant.

FRITZ   What does he do about his girl? We mustn't neglect our physiology.

BUTTRESS   With girls it's not our coats that count, it's . . .

SQUINT   Our heads, Berg. In my case it doesn't really matter, because my girl doesn't know me.

FRITZ   You mean it's all imagination?

BUTTRESS   He dreams about her. And his bed sheet gets it all. What I say is: Tell me the girl you dreamed about and I'll tell you the girl you didn't sleep with. But now we've invited Insterburg for coffee. Where in blazes is the coffee? (*He stamps his foot*) Mrs. Blitz! Damn it, Mrs. Blitz, we paid you, didn't we?

(*Mrs. Blitz comes in with a serving of coffee*)

BUTTRESS   Where on earth have you been, ma? Mr. Squint has been waiting for an hour.

MRS. BLITZ   (*to Squint*)   What? You good-for-nothing tramp, you alley-cat! What are you hollering about? I'll take the coffee away this minute, I'll—

BUTTRESS   Biscuits.

MRS. BLITZ   There aren't any. (*Referring to Squint*) Do you think I have nothing else to do than give that bald-headed lout his biscuits every afternoon?

BUTTRESS   Why him? I need biscuits! You know I never touch coffee without biscuits—what am I paying you for?

MRS. BLITZ   (*hands him biscuits out of her apron*)   Now are you satisfied, you trombone? Mr. Buttress has a voice like a whole regiment. *(To Squint)* Put your books away, they're no good anyway. All those beautiful, expensive books and you still don't know which way is up! Well, is the coffee all right? Is it? Tell me this minute or I'll tear the last hair out of your bald head.

SQUINT *(drinks)*   Incomparable! Really, I never had better in all my life.

MRS. BLITZ   You see, you young rascal. If Ma Blitz didn't take care of you and give you food and drink you'd starve by the wayside. Just look at him, Mr. von Berg, the way he goes around, without a coat to his name and his dressing-gown looking as if he'd been hanged in it and fallen off the gallows. This is the fourth year he's failed in philosophy. Why? Because he just can't get that stuff into his head. I feel sorry for his mother. She's a widow too. And now all the widows' and orphans' pensions have been reduced because of the glorious war. But you seem to be a nice, well-bred gentleman, I don't see how you can be friends with that lout. Well, I suppose it's coming from the same district that makes for a kind of family feeling. That's why I keep saying that Mr. von Berg should move in here. Then we might make something of you. That's what I say. *(Goes out)*

SQUINT   You mightn't think so, Berg, but she's really a good soul.

FRITZ   What's this about your failing all the time, Squint?

SQUINT   I'm studying under Professor Wolffen. He detests Mr. Kant of Königsberg. And Kant is my man.

BUTTRESS   Your Mr. Kant is a muddlehead. Listen to this—*(he picks up a book)*—"When peace is concluded after a war, it might not be amiss for a nation to let the thanksgiving celebrations be followed by a day of repentance, on which day the people, in the name of the state, would implore heaven's forgiveness for the great sin which mankind persists in committing—the utilization of the barbaric instrument that is war."—Imagine teaching stuff like that at a German university.

FRITZ   It doesn't seem so wrong to me.

BUTTRESS   Altogether wrong. Take the title: "Eternal Peace." If we stopped fighting old Blitz for one day, her coffee would be pure barley. For four years now our friend here has been reeling off Mr. Kant's absurdities in Wolffen's classroom. Naturally he flunks. Repeat after me: Mr. Kant is an idiot.

FRITZ   Couldn't you say it just to get your degree?

SQUINT   *(has carved something on the table top with his pocket knife)* Here, read what I've carved.

FRITZ   "No."

SQUINT   I'll say it a fifth time if I have to. And my "No" applies equally to every aspect of German servility. As long as Germans find their only happiness in obeying orders, they will go on serving, preferably as soldiers, and sacrificing themselves to some supreme leader.

BUTTRESS   I call it strength of character. You appall me. Squint, the upright! Squint, the fearless!

SQUINT   Who is Wolffen anyway? He hates Kant's writing on freedom as the capon hates the cock's crow.

FRITZ   I take it, Mr. Buttress, that you're not interested in these battles of minds.

BUTTRESS   No. I'm going to be a tutor, I'll be shut up in some god-forsaken hole. In the meantime I've got to get in a lifetime of loving.

FRITZ   This coffee tastes like barley.

BUTTRESS   What's that? *(He tastes it)* So it does. With the biscuits I hadn't—*(Looks into the pot)* God damn it! *(Throws the coffee things out the window)* Barley coffee for five hundred guilders a year! It's an insult to Squint the upright!

SQUINT   Buttress, you're raving, my dear Buttress!

MRS. BLITZ   *(rushes in)* What's this? What in the devil is going on? *(To Squint)* Are you raving, sir, or has the devil got into you?

SQUINT   Calm down, ma, I'll pay for it.

MRS. BLITZ   *(with a horrible scream)* Where are my coffee things? Heavens alive, out the window!—I'll scratch your eyes out!

SQUINT   There was a spider in the coffee; in my fright I threw it—is it my fault if the window was open?

MRS. BLITZ   I wish you'd choked on that spider. If I sold you and all your belongings, it wouldn't pay for my coffee set, you worthless dog! Rack and ruin is all I get from you. I'll have you prosecuted, I'll have you locked up.

SQUINT Let it go for once, Mrs. Blitz. It won't happen again. Please, Mrs. Blitz.

MRS. BLITZ And what's that on my table, you monster? Don't cover it up. He's been carving. Some obscenity. "No."

SQUINT It's in reference to Immanuel Kant.

MRS. BLITZ On my table! I'll call the constable. I—

BUTTRESS That'll do, Ma Blitz. Don't frighten Squint the fearless. The coffee was inadequate. Get thee hence, woman!

MRS. BLITZ *(intimidated)* Well, I must say—throwing my coffee set out in the snow drifts . . . *(Goes out)*

SQUINT I fear nothing but that woman. She is devoid of understanding.

BUTTRESS What would you do without Buttress? You'd pay through the nose and starve to death.

FRITZ I'm thinking of taking up philosophy myself.

BUTTRESS Mr. von Berg, I only hope philosophy can stand it. Everybody's taking up philosophy. I'll have to change now, I'm going to the new comedy tonight. They're playing *Minna von Barnhelm*. I have a weakness for actresses.

FRITZ Can I come along? It's a nice play. If only I could take my Gussie to see it.

SQUINT I wish I could go too. But I haven't got a coat!—So her name is Gussie? I'll be glad to show you my girl. Now I really need a coat.

BUTTRESS You haven't got one, though. So I'll show him your girl. She's the daughter of Swandown the lutenist. She gets a free place in the standing room, thanks to her father. A footnote to the history of the war. Let's go, Berg. And mind you, don't neglect your physiology. *(Buttress and Fritz go out)*

7

Insterburg, in March. Gussie's room.

Gussie, Hasty.

GUSSIE   I believe that God created me.
HASTY   If only He hadn't! *(Helping her along)* And all . . .
GUSSIE   And all other creatures . . .
HASTY   And has given me . . .
GUSSIE   And has given me, and keeps my body and soul . . .
HASTY   Body too . . .
GUSSIE   Eyes, ears, and all my limbs, my reason and all my senses . . .
HASTY   And that . . .
GUSSIE   And that he bestows upon me each day clothing and shoes, meat and drink, house and home, wife and child, fields and cattle, and all my goods . . .
HASTY   And supplies in abundance all needs and . . .
GUSSIE   Necessities of my . . .
HASTY   Body . . .
GUSSIE   And life . . .
HASTY   And protects me . . .
GUSSIE   From all perils, and guards and defends me from all . . .
HASTY   Bodily harm . . .
GUSSIE   What's the matter with you?
HASTY   Without any merit or worthiness in me.
GUSSIE   Amen.
HASTY   Weren't we supposed to draw from nature? You had a good laugh, didn't you, at the thought of that silly tutor waiting for you at the mill. And how many more fine March mornings will there be? *(Hasty slaps his palm with the ruler)*
GUSSIE   Ha, ha, ha, my dear tutor. Really, I had no time.

HASTY   Don't be cruel.

GUSSIE   But what *is* the matter with you? I never saw you so deep in thought. And I've noticed that you don't eat.

HASTY   You have? Really? You're a paragon of compassion.

GUSSIE   Oh, Mr. Hasty—

HASTY   Would you care to draw from nature this afternoon?

GUSSIE   *(touches his hand)*   Oh, dearest tutor, forgive me for disappointing you yesterday. It was quite impossible for me to come. I was so amazingly enrhumée.

HASTY   I suppose it's the same today. Perhaps we had better stop drawing from nature altogether. It doesn't amuse you any more.

GUSSIE   *(half in tears)* How can you say that, Mr. Hasty? It's the one thing I like to do.

HASTY   Or find yourself a drawing master. Because I believe I shall ask your father to remove the object of your aversion, your hatred, your cruelty, from your sight. I can see that instruction from me is becoming more and more repellent to you.

GUSSIE   Mr. Hasty—

HASTY   Let me be. I must find a way of putting an end to this miserable life, since death is denied me.

GUSSIE   Mr. Hasty—

HASTY   You're torturing me. *(He tears himself away and rushes out)*

GUSSIE   Oh, how sorry I feel for him!

8

Privy Councillor von Berg's ornamental garden.

Privy councillor, Pastor Hasty, Hasty.

PRIVY COUNCILLOR   I'm sorry for him and even more sorry for you, reverend. But intercede with my brother on behalf of your son—no!

PASTOR   But think of it, only three hundred thalers! Three hundred miserable thalers! The major promised him four hundred. Then, after the first six months, he paid him a hundred and forty. And now, at the beginning of the second half year, while more and more work is being piled on my son, he speaks of two hundred as his annual wage. That is unjust. Begging your pardon.

PRIVY COUNCILLOR   Why? A tutor! What does he do? Lolls about and gets paid for it. Wastes the best hours of the day with a young master who doesn't want to learn anything and has no need to. Spends the rest of his time bowing to madame's whims or studying the lines in the major's face. Eats when he's full and fasts when he's hungry, drinks punch when he wants to piss and plays cards when he has the colic. Without freedom life goes backward. Freedom is to man what water is to fish. A man who forfeits freedom poisons his noblest impulses, smothers the sweetest joys of life in their bloom, and murders himself.

PASTOR   But—oh my! Those are the things a tutor must put up with. No one can do what he likes all the time, my son understands that, but—

HASTY   It was about the horse, your worship.

PRIVY COUNCILLOR   So much the worse if he puts up with it, so much the worse. Blast it, reverend, you didn't raise your son to be a common servant. And what is he now but a servant?

PASTOR   But, your worship! Goodness gracious!

HASTY   Stick to the horse, father.

PASTOR   Good God, sir! There have to be tutors in this world.

PRIVY COUNCILLOR   In my opinion tutors are not needed in this world. Worthless trash, that's what they are.

PASTOR   Your worship, I didn't come here to be insulted. I was a tutor myself once. Good day.

HASTY   Father!

PASTOR   I'm not a hot-headed man, but how can I listen to such absurdities? Tutors are useless, you say. I hear your son is studying at the university of Halle. Who taught him sense and good manners?

PRIVY COUNCILLOR   Why, I had the good judgment to send him to public school. And the few principles he needs to conduct himself as a scholar and a gentleman, he got from me. We talked it over at the dinner table.

PASTOR   I see—*(takes out his watch)*—alas, your worship, I haven't time for prolonged disputations. I'm a plain pastor, a shepherd of souls, and when once in a blue moon I come all the way from Ingelshausen I have errands to do.

HASTY   Your worship, couldn't you . . .

PASTOR   Forget it, son. Come along!

HASTY   The horse. Couldn't you put in a word with your brother? The worst of it is that I never get away from Insterburg. For six whole months—I'm coming, father—I haven't left . . . I was promised a horse to ride to Königsberg every three months!

PRIVY COUNCILLOR   What do you want to go to Königsberg for?

HASTY   Visit the libraries, your worship.

PRIVY COUNCILLOR   The brothels seems more likely. Been feeling your oats? *(The pastor goes out)*

HASTY   Your worship . . . Something terrible may happen . . . *(Follows his father)*

PRIVY COUNCILLOR   *(calling after them)* My brother hasn't enough horses for his farm, and here you are, wanting one for your dissipations.

ACT THREE

Halle.

Squint, Fritz.

FRITZ   Look what she's sent me. She copied it out of the Klopstock I gave her:

"Oh thou, to find thee I learned love,
Which has exalted my swelling heart
And now, in ever sweeter dreams,
Is wafting me to Paradise."

And this one:

"Great, O Mother Nature, is the glory of thy invention
On every field and meadow . . ."

And now she's drawing from nature. But what are you brood-
ing about?

SQUINT   A metaphysical problem, brother, a philosophical
problem. I'll dissect it for you. Let us assume that a woman's
body and senses are directed toward an object—a particular
man—and so likewise are her soul and mind—in other words
that the thought of her mind and the desires of her body
coincide, then everything is as it should be and without philosophical interest. Agreed?

FRITZ   Agreed. But what are you driving at?

SQUINT   That it becomes of philosophical interest when she loves one man A and desires, or gives her body to, another man, B.

FRITZ   Is that an actual case?

SQUINT   A hypothetical case. But what is the solution? Is it the body or the spirit that counts? You see that the problem is philosophical.

FRITZ   You mean: should we say that she loves A or that she's sleeping with B?

SQUINT   Precisely. And what's the answer?

FRITZ   I suppose you want me to say that the spirit counts. But why are you trembling? Has it anything to do with you?

SQUINT   Berg, there are times when I feel almost weary of philosophy. *(He bursts into tears)* Oh, Buttress, Buttress! Why did you have to take my place at the meeting with Miss Swandown? Why did you take her to the shooting gallery to put in a word for me? If only I had had a coat! It was for me, for me that you fondled her and got her with child!

FRITZ   So that's it. Has Buttress confessed? Poor Squint.

SQUINT   Poor Squint! Doubly poor, for he lacks the wherewithal to help the unhappy creatures. Poor Squint, always flunking, ruined by his perseverance in antagonizing Professor Wolffen. So that now he is unable to do his duty.

FRITZ   What duty?

SQUINT   Don't you see? The surgeon wants twenty thalers.

FRITZ   But good Lord, not from you. It wasn't you that . . .

SQUINT   But it was done for my sake and no one else's. I'm the one she loves. If he hadn't gone in my stead, she'd never have . . . Her tear-drenched face haunts my dreams: when Buttress brought her to me, she took my hand and whispered: "We talked of nothing but you the whole time." How can I abandon her?

FRITZ   *(embraces him)* Magnanimous Squint. I understand. What will you do? What shall we do? Yes, we. Am I not your friend? Your duty is my duty. Command my purse.

SQUINT   Fritz, oh Fritz, can it be true? Is the earth peopled by a race of philosophers?

FRITZ   *(gives him money)* Quick, take it. I had it on me because I was going to Insterburg for the holidays.

SQUINT   Then I won't accept it. Your Gussie! I shouldn't wonder if she needed you badly, straining her eyes for the sight of you. And no Fritz appears to embrace her. He sacrifices his travel money for Miss Swandown . . .

FRITZ Forget it, Squint, let's say that I am not overcome by emotion but guided by reason. My girl expects me for the holidays, she says so in her letter. *(Reads)* "In your Easter holidays you will find a bolder Juliet!" Frankly, Squint, those words frightened me. No, believe me, I shall do better not to go home this year. I'm not the chaste Joseph I used to be. I too have developed in this Halle of yours.

SQUINT How can I ever repay you, brother?

FRITZ By teaching me more about your rebellious Immanuel Kant during the holidays. I'll have got the better of the bargain.

SQUINT I will—though his rebellion is limited to the realm of ideas. *(The doorbell rings)*
(Squint leaps to the window)

SQUINT Here they are!
(Enter Buttress and Miss Swandown)

BUTTRESS Well, we're back. The Hunold woman wants thirty thalers.—Miss Swandown is indisposed. A glass of water would help.

SQUINT My dear, adorable child, you find me—my friend here too, he knows all—overcome with tenderness.

BUTTRESS Tenderness is all very well, but how about some cash?

SQUINT Everything will be all right. But first that glass of . . .

BUTTRESS All right, you say? You'll cough up? You've got money? Don't run away! You've got it?

SQUINT Miss Swandown, I won't keep you in suspense another minute. I shall do my duty without reserve or delay.

BUTTRESS Twenty thalers?

SQUINT *(counts out the money on the table)* Rendered liquid by the profound influences of philosophy!—Twenty thalers!

MISS SWANDOWN You're very kind, Mr. Squint, seeing you didn't get anything out of it for yourself.

BUTTRESS Don't say that. But you've done a good deed. Kiss her, honest Squint, you deserve it.

SQUINT *(with a deep bow)* Your humble servant, Miss Swan-down.

(Buttress and Miss Swandown leave)

SQUINT There must be something good in Buttress, or he wouldn't be so crude. He's eating his heart out. *(Returns the purse to Fritz)* You have acted on the principles of Immanuel Kant, Brother Berg. *(Looks for something in a book)* "So act that you can will the maxim of your action to become universal law." Writings on Morals, Part One, Fundamental Principles of the Metaphysics of Morals, Chapter Two.

10

Insterburg, Gussie's room.

Gussie and Hasty, in bed.

HASTY Your father's been to blame from the start. Why did he have to scrimp on a teacher for you? Then in the same burst of avarice he reduced my pay. And now he wants to cut me down to a hundred and twenty thalers for next year. I shall have to quit.

GUSSIE But what will I do then?

HASTY Get them to send you to my father's rectory in Ingels-hausen.

GUSSIE My uncle would never let my father send me to your father's house.

HASTY Confound his beastly nobleman's pride!

GUSSIE *(takes his hand)* Don't be angry, Hermann! *(Kisses him)* Oh, dear teacher, how does your pupil look? As pale as death?

HASTY As fit as a fiddle. Now, I need your advice.—Yesterday your brother slapped my face again.

GUSSIE You must bear it for my sake.

HASTY Then maybe I needn't regret my failure to control myself. I suppose I'm being fed too well for a slave. The celery, the turkey, the chocolate—how can a body so pampered help succumbing to sin?

GUSSIE   Faugh! Is that the language of love? It was fate, my dear teacher.

HASTY *(as she continues to raise his hand intermittently to her lips)* Let me think . . . *(Sits up in thought)*

GUSSIE *(in the pantomime described)*   Oh, Romeo, if this were thy hand!—Why hast thou abandoned me, ignoble Romeo? Dost not thou know that thy Juliet is dying for love of thee—hated, despised, rejected by all the world, by her whole family? *(Presses his hands to her eyes)* Cruel Romeo!

HASTY *(looks up)*   What are you raving about?

GUSSIE   It's a soliloquy from a tragedy that I like to recite when I'm upset.

HASTY   I don't care for tragedies.

GUSSIE   Oh, Halle, worlds away!—Maybe I shouldn't blame it all on you. Your father forbade you to write to me—but love surmounts all obstacles.—You've forgotten me . . .

HASTY *(suspiciously)*   Even in bed I have to decipher everything you say.

GUSSIE *(kisses Hasty's hands with abandon)*   Oh, heavenly Romeo!

HASTY *(crossly)*   I'm not Romeo, I'm Hasty, if you don't mind. *(Gussie turns to the wall, weeps. Hasty remorsefully kisses her hand and gazes at her for a while)* What happened to Abelard could happen to me. I seem to recall that you've read the romance, Miss von Berg. Would you recapitulate what you know of Abelard and Héloise?

GUSSIE   When it became known that Abelard and Héloise had secretly married, her uncle, Monsignor Fulbert, canon in Paris, had him seized and deprived of his manhood.

HASTY   I hear footsteps in the hall!

GUSSIE   My father—Oh God—you've stayed three-quarters of an hour too long. *(Hasty hurries away)* Oh Fritz, my love!

11

Mrs. von Berg's parlor. August.

Mrs. von Berg, Count Vermouth, the major.

MRS. VON BERG *(at the spinet)*   Ah, dear count, so many talents are doomed to hide their light. They find no scope in this
· narrow world. Oh, to be a singer! With the candles shining on me, perhaps even the footlights. It's denied us, our station doesn't permit of such liberties. Do you like this one? *(She sings a languishing air)*

COUNT   Superb!

MRS. VON BERG   Flatterer! I'm not in good voice today. This one
. . . *(Sings another)*

COUNT   A natural talent. Some have it, some don't. And if they don't, nothing helps.

MRS. VON BERG   Believe me, it's training and hard work as well. Sheer will power.

COUNT   I wish Miss Gussie had inherited such genius. Where is she?

MRS. VON BERG   Ah, yes. *(Hums)* I see I'm keeping you. Is there anything more ghastly than an artist—however talented—who doesn't know when to stop? Just one more, may I? *(She sings)*

COUNT   Charming. But, madame, am I never to see Miss Gussie again? Has she been well since the hunt the other day?

MRS. VON BERG   Thank you for asking. She had a toothache last night, that's why she must keep out of sight today. And your stomach, count, after the oysters?

COUNT   Oh, I'm used to it.—I must say that Miss Gussie has developed magnificently—blossomed out like a rose since last fall.

MRS. VON BERG   These modern young girls . . . they change from day to day. Those sentimental books they read give them consumptive shadows under their eyes; but then a little drawing from nature brings back the bloom . . . I always say that proper health begins at forty.

COUNT   And health is the true source of beauty. *(Mrs. von Berg plays the spinet again)* If Miss Gussie were to come down, I should like to take a stroll in the garden with her. I can't ask you, dear madame, because of the fontanelle on your leg.

MRS. VON BERG   If only certain people were as concerned about my well-being . . . Since the war the major has had only one interest, his damnable farm. All day he's in the fields, and when he comes home he sits there like a stick.—Oh, dear count . . . A few days ago he took it into his head to sleep with me again, but in the middle of the night he jumped out of bed and started . . . ha, ha, ha, I shouldn't be telling you this, but you know how ridiculous my husband can be . . .

COUNT   Started . . . ?

MRS. VON BERG   Poring over his account books. And groaning something dreadful. I could hear him down in his study. But his foolishness is nothing to me. Let him turn Quaker or Pietist if he wants to. It won't make him any uglier or more amiable in my eyes than he is now. *(She looks roguishly at the count)*

COUNT   *(chucks her under the chin)* What wicked things you say! —But where is Gussie? I'd really like to take a stroll with her.

MRS. VON BERG   Hush! Here comes the major . . . Why don't you go out with him, count? He'll show you his hothouse.

COUNT   Fancy that!—But it's your daughter I want to see.

MRS. VON BERG   I dare say she's not dressed yet. The girl is insufferably lazy.

(Major von Berg comes in, his coat bespattered with mud)

MRS. VON BERG   *(plays Handel's* Largo *on the spinet)* Well, husband? What have you been up to now? I don't lay eyes on you from morning to night, and now look at him, count. Doesn't he look exactly like Terence's Self-Tormentor in Madame Dacier's edition? I do believe you've been carting manure, Major von Berg.

COUNT   It's true, major, you've never looked so horrible. I'd never have expected farming to go to your head like this.

MRS. VON BERG   Avarice, pure, execrable avarice. He thinks we'll starve if he doesn't go burrowing in the muck like a mole. He spades, he plows, he harrows. If you must turn peasant, couldn't you find me another husband first?

MAJOR   Zounds, woman, you forget that wars have to be paid for. But it's true, I never see you ladies any more. Where's Gussie?

MRS. VON BERG   *(still playing)*   Gussie! Gussie! Gussie! That's all I ever hear! The mole, there's nothing else left in his head. Only Gussie. His Gussie, always his Gussie.

MAJOR   Yes, and you keep her away from me because you're jealous of her.

MRS. VON BERG   How the man speaks to me! As if I kept her locked up. I'm sick of it. She should come down when there are visitors. *(Goes out)*

COUNT   I am embarrassed, Major von Berg. Permit me to take my leave.

MAJOR   Just hang around.

COUNT   *(after a pause)*   Speaking of economics, have you seen a gazette recently? There's been quite a stir about the king founding a bank in Berlin on the French . . .

MAJOR   Berlin!

COUNT   Don't say anything against Berlin. We are definitely making progress, all Europe is watching us. First the ballet and now the bank, à la bonne heure!

MAJOR   A bank! It's a rotten business, count, take it from me. We can perish like Sodom without any need for banks and such-like novelties, indeed we can.

COUNT   But think of the ballet. Between you and me, major, I've always felt that a brief excursion to Sodom now and then is good for the blood.

(Mrs. von Berg rushes in)

MRS. VON BERG   Help! Help! Husband—we're lost—the family! The family!

COUNT   Madame, what on earth . . . ?

MRS. VON BERG   The family—the infamy—oh, I can't go on. *(Falls on a chair)* Your daughter!

MAJOR   *(goes toward her)*   What's happened? Out with it! Speak up or I'll wring your neck!

MRS. VON BERG   Your daughter—the tutor—hurry! *(She faints)*
MAJOR   Has he made a whore of her? *(Shakes her)* Is this what
I burrow in the earth for? What's the good of collapsing? This
is no time to collapse. Made a whore of her? Is that it? All
right. Let them turn the whole world into a whore, with
ballets, banks and spinets. And you, Berg, take up your pitchfork. *(To his wife)* Come on, you're a whore too! Watch me!
(Tears the doors open) I'll set an example. That's what God has
preserved me for to this day—to make an example of my wife
and children.—Burn it all, burn, burn, burn! *(Carries his wife,
who is still in a faint, off the stage)*
COUNT   Parbleu!

12

Village school near Insterburg.

Wenceslas, Hasty, Lisa.

WENCESLAS   *(sitting at a table, spectacles on his nose, ruling sheets of
paper)*   Who's there? What is it?
HASTY   *(who has rushed in breathlessly)*   Help! Save me! Dear
schoolmaster! They'll kill me!
WENCESLAS   Who are you?
HASTY   The tutor at the castle. Major von Berg is after me with
all his servants. He wants to shoot me.
WENCESLAS   God forbid!—Just sit down quietly.—You'll be
safe with me, here's my hand on it. Tell me all about it while
I write out these exercises.
HASTY   Let me collect my wits first.
WENCESLAS   All right. Get your breath. But tell me this—tutor
—*(puts his ruler aside, takes off his spectacles and looks at him for
a while)* what on earth can have made your master so angry
at you?—Would you kindly pass me the sand box?—You see,
I have to rule out the lines for my boys, because nothing is

harder for them to learn than to write straight, to write evenly.—The main thing, I always say, is to write not elegantly or quickly, but straight, because handwriting has its effect on everything else, morals, thought, in short everything, my dear Mr. Tutor. A man who can't write straight, I always say, can't act straight either.—Where were we? Would you put these sheets over there?

HASTY *(who has done so)* May I ask you for a glass of water?

WENCESLAS Water?—You shall have beer. But—yes, what were we talking about?

HASTY About writing straight.

WENCESLAS No, about the major. Ha, ha, ha. Now let's see. Do you know, Mr.—what is your name?

HASTY Name—my name is—Midge.

WENCESLAS Mr. Midge.—Forgotten it, hadn't you? Strange how our thoughts can give us the slip.

HASTY May I open the window? Oh God, there's Count Vermouth.

WENCESLAS *(severely)* I need the sand box again, if you please. *(Hasty, shaking, hands it to him. Count Vermouth comes in with some servants brandishing pistols. Hasty dashes into another room)*

WENCESLAS Nervi corrupti!

COUNT I'm looking for a certain Hasty. A student with a brown braided coat.

WENCESLAS Sir, in our village it is customary to remove your hat when addressing the master of the house.

COUNT The matter is urgent.—Is he here or not?

WENCESLAS What can the man have done that you should be looking for him with pistols? *(The count is about to enter the side room; Wenceslas blocks the door)* Stop, sir. That is my room. Leave my house this instant, sir, or I shall pull the bell cord and half a dozen sturdy peasants will beat you to a pulp, pistols and all! If you behave like a bandit, you shall be treated like a bandit, sir! The way out is the same as the way in, but in case you've forgotten—*(He takes him by the hand and leads him out the door)*

HASTY *(peeps out of the side room)* Happy man! Enviable man! I admire you . . .

WENCESLAS Now sit down and have some knackwurst and

potato salad after your fright. Lisa! *(Lisa comes in)* Bring Mr. Midge a pitcher of beer. *(Lisa goes out)* She's my ward.—While you're waiting for your beer, you may as well earn your supper and help me to rule these sheets. It will improve your morals. *(Hasty sits down to do the ruling)* Who was that rude fellow who wanted you?

HASTY   A certain Count Vermouth, the major's son-in-law to be. He's jealous of me, because the young lady can't stand him. That's all.

WENCESLAS   But what's the sense in it? What does the young lady want of you, monsieur ladykiller? Better get that sort of thing out of your head and stick to knackwurst. Go ahead, eat! But don't make grease spots. And draw the lines evenly, if you please.—I dare say there's a difference between the major's table and mine. But when schoolmaster Wenceslas eats his supper, a clear conscience helps him digest it, and when Mr. Midge was eating pheasant with mushroom sauce, his conscience prompted moral qualms that drove every bite he swallowed back into his throat.

HASTY   Very true, but that's not all. You don't realize how fortunate you are. Have you never seen a slave in a braided coat? Oh, freedom, golden freedom!

WENCESLAS   *(motioning him back to his ruling)*   That churl wanting to break into my room without so much as a by-your-leave! Just let him come back, with all the majors in the world! Zooks! Now you've finished your knackwurst, and the beer isn't here yet.—Won't you smoke a pipe with me?

HASTY   I'll be glad to try. I've never smoked in all my life.

WENCESLAS   Of course not, you fine gentlemen, it discolors your teeth, is that it? I started smoking when I was barely weaned. Exchanged my mother's nipple for the mouthpiece. Ha, ha, ha. Smoke is good for foul air, and for foul cravings as well. Here's my program: on rising, cold water and a pipe, school till eleven, then another pipe until the soup's ready. My Lisa's soup is as good as any French chef's. Then another pipe, then school until four. Then I write out exercises until supper time. Most usually I have a cold supper, sausage with salad, a piece of cheese, or whatever the good Lord may provide. And then a last pipe before bed.

HASTY   God help me, I've come to a smoking den!

WENCESLAS   And with all that I'm fat and healthy and cheerful, and I haven't even begun to think about death.

HASTY   You earn good wages, I presume?

WENCESLAS   Wages? That's a stupid question, Mr. Midge. Forgive me, did you say wages? My wages are from God, a good conscience. Have you any idea what it means to be a schoolmaster? *(He struts awesomely to and fro)* I shape human beings in my own image. German heroes! Healthy minds in healthy bodies, not French monkeys. On the one hand, as it were, mental giants, on the other hand, good subjects. And what does that mean? Does it mean subjected giants or gigantic subjects? It means: reach for the stars, but God help you if you kick against the pricks!—Won't you have a smoke? Go on, have a pipe. Conquer yourself—no, not you, the German hero —if you would conquer the world. I'll take the cane to you if ever you . . .Oh dear *(he snatches the goose quill which Hasty has been picking his teeth with)* what are you doing! A grown man! Haven't you even learned to take care of your own body? Picking the teeth is suicide. There. If something gets stuck in your teeth *(takes water and rinses his mouth)* this is the thing to do, if you want to have sound teeth. Go on, do it! *(Hasty does so)*

HASTY   He's going to schoolmaster me to death.

WENCESLAS   You don't care for the pipe? Just spend a few days with old Wenceslas, and I'll wager this hand will shape you so you won't know yourself.—I assume, young man, that without a reference your tutoring days are over. And you can't hope for a position in a village school because the king, now that his war is over, is putting in his disabled sergeants as schoolmasters. Yes, that's how it is. You're probably weak in Latin, but as a tutor you must have a likely handwriting. You could lend me a hand in the evening. It's time I began to spare my eyes. You could write out the exercises for my boys. But you will have to work hard, I can tell you that!

HASTY   The humiliation!

(The major, the privy councillor and Count Vermouth enter with servants)

MAJOR   *(with pistol drawn)*   The deuce . . . ! There he sits like a rabbit in the cabbage patch. (*He shoots and hits Hasty in the arm. Hasty tumbles from his chair*)

PRIVY COUNCILLOR (*has vainly tried to restrain the major*)   Brother! (*Pushes him angrily*) Now you've done it, you fool!

MAJOR   Hey! Are you dead? Speak to me! Where is my daughter?

WENCESLAS   Your lordships! Is the last judgment on its way? (*He reaches for the bread knife*) I'll teach you to assault a Christian in his own house!

HASTY   Don't, I implore you!—It's the major. I deserved it for what I did to his daughter.

PRIVY COUNCILLOR   Worthy schoolmaster, is there a surgeon in the village? He's wounded in the arm. I want to have him cared for.

WENCESLAS   Cared for! You bandits! Do you think you can shoot people down because you're rich enough to have them cared for? He's my assistant. He's been in my house exactly one year. A quiet, peaceful, industrious man. And you barge in and shoot down my assistant before my very eyes!—I'll be avenged!

PRIVY COUNCILLOR (*motions a servant to bandage Hasty*)   What's the good of lying, my dear man? We know the whole story. (*To the major*) I shall send Fritz to Italy, he must never hear of this.—He'll bleed to death. Run for a surgeon!

WENCESLAS   Nonsense! If you make wounds, you can heal them yourselves, you bandits! I'm not running to get the surgeon, I'm running to ring the tocsin. (*Leaves*)
(*Servants put Hasty back on his chair. Hasty comes to*)

MAJOR   And now to you! If it takes red-hot pincers: Where is my daughter?

HASTY   If your worship had only granted me a horse to ride to Königsberg, as you agreed to!

MAJOR   What's the horse got to do with it, you scoundrel? Where's my daughter?

HASTY   I don't know.

MAJOR   You don't know? (*Draws another pistol*)

LISA (*comes in with the beer*)   Don't shoot! Poor Mr. Midge! (*Throws herself in front of Hasty*)

PRIVY COUNCILLOR (*snatches the pistol from the Major and fires it out the window)* Do we have to put you in chains, you . . . *(To Hasty)* Answer us!

HASTY I haven't seen her since I escaped from your house. I swear to God before whose judgment seat I may soon stand.

MAJOR *(about to assault him again)* Another charge of powder wasted! Swine, I wish it had gone straight through your body, seeing we can't get any sense out of you!

PRIVY COUNCILLOR Berg!

LISA Are you Major von Berg? Oh, your grace, there was a lady at the inn, she ordered coffee. As she was paying she said to the landlord, "If my father comes asking for me, don't tell him I went to the pond by the elm trees. Tell him, good people, that I send him my love."

MAJOR To the pond? To the pond! To the pond! *(Goes out)*

PRIVY COUNCILLOR The man can't swim.

COUNT If only I could!

PRIVY COUNCILLOR I mustn't lose sight of him. *(Throws Hasty a purse)* Use it to get well and remember you wounded my brother a good deal worse than he wounded you.

(The privy councillor and the count leave quickly)

HASTY *(with bitterness)* What's the horse got to do with it! My vita sexualis can go hang!

13

Near Insterburg.

Gussie at the edge of a pond surrounded by bushes. Major, privy councillor, Count Vermouth, servants.

GUSSIE Nobody's coming. Must I die here? Fritz, oh Fritz! Why didn't you come home for the holidays? Then I was still . . . Clouds are passing over the moon. No one will ever find me.

MAJOR *(from a distance)* Gussie! Gussie!

(Gussie puts down her shoes and wades into the pond, her face turned back)

MAJOR *(appears, followed by the privy councillor and Count Vermouth)* Heigh-ho! Somebody's gone into the pond—there, look, it's a woman. After her, Berg! I'll save her or go to hell. *(Wades after her)*

PRIVY COUNCILLOR   God Almighty, he's going to drown too.

COUNT   Let's hope it's shallow.

PRIVY COUNCILLOR   To the other side! *(To the servants who are carrying long poles)* After them, fellows!—I think he's grabbed her . . . There . . . back there, by the bushes.—Don't you see? He's wading along the shore. God preserve our wits! On the other hand, can one help being moved by human . . .

(The servants probe the pond with their poles)

MAJOR *(backstage)*   Help! This way! It's my daughter!

PRIVY COUNCILLOR *(to Count Vermouth)*   The tragedy of it all! The tragedy! The poor man; for all we know, he's saving two lives.

COUNT *(to privy councillor)*   I feel so helpless. Those crude fellows *(pointing at the servants)* are better at it.

MAJOR   Odds bobs, zookers and bodkins! Give me a pole! The plague . . .

PRIVY COUNCILLOR *(kicks a servant in the behind, making him fall in the water)*   Get out there, you rascal. Don't just think of yourself!

(Major Berg carries Gussie on to the stage)

MAJOR   There! *(Puts her down and kneels down beside her)* Gussie! Why did you do it?—If only you had breathed a word to me. I'd have bought the swine a title, then you could have crawled into bed with him to your heart's content.—For God's sake, do something. She's only fainted.

PRIVY COUNCILLOR   I wish I knew where that goddam surgeon was.

GUSSIE *(in a feeble voice)*   Father!

MAJOR   What do you want?

GUSSIE   Your forgiveness.

MAJOR   Forgiveness be damned, you spoiled brat.—No, don't collapse. I forgive you—and you forgive me. I've put a bullet through that scoundrel's brains.

PRIVY COUNCILLOR   I think we'd better carry her.
MAJOR   Let her be! What concern is she of yours? Worry about
your own flesh and blood at home! *(Carrying her in his arms)*
There, my girl—really, I ought to walk back into the pond
with you *(swings her toward the pond)*—but maybe we shouldn't
try to swim until we've learned how.—*(Presses her to his heart)*
Godless hussy! *(Carries her out)*

Interlude

To the accompaniment of a music box which misses a few notes,
the stage revolves to show the passing of a year and how our
characters are spending it. Winter: Fritz von Berg strolling
under lemon trees in Italy; spring: Squint marrying his Caroline in Halle; summer: Gussie sewing diapers in Insterburg;
autumn: Hasty still writing out exercises at the village school.

ACT FOUR

14

Village school.

a)

Stormy night in November. Hasty is correcting papers. Lisa comes in.

LISA I've frightened you. I only wanted to ask you if you—needed anything, Mr. Midge.

HASTY Me? Need anything? Why, I never do. What should a wretch like me need? I have everything. And I'll be going to bed soon.

LISA I shouldn't have disturbed you. I'll go, Mr. Midge. You're always writing.

HASTY Heavenly apparition!

LISA I thought the lamp might be smoking.

HASTY I see.

LISA But it isn't.

HASTY You're cold, my child. Let me put my scarf on you. Now go.

LISA A pot of coffee, Mr. Midge, to keep you warm?

HASTY No. Yes, make some coffee. *(Lisa goes out)* Have I gone mad? What has happened to me? This innocent creature. This angel of kindness. And I, in these few minutes assailed by contemptible instincts! Whence this hurricane rising from a mere nothing? She shows an innocent solicitude—is my lamp smoking?—I requite her with carnal lust! Under my benefac-

tor's own roof, in sight of the objects—this chair, this bed—
with which he has surrounded me in his loving kindness.
That is how I repay the man who taught me what it is to
teach. Monster that I am, shall I never mend my ways? Is it
to start all over again? Haven't I already . . . ? My head's in
a whirl. Ravished. Fished out of the pond by a despairing
father, pushed in by me. And now, is it to be Lisa? Never!
Never! *(He bars the door)* Midge, get back to work! *(He works
again)* Write straight, live straight. What am I coming to with
this hurricane in my heart? How long does it take to make a
pot of coffee? Grade papers, correct spelling, a bodice is made
for concealment, stop trying to look through it. Scoundrel
without a reference, without a future. *(A knocking at the door)*
Don't move! The latch will hold. Angel, turn back! *(He opens
the door)*

LISA *(comes in with a pot)* Why do you lock yourself in? No
evil-doer would come this way at night. Here's your hot
drink.

HASTY Thank you. *(Takes it from her and pushes her out)* That's
done. *(Sinks onto a chair)* Go in peace, Lisa, you're saved.
(Another knock) The latch! *(Lisa comes in)*

LISA I'm back again, Mr. Midge. Do you mind?

HASTY Yes, I mind.

LISA I've come because you said there would be no catechism
tomorrow—because you—that's why I've come—you said—
I've come to ask if there'd be catechism tomorrow.

HASTY Oh!—Those cheeks, angels of heaven! See how they
burn with the fire of innocence, then condemn me if you can
—Lisa, why are your hands trembling? Why are your lips so
pale and your cheeks so red? What do you want?

LISA To know if there'll be catechism tomorrow.

HASTY Come, Lisa, sit down.—Who puts your hair up when
you go to church? *(Makes her sit down on a chair beside him)*

LISA *(wants to get up)* Excuse me. My cap must be crooked.
There was such a wind when I went to the kitchen.

HASTY *(takes both her hands in his)* Oh you are—How old are you,
Lisa? Have you ever—what was I saying—have you ever been
courted?

LISA *(gaily)* Oh yes, and Greta at the Sheepshead Inn was

envious. "How can he be so interested in that stupid girl?" that's what she used to say. And then I knew an officer too, before you came here.

HASTY   An officer?

LISA   Oh, yes. And most distinguished, with three stripes on his arm. But I was too young, my mother wouldn't let me have him.

HASTY   And then?

LISA   Because of the life soldiers lead, always moving about, and in the end they have nothing.

HASTY   And me? What have I got?

LISA   But you're in trouble, Mr. Midge.

HASTY   Would you—would you really—*(slaps his hand with the ruler)*

LISA   Oh yes, with all my heart. *(Hasty throws himself on her and kisses her hand. Lisa takes it away)* Oh, you mustn't. My hand is all black from the stove.—Shame on you, what are you doing? You know, I always thought I wanted a clergyman. Even as a child I liked educated gentlemen, they're so gentle and polite, not slam-bang like soldiers, though in a way I like them too, I can't deny it, because of their gay coats. If clergymen wore such gay coats, really it would be the end of me.

HASTY   *(leaps at her and seizes her)*   Oh, Lisa! You don't know how unhappy I am.

LISA   For shame, sir, what are you doing?

HASTY   Once more. And then never never again! *(Kisses her)*

LISA   No, no, no . . .

WENCESLAS   *(bursting in)*   What's going on? Is this the attention you owe to your flock? A rabid wolf in sheep's clothing? Seducing the innocence it's your duty to protect!

HASTY   Master Wenceslas!

WENCESLAS   Not a word! You've shown your true colors. Leave my house, you seducer!

LISA   *(kneels before Wenceslas)*   Dear godfather, he's done me no wrong.

WENCESLAS   He's done you more wrong than if he were your worst enemy. He has seduced your innocent mind.

HASTY   I confess my guilt.—But how could anyone resist such charms? Unless you tear the heart out of my body . . .

WENCESLAS   Do you mean to go on seducing innocent girls? Is that your plan?

HASTY   No, no. God is my witness, if I sealed these innocent lips with my kisses, it was only to stop them from inciting me to far greater crimes with the magic of their speech.

WENCESLAS   And how would you support her, you pauper?

HASTY   That's what I told her.

WENCESLAS   Do you think that will keep her fed? You, get up, innocent victim. You're a disgrace to your profession. Where are your references? Where can you show your face? Out of my sight, you reprobate! (*Takes the copy books away*) You will corrupt my good children no longer. Tomorrow morning you leave my house! (*He drags Lisa out*)

b)

Hasty, at the open window.

HASTY   There I go again!—Roar, ye night winds! And you, unworthy fiend, out into the storm with you! Did you think you could shape little children in your own image? Behold your face in this window glass, and tremble! Does a nursery-man pull up his seedlings? Guardian, where is your guardian? All your life you've been an outcast. After what you have done will you go to him and say: Unfortunate man—unfortunate because you trusted me—give me the hand of your ward whom I have abused. You can ruin her, but can you feed her? And yet, is it so reprehensible to be human? Carnal or not, are such impulses unnatural? A curse on nature for not making me a stone in the presence of her creation! What's wrong with me? A stablehand is allowed to be a man. Not I. Shall I pluck out the eye that offends me? Shall I stand up to you, spirit of creation, and say: I reject your purposes? The face you gave me is disfigured, I myself disfigured it because it did not fit. And say to the wind, when you come back tomorrow, I shall be here no longer. So be it. I must. I will set an example to make you tremble! (*Tears off his coat*)

c)

Hasty, in bed. Wenceslas comes in.

WENCESLAS Holy God! What is it now? Why have you called me away from my work? This room!—It looks like a battlefield. Why are you still in bed? I've told you to leave my house. You should have been on your way to Heidebühl long ago.

HASTY I believe I'm on my way somewhere else.

WENCESLAS Why those fearful glances? They make my blood run cold. Frigidus per ossa—What is it?—As if you had killed a man.—Why are you making such a face?

HASTY Master Wenceslas, I don't know if I've done right.—I've castrated myself.

WENCESLAS What?—Emasculated?—But that's . . .

HASTY I hope you'll grant me a few more days under your desecrated roof.

WENCESLAS Say no more. You shouldn't have done it. Why, you're a second Origen! Let me embrace you, young man, oh precious chosen vessel. A deed like this can make you a beacon of the school system, a shining star of pedagogy. I congratulate you. Wenceslas salutes you with a Jubilate and Evoë —my spiritual son!

HASTY And yet, dear schoolmaster, I regret it.

WENCESLAS What, regret it? Not for one moment, my dear colleague! Will you darken your noble deed with foolish regrets and sully it with sinful tears? Do I see tears welling up in your eyes? Swallow your tears and intone a joyful song: I have freed myself from vanity, and need but wings to fly. Are you going to behave like Lot's wife, looking back at Sodom when you've already reached the peace and safety of Zoar? No, no. I prefer our blessed Doctor Luther: Whatsoever rises is for our dear Lord, whatsoever descends is for Beelzebub.

HASTY I'm afraid my motives were of a different kind . . . Repentance . . . Concern for my livelihood.

WENCESLAS That's taken care of now. Who can be better fitted for a teaching career than you? Now you have the highest qualifications of them all. Haven't you destroyed your rebellious spirit, subordinated everything to duty? No longer will your private life deflect you from shaping human beings in your own image. What more could you have done? As to your future, don't let it worry you. You've done your duty. Your prospects are of the brightest.

HASTY   I've written a letter to Major von Berg. It's there on the table, beside the knife. Would you read it and send it off if you approve?

WENCESLAS (reads)   ". . . And so, by my own decision—a cruel one, I can assure you—I have eliminated any danger that may have arisen from my manhood . . . Between Scylla and Charybdis, between nature and my profession, I have chosen my profession, and venture to hope that you will most mercifully vouchsafe me a testimonial permitting me the exercise of that profession. All the more so, most gracious lord, as I shall endeavor must dutifully, in all other respects as well—I repeat, in all respects—to do and to teach exactly what is desired of me, for my own good and that of my fellow men . . . I am, most gracious etc. . . . Your most humble and obedient servant . . . Postscript: Furthermore I promise always to teach the martydom of our Hero-King without omissions."

HASTY   Is it still storming?

WENCESLAS   No.

HASTY   No.

WENCESLAS   Everything's covered with snow.

HASTY   Safely tucked away.

WENCESLAS   Great-hearted sufferer, any teaching position, I assure you, any teaching position in the district is open to you.

ACT FIVE

15

Halle, winter.

Squint in slippers, smoking his pipe. Fritz in traveling habit.

SQUINT Let me quote what Immanuel Kant has to say: "Matrimony (matrimonium) is a contract between two persons providing for the lifelong use of each other's sexual organs." And here: "Hence, though based on the supposition of pleasure through the mutual use of the sexual attributes, that is to say, the sexual organs, the marriage contract is no arbitrary contract, but one made necessary by the laws of mankind, that is, if man and woman desire to derive pleasure from one another in accordance with their sexual attributes, they must of necessity marry, and this necessity follows from the laws prescribed by pure reason." You see.

FRITZ I thought you'd given up Kant.

SQUINT Only in public. How else could I have obtained a teaching position? And without a position, how could I have married my Caroline—you haven't met her yet, the dear. And as you see right here, I had to.

FRITZ So your favorite philosopher has proved to you that you had to give him up, and you've given him up by following his precepts. What a world!

SQUINT An antinomy, that's all. He could have resolved it in a twinkling.

FRITZ What was the subject of your thesis?

SQUINT I was clever, Berg. I left philosophy well alone. "War, Father of all Things"—still, I managed to slip in a suitably

obscure phrase implying that the paternity is not always de-
monstr . . .

FRITZ   Speaking of Caroline, what became of Miss Swandown?

SQUINT   She sank lower and lower.—Caroline is very different.
She was made for marriage. Incidentally, she's the rector's
daughter.

FRITZ   So the two of you live here beside the stove, happy.—Do
you ever see Buttress?

SQUINT   I find that I've rather cooled toward him, Berg. Now
that we're both schoolmasters. There's some good in him,
but . . . Caroline finds him attractive and I've forbidden her
to see him. Women have got to be kept in hand, Berg . . . How
was Italy?

FRITZ   Divine. It's made a man of me.

SQUINT   Half a year in Italy!—There's a father after Rousseau's
own heart.

FRITZ   I don't know, Squint. Sending me to Italy like that and
giving me that curious piece of advice, not to write to Gussie
—I was too excited about the trip to wonder why. Down
there, among the lemons and olives, I began to worry, but
consoled myself with the thought that he was putting our
love to the test. And then in Pompeii a sudden fear sent me
flying back—covering as much as eighty miles a day. Here in
Halle the same emotions made me interrupt my headlong
journey. It seemed to me that perhaps I had better not return
too quickly to my beloved Insterburg. And here I find this
letter, I'm afraid to open it. My hand shakes every time I try
to break the seal. You break it, brother, and read it to me.
(Throws himself into an easy chair)

SQUINT   Who is it from? Is it your father's hand?

FRITZ   No, it's from a certain Soapbubble. A neighbor.

SQUINT   (reads)   "In view of the friendship I have had the honor
of enjoying in your father's house—" (Stops) the fellow's
spelling is insane! (Reads on) "—I feel obliged, considering
that having long been out of communication with our delightful Insterburg you can hardly be aware of the incident
concerning the tutor who has been put out of your esteemed
uncle's house . . . (Stops)

FRITZ   Go on!

SQUINT   ". . . for ravishing your cousin, whereby her spirits were so shaken that she jumped into a pond, which calamity threw your family into the utmost . . ." *(Fritz faints)* Berg! What's the matter? *(Pours lavender water on him)* Berg, Berg, speak to me!—Damn letter, if only I hadn't . . . It must be a fabrication—Berg! Berg!

FRITZ   Leave me alone. It will pass.

SQUINT   Shall I get someone to bleed you?

FRITZ   Faugh! Don't be so French! Read it again.

SQUINT   Certainly not.—It's a disgusting, malicious letter, I'll . . . *(Tears it up)*

FRITZ   Ravished—drowned—*(Strikes his forehead)* My fault. All my fault.

SQUINT   You're out of your mind.—Is it your fault if she lets that tutor seduce her?

FRITZ   Squint, I swore to go back home for the holidays! And I went to Italy. Damn picturesqueness! She despaired of me. Grief. You know her melancholy bent. Loneliness, disappointed love. It's as plain as day: I'm a villain. I'm to blame for her death. *(Throws himself back into the chair and covers his face)*

SQUINT   Pure imagination!—It's not true, it wasn't like that at all. *(Stamps his foot)* 'Sblood! How can you be stupid enough to believe all this, she can't have been all that innocent. Women! We know what they are. They don't want it, but they do it. When they itch, they look for someone to scratch them.

FRITZ   I beg of you, Squint, she is no more.

SQUINT   Berg, look me in the eye and tell me women are not as I say.

(Caroline Squint comes in)

SQUINT   Here she is, my beloved wife. This is Berg, an old school friend.

CAROLINE   I've heard about you. You're a companion of Squint's rebellious youth.

SQUINT   Yes, indeed. Make him some coffee, he needs it. He's just had a terrible letter from home.

CAROLINE   Oh, it can't be so terrible that a good cup of coffee . . .

FRITZ Please, don't trouble. I must hurry home. My friends, my place is at a grave-side. *(Leaves)*

SQUINT Sad.—But it's no concern of ours. Come, Caroline, come and warm yourself by the stove.

16

Insterburg, Mrs. von Berg's parlor.

Mrs. von Berg, the major, Gussie, privy councillor, Leopold. A baby in a cradle.

PRIVY COUNCILLOR My dear sister-in-law, my dear brother, dear Gussie, dear Leopold! Let us drain a glass of grog in honor of St. Nicholas and the first snow that decks the streets so gloriously. But first it seems fitting to ask the servants in to share the hot spirits with us and admire the landscape so beautifully transformed.

GUSSIE I'll call them. *(Leaves)*

PRIVY COUNCILLOR Oh yes, there's a letter for you from Hasty, in which he proclaims his contrition and swears to change for the better. He encloses a medical certificate to the effect that he, with his own hands, has so corrected his God-given corpus as never again to be a menace to his female pupils.

MRS. VON BERG Disgusting!

PRIVY COUNCILLOR I agree, sister-in-law. And he asks you, dear Berg, in exchange for his certificate to give him a reference that will enable him to pursue his profession.

MAJOR *(laughs)* He ought to be all right now.

PRIVY COUNCILLOR Say what you will, he's a man of principle.

MAJOR A rare disciplinarian!

PRIVY COUNCILLOR A true pedagogue, by the grace of God.

MAJOR He shall have his reference.

PRIVY COUNCILLOR Thou shalt not muzzle the ox—ha, ha, ha, the ox—when he treadeth out the corn. *(They laugh uproariously)*

MRS. VON BERG   Disgusting!—

(*Maid comes hurrying in*)

MAID   Sir! Madame! The young master. (*She sobs*)

MAJOR   Which young master?

MAID   Master Fritz!

PRIVY COUNCILLOR   Fritz back from Italy?

MAID   He's downstairs. What a thing to happen! They'll put it in the gazette. He comes in in his traveling clothes. He sees Miss Gussie. Stares at her like she's a ghost. Cries out: "Gussie, you're not dead? My own Gussie, not dead?" She's in his arms. "Oh Fritz, you've come?" And all is love. But then: "Poor me, don't touch me, I'm your Gussie no longer." And he, you should have heard his voice . . . "Oh yes, you are!"— and she: "No, you don't know." And him so loud they could hear him in the kitchen: "I know all about it, and all I want is—to beg your forgiveness. My Gussie!" Oh, here they come.

MRS. VON BERG   Gussie and Fritz?

MAJOR   'Ods bodkins!

(*Fritz and Gussie enter*)

FRITZ   Father! And my second parents! I'll fight for my Gussie to the last drop of blood.

MAJOR   You mean you want to marry her? In spite of everything?

FRITZ   In spite? No, not in spite, because of. Let me tell you, Gussie, how a strange experience in Halle opened my eyes to the glory and weakness of your sex. A young lady, to make a long story short, was in love, passionately in love, with a splendid fellow, conscientious, devoted to philosophy, though perhaps somewhat unworldly. Nevertheless—perhaps, my friends, I should say for that very reason—she gave herself to a man of far less consequence. But while in his arms she never for one moment—she told me so herself—thought of anyone but the man she truly loved. Yes, dear father, you may not understand it but I do, and now more than ever; in reality, in spirit, she gave herself to her true beloved. Nothing, my friends, would have happened to Gussie, if oddly enough because of my involvement in this very affair, I hadn't stayed away during the holidays.

PRIVY COUNCILLOR   Or if a certain young scoundrel had been given a horse.

GUSSIE   Oh, Fritz, that's how it was, just like that.

FRITZ   Papa, I thought she was a ghost when I saw her on the stairs. But she's real.

PRIVY COUNCILLOR   Always stick to reality—isn't that what I've always taught you?—unless it contradicts the inner image.

MAJOR   Come! *(Takes Fritz to the sofa)* Are you a philosopher?

MRS. VON BERG *(referring to the baby)*   Do you recognize this?

PRIVY COUNCILLOR   My son, having justified the cause, you must not shrink back from the effect. Having climbed a tall tree, will you climb down again to retrieve your hat that has blown away? What have you studied logic for?

FRITZ *(kisses the baby and hands it to Gussie)*   Now the child is mine too. I love it already. It has your angelic features.

GUSSIE   Fritz!

PRIVY COUNCILLOR   You're right!

MRS. VON BERG   Oh dear!

(The servants appear)

MAJOR   Don't gape, you people, don't gossip, don't judge. Join a happy father in a drink. To the young couple!

LEOPOLD   And to the little one!

MRS. VON BERG   Leopold!

PRIVY COUNCILLOR   And to the first snow!

MRS. VON BERG   Berg, I suspect you would like me to contribute something in the popular vein. *(She sings at the spinet while all others drink)*

Oh silent winter snow
That cloaks the earth below.
Men sit and idly gaze
Upon the snow-clad days.
And in the barn the silent cows
Hark to the silence as they drowse.

17

Village schoolhouse.

Wenceslas, Hasty, both dressed in black. Lisa.

WENCESLAS   What did you think of my sermon, colleague? Did you find it edifying?

HASTY   Oh yes. Yes indeed. *(Sighs)*

WENCESLAS *(takes off his wig and puts on a nightcap)* That won't do.—Tell me what part of it your heart most favored. Listen to me—sit down—I have something to say to you: in church just now I saw something that troubled me. Your gaze as you sat there was so shifty that, to tell you the truth, I felt ashamed of you in the eyes of the congregation. Several times I nearly lost the thread of my discourse. I said to myself: Is this the young warrior who fought so bravely and triumphed, as it were, in the hardest of battles?—And I must confess, you made me angry. I saw the direction of your thoughts, I saw it only too clearly. Toward the center door, down by the organ. Did you for one moment hear what I was saying? Can you repeat one word of my sermon? It was all for your benefit, you know, designed to fit your particular case.—Oh, oh, oh!

HASTY   I was delighted with your idea that the rebirth of our souls can be likened to the raising of flax and hemp, and that just as hemp must be freed of its husks by vigorous beating, so our spirits must be prepared for heaven by suffering, hardship, and the eradication of all sensuality.

WENCESLAS   It was designed to fit your case, my friend.

HASTY   However, I can't deny that your list of the devils expelled from heaven and the whole story about the revolt and about Lucifer regarding himself as the most beautiful strikes me as sheer superstition—our age has outgrown all that!

WENCESLAS That's why this rational world of ours will go to the devil. Take the devil away from the peasant and he'll turn against his master like a devil, so proving that devils exist. But enough of that—what was I saying? Yes. Just tell me, whom were you looking at all through my sermon? Don't deny it. You certainly were not looking at me, or you'd have had to squint disgracefully.

HASTY I don't know what you mean.

WENCESLAS You were looking down toward the girls who get their catechism from you.—My dear friend, can a pinch of the old Adam have lingered in your heart? I ask you—the very thought makes my hair stand on end—what will become of you if you yield to the old evil promptings when you lack the means of satisfying them? *(Embraces him)* I beg you, my dear son, by these tears that I'm shedding out of the most heartfelt concern for you: Don't go back to the fleshpots of Egypt when you have come so close to Canaan! How can you keep leering at my ward as if you were dying of thirst? As if she would content herself with a capon.

(Lisa steps forward)

LISA Oh yes, dear godfather, I'm perfectly content with him.

HASTY Woe is me!

LISA Believe me, dear godfather, I shall never let him go.

WENCESLAS Oh.—The devil—Lisa, you don't understand—Lisa, I can't tell you why, but you can't marry him, it's impossible.

LISA Why is it impossible, dear godfather? You always said I might marry a clergyman some day.

WENCESLAS The devil take you, he can't—God forgive me my sins, can't you take my word for it?

HASTY Maybe that's not what she's asking for.—Lisa, I cannot sleep with you.

LISA But you can wake with me. If only we can be together in the daytime and smile at each other and kiss each other's hands now and then, because, by God, I'm fond of you. God knows, I'm fond of you.

HASTY You see, Master Wenceslas! All she wants of me is love. Does a happy marriage really require the satisfaction of animal lusts?

WENCESLAS   Heaven help us.—Be fruitful and multiply, says the Good Book. Where there is marriage there must be children.

LISA   No, dear godfather. I swear that I want no children as long as I live. You've got plenty of ducks and chickens for me to feed every day: must I feed children too?

HASTY *(kisses her)*   My divine Lisa!

WENCESLAS *(pries them apart)*   I declare! What's this? Before my very eyes?—All right, go ahead, crawl into bed, it's better to marry than to burn.—But, Mr. Midge, it's all over between you and me. The high hopes I set in you as a paragon without compare—the expectations aroused by your heroism—merciful heavens! To me you're just another hybrid, neither fish nor flesh. *(Goes out)*

HASTY   And I feel sure their lordships at Insterburg will help me—in my present state—to find a good position that will enable me to support my wife.

Epilogue

Spoken by the actor who played the tutor.

That's the conclusion of our play
We hope it's brought you some dismay.
You've seen the sorry state of mind
To which the Germans were resigned
A hundred years and even ten years ago—
It still prevails in many parts, you know.
You've seen a tutor of the German school
Led to his calvary of ridicule—
Poor devil whom they so browbeat
He can't distinguish hands from feet.
Enacting a parable bigger than life
He finally has recourse to the knife
Exterminating his virility
Which only brought him misery.
For when he did as nature meant
The higher-ups were not content
And when he crawled as best he could
They cut down on his livelihood.
His sterling value they proclaimed
Only when he was cut and maimed.
His backbone broken, he would do
His duty by breaking his pupils' too.
The German schoolmaster, if one reflects
Is the product and origin of our defects.
Pupils and teachers of this century:
Consider his servility
And let it teach you to be free.

Coriolanus

by Shakespeare

Adaptation

Translator: Ralph Manheim

CHARACTERS

CAIUS MARCIUS, later called
  CORIOLANUS, a Roman
  general
VOLUMNIA, his mother
VIRGILIA, his wife
YOUNG MARCIUS, his son
MENENIUS AGRIPPA, his friend
COMINIUS, TITUS LARTIUS,
  generals against the
  Volscians

SICINIUS VELUTUS, JUNIUS
  BRUTUS, tribunes of the
  people
VALERIA, friend of Virgilia
VIRGILIA'S SERVANT
THE MAN WITH THE CHILD
TULLUS AUFIDIUS, general of the
  Volscians
ONE OF AUFIDIUS' CAPTAINS

ROMANS AND VOLSCIANS: (SENATORS, CON-
SULS, AEDILES, PATRICIANS, CITIZENS—
PLEBEIANS—OFFICERS, SOLDIERS, A HER-
ALD, ATTENDANTS, SERVANTS, MESSEN-
GERS)

ACT ONE

1

Rome. A public square.

Enter a group of rebellious citizens to whom clubs, knives, and other weapons are distributed; among them a man with a child; the man is carrying a large bundle.

FIRST CITIZEN Before we go any further, let me speak.

CITIZENS Speak, but be brief.

FIRST CITIZEN Are all of you resolved to die rather than starve?

CITIZENS Resolved. Resolved.

FIRST CITIZEN Are you prepared to stand fast until the senate agrees that it's us citizens who decide the price of bread?

CITIZENS Yes. Yes.

FIRST CITIZEN And the price of olives?

CITIZENS Yes.

FIRST CITIZEN Caius Marcius will meet us with force of arms. Will you run away or will you fight?

CITIZENS We'll knock him dead.—He's the people's main enemy. No need to ask us that.

FIRST CITIZEN Because if you're not prepared to see this thing through, you can count me out. Why have you brought that sack? And the child?

THE MAN WITH THE CHILD I want to see how far you get. If you fail, I'm going to leave Rome with those people from the third district.

FIRST CITIZEN Regardless of the fact that the plain where they're going to settle is as arid as stone?

THE MAN WITH THE CHILD Regardless. We'll have water, fresh
air and a grave. What more is there for us plebeians in Rome?
At least we won't have to fight rich men's wars. *(To the child)*
Will you be good, Tertius, if there's no goat's milk for you?
(The child nods)

FIRST CITIZEN You see, that's the kind of people we've got. He
fears Caius Marcius more than the wilds of the Allegi Mountains. Aren't you a Roman citizen?

THE MAN WITH THE CHILD Yes, but a poor one. They call us
plebeians the poor citizens, but they call the patricians the
good ones. The unnecessary food the good citizens stuff into
their bellies could save us from starvation. Even if they gave
us their leftovers, we'd be saved. But they don't even think
that much of us. Their food tastes better when they see us
starving. *(To the child)* Tertius, tell him you don't want to be
a citizen of such a city.
(The child shakes his head)

FIRST CITIZEN Then make off quickly, you cowardly dog, but
leave the child here; we'll fight and make a better Rome for
Tertius.

CITIZENS What's that shouting?—The sixth district has risen.
—And we hang around here, squabbling among ourselves.
To the Capitol! Who's this?
(Enter Menenius Agrippa)

FIRST CITIZEN It's Menenius Agrippa, the senator and silver-
tongued orator.

CITIZENS Not the worst of them.—He has a weakness for the
people.

MENENIUS
My dear fellow citizens, what's this? Where are you going
With bats and clubs? What's wrong, I pray you?

FIRST CITIZEN Our business is not unknown to the senate.
They've been hearing rumors of it for a fortnight. Your Caius
Marcius says our smell takes his breath away. He says poor
pleaders have strong breaths; he'll see that we have strong
fists too.

MENENIUS
Citizens, my good friends and honest neighbors
Are you determined to destroy yourselves?

FIRST CITIZEN We can't do that, sir. We're destroyed already.

MENENIUS

I tell you, friends, the senate has for you
Most charitable care. For your grievances—
The rising cost of food—you may as well
Strike at the heavens with your staves as lift them
Against the senate; you see, the soaring prices
Come from the gods and not from man. Alas
Your misery is driving you to greater
Misery. You remind me of a babe that
Bites at the empty breast of its unhappy
Mother. You curse the senate as an enemy
And yet it cares for you.

FIRST CITIZEN Cares for us! A likely story! They've never cared
for us. Leave us to starve when their storehouses are crammed
full of grain. Issue decrees against usury that benefit no one
but the usurers! Every day they repeal another good law
against the rich and every day they grind out another cruel
regulation to chain the poor. If the wars don't eat us up, they
will. That's all the love they bear us.

MENENIUS

Either you must
Confess yourselves wondrous malicious
Or be accused of folly. I shall tell you
A pretty tale. It may be you have heard it
But it's appropriate. Well, will you listen?

FIRST CITIZEN It's hardly a time for stories. But I for my part
have long wished to learn how to make a pretty speech. And
that can be learned from you, Agrippa. Fire away!

MENENIUS

There was a time when all the body's members
Rebelled against the belly, thus accused it:
That only like a gulf it did remain
In the midst of the body, idle and inactive
Yet storing up the victuals, never bearing
Equal labor with the rest, whereas the other organs
Did see and hear, devise, instruct, walk, feel
And, mutually participating, minister

Unto the appetite and affection common
To the whole body. The belly answered . . .

FIRST CITIZEN

Well, sir, what was the belly's answer?

MENENIUS

Sir, I shall tell you. With a kind of smile
That came not from the heart, a dismal smile—
For you see, I can make the belly smile
As well as speak—it tauntingly replied
To the discontented members, the mutinous parts
That envied its receipts . . .

FIRST CITIZEN

What did he say?
The lazy belly, sink and cesspit of
The body? What did he say?

MENENIUS

What? No—how!
That is the crux of the matter.

FIRST CITIZEN

No, tell us what your gluttonous belly said.
What could he say?

MENENIUS

You soon shall hear.

FIRST CITIZEN

With you "soon" means "tomorrow."

MENENIUS

Your most grave belly was deliberate
Not rash like his accusers, and thus answered:
"It is true, my incorporate friends," he said
"That I am the first to receive the general food
You live upon, and this is necessary
Because I am the storehouse and the shop
Of the whole body. But if you will remember
I send it through the rivers of your blood
And through the corridors and pantries of the body.
The strongest sinews and the finest veins
From me receive their proper sustenance.
And though, my friends, you may not all at once"—
This is the belly speaking, mind you . . .

FIRST CITIZEN
  Stop, sir.

MENENIUS
          "Though you may not see all at once
  What I deliver out to each of you
  Still, my account books show that I
  Distribute to you all the finest flour
  Retaining only the bran." Well then, what do
  You say to that?
  (Enter, unnoticed except by Menenius, Caius Marcius escorted by armed men)

FIRST CITIZEN
  An answer of sorts. But now the moral?

MENENIUS
  The senators of Rome are this good belly.
  You are the mutinous members. Think!
  That's all you have to do. Think, think, think, think!
  Then you will fathom how the worthy fathers
  Intent upon the common weal, distribute
  The public bounty to each citizen.
  Whatever you receive is given you
  By them alone. Well, what do you think now?
  You, the great toe of this assembly?

FIRST CITIZEN
  I the great toe? Why the great toe?

MENENIUS
  Because you, the lowest, basest, poorest
  Of all this rabble, take the lead.
  You scoundrel, you infectious rotten apple, you
  Self-seeking bandit—very well, swing your clubs!
  Rome will make war upon its rats. Once and
  For all it will . . . Hail, noble Marcius!

MARCIUS
  Thanks. What's the matter? Got the itch again?
  Scratching your old scabs?

FIRST CITIZEN
                          From you we can
  Always expect a gracious word.

MARCIUS
                              You curs
That like nor peace nor war. War frightens you
Peace makes you insolent. Anyone who trusts you
Finds hares when he wants lions, geese when he looks
For foxes. You hate the great because they are great.
To depend upon you is to swim with fins
Of lead and hew down oaks with rushes. Hanging's
The only hope! You've got the appetite
Of a sick man who devours what makes him sicker.
You curse the senate who with the help of the gods
Maintain some little order. If they didn't
You'd feed upon each other.

MENENIUS
                              They're demanding
The right to set the price of grain. They say
The granaries are overflowing.

MARCIUS
                              They say! Hang 'em!
They sit by the fire and presume to know
What's happening on the Capitol, what there is
And what there isn't. Waste grain on them!
If only the senate dropped its moderation
For which I have a very different name—
They say there's grain!—they'd get their answer
From my sword. And with my lance I'd measure
Not grain but their corpses by the bushel
In the streets of Rome.

MENENIUS
Let be. I've won these fellows over, stopped them
With a fairy tale. Though to be sure, it was not
The sword of my voice but rather the voice of your sword
That toppled them. But what of the other troop?

MARCIUS
Dissolved. I broke it up. Hang 'em! Damnation!
They shouted they were hungry, bellowed slogans
That hunger breaks stone walls, that dogs must eat
That bread is made for mouths, that the gods don't send
Fruit for the rich alone. And more such nonsense.

And when I fell upon them, while retreating
They shouted: "Then we'll emigrate." And I
Wished them a pleasant journey.
(A messenger enters)

MESSENGER   Where's Caius Marcius?

MARCIUS
Here. What's the matter?
(The messenger whispers in his ear)

MARCIUS
                Menenius, in the forum
They're tossing up their caps into the air
As if they wished to hang them on the moon:
The senate has allowed them their demand.

MENENIUS
Allowed them what?

MARCIUS
             Two tribunes
To represent the wisdom of the rabble.
The one is Junius Brutus, then Sicinius
And heaven knows who else. I'd sooner
Have seen the rabble tear the city's roofs off
Than granted that. They'll be
More insolent than ever. Soon they'll threaten
Revolt for every pound of olives.

MENENIUS
                It is strange.
(A citizen comes running)

SECOND CITIZEN   Long live Junius Brutus! The senate has
   granted all our demands! Two tribunes appointed! With the
   right to attend all sessions and veto decisions!

CITIZENS
Hurrah for Junius Brutus!

SECOND CITIZEN
            And Sicinius Velutus!

MARCIUS
Go home, you fragments!

MENENIUS
        The worthy fathers!

MARCIUS

And the newly baked
Tribunes are coming too. With faces
Such as you'd cut down from the gallows!
(Enter Cominius, Titus Lartius and other senators, Brutus, and Sicinius)

CITIZENS

Long live Sicinius!—And Junius Brutus!

MARCIUS

Most worthy fathers, I've heard ugly news
And I see an ugly sight . . .

FIRST SENATOR

Noble Marcius
The Volscians are in arms, encouraged by
Reports of shortage and rebellion here.

COMINIUS

War!

MARCIUS

I'm glad to hear it.
That ought to help us here in Rome
To use our surplus that is growing moldy.

FIRST SENATOR

Tullus Aufidius is leading them.

MARCIUS

I know him.

COMENIUS

You've fought together.

MARCIUS

An enemy like him
Makes the whole war worth fighting.

FIRST SENATOR

You will fight under Cominius.

COMINIUS

As you once promised.

MARCIUS

Agreed. And Titus, what of you?
Stiff in the joints? Will you stay home?

LARTIUS

Never, Marcius.

I'll lean upon one crutch and fight with the other
Before I miss this business.

FIRST SENATOR

     To the Capitol!

LARTIUS

 Lead on, Cominius.

COMINIUS

    After you.

LARTIUS

      You first.

MARCIUS

 After you.

FIRST SENATOR

   Citizens, go home.

MARCIUS

     No, let them follow.
The Volscians have much grain; take these rats with you
To gnaw their garners. Worshipful mutineers
Your courage can now prove itself. Do follow!
(All go out except for the tribunes and citizens)

BRUTUS

 Follow him, friends. Inscribe your names in the lists!
Be valiant soldiers for a better Rome.
As for the struggle waged within its walls
Over grain, olives, and the remission of debt
We will keep watch while you are in the field.

CITIZENS

 The Volscians are in arms!—War!
(The citizens go out)

BRUTUS

 We'll have to. Did you see Marcius' eye
When we, the tribunes of the people, approached him?

SICINIUS

 I heard him speak. A man like him's a greater
Danger to Rome than to the Volscians.

BRUTUS

 I don't believe that. The valor of his arm
Outweighs his vices and makes good their harm.
(Both go out)

<h1 style="text-align:center">2</h1>

Rome. The house of Caius Marcius.

Volumnia and Virgilia are standing on the balcony looking after the departing soldiers. Martial music.

VOLUMNIA   If my son were my husband, I should rejoice more in an absence that won him honor than in the fondest embraces of his bed. When he was still tender of body, the only son of my womb, when the comeliness of his youth attracted every eye, when a king might have entreated me all day before I'd have let him out of my sight for an hour, I bade him seek danger where he was likely to find fame. I sent him to a cruel war. He came back crowned with oak leaves. I tell you, daughter, I didn't leap more for joy at first hearing he was a man-child than on the day when he first proved himself to be a man.

VIRGILIA   But if he had died in the battle, madam, what then?

VOLUMNIA   I tell you sincerely that if I had a dozen sons, none less dear to me than your Marcius and mine, I would rather see eleven die on the battlefield than one wallow in peace.

VIRGILIA   Heaven protect my husband from Aufidius.

(Enter a serving woman)

VOLUMNIA

Virgilia, I seem to hear your husband's drum.
I see him slaughter this Aufidius and go
His way like a reaper after a day's work.
Upon his neck, as it says in the *Iliad*
He sets his bloody foot.

VIRGILIA

                 Oh no, no blood!

SERVING WOMAN   Valeria.

(Enter Valeria. The servant woman goes out)

VALERIA   How is your little son?

VIRGILIA   Thank you, my dear; he is well, my dear.

VOLUMNIA   He would rather look at swords and hear a drum than listen to his teacher.

VALERIA   Every inch his father. A darling child. On Wednesday I watched him for half an hour on end. What a resolute little boy! I saw him run after a gilded butterfly. And when he caught it, he let it go again. And over and over again he caught it and let it go. Then he fell down. And perhaps because his fall made him angry, or something else, he suddenly set his teeth and tore it apart. My word, he tore it into little pieces!

VOLUMNIA   One of his father's rages!

VIRGILIA   A lively lad, madam.

VALERIA   You must play grass widow with me this afternoon.

VIRGILIA   No, my dear. I have no wish to go out.

VALERIA   No wish to go out?

VOLUMNIA   She shall. She shall.

VIRGILIA   No, by your leave, I won't set foot over the threshold until my lord returns from the wars.

VALERIA   Faugh! It's not reasonable to shut yourself up like that. She wants to be another Penelope. But they say all the yarn she spun in Ulysses' absence only filled Ithaca with moths. Leave her alone; in her present mood she would only spoil a pleasant evening.

(All go out)

3*

a)

Before Corioli.

Enter with drums and banners Marcius, Titus Lartius, captains, and soldiers. To them a messenger.

MARCIUS
A messenger. I wager they have met.

LARTIUS
My horse to yours they haven't.

MARCIUS
                              Done.

LARTIUS
                                        Agreed.

MARCIUS
Say, has our general met the enemy?

MESSENGER
They are in view, but haven't spoken yet.

LARTIUS
Then the good horse is mine.

MARCIUS
                              I'll buy him from you.

LARTIUS
No, I won't sell or give him, I'll lend him to you
For fifty years.—Call on the city to yield.

*For scene 3, Act One of his adaptation Brecht intended to combine Shake-speare's scenes 4–10 into a big battle scene. He planned to write this new scene 3 in the course of production because he thought it necessary to study the positions and movements of the actors in rehearsal. He did not live to do this work. Consequently Shakespeare's scenes 4 to 10 are given here in Dorothea Tieck's translation as scenes 3 a–g. (Note to German edition.)

    In the English of these scenes Shakespeare's text is somewhat modified to accord with the style employed in the translation of the rest of the play. (R.M.)

MARCIUS

How far away are the armies?

LARTIUS

Less than a mile and a half.

MARCIUS

Then we shall hear their trumpets, and they ours.
Now Mars, I pray you, help us to work quickly
And then with smoking swords we shall march off
To aid our embattled friends! Come, blow your blast!
(They sound a parley. Enter two senators, with others on the walls)
Tullus Aufidius, is he within your walls?

FIRST SENATOR

No, nor any man who fears you less than he,
Which is less than little. *(Drum afar off)* Hear that!

Our drums
Are calling out our youth. We'll break the walls
Rather than let them close us in. Our gates
Which still seem shut, are only pinned with rushes;
They'll open of themselves. *(Alarum far off)* Listen out there.
That is Aufidius. Hear what he is doing
To your divided army.

MARCIUS

Ha, they're at it!

LARTIUS

Their noise will keep us informed. Ladders, ho!

MARCIUS

They're not afraid. They're coming out to meet us.
Now put your shields before your hearts and fight
With hearts more staunch than shields. Advance, brave Titus!
I never expected to see them despise us so;
It makes me sweat with rage. Come on, men. If
Any of you retreat, I'll take him for a Volscian,
And he shall feel my sword.
(Alarum. The Romans are beaten back to their trenches. Re-enter Marcius, cursing)

MARCIUS

All the contagion of the south light on you,
You shame of Rome! You herd of . . . ! Boils and plagues

Plaster you over till you can be smelled
Further than seen, and one infect another
Against the wind a mile! You souls of geese,
That bear the shapes of men, how can you run
From slaves that apes could beat! Pluto and hell!
Wounded behind! Backs red and faces pale
With flight and palsied fear! Turn back and charge,
Or, by the fires of heaven, I'll leave the foe
And make my war on you. Look to it; come on!
If you'll stand fast, we'll beat them to their wives
As they have beaten us to our trenches.
(Another alarum. The Volscians fly, and Marcius follows them to the gates)
The gates are open; now show yourselves good soldiers.
Fortune has widened them for the pursuers,
Not for the fugitives. Watch me, and follow.
(He enters the gate)

FIRST SOLDIER
The man's insane; not I.

SECOND SOLDIER
                        Nor I. *(Marcius is shut in)*

FIRST SOLDIER
Look, they have shut him in. *(Alarum continues)*

ALL
That's the end of him, I warrant.
(Re-enter Titus Lartius)

LARTIUS   What has become of Marcius?

ALL
                                Killed, sir, doubtless.

FIRST SOLDIER
Pursuing the fugitives at their very heels,
With them he enters; whereupon they
Suddenly slam the gates. He's left alone
To fight the entire city.

LARTIUS
                    O noble soldier!
Who sensibly outdares his senseless sword,
And when it bends stands straight. You are lost, Marcius;
The purest diamond, as big as you are,

Would not be so rich a jewel. You were a soldier
After Cato's heart, not fierce and terrible
Only in blows; but with your grim looks and
The thunder-like percussion of your sounds,
You made your enemies shake, as if the world
Were feverish and trembling.
(Re-enter Marcius, bleeding, assailed by the enemy)

FIRST SOLDIER

                    Look, sir.

LARTIUS

                            O, it's Marcius!
Let's carry him off, or stay and die with him.
(They fight and all enter the city)

b)

Corioli. A street.

Enter certain Romans with loot.

FIRST ROMAN   I'll carry this to Rome.
SECOND ROMAN   And I this.
THIRD ROMAN   A plague on it! I took this for silver.
   (They go out. Alarum continues still far off)
   (Enter Marcius and Titus Lartius with a trumpeter)

MARCIUS

Look at these thieves whose hours are no more worth to them
Than a cracked drachma! Cushions, leaden spoons,
Halfpenny irons, doublets that the hangman would
Bury with those that wore them, these base slaves
Pack up before the fight is done. Cut them down!
But listen to the general's battle cry!
And there's the man I hate, Aufidius,
Piercing our Romans; therefore, brave Titus, take
What numbers you may need to hold the city;
While I, with those who have the spirit, will hurry
To help Cominius.

LARTIUS

                    Worthy sir, you're bleeding.
Your exercise has been too violent
To let you fight again.

MARCIUS

                    Sir, do not praise me,
My work has not yet warmed me; fare you well,
The blood I drop is far more curative
Than dangerous to me. Now I'll go
To fight Aufidius.

LARTIUS

                    May the fair goddess Fortune
Fall deep in love with you, and her great charms
Misguide your opponents' swords! Brave Marcius, may
Prosperity attend you.

MARCIUS

                    And be your friend no less
Than those she places highest. So, farewell.
(Marcius goes out)

LARTIUS

O worthiest Marcius!
Go, sound your trumpet in the marketplace
And summon all the officials of the town:
There they shall know our mind.

c)

Near the camp of Cominius.

Enter Cominius, as though in retreat, with soldiers.

COMINIUS

Rest awhile, friends. Well fought. We have come off
Like Romans, neither foolhardy in our standing
Nor cowardly in retreat. Believe me, sirs,
We'll be attacked again. While we were fighting,
At intervals, borne by the wind, we heard

The battle cry of our friends. O Roman gods!
Lead them to victory and ourselves as well
That both our armies may meet with smiling faces
And give you thankful sacrifice.
(Enter a messenger)

COMINIUS

                        Your news?

MESSENGER

The citizens of Corioli have sallied
And given battle to Marcius and Titus;
I saw our party driven to their trenches,
And then I came away.

COMINIUS

                The truth perhaps
But most unwelcome. How long ago was that?

MESSENGER

More than an hour, my lord.

COMINIUS

It's not a mile; we heard their drums a moment.
How could you take an hour to cover a mile
And bring your news so late?

MESSENGER

                      Volscian scouts
Pursued me, forcing me to make
A three or four mile circuit. Otherwise
I would have been here half an hour since.
(Enter Marcius)

COMINIUS

                        Who's that,
Looking as if they'd flayed him? Gods above!
He has the stamp of Marcius, and I've seen
Him looking thus before.

MARCIUS

                Am I too late?

COMINIUS

A shepherd would sooner take thunder for a tabor
Than I mistake the sound of Marcius' voice
For that of any lesser man.

MARCIUS

Am I too late?

COMINIUS

Yes, if you come not in the blood of others
But mantled in your own.

MARCIUS

O, let me clasp you
In arms as sound as when I wooed, in heart
As merry as when our wedding day was done
And tapers burned to bedward.

COMINIUS

Flower of warriors,
How is it with Titus Lartius?

MARCIUS

As with a man who's busy with decrees:
Condemning some to death and some to exile;
Mercifully ransoming one, threatening another;
Holding Corioli in the name of Rome,
As one holds a fawning greyhound in the leash,
To let him slip at will.

COMINIUS

Where is that slave
Who told me that he beat you to your trenches?
Where is he? Call him.

MARCIUS

Let him alone.
He told the truth. But for our gentlemen,
The rank-and-file—a plague! Tribunes for them?
A mouse never fled from a cat as those knaves ran
From rascals worse than they.

COMINIUS

But how did you come through?

CORIOLANUS

Is this a time for telling? I think not.
Where is the enemy? Are you lords of the field?
If not, why stop until you are so?

COMINIUS

Marcius,
We've fought at a disadvantage. We retired
To win our purpose.

MARCIUS
  What is their battle order? Do you know
  On which side they have placed their trusted men?
COMINIUS
  In the vanguard, Marcius, I believe they've placed
  The Antiates, their best troops, led by Aufidius,
  Their very heart of hope.
MARCIUS
                      Then I beseech you,
  By all the battles you and I have fought,
  By the blood we've shed together, by the vows
  Of friendship we have made, that you directly
  Set me against Aufidius and his Antiates.
  Delay no longer, but let us,
  Filling the air with clashing swords and darts,
  Attempt our chance at once.
COMINIUS
                          Although I wish
  You might be taken to a gentle bath
  And balms applied to you, I would never dare
  Refuse your asking. Take your pick of those
  Who best can aid your action.
MARCIUS
  Those are the most willing. If any such be here—
  It would be a sin to doubt it—who love this paint
  You see me smeared with; if any of you fear
  Harm to his person less than ignominy;
  If any think brave death outweighs bad life,
  And that his country's worth more than himself;
  Let him alone, or all that are so minded,
  Wave thus to express his disposition,
  And follow Marcius.
  *(They all shout and wave their swords, take him up in their arms and
  throw up their caps)*
  O, me alone! Come, make a sword of me!
  If this is not an outward show, which of you
  Isn't equal to four Volscians? Each of you
  Is able to oppose to the great Aufidius
  A shield as hard as his. I thank you all,
  Yet I must choose a certain number from

Your ranks; the rest will fight another time
As occasion may require! forward, friends!
And four of you, whichever prove the fittest
Shall be my captains.

COMINIUS

                                        March off, men,
Make good your boast, and all of you
Shall share with us alike.
    (*They go out*)

---

d)

The gates of Corioli.

Titus Lartius, having set a guard upon Corioli, going with drum and trumpet toward Cominius and Caius Marcius, enters with a lieutenant, other soldiers, and a scout.

LARTIUS

So, let the gates be guarded; do your duties
As I have ordered. If I send word, dispatch
Those companies to our aid; the rest will serve
To hold here briefly. If we lose the field,
We cannot keep the city.

LIEUTENANT

                                        You can trust me.

LARTIUS

Go then! And shut the gates behind us.
Come, guide; and lead us to the Roman camp.
    (*They go out*)

e)

A battlefield.

Battle cries. Enter Marcius and Aufidius from different directions.

MARCIUS

    I will fight none but you, for I hate you
    Worse than a perjuror.

AUFIDIUS

                 We hate alike.
    Africa has no serpent I abhor
    More than your envied fame. Stand fast.

MARCIUS

    Let the first to yield ground die the other's slave,
    And the gods doom him after!

AUFIDIUS

              If I run, Marcius,
    Hunt me down like a hare.

MARCIUS

              Within these three hours, Tullus,
    I fought alone within your Corioli's walls,
    And struck what blows I pleased. It's not my blood
    You see me masked in; for your revenge
    Screw up your power to the utmost.

AUFIDIUS

              If you were Hector,
    Champion of your boasted ancestors,
    You'd not escape me here.
    (They fight. Some Volscians come to the help of Aufidius)
    Zealous but not valiant, you have shamed me
    With your detested succor.
    (They go out)

f)

The Roman camp near Corioli.

*Flourish. Alarum. A retreat is sounded. Enter from one side Cominius
with the Romans; from the other side, Marcius with his arm in a sling.*

COMINIUS

    If I should tell you about this day's work,
    You'd not believe your deeds; but I'll report it
    Where senators will mingle tears with smiles,

Where great patricians hearing it will shrug,
But then be struck with wonder; where ladies thrilled
With fright will ask for more; where the dull tribunes,
Who like the stinking plebs abhor your honors,
Will say despite themselves: "We thank the gods
That Rome has such a soldier."
But you have barely come for the end of this feast,
Having fully dined before.
(Enter Titus Lartius with his men)

LARTIUS
                    O general,
Here is the steed, we the caparison.
If you had seen . . .

MARCIUS
                    Come, come. No more. My mother,
Who is entitled to extol her blood,
Annoys me with her praises. I have done
What you have done, to wit, my best; induced
As you have been by love of country.
Anyone who has done his utmost
Has done as well as I.

COMINIUS
                    You shall not
Stifle your glory; Rome must know
The value of her own. It would be concealment
Worse than a theft, no less than a betrayal,
To hide your doings, and to silence what,
If carried to the pinnacle of praise,
Would still seem slighted; therefore, I beseech you—
In token of what you are, not to reward
What you have done—let me address the army.

MARCIUS
I have some wounds upon me, and they smart
To hear themselves remembered.

COMINIUS
                    Should they not,
Well might they fester with ingratitude
And plague themselves to death. Of all the horses
We've taken, and we've taken good ones, of all

The treasure captured in the fields and city,
We render you the tenth, to be selected
Before the general distribution, at
Your choice alone.

MARCIUS

               I thank you, general, but
I cannot make my heart consent to take
A bribe to pay my sword. I must refuse it,
I'd rather take an equal share with those
Who only looked upon the doings.
(*A long flourish. All cry: "Marcius! Marcius!" and throw up their
caps and lances. Cominius and Lartius stand bareheaded*)
Let these same instruments which you profane
Never sound again! If drums and trumpets
Are flatterers in the field of war
Then courts and cities are but lies and sham.
When steel grows soft as the parasite's silk,
Let it no longer serve as a warrior's shield.
No more, I say! Because I have not washed
My nose that bled, or downed some feeble wretch—
As many others here have done unnoticed—
You glorify me with fulsome acclamations,
As if I wished to feed my humble person
On praises spiced with lies.

COMINIUS

               You are too modest,
More cruel to your just repute than grateful
To us who represent you truly. By your leave,
If you are angry at yourself, we'll put you
Like one intent upon his harm, in manacles,
So we can speak with you more safely. Be it known
To all the world as it is to us that Caius Marcius
Has won the laurels of this war, in token of which,
My noble steed, known to the camp, I give him,
With full equipment. And from this time on,
For what he did before Corioli, call him,
With all the applause and clamor of the army,
Caius Marcius Coriolanus! Bear

Your new name forever nobly!
(*Flourish. Trumpets sound, and drums*)

ALL

Caius Marcius Coriolanus!

CORIOLANUS

       Now I'll go wash;
And when my face is clean, you'll see
Whether I blush or not. However, thank you;
I mean to ride your horse, and at all times
Show myself worthy of my new name
As best I'm able.

COMINIUS

      Come to our tent
Where, before lying down to rest, we'll write
To Rome of our success. You, Titus Lartius,
Return to Corioli. Send their leaders
To us in Rome, that we may draw up articles
Of peace, for their own good and ours.

LARTIUS

I will, my lord.

CORIOLANUS

The gods begin to mock me, I who have just
Declined most princely gifts am compelled to beg
A favor of my general.

COMINIUS

Take it; it's yours. What is it?

CORIOLANUS

I lodged some years ago in Corioli
At a poor man's house. He was kind to me.
He called out to me—I saw him prisoner—
But then Aufidius came within my view
And rage overwhelmed my pity. I request you
To give my poor host freedom.

COMINIUS

       A handsome plea!
Were he the butcher of my son, he should
Be free as the wind. Deliver him, Titus.

LARTIUS

Marcius, his name?

CORIOLANUS

                    By Jupiter, forgot!
I am weary; yes, my memory is tired.
Have we no wine here?

COMINIUS

                    Let us go to our tent.
The blood upon your face is drying; it's time
Your wounds were cared for. Come.
(They go out)

g)

The Volscian camp.

*A flourish. Trumpets. Enter Tullus Aufidius, bloody, with two or three
soldiers.*

AUFIDIUS
The town is taken.

FIRST SOLDIERS
It will be given back on certain terms.

AUFIDIUS

                    Terms?
I wish I were a Roman, for I cannot,
Being a Volscian, be what I am. Terms?
What sort of terms can be expected by
The party that sues for mercy. Five times, Marcius,
I've fought with you; five times you've beaten me,
And will continue, I think, if we should fight
As often as we eat. By the elements,
If ever again I meet him face to face
He's mine or I am his. My ambition
Has lost a measure of its honor, for once
I hoped to vanquish him on equal terms,
Sword against sword, but now I'll strike him as
I can; by wrath or craft I'll get him.

FIRST SOLDIER
  He's the devil.
AUFIDIUS
  Bolder, though not so subtle. My valor is poisoned
  With letting him stain it; for him it will
  Bely itself. Neither sleep nor sanctuary,
  Being naked or sick; nor temple nor capitol,
  Nor prayers of priests nor times of sacrifice—
  All obstacles to fury—shall assert
  Their worn-out privilege and prerogative
  Against my hate of Marcius. Wherever
  I find him, even at home under my brother's
  Protection, in defiance of the laws
  Of hospitality, I'll wash my angry
  Hands in his heart. Go now to the city;
  Learn how it's held and who are being sent
  To Rome as hostages.
FIRST SOLDIER
                Will you not go?
AUFIDIUS
  I am expected at the cypress grove. I pray you—
  It's south of the city mills—to bring me word
  How the world goes, so I may adjust my step
  To its pace.
FIRST SOLDIER
          I will, sir.
  (They go out)

ACT TWO

1

Rome. A public place.

Enter the tribunes Brutus and Sicinius.

BRUTUS   The augurs, I hear, have received news from the field this morning.

SICINIUS   The worthy priests do not honor me with more confidences than you, Brutus, but I know the news is bad.

BRUTUS   Why necessarily bad?

SICINIUS   Because either the Volscians have won, and then they will be the masters of Rome, or Caius Marcius has won, and then he will be master.

BRUTUS   That's the truth. Here comes Menenius Agrippa.
   (Enter Menenius)

MENENIUS   How goes it, herdsmen of the plebeian cattle?

SICINIUS   Food is in short supply on the banks of the Tiber. But it seems you have had news.

MENENIUS   Yes, from Caius Marcius, but you don't love him. Tell me: whom does the wolf love?

SICINIUS   The lamb.

MENENIUS   Yes, to devour him; as the hungry plebeians would the noble Marcius.

BRUTUS   He's a lamb that roars like a bear.

MENENIUS   No, he's a bear that lives like a lamb. Do you know how you are judged in the city? I mean by us, the upper classes?

BRUTUS   Well, how are we judged this morning?

MENENIUS   As a pair of conceited, violent, unpatriotic rogues, not good enough to serve beer to a fishwife.

SICINIUS   Come, sir, come, we know you.

MENENIUS   You know neither me, nor yourselves, nor anything else.

BRUTUS *(to Sicinius as they leave)*   Now it's clear what the news is. Marcius has conquered. Otherwise the fellow wouldn't be so insolent.
(Enter Volumnia, Virgilia, and Valeria)

MENENIUS   Where are you going, my noble ladies?

VOLUMNIA   Honorable Menenius, my boy is on his way. Don't delay us.

MENENIUS   Marcius coming home?

VOLUMNIA   Yes, and with the highest honors.

MENENIUS   Marcius coming home!

VOLUMNIA AND VIRGILIA   Yes, it's true.

VOLUMNIA   Here's a letter from him; the senate has one, his wife has one, and I think there's one at home for you.

MENENIUS   A letter for me?

VIRGILIA   Indeed there's a letter for you. I've seen it.

MENENIUS   A letter for me? That will keep me in good health for seven years; I'll spit in my doctor's face. But—isn't he wounded? Usually he comes home wounded.

VIRGILIA   Oh no, no, no.

VOLUMNIA   Oh, he's wounded, I thank the gods for it.

MENENIUS   And so do I, if it's not too bad. Is he bringing victory in his pocket?—If so, his wounds become him.

VOLUMNIA   Yes, on his brows, Menenius. For the third time he's coming home with the oaken garland.

MENENIUS   Has he given Aufidius a lesson?

VOLUMNIA   Titus Lartius writes that they fought together but Aufidius escaped.

MENENIUS   Indeed, Caius Marcius is not the man to cross, not for all the chests in Corioli and all the money in them. Has it been reported to the senate?

VOLUMNIA   Ladies, we must go. Yes, yes, yes. The senate has received letters from the general, giving my son full credit for the capture of Corioli.

MENENIUS   Splendid!—Where is he wounded, ladies?

VOLUMNIA   In the shoulder and in the left arm. There will be large scars to show the people when he runs for office. And in the battle against Tarquin he received seven body wounds.

MENENIUS   One in the neck and two in the thigh. That makes
nine that I know of.

(Trumpets)

MENENIUS   They're coming.

VOLUMNIA

And under the step of the mighty
The same earth trembles both in fear and joy.
And many are no more, and home comes the victor.

*(Enter Cominius and Titus; between them, crowned with an oaken
garland, Coriolanus)*

HERALD

To all and sundry be it known
That Caius Marcius fought his way unaided
Into the fortified city of Corioli.
For which deed, his name and title
Shall henceforth be Coriolanus.

MENENIUS

Welcome to Rome, renowned Coriolanus!

CORIOLANUS

No more of that, I beg you.

COMINIUS

Look, sir, your mother.

CORIOLANUS

Oh!

(Goes to her)

I know you have petitioned all the gods
For my success.

(He kneels down before her)

VOLUMNIA

No, stand up, soldier. My dear Caius
My worthy Marcius, and—what was it, how
Son, must I call you now? Ah yes, Coriolanus.
But oh, your wife!

CORIOLANUS

                                Hail, my dear silence!
Would you have laughed if I'd come home in a coffin,
That you weep to see me triumph? Ah, my dear
The widows in Corioli have such eyes

And the mothers who lack sons.

MENENIUS

Now the gods crown you.

CORIOLANUS

You still alive? *(To Valeria)* Forgive me!

MENENIUS

A hundred thousand welcomes! I could weep
And I could laugh, I am light and heavy. Welcome!
Rome ought to deify all three of you
But even now we've got some crab trees here
That no amount of grafting will make sweet
To your taste.

COMINIUS

The old man hasn't changed.

CORIOLANUS

Still the old Menenius, eh? *(To Volumnia and Virgilia)* Your
    hand!
And yours.

VOLUMNIA

I've lived to see my wishes granted.
There's only one thing wanting, and now Rome
Will give you that.

CORIOLANUS

Good mother,
I'd rather be their slave in my own way
Than their master in theirs.

COMINIUS

To the Capitol!

(All go out except the tribunes)

SICINIUS

What a to-do!
As if a god had come down on the earth!
Believe me, he'll be consul before you know it.

BRUTUS

For us tribunes that would be good night.

SICINIUS

His mission was to turn away the Volscians.
No more. You might as well command the wolf
To chase the fox away from the chicken house
And stop at that. He's taken Corioli.

BRUTUS
>And by so doing stirred the Volscians up
>Against us for years to come.

SICINIUS
>Now listen how a city drunk with triumph
>Echoes the praises of that lawless man!
>Today every saddler's boasting to his wife
>That Corioli's been given him as a bonus.
>How will he ever find room for three or four
>Patrician villas in his cellar? That's all
>They want to know. And we're just spoil-sports.

BRUTUS
>On the other hand
>He breaks the rules of every game he plays.
>I've heard that if he deigns to stand for consul
>He will not speak in the market as customary
>Or show himself in a worn-out toga, or
>Display his wounds to the people. That, he says
>Would be to beg for votes. Yet if he did it
>He'd likely hit the mark.

SICINIUS
>   I hope he stands
>By his proud purpose.
>*(Enter a messenger)*

BRUTUS
>   What's the matter?

MESSENGER
>You're summoned to the Capitol. Everyone thinks
>That Marcius will be consul. I have seen
>The deaf crowding to see him, the blind
>To hear him. Ladies are flinging gloves
>Young girls are tearing off their scarves and tossing
>Them down upon him. The patricians
>Are bowing to him as if he were Jupiter's statue.
>The commoners are clapping their rough hands.
>I never saw the like.

BRUTUS
>   To the Capitol!
>*(All go out)*

2

Rome. The Capitol.

Attendants are laying cushions.

FIRST   Come, come, they'll soon be here. How many are standing for the consulate?

SECOND   Three, so they say; but everyone thinks Coriolanus
will carry it off.

FIRST   A good man, but damnably proud; he has no love for the
common people.

SECOND   There have been great men who flattered the people
more, yet didn't love them. And there are some that the
people have loved, without knowing why. In other words,
when they love, they don't know why, and they hate for no
better reason. Consequently, if Coriolanus doesn't care
whether they love him or hate him, it only shows his intelligence. They're coming.

*(Enter Cominius, the consul, Menenius, Coriolanus, senators,
Sicinius, and Brutus)*

MENENIUS
Now that the matter of the Volscians is settled
The main business before this second session is
To glorify the man who conquered them
For Rome. Permit, then, noble elders, that
The present consul and recent general
Should say a few words of the warlike valor
Displayed by our Caius Marcius Coriolanus.

SENATOR
Speak, consul, and your words need not be few.

Tribunes, lend ear, and presently in the assembly
Of the people, argue to obtain approval
Of what is here decided.

SICINIUS
                                        We are here
Amicably disposed, not disinclined
To honor and support the object of
This session.

BRUTUS
                        Most particularly if he shows
A little more respect for the common people
Than hitherto.

MENENIUS
                        That's out of place.
You'd have done better to say nothing. Would
You hear Cominius speak?

BRUTUS
                                        Most willingly.
And yet my warning was more pertinent
Than your rebuke.

MENENIUS
                            He loves your people surely.
Just don't press him to be their bed-fellow.
Speak, Cominius.
(Coriolanus stands up and wants to go)
Come, come, sit down.

SENATOR
                            Don't be afraid to hear
Of things that you were not afraid to do.

CORIOLANUS
Forgive me, I would rather cure my wounds
Than hear tell how I came by them.

BRUTUS
                                            I hope
My words are not driving you away, sir.

CORIOLANUS
                                    No, sir. Often
When blows have made me stay, I've fled from words.
Since you don't flatter me, you don't offend

Me either. And as for your people, I love them
As much as they deserve.

MENENIUS

Come, be seated.

CORIOLANUS

I'd rather have someone scratch my head in the sun
When the alarm is sounded, than sit idly
While such a fuss is made about my nothings.
(Coriolanus goes out)

MENENIUS

You see the kind of man he is.
He'd rather venture all his limbs for honor
Than risk an ear to hear about it. Proceed, Cominius.

COMINIUS

My voice will be inadequate. In times
Like these such deeds as Coriolanus does
Should not be uttered feebly. At sixteen
When Tarquin marched on Rome, he went to battle.
With beardless chin he drove the bristled lips
Before him. At an age when he might have played
The parts of women on the stage, he won
The crown of oak. Then, grown to manhood
He bore the brunt of seventeen battles
And robbed all swords of the garland. To his prowess
Before and in Corioli, I cannot
Do justice. Those who were taking to their heels
He stopped, and by his rare example made
The last of cowards exult in war as a sport.
Like rushes before a vessel under sail
Battle lines swayed and fell before his prow.
He was a bloody instrument, whose every movement
Brought cries of death. Alone, he entered
The deadly city gate, almost unaided
Returned, and then with sudden reinforcement
Struck Corioli like a meteor.

MENENIUS

There's a man!

SENATOR

In fullest measure he deserves the honors
That we propose.

COMINIUS

                    He kicked away the spoils
As other men would kick the dust from their path.

MENENIUS

  Call him! Call him!

SENATOR

                    Call Coriolanus.
(An attendant brings Coriolanus in)

MENENIUS

  Coriolanus, the senate unanimously
  Elects you consul.

CORIOLANUS

                    I still owe them
  My life and service.

MENENIUS

                    Then you have only to
  Address the people.

CORIOLANUS

                    I beseech you
  Let me omit that custom. I cannot
  Unbutton my coat, stand naked and entreat them
  To elect me for my wounds. I beg you
  Let me forgo that usage!

SICINIUS

                    Sir, the people
  Must have their voice, and they will not forgo
  One jot of ceremony.

MENENIUS

  Incline please to the custom. Do as all
  Consuls have done before you.
  No more nor less.

CORIOLANUS

                    It's a part
  I blush to play. The people should be made
  To do without such spectacles.

BRUTUS

                    Did you hear that?

CORIOLANUS

  To stand before them bragging: I did this
  And that could not have been done without me.

And show my mended wounds and say: My friends,
I came by these to make you vote for me.

MENENIUS
Better give in. Now, tribunes of the people
Make our decision known.—To the new consul
We wish all joy and honor.

SENATORS
                          All joy and honor!

(The senators go out with Coriolanus)

BRUTUS
You see how he means to treat the people.

3

Rome. The Forum.

Enter citizens.

FIRST CITIZEN   Once and for all: if he asks for our votes, we can't
deny them.

SECOND CITIZEN   We can if we want to, friend.

FIRST CITIZEN   Yes, we have the power, but it's a power we
haven't the power to use. Because if he shows us his wounds
and tells us his noble exploits, we've got to show a certain
amount of noble appreciation. He's indispensable.

SECOND CITIZEN   Like a neck with a goiter.

FIRST CITIZEN   What do you mean by that?

SECOND CITIZEN   A neck is indispensable even if it has a goiter.
The goiter is his pride.

FIRST CITIZEN   I still say that if he were friendlier there'd be no
better man.

SECOND CITIZEN   Here he comes.

FIRST CITIZEN   And in a plain toga as the law requires.

SECOND CITIZEN   Let's see how he behaves.

FIRST CITIZEN   Let's wait until he stops and then pass by him

singly or by twos or threes. He will have to make his request
of each one of us, and then each one of us will give him his
vote.

SECOND CITIZEN   If he wants to.

(Coriolanus has entered with Menenius Agrippa)

MENENIUS

No, sir, you are not right. You're well aware
The greatest men have done it.

CORIOLANUS

What must I say?
Please, sir! No, damn it, my tongue
Sticks in my throat. Look, sir, my wounds.
I got them in my country's service, when
Some of you fellows howled and fled
From the sound of your own drums.

MENENIUS

Ye gods, not that!
Don't take that tone. Remind them of your deeds
Not your opinions!

CORIOLANUS

Let them forget me as
They've always forgotten honor and gratitude.
Hang 'em!

MENENIUS

Don't spoil it all, I beg you.
Speak to them. And please, please, speak sensibly.

CORIOLANUS

Tell them to wash their faces
And clean their teeth.

(Menenius goes out)

Well, here comes
The first batch.
You know, friends, why I'm standing here?

FIRST CITIZEN   Yes, sir, we know. Tell us what brought you to
it?

CORIOLANUS   My own merit.

FIRST CITIZEN   Your own merit?

CORIOLANUS   Yes, not my own desire.

FIRST CITIZEN   What? Not your own desire?

CORIOLANUS
    No, it was never my desire
    To beg from the poor.

SECOND CITIZEN   The poor?

FIRST CITIZEN   To beg? Don't let that worry you. If we give you
    something, it's because we hope to get something in return.

CORIOLANUS
    Very well, then what's the price of the consulship?

SECOND CITIZEN
    The price is that you ask for it politely.

CORIOLANUS
    Politely?
    Sir, let me have it. I have wounds
    That I can show you in private. Sir, your vote!
    Well, what's your answer?

FIRST CITIZEN
                        You shall have it, sir.

CORIOLANUS
    Is it a deal, sir?
    There, that's two worthy voices begged.
    I've got your pennies! So good-bye!

FIRST CITIZEN
    This is very odd.

SECOND CITIZEN
    If I had to give again . . . But never mind.
    (Both go out. Enter the man with a child)

CORIOLANUS
    Sir, I should like to be consul.

THE MAN *(pointing out Coriolanus' toga to the child)*   That's the
    plain toga, Tertius, they've got to wear it when they plead in
    the marketplace. It has no pockets, that's to keep him from
    buying votes, ha ha ha. Otherwise, you see, he might buy
    them. Ha ha ha. But he'll get my vote because he's taken one
    more city for Rome. He'll get it. *(Goes out)*

CORIOLANUS   Many thanks, sir.
    (Enter two citizens)
    A word, sirs. It's the regulation
    That all should see how for a high honor
    I wear my shoes out in the market place . . .

THIRD CITIZEN I'm glad to see that, sir, if only because of my trade.

CORIOLANUS What is your trade, sir?

THIRD CITIZEN To tell you the truth, sir, it's mere patchwork compared to yours.

CORIOLANUS What is your trade then?

THIRD CITIZEN *(archly)* A trade I can practice with a clearer conscience than certain noble lords can practice theirs. It consists in improving the wretched walks of life.

CORIOLANUS Your trade.

FOURTH CITIZEN Begging your pardon, sir, he's a shoemaker. And you have his vote because war raises the price of shoes and you are the living embodiment of war, sir.

(Another citizen joins them)

CORIOLANUS Ha ha ha! I'm studying the trades here. This gentleman is a shoemaker, and what are you, sir?

FIFTH CITIZEN I'm a gardener, sir.

CORIOLANUS And what does your trade teach you about the state? Because you are being asked to make a decision concerning the state.

FIFTH CITIZEN

My garden, sir, that little realm
Of flowerbeds and turnip patches, has taught me
That even the noble rose of Corinth must
Be pruned of undue pride of growth, or else
It cannot thrive. Moreover, it must humble
Itself to having leeks and cabbages and
Such plants of low descent, but passing useful
Watered and cultivated by its side.

CORIOLANUS

What does all that mean, vote?

FIFTH CITIZEN

It seems to me the garden would grow wild
If one thought only of the royal rose.

CORIOLANUS

Thanks for the lesson. But just one thing more:
Your vote! Your vote!

(Three more citizens have joined them)

Good day, gentlemen! If you have no objection to my face,

I'd like to be consul. I'm wearing the customary dress.

SIXTH CITIZEN You've deserved nobly of your country, and you have not deserved nobly.

CORIOLANUS The answer to your riddle?

SIXTH CITIZEN You've been a scourge to her enemies and a rod to her friends. To put it plainly, you haven't loved the common people.

CORIOLANUS I love them according to their deserts. But you hold that I haven't made myself common with my love for the common people. I understand. There are certain needs, and to meet them you need public establishments and public men. However, if you set more store by my hat than by my heart, I will tear out my heart, remove my hat, and pray you humbly: let me be consul.

THIRD CITIZEN You have received many wounds for your country?

CORIOLANUS I won't bother you to look at them. But if you demand entertainment, I can sing you a song about the gratitude of the she-wolf. (To the tune of a bagpiper who has begun to play for small coins)

Here stands C. Marcius Coriolan
Trying to please the common man
He's selling the Roman eagle here
(Don't fight over the feathers, children dear!)
Gentlemen, my wounds. These. And these.
Look closely. Touch them if you please.
I'll serve you for a penny; I'll dance
Attendance. Gather round! Step up! Last chance!
(More citizens step up)
Here come more votes.
Your votes! I went to battle for your votes.
Stood sleepless for your votes. For your votes
I've got two dozen scars. I've fought
In eighteen battles. For your votes I've done
All manner of things and not done others.
Give me your votes and I'll be consul.

THIRD CITIZEN (frightened) Of course. Of course. Calm down.

FOURTH CITIZEN Let him be consul if that's what he wants. Bravery is the one thing that counts in these warlike times.

FIFTH CITIZEN Amen.
  (Coriolanus bows low)
  (Enter senators and tribunes)
MENENIUS
  You've carried out the program.
CORIOLANUS

                      Then I'm through?
SICINIUS
  You've pressed your candidacy singly and
  In person, no objection has been raised.
  The senate and the tribunes can confirm you.
CORIOLANUS
  Where? In the senate?
SICINIUS

                  Yes.

CORIOLANUS

                  But can I change
  This toga now?
SICINIUS

                  Yes, that you may. One thing perhaps
  Remains: before the assembled people to
  Question the candidate concerning
  His program and his general opinions.
MENENIUS

                                No!
  That's not provided in the charter.
SICINIUS

                                The tribunes
  Aren't mentioned in the charter either. The people
  Have won a new law in the field, and now
  In victory they want to use it, sirs.
FIFTH CITIZEN
  That's right.
SICINIUS

          Coriolanus
  You are descended from the noble house
  Of Marcius, from which house sprang also
  That Ancus Marcius, Numa's daughter's son
  Who followed great Hostilius as our king.

Of the same house were Publius and Quintus
Who brought us our best water with their conduits.
And now, before I put my questions in
The people's name, I ask you to look back
Most earnestly upon your beloved ancestors.
Coriolanus, ships from conquered Antium
Have just put into port. Their cargo is grain
Tribute and booty taken in the bloody
War with the Volscians. Noble Marcius, what
Will you do with this grain if chosen consul?

MENENIUS
Easy does it, Marcius.

CORIOLANUS
This is a plot.

BRUTUS
Call it a plot! The people are crying for grain.
When free grain was apportioned to the people
Some seven months ago, you, Marcius, literally
Reviled all those who took it as lazy scoundrels.

CORIOLANUS
Yes, yes, it's long since known.

SICINIUS
But not to all.

CORIOLANUS
Then tell the others!

MENENIUS
Easy now.

COMINIUS
You're stirring up the people!

CORIOLANUS
Speaking to me of grain! Would it please you
To hear it again? It would? Then I'll repeat it.

MENENIUS
Not now. Not here.

COMINIUS
Not now and in this heat.

CORIOLANUS
Here and at any time. I say what I think.
You don't feed virtue when you give free grain.

You're feeding disobedience, fattening it
For insurrection, for with every wish
You satisfy, you give the filthy rabble
New wishes.

FIFTH CITIZEN

       Oho!

MENENIUS

           Let well enough alone.

SICINIUS

Let me ask you this: why should the people vote
For a man who speaks of them like that?

CORIOLANUS

Was it then children's votes I got by my begging?

COMINIUS

Keep calm!

BRUTUS

           You've not yet been confirmed in office.

CORIOLANUS

Whoever suggested that the granaries
Be emptied free of charge, as may perhaps
Be customary in Greece . . .

BRUTUS

                Where the people
Are really consulted, and not just on paper!

CORIOLANUS

In Greece? Then go to Greece.
This city's name is Rome.

COMINIUS

       Enough!

SICINIUS

And then some.

CORIOLANUS

       No, I'll give you something more
For your constituents. It's free. I happen
To know that when war threatened this city
With sudden doom, the scum who live in
The stinking districts by the lower Tiber
Demanded grain before they'd take up arms.
Some people thought the time had come to feather

Their nests by blackmailing the state.

COMINIUS
No more, I beg you, sir.

FOURTH CITIZEN
Instead of blackmail, certain others steal.
Where, Coriolanus, are the spoils
Of Corioli?

MENENIUS
                    Be still!

CORIOLANUS
That's dual sovereignty, where one part
Despises with good ground and the other part
Flings groundless insults, where greatness, power and wis-
    dom
Can't move a step without the yes or no
Of the unreasoning mob.

CITIZENS
                    It's us he means.

BRUTUS
He's said enough.

SICINIUS
                    He's spoken as a traitor.
He'll answer for it as a traitor should.

CORIOLANUS
You dogs, you crippled sons of turmoil
Because you were confirmed in time of turmoil
When not what's right, but only what cannot
Be helped becomes the law. But now that Rome
No longer has the Volscians at its throat—
And thanks to me—Rome will know how to laugh
And wash away this scurf.

BRUTUS
Manifest treason!

SICINIUS
                    This a consul? Never!

BRUTUS
The aediles, ho!—Arrest this man.

SICINIUS
Summon the people. In their name
I apprehend you as an innovator

Rebel and enemy of the state.
(Brutus goes out)

CORIOLANUS
Go away, old goat!

MENENIUS
Hands off, old man!
(Coriolanus takes Cominius' shortsword)

CORIOLANUS
      Or else I'll shake your bones
Out of your clothes.

CITIZENS
Careful, Sicinius!—Watch out for his sword!

CORIOLANUS
A plot, I knew it, to end
The rule of the patricians.

SICINIUS
      This way!
(Brutus re-enters with aediles and citizens)

BRUTUS
He's drawn the shortsword now!

COMINIUS
      Stand back!
Here stands the victor of Corioli.

SENATOR
      Put that sword away.

SICINIUS
Here stands a usurper of the people's sovereignty.

MENENIUS
On both sides more respect.

BRUTUS
      Seize him, aediles!

CITIZENS Down with him.—Down with the grain robber!—
Weapons, weapons!
(The patricians crowd around Coriolanus)

PATRICIANS
You'll take him over our dead bodies!—
Lead him away!—Menenius
You speak to them!—Away!

MENENIUS
     I can't.

Tribunes, speak to the people.
Coriolanus, quiet! Speak, friend Sicinius!

SICINIUS

Hear me, citizens! Quiet!

CITIZENS

Hear the tribune!

SICINIUS

           The man you see before you has
Outraged the tribunes.

MENENIUS

That's stirring up the fire, not putting it out.

FIRST SENATOR

That's making war on Rome!

BRUTUS

                Who's Rome? You or
Its people?

SICINIUS

For laying hands on a tribune, the penalty
Is death. Take him away. Take him to
The Tarpeian Rock.

BRUTUS

          Aediles, go seize him.

CITIZENS

Surrender, Marcius.

MENENIUS

         Patricians! Here! Defend our Marcius!

CITIZENS

Down with him—To the Rock!

FIRST SENATOR

             The man's his own worst enemy!
Quick! Let's be going! Hold him up! Oh, why
The devil couldn't he speak gently!
(*The patricians push the bewildered Coriolanus out. The citizens
follow*)

BRUTUS

                Seize the viper
Who's ready to depopulate a city
To be its one and all.

ACT THREE

1

Rome. Coriolanus' house.

Volumnia, Coriolanus, and a few friends.

CORIOLANUS
Only one thing surprises me, that my mother
Is not more pleased with me. She used to call
Them churlish vassals, creatures made
To sell themselves for pennies, and to stand
Bareheaded in assemblies, yawning and
Scratching their heads in puzzlement when one
Of my rank stood up and spoke for peace or war.
Why would you wish me milder? Would you want me
To make a dovecote of my heart? I play
The man I am, and that's the end of it.

VOLUMNIA
Son, son. I only wish
You'd taken time to put your power on
Before you wore it out.

CORIOLANUS
                              Forget it.

VOLUMNIA
You could have been the man you are more fully
If you had shown it less. When once you hold
The power, they'll no longer have
The power to defy you.

CORIOLANUS
                              Hang 'em!

VOLUMNIA

                              Yes,
And burn them too.
(Enter Menenius and senators)

MENENIUS
Come, come, you have been too rough, a bit too rough.
Come back with me and make amends.

SENATOR

                              It can't be helped.
Our city, if you don't, will break in two
And perish.

VOLUMNIA

              Son, my heart is no more faint
Than yours; my brain, however, tells
Me when it's time for anger and when not.
Take my advice.

MENENIUS

                  That's it. A little time
Will turn the trick. If not, I'd put
My armor on that I can scarcely carry
Sooner than see you grovel to the mob.

CORIOLANUS
What must I do?

MENENIUS

                  Return to the tribunes.

CORIOLANUS
Very well. But what then? What then?

MENENIUS
Repent of what you said.

CORIOLANUS

                  To them? To the gods I cannot.

VOLUMNIA
You're too unbending. I have heard you say
That guile and honor are compatible
In war. Why not in peace?

CORIOLANUS

              Be still.

MENENIUS

                        Well questioned.

VOLUMNIA

    If in your wars it brings you honor to seem
    What you are not—and that you've always done
    When great ends could be won by it—then why
    Should that same policy dishonor you
    In peace?

CORIOLANUS
            Why do you press me so?

VOLUMNIA

    Because your duty now is to address
    The people, to speak to them with words
    That bubble from the surface of your tongue
    Bastards, mere sounds and syllables
    That bear no kinship to your heart.
    It will dishonor you no more
    Than with soft words to take a city
    Against which you would otherwise be forced
    To tempt your luck and risk great loss of blood.
    Be reasonable. Your friends and family are
    In danger. That's the honorable course.
    But you would rather show this stinking rabble
    How splendidly you frown than smiling cheat
    Them of their votes, and save what otherwise
    Will go to ruin.

MENENIUS
           Come, go with us.
    Just a few friendly words. That's all.

VOLUMNIA
                    Son,
    I beg you, go to them. Just stand bare-headed
    Holding your hands out so (see, here you are)
    Your knees nearly touching the pavement (for in such cases
    Posture counts more than words) and wag your head.
    Just tell them you're a soldier, reared in the noise
    Of battle, unaccustomed to the gentle
    Manners which they, as you must now admit
    Have every reason to expect. Then tell them
    From this day on they will not find you wanting.

MENENIUS
    If you'd do that, speak as your mother has spoken
    By the gods, you'd win all hearts.

VOLUMNIA
    I beg you, go. I know you'd sooner follow
    Your enemy into a fiery pit than gently
    Into a tavern.

MENENIUS
                    Cominius!
    (*Enter Cominius*)

COMINIUS
    I've come from the Forum, Marcius, and advise you
    To place a strong guard round your house. Or else
    Take flight.

MENENIUS
                A gentle word would do it.

MENENIUS
    Of course it would, if he could squeeze one out.

VOLUMNIA
                                            Son,
    I beg you, just say yes, and go.

CORIOLANUS
                        Shouldn't
    I have my face shaved first? All right, I'll do it.
    Why fret about this bag of dust named Marcius?
    Scatter it to the wind! Come, to the Forum!
    Good-bye, my spirit, let some harlot's spirit
    Possess me, let my warlike voice
    Pipe like a eunuch's, let my eyes be filled
    With schoolboy tears, and let my armored knees
    That never bent except in stirrups, bow
    Like a beggar's stooped for coins. I will not do it.
    I will not cut the truth within me down
    Or let base gestures vitiate my mind.

VOLUMNIA
    You will decide. I'd call it more dishonor
    For me to beg of you, than you of them.
    Let ruin fall upon us. Do as you please.
    You sucked your courage from my breast, but not
    Your pride.

CORIOLANUS

Calm down. I'm going to the marketplace. Stop scolding.
I'll cheat them of their hearts. When I come back
I'll be the idol of every shopkeeper in Rome
And consul too. Commend me to my wife.

VOLUMNIA

Do as you like. *(Goes out)*

COMINIUS

Come, now the tribunes are waiting.
And arm yourself with mildness. They have heaped up
Still stronger accusations than before.

CORIOLANUS

"Mild" is the word. Come, let's be going.
Inventive as may be their accusations
My repentance will be more so.

MENENIUS

Yes, but put it mildly.

CORIOLANUS

Right. Mildly does it. Mildly, mildly.
(All go out)

2

Rome. The Forum.

Sicinius, Brutus, citizens, an aedile.

BRUTUS   Are these the chairmen of the electoral districts?

AEDILE   Yes.

BRUTUS   Have you a list of all the voters they represent?

AEDILE   Yes, here it is.

SICINIUS   And here he comes.

(Enter Coriolanus, Menenius, Cominius, and senators)

MENENIUS

Speak calmly now, I beg you.

CORIOLANUS

Yes, like a stable boy, who for a tip

Puts up with any insult. May the gods
Keep Rome in safety and its seats of justice
Supplied with worthy men. Let love be our
Rallying cry. Peace to the city!

FIRST SENATOR
                              Hear, hear!

MENENIUS
  A noble greeting.

SICINIUS
                      Chairmen, be seated.

AEDILE
                                      Hear
  Your tribunes!

CORIOLANUS
                      Hear me speak first!

CITIZENS
  Him first! The same old story! Him first!

SICINIUS
  Very well, speak.

CITIZENS
                      First me and then the law!—
  The forms be damned.

AEDILE
                          Silence, please.

CORIOLANUS
  Shall I be further prosecuted elsewhere?
  Will everything be settled here?

SICINIUS
                                  I must
  First ask you this: Do you submit
  To the people's voice? Do you recognize
  Their representatives? Do you consent
  To suffer punishment for such offense
  As may be proved against you?

CORIOLANUS
                                  I do.

MENENIUS
  Hear that? He does. Consider his services

In war. He speaks here not as a citizen
But as a soldier.

COMINIUS

                That's enough now, friend.

CORIOLANUS

How comes it that no sooner voted consul
I am dishonored and expelled from office?

SICINIUS

You are on trial, not we.

CORIOLANUS

                Well, try me then.

SICINIUS

You are accused of trying to overthrow
The tribunes of the people and to seize
A tyrant's power. Hence of treason
Against the people.

CORIOLANUS

           Treason!

MENENIUS

              Easy, now!

COMINIUS

You promised!

CORIOLANUS

            Let the fires of bottommost hell
Swallow up the people.

SICINIUS

           Did you hear that?

CORIOLANUS

Call me a traitor! Why, you dog
Of a tribune, you tribune of dogs. You lump
Of filth! You scoundrel hungry for my death!
You throat clogged fast with lies!

CITIZENS

              Enough!

SICINIUS

No need of adding further evidence
To our complaint. What you've just seen . . .

CITIZENS

                To the Rock!

SICINIUS

  And heard . . .

CITIZENS

            Come. Take him to the Rock!

SICINIUS

  Beating the tribunes, cursing you, the people
  Opposing law with violence, and now
  Arrogantly defying those empowered
  To judge him. Such offences warrant the
  Death penalty.

CITIZENS

          Right! Right! Put him to death.

BRUTUS

  But since he has served Rome well . . .

CORIOLANUS

                   What is this talk
  Of serving well?

BRUTUS

        I'm saying what I know.

CORIOLANUS

  What you know!

MENENIUS

       Is this the promise
  You made your mother?

COMINIUS

           Calm yourself. You know . . .

CORIOLANUS

  Don't tell me what I know. Let them hurl
  Me down from the steep Tarpeian Rock, or send
  Me off to exile, or whatever else they
  Can think of. I'll not buy their mercy with
  So much as one soft word, not even a
  "Good morning."

SICINIUS

        That condemns you. In the people's
  Name, we the tribunes banish you from Rome
  And warn you on pain of being hurled
  From the Tarpeian Rock, never again
  To enter the city gates.

CITIZENS

                    Well done!

(All stand up, to go)

COMINIUS

  Hear me!

SICINIUS

              He's sentenced. The session's closed.

COMINIUS

  No, let me speak. I have been consul. Rome
  Can see the marks of her enemies on me. When
  I say . . .

SICINIUS

            We know what you will say.

BRUTUS

  He's banished. That's the end of it.

COMINIUS

                              The end?

CORIOLANUS

  You pack of common curs, I hate your breath
  More than the reek of putrid swamps, and value
  Your love no more than the carcasses of unburied
  Enemies. I banish you!
  Stay here in Rome, shaking with fear, shitting
  In your pants whenever a plume of unfamiliar
  Color appears outside the gates. Maintain
  The power to banish your defenders till
  Your ignorance (which sees no farther than
  Its nose) sends everyone away but you
  Who have always been your cruelest enemies
  And in the end delivers you to some
  Nation that takes the city without striking
  A blow. Despising Rome on your account
  I turn my back on it. There's a world
  Elsewhere.

(Coriolanus goes out with Menenius, Cominius, and senators)

CITIZENS

  The enemy of the people's gone! He's gone!

(They fling their hats into the air)

3

Rome. Outside the gates.

Coriolanus, Volumnia, Virgilia, Menenius, Cominius, and senators.

CORIOLANUS
  Come, come. Don't cry. Good-bye. The many-headed
  Beast has butted me out. No, mother
  Where's the old pluck? Who was it taught me
  That common fortune and misfortune were
  For common people? That when the sea was calm
  All ships show equal mastery in sailing
  But that to bear the hardest strokes of fate
  And not get hurt requires noble skill?

VIRGILIA
  O heavens! O heavens!

CORIOLANUS
                    Stop, woman, please . . .

VOLUMNIA
  A plague on all the guilds of Rome!

CORIOLANUS
                            What! What! What!
  They'll love me when they need me. No, mother
  Remember how you used to say
  That if you'd been the wife of Hercules
  You'd have done six of his labors and so saved
  Your husband all that sweat. Cominius
  Chin up. Good-bye. Good-bye, wife. It's nothing, mother.
  I'll get along. Take care, Menenius.
  At your age tears are saltier than when
  You're young; they're not good for the eyes.
  You, general, I've know you to be staunch.
  Heartrending scenes are nothing new to you.

Tell these sad women that it's just as foolish
To cry at blows that cannot be avoided
As it is to laugh. The dangers I have faced
Have kept you youthful, mother, you know that.
Believe me if you can: although he now
Goes forth like a lone dragon which his cave
Makes feared and talked of more than seen, your son
Will either do uncommon deeds or fall
A victim to the petty treachery of
The common herd.

VOLUMNIA

              Dear son, where will you go?
Take Cominius with you for a while. Discuss
With him your future course, for fear blind chance
Should be your guide.

CORIOLANUS

           O heavenly gods!

COMINIUS

I'll stay with you a month. We'll talk things over
Decide where you're to go, so you may hear
From us and we from you.

CORIOLANUS

              Thank you, old man. But
You're not as young as you have been. Too old
To roam the country with a man—forgive me—
Who still has ample plans. Just bring me to
The gate. Come, come! And once outside
We'll smile and say good-bye. As long as I
Remain above the ground you'll hear from me
But only news recalling the old Marcius.
(*All go out through the gate*)

4

Rome. A street near the gate.

Sicinius, Brutus, and an aedile.

SICINIUS
Send them all home. He's gone. The thing is done.
The nobles who, as we see, have sided with him
Are thrown into confusion.

BRUTUS
                    Now we've shown
Our power, we can take a humbler attitude.

SICINIUS
Make them go home. Their great enemy
Is gone.

BRUTUS
        Yes, send them home. Here comes his mother.
(Enter Volumnia, Virgilia, and Menenius)

SICINIUS
Quick. Let's be going.

BRUTUS
                Why?

SICINIUS
                    They say she's mad.

BRUTUS
They've seen us. Quick.

VOLUMNIA
                    Well met. God damn your souls!

MENENIUS
Sh! Gently, gently. Not so loud!

VOLUMNIA
                        If only
My tears would let me speak, you'd hear
A thing or two. No, stay. You shall hear. Stay there!

VIRGILIA

And you stay too. I wish I had the power
To say that to my husband.

SICINIUS

Bear up like a man.

VOLUMNIA

She's not a man. That's no disgrace for her.
I only wish that you were not a fox.
Then he would still be here who's struck more blows
For Rome than you've made slanderous speeches. Go
Now. No, I've something more to say. I wish
My son were in Arabia, and you
With all your tribe before him in the desert.

SICINIUS

What then?

VIRGILIA

What then? The entire breed
In wedlock born and bastards, you would all
Be soon exterminated. There's revenge!

MENENIUS

Be still!

SICINIUS

If only he had gone on serving
His country as he did at first.

BRUTUS

I wish he had.

VOLUMNIA

"I wish he had?" But you stirred up the mob.

BRUTUS

We'll leave you now.

VOLUMNIA

High as the Capitol
Towers above the meanest hut in Rome
So towers my son (this lady's husband, here
Do you see her?) whom you've banished
Above you all.

BRUTUS

That may be so. Come let's
Be going.
(Brutus, Sicinius, and the aedile go out)

MENENIUS

You've sent them packing
And upon my word you had every reason to.
Will you sup with me?

VOLUMNIA

No, not tonight.
Anger's my meat. I'll sup upon myself.
And so shall starve with feeding. Come, let's go.
(*All go out*)

ACT FOUR

1

Highway between Rome and Antium.

A Roman and a Volscian meet.

ROMAN Why are you turning back? I've come from Rome, but I'm not a bandit.

VOLSCIAN If it isn't Laetus, the tanner on Sandalmaker Street!

ROMAN Piger! Where have you been keeping yourself? *(They embrace)*

ROMAN How's the old lady? Still making those millet cakes?

VOLSCIAN Still making them; she can get the raisins, but I've got no hemp for my rope shop. That's what I'm going to Rome for.

ROMAN And I'm going to Antium to see if they can use any of my leather hassocks.

VOLSCIAN Did you pass through Corioli—the place you stole from us? How is it?

ROMAN You'll see. Hasn't changed much. People eat, sleep and pay taxes. How is it in Antium?

VOLSCIAN We eat, sleep and pay taxes. And in Rome?

ROMAN We eat too, and sleep and pay taxes. But we've had an uprising and thrown Coriolanus out.

VOLSCIAN Really? You've got rid of him? I can tell you one thing: that makes me happier about going there.

ROMAN I was less worried about leaving.

VOLSCIAN Man, to think we've got peace again!

ROMAN Have a good trip, Piger. I hope you make out all right in Rome.

VOLSCIAN   I hope you make out all right in Antium, Laetus.
  (They take leave and go their ways)
  (A disguised man comes from the direction of Rome. It is Coriolanus)

2

Antium. Outside Aufidius' house.

Enter Coriolanus shabbily dressed and muffled.

CORIOLANUS
  Not a bad town, this Antium. City, I'm
  The man who turned your wives to widows. Many
  A citizen would have inherited
  A house like this had he not groaned and fallen
  In my wars. It's better for you not to know me.
  Your women would belabor me with buckets
  Your little boys with stones.
  (Enter a citizen)
                                Good evening, sir.
  Can you inform me where the great
  Aufidius lives? Is he in Antium?

CITIZEN
  Yes, he's at home and entertaining
  The nobles of the city.

CORIOLANUS
                          Where is his house?

CITIZEN
  Right here before you.

CORIOLANUS
                          This one? Thank you, sir.
  Good evening.
  (The citizen goes out)
  O world, your slippery turns! Two loving friends
  Who seem to bear one heart within two breasts
  Sharing their hours, their bed, their meals, their sports

Inseparable twins, will between twelve and noon
Break into bitterest enmity for less than nothing.
Likewise, the most deep-rooted enemies
Whose hate keeps them awake at night devising
Ways to exterminate each other, will
By some stupid trick of chance, not worth an egg
Be turned to staunchest comrades who betroth
Their children. So it is with me. I hate
My birthplace and I love this enemy town.
I'll enter. If he kills me, it's his good
Right. If he welcomes me, I'll serve his country.

SERVANT *(stepping out of the house)*   What are you gaping at?

SECOND SERVANT   Hey, where's the wine? Call that service? Are
you fellows asleep?
(First servant goes out)

THIRD SERVANT   Cotus! The master's calling Cotus. *(Goes out)*

CORIOLANUS   A nice house. That dinner smells good too.

SECOND SERVANT   What do you want, friend? Where are you
from? There's no room for you here. Would you kindly . . .

CORIOLANUS   All right. I don't deserve a better reception: I am
Coriolanus.

FIRST SERVANT *(comes back)*   You still here? Hasn't the gatekeeper any eyes in his head, letting such people in? Get going
now.

CORIOLANUS   Get going yourself.

FIRST SERVANT   Me? Let's not be insolent.

CORIOLANUS   You're getting troublesome, friend.

SECOND SERVANT   Sir, you've been asked politely to leave. So
leave.

THIRD SERVANT *(comes back)*   Who's this character?

FIRST SERVANT   A freak. I can't get rid of him. Call the master.

THIRD SERVANT   Get a move on!

CORIOLANUS   Just let me stand here. I won't harm your hearth.

SECOND SERVANT   But who are you?

CORIOLANUS   A man of some renown.

FIRST SERVANT   But very poor.

CORIOLANUS   Yes, that I am.

THIRD SERVANT   May I then ask you, poor man of some renown,
to stand somewhere else? In short: clear out!

CORIOLANUS   Do as you've been told. And make it quick or someone else will eat your scraps. *(Pushes him)*

SECOND SERVANT   Get the master!

(Third servant goes out)

FIRST SERVANT   Where do you live anyway?

CORIOLANUS   Under the canopy.

SECOND SERVANT   Under the canopy?

CORIOLANUS   Yes.

FIRST SERVANT   Where's that?

CORIOLANUS   In the city of kites and crows.

FIRST SERVANT   A fool. Then you must live with the feather brains?

CORIOLANUS   No. I don't serve your master.

FIRST SERVANT   You . . . !

SECOND SERVANT   Have you any business with our master?

CORIOLANUS   Yes, and you'd better be glad it's with him and not with your wife. You stand here and prattle. Out to your platters!

(Enter Aufidius with the third servant)

AUFIDIUS   Where is the man?

FIRST SERVANT   Here, sir. I'd have whipped him like a dog but I didn't wish to disturb the company inside.

AUFIDIUS   Where do you come from? What do you want here? Your name? Why don't you speak? Speak, man. What's your name?

CORIOLANUS
A name unmusical to Volscian ears
And harsh to your ears too.

AUFIDIUS
                              Your looks are rude
And yet there's something in your eye as if
You'd lifted up your voice in times gone by.
The tackle's torn and yet the vessel
Was surely noble.

CORIOLANUS
                    Prepare to frown. Do you
Really not know me?

AUFIDIUS
                    I don't know you. Your name!

CORIOLANUS

My name is Caius Marcius, who has done
To you particularly and to all the Volscians
Great hurt and mischief, as my surname bears
Witness: Coriolanus. That name embodies
My arduous service, the mortal dangers faced
The drops of blood I've shed for an ungrateful
Rome. It must surely waken to your mind
The hate you owe me. Only the name is left.
The cruelty and envy of the people
The cowardice of the nobles, who have all
Betrayed me, have devoured the rest.
The voice of slaves has whooped me out of Rome
And this calamity has sent me to your door
Not hope to save my life—no, don't mistake me—
For had I been afraid of death, it's you
Of all men in the world I'd have avoided.
Sheer hatred, lust to be avenged on all
That rabble brings me here before you. If you
—I don't know you—wish to repay the wrong inflicted
Upon you in particular, and the shameful
Scars to be seen throughout your country
Employ me. Put my misery to use.
Harness the vengefulness that burns my entrails
To your own purposes. Your purposes
Are mine. I'll turn the malignant fury of
My sword against my cankered country.
However, if this venture frightens you
If weariness has tamed your enterprise
Then, in a word, I too am tired of living
I offer you my throat and call you fool
If you hesitate to cut it. I have always
Pursued you with my hatred, I have drawn
Barrels of blood from your country's heart. Therefore
My life must cover you with shame, unless
I live to serve you.

AUFIDIUS

O Marcius, Marcius
Each word you've said has weeded from my heart

A root of ancient envy. Let me now
Vie for your love as formerly
I battled with your valor. A dozen times
You've drubbed me so that ever since I've dreamed
Each night of fighting you, unbuckling helmets
Clutching each other's throats—and waked with nothing.
Worthy Marcius, if we had no other quarrel
With Rome except that they have banished you
We'd muster every man from twelve to seventy
And hurl them at the city. Come in. Come in.
Some senators, my friends.

CORIOLANUS
                              O gods, how kind

You are today!

AUFIDIUS
                    And so, sir, if you wish
To pay your debt in person, take one half
My army, and, since you have the experience
And know the strength and weakness of your country
Proceed as you see fit. Choose if you will
To knock directly on the gates of Rome
Or visit more outlying spots. You know
The rule: first frighten, then destroy. But now
Come in! Let me commend you to my friends
Who will approve your wishes. Come!
A thousand welcomes! More a friend than ever
An enemy. And, Marcius, that is saying
Quite a good deal. Come in!

3

Rome. The Forum.

Sicinius and Brutus.

SICINIUS
No news of him. No need to fear him now.
We've made his friends in the senate blush, to see
The world goes on without the hero. It
Grieves them to hear our bakers, ropers, sandal-
Makers all singing at their work.

BRUTUS
We struck before it was too late.

SICINIUS
Menenius.

BRUTUS
His manners are improving too.
(Menenius enters. Greetings are exchanged)

SICINIUS
Your Coriolanus isn't greatly missed.
By a few friends perhaps. The state, however
Endures, and even if he hated it far more
Would still endure.

MENENIUS
Yes, all is well
And might have been still better had he learned
To temporize.

SICINIUS
Where is he? Have you heard?

MENENIUS
No news. His wife and mother have no word of him.
(A few citizens pass by)

CITIZENS
  The gods preserve you both!

BRUTUS
                          Good evening, neighbors.

SICINIUS
  Good evening all! Good evening!

FIRST CITIZEN
  Let me say this: our wives and children too
  Should get down on their knees and pray
  The gods to give you both good health.

BRUTUS
  The gods protect you, neighbors!
  (The citizens go out)

SICINIUS
  Aren't we all much better off than in the days
  When they detested you?

BRUTUS
                        Caius Marcius was
  A worthy soldier in the field, but insolent
  Puffed up with pride, ambitious beyond measure
  Self-loving . . .

SICINIUS
                  Yes, he aimed to make himself dictator.

MENENIUS
  That seems unlikely.

SICINIUS
                  We'd have found out to
  Our sorrow, had he been chosen consul.

BRUTUS
  The gods prevented that. Now Rome
  Is breathing easier.
  (Enter an aedile)

AEDILE
                  Tribunes!
  A slave—we've thrown the man in prison—reports
  The Volscians with two separate armies have
  Invaded Roman territory, destroying
  Everything in their path.

MENENIUS

Aufidius

Who, hearing we had banished Marcius
Is putting out once more the feelers that
He'd anxiously retracted when he knew
Marcius was here with us.

SICINIUS

Come, come, why bring up Marcius?

BRUTUS

Have him whipped!

The rumor monger! That's not possible!
The Volscians wouldn't dare to break with us!

MENENIUS

Not possible? It's more than possible.
Three times it's happened in my lifetime.
Question the man before you punish him
And find out where he heard it. Otherwise
You will be whipping information.

SICINIUS

Don't tell

Me that. I know it can't be so.

BRUTUS

Impossible.

(Enter a messenger)

MESSENGER

The nobles are meeting in the senate.
Bad news has come in from the mountains.

SICINIUS

That slave again! A provocation! Whip him!

MESSENGER

No, sir. He told the truth. Except it's worse.

SICINIUS

What's worse?

MESSENGER

I don't know if it's true, but all
Reports concur in saying that Marcius
Joined with Aufidius is leading
An army against Rome, and swears to take

Such vengeance on the city that neither young
Nor old . . .

SICINIUS
                    A likely story!

BRUTUS
                            Trumped up to make
Our weaker sisters wish for Marcius'
Return.

SICINIUS
          No doubt about it.

MENENIUS
                    Most unlikely:
He and Aufidius! That's mixing oil and water.
    (Enter another messenger)

SECOND MESSENGER
    They want you in the senate, sir.
    A fearful army led by Caius Marcius
    In league with Aufidius is driving on Rome.
    Corioli's in flames and fallen to
    The enemy.
    (Enter Cominius)

COMINIUS
          Good work you've done!

MENENIUS
                        What news? What news?

COMINIUS
    You've helped to ravish your own daughters
    And melt the leaden roofs on your own heads.

MENENIUS
                            What news?

COMINIUS
    And burn your temples down to their foundations.
    Now you can take your precious bill of rights
    And stuff it in a mouse hole.

MENENIUS
                    In the gods' name, what news?
If Marcius should indeed have joined the Volscians . . .

COMINIUS
    If? Why, he's their god. He leads them like a thing

Made by some other deity than nature
That turns out better men. They follow him
With no less confidence than boys pursuing
Summer butterflies or butchers killing flies.

MENENIUS

Good work you've done! You and your apron men
And garlic eaters, with the mighty voice
Of the Roman working class!

COMINIUS

                      He'll shake your Rome
About your ears.

BRUTUS

             But is this true, sir?

COMINIUS

Yes! "Is this true, sir?" All the cities
Laugh and rebel against us. Those who choose
Not to rebel are mocked for their brave innocence
And die like fools.

MENENIUS

              We're lost unless the great man
Takes mercy on us.

COMINIUS

             But who will plead with him?
The tribunes of the people can't; the people
Deserve his pity as the wolf deserves
The pity of the shepherd. As for his friends
If they should come and say "Be kind to Rome"
They'd merely prove themselves his enemies.

MENENIUS

That's true. If he were here now with a torch
To set my house on fire, I wouldn't have
The gall to say: "Please don't." This thing will cost you
Your cowhide aprons and your hides as well.

COMINIUS

We love him, but like stupid cattle we
Betrayed him to you and your salt of the earth.
And when he comes, he'll meet not armed resistance
But a despairing mob.
(Enter a group of citizens)

MENENIUS

                    Here comes the salt.
You threw your greasy caps into the air
To drive him from your city. Now he's coming.
He'll take himself as many heads as you
Threw caps. But all of us are in for it.
If he could burn us all to cinders
I'd say we had it coming. Shall we go to the Capitol?

COMINIUS
What else is there to do?
(Cominius and Menenius go out)

CITIZENS
They say he's burning every foot of ground
He steps on.

SICINIUS

                    Don't be discouraged. There are dogs in Rome
Who'd gladly see confirmed what they pretend
To fear. Now go, my friends, I didn't say
Run. Go back to your districts
And show you're not afraid.

SECOND CITIZEN

                              I'd rather have
A sword to show than courage. Was it wise
To banish him?

SICINIUS

            Yes.
(The citizens go out slowly)
                    To the Capitol!

4

Camp near Rome.

Aufidius and a captain.

AUFIDIUS
Are they still flocking to the Roman?

CAPTAIN

    I can't make out what witchcraft he has in him.
    But to your soldiers he is grace before meat
    Their talk at table and their thanks before rising.
    You are overshadowed in this action, sir
    In your own army.

AUFIDIUS

                I can't help that now.
    If I should try to, it would halt the whole
    Campaign before it's fairly started.

CAPTAIN

                      Sir
    I wish you had not shared the high command
    With him, but taken it yourself, or else
    Left it to him entirely.

AUFIDIUS

    I understand you well. But rest assured
    When the time comes to settle up accounts
    He doesn't know what I can urge against him
    Although it seems, and so he thinks, and so
    Do people generally think, that he is
    Loyal in all his actions. Still, there's
    Something he will not do, and if it's left
    Undone, it will break my neck, and that in turn
    Will break his neck.

CAPTAIN

            Do you think he will take Rome, sir?

AUFIDIUS

    Cities surrender to him before he even
    Lays siege to them. The Roman nobles
    Are for him. The tribunes are
    No soldiers. He has spread the word in Rome
    That to prevent unprofitable slaughter
    A smoke cloud sent up from the Capitol
    Should signal unconditional surrender.
    Smug as the ocean whale he calmly waits
    For lesser fish to swim obligingly
    Into his jaws, but one thing he forgets:
    Once he has Rome, I will have him.
    For anything he does then will be wrong

Because he does it. If he's hard on the nobles
He's done for—the Volscian nobles will object.
And if he's easy on the nobles, he's done for—
Then too the Volscian nobles will object.
This man was fortune's child and yet unable
To use his fortune. He could not exchange
The saddle for the seat of government
Or war for peace. His deeds are great
But he dwarfs them by extolling them. Our merit
Depends upon the use our epoch makes of us.
Our power has no tomb so everlasting
As the speaker's platform on which it is praised.
The storm puts out the fire it has fanned
Nail drives out nail and power by power's unmanned.

ACT FIVE

1

Rome. The Forum.

Menenius, Cominius, and other senators. Sicinius and Brutus.

COMINIUS
  He didn't seem to know me.

MENENIUS
                         His
  Former commander!

COMINIUS
                    Coriolanus, I said.
  He forbade that name and every other, shouted
  He was a king of nothing, titleless
  Until he forged himself a new name in
  The fire of burning Rome.

SICINIUS
                 Or fails to.

MENENIUS
  Will he be prevented by a pair of tribunes
  Expert at bringing down the price of corn cakes?

BRUTUS
  Whereas you are expert
  At bringing down the price of Rome. Send up
  Smoke from the Capitol, let your crony know
  He's welcome. Fall upon your knees before
  His tent. No, do it a mile away
  And on your knees crawl into his good graces.
  Make up your minds! Who wants to see the smoke?
  (Pause)
  Good. No one. Then distribute arms, or else
  Those who reject the little smoke

Will see a big smoke from the blaze of Rome.
(Pause)
(Sicinius and Brutus go out)

COMINIUS

I pointed out
That mercy is more worthy of a king
The less it is expected. To which he
Replied that coming from a city which
Had banished him, my plea was rather tawdry.

MENENIUS

                                        Indeed.

COMINIUS

I spoke of consideration for his friends.
He said he hadn't time to pick them out
From a pile of noisome musty chaff. He said
It was foolish for one poor grain or two
To leave the heap unburned to go on stinking.

MENENIUS

For one poor grain or two? I'm one of those.
His mother, wife and child, and this brave man
We are the grains.—They are the musty chaff
That stinks above the moon. And we must burn
On their account. All right, I'll go to him.
You tackled him too early in the morning
He hadn't had his breakfast. That, perhaps
Is why you found him in so sour a mood.
I'll wait till he has eaten.
(Menenius goes out)

COMINIUS

                        He'll never gain a hearing.

2

The Volscian camp near Rome.

Sentries. Enter to them, Menenius.

FIRST SENTRY

Halt! Where are you from?

SECOND SENTRY

Go back! Go back!

MENENIUS

I am a messenger of state. I come
To speak with Coriolanus.

FIRST SENTRY

You're a Roman?

MENENIUS

Yes.

FIRST SENTRY

You can't go through. Turn back. Our general
Wants no more truck with Rome.

SECOND SENTRY

You'll see
Rome burning long before you speak to him.

MENENIUS

Men, if you've heard your general speak of Rome
Or of his friends there, I'll lay ten to one
He mentioned my name too—Menenius.

FIRST SENTRY

We're glad to hear it, but you can't go through.

MENENIUS

The general's my friend, I tell you.

FIRST SENTRY

Then
Friend of my general, go back!

MENENIUS   But my dear fellow, haven't I told you my name is
Menenius, a member of your general's party from way back.
—Has he had his breakfast? Do you know that? I don't intend
to speak to him before he's had his breakfast.

FIRST SENTRY   You're a Roman, aren't you?

MENENIUS   I'm what your general is.

FIRST SENTRY   Then you should hate Rome as he does. Let me
tell you something. You've driven the man out of your city,
the same man who defended it for you. You've thrown your
shield to the enemy. Do you think you can stop what's coming now with old women's sighs, with a few virgins wringing
their hands, or with the gouty kneeling of a doddering old
fool like yourself? Do you, with your weak breath, expect to

blow out the fire intended for Rome? Don't make me laugh.
Go back to Rome and wait for your execution!

MENENIUS   Sir, if your general knew . . .

(Enter Coriolanus and Aufidius)

CORIOLANUS   What's going on?

MENENIUS   Now, fellow, you've got yourself in a fix. Judge by
his manner of speaking to me whether or not you're ripe for
the gallows.—My son, you are preparing a fire for us. Here's
the water to quench it.

(Coriolanus looks to see if smoke is going up)

MENENIUS   I was not easily moved to come here. They know
that I alone can move you. Sighs, my son, blew me out of the
city gate. And now I beseech you, let Rome live! Turn back,
my son!

CORIOLANUS   Go away!

MENENIUS   What's this? Go away?

CORIOLANUS

I don't know you or any other Roman.
What I do now serves others. Moreover
I am entitled to revenge. The power to pardon
Is with the Volscians. Let it rather be
Consigned to forgetfulness that we were friends
Than sorrowfully recalled how much so. Go.
My ears are better fortified against
Your pleas than are your gates against my troops.
And yet, because I loved you, take this letter
I've written you. I would have sent it.
And now, Menenius, not another word.
This man, Aufidius, was dear to me in Rome
And yet you see . . .

AUFIDIUS
                                You have stood firm.

(Coriolanus and Aufidius go out)

FIRST SENTRY   Well, sir, so your name is Menenius.

SECOND SENTRY   It does wonders, doesn't it? You know the way
home.

FIRST SENTRY   Did you hear how we were raked over the coals
for not admitting a messenger of state?

3

Rome. One of the gates.

Cominius and senators are waiting for Menenius. He enters.

MENENIUS   I told you there's no hope. Our throats are sentenced and waiting for the executioner.

SENATOR   Is it possible that a man can change so in so short a time?

MENENIUS   This Marcius has changed from man to dragon. His face turns ripe grapes sour. He moves like a war machine and the ground shrinks under his tread. I'm painting him from life.

(Sicinius and Brutus have entered. With them citizens)

COMINIUS   The gods take pity on our poor city!

MENENIUS   No, this time the gods will not take pity on us. When we banished him, we disregarded them, and now that he's coming back, they will disregard us. *(To Brutus)* And it's you we have to thank for all this.

(He goes out with the senators except for Cominius)

BRUTUS   They've gone to pack. They prefer to die on their estates. *(To the citizens)* It's just as we told you. The city fathers are leaving Rome to its fate. How do things stand in your districts?

A CITIZEN   The majority have reported for military duty. The ones who were still waiting to see if Menenius would get anywhere with Coriolanus will report now.

BRUTUS   Good. If the people who live off Rome won't defend it, then we, whom Rome has lived off up to now, will defend it. Why shouldn't masons defend their walls?

COMINIUS   A few of us are with you. Arms will be distributed. On my responsibility.

CITIZENS   Long live Cominius!

(A second citizen enters)

SECOND CITIZEN   Volumnia, his mother, and four women of the foremost families request a pass to see Caius Marcius. They want to plead with him to turn back.

SICINIUS   Request rejected.

BRUTUS   Granted.

SICINIUS   You mean to let those traitors out of the city?

BRUTUS   A few patrician families are living in fear of being stoned for their connection with him. They seem to have appealed to her. I don't believe the old lady is afraid of us, but I doubt if she wants to see the Volscian senate meeting on the Capitol. She's a patriot in her way: she'd rather see us plebeians trampled on by Romans than by Volscians. What do you think, Cominius?

COMINIUS   Let them go, but . . . Do you see that cornerstone on the Capitol?

SICINIUS   Why, what of it?

COMINIUS   If you can move it with your little finger, there is some hope that the ladies of Rome will get somewhere with him.

BRUTUS   Her words may be powerless to move him—though that's not so sure, she will be able to tell him certain things that are new to him. That stone you see there is immovable. Give me an earthquake and perhaps I'll move it after all.

COMINIUS   There's no more mercy in him than milk in a male tiger.

SICINIUS   They say he loved his mother.

COMINIUS   He loved me too. And he no more remembers his mother now than an eight-year-old horse would remember his.

BRUTUS   The interview may give us a breathing spell. Tonight and tomorrow we'll be short of men to defend the walls. (To the citizen) They can go. But send one of their serving women with them, one you can trust, to report their conversation. Agreed?

SICINIUS   Agreed. Two hard days ahead of us.

BRUTUS
I have the feeling, shared, I'm told, by many
Others, that Rome's a better place
With that man gone, a city worth defending
Perhaps for the first time since it was founded.
(All go out)

4

The Volscian camp.

Coriolanus, Aufidius, a sentry.

SENTRY
  No, sir, no smoke.
AUFIDIUS
                How long do you mean to wait?
CORIOLANUS
  We'll camp tomorrow before the walls of Rome.
AUFIDIUS
  Why not today?
CORIOLANUS
                You are my partner in this action.
  You must inform the lords in Antium
  How loyally I've gone about this business.
AUFIDIUS
  Of course. Of course. You've been the very soul
  Of loyalty.
CORIOLANUS
                That old man now, whom I sent
  Back to Rome broken-hearted, loved me more
  Than had he been my father, worshiped me as
  A god—sending him was their last resort.
AUFIDIUS
  Yet even that old man who worships you
  Showed no submission, only entreaty and
  An invitation to go and hang yourself.
  (Shouts backstage)
CORIOLANUS
  What's the noise?
  (A soldier enters)
SOLDIER
                A delegation, sir
  Some ladies of the foremost Roman families

Are here in camp. It may be rumor, but
They say your mother's here, sir, and your wife
And little boy.

CORIOLANUS *(looking Aufidius in the eye)*

Control your feelings! Clench
Your teeth, for fear the gods above will laugh
And say this scene's unnatural. The
Volscians can plow up Rome and harrow Italy
Before you'll see me bow to nature or
Grovel before my instinct.

*(Volumnia, Virgilia with young Marcius, and four Roman ladies
have entered)*

VIRGILIA

My lord and husband!

(Coriolanus approaches and greets them)

CORIOLANUS

Woman, these eyes are not the same as
They were in Rome.

VIRGILIA

Yes, troubles change a man.

VOLUMNIA

You know this lady?

CORIOLANUS

Young Publicola's
Illustrious sister. Rome's chaste Luna.
My dear Valeria!

VIRGILIA

Here's a small extract of yourself, which by
The interpretation of the years may grow
To be entirely like you.

CORIOLANUS

Yes, my boy
The gods, I trust, are busy making you
A fighter, who amidst the battle's tumult
Will stand, for all who see you, like a beacon
Invulnerable to shame as well.

VOLUMNIA

Kneel, child.

CORIOLANUS *(preventing him from kneeling)*

That's my good boy, and now don't ask me to

Call off my soldiers and negotiate
Again with Rome's bricklayers. And don't tell
Me that my conduct is unnatural.
Aufidius, and you Volscians, listen closely:
We want no private word from Rome. Your business!

VOLUMNIA

If silence were possible, I should keep silent
For then I should say nothing that would stir
You or destroy you. Nor should I waste my words.
For I have not set out like other mothers
To save her child, but rather to corrupt him
That is, if he's still human—and if he's not
He'll turn against me. Son, I cannot pray
The gods to give you victory, as under
Usual circumstances would be my duty
Nor to give victory to our city, as would also be
My duty. I must either forfeit Rome
Our family's cradle, or forfeit you, our mainstay
In Rome. To me the outcome's fatal
In either case, for either you'll be led
Through Rome in chains as a traitor, or else in triumph
You'll tread the orphaned ruins of your city
And thereupon be crowned with bronze for shedding
Your wife's and children's blood. For my part, son
I shall not wait until the war decides which
Misfortune is to strike me. If I can't
Persuade you, you will not set foot in Rome
Before you've trampled on the womb of
The mother who bore you.

VIRGILIA

                          And on mine
That brought you forth this boy to keep your name
Living in time.

YOUNG MARCIUS

                    You will not trample me.
I'll run away until I'm bigger, then I'll fight.

CORIOLANUS

                                  Aha!
If you would not turn womanish and mild
Don't look upon the face of woman or child.

I've sat too long.
(He stands up)

VOLUMNIA
                    Not only in our presence.
Forget my petty trouble, that I'll find
It hard to veil my face from this day on
Whenever I go out, because your father
Never gave me reason to. Enough of
Your childish sentiment. I've something else
To say. The Rome you will be marching on
Is very different from the Rome you left.
You are no longer indispensable
Merely a deadly threat to all. Don't expect
To see submissive smoke. If you see smoke
It will be rising from the smithies forging
Weapons to fight you who, to subject your
Own people, have submitted to your enemy.
And we, the proud nobility of Rome
Must owe the rabble our salvation from the
Volscians, or owe the Volscians our
Salvation from the rabble. Come, we'll go now.
The fellow had a Volscian for a mother
His wife is in Corioli, and this child
Resembles him by chance.
(The women go out)

CORIOLANUS
    O mother, mother! What have you done?

                    5

Rome. A guarded gate.

Brutus and Sicinius. A messenger.

MESSENGER
    News!
    The Volscians have withdrawn and Marcius with them!

BRUTUS
  The stone has moved. The people takes
  Up weapons, and the old earth shakes.
  (Both go out)

6

Corioli. The city gate.

Aufidius with attendant and officers.

AUFIDIUS
  Stand over there and give the senators
  This paper when they come to welcome me.
  Tell them I'll vouch for the truth of what it says
  Before them and before the people. Right
  Here at the gate I will accuse him, when
  He comes to clear himself with empty words.
  Go now.
  *(The attendant stands off to one side and gives the arriving senators
  Aufidius' paper)*
SENATORS
          Most welcome home!
AUFIDIUS
                        Why welcome?
  I haven't earned your welcome. Have you read
  My message?
FIRST SENATOR
          Yes.
SECOND SENATOR
                  And with dismay. His old
  Misdeeds can pass. But stopping where he should
  Have started, throwing away the advantage
  Leaving us nothing but the bill to pay
  That's unforgivable.

AUFIDIUS

He's coming. Hear what he says.
(Enter Coriolanus with drums and banners. Citizens with him)

CORIOLANUS

Hail, gentlemen. I'm back. Your soldier
No more infected with the love of my country
Than when I marched off under your
Supreme command. Through bloody fields I've carried
Your battle to the very gates of Rome.
The spoil that we've brought back accounts for more than
A third of what the campaign cost.

AUFIDIUS

Don't read
The inventory. Tell the traitor he has grossly
Abused your trust, and . . .

CORIOLANUS

Traitor? Why? What's wrong?

AUFIDIUS

Yes, traitor, Marcius.

CORIOLANUS

Marcius?

AUFIDIUS

Did you think
I'd bow to your theft, your stolen name, and call
You Coriolanus in Corioli?
You lords and senators of this state, this man
Is perjured. He has betrayed your cause. For a
Few drops of salt he has given away your Rome
(Your Rome, I say) to his wife and mother
Breaking his oath like a thread of rotten silk.
Without so much as calling a council of war
At the mere sight of his nurse's tears, he whimpered
And whined away your victory. The drummer
Boys blushed, the men
Looked at each other in silence.

CORIOLANUS

I whimpered?

AUFIDIUS

Like a milksop.

CORIOLANUS

                    Oh, you barefaced liar!
Milksop! Forgive me, gentlemen, I've never railed
Before in public. Worthy gentlemen
I've thrashed such welts into this cur
He'll take them to his grave.

SECOND SENATOR

                                Peace, both of you!

CORIOLANUS

Cut me to pieces, Volscians. Let the children
Redden their penknives in me. Milksop!
You lying dog! If ever your chronicles
Should tell the truth, they'll say that like
An eagle in a dovecote, I fluttered
Your Volscians in Corioli. Milksop!

AUFIDIUS

Enough! More than enough! Gentlemen
Will you allow this braggart to remind you
Of his luck in battle that was your disgrace?

OFFICER   That's his death warrant!

CITIZENS   Tear him to pieces.—He killed my son.—My daughter.—He killed my cousin Marcus.—He killed my father.

AUFIDIUS

Kill him!

(Aufidius' officers draw and kill Coriolanus)

7

Rome. The senate.

Consul, senators, tribunes.

CONSUL

The tribunes' motion to restore the lands
Taken from the inhabitants of Corioli
To their owners, is enacted into law.

SENATOR
   Motion: that we construct an aqueduct
   From the third hill to the eastern gardens.
   (*A messenger brings in a dispatch*)

CONSUL
   This message says that Caius Marcius
   Was stabbed to death in Corioli
   Yesterday morning.
   (*Silence*)

MENENIUS
   Motion: He's dead now, therefore let his name
   So great before misfortune fell upon
   It, be inscribed in the Capitol
   As that of a Roman and a . . .

BRUTUS
   Motion: let the senate proceed
   With current business.

CONSUL
                     Question:
   His family has petitioned that its women
   As stipulated in the law of Numa
   Pompilius concerning the survivors
   Of fathers, sons and brothers, be permitted
   To wear mourning in public for ten months.

BRUTUS
   Rejected.
   (*The senate resumes its deliberations*)

The Trial of Joan of Arc
at Rouen, 1431

After a Radio Play by Anna Seghers

Collaborator: B. Besson

Translators: Ralph Manheim and Wolfgang Sauerlander

The proceedings were recorded day by day in the Latin language. The original of the trial record was prepared for Bishop Cauchon of Beauvais and is preserved at the Chamber of Deputies in Paris. The radio play is based on these trial records as well as on the testimony and information furnished by contemporaries. Bertolt Brecht used the radio play for his dramatization for the Berliner Ensemble.

A. S.

CHARACTERS

JOAN OF ARC	JACQUES LEGRAIN
BISHOP CAUCHON OF BEAUVAIS	PEASANT
JEAN BEAUPÈRE	PEASANT WOMAN
JEAN DE LA FONTAINE	SON
JEAN DE CHATILLON (CHATION)	SISTER-IN-LAW
GUILLAUME ERARD	CHILD
NICOLAS MIDI	FISHWIFE
GUILLAUME MANCHON	DR. DUFOUR
JEAN D'ESTIVET	HIS TWO NIECES
JEAN LEFÈVRE	WELL-DRESSED GENTLEMAN
JEAN MASSIEU	LOOSE WOMAN
RAOUL DE RINEL	WINE MERCHANT
A CLERK	INNKEEPER
THE EXECUTIONER	YOUNG CURATE
NUNS	WAR CRIPPLE
AN ENGLISH OBSERVER	GRANDFATHER BREUIL and HIS
HIS ADJUTANT	GRANDSON
GUARDS OF JOAN OF ARC	CHILDREN
ENGLISH SOLDIERS	PEOPLE
TWO PEASANT GIRLS	

1

Autumn, 1430. For eight years war has been raging between England and France. Recently France has undertaken two bloody campaigns under the banner of a seventeen-year-old girl, Joan of Arc, in a desperate attempt to ward off the English conquerors who still occupy more than two-thirds of the country. A village in Touraine, in the unoccupied part of France, gets bad news.

In front of a peasant house in Touraine two young girls are pressing grapes. Children are helping.

YOUNG GIRLS *(singing)*
　　Oh wondrous maiden of Lorraine
　　Barely sixteen and daughter of a frugal hearth
　　Upon your shield the enemy strikes in vain.
　　War is your strength, your resting place the naked earth.
　　Your boldness has its equal in your guile
　　Your enemies fall back in panic fear
　　None dares to stand, they run full many a mile
　　And countless eyes look on from far and near.
SECOND GIRL *(to the children)*　Don't eat them all.—They're worse than woodpeckers.
A BOY　You haven't filled a single vat yet.
THE GIRLS *(sing)*
　　Many, it's true, are so cast down with woe
　　They cannot understand the Maid. For he
　　Who weeps is blinded. Though in the brightest glow
　　His eyes are powerless to see.
　　But many now have joined the Maiden's ranks

As though to dance they're marching off to fight
The Loire has shaken the enemy from its banks
The sun of France shines with a clearer light.

FIRST GIRL   Where's Jacques?

SECOND GIRL   Gone to town again.

FIRST GIRL   He ought to go easy on his leg.

SECOND GIRL   I can't hold him back.—How much more is there
to pick in the upper vineyard?

FIRST GIRL   Two acres.

THE GIRLS (*sing*)
Oh, all ye villains, traitors all
Suffered too long by this long-suffering folk
You who have fostered England's joy and France's fall
Her poverty and shame and captive yoke:
You have been fighting for an unjust cause.
It's not too late for you to mend your ways.
If you go on supporting France's foes
A bitter end will strike your evil days.

JACQUES LEGRAIN (*joins them*)   They've captured her, near Compiègne. They've put her in a cage and they're taking her to
Rouen.

FIRST GIRL   No?!

LEGRAIN   Get my pack ready.

SECOND GIRL   Where are you going?

LEGRAIN   To Rouen, to buy a pound of mackerel.

2

February 21, 1431. In the market place of English-occupied Rouen a crowd looks on as English noblemen and French renegade churchmen lead the resistance fighter to her trial.

Market place at Rouen. Among the crowd a peasant family (father, mother, sister-in-law, son, and child), a fishwife, Legrain with his pack, a well-dressed gentleman, a loose woman, a wine merchant, a physician, the executioner in his everyday clothes. Two English soldiers. Church bells and drumrolls.

WELL-DRESSED GENTLEMAN   That's the Duke of Bedford.

FISHWIFE   Look at his white horse. As sleek and fat as his master.

PEASANT WOMAN   Hey, Johnny, are you sure she'll come this way?

SON   Or is she already inside?

FISHWIFE   Don't worry, madame, she's sure to come this way.

PEASANT WOMAN   Eugene, have you got the food parcel?

CHILD   Who's that all in silk?

WELL-DRESSED GENTLEMAN   Bishop Cauchon of Beauvais.

DR. DUFOUR   A French bishop walking behind an English duke! I'm surprised the Englishman hasn't got him on a leash.

LOOSE WOMAN *(sings in an undertone)*
Bishop Cauchon of Beauvais
Is an Englishman now, they say
On sentimental grounds
And for five thousand pounds.

FISHWIFE   That's no joke for the Maid.

LOOSE WOMAN   They say she has voices and visions. I wonder if it's true.

PEASANT WOMAN   Did you hear that? She has visions.

PEASANT   Ssh.

WINE MERCHANT   The learned doctors will see about that.

WELL-DRESSED GENTLEMAN   The papal nuncio.

(The peasant woman crosses herself)

LOOSE WOMAN   Look at his hat!

(All laugh, including the peasant woman)

SISTER-IN-LAW   Too bad about the girl. Nobody likes the English.

WELL-DRESSED GENTLEMAN   I wouldn't say that too loud, madame, not today.

PEASANT   She's always shooting her mouth off.

LOOSE WOMAN   Johnny, there's somebody here that doesn't like you.

FISHWIFE   Forget it, they don't understand French.

WINE MERCHANT   Maybe it's all for the best. She was a trouble-maker.

FISHWIFE   The English give you plenty of business, don't they?

DR. DUFOUR   Well said!

(Loose woman laughs)

WELL-DRESSED GENTLEMAN   I beg your pardon!

PEASANT WOMAN (to child)   Isn't it a lovely holiday, Jacqueline?

WINE MERCHANT   I've already seen one of these witches burnt.

EXECUTIONER   When was that?

WINE MERCHANT   Four years ago, in Beauvais, in the spring of twenty-seven.

EXECUTIONER   I see.

FISHWIFE   That's Monsieur Dujardin, the executioner.

PEASANT WOMAN   Where?

(All turn around to look at the executioner)

LOOSE WOMAN   Dear me!

WELL-DRESSED GENTLEMAN   Seems like he's taking her measurements.

DR. DUFOUR   Look, there are the doctors from Paris.

SON   Why can't the English try her themselves?

DR. DUFOUR   They'd rather let the French do it for them.

SON   But the French have no reason to.

DR. DUFOUR   All those doctors ought to be able to find one.

LEGRAIN   As long as she answers boldly. That's the main thing.

SISTER-IN-LAW   Boldly! How can a girl stand up against so many?

LOOSE WOMAN   What did she have to stick her neck out for? Why didn't she stay home?

(Well-dressed gentleman assents)

LEGRAIN   Because the English came to France. Because the English occupied all France as far as the Loire. Because they're gobbling up the whole country. Because they've dethroned the king. Because before she came along the king was too lazy to defend himself.

PEASANT WOMAN   Because—because—because, is that a reason to get crazy ideas and run around in men's clothes in front of soldiers?

PEASANT   Shut up!

WELL-DRESSED GENTLEMAN   She says she owes it to her country, madame.

DR. DUFOUR   Country? What do you mean by country?

FISHWIFE   Her voices told her to drive the English out of the country, Dr. Dufour.

DR. DUFOUR   Country! What difference does it make to the country who's on the white horse that's trampling it into dust? The Duke of Bedford or the Duke of Orléans? What difference does it make to the country who gobbles up its wheat and its wine, its venison and fruit, its taxes and tithes? The Lord of Beauvais or the Duke of Gloucester?

FISHWIFE   It's easier to give a French lord a piece of your mind. Those English gentlemen don't even understand our curses.

CHILD   Is that the king?

SISTER-IN-LAW   No, that's an English trumpeter.

(Drumrolls)

LOOSE WOMAN   Here she comes! Here she comes!

ENGLISH SOLDIER   Move back! Back, I say!

PEASANT WOMAN   Careful with the eggs, Eugene!

LOOSE WOMAN   My, she's little.

SISTER-IN-LAW   Those chains must be heavy on her. No bigger than an apple.

(The wine merchant laughs)

LEGRAIN   That little apple had the English on the run.

DR. DUFOUR   The Duke of Bedford paid the Duke of Luxemburg twelve thousand pounds for that little apple.

PEASANT   Why did he do that?

FISHWIFE   To make his Englishmen stop running.

3

At the first session of the great ecclesiastical trial in the Chapel Royal of the castle, Joan cleverly eludes the trick questions of the churchmen who are out to convict her of heresy, and boldly reminds them of the wretched state of France.

The Chapel Royal of the castle. The churchmen, Beaupère, Chation, La Fontaine, d'Estivet, Manchon, Midi, Lefèvre, Massieu, Brother Raoul and the clerk. Enter the English observer with his adjutant and the Bishop of Beauvais. The churchmen kneel.

BISHOP   Praised be the Lord.

ALL   For ever and ever. Amen.

THE ENGLISH OBSERVER *(to the bishop)*   Splendid crowd of doctors.

BISHOP   Thank you.

THE ENGLISH OBSERVER   Pleasant chapel, even if not one of the oldest.

BISHOP   Nor one of the newest. Built by Charles the . . . *(He raises five fingers)*

THE ENGLISH OBSERVER   Oh, the fifth, I see. Don't let me keep you.

(All take their seats)

BISHOP   We, Bishop Cauchon of Beauvais, and our illustrious assessors, the noble lords and doctors here present, have gathered this day to conduct a trial which we hereby declare opened. Milord, have you conveyed to the accused the summons to appear before us and answer our questions in accordance with the law?

ADJUTANT   Said woman has answered the summons and is waiting outside. She requests, however, to be admitted to confession before the trial.

(The bishop consults the assessors. They nod)

BISHOP   The request must be denied. In view of the gravity of the charges and the refusal of the accused to relinquish her male clothing. Monsieur Massieu, bring in the accused.

MASSIEU   The accused may be brought in.

ADJUTANT   Bring her in.

(Joan is led in by two English soldiers)

BISHOP   This woman now appearing before us, Joan, popularly called the Maid, has been apprehended in the jurisdiction of our diocese. As a suspected heretic she has been turned over to us by our Most Christian Lord, the King of England and France. And inasmuch as rumors concerning her offenses against the faith have spread far beyond our diocese and indeed throughout France and the whole of Christendom, we have brought her before this court in order that she may justify herself. We admonish you, Joan, to touch these Most Holy Gospels and swear to reply truthfully to all questions. Monsieur Massieu!

(At a sign from Massieu Brother Raoul brings the Bible)

BISHOP   Now swear by these gospels. Place both hands on the book.

JOAN   But I don't know what you're going to ask me. Maybe you want to know something that I won't tell you.

BISHOP   Come, come, just swear to tell the truth in all matters concerning the faith.

JOAN   I'll gladly swear to tell you about my family and my home and anything that happened before I came to Chinon, but I will not say one word about my voices and revelations, not even if you cut my head off.

BISHOP   Very well, Joan. We ask you only to tell the truth in matters of faith, as the law requires in proceedings of this kind. Go on.

JOAN   *(kneels)*   I swear to tell the truth in matters of faith. *(She sits down)*

BISHOP   Tell us your first and last name.

JOAN   At home they called me Jeannette and in France Jeanne. I know of no other name.

BISHOP   Where were you born?

JOAN   In Domrémy on the Meuse.

BISHOP   Who are your parents?

JOAN   Jacques d'Arc and Isabeau.

BISHOP   How old are you?

JOAN   About nineteen, I think.

BISHOP   Who instructed you in the faith?

JOAN   My mother taught me everything: the Lord's Prayer, the Hail Mary, and the Creed.

BISHOP   Say the Lord's Prayer.

JOAN   Hear my confession and I'll say the prayer.

BISHOP   In men's clothes? Come now, just say the Lord's Prayer.

JOAN   I will not say it unless you hear my confession.

BISHOP   Joan, we, your bishop, forbid you to leave the prison for whatsoever purpose except by our permission. To do so would be disobedience to the church and a grave offense against the faith.

JOAN   I can't accept that ruling. No one can accuse me of breaking my word if I escape, I haven't given it to anybody. What's more, I protest against these chains and shackles you've loaded me down with.

BISHOP   You have made several attempts to escape. Hence our severity.

JOAN   Naturally I tried to escape. Like any captive. I'd escape right now if I could.

BISHOP   Have your voices given you permission to escape from prison whenever you feel like it?

JOAN   I've asked their permission more than once, but never received it.

BISHOP   I see.

JOAN   But then they say that "God helps those who help themselves."

BISHOP   *(to the English observer)*   With your permission, my lord. *(To the guards)* We enjoin you most urgently, you, John Grey, and you, William Talbot, to guard her closely and permit no one to speak to her.

GUARDS   Yes, sir.

BISHOP   Monsieur Jean Beaupère, Professor of the Faculty of

Theology at the University of Paris, you may question the
accused.

BEAUPÈRE *(after having bowed to the English observer)* First of
all, I must once again exhort you, Joan, to answer my questions with nothing but the truth. Have you learned a
trade?

JOAN Yes. Sewing and spinning.

BEAUPÈRE What work did you do at home?

JOAN I did the housework. Sometimes I helped to drive the
cows into the fortress to prevent the English from stealing
them.

MIDI Monsieur Beaupère, may I interrupt? Are the people of
Domrémy loyal to our Most Christian Lord, the King of
England and France, or do they follow the man whom you
call King of France?

JOAN I know of only one person in Domrémy who's in favor
of the English. I'd gladly have seen his head cut off if it had
so pleased the Lord.

(Commotion among the assessors)

BISHOP Monsieur Beaupère, pray continue.

BEAUPÈRE When did you first hear what you call your voices?

JOAN When I was thirteen I heard a voice that came from God.
That was the first time, and I was really frightened. The voice
came to me in my father's garden, one summer afternoon. I
heard it somewhere behind me, from the direction of the
church. A great light came with the voice.

BEAUPÈRE How could you see the light if it was somewhere
behind you?

JOAN When I heard the voice for the third time, I knew it was
the voice of an angel.

BEAUPÈRE What did it say?

JOAN It has always protected me. It told me to be good and go
to church often. And two or three times a week it told me to
leave everything and go to my king. It said I would raise the
siege of Orléans.

BEAUPÈRE What was your answer?

JOAN I said: I'm a girl, I've never ridden a horse, I don't know
a thing about war. But the voice pressed me cruelly and gave
me no peace. It told me to go. So I went.

D'ESTIVET Question: Hadn't you left home once before?

JOAN   Yes, when the English attacked our village, we all ran away, and then two weeks later we came back. Everything had been burned to the ground.

BISHOP   Let's get on.

LA FONTAINE *(intervenes)*   Was it right to leave secretly? Are we not enjoined to honor our father and our mother?

JOAN   Yes, but even if I'd had a hundred fathers and mothers, I'd have gone.

BEAUPÈRE   What kind of clothes were you wearing when you arrived in Chinon?

JOAN   I went to my king in Chinon in men's clothing. I had a sword, but no other weapons.

BEAUPÈRE   Who told you to wear men's clothes?

JOAN   Ask me something else.

D'ESTIVET   Your Eminence, we must insist on being told who advised the accused to wear male attire.

CHATION   Absolutely.

JOAN   Ask me something else.

BISHOP   Don't you know that the Scriptures say: The woman shall not wear that which pertaineth unto man, neither shall a man put on a woman's garment?

JOAN   I had the best of advice and I trusted it.

BEAUPÈRE   How did you get to this man whom you call your king?

JOAN   No trouble at all. I arrived in Chinon around noon and went to an inn. After dinner I went to the castle. I recognized the king right away, with the help of my voice. I told him I wanted to go out and fight the English.

MANCHON   May I interrupt?

BISHOP *(to Beaupère)*   Monsieur Manchon!

MANCHON   Did the king have voices too?

JOAN   Ask him, maybe he'll tell you.

LEFÈVRE   Question: How far away from the king were you standing?

JOAN   About a lance's length, I think.

LEFÈVRE   When you first saw the man whom you call your king was there an angel beside him?

JOAN   God forbid, I didn't see one.

BISHOP *(to Beaupère, with contempt)*   Monsieur Lefèvre!

D'ESTIVET   Was there a halo around his head?

JOAN   There was a splendid gathering of knights around him. Close to three hundred knights. And about fifty torches were burning, not to mention the spiritual light.

MANCHON   By your leave. Do you still hear your voice?

JOAN   Not a day goes by without my hearing it and I'm badly in need of it too.

LA FONTAINE   What do you ask of your voice?

JOAN   Victory for my side.

CHATION   The day when you fought before Paris was a feast day.

JOAN   Possible.

CHATION   Was it right to fight on a feast day?

JOAN   Ask me something else.

LA FONTAINE   When you came to Compiègne, before you were taken prisoner, would you have gone on fighting if the voice had foretold that you would be captured?

JOAN   With a heavy heart. I would always have done what it told me.

MIDI   How long were you a prisoner in the tower of Beaurevoir?

JOAN   Four months. When I found out I'd been sold to the English and they were going to take me away, I became very downcast. My voices gave me no counsel and at first I was scared. But then I was more scared of the English, so I forced myself to jump.

MIDI   Did you say at the time that you would rather die than fall into the hands of the English?

JOAN   I'd certainly rather be in the hands of God than of the English.

BEAUPÈRE   When was the last time you heard your voices?

JOAN   Today.

BISHOP   What did they say?

JOAN   They said I should answer you judges boldly. You, Bishop of Beauvais, call yourself my judge. I don't know if that is true. But I must tell you that you will be putting yourself in great peril if you judge me wrongly.

BEAUPÈRE   Was it saints that spoke to you, or angels, or God Himself?

JOAN   Saint Catherine and Saint Margaret.

BISHOP   Anyone else?

JOAN   Saint Michael.

BEAUPÈRE   Which was the last?

JOAN   Saint Michael. He's the one who sent me to Chinon.

BEAUPÈRE   What is he telling you now?

(Midi is shaking with repressed laughter)

JOAN   Always to show you a friendly face and to answer you boldly.

MASSIEU   Was Saint Michael naked?

JOAN   Naked? Do you think God can't afford to clothe him?

LEFÈVRE   Did he wear his hair cut short?

JOAN (for the first time slightly impatient)   Why should Saint Michael have his hair cut short?

THE ENGLISH OBSERVER   Let her be asked whether Saint Margaret speaks English.

ADJUTANT (to Massieu)   My lord wishes to know whether Saint Margaret speaks English.

MASSIEU (to Joan)   Does Saint Margaret speak English?

JOAN   Why would she speak English when she's against the English?

(The English observer laughs)

CHATION   How could you be sure it was Saint Michael and not the devil pretending to be Saint Michael?

JOAN   By the way he spoke, and because he taught me a lot of good things.

CHATION   What did he teach you?

JOAN   Most of all that I must come to the help of my people, which so many have abandoned. And he told me about the great misery in France.

BEAUPÈRE   I see. Did you wear a sword?

JOAN   The sword from Vaucouleurs. I had a sheath made for it out of strong leather.

BEAUPÈRE   Did you carry a flag?

JOAN   I had a banner, snow-white.

LA FONTAINE   Which did you like more, your sword or your banner?

JOAN   My banner, much more. At least forty times more. Holding it high, I led the troops against the enemy. I never killed anybody myself.

D'ESTIVET   Were you never present when Englishmen were killed?

JOAN *(laughing)* I sure was. You talk like a ninny. On battlefields there are dead people. They should have stayed home.

BEAUPÈRE   Why did you never negotiate with the enemy?

JOAN   My side sent word to the English that no delay would be tolerated, no postponement granted. They should clear out then and there. I shouted over to them myself to beat it on the spot, without bothering to dress, with no other baggage than their bare lives.

THE ENGLISH OBSERVER *(pushing the adjutant)*   Go and tell him.

ADJUTANT *(aside)*   Your Eminence.

BISHOP   What's up?

ADJUTANT   The Duke of Bedford will be angry; he specifically asked for a speedy trial. We consider this additional questioning superfluous.

BISHOP   The Duke of Bedford will have to accept the fact that this is an ecclesiastical court, not a court martial. Not that the Duke of Bedford has anything to worry about.—Monsieur Beaupère!

MANCHON   Question: What do you believe will happen to your side?

JOAN   It will win. The English will have to give up every last shred of French soil. Not a single man will remain.

MIDI   Remember where you are, girl.

BISHOP   How can you know such things unless the devil told you?

JOAN   The devil doesn't know anything. I know the English are out to kill me. They figure that once I'm dead they'll conquer the rest of France. But even with a hundred thousand more men, they will never get France.

(The English observer rises)

BEAUPÈRE   That shouldn't be in the record.

MASSIEU   It cannot be stricken. I protest, Professor Beaupère.

BEAUPÈRE   Do you believe God hates the English?

JOAN   Whether God hates or loves the English or what He may have in mind for their souls, I don't know. What I do know is that they're going to be driven out of France, except for the ones who die here.

THE ENGLISH OBSERVER   Incompetent. *(Goes out with his adjutant)*

BISHOP   D'Estivet! I wish the Duke would realize that this trial must proceed strictly according to law. The eyes of the world are upon us. Monsieur Massieu!—Monsieur Beaupère, please continue!—Brother Raoul! Go and advise my lord that we have observers here from all over, from the council at Basel, from Rome, from every chancellery in Europe. *(Brother Raoul leaves)* Monsieur Beaupère!

BEAUPÈRE *(peevishly)*   Did God command you to wear male attire?

JOAN *(lustily)*   Why do you keep asking about my clothes? Clothes are nothing, they don't matter at all. Why don't you say you want to burn me because I'm against the English?

BEAUPÈRE   Did you receive the sacraments in male attire?

JOAN   Unarmed, in men's clothes.

BISHOP   Hm, in view of what we have just heard, we declare today's session closed. Monsieur Massieu, conduct the accused back to prison.

(Joan is taken away)

BISHOP   Gentlemen, from now on we shall question the accused in her cell, myself and two assessors from our number; the public will be excluded. Make use of your time, gentlemen, and study the transcripts. And I remind you once more that no one is permitted to leave Rouen until the trial is over.— Praised be the Lord.

ALL   Forever and ever. Amen.

4

Bishop Cauchon of Beauvais visits Joan in the prison of La Tour des Champs and asks her a strange question.

The prison of La Tour des Champs. Joan is lying on a cot. Two English guards are playing dice.

FIRST GUARD   Joan!

JOAN *(tired)*   What is it now?

FIRST GUARD *(mocking her)*   I'm Saint Catherine.

JOAN   A very brave soldier, that's what you are.

SECOND GUARD   I'm Saint Margaret.

JOAN   You're a swine. Shut up!

SECOND GUARD   It's me, Saint Michael.

(Joan strikes him)

SECOND GUARD   The bitch. Did Saint Michael wake you like this? Did he hold you like this?

(Enter Jean de la Fontaine)

LA FONTAINE   What's going on?

(The guards let Joan go. She gets up)

FIRST GUARD   Halt! No one can come in here. It's forbidden.

LA FONTAINE   I'm in charge of this interrogation.—Why are you crying, Joan?

JOAN   I'm not crying. Leave me alone.

LA FONTAINE   How have you been getting along since Saturday?

JOAN   You can see for yourself how I've been getting along, Father. As best as I can. The bishop sent me a piece of carp, but it made me sick.

LA FONTAINE   Oh, I'm sorry to hear that. *(He motions the guards to step aside)* Listen to me. You've got to accept my advice; don't be so obstinate. Several among us assessors wish you well. Do you understand?

JOAN   No.

LA FONTAINE   Get ready, Joan, the interrogation is about to start.

JOAN   All over again?

LA FONTAINE   You have no one but yourself to blame if it's taking a long time. Here is your bishop.

(Enter the bishop, Massieu and the clerk)

LA FONTAINE   *(in a low voice to the entering churchmen)*   The conditions here are intolerable. These English guards . . .

BISHOP   Tush. The child is used to soldiers' company. I trust she can handle them. Monsieur Massieu!

(At a sign from Massieu the guards and the clerk leave)

BISHOP   Well then. You have said that we, your bishop, would be putting ourselves in great peril if we called you to account. What did you mean? What would that peril be? For us, your bishop, and the others?

JOAN   You'll find out soon enough.

BISHOP   Did your voices tell you something about it?

JOAN   This has nothing to do with your trial. But it's quite possible that the people who want me out of the world will be leaving it before me.

BISHOP   Did your voices promise a turn for the better?

JOAN   I've answered that before.

BISHOP   When will it be?

JOAN   I don't know the day and the hour.

BISHOP   The year then.

JOAN   I won't tell you just yet.

BISHOP   Before Saint John's day?

JOAN   Ask me something else.

(Massieu whispers in the bishop's ear)

BISHOP   What did you say to Grey of the guards?

JOAN   That something might happen to them before All Saints' Day.

BISHOP   Monsieur La Fontaine.

(At a sign from Massieu the clerk returns)

LA FONTAINE *(stepping close to Joan)*   Have your voices promised that you would be rescued from prison?

JOAN *(with sudden gaiety)*   My voices promised me help. But I don't know if it means that I'll be rescued from prison, or not until the day of the execution, when a great turmoil will make it possible for me to escape. My voices keep telling me that a great victory will set me free.

LA FONTAINE   I take it you know that others have claimed to hear voices.

(Joan is silent)

LA FONTAINE   You have met a certain Catherine of La Rochelle, have you not?

JOAN   I have. She told me a white lady in a golden robe appeared to her; she said the lady commanded her to ask the king for heralds and trumpeters. They were to go from city to city proclaiming that anyone possessing gold or silver or hidden treasures must hand them over at once. She said she could tell who was holding back and find all the treasure anyway. Catherine said she'd use the money to pay my infantry.

LA FONTAINE   What was your answer?

JOAN   I told her to go home to her husband and take care of her house and feed her children. But to make perfectly sure I talked it over with Saint Catherine and Saint Margaret and they said Catherine La Rochelle's talk was nonsense. Nothing in it. I wrote my king a report, telling him just that.

LA FONTAINE   Did you discuss anything else with her?

JOAN   Oh yes. She wanted to go to the English and arrange for peace. I told her I didn't think they'd give us any peace except at lance's point.

BISHOP   I see.

JOAN   I also asked Catherine if her white lady came every night, because then I'd spend a night with her. I did. I stayed awake until midnight and I didn't see a thing. Then I fell asleep. In the morning I asked Catherine if the white lady had come. Yes, she said, while I was asleep. But she hadn't been able to wake me. I asked her if the lady would come the next night and she said yes. So I slept all day so as to stay awake at night. And I stayed awake all night but I didn't see a thing. I asked her several times if the white lady would come soon. Catherine always answered, yes, soon.

LA FONTAINE   Then you believe you are in a state of grace?

JOAN   If I am not, God will put me in it; if I am, God will keep me in it. I would be the unhappiest creature in the whole world if I knew I wasn't in God's grace.

LA FONTAINE   But when you jumped from the tower, you wanted to kill yourself, did you not?

JOAN   No. To escape.

LA FONTAINE *(with extreme insistence)*   Then you believe you can never again commit a deadly sin?

JOAN   I firmly believe in my salvation.

BISHOP   If you are confident of your salvation, why then would you wish to confess?

JOAN   A body can never keep her conscience clear enough, bishop.

LA FONTAINE *(no longer kindly, almost furious)*   Wouldn't you say it was a deadly sin to capture a man by ruse, and then to kill him?

JOAN   I never did any such thing.

LA FONTAINE   You did not? What about a certain Franqué of Arras who was murdered in Lagny at your command?

JOAN   Him? He deserved it. By his own admission he was a

scoundrel, a thief, and a traitor. I wanted to exchange him for one of our people, a good man, Monsieur de l'Ours in Paris. But the man died on us in the meantime. It would have been stupid to let that no-good Franqué go.

LA FONTAINE   Did you give money to the man who captured Franqué?

JOAN   I have no mint or treasury in France; how would I pay out large sums of money?

BISHOP   Joan, in summation, we charge you as follows:
1. You fought before Paris on a feast day.
2. You jumped from the tower at Beaurevoir with intent to commit suicide.
3. You brought about the death of Franqué of Arras.
4. You have worn men's clothes.

LA FONTAINE   Is it possible that you see no mortal sin in all this? Joan!

JOAN   Bishop of Beauvais, you'd better watch what you're doing. This trial of yours is crooked. First, this thing about Paris —what if it was a feast day? Sin or not, it has nothing to do with this trial, the confessional's the place for it. Secondly, I jumped from the tower in hope and not despair.

BISHOP   And the men's clothes?

JOAN   As long as I'm here, I have to wear them. If you give me women's clothes and let me go back to my mother, I'll put them on and go home.

MASSIEU   Joan, what would you prefer, to forgo mass or to attend it in women's clothes?

JOAN   Dress me in women's clothes like any burgher's daughter, I'll even wear a long train and a big hat if that's the only way I can hear mass. When it's over I'll tear them off. But with all my heart I beseech you, let me be as I am.

BISHOP   I have been told that your only reason for not removing your men's clothes is that you have heard of a plan to rescue you.

JOAN   I won't answer any more questions. You'll find my answers in the record. (She throws herself on the cot)

BISHOP   Very well. Let us close the proceedings. Transmit the bill of particulars to the court for engrossment.

5

The weekly market in Rouen.

Two stalls. The peasant woman and her son are selling cheese, butter, and eggs, the fishwife is selling fish. A war cripple is playing the bagpipes. Customers, among them Dr. Dufour and his two nieces.

An English soldier, already loaded down with merchandise, points at the wares in the peasant woman's stall. He makes her sell him twenty eggs, four cheeses, and two prints of butter. He allows the peasant woman to fish the money out of his purse.

PEASANT WOMAN (counting)   Twenty, twenty-two, twenty-four.

THE ENGLISH SOLDIER   Stop.

A SHABBILY DRESSED WOMAN   Two eggs, madame.
   (The soldier lumbers to the fishwife's stall and buys the biggest fish. He takes out his purse, the fishwife takes out the money)

THE ENGLISH SOLDIER   Stop. *(With a friendly grin he leaves)*

FISHWIFE   Hope it poisons you. *(To Dr. Dufour)* Nice mackerel today, doctor.

DR. DUFOUR *(choosing one)*   This one with the soulful eyes. No doubt she heard voices too. I suppose they advised her to take the bait.

FIRST NIECE *(from the peasant woman's stall)*   Uncle!

PEASANT WOMAN   People shouldn't joke about religion. The girl is a witch and that's that.

FISHWIFE   Too bad she's a witch if she's against the English.

PEASANT WOMAN   Her voices come from the devil.

FISHWIFE   Bah, her voices seem to say what we're all saying. I mean, that the English should get out of France.

SON   She's a saint.

PEASANT WOMAN   You shut up!

DR. DUFOUR *(addressing his mackerel)*   You may have been a saint and you may have been a witch, but now you've been caught and you're going to be fried.

FISHWIFE   Very true, doctor, witch or not, she's being tried because the English want to swallow up the rest of France.

FIRST NIECE   Come along, uncle, you'll get into trouble. *(Leaves, anxiously looking over her shoulder)*

DR. DUFOUR *(with a negative gesture to his niece)*   Ah, madame, you're against the Maid because she's a witch. If she weren't a witch, Madame Braillard would be for her because she's a good Frenchwoman. Madame, I'm now going to buy one pound of your certified Catholic butter, and a minute ago you saw me buying a certified French fish from Madame Braillard. These opposites, dear ladies, will be united in my frying pan to make a mouth-watering dish.

FISHWIFE   You never change, Doctor Dufour.

DR. DUFOUR   Why should I change, Madame Braillard?

FISHWIFE   The Maid might be able to tell you why, Dr. Dufour.

SON   They say she's giving the court a hard time.

(Four priests, Beaupère, d'Estivet, Manchon, and Lefèvre, in conversation, cross the market)

MANCHON   Well, what's next?

BEAUPÈRE   It's all over.

MANCHON   What do you mean?

BEAUPÈRE   The report of the Paris faculty has come in.

D'ESTIVET   Fuel for the fire, crushing for the accused.

BEAUPÈRE   Schismatic and heretical on twelve counts.

LEFÈVRE   Of course people will say that Paris is occupied by the English, just as much as Rouen.

MANCHON   No, Paris is Paris!

LEFÈVRE   I understand there's another report from old Gerson —favorable to the accused. There's no denying that for years now the man has been Europe's leading luminary. His opinion has been decisive in all ecclesiastical trials.

BEAUPÈRE   The old fox has always made his decisions with an eye to the common people. In Constance he sent Hus to the stake, but this time it's a child of the people.

MANCHON   Child of the people, indeed! As subtle as ten theologians. How careful she is, for instance, not to say that her voices advised her to wear men's clothes. She knows that would finish her, because it would show incontestably that her voices came from the devil.

LEFÈVRE   Even then we wouldn't have been able to prove that she's in league with the devil. Maid who doth the devil see can no more a maiden be. I understand that Lady Bedford in person has established her virginity.

D'ESTIVET   And I understand that her husband, our beloved Duke of Bedford, has done likewise, thanks to an aperture in the floor, made for that express purpose.

(Laughter. They move on)

(Dr. Dufour has whispered to the war cripple. The latter nods and plays the well-known song lampooning Cauchon of Beauvais. Manchon drops him a coin, but is informed by d'Estivet that the song is not intended to be friendly)

D'ESTIVET   *(to the war cripple)*   Scoundrel.

(Indignantly the churchmen leave)

FISHWIFE   *(joins in the singing)*

Bishop Cauchon of Beauvais
Is an Englishman now, they say
On sentimental grounds
And for five thousand pounds.

6

May 9, 1431. In the armory of the royal castle. Joan is threatened with torture.

Armory in the great tower of the royal castle. The Bishop of Beauvais, all the assessors, Brother Raoul, the clerk, the executioner, Joan, and the guards.

BISHOP   Praised be the Lord.

ALL   Forever and ever. Amen.

BROTHER RAOUL   Your Eminence, this is Monsieur Dujardin, the executioner.

(The executioner kneels before the bishop and kisses the hem of his cassock. The bishop blesses him)

BISHOP   Monsieur Jean de Chation, Professor at the Theological Faculty of Paris.

CHATION   Joan, in humility and moderation, with no thought of vengeance or punishment, solely intent on your salvation and instruction, we shall make a last attempt to save your body and soul.

JOAN   Just reel off your speech, then I'll answer you.

CHATION   Is that all you wish to say?

JOAN   Don't beat about the bush. Read the indictment.

CHATION   Joan, we have meticulously examined your acts and deeds as recorded in these minutes. We have found grave trespasses.

JOAN   How do I know what extra tidbits you've worked into the minutes?

CHATION   Do you mean to say that you do not recognize us as your secular judges appointed by the church?

JOAN   Exactly.

CHATION   Joan, if as you indicate you refuse to recognize the article Unam Sanctam Ecclesiam Catholicam, the court must send you to the stake.

JOAN   Even in the fire I couldn't say anything else.

CHATION   Joan, we have shown you how hazardous, nay dangerous it is to direct one's curiosity to things that transcend the capacity of human understanding, to place one's faith in new things and even invent new and unheard-of things, for the demons find ways of insinuating themselves into our curiosity. All the learned masters and doctors of the University of Paris have recognized your statements concerning your voices and apparitions to be pure lies. Heedless of our admonitions, you in your pride have deemed yourself worthy to receive voices and inspirations directly from God. Forgetting that God tempts prideful persons like you with diabolical visions, you yourself have invented these voices. We therefore exhort you to subdue your vanity and cast off your lies. If you will not submit to the church today your soul will be consumed by eternal fire and your body by temporal fire.

JOAN   Do you think you can intimidate me with such talk and win me over to your side?

BISHOP   Monsieur La Fontaine!

LA FONTAINE   Joan, dearest sister. I beg you, don't let the worst happen. If you really heard voices, dear sister, accept the opinion of the University of Paris which declares your voices to be imaginings and nonsense. What would you have done if one of your soldiers had said, I refuse to obey the orders of my king's officers? So what can you think of yourself when you refuse to obey the representatives of your church? Abandon your resistance, dear sister, or your soul will suffer eternal torments. Moreover, I am very much in fear for your life. Submit, I implore you, in order that we may save your body and your soul.

JOAN   I have submitted to God, isn't that enough?

LA FONTAINE   You should know, Joan, that we distinguish the church triumphant from the church militant. The church triumphant consists of God, his saints and all redeemed souls; the church militant of the Holy Father, the cardinals, prelates, bishops, priests and all Christians. This church, congregated upon earth, led by the Most Holy Ghost, is infallible. Will you submit to it?

JOAN   I won't answer any more questions.

BISHOP   Joan, for the last time I ask you, will you submit to the church?

JOAN   What *is* the church? No. I will not submit to you judges.

BISHOP   Will you submit to the pope?

JOAN   Take me to him and I'll tell him.

BISHOP   Will you submit to the Council of Basel?

JOAN   The Council of Basel? What's that?

LEFÈVRE   It is an assembly representative of the entire church. In other words, it includes members of the English party as well as your own.

JOAN   I think I'd rather submit to them.

CHATION   Basel!!

LEFÈVRE   She has every right to do so.

CHATION   It's out of the question.

BEAUPÈRE   What an idea!

BISHOP   Who has been advising her since our last session?

MASSIEU   No one.

MANCHON   Why, then, is she being asked?

CLERK   Can her submission be recorded as final?

BISHOP   No, wait.

JOAN   You're not letting him record anything in my favor.

BISHOP   Be still!—Inasmuch as you, Joan, are unresponsive to our admonitions and continue to deny the truth, we are obliged to subject you to torture. Monsieur Massieu, show the accused the instruments.

(*The guards lead Joan to the table where the instruments are displayed*)

MANCHON   Pray answer us, Joan!

LEFÈVRE   Pray submit!

D'ESTIVET   Won't you give in, girl?

LA FONTAINE   You're not helping anyone.

CHATION   Joan, the torturers are ready to lead you to the truth by force, for the salvation of your soul.

(*Joan faints; she is brought front stage again*)

JOAN   If you break my bones with these instruments and squeeze my soul out of my poor body, I will not say anything different. And if I do say something different, I'll say afterwards that it was torn from me by force.

MASSIEU   (*in an undertone*)   Should we?

LA FONTAINE   (*in an undertone*)   Let us spare her.

BISHOP   (*in a loud voice*)   In view of the obstinacy of the accused and the insolence of her answers we, the judges, fear that torture can no longer benefit her. We shall therefore dispense with it. Take her back to prison.

(*Joan is dragged out*)

7

Sunday in the prison of La Tour des Champs. Joan
hears a song, but does not understand the words.

*Prison. Joan is lying on the cot. The two English guards. In the distance
a bagpipe is playing "Bishop Cauchon of Beauvais."*

JOAN   Why are the people so gay?
GUARD   Because it's a holiday. Why shouldn't people be gay?
JOAN   Yes.

8

Joan thinks the people have forgotten her. But in the
markets and taverns they are beginning to understand her.

*The "St. Peter's Catch" tavern. The peasant family from the outskirts
are eating their lunch. A young, shabbily dressed curate. The loose
woman. The well-dressed gentleman. The innkeeper. Bagpipe music.*

LEGRAIN   I see there are decent people here. Anybody who can
read?
YOUNG CURATE   What is it?
LEGRAIN   It's a copy of the letter she wrote to the English before
she raised the siege of Orléans. I don't know if you'd care to
read it.
YOUNG CURATE   Does my cassock look as if it were paid for
by English money? *(He reads)* "Jesus Mary! You, King of

England, and you, Duke of Bedford, who call yourselves re-
gents of the kingdom of France, and you, William Pole, Earl
of Suffolk, John Talbot, Thomas Lord of Scales, who call
yourselves lieutenants of the said Duke of Bedford: render
His due to the King of Heaven and give back the keys of all
the fortified cities of France which you have taken and ravished. The Maid has come in the name of God. She is ready
to make peace as soon as you leave France and pay for your
presence here. And you, all the rest of you, archers, soldiers,
and so on, who are here before our city of Orléans, go back
to your country, in the name of God. If you do not, you may
expect the Maid, who will visit you very soon to your great
grief."

LOOSE WOMAN   She's good.

YOUNG CURATE   "King of England, wherever I find your men
on France's soil, I will drive them away, whether they will or
not. And if they will not, I will have them all killed. Wherever
we find you we will strike you and raise a clamor the like of
which has not been heard in France for at least a thousand
years. Written this day, Tuesday of Holy Week . . .

Joan."

Unconquerable.

ENGLISH SOLDIER *(comes in and demands a drink)*   Evening. Some
wine!

YOUNG CURATE   Praised be Jesus Christ.

PEASANT *(tipsy, plants himself in front of the English soldier)*   If you
are a servant of the Duke of Bedford, then listen to this: the
Duke of Bedford's a drunk.

WELL-DRESSED GENTLEMAN   Come along, Blanche. *(They leave the
tavern)*

PEASANT WOMAN   Guillaume!

PEASANT   He drinks from morning to night, and all he ever
thinks of is hitting us with taxes and grinding down the
people.
*(The English soldier leaves, looking back over his shoulder. A roar of
laughter)*

YOUNG CURATE   Give me the letter.

9

In the chapel of the graveyard of Saint-Ouen. Threatened with the stake and worn down by a feeling of utter forsakenness, Joan signs a recantation. It is May 24, 1431.

The chapel of the graveyard of Saint-Ouen. La Fontaine. Joan is carried in. Guards and an English officer. Church bells and the noise of a crowd are audible while Joan is being carried in.

LA FONTAINE   Joan, you are in the chapel of the graveyard of Saint-Ouen. Collect yourself, dear sister. Out on the square the stake is ready.

JOAN *(barely audible)*   Saint Michael.

LA FONTAINE *(steps up to her)*   Believe me, Joan, it is not too late for your salvation.
(Enter the bishop, Maître Erard, Massieu, Beaupère, Brother Raoul. Once more bells and the noise of crowds are heard)

BISHOP   Maître Erard, we are obliged to you for postponing your journey. You say you had a better impression of her yesterday?

MAÎTRE ERARD   God will help.—Her physical condition is not of the best. She keeps asking how the people are reacting to her trial—with sympathy or indifference. Attempts by her partisans to communicate with her have been thwarted. She is upset because her voices have abandoned her. Has it been sufficiently impressed on her that today . . .

LA FONTAINE   She was told at five o'clock this morning.

MASSIEU   Here are the three documents. This is the sentence in case she recants. *(Hands it to the bishop who gives it to Brother Raoul)* This is the sentence if she fails to recant. *(He keeps it)* This is the recantation. *(Gives it to Maître Erard)* Bid her sign the recantation in order that this sentence *(the document in his hand)* may not become effective.

BISHOP   Maître Erard! Monsieur Massieu!

MAÎTRE ERARD   The ground has all been covered, dear sister.
Your king is a heretic; moreover, he has forgotten you. Your
apparitions are illusions; the professors have said so and they
know; you know nothing. You may as well take off your male
attire, nobody has come with a horse to set you free. Your
voices have deceived you, and what's more, they have stopped
coming. I know they have. Were they here today? Did they
come yesterday?

JOAN   No, not yesterday.

MAÎTRE ERARD   And the day before, my child?

JOAN   No.

MAÎTRE ERARD   You see, they have abandoned you, but the stake
is ready. And here I have a document; if you submit and sign
and recant, you will be released from prison.

JOAN   (in tears)   I have done nothing wrong.

MAÎTRE ERARD   If you don't recant, it will be the fire, dear sister.
(At a sign from him the door is thrown open and the bells and the
noise are heard)

MAÎTRE ERARD   Would you not rather stay with your mother,
the church, for it is written, "The branch cannot bear fruit
of itself, except it abide in the vine."
(Joan does not answer)

MAÎTRE ERARD   Joan, it's to you I am speaking.
(At a sign from Massieu the door is closed)

MASSIEU   Forgive me if I should be mistaken, but I believe I
heard her say "Then I will."
(All gather around Joan)

MASSIEU   She says that if the Council at Basel decides she must
sign she will do so.

BEAUPÈRE   No, dear sister, you must do it now.

JOAN   I can't get up.

BEAUPÈRE   I'll help you.

CHATION   Sign here.

JOAN   I can't write.

LA FONTAINE   I'll guide your hand.

CHATION   Quick, sign.

JOAN   I've got to think it over.

BEAUPÈRE   The executioner is outside. He's got his torch ready.

LA FONTAINE   Sign! Sign!

JOAN   I feel sick.

LA FONTAINE   Courage, Joan.

CHATION   You must sign.

JOAN   Where? I can't see.

(La Fontaine guides Joan's hand. She signs)

JOAN   I'd sooner sign than be burned.

BISHOP   A great day, my girl. Your body and soul are saved. *(To Brother Raoul)* Give me the sentence.

BEAUPÈRE   Your voices led you astray, my child.

JOAN   Yes, I guess they deceived me.

BISHOP   Give the prisoner women's clothes.

(Two nuns have entered. A screen is brought in. The nuns dress Joan, who is tottering, in female clothes)

BISHOP   Brother Raoul, send a message to my lord that she has recanted. *(Reads the sentence very quickly)* You, Joan, having been repeatedly and patiently admonished by us, have now recanted your errors by word of mouth and publicly abjured them. Consequently, you are hereby readmitted to the church. However, since you have most gravely sinned against the church, we condemn you to imprisonment for life, to the bread of sorrow and the wine of tears, albeit constantly in the shelter of our compassion. This is the final decision of the court.

(The English observer and the adjutant have come in)

THE ENGLISH OBSERVER   Goddam! The witch has to be burned at once!

ADJUTANT   What's going on here?

BISHOP   She has recanted.

ADJUTANT   This is high treason.

BISHOP   I'm being insulted. I demand satisfaction.

ADJUTANT   You're letting the girl get away.

BISHOP   That's a lie.

ADJUTANT   The girl must be executed at once.

BISHOP   That decision rests with me.

THE ENGLISH OBSERVER   No. *(Goes out with his adjutant)*

MASSIEU   Where is she to be taken?

BISHOP   Same place you took her from. *(Out)*

MASSIEU   Take her back to prison. *(Out)*

JOAN   But you said I would be free!
GUARD   Just come along quietly, little girl. How pretty you look
in your nice dress.

10

In the graveyard of Saint-Ouen an expectant crowd
hears of Joan's recantation.

Market place in Rouen. A crowd, waiting. English soldiers.

WAR CRIPPLE   Are they going to burn her today or not?
(*An English soldier shrugs*)
SECOND SOLDIER   The time it takes. Do they expect us to eat our
dinner out here?
FIRST SOLDIER   Goddam!
SISTER-IN-LAW   You can't get her down, can you? She holds her
head high.
LITTLE GIRL   Why have the bells stopped?
PEASANT WOMAN   Don't know.
FIRST SOLDIER   The "Red Lion" costs more, but at "St. Peter's
Catch" they cook with garlic.
SECOND SOLDIER   They cook with garlic because they don't want
us.
(*A third English soldier joins the other two and tells them something.
They laugh*)
SISTER-IN-LAW   What are the English soldiers laughing about?
(*The soldiers go off, laughing*)
LOOSE WOMAN   Henry, what's happened?
FIRST SOLDIER   You can all go home. Your Maid has recanted.
SECOND SOLDIER   Not that she is one.
LEGRAIN   Some new piece of skulduggery.
LOOSE WOMAN   It's all over. The bells have stopped ringing.
SISTER-IN-LAW   You mean they're not going to burn her after
all?

SON   How can she recant the truth? How can she betray us like this?

WAR CRIPPLE   She's recanted all right.

INNKEEPER   To save her skin.

PEASANT WOMAN   Is this the end of it all?

PEASANT   She's recanted. Let's go home.

PEASANT WOMAN   Eugene.

WINE MERCHANT   Ha, ha! Not that she is one. Ha, ha, ha! *(He is jostled by the son)*

FISHWIFE   What can they have done to the girl?

11

At the "St. Peter's Catch" tavern, opinions are divided.

The "St. Peter's Catch" tavern. The innkeeper. The fishwife. The well-dressed gentleman. The loose woman.

WELL-DRESSED GENTLEMAN   I'm not for the English. I only said that it's no good trying to crack a nut with a sledgehammer —you might need the nut. The tripe vendors and sewer workers are full of patriotic fervor, that's fine. Jostling the English guards, splendid. But what will it lead to? After all, there's no great difference between the door of a guardroom and the door of my hotel. The English are boors, not much culture, they've blundered unforgivably in their dealings with the population, I grant you that, but for the moment they are responsible for law and order.

LOOSE WOMAN   *(to fishwife)*   Law and order, he says. I like that. He hasn't paid my rent in weeks.

FISHWIFE   *(calms her)*   Take it easy, Blanche.

WELL-DRESSED GENTLEMAN   We've got to keep cool. What I say is: everything in its place. I don't ask my butcher to cook my supper.

LOOSE WOMAN   Pay my rent.

LEGRAIN *(enters)*   Monsieur François, un petit blanc! There's been a riot in the harbor. The stevedores have refused to unload two siege machines from the corvette "Glorious." The Duke of Bedford has let loose his watchdogs, but the dockers are fighting back.

INNKEEPER   Maybe I'd better close the place. They've already smashed it up once.

FISHWIFE *(laughs)*   What will the bishop do now?

WELL-DRESSED GENTLEMAN   How can you laugh, madame? I've had as much as I can take. I'm telling you straight: This town has got to be cleaned up. Sneers, whispering, dirty looks. Pretty soon it won't be safe for a man to show himself in a clean shirt.

LOOSE WOMAN   Especially if the laundress hasn't been paid.

WELL-DRESSED GENTLEMAN   There you have it! Insurrection.

LOOSE WOMAN   You mean you won't pay?

WELL-DRESSED GENTLEMAN   These people are taking me for all they can get.

INNKEEPER   Say!

LOOSE WOMAN   You aren't that pretty. You think going to bed with you is a pleasure? And listening to your hogwash day and night? Pay up and clear out. A peasant girl! What does that make me? A dockside whore, I suppose. Pay if you want to have fun, pay, pay, pay!

WELL-DRESSED GENTLEMAN   Suppose I haven't got it?

LOOSE WOMAN   Pluck your hat and sell the feathers, you sissy.

WELL-DRESSED GENTLEMAN   Let me explain . . .

LOOSE WOMAN   Don't explain, pay!

WELL-DRESSED GENTLEMAN   That's the last straw. There's only one thing to be done with you scum, your Maid included: root out, burn to the ground, drown in blood, hang, crush underfoot, exterminate. *(The loose woman slaps his face. He leaves)*

FISHWIFE   You shouldn't have done that. He'll give you a bad name in the taverns.

LOOSE WOMAN   All this is getting me down.

INNKEEPER   You're not the only one, mademoiselle. You're not the only one.

12

Rioting in Rouen. The Bishop of Beauvais receives distressing news.

In the bishop's house. The bishop at dinner. Massieu.

BISHOP   Those English blockheads don't realize how well I've served them. They may know all about invading France, but they fail to understand the French mind.

MASSIEU   Thanks to your great skill they have one less enemy, and the church has lost a martyr.

BROTHER RAOUL *(entering)*   Your Eminence. The city is in a turmoil. The people are crowding into the harbor and beating up the English sailors. Several guard posts have been attacked. The English are demanding satisfaction.

BISHOP   I can't be bothered with street brawls. The English can reinforce their guards.

BROTHER RAOUL   Your Eminence, they're putting the blame on us and the way we conducted the trial. I hear the Duke of Bedford is sick with rage.

BISHOP   The Duke of Bedford has all the doctors he needs. Besides, he's always had trouble with his liver. It's the life he's been leading. Anything else?

BROTHER RAOUL   The English report that she put on men's clothes this morning.

MASSIEU   She must have heard about the riots on her account.

BISHOP *(aghast, puts his napkin down)*   Water!
   (Brother Raoul hands him the bowl to wash his hands in)

13

The prison of La Tour des Champs. Joan has heard
the voice of the people and resumes her struggle.

*Prison. Joan, again in men's clothes. Enter the Bishop of Beauvais and
La Fontaine.*

BISHOP   You are wearing men's clothes again!

LA FONTAINE   Why have you caused us this sorrow? Dearest
sister, it's too late to save you. You've broken your promise;
you've relapsed, now you're lost forever.

JOAN   What did I promise you?

BISHOP   Have you heard your voices again?

JOAN   Yes.

BISHOP   And they told you . . .

JOAN   That I betrayed my cause.

BISHOP   But you have publicly recanted.

JOAN   Yes. Because I didn't know what a public recantation
meant. I only recanted because I was afraid of the fire. In
battle I was never afraid of fire, because I wasn't alone, I had
my men around me. But then I doubted the people; I thought
they wouldn't care if I died, and would just go on drinking
their wine. But they knew all about me the whole time, and
nothing I did was in vain.

BISHOP   What does it matter what the coopers and fishwives
know?

JOAN   Bishop, a day will come when the vintners of Touraine
and the sailors of Normandy will sit together, and you people
won't be here any more.

BISHOP   In other words you are obstinate and guilty of a relapse.

JOAN   I am.

BISHOP   Joan, you have reverted to your old errors and trespasses as a dog returns to its vomit. The church can no longer
defend you. Farewell, farewell! *(Goes out with La Fontaine)*

14

On May 30, 1431, Joan is handed over to the executioner.

Prison. Joan. In the background the executioner, a nun, an English officer, English soldiers, the two guards. Enter Massieu.

MASSIEU   Joan, the Bishop of Beauvais has sent me to prepare you for death.

JOAN   Yes.

MASSIEU   Are you afraid of death?

JOAN   Yes, very much afraid.

MASSIEU   Then you repent?

JOAN   No.

MASSIEU   Joan, in the face of death do you persist in considering your voices true?

JOAN   Yes.

MASSIEU   But, Joan, haven't those voices promised that you would be freed from prison forever?

JOAN   Won't I be freed from prison forever today?

MASSIEU   Joan, did they not foretell your impending release?

JOAN   Am I not being released from the fear of death? Am I not being released from fear of the powerful?

(Solemn entry of the Bishop of Beauvais with all the judges and assessors of the trial)

BISHOP   We have come to the end. Joan, have you anything more to say?

JOAN   Yes. If the fire were to be lit right now and the faggots were burning and the executioner fanning the flames, I would say nothing different from what I have always said.

BISHOP   Conduct her to the stake.

(The executioner steps forward)

MASSIEU   This is irregular, my lord. You must proclaim the
reasons for your order.

BISHOP   Take her away, take her away!

(The executioner takes Joan away)

15

**In the market place of Rouen, in the presence of an
immense crowd, the Maid is burned at the stake.**

Market place in Rouen. A large crowd. English soldiers.

SISTER-IN-LAW   She looks so little among the men.

PEASANT WOMAN   Lift the child up!

SON *(to the curate)*   Do you think she's afraid?

YOUNG CURATE   We are afraid, she isn't.

CHILD   It's daylight. Why has that man got a torch?

OLDER NUN   That's the executioner, little girl. He's ready with
his torch to light the fire for the witch.

FISHWIFE   Look at the Duke of Bedford, he's laughing and enjoying himself. Those twelve thousand pounds for the Maid
have paid off.

SON   Cardinals and dukes, birds of a feather. English and
French lords, birds of a feather.

PEASANT   Hold your tongue.

SOLDIER   Who was that?

FISHWIFE *(drops her basket to cover up the flight of the young peasant)*
My fish, my mackerel!

WINE MERCHANT *(to the soldier)*   Someone pushed me from behind.

YOUNG CURATE   That's right, I saw it myself.

LOOSE WOMAN   Henry, go home.

BISHOP'S VOICE   We, Bishop of Beauvais, hereby declare you,
Joan, a heretic and relapsed sinner and by this same declara-

tion excommunicate you. At the same time we pray that divine judgment upon you may be mitigated after your death and the imminent destruction of your body.

FIRST SOLDIER   Took a long time!
(Church bells)

SECOND SOLDIER   Don't push. The wood's piled high enough, everybody can see her.

FISHWIFE   Swine! They've piled it high to make her suffer more.

SECOND SOLDIER   Why do they let the people come so close?

FIRST SOLDIER   Don't worry, you've got a pike. Let them get a taste of the smoke.

LOOSE WOMAN   Now!
(Nuns recite the Hail Mary)

FIRST SOLDIER   It's all over, let's go home. What are you people gaping at? She can't do any more than burn.

PEASANT (to his wife)   Don't cry now. She can't feel anything now.

LOOSE WOMAN   She's still screaming.

SECOND SOLDIER   Got to sound off to the bitter end.

SISTER-IN-LAW   She's stopped screaming.

16

Five years later the ultimate liberation and unification of France is initiated by the revolt of the people in Paris. At the head of the popular movement walks the legendary figure of little Joan of Arc.

The village in Touraine. Jacques Legrain is hammering a wine barrel. Grandfather Breuil, an old man from a neighboring village, steps up, leading a child by the hand.

GRANDFATHER BREUIL   Well, Jacques, that was a long visit you had with François at the "St. Peter's Catch." Something like five years.

LEGRAIN   One thing led to another, Grandfather Breuil.

BREUIL   A man sets out for Rouen and ends up in Paris, hein? The English are there too, I suppose.

LEGRAIN   Not any more, grandfather, not any more.

BREUIL   What do you mean, not any more?

LEGRAIN   The artisans from the suburbs, the drapers and tanners, the vegetable women from the market have driven them out.

BREUIL   And fellows like Jacques Legrain, I daresay. I suppose they're still in Compiègne?

LEGRAIN   Not there either. Nor in Rheims or Châlons. They're still in Calais, though, and down in Bordeaux; but not for long.

BREUIL   *(to the child)*   Did you hear that? The French are making themselves at home in France.

CHILD   Did you see her, Monsieur Legrain?

LEGRAIN   I saw her burn, Pierre.

BREUIL   She led France.

LEGRAIN   Yes, but France led her as well.

BREUIL   I thought she was led by voices.

LEGRAIN   Yes, our voices.

BREUIL   What do you mean?

LEGRAIN   Well, it was like this: First she led the people against the enemy, that's how she was captured. Then when they locked her up in the tower in Rouen, she didn't hear from us and became weak like you and me. She even recanted. But when she recanted, the common people of Rouen got so angry at her that they went to the docks and beat up the English. She heard about it, nobody knows how, and her courage came back. She realized that a law court is as good a battleground as the earthworks before Orléans. So she turned her greatest defeat into our greatest victory. After her lips were silenced, her voice was heard.

BREUIL   Well, well. The war isn't over yet.

CHILD   Will the English soldiers come back, grandfather?

BREUIL   I doubt it. How's the wine at your place this year?

LEGRAIN   I wasn't there last year, but the girls say it's as sweet as in twenty-eight.

(The girls are heard singing as they pick the grapes)

GIRLS *(singing)*
    The Maid stood trial for half a year
    All France was waiting until May.
    And those she spoke to did not hear.
    Then she was taken out into the day.
    And as they dragged her to the stake,
    As torches hissed and the wind blew shrill
    She cried out: Frenchmen, Frenchmen, wake
    And fight for France, for the soil you till!

LEGRAIN   They're singing that song in both halves of France
    now, ours and theirs.

Don Juan

by Molière

Adaptation

Collaborators: B. Besson, E. Hauptmann

Translator: Ralph Manheim

CHARACTERS

DON JUAN, son of Don Luis Tenorio

SGANARELLE, Don Juan's servant

DON LUIS TENORIO

DONNA ELVIRA, Don Juan's wife

DON CARLOS and DON ALONSO, Donna Elvira's brothers

THE STATUE OF THE COMMANDER

ANGELICA, the commander's daughter

MR. DIMANCHE, a tailor

GUZMAN, Donna Elvira's equerry

LA VIOLETTE, servant to Don Juan

RAGOTIN, Don Juan's equerry

PIETER, a fisherman

BERTHELOT, ANGELOT, COLIN, boatmen

CHARLOTTE and MATHURINE, fisher maidens

MARPHURIUS, a physician

A BEGGAR

SERAPHINE, Don Juan's cook

The action is laid in Sicily.

ACT ONE

Entrance of an elegant town house. In front of it, pieces of baggage.

1

Sganarelle. Guzman.

SGANARELLE *(fishes a snuffbox out of Don Juan's baggage and looks at it)* Whatever Aristotle and the other philosophers may say, there's nothing better than tobacco. It's a passion with the nobility. Ah, they choose their passions wisely! To live without tobacco in this day and age is not to live at all. Not only does it cleanse and rejoice the brain, but above all it confers that divine peace of mind without which a nobleman cannot be a nobleman. Tobacco alone allows a nobleman to forget sufferings, especially other people's. One or two of our farms are on the rocks? We take a pinch of snuff and things don't look half so bleak. A petitioner makes a nuisance of himself, a creditor importunes us? Take a pinch of snuff, my friend, be a philosopher! A pinch of snuff satisfies the giver as well as the taker. The mere gesture of offering: you don't wait to be asked, you anticipate your fellow man's desires—tobacco is what he wants—you satisfy them with a smile. Take a pinch, friend Guzman, help yourself.

GUZMAN   Thank you kindly. But let's get back to the subject. Perhaps I haven't made myself quite clear.

SGANARELLE   Oh yes you have. Donna Elvira has hurried after us, overpowered by love for my master. She can neither live nor die without him. In short, you are here.

GUZMAN   But tell me this: What sort of reception can we expect?

SGANARELLE   Shall I tell you what I think? I am afraid that her love will be ill-rewarded, that her journey will do her no good. She would have done better to stay at home.

GUZMAN   Why? Has your master intimated that his love has grown cold so soon? Is that the reason for his sudden departure?

SGANARELLE   Oh no! What do you imagine? We never discuss our love affairs. To tell you the truth, I've known him so long, I can see how the land lies without his breathing a word. Sometimes I know better than he does himself. Experience!

GUZMAN   What! Then this sudden journey of his was merely a contemptible betrayal? And Don Juan has miserably deserted Donna Elvira after only a few weeks of marriage? Without a word of explanation?

SGANARELLE   (takes a pinch of snuff)   Oh! We're still young and short on courage . . .

GUZMAN   A man of his station!

SGANARELLE   Station, my foot! His station won't stand in his way. Do you really think he would deny himself the slightest pleasure for the sake of his station?

GUZMAN   But the holy ties of matrimony?

SGANARELLE   Ah, my dear Guzman, my poor friend! Even holy ties are—ties. You don't know Don Juan.

GUZMAN   I am beginning to fear that I don't. Those sacred oaths, those ardent letters, his impatience until he had lured her out of her pious refuge at the convent of Santa Regina! How can he abandon her after all that? I don't understand.

SGANARELLE   If you knew the fellow, you would know that such things give him no trouble at all. Incidentally, I haven't said a word. I had to come here ahead of him to make certain arrangements, and since his arrival I haven't spoken to him. I don't know anything definite. But to be on the safe side, I'd better inform you that my master, Don Juan, is the biggest scoundrel that ever walked the earth, a madman, a devil, a heathen, who believes neither in heaven nor in hell, who lives like a wild beast, an Epicurean pig, a Sardanapalus! Very well, he married your mistress. To get what he wanted he'd have married you too and the priest and the dog and the cat. What's a marriage to him? It's simply the trap in which he catches them all. He is the greatest of all marriers before the Lord: housewife or virgin; noble or shopkeeper; countess or peasant woman; mayor's wife or novice—nothing's too hot or too cold for him. If I were to list all the women he had married in various parts of the world, we'd still be standing here tomorrow morning. But there's one thing I've got to admit: he attracts women as jam attracts flies. He's a magnet that none can resist. His poor old father endures disgrace after disgrace and wonders how he can go on. And the debts! But what can we do? Nothing. One day heaven in its wrath will crush him.

GUZMAN   Sh-h! Here he comes. What shall I tell my mistress?

SGANARELLE   (*shrugs his shoulders*)

GUZMAN   (*goes off in despair*)

2

Don Juan. Sganarelle.

SGANARELLE   (*reporting*)   The light campaign baggage.

DON JUAN   Whom were you talking to just now? Wasn't that Donna Elvira's equerry? Guzman?

SGANARELLE   Mm, someone of the sort.

DON JUAN   (*threatening him with his stick*)   Was it or wasn't it?

SGANARELLE   It was.

DON JUAN   How long has he been in this city?

SGANARELLE   Just arrived.

DON JUAN   What brings him here?

SGANARELLE   You ought to know.

DON JUAN   Our journey?

SGANARELLE   He wanted to know the reason for it.

DON JUAN   What did you tell him?

SGANARELLE   That you hadn't confided in me.

DON JUAN   And what is your opinion?

SGANARELLE   Mine? Begging your pardon, I think we're after another young lady.

DON JUAN   That's what you think?

SGANARELLE   Yes.

DON JUAN   You're not mistaken. We are. Another has banished Elvira from my thoughts.

SGANARELLE   I know my master like my little finger. Your heart is insatiable.

DON JUAN   Can it be that you don't approve?

SGANARELLE   Well, my lord . . .

DON JUAN   Well, what?

SGANARELLE   Of course I approve if that's what you want. In that case I haven't a word to say. But if you wanted something different, it might be different.

DON JUAN   Never mind that. Just tell me what you think. I authorize you.

SGANARELLE   In that case, my lord, I'll put it plainly. This indiscriminate loving is abominable.

DON JUAN   What? Would you wish me to chain myself to the first one who comes along and have no eyes for others? Fidelity—what an absurd notion! All the beauties in the world have the right to bewitch us. If in justice to one I succumb to her charms, does it mean that I should be unjust to the others? Is it right that one who has had the good fortune to cross our path should deprive all others of their just claims to our heart? My eyes are open to every woman's qualities; I am resolved to pay each one the tribute that nature imposes. A chair! (*Sganarelle brings him the folding traveling chair. Don Juan sits down*) What ineffable pleasure it is to invent the thousand flatteries that subjugate a young beauty's heart! To take note each day of the progress one has made. How gratifying to lay siege, with protestations, tears, and sighs, to a chaste soul reluctant to surrender. Step by step to overcome her tender resistance, to surmount the pangs of conscience on which she prides herself, and to lead her gently where we want her. Once the fortress is ours, we have nothing more to say or desire: we fall asleep. In this domain, my friend, I have the ambitions of a conqueror, who races eternally from one victory to the next, recognizing no boundary to his wishes. Nothing, nothing can halt my impetuous desires. This heart that beats within me aspires to love the whole world. Like Alexander of Macedon, I long for still other worlds to subject to the power of my love. What do you say to that, Sganarelle?

SGANARELLE   Well, my lord . . . your way of life . . . I just don't like the way you live.

DON JUAN   What do you mean? How do I live?

SGANARELLE   Oh, splendidly. Excellently. Except—well, this business of getting married every few weeks.

DON JUAN   But it's delightful!

SGANARELLE   Undoubtedly. I wouldn't mind doing it myself if only it weren't so sinful. Making a mockery of such a sacred institution!

DON JUAN   Come, come. That's between me and heaven.

SGANARELLE   Oh, sir. They say that the vengeance of heaven is terrible. People who mock it . . .

DON JUAN   Hold your tongue! Don't you know that I can't abide sermons? Blockhead!

SGANARELLE   God forbid. I wasn't referring to you. You can't help it. You have your justifications. Such power to attract! So full of fire! It grieves me to say that there are men who take morality lightly without such excellent justifications. If I had that kind of master, I'd say it to his face: You earthworm, I'd say, you crawling louse, how dare you make a mockery of something that all mankind holds sacred! Do you think because you're a nobleman with a blond, prettily curled wig, and feathers on your hat—that's what I'd say to *him*—do you think because you wear a gold-embroidered coat with dashing red braid that you can do anything you please?—that's what I'd say to *him* . . .

DON JUAN   (*smiling*)   Rascal.

SGANARELLE   It would be my duty to tell that kind of man what I thought of him.

DON JUAN   That's enough. We haven't much time. Now we must speak of the beauty who has brought us here . . .

SGANARELLE *(aside)*   Brought!

DON JUAN   . . . by bringing herself.

SGANARELLE   That's just it! Must I remind you that you killed the Commander, Don Rodrigo, here in this province? Aren't you afraid?

DON JUAN   What is there to be afraid of? I killed him, didn't I? According to all the rules of the art.

SGANARELLE   That is true. He can't complain on that score.

DON JUAN   Who's afraid of the dead? Anyway, I was tried, my father interceded for me, I was pardoned. The affair is dead and buried.

SGANARELLE   Yes, dead and buried. But there are friends, close relations, a young daughter—do you suppose those friends and relations were overjoyed to see you pardoned?

DON JUAN   That's enough. It's time to think of the pleasures that lie *ahead* of us. The beauty I referred to is a young . . . *(He catches sight of Donna Elvira)* Donna Elvira! A most unwelcome sight. Scoundrel! Traitor! Why didn't you tell me she was here?

SGANARELLE   You didn't ask me, my lord.

DON JUAN   Has she lost her mind? Traveling around in evening dress!

3

Don Juan. Donna Elvira. Sganarelle.

DONNA ELVIRA   Don Juan! May I ask you to recognize me? May I hope at least that you will deign to look my way?

DON JUAN   My lady, I must own that I am surprised. I wasn't expecting you here.

DONNA ELVIRA   Yes, I can see you were not expecting me. Your surprise is not of the kind I had hoped for. It convinces me of what I had refused to believe. And now I am amazed at my simplicity and the folly of my heart that led me to doubt your treachery despite so many proofs. I was good, or rather stupid, enough to deceive myself. I thought up a hundred reasons for your sudden departure. In order to acquit you of the crime of which my reason convicted you, I gave ear to a thousand fantastic whisperings that proclaimed your innocence. But this reception dispels all doubt; your look when you saw me revealed more than I wished to know. And yet I should be glad to hear from your own lips the reasons for your sudden departure. Speak, Don Juan, I implore you. I am curious to see how you will justify yourself.

DON JUAN   Sganarelle here will tell you why I went away, my lady.

SGANARELLE *(in an undertone to Don Juan)*   I, my lord? Begging your pardon, sir, I don't know a thing.

DONNA ELVIRA   Speak, Sganarelle. It makes no difference from whom I learn the truth.

DON JUAN *(motions Sganarelle to approach Donna Elvira)*   Go ahead, tell the lady.

SGANARELLE *(in an undertone)*   What should I say?

DON JUAN   Speak up!

SGANARELLE   My lady . . .

DONNA ELVIRA   Well?

SGANARELLE *(to Don Juan)*   My lord . . . what . . . *(A stern look from Don Juan)* Well . . . my lady . . . the great conquerors . . . Alexander of Macedon . . . and the other worlds . . . were to blame for our departure . . . that's as much as I know.

DONNA ELVIRA   Don Juan, may I ask you to explain your puzzling explanation?

DON JUAN   To tell the truth, my lady . . .

DONNA ELVIRA   Heavens, how clumsily you defend yourself! Didn't they teach you anything at court? Couldn't you simply swear that your feelings for me are unchanged, that you still love me with the same matchless ardor, and that death alone can part you from me? Couldn't you tell me that an affair of the utmost importance obliged you to slip away without taking leave of me, that you are compelled, quite against your will, to stay here for a time, that I should return home in the certainty that you will follow as soon as possible, and that in my absence you suffer like a body separated from its soul.

That's how you should defend yourself instead of just standing there!

DON JUAN   My lady, I must own that I have no talent for dissimulation. I can only tell the truth. I will not say that I still harbor the same feelings for you, that I am burning with desire to be reunited with you, when it is plain that I fled from you. Not for the reasons you suppose, but for reasons imposed by my conscience. To continue living with you would be a sin. Today I see what I have done through the eyes of my immortal soul. Today I see that in order to marry you I ravished you from the holy seclusion of the convent. That you have broken the vows that bound you to another. Heaven, as everyone knows, is extremely jealous in such matters. I fear, my lady, that our marriage is adultery in disguise. I fear the wrath of heaven for both of us. I am trying to forget you. It is my duty to let you return to your former bonds. My lady, would you oppose so pious a thought? Would you have me, by remaining with you, bring down the wrath of heaven on my head? My lady, our obligation to heaven and our fellow creatures often demands painful sacrifices . . .

DONNA ELVIRA   Ah, scoundrel! Now I know you. To my misfortune, I have come to know you too late. What use is my knowledge to me now? It only hurls me into deeper despair. But know this: your crime will not go unpunished. The heaven you scoff at will avenge me.

DON JUAN   Sganarelle. Heaven!

SGANARELLE   Heaven, indeed! Do they expect us to fall for that?

DON JUAN   My lady . . .

DONNA ELVIRA   Enough. I won't listen. I have heard too much. Don't expect me to indulge in reproaches and abuse. I will not waste my fury in words. But I repeat, Don Juan: Heaven will punish you. (Goes out)

4

Don Juan. Sganarelle. Later the boatmen.

DON JUAN   Well, the beauty I wished to speak of is engaged to be married. I caught sight of her a few days ago: the loveliest thing that eye has ever looked upon. She was strolling arm in arm with her betrothed. I have never seen a couple so happy and so pleased with themselves. They made no attempt to conceal their feeling for each other, and that moved me deeply, indeed, it struck me to the heart. I found it utterly intolerable to see them so happy together. To destroy this union that so offended my sensitive heart seemed a voluptuous duty.

SGANARELLE   I understand.

DON JUAN   You understand nothing. Something has happened that defies understanding. The lady refuses to be parted from her bumpkin.

SGANARELLE   Well . . .

DON JUAN   So that I find myself obliged to take the necessary steps.

SGANARELLE   What about our letters? Our gifts?

DON JUAN   All returned.

SGANARELLE   What? The lady detests you!

DON JUAN   So she thinks. She actually intends to marry the fellow tomorrow. That calls for extreme measures. She must be abducted.

SGANARELLE   Oh no!

DON JUAN   What! The lout is already playing the husband, planning to entertain her with a boat ride on the sea. I have hired a fast boat and several strong boatmen.

SGANARELLE   Oh, my lord! Last night I dreamed of dead fish and cracked eggs, and our cook Seraphine always says that means . . .

DON JUAN *(threatens him)*

SGANARELLE   Oh, my lord! This is going to be another of your . . .

DON JUAN   Of my . . . ?

SGANARELLE   . . . great adventures!

DON JUAN   You of course will accompany me. Test your weapons carefully, your life will depend on it. And don't forget the wine.

(The boatmen enter with their oars)

DON JUAN   Let's get going.

5

Don Juan. Sganarelle. Berthelot. Angelot. Colin.

DON JUAN   Give these men their instructions.

SGANARELLE   Money would be the best instructor, my lord.

DON JUAN *(throwing him a purse)*   Here you are. But no more.

SGANARELLE *(examines the purse)*   Twenty ducats. That will do it. *(He puts the purse away)* This way, men. We'll pay you two ducats each for your services.

(The boatmen are overjoyed)

COLIN   Many thanks, sir.

SGANARELLE   Just a moment. For special pay we expect special services. Can you handle an oar?

ANGELOT   Nowhere on this whole coast . . .

SGANARELLE   Not just this way. *(He makes the gesture of rowing)* This way as well! *(He makes the gesture of striking with an oar)*

COLIN   Oh, it's that kind of job!

ANGELOT   We're peaceful fishermen, sir. If people are going to get hit . . .

SGANARELLE *(sternly)*   Oh, so you don't know how to fight. Then I'll have to teach you.

ANGELOT   Teach us how to kill people? These men don't seem to have any religion.

SGANARELLE   We don't pay two ducats for rowing.

BERTHELOT   It can't be done, sir. I know him. *(Pointing at Angelot)*

ANGELOT *(to the two others)*   Would you want to kill your fellow men for two ducats?

BERTHELOT   He's right, sir. Two ducats aren't enough for that kind of thing.

COLIN *(to Angelot)*   You wouldn't even do it for three, would you, Angelot?

ANGELOT *(shakes his head)*

BERTHELOT *(to Angelot)*   For four?

SGANARELLE   Three ducats are out of the question.

ANGELOT   Four ducats is a lot of money. *(But he continues to shake his head)*

COLIN   He's too soft-hearted, you see.

SGANARELLE   Trying to gouge three ducats out of us—is that what you call soft-hearted?

BERTHELOT   Under five ducats nothing doing.

DON JUAN *(calling to Sganarelle)*   How about it?

SGANARELLE *(furious)*   Very well, I will pay you the outrageous sum of four ducats . . .

ANGELOT   Five!

SGANARELLE   Very well. But you've lost my respect; we're not friends any more. *(Driving the boatmen upstage)* You might as well show me what you can do. *(Upstage Sganarelle instructs the boatmen in "oarsmanship," he himself using his sword. He shouts commands of: "Parry left!" "Parry right!" "Lunge!")*

SGANARELLE   My lord, we will do our part, but . . .

DON JUAN *(to Angelot)*   Lift up that oar, fellow!

ANGELOT   No, no, no. My conscience won't let me. *(He runs off)*

SGANARELLE   Go to the devil!

COLIN   But two of us won't be enough.

DON JUAN *(to Sganarelle)*   Raise the pay.

COLIN *(calls after Angelot)*   Six ducats. Come back here.

ANGELOT *(slowly coming back)*   Now it's gone up to six. I'm sorry.

SGANARELLE   Let's be going. *(To Don Juan)* Oh, my lord, here comes your father!

DON JUAN   Everything seems to be conspiring against me today.

(Enter Don Luis. During the following the fencing exercise dies down whenever Sganarelle is required to wait on Don Juan)

6

Don Juan. Don Luis. Sganarelle. Boatmen.

DON LUIS   I am well aware that my presence is unwelcome to you. But if you are weary of the sight of me, I am no less weary of your excesses. How, on top of everything else, can you expect me to put up with your latest sacrilege? Snatching the only daughter of our noble friend Don Filipo away from the holy seclusion of the convent! When will you cease to bring grief upon my head grown gray in the service of king and country? Must you heap crime upon crime?

(Sganarelle discreetly presents Don Juan two swords from which to choose. Don Juan imperiously indicates one of them. Sganarelle goes out)

DON LUIS   To cover up your scandalous doings I am obliged to wear out the mercy of our king. A time comes when the most benevolent mercy is at an end. While you gratify your whims, I am forced to squander the credit my services have built up.

DON JUAN   Won't you be seated, sir? It's easier to talk sitting down.

DON LUIS   No, you blackguard, I will not be seated. Ah, how heedless we are when we beget sons! How passionately I desired a son, how obstinately I begged for one—here he stands, the son for whom I importuned heaven with my prayers: a monster! He scoffs at my remonstrances, laughs at my legitimate wishes!

(During this tirade Sganarelle points smilingly at the performance of the fencing boatmen)

DON JUAN   Not at all, father. Inform me of your wishes regarding the lady in question, and I shall do my best to comply.

DON LUIS   Be still! Don't remind me that I am your father. Too many people do so to wound me. Are you really not ashamed to be so unworthy of your birth? What have you ever done to glorify the name you bear?

DON JUAN *(while Sganarelle shows him a basket filled with bottles of wine)* More of that kind. *(Sganarelle withdraws upstage)*

DON LUIS You're living on the reputation of your ancestors. But their heroic deeds will not help you. On the contrary, their glory is a torch that shows up your disgrace.

DON JUAN Sir, you will not find me as disobedient as you seem to think. There are situations in which a nobleman has no choice. Certain obligations must be met, regardless of the cost.

SGANARELLE *(aside)* Regardless of the cost to his father.

DON JUAN I will allow Donna Elvira to return to the seclusion from which I should never have snatched her. In view of which change of heart I venture to hope that you will resume your past generosity toward me. My creditors . . .

DON LUIS Wretch, not a word about your creditors! You have more to fear from the wrath of heaven! *(Goes out)*

7

Don Juan. Sganarelle. Boatmen.

DON JUAN *(motions Sganarelle to approach)* I want you to have a coach ready when we return in the boat.—How revolting it is to see fathers who live as long as their sons.

SGANARELLE *(who has lined up the boatmen and loaded them with baggage and weapons)* My lord, you should have thrown the old man out. I admire your patience.

DON JUAN Patience? That is exactly what I haven't got. You rascal, I am thirty-one. Alexander died at the age of thirty-three. He had taken six hundred and eighteen cities. Which means I've got to hurry. Time to get going! The boat! *(They go out)*

ACT TWO

Ocean beach. Don Juan's and Sganarelle's coats have been hung up to dry.

1

Charlotte. Pieter.

CHARLOTTE It was lucky for them that you happened to be here.

PIETER Yer dern tootin'. They'd have drowned.

CHARLOTTE Was it that little squall this morning that upset their boat?

PIETER I can see I'll have to tell you the whole story from the beginning. Well, the two of us, me and Tubby, were on the beach horsing around, throwing sand at each other, when all of a sudden I see somebody paddling around way out in the ocean. I seen them plain as day and then all of a sudden I seen that I couldn't see nuthin'. Tubby, says I, it looks to me like somebody's swimmin' out yonder. Piffle, says he. Consarn it, says I, there's somebody swimmin' out there. Fiddlesticks, says he, you're seein' ghosts. Do you want to bet, says I, that I'm not seein' ghosts and it's hoomans swimmin' this way. Consarn it, says he, I bet it isn't. All right, says I, this dime says it is. All right, says he, here's my money, says he. I'm nobody's fool, I throw in a dime and then another nickel, I knew what I was doin'. Well, we'd no sooner made our bet than we see these two men plain as day, wavin' like all get-out for us to come and save them. So first I rake in my money.

Come on, Tubby, says I, can't you see they're shoutin' for help? Let's get a move on. Naw, says he, they've cost me too much already. Well, to make a long story short, I kept at him till he jumps in the boat with me, and in three shakes we fish them out of the water. They were all blue. So I take them home and sit them down by the fire, they take their clothes off to dry, they're sittin' there mother-naked and then Mathurine comes in, and right then and there one of them starts makin' eyes at her. And that's my story.

CHARLOTTE *(all curiosity)* But Pieter, didn't you say one was much better looking than the other?

PIETER   That's the master. Must be some bigwig. There's gold all over his coat. *(He points to the coat hung up to dry)* From top to bottom. And his servant looks like a lord too. But bigwig or not, he'd have drowned if I hadn't been there.

CHARLOTTE   You don't say so?

PIETER   Consarn it! If I hadn't been there, he'd have been up split creek.

CHARLOTTE *(burning with curiosity)* Is he still sitting naked by your fire, Pieter?

PIETER   Naw, his servant dressed him and we all looked on. Bless my soul, I'd never seen one of them fancypants gettin' dressed. The gear they hang on those courtiers! Listen to this, Charlotte. They got hair that don't grow on their head, it's like oakum and they put it on like a great big hat. Their shirts —the two of us would fit into one of the sleeves! Instead of pants they wear an apron that's as wide as from here to Christmas. Instead of a jerkin, they wear a wee little vest that hardly reaches down to their belly button. Instead of a regular collar they wear a neck cloth *(makes a motion)* as big as this, with four big tufts of lace that hang down to their stomachs. *(Sganarelle enters briefly upstage and takes the coats)* On their wrists they got more collars, and on their legs big braided funnels. And they're covered with ribbons, ribbons, ribbons, enough to drive you crazy.

CHARLOTTE   Goodness me, Pieter, I want to get a look at that. *(Stands up)*

PIETER *(makes her sit down again)* Listen to me first, Charlotte. I've got something else to tell you.

CHARLOTTE *(in a hurry)* Well, go ahead.

PIETER Well, Charlotte, you see, I've just got to pour out my heart, as they say. I like you, you know I do, I'm all for our teaming up, but dern it, I'm not rightly pleased with you.

CHARLOTTE Why? What's wrong?

PIETER What's wrong? You just make me miserable.

CHARLOTTE Miserable?

PIETER Dern it, you don't love me.

CHARLOTTE Is that all?

PIETER That's all. Ain't it enough?

CHARLOTTE Shucks, Pieter, you always come around with the same old story.

PIETER I always come around with the same old story 'cause it's always the same old story. If it warn't the same old story I wouldn't come around with the same old story.

CHARLOTTE What do you want of me?

PIETER I want you to love me, dern it.

CHARLOTTE Who says I don't?

PIETER No. You don't love me. I can stand on my head, I buy you ribbons from every peddler that comes along, I dern near break my neck bringin' you blackbirds fresh out of the nest, I pay the organ grinder to play for you on your saint's day —where does it get me?

CHARLOTTE But shecks, Pieter, I do love you. What do you want me to do?

PIETER I want you to do what people do when they really love each other.

CHARLOTTE I really love you.

PIETER Naw. Anybody can see when it's real. Take Thomasine, she's plumb crazy about her Benjamin. Pesters the life out of him from morning to night, she never leaves him alone. Only the other day . . . he was sittin' on a stool . . . so she sneaks up behind him and pulls it out from under his ass. That's the right way to love somebody. You never do anything like that, you just stand around like a block of wood. I could pass you twenty times, you wouldn't even bother to poke me in the ribs. Consarn it! That's no good. You're cold.

CHARLOTTE That's the way I am.

PIETER But you shouldn't be. When you love somebody, you should show it somehow or other.

CHARLOTTE   Well, I love you as best I can. If it doesn't suit you, you can find yourself somebody else.

PIETER   See? What did I tell you? Consarn it, you wouldn't say that if you loved me.

CHARLOTTE   Why must you always keep after me?

PIETER   All I want is a little love.

CHARLOTTE   Don't prod me. Maybe if we stop thinking about it, it'll come all by itself.

PIETER   All right, Charlotte. *(Gives her his hand)*

CHARLOTTE   All right. *(Taking his hand)* There.

PIETER   Try to love me more. Promise.

CHARLOTTE   I'll do my best, but it's got to come by itself. Pieter, is that his lordship?

PIETER *(proudly)*   That's him.

CHARLOTTE   Gracious me, how handsome he is! What a shame if he'd been drowned!

2

Charlotte. Pieter. Don Juan. Sganarelle.

DON JUAN *(motions Pieter to come closer)*

PIETER *(to Charlotte)*   See? He knows me. *(While Pieter, proudly smiling, approaches the man he has rescued, Charlotte stares at the nobleman)*

DON JUAN   My good man, I'm sure you'd be glad to do me another little service. Run up to the village and give that girl —I believe her name is Mathurine—my best greetings. Tell her I wish to speak to her here on a matter of the greatest importance. And don't tell anyone else. Understand?

PIETER   She'll be here in a minute, your lordship. Yes, your lordship. *(Running past Charlotte)* I'll be right back. I'm running an errand for his lordship. *(Goes out)*

3

Charlotte. Don Juan. Sganarelle.

SGANARELLE   We'd better be getting out of here, my lord. Those
damned boatmen may have righted their boat and somehow
reached the shore.

DON JUAN   Be still! I'm thinking.

SGANARELLE   Remember, when the storm was coming up, they
wanted to go home and you doubled their pay three times.
But the sea has swallowed up our treasury.

DON JUAN   Sganarelle, we've had bad luck. That storm this
morning upset not only our boat but our plans as well. And
yet, I must confess, that fisher maiden we saw just now makes
up for it all. I discerned charms which, I suspect, will make
up to me very amply for our unfortunate accident. That heart
must not evade me. And I believe I have already softened it
to the point where only a few sighs will be necessary.

SGANARELLE   I can hardly believe it: here we've escaped death
by a miracle and instead of thanking heaven for its mercy
you start bringing down its wrath on our heads by your
usual . . .

DON JUAN *(threatening him)*   Hold your tongue! You don't know
what you're saying. Your master knows what he's up to.
(Notices Charlotte) Ah! Ah! Another fisher maiden. Where has
she come from? Sganarelle! Have you ever seen anything so
charming? Seriously, isn't she at least as beautiful as the other
one?

SGANARELLE   Of course. *(Aside)* Here we go again.

DON JUAN *(to Charlotte)*   Lovely child, to what good fortune do
I owe this delightful meeting? Can it be? Can there really be
creatures like you in these remote regions, in the midst of
trees and cliffs?

CHARLOTTE   Yes, my lord.

DON JUAN   Are you from this village?

CHARLOTTE   Yes, my lord.

DON JUAN   And you live here?

CHARLOTTE   Yes, my lord.

DON JUAN   And your name?

CHARLOTTE   Charlotte, my lord, at your service.

DON JUAN   Ah, what a lovely creature! What irresistible eyes!

CHARLOTTE   You make me blush, my lord.

DON JUAN   Ah, never blush to hear the truth about yourself! Sganarelle, what do you say? Can you conceive of anything more lovely? Turn around—I beg you. Oh, what a graceful back! The head a little higher—I implore you. Oh, what an adorable little face! Open your eyes. Wider! How beautiful they are! Grant me a glimpse of your teeth—please! Oh, how loving they are! Oh! And the lips, those precious lips! I'm overwhelmed. Never in all my life have I seen so lovely a child!

CHARLOTTE   I don't know if you're making fun of me or not, my lord.

DON JUAN   I make fun of you! God forbid! I love you far too much, my words spring from a full heart. Sganarelle, just look at her hands!

CHARLOTTE   Phoo, my lord, they're all black with tar.

DON JUAN   What are you saying? They are the most beautiful hands in all the world. Let me kiss them—I beg you.

CHARLOTTE   You do me too much honor, my lord. If I'd only known, I'd have scrubbed them with sand.

DON JUAN   Oh!... Tell me, lovely child. You're not married yet, I presume?

CHARLOTTE   No, my lord, but soon, to Pieter. He's the son of our neighbor Simonette.

DON JUAN   What! A creature like you marry a common fisherman? No, no, that would be a crime against your marvelous beauty. You were not born to spend your life in a village. You are destined to higher things. Heaven has sent me here to prevent this marriage and do justice to your charms. You have only to say the word, my dear child, and I shall save you from a wretched fate and set you in the place you deserve. Perhaps you will say that my love is rather sudden. Ah, but Charlotte, that is the miraculous effect of your beauty; you inspire more love in ten minutes than another in six months.

CHARLOTTE Really, my lord, I don't know what to say. Your words give me pleasure and I'd like to believe them, but they tell me I should never trust a noble gentleman because all his fine talk is just a trap to take a poor girl in.

DON JUAN I'm not one of those.

SGANARELLE *(aside)* God forbid!

CHARLOTTE It's no joke to be taken in. I'm only a poor fisher maiden, my honor means a lot to me, I'd rather be dead than dishonored.

DON JUAN By me? I vile enough to dishonor you? No, never. My conscience is much too delicate. Believe me, dear child, I have no other design than to marry you in all honor. I am ready. Whenever you wish. This man here is a witness to my promise.

SGANARELLE No, no, you needn't worry. He'll marry you as much as you like.

DON JUAN Ah, Charlotte, you're not the kind one deceives. Your beauty is your safeguard.

CHARLOTTE My goodness, I don't know if you're telling the truth or not, but the way you talk makes a body believe you.

DON JUAN Do you wish to be my wife?

CHARLOTTE Oh yes, if my aunt doesn't mind.

DON JUAN Give me a kiss in pledge . . .

CHARLOTTE Oh, my lord, wait until we're married. Then I'll kiss you all you want.

DON JUAN Ah, child, I want only what you want. Just give me your hand and on it permit me, with a thousand kisses, to express my ineffable delight.

4

Charlotte. Don Juan. Sganarelle. Pieter.

PIETER *(calling in the distance)* Your lordship! Your lordship! Mathurine will be . . . *(He comes closer and sees Don Juan caressing Charlotte. He pushes Don Juan aside)*

PIETER   Hey, sir, take it easy! You're all in a lather, you'll catch cold.

DON JUAN *(pushing him back)*   How did he get here?

PIETER *(placing himself between Don Juan and Charlotte)*   I'm telling you to watch your step. Keep your paws off our womenfolk.

DON JUAN *(pushes him away again)*   Oh! So much noise!

PIETER   Consarn it! I'll teach you to push me around!

CHARLOTTE *(intervenes)*   Leave him be, Pieter.

PIETER   What? Leave him be? I won't have it.

DON JUAN *(menacingly)*   Ah!

PIETER   Dag nab it! Just because you're a lordship do you think you can smooch our women under our nose? Go smooch your own.

DON JUAN   What did you say?

PIETER   You heard me. *(Don Juan slaps his face)* Don't you dare touch me! *(Don Juan slaps him again)* Consarn it! Is that a way to repay me for pulling you out of the water?

CHARLOTTE   Don't get excited, Pieter.

PIETER   I want to get excited. And you're a no-good fly-by-night, letting him pet you like that.

CHARLOTTE   Oh, Pieter, you're stupid. It's not what you think. His lordship wants to marry me; that's nothing to get sore about.

PIETER   What? Gee willickers! You're engaged to me!

CHARLOTTE   What of it, Pieter? If you love me, you ought to be glad I'm going to be a lady.

PIETER   No, goldarn it, I'd rather see you dead than married to someone else.

CHARLOTTE   Now now, Pieter, don't worry. When I'm a lady I'll help you make money, you can bring all your fish and crabs to the castle.

PIETER   Consarn it! I won't bring you anything even if you pay double. You going to listen to him? Huh! Holy mackerel! If I'd known I'd have thought twice before pulling him out of the water, I'd have given him one on the bean with my oar. *(Don Juan approaches Pieter as if to strike him)*

PIETER   Jumping Jehoshaphat! Do you think I'm afraid of you?

DON JUAN *(coming toward him again)*   That we shall soon see.

PIETER   I've taken care of better men than you.

DON JUAN   Indeed?

SGANARELLE   Oh, my lord, leave the poor devil alone. He helped us, you know. *(To Pieter)* Stop hollering, son, and make yourself scarce.

PIETER   But I want to holler.

DON JUAN *(raises his hand to slap Pieter again)*   Ha! Let this be a lesson to you! . . .
   (Pieter ducks and Sganarelle gets the slap)

SGANARELLE *(furious)*   You young snotnose! You can go to the devil! *(Goes to one side)*

DON JUAN *(to Sganarelle)*   You asked for that, you humanitarian!

PIETER *(to Charlotte)*   All right, I'll be going. But I'll tell your aunt. *(Goes out)*

DON JUAN *(to Charlotte)*   What heavenly bliss when we are man and wife!

5

Don Juan. Charlotte. Sganarelle. Mathurine.

SGANARELLE *(catching sight of Mathurine, laughs)*   Ha ha!

MATHURINE *(to Don Juan)*   My lord, what are you doing with Charlotte? Have you been talking love to her too?

DON JUAN *(aside to Mathurine)*   No, of course not. She's been buzzing in my ears. She wants to be my wife. I've just told her I was engaged to you.

CHARLOTTE *(to Don Juan)*   What does Mathurine want?

DON JUAN *(to Charlotte)*   She's jealous because I was talking to you. She wants me to marry her. But I've told her I was going to marry you.

MATHURINE   It's not nice of you, Charlotte, to poach on other people's preserves.

DON JUAN *(aside to Mathurine)*   There's no point in talking to her; she won't listen to reason.

CHARLOTTE   It's not nice of you, Mathurine, to be jealous when his lordship talks to me.

DON JUAN *(aside to Charlotte)* You're wasting your breath. She's got an idea in her head, you'll never get it out.

CHARLOTTE   Oh yes, I will. *(Removes one of her clogs)*

MATHURINE   You underhanded slut!

DON JUAN *(to Mathurine)* Ignore her. She's possessed by a devil.

MATHURINE   Then I'll drive it out of her. *(Also picks up a clog)*

CHARLOTTE   Sneak!

DON JUAN *(to Charlotte)* Don't arouse her. She's dangerous.

MATHURINE   No, no, I want to give her a piece of my mind.

CHARLOTTE   I've got to find out what she thinks.

MATHURINE   What I think? Of you? *(She strikes; Charlotte strikes back)*

DON JUAN *(aside to Mathurine)* I'll wager she tells you I promised to marry her. *(Aside to Charlotte)* I'll wager she claims that I promised to make her my wife.

MATHURINE   He saw me first!

CHARLOTTE   But then he saw me and promised to marry me.

DON JUAN *(to Mathurine)* What did I tell you?

MATHURINE *(to Charlotte)* He promised to marry me, not you.

DON JUAN *(to Charlotte)* Wasn't I right?

CHARLOTTE   Fiddlesticks! He wants me, not you!

MATHURINE   Hussy! He wants me, not you!

CHARLOTTE   Hussy yourself. He'll tell you I'm right.

MATHURINE   Don't make me laugh! He'll show you who's right.

CHARLOTTE   My lord, did you promise to marry her or didn't you? She claims you did.

DON JUAN *(aside to Charlotte)* Let her claim what she likes.

MATHURINE   My lord, is it true you promised to make her your wife? She says you did.

DON JUAN *(aside to Mathurine)* Let her say what she likes.

CHARLOTTE   No, no. I want to know the truth.

MATHURINE   This has got to be settled.

CHARLOTTE *(to Mathurine)* Exactly. His lordship will show you that you're still wet behind the ears.

MATHURINE   Exactly. His lordship will stop your impudent mouth.

CHARLOTTE *(to Don Juan)* My lord, settle the argument.

MATHURINE *(to Don Juan)* Decide between us.

CHARLOTTE *(to Don Juan)* Go ahead!

MATHURINE *(to Don Juan)* Speak up!

DON JUAN   Ladies, what can I say? You both claim that I promised to make you my wife. Doesn't each of you know what
actually happened without my going into details? Everything
has been said. I promised marriage. So far so good. If you have
my promise, you can rest easy, no need to be put off by idle
chatter. The one to whom I have given my promise will be
my wife. It's actions that count, not words. When I marry,
you will see whom I marry. *(Aside to Mathurine)* Let her think
what she likes. *(Aside to Charlotte)* Let her lull herself in hope.
(Aside to Mathurine) I adore you. *(Aside to Charlotte)* My heart
is yours alone. *(Aside to Mathurine)* All beauty pales before
yours. *(Aside to Charlotte)* One who has seen you can have eyes
for no other. *(Aloud)* I have a little matter to attend to. I'll be
back in a moment. Sganarelle, entertain the ladies.

SGANARELLE *(with a dismayed look at the one bottle of wine that has
been saved)* I've only saved one.

DON JUAN   Knock the neck off. *(Goes a few steps away)*

6

Charlotte. Mathurine. Sganarelle. Don Juan.

MATHURINE *(to Charlotte)* I say it's me he's going to marry.

CHARLOTTE *(to Mathurine)* All I say is it's me he loves.

SGANARELLE *(offering wine)* Poor things! Don't let him hornswoggle you. Him! Naturally he can turn your heads. Nothing to it.
(Don Juan comes closer)

SGANARELLE   Give me his coat, his ribbons, and his feathers and
I'll seduce you without trying; but then at least you'll
get something out of it. Take my advice: don't trust him. *(Sees
Don Juan)* Don't trust the fellow who speaks ill of my
master . . .

DON JUAN   Sganarelle . . . *(Grabs him by the ear)*

SGANARELLE   You don't know my master.
(Someone is hurrying in)

7

Charlotte. Mathurine. Don Juan. Sganarelle. Marphurius.

SGANARELLE   What's up? What's the hurry?

MARPHURIUS *(panting)*   Is this where the duel is to take place?
(Introducing himself) I am Dr. Marphurius, the medical authority of this humble village.

SGANARELLE   What duel?

MARPHURIUS   Between the noble brothers Don Alonso and Don Carlos on the one hand and the noble Don Juan Tenorio on the other.

SGANARELLE   Donna Elvira's brothers! Are they here?

MARPHURIUS   They will be here in a moment. They combed the village for a whole hour, inquiring after this noble Don Juan Tenorio. Then a young fisherman informed them that he was indeed here. *(To Don Juan)* Is it you, sir? I have come posthaste to offer you my services for the impending duel. I shall be greatly honored to attend your lordship. Foresight is better than hindsight. When the blood flows, we must be prepared. *(To the girls)* Bring shirting and basins of water.

CHARLOTTE   Heavens, they're going to stab each other.

MARPHURIUS   Yes, they are going to stab each other. *(To Don Juan)* In these humble villages, your lordship, a stab wound is seldom seen nowadays. Ah! The golden age of dueling is past. In those days surgery made greater progress in ten years than in the preceding three centuries. The stab wound flourished, the cleanest, the most elegant of all wounds. Nowadays all they ever bring me is an occasional arm crushed between fishing boats. I am not speaking of the money but of the healer's art. Duels trained the surgeon's hand, they perfected his instruments. With this probe, for example, I treated Don

Malaga after his glorious duel with the Duke of Estramadura.
The wound was all of two feet long. The family gave me this
purse! There were once fifty ducats in it, your lordship. I am
not speaking of the money but of the healer's art. How manners have degenerated and the arts with them! *(While pacing
off the distance between the duelists)* I can see the day coming
when our grandees will belabor each other with fish buckets.
They will settle their delicate quarrels with flails and avenge
their ladies with butcher knives.

DON JUAN   My dears, one of those affairs which honor makes
incumbent on those of my class obliges me to remain here
alone.

MARPHURIUS   O tempora, O mores! O times, O customs! The
stab wound vanishes, the bashed-in skull takes its place.

DON JUAN   If it pleases heaven to preserve my life, I entreat you
to remember my promise. You will hear from me before
nightfall.

MARPHURIUS   A robust but uncultivated population is preparing to force its barbarous ways upon the nation.

DON JUAN *(to Sganarelle)*   Escort these sweet young ladies to the
village and see to it that no evil befalls them.

MARPHURIUS   Ah yes, those boatmen I just met . . .

SGANARELLE   What boatmen?

MARPHURIUS   Three boatmen who escaped this morning's
storm by a hair's breadth. They have been going about complaining with the utmost insolence that a noble lord owes
them fifty-four ducats. Brandishing their oars in blind fury
and letting everyone know that they have been taught how
to handle them.

SGANARELLE   The rogues! Fifty-four ducats!

CHARLOTTE   Are they looking for you, my lord? You'd better
run.

SGANARELLE   Yes, my lord, you'd better run.

MARPHURIUS   Cut the knaves down and basta!

SGANARELLE *(to the girls)*   Beg him on your knees or we'll all be
lost.

MARPHURIUS   Exterminate them! Wipe them off the face of the
earth!

MATHURINE *(kneeling)*   Run, my lord.

CHARLOTTE *(kneeling)*   Yes, my lord, run! One of them must be that brute Berthelot from the next village. Run, run!

MARPHURIUS *(kneeling)*   And I implore you to cut them down.

MATHURINE   Run, my lord. A fine gentleman like you can't let his nose be bashed in.

SGANARELLE   They're coming, they're coming!

MARPHURIUS   Do you vulgarians suppose that a Don Juan Tenorio handles his affairs like you loutish fisherfolk? *(He tears linen for bandages and brandishes his instruments)*

MATHURINE AND CHARLOTTE *(at once)*   Run, my lord. They'll beat you to a pulp.

DON JUAN   Indeed, the contest seems too unequal. I will have no truck with brute force. Fate has come between us. Ah, my fair maidens, I cannot ignore your entreaties. Sganarelle, I find myself in a position to fulfill your heartfelt wish. You may put on my coat, give me your rags.

SGANARELLE   You are joking, my lord. Do you want me to die in your clothes?

DON JUAN   Not if it can be helped. Make ready for the journey home. *(Don Juan goes out with Sganarelle. The doctor runs after them)*

MARPHURIUS   Your lordship! Your lordship! The duel! The duel!

(The fisher maidens look at each other, start laughing, and laugh so hard that they have to sit down on the ground)

ACT THREE

An overgrown park. Among the trees a white building.

1

Don Juan in Sganarelle's clothes. Sganarelle in Don Juan's clothes.

DON JUAN Tell me, Sganarelle, haven't we come this way before? These trees, these bushes, these paths look familiar. This ancient tree—was it not a witness to passionate oaths?

SGANARELLE There have been so many trees, my lord, in so many different places. I can't keep them apart. Permit me to sit down a while, my lord. The excitement, the weight of your clothes, not to mention this basket, have tired me out.

DON JUAN Blockhead, why did you have to take the basket? Did I order you to take it? Don Juan does not carry baskets.

SGANARELLE Your clothes have not changed me enough to make me forget my duty of catering to Don Juan's stomach. Shall we eat, my lord?

DON JUAN Knave! A nobleman doesn't bite into a piece of pie on the roadside like a dog. Show my garments more honor. You must behave like me. I will force myself to imitate your manners. And you, knave, will not touch a single bite! (*Don Juan eats and drinks*)

SGANARELLE (*while Don Juan eats*) I'm still thinking about that doctor. Perhaps I should have gone to him for treatment. I feel extremely weak and my stomach is beginning to toss so strangely: from left to right. God knows my health is not of the best, my lord. *(Don Juan gives him a severe look)* I think I could really use a doctor.

DON JUAN   What for?

SGANARELLE   To cure me.

DON JUAN   A doctor to cure you? The time to see a doctor is when you want to die.

SGANARELLE   Don't you believe in senna leaves?

DON JUAN   Why should I believe in senna leaves?

SGANARELLE   *(shakes his head in despair)*   All right, never mind medicine. If you don't believe in it, you don't. Let's talk about something else. *(Serves him wine)* What about heaven? Don't you believe in that either?

DON JUAN   Never mind.

SGANARELLE   Hm, that means you don't believe in it. And hell?

DON JUAN   Bah!

SGANARELLE   So it's no again. And the devil?

DON JUAN   Yes, yes.

SGANARELLE   So you don't believe in him either. What about the other world?

(Don Juan laughs loudly)

SGANARELLE   But how do you feel about the black bishop?

DON JUAN   The plague take you!

SGANARELLE   That's too much. A fact is a fact. Who else do you suppose sucks the blood out of February babies? Who do you believe in if you don't believe in him?

DON JUAN   What I believe in?

SGANARELLE   Yes.

DON JUAN   I believe that two times two is four.

SGANARELLE   That's a lovely thing to believe. A fine article of faith. So your religion is the multiplication table. As for me, my lord, I haven't studied like you. No man can boast of having taught me anything. But I can see that things aren't so simple. For instance, I'd be glad to have you tell me who made those trees and those rocks; who made the earth and the sky up there. Did they all make themselves? Take yourself, for instance. You're here, aren't you? Well, did you make yourself? Didn't his lordship your father have to get her ladyship your mother pregnant in order to make you? Don't you marvel at how everything in a man works, how everything hangs together—the nerves, the bones, the veins, the arteries, these—these lungs, the heart, the liver and all the trimmings which . . .

DON JUAN   Are you almost finished?

SGANARELLE   So there is something wonderful about man, whatever you may say. Isn't it a wonder that I'm here? That I have something in my head, something that can think a hundred things at once and move my body the way I want. I want to clap my hands, *(demonstrating)* lift my arm, raise my eyes, lower my head, move my feet, go to the right, to the left, forward, backward, about face! *(Turns around and falls down)*

DON JUAN   Lovely. But now we've got to be thinking about how to get to the city.

SGANARELLE   Here comes a man. We'll ask him the way.
(Enter a beggar)

SGANARELLE   Hey, you! Hey!

DON JUAN   Eat properly at least. Don't forget that you're me.
(Sganarelle starts to eat. He eats wastefully like Don Juan)

2

Don Juan. Sganarelle. The beggar.

SGANARELLE   Which is the quickest way to the city?

BEGGAR   *(to Sganarelle)*   You just have to take this path, turn right, and then straight ahead. But I advise you to be on your guard, my lord. A little while ago some dangerous-looking men passed by, they were brandishing big cudgels and shouting terrible threats against noblemen.

SGANARELLE   I'm very much obliged to you, my friend.

BEGGAR   *(to Sganarelle)*   I am a poor beggar, your lordship. A trifling gift, if you please.

DON JUAN   Ha, I see your helpfulness was not entirely disinterested.

BEGGAR   *(to Sganarelle)*   I am a poor man. I shall not fail to pray heaven to send you riches.

SGANARELLE   Thank you, my friend.

DON JUAN   My foot! Why doesn't he pray heaven to send him a coat without holes in it?

SGANARELLE   My friend, you don't know his lordship. He only believes in "two times two is four."

DON JUAN   How do you spend your time in the woods?

BEGGAR *(to Sganarelle)*   All day long I pray heaven to increase the prosperity of the good people who treat me generously.

DON JUAN   Then you must be doing very well.

BEGGAR *(to Sganarelle)*   Oh, your lordship, I'm as poor as a church mouse.

DON JUAN   You must be joking. If you pray all day your affairs are sure to prosper.

BEGGAR   I assure you, your lordship, that most of the time I haven't even a crust of bread for my toothless mouth.

DON JUAN *(to Sganarelle)*   Strange, very strange, your lordship. *(To the beggar)* Your efforts are ill rewarded. *(He laughs loudly)* His lordship will give you a louis d'or, his last, but only on one condition: you must curse.

SGANARELLE   Your lordship, please!

BEGGAR *(to Sganarelle)*   Oh, your lordship, don't lead me into temptation.

DON JUAN   Make up your mind: do you want to earn a louis d'or or don't you? Here it is. *(To Sganarelle)* In the left-hand pocket, knave. *(He takes a louis d'or from Sganarelle's pocket. To the beggar)* Go on. Take it, but curse!

SGANARELLE   But your lordship . . .

BEGGAR *(to Sganarelle)*   Your lordship . . .

DON JUAN   Or you don't get anything. *(Aside to Sganarelle, giving him a shove)* Sganarelle!

SGANARELLE   Just a little curse! There's nothing to it . . .

DON JUAN   Go ahead, in the devil's name take it, but curse!

BEGGAR   No, your lordship, I'd rather starve and go to heaven.

DON JUAN *(gives him the louis d'or)*   You idiots! There! I give it to you for love of humanity.

(The beggar takes the gold piece and goes off in a fright)

SGANARELLE   Your lordship, we must be going! Night is coming on.

3

Don Juan. Sganarelle. Angelica. Nurse.

Accompanied by her nurse, Angelica, a young girl in mourning, steps out of the park carrying a basket of flowers. They go into the mausoleum.

DON JUAN   Oh, what a divine apparition!

SGANARELLE *(holds him back)*   Your lordship! Pull yourself together. How can you take the field of love in such a ridiculous outfit?

DON JUAN   You're perfectly right. Only a great beauty could make me forget my disguise. Quick, my clothes. Hurry, knave, she'll soon be coming out.

SGANARELLE *(begins taking his coat off. Grumpily)*   Oh . . . *(He has barely unbuttoned his vest when a great uproar is heard. Amid shouts the boatmen are besetting a young nobleman)*

DON JUAN   What's this? A noble assaulted by three oafs!

SGANARELLE   The boatmen!

DON JUAN   The contest is too unequal; such cowardice is more than my eyes can bear. Go to the man's help immediately. I myself do not fight with ruffians who brandish cudgels. Get in there and fight, knave! *(He gives Sganarelle a kick which sends him into the mêlée, and goes off to one side)*

4

Don Juan. Sganarelle. Don Carlos. Boatmen. Angelica. Nurse.

Pantomime: Fight. Struck by a boatman, the nobleman falls unconscious to the ground. Sganarelle's roars put the boatmen to flight. Angelica and her nurse emerge from the mausoleum, see the limping half-naked and groaning Sganarelle, and take flight. While Sganarelle tries to revive the young nobleman with wine, Don Juan looks after the fleeing young girl in dismay.

5

Don Juan. Sganarelle. Don Carlos.

DON JUAN   Hurry, knave, hurry! She's feeding the does in the clearing!

SGANARELLE *(busy dressing Don Juan, apologizes to the moaning Don Carlos)*   Patience, sir. As soon as his coat is buttoned you shall have wine.

DON JUAN   Button it properly, he'll come to by himself. *(The coat is buttoned, Sganarelle wants to go to Don Carlos)* Sash! *(Sganarelle puts on Don Juan's sash)* Bandolier! *(Sganarelle continues to busy himself with Don Juan)*

SGANARELLE *(to Don Carlos who staggers to his feet)*   Nothing serious, young sir. You were hit by an oar! I got it in the knee.

DON JUAN   Wig!

DON CARLOS *(to Don Juan as Sganarelle adjusts his wig)*   Sir!

DON JUAN *(whose accoutrement is not yet fully in order, motions him to wait)*

DON CARLOS *(when Don Juan is fully dressed)*   Permit me, sir, to tender my thanks for your magnanimous assistance and your . . .

DON JUAN *(looking around impatiently)*   Sir, I only did what you would have done in my place.

SGANARELLE *(aside)*   Meaning, nothing.

DON CARLOS   Indeed, your mere presence sufficed. Your look of authority, your voice accustomed to command. You are wondering, sir, why those devils flung themselves upon me. An unfortunate accident separated me from my brother in whose company I set out this morning to settle a certain affair. While looking for him, I came across these bandits. Though I was a total stranger to them, they importuned me with a story about some nobleman who owed them money, so they claimed, and slandered him most abominably. When I remonstrated with them over their disgraceful maligning of our station, they unleashed such a storm of insults that despite their superior number I resolved to punish them. Their only weapons were oars. But they handled them with such dexterity *(Sganarelle bows complacently)* that I should have succumbed but for your exemplary courage.

DON JUAN   Are you on your way to the city?

DON CARLOS   No, my elder brother and I are involved in one of those affairs with which our families are so painfully afflicted and which constrain us noblemen to the most extreme sacrifices. O honor, thou inexorable taskmaster!

DON JUAN *(to Sganarelle)*   Quick! Run! Find that girl!

DON CARLOS   Indeed, the outcome of a duel is bitter in either case. If we do not leave our life on the field, we have to leave the country. We noblemen have a hard lot. Neither caution nor blameless conduct can help us. Our laws of honor make us the victims of other men's transgressions. Our life, our peace of mind depend on the whims of any scoundrel who sees fit to inflict upon us, out of the clear blue sky, one of those insults that a nobleman can expunge only with his sword.

DON JUAN   At least we have the advantage of being able to inflict the same inconveniences on anyone who annoys us. If I am not being indiscreet: what sort of affair are you involved in?

DON CARLOS   The matter has gone so far that there is no further need of secrecy. Since the insult has become public knowledge, our honor commands us not to overlook it but to avenge it. Accordingly, my dear sir, I need not hesitate to inform you that the disgrace we are resolved to avenge is that of a sister wrested from the holy seclusion of a convent and seduced. The offender is a certain Don Juan Tenorio, son of the venerable Don Luis Tenorio. We have been tracking him since this morning.

DON JUAN   Do you know this Don Juan you speak of?

DON CARLOS   I myself do not. I have never seen him. But my

elder brother has given me a description of him. The life he leads is utterly . . .

DON JUAN   If you please, sir, not another word. Don Juan is my best, to tell you the truth, my only friend. I will hear no evil said of him.

DON CARLOS   To oblige you I will say no more. That is little enough to ask of a man who owes you his life. But despite your friendship with this Don Juan, I venture to hope that you will frown on his conduct and therefore find it no more than natural that we mean to wreak bloody vengeance on him.

DON JUAN   I am Don Juan's friend, I cannot alter the fact, but even he may not with impunity transgress against the honor of our station. To spare you the trouble of tracking him down, I shall impel him to give you satisfaction where and when you desire. You have my word of honor.

DON CARLOS   What high hope you arouse in us! We are most obliged to you, sir, though it would grieve me to see you involved in this affair.

DON JUAN   I am so close to Don Juan that he would never fight without my consent.

DON CARLOS   O cruel fate! Why must I owe you my life when Don Juan is your friend?

6

Don Juan. Don Carlos. Don Alonso.

DON ALONSO *(speaking to someone behind him, does not see Don Juan and Don Carlos)*   Water the horses and bring them after me. I wish to walk a while. *(He sees the two)* What do I see? You, my brother, with our family's deadly enemy?

DON CARLOS   Deadly enemy?

DON JUAN *(his hand on his sword)*   Yes, I am Don Juan. Your superior number cannot move me to conceal my name.

DON ALONSO (*drawing his sword*)   Ah! Scoundrel! Now you must die!

DON CARLOS   Stop, brother, stop! I owe him my life. If not for him, ruffians would have killed me.

DON ALONSO   Will you permit such a consideration to hamper our vengeance? Such gratitude is absurd. Since honor is far more precious than life, if we owe our life to the man who has robbed us of our honor we owe him nothing.

(*Sganarelle appears between the trees. He beckons excitedly to attract Don Juan's attention*)

DON JUAN   Gentlemen, I have but one request to make of you: that you decide quickly. I am in a hurry.

DON CARLOS   Brother, I know what I owe to our honor. Shall I permit this gentleman to carry with him to the other world a debt that I have failed to redeem?

DON ALONSO   Heaven has given us an opportunity to take vengeance here and now. If you do not wish to fight, then go. I alone will make the holy sacrifice.

DON CARLOS   Brother, I implore you . . .

DON ALONSO   No, he must die . . .

DON CARLOS (*placing himself in front of Don Juan*)   Stop, brother; stop, I say. I will not suffer you to take his life in this place where he defended mine. If you wish to kill him, you will first have to pierce my heart.

(*Pause*)

DON ALONSO   O unforgiveable weakness!

DON CARLOS   Grant me a delay, brother.

DON ALONSO   The interests of our family . . .

DON CARLOS   Will be safeguarded. Don Juan, you see that I am doing my utmost to repay my debt to you. From which I bid you infer that tomorrow I shall requite your offense with the same zeal as today I requite your succor.

DON JUAN   Sir, I have given you my word. Rest assured, I do not fear this encounter, but I must own to you that I should find it rather inconvenient at the present moment. I am thankful to you for the postponement.

DON CARLOS   Come at midnight to the dark alley leading to the convent.

DON ALONSO   There we shall make amends for our present neglect.

DON CARLOS   Let us go, brother.

(Both go out)

. *7*

Don Juan. Sganarelle.

DON JUAN   Well, knave, where is she?

SGANARELLE   Your lordship!

DON JUAN   The devil take you, speak! Why are you standing there as if you'd been struck by lightning?

SGANARELLE   Your lordship, I have! Do you know what that white building is?

DON JUAN   Blockhead, what's a white building to me? Where's the girl?

SGANARELLE   Your lordship, that white thing among the trees is—his tomb.

DON JUAN   Whose tomb?

SGANARELLE   The man you killed according to all the rules . . .

DON JUAN   The Commander?

SGANARELLE   Heaven protect you!

DON JUAN   Oh!—But let's get back to essentials: who is the girl?

SGANARELLE   The girl is . . . the Commander's daughter.

DON JUAN   His daughter! My word.

SGANARELLE   Robbed by you of her father and mother! Your lordship, I implore you, we must leave this place of doom. To stay is to bring the dead man's wrath upon us.

DON JUAN   What, coward? Afraid of stones when I'm here beside you? I'll drive this fear out of you. I'll pay the Commander my respects, and you'll come with me.

SGANARELLE   Your lordship, please don't go in, please.

DON JUAN   I order you not to be afraid! I owe the gentleman a

visit. If he's a gentleman, he'll receive us politely. Come.
(They approach the mausoleum among the trees)
(Music. The mausoleum opens. Don Juan and Sganarelle stand before the statue of the Commander)

8

Don Juan. Sganarelle. The statue of the Commander.

SGANARELLE   There! There he is.

DON JUAN   Good Lord! Done up as a Roman emperor.

SGANARELLE   Your lordship, he looks so real. As if he were alive and wanted to speak. He's looking at us—I'm . . . *(Don Juan gives him a menacing glance)* I'd be afraid if you weren't here. You know, your lordship, I think he's unfriendly to us.

DON JUAN   That would be most unjust of him. It would suggest that he failed to appreciate the honor I'm showing him. Invite him to dinner at my house.

SGANARELLE   I don't think that's of much use to him now, your lordship.

DON JUAN   Go on. Invite him, I said.

SGANARELLE   You're joking, my lord, a stone can't hear.

DON JUAN   Exactly. Do as you're told.

SGANARELLE   Lord Commander—*(aside)* this is idiotic!—*(aloud)* Lord Commander, my master Don Juan Tenorio bids me ask whether you will do him the honor of dining with him this evening.

(The statue nods)

SGANARELLE   Oh!

DON JUAN   Now what's wrong with you? Say something.

SGANARELLE   *(mimics the statue's nod)* The statue . . .

DON JUAN   Idiot! Speak up!

SGANARELLE   The statue!

DON JUAN   The statue what? Speak or I'll strike you dead.

SGANARELLE   The statue nodded.

DON JUAN   The plague take you!

SGANARELLE   He nodded. Really. Speak to him yourself.

DON JUAN   Blockhead. Lord Commander, will you do me the honor of dining at my house—in pleasant company?

(The statue nods)

SGANARELLE   Oh!

DON JUAN *(takes a pinch of snuff)*   Time to be going.

(Both go out)

ACT FOUR

The terrace of Don Juan's castle.

1

Sganarelle. Ragotin.

RAGOTIN *(holding a letter in his hand, passes Sganarelle; he is wearing riding boots and breeches)* This'll be the fourth letter I've taken over there.

SGANARELLE Ragotin! Is she coming or not?

RAGOTIN Yes.

SGANARELLE Yes, what?

RAGOTIN She's either coming or she's not. How do I know? Why shouldn't she come? You might say she's still in mourning for the commander. But what's that to me? I've got my hands full: knock off a gate keeper, poison a dog, bribe a governess. Letters, letters—back and forth! Two horses worn to a frazzle! Only three left in the stable. Are they my horses? Well then. Is she coming or not? I don't ask, I don't know, my business is riding. *(Goes out)*

2

Sganarelle.

SGANARELLE   Happy man! My trouble is that I know too much. I can feel a terrible tempest brewing over this house, and I'm very much afraid that the lightning will strike the servant along with the master. I'll ask the cook to read my palm. She's good at it. *(Calls)* Seraphine! Seraphine!

3

Sganarelle. Seraphine.

SERAPHINE   What is it? I've got a big dinner to cook.

SGANARELLE   That's just it.

SERAPHINE   What's the dinner to you?

SGANARELLE   That's just what I want you to tell me. Seraphine, I've got a feeling that a terrible storm is gathering over this house and I want you to read my palm. Seraphine, is my fate tied up with the fate of a great lord? Watch your step.

SERAPHINE   Let's see!

SGANARELLE   *(hesitates)*   I want the whole truth.

SERAPHINE   *(taking his hand)*   I always tell the whole truth.

SGANARELLE   *(withdraws his hand)*   But you can make mistakes.

SERAPHINE   If you think I can make mistakes, I'll go back to my hors d'oeuvres. I'm sick of reading you people's palms anyway. The other day Josephine fainted and that made Ragotin cut me.

SGANARELLE   *(suspiciously)*   So you think I'll faint if you tell me the whole truth?

SERAPHINE I haven't even looked yet.

SGANARELLE Oh yes, you have.

SERAPHINE I say I haven't. And now I'm going back to my carp.

SGANARELLE Damn the carp. Don't be so touchy. Here's my hand. Just tell me if my fate is tied up with the fate of a great lord. Watch your step. *(After a pause)* It isn't, is it? *(Jangles coins in his pocket)* Look carefully.

SERAPHINE Your fate is . . .

SGANARELLE Watch your step, now.

SERAPHINE Not tied up with the fate of a great lord!

SGANARELLE Right! You really are a good palm reader. *(Suddenly distrustful)* Do you really see that, or are you just trying to make me feel good? I want you to tell me exactly what my hand says. Not what it gives me pleasure to hear. My life line —would you say it was long?

SERAPHINE *(inspects his hand for some time)* Long, yes . . .

SGANARELLE What do you mean "long, yes . . ."? Now you're trying to scare me.

SERAPHINE I told you you wouldn't be able to take it. Now I'm going back to my ducks in orange sauce. They don't interrupt me all the time.

SGANARELLE Don't try to cut me short when I want to know about my life line. When everybody knows that palm reading is unreliable. If you want to know the truth about the future, what you need is a horoscope. It's expensive but you can rely on it.

SERAPHINE You only say that because you're afraid. You're not a man. And it shows in your life line.

SGANARELLE You said yourself it was long.

SERAPHINE Yes, long. But thin.

SGANARELLE Hm. Then let it be thin.

SERAPHINE It's thin all right.

SGANARELLE But long.

SERAPHINE Yes.

SGANARELLE Seraphine, what are we fighting for? All I want you to tell me is this: does it say if there's something special I should watch out for?

SERAPHINE But if I tell you you'll start yelling at me again.

SGANARELLE   No, I promise.

SERAPHINE   Veal.

SGANARELLE   Don't be silly, Seraphine. Veal doesn't hurt me in the least.

SERAPHINE   You're Aries, aren't you?

SGANARELLE   No, Cancer.

SERAPHINE   In that case veal really can't hurt you.

SGANARELLE   Take another look: should I watch out for stone?

SERAPHINE   Stone?

SGANARELLE   Yes or no?

SERAPHINE   *(hears Don Juan coming)*   His lordship! *(She runs away)*

SGANARELLE   *(shouts after her)*   Stone? Yes or no?

4

Sganarelle. Don Juan.

DON JUAN   What's all the shouting?

SGANARELLE   Oh, your lordship, I can't get that talking statue out of my mind.

DON JUAN   Forget it. Maybe a shadow deceived you, or a blood stoppage could have clouded your eye.

SGANARELLE   No, your lordship, you can't deny it, that nod was real. It was a miracle wrought by heaven itself because your way of life has . . .

DON JUAN   Listen to me: you stop bothering me with your idiotic sermons or I'll call a stable boy with a whip. Three men will hold you down, or maybe four would be better, and you'll be beaten like a carpet. Understand?

SGANARELLE   I understand, your lordship. You express yourself very plainly; that's the best thing about you, you don't beat about the bush, you make things so beautifully clear.

DON JUAN   Hm.—What's Ragotin doing?

SGANARELLE   Riding.

5

Don Juan. Sganarelle. La Violette.

LA VIOLETTE   Your lordship, Mr. Dimanche your tailor is here; he insists on seeing you.

SGANARELLE   A creditor! That's all we needed. Coming to us for money! The idea! Why don't you tell him his lordship is out?

LA VIOLETTE   That's just what I've been telling him for a whole half hour, but he won't believe me. He's sat down in the antechamber and he's waiting.

SGANARELLE   Then let him sit in the antechamber till he rots.

DON JUAN   No. That won't do. Bring him in. It's bad tactics to hide from creditors; it's much better to give them something. *(La Violette brings in Mr. Dimanche)*

6

Sganarelle. Don Juan. Dimanche. La Violette.

DON JUAN   Ah, my dear Dimanche, how kind of you to call! You are my first visitor since my return. I shall never forgive my servants for not bringing you in at once. I had given orders to admit no one, but they ought to realize that such orders don't include you. To you my door is at all times open.

DIMANCHE   I'm much obliged to you, your lordship.

DON JUAN   *(to La Violette and Sganarelle)* Scoundrels! I'll teach you to let Mr. Dimanche cool his heels!

DIMANCHE   It's nothing, your lordship.

DON JUAN   Nothing? Telling you, my best friend, that I'm out?

DIMANCHE   Your lordship, I have come to . . .

DON JUAN   Quick, a chair for Mr. Dimanche.

DIMANCHE   I don't mind standing, your lordship, if . . .

DON JUAN   When you're in my house, I want to see you comfortably seated.

DIMANCHE   It's quite unnecessary. (*He begins to sit down*)

DON JUAN   Take that stool away! A chair, I said.

DIMANCHE   Your lordship pleases to joke. I . . .

DON JUAN   No, no. I know what I owe you. I wish to see no distinction between us.

DIMANCHE   Your lordship . . .

DON JUAN   Come, come. Do sit down.

DIMANCHE   It's really unnecessary, I shall be very brief. I've come to . . .

DON JUAN   Sit down, I say.

DIMANCHE   No, no, your lordship. Don't put yourself out. I only wished to . . .

DON JUAN   No, I refuse to listen unless you sit down.

DIMANCHE   If you insist, your lordship. (*Sits down*) I . . .

DON JUAN   You're looking well, Mr. Dimanche.

DIMANCHE   Thank you, your lordship. Your humble servant. I've come . . .

DON JUAN   Your health is your most precious possession—full lips, rosy cheeks, sparkling eyes.

DIMANCHE   I should like . . .

DON JUAN   Madame Dimanche is well, too, I hope.

DIMANCHE   Tolerably well, your lordship, thank heaven. I thought . . .

DON JUAN   An excellent woman!

DIMANCHE   Thank you, your lordship. I hoped . . .

DON JUAN   And your daughter Claudine?

DIMANCHE   In the best of health.

DON JUAN   Ah, the sweet little pigeon. Charming!

DIMANCHE   You do me too much honor, your lordship. I wished . . .

DON JUAN   And Paolo, your little boy? Still making such a hubbub with his little drum?

DIMANCHE   He's still at it, your lordship . . . I . . .

DON JUAN   And Pippo, your little dog? Does he still growl and nip your visitors' legs?

DIMANCHE   More than ever, your lordship, we can't seem to break him of the habit.

DON JUAN   My inquiries seem to surprise you. You forget the deep interest I take in your family.

DIMANCHE   We're very much obliged, your lordship. I . . .

DON JUAN   Give me your hand, Mr. Dimanche. If I have any friend in the world, it's you.

DIMANCHE   Your humble servant!

DON JUAN   And I am yours with all my heart!

DIMANCHE   You do me too much honor. I . . .

DON JUAN   There's nothing I wouldn't do for you. But you know that. Nothing . . .

DIMANCHE   You are too kind, your lordship . . .

DON JUAN   Without thought of my own advantage.

DIMANCHE   You put me to shame. But, your lordship . . .

DON JUAN   Ah, Mr. Dimanche . . . without mincing words . . . will you stay for dinner?

DIMANCHE   No, your lordship. I really must be going. I . . .

DON JUAN   (stands up) Servants! Quick! Bring torches. Escort Mr. Dimanche. Four of you, no, five. With muskets.

DIMANCHE   (likewise stands up) Oh but your lordship, it's not necessary, I'll find my way. But . . .

   (Sganarelle immediately removes his chair)

DON JUAN   Not a word. I insist on giving you an escort. I always said you'd go far and I mean to see that you do. I am your servant and what is more your debtor.

DIMANCHE   Oh, your lordship!

DON JUAN   I make that clear to anyone who is willing to listen.

DIMANCHE   If you . . .

DON JUAN   Oh, you'd like *me* to escort you?

DIMANCHE   Oh, your lordship. Now you're making fun of me. Your lordship . . .

DON JUAN   Embrace me, I beg you. And once again I ask you to believe that I am always at your disposal, and that there is nothing I wouldn't do for you.

   (Dimanche is led away by the armed servants bearing torches)

DIMANCHE   Your lordship. I wished . . .

DON JUAN   (calling after him) Send me two of the usual coats. I'm getting engaged.

DIMANCHE   Oh! *(Goes out)*

DON JUAN   What is it, La Violette?

LA VIOLETTE   A lady! Heavily veiled.

DON JUAN   Bring her in. *(To Sganarelle)* Blockhead! Why are you looking at me like that? Still afraid of that chunk of stone?

7

Don Juan. Donna Elvira. Sganarelle. La Violette.

DONNA ELVIRA   It may surprise you, Don Juan, to see me here at this late hour and thus attired. But what I have to say cannot be put off. I have not come in anger as I did yesterday morning. I am no longer the woman who cursed you and thirsted for vengeance. Heaven has banished all earthly passion from my heart. What I feel for you now is a devout tenderness, an affection freed from the lusts of the flesh, which knows no self-interest and whose sole concern is for your immortal soul.

DON JUAN *(to Sganarelle)*   No, really! I believe you're crying.

SGANARELLE   For joy, your lordship.

DONNA ELVIRA   This new love has made me the messenger of heaven, come to snatch you if I can from the brink of the abyss. Yes, Don Juan, your crimes are known to me. Heaven has sent me to say that its patience is worn thin and that its terrible wrath hangs over your head. You can avert this by repenting before it is too late. You may have only a few hours in which to escape your doom. As for me, my fate is decided. I shall withdraw into the holy seclusion of the convent of Santa Regina. It would be a source of the utmost grief to me in my retirement if heaven should be forced to make a terrible example of the man I loved so dearly. But what bliss it would be for me if I could move you to ward off the fearful blow that threatens you. Don Juan, grant me this sweet consolation; don't refuse me the salvation of your soul; spare me the sorrow of seeing you condemned to the eternal torments of hell.

SGANARELLE *(aside)* Poor woman!

DONNA ELVIRA I loved you very dearly. Nothing in this world was so dear to me as you. For you I forgot my duty; for you I gave all I had to give. And now I ask only one thing of you: don't let yourself be damned. Save yourself, I implore you, for your sake or for mine. I beseech you by everything that is capable of touching your heart!

SGANARELLE *(aside)* The heart of a tiger!

DONNA ELVIRA I'm going now. I have said my say.

DON JUAN It's late, my lady. Don't go. We shall do our best to make you comfortable here.

DONNA ELVIRA No, Don Juan, don't try to detain me.

DON JUAN My lady, believe me, it would give me pleasure if you stayed.

DONNA ELVIRA No, there is no time to waste in needless talk. Let me go. No, don't accompany me. And take my words to heart. *(Goes out)*

8

Don Juan. Sganarelle.

DON JUAN Sganarelle, what's to become of our reputation? In love as in war that's what counts the most. A fortress will surrender to the man other fortresses have surrendered to. It accepts surrender as a law of nature. Alexander's reputation conquered more cities for him than his army. A general without a reputation has no other resort but to fight like a madman. Every defeat must be followed by a victory. Have you made the preparations for the dinner as I wished? The musicians? And Belisa, the famous singer? I want her to embellish our banquet with a serenade. And send for those fisher maidens. Have them come in at midnight with their oysters and crabs. I'll sample the wines.

SGANARELLE Oh, your lordship. Heaven forgive you. *(Strange beat lightning on the horizon. Sganarelle is terrified and Don Juan laughs)*

DON JUAN   Still no news of Ragotin?

SGANARELLE *(trembling)*   No.
   (Enter La Violette)

9

Don Juan. Sganarelle. La Violette.

LA VIOLETTE   Your lordship, your father is here. On the way he fell in with some boatmen who were turned away by the gate keeper and have been making a disturbance outside. They have been telling him all sorts of stories.

DON JUAN *(to La Violette)*   Keep him busy for a few minutes. *(To Sganarelle)* Make me up. A little white.
   (Sganarelle makes him up)

DON JUAN   Do you know that I felt a slight surge of feeling for Donna Elvira? That this bizarre new situation has given me a kind of pleasure, and her careless dress, the mildness of her look, and her tears have rekindled the sparks of a flame that was almost spent?

SGANARELLE   In short, her words made no impression on you?

DON JUAN   A touch under the eyes.

SGANARELLE   As you wish.

DON JUAN   Sganarelle, we ought to think of mending our ways.

SGANARELLE   Oh yes.

DON JUAN   Yes, it's a fact, we've got to mend our ways. Another twenty or thirty years of this life and we shall start thinking of our immortal soul.
   (Heat lightning in the sky)

SGANARELLE   Oh, your lordship, heaven is nodding agreement. Don't harden your heart. There's still time. Repent.

DON JUAN   That's just what I mean to do—in a manner of speaking. Go.
   (Sganarelle goes out)

10

Don Juan. Don Luis. Then Sganarelle.

DON LUIS   Scoundrel! What is this new exploit I hear of? How base! How contemptible! Am I to cover such conduct with my name? I can do so no longer. By what right do you enjoy our privileges? What have you done in the world to deserve the name of nobleman? Do you suppose that your blood ennobles you when you lead the life of a villain? Have you forgotten how to blush? Shall it be said that a nobleman is a monster? Shall it be said that the sons of common laborers are more virtuous than ours?

DON JUAN   Father, an inner voice must have told you how much I needed you; that must be why you leaped into your carriage. I have had an experience that I can speak of to no one but you. You are a soldier, you are a pious man, you will understand me. Father, you see me miraculously transformed. Let us not speak of the shameful lusts that made me put out to sea to ravish a woman. In the bleak dawn, as the wind howled about my craft, I heard you, my father, crying out to me in a terrible voice: "Turn back!" I fled to the shore.

DON LUIS   To the shore! Oho!

DON JUAN   Some pious fisher maidens took me in and vied with one another in caring for me. Their simple chatter moved me deeply. *(Ragotin has entered with a letter)* What is it? *(Ragotin hands Don Juan the letter. Don Juan reads it with every sign of satisfaction and tosses Ragotin a purse)* Excuse me, father. Heaven has sent me another sign. But let me continue. A little later, deep in the woods, I met a child of angelic beauty who seemed to know me. She took me by the hand and led me to a white mausoleum in the Roman style. We entered. I found myself standing before the stone effigy of the man whom I had robbed of everything he had in the world, his wife, his honor, and finally his life. "My father," said the little girl. "He wishes to forgive you."

DON LUIS   Forgive you!

DON JUAN   And what do you think it says in this letter? To make his forgiveness complete, that angelic child, the Commander's daughter, announces her visit. I must show myself worthy of her.

(Sganarelle has come back with two jugs of wine)

DON LUIS   Can it be?

DON JUAN   Yes, father. Everyone will see my sudden transformation. I will repair the harm done by my deeds and strive for one thing only: full forgiveness. That shall be my life from this day on, and I beg of you, my father, to help me tread the path I have chosen.

DON LUIS   *(embraces him)*   I came to speak of your latest escapade, which some crude fishermen have brought to my attention. But how quickly a father's reproaches are dispelled by the least sign of repentance! I have already forgotten the cares you've caused me, your words have scattered them to the winds. My cheeks are stained with tears of joy. *(Don Juan begins to lead him away)* Persevere in this admirable attitude and you may ask anything you wish of me. But now I must rush to tell your mother; she too must share in this heavenly news. *(Goes out)*

11

Don Juan. Sganarelle.

During this scene the servants finish setting the table. Musicians arrive with their instruments and the servants show them their places amid the foliage.

SGANARELLE   Ah, your lordship, I've been waiting a long time to hear those words. Is it possible? You repent? The Lord be thanked, now I have nothing more to wish for.

DON JUAN *(selecting wine)*   Idiot!—This one.

SGANARELLE   Idiot?

DON JUAN   Did you suppose I really meant what I said?

SGANARELLE   What? It isn't . . . You're not going to . . . Your . . . Oh, what a man! What a man!

DON JUAN   If I said I was going to mend my ways, it was only a stratagem, a bit of dissimulation which I must submit to in order to regain the sympathies of my father and certain others whom I need.

SGANARELLE   What? You believe in nothing and you are going to play the part of virtue! What a man! What a man! What a man!

DON JUAN   A wise man knows how to exploit the vices of his times. The fashionable vice today is hypocrisy, and when a vice is in fashion it always passes for a virtue. The role of the hypocrite presents marvelous advantages. A grimace or two is all it takes to join the pious club and then, behind the screen of piety, you are free to pursue your own interests. If I run into trouble, no need to stir a finger; the whole pious crew will come to my rescue and defend me against all comers. An honest man is forbidden to blow his nose, a hypocrite can make off with a whole city. Which is just what we're going to do. Listen to me, Sganarelle. Angelica, the Commander's daughter, has consented to come here for dinner. We shall prepare for the meeting with steadfast heart. This is going to be one of the most glorious and delightful feats of my whole career.

SGANARELLE   She has consented? But your lordship, does she know who you are?

DON JUAN   She will find out. From my lips.

SGANARELLE   That you seduced her mother and killed her father? Your lordship, she is the only surviving avenger . . .

DON JUAN   Of a dead but, as you suppose, highly indignant father. Ah, to overcome such almost superhuman obstacles, to subjugate a heart that has such good reasons to resist me— there's an exploit that seems worthy of me.

SGANARELLE   Your lordship, I have never given up hope that you would be saved, but this is worse than anything you've ever done. Heaven will never stand for such outrageous defiance.

DON JUAN   Come, come. Heaven isn't such a stickler as you think. I can see her coming in, light-footed, lovely, blushing ever so slightly. Sorrow for her dearly beloved father casts a charming shadow over her smooth brow. *(To the musicians who have taken their positions among the trees)* Are my little birds all ready in the branches of my trees? Gentlemen, the music! *(The music sounds)*

DON JUAN   "My dear señorita, you do not know me. But I know you well, and furthermore I know your family to which I am bound by the closest ties of blood and love. For I am Don Juan Tenorio."

SGANARELLE   I hope she scratches his eyes out.

DON JUAN   Sganarelle, I would like her to try—"Señorita, spare me nothing. Wound me however you wish, but leave me my eyes; now that I have met you, I need them." Even the dead are moved by flattery, Sganarelle.—"Ah, God is cruel to have created beauty like yours. But He knows what He's doing. Señorita, when I saw you, when I heard who you were, I forgave your father."

SGANARELLE   What? You? Forgiving the Commander, the man you killed?

DON JUAN   Yes, forgave. Don't interrupt me.—"Alas, señorita, alas, I killed him. There it is again, the reproach he brought upon me by dying. All he had to do to destroy me was die." Ingenious to be sure, but confusing. "If only your father had defeated me in that duel which I did not ask for! I should no longer be alive. How much better for me than to live and be detested by you!" Now the final thrust: "Can you rebuff a desperate man who stands on the brink of nothingness? If you can, then free me at least from a life that has lost all purpose." Something along those lines.

SGANARELLE   And honesty is the worst policy, and lies have seven-league boots, and he who laughs first laughs best, and last come first served, and vice is its own reward, and forgive us our innocence, and camels pass through needles' eyes. Ah, to think that a man of your social position can do whatever he pleases and that no power on earth can stop him! Is there indeed no one to do the will of heaven? No one?

DON JUAN   Exactly: there's no one.

SGANARELLE   To think of all the people who were praying only today that heaven would crush you!

DON JUAN   Yes, I could even see it in Mr. Dimanche's eyes. As for my father, it took all my hypocrisy to disarm him. Donna Elvira's brothers are out for my blood. And there must be others who escape my mind. But you're quite right: what can they do?

(Lightning on the horizon. Thunder. The light grows somber)

SGANARELLE   Oh, your lordship! That's the third time. And now I'm sure of it. Heaven is speaking to you. Heaven is giving you a sign.

DON JUAN   If heaven wants to give me a sign, it should express itself a little more clearly.

(Knocking)

DON JUAN   She's come. Go on. Open the door.

(Sganarelle goes)

DON JUAN   Bring on the dinner. *(To the musicians)* Twitter, my dicky birds.

(Belisa sings a serenade. Don Juan waits in vain for Angelica to appear. Sganarelle returns, pale as death)

12

Don Juan. Sganarelle. The statue of the Commander.

DON JUAN   What is it?

SGANARELLE *(nodding like the statue)*   He . . . he's here.

DON JUAN   Oh! Not she? Well, I must say, I'm disappointed. Bring him in!

(The statue of the Commander enters)

DON JUAN   My lord Commander, I had hoped that both of you would come. But do be seated.

(The statue of the Commander does not sit down)

COMMANDER   Don Juan, I have come to invite you to sup with me. Have you the courage to accept?

DON JUAN   Yes. Where?

COMMANDER   Give me your hand.

DON JUAN   Here it is. If somebody wants to find me, where should he go?

COMMANDER   In the place to which I am taking you you will not be found so easily—should anyone wish to meet you.

DON JUAN *(to Sganarelle)*   Bring a lamp.

COMMANDER   No light is needed when heaven leads the way.
(Sganarelle faints)

COMMANDER   Don Juan, a terrible end awaits those who harden their hearts in sin. To exhaust the mercy of heaven is to invite its lightnings.

(The statue of the Commander leads Don Juan downstage)

DON JUAN   O heaven! The pain! I am scorched by fire! Stop! Oh!
(Amid loud thunder the earth opens. One hand in the Commander's clasp, vainly trying to hold his hat with the other, Don Juan sinks into the depths. Tall flames flare from the hole into which they vanish. The music has stopped. Various persons rush out on the stage, one after another)

13

Sganarelle. La Violette. Seraphine. Angelica. Dimanche. Elvira's brothers, Don Alonso and Don Carlos, followed by Dr. Marphurius, Don Luis, the boatmen, the fisher maidens accompanied by their fiancés.

LA VIOLETTE   What a disaster! He's gone!

ANGELICA   I'm a little late. *(Sees the hole)* Oh! How awful!

DIMANCHE *(bringing in two coats)*   It's blackmail! Your two coats, your . . . Oh! My best customer!

ELVIRA'S BROTHERS   The scoundrel! Where is he?—Oh! The honor of our family stained forever!

SERAPHINE   Oh! Now who's going to eat my ducks in orange sauce?

MARPHURIUS   Oh! The duel!

DON LUIS   Oh! My son! My heir!

THE BOATMEN   Oh! Where is he?—Fifty-four ducats down the drain!

THE FISHER MAIDENS   Oh! Who's going to take our oysters?— The handsome young gentleman!

(All stand at the edge of the hole. Slowly Don Juan's hat flutters down from above)

ŠGANARELLE   My wages! My wages!

Trumpets and Drums

Adaptation of George Farquhar's
The Recruiting Officer

Collaborators: B. Besson and E. Hauptmann

Translators: Rose and Martin Kastner

CHARACTERS

CAPTAIN WILLIAM PLUME

CAPTAIN BRAZEN

SERGEANT KITE

MR. BALANCE, justice of the peace

VICTORIA, his daughter

MR. WORTHY, a shoe manufacturer

MR. SMUGGLER, a banker

SIMPKINS, butler to Mr. Balance

MELINDA MOORHILL

LADY PRUDE

ROSE, a country girl

LUCY, Melinda's maid

MAGGIE

SALLY

THOMAS APPLETREE

COSTAR PEARMAIN

BULLOCK, Rose's brother

WILLIAM

MIKE, a potboy

JENNY, a soldier's wife

MRS. COBB, a dead soldier's mother

BRIDEWELL, a constable

A BROAD-SHOULDERED MAN

AN UNEMPLOYED MAN

THE UNEMPLOYED MAN'S WIFE

A MINER

THE MINER'S WIFE

A PIMP

KITTY, of Chicken Road

A PICKPOCKET

A COURT ATTENDANT

A DRUMMER

A SERVANT

The action takes place in England during the American War of Independence.

Prologue

Spoken by Sergeant Kite, who steps in front of the curtain with his drummer.

I'm Sergeant Barras Kite, now gathering a company
To help our good King George. For across the sea
In His Majesty's colony America
There's rebellion such as no man ever saw.
If anyone here should crave to join the forces—
Veterans of previous wars, or heroes without horses
Wild about living out of doors
Or footloose, eager to see foreign shores
Apprentices whose masters are too mean
Sons of parents you have never seen
A working man, who leads a hungry life
A husband suffering from a nagging wife—
Come to the Raven, apply to Sergeant Barras Kite
An honest man who'll set you right.
Now, gentlemen: Who among you, in exchange for a hand-
    some uniform and plenty of fodder
Will defend our dear old England (to the exclusion, of course,
    of his sister, his brother, his father and his mother)?

1

Market place in Shrewsbury.

To one side Judge Balance's house, on the other a recruiting booth. Sergeant Kite steps up to the farm boys Pearmain and Appletree who are looking at the pictures outside the recruiting booth.

KITE Gentlemen, I take it you know the Severn, but do you know the Mississippi? *(He pulls a small field table from the recruiting booth and sets a soldier's cap on it)* Gentlemen, observe this cap. It's a cap of honor; it makes a gentleman out of you as fast as you can pull a trigger. Anyone who has had the good fortune to be born six feet tall was born under Uranus and is destined to become a great man. *(To Thomas Appletree)* Allow me, sir; I just want to see how your head looks in this cap.

APPLETREE There's a trick to this. Won't that cap enlist me?

KITE No, no, the cap can't do that, and neither can I. *(Since Appletree refuses he turns to Pearmain)* What about you? Come, let me see how it looks on you.

PEARMAIN It's a very nice cap, but I suspect you're up to something.

KITE Oh no, friend. Don't be afraid now. *(He manages to get the cap on Pearmain's head)*

PEARMAIN It stinks of sweat and powder.

APPLETREE What's that on the front?

KITE The golden emblem, two fingers wide, over a G for King George. A badge of honor, brother.

PEARMAIN Brother?—Look 'ere, sergeant; no coaxing and wheedling. You can't pull the wool over my eyes. Take back your cap and your brothermanship, because I ain't in the mood today. Let's be going, Tummas.

(They go off laughing. Kite hangs the cap on the wall of the booth. Sounds of approaching horses. Captain Plume enters)

KITE   Welcome to Shrewsbury, captain! From the banks of the Delaware to Severn side.

PLUME   *(strolling about)*   Shrewsbury! *(Sighs)* How goes the recruiting? What reception has Shrewsbury given her military suitors this year?

(Kite makes a disparaging gesture)

PLUME   No luck?

KITE   None to speak of, captain. I ask this rabble, as is my bounden duty: Doesn't your English blood boil in your veins when those American dirt farmers and fur trappers refuse to pay taxes to our good King George?

PLUME   Well?

KITE   Their answers weren't nice. I've been here a full week and only recruited five.

PLUME   Five. *(Pause)* What sort?

KITE   A poacher. The Strong Man of Kent—once famous as a boxer. A Scottish peddler. A disbarred lawyer and an unfrocked Welsh parson.

PLUME   A lawyer? Have you taken leave of your senses?

KITE   Why?

PLUME   Mr. Kite, I will have no one in my company who can write. A fellow that can write can draw up petitions and submit complaints—let him go, I say! Discharge him at once!

KITE   What about the parson? He plays the fiddle.

PLUME   He can probably write too. Well, keep him for his fiddle. Go on.

KITE   Go on! That's the lot!

PLUME   Damnation!

KITE   There's one more recruit, captain. One you didn't expect.

PLUME   Who's that?

KITE   One you drummed in last time you were here. You remember Molly at the Raven?

PLUME   She's not with child, I hope?

KITE   Not any more, sir, she's got it.

PLUME   Kite, it's your duty to father the child.

KITE   I'd rather not, sir. You know I'm married already.

PLUME   How many times?

KITE   I haven't got it by heart.—I've put them down here on the back of the muster roll. *(Pulls out the muster roll)* Miss Sheely

Snickereyes, she sells fish in Dublin harbor; Peggy Guzzle, the brandy woman at the Horse Guards in Whitehall; Dolly Waggon, the carrier's daughter in Hull; Mademoiselle Van Bottomflat at the Sly Kiss. Then there's Jenny Oakum, the ship's carpenter's widow in Portsmouth, but I don't usually count her, because she was married at the same time to two marine lieutenants and a man of war's boatswain.

PLUME   Five. Make it half a dozen, Kite. Is it a boy or a girl?

KITE   A boy.

PLUME   Put the mother down on your list and the boy on mine. Enter him as Francis Kite, grenadier on unlimited furlough. I'll allow you a man's full pay for his keep. But now go comfort the poor wench in the straw.

KITE   *(with a sigh)*   Yes, sir. Have you any further commands?

PLUME   Not for the present.

KITE   There comes someone you must remember from last year. Mr. Worthy, the shoe manufacturer. *(Goes out)*

PLUME   For a fact, it looks like Worthy—or maybe Worthy's ghost.

WORTHY   Plume! Back again safe and sound?

PLUME   Safe from the battlefields of the New World and sound, I hope, from London's ale houses.

WORTHY   You're a happy man, Plume.

PLUME   What's wrong? Has your father risen from the dead and climbed back into the business?

WORTHY   No. No.

PLUME   Married?

WORTHY   No, no.

PLUME   Well then, who is it? Do I know her?

WORTHY   Melinda.

PLUME   Melinda Moorhill? But she began to capitulate a year ago, and, if I recall correctly, offered to surrender on honorable terms. I believe I advised you to propose an elopement to suit her romantic nature.

WORTHY   And so I did. She asked for time to consider. But then suddenly, and most unexpectedly, the fortress received fresh supplies and I was forced to turn the siege into a blockade.

PLUME   Details, if you please.

WORTHY   Her aunt in Flintshire died, leaving her twenty thousand pounds.

PLUME   My dear Worthy, I see you haven't mastered the rules of warfare. Your blockade was foolish. You should have redoubled your attacks, taken the fortress by storm, or died on the ramparts.

WORTHY   I did make one general assault, throwing in all my forces. But I was repulsed with such vigor that I had to abandon all hope of making her my mistress. For the past six months, I have been courting her with the utmost tenderness and devotion: my intention is marriage.

PLUME   And while you worship her like a goddess, she treats you like a dog. Is that it?

WORTHY   Exactly.

PLUME   My dear Worthy, if you want to give her a better opinion of you, you must bring her to a lower opinion of herself.

WORTHY   How?

PLUME   Let me think.—My first thought would be to sleep with her maid. Or I might hire three or four wenches in the neighborhood to spread the rumor that I'd got them all with child. Or, we could run verses in the gazette about every pretty woman in Shrewsbury, and leave her out. Or we could arrange a ball, neglecting to invite two or three of the town's worst scarecrows, and overlooking Melinda as well.

WORTHY   Those would be telling blows, I admit. But Shrewsbury is such a dull Tory stronghold—balls or verses in the gazette are out of the question.

PLUME   And bastards as well? With all these recruiting officers in town? I thought it was our principle to leave as many recruits behind as we carry off.

WORTHY   My dear captain, no one questions your determination to serve your country with all you've got. Molly at the Raven can testify to that.

    (Kite has re-entered)

PLUME   What now?

KITE   You sent me to comfort that poor woman in the straw— Mrs. Molly, my wife, Mr. Worthy.

WORTHY   Splendid! I wish you joy, Mr. Kite!

KITE   Well you may, sir, seeing as how I came by wife and child in half an hour. Captain, sir, someone else had been comforting her before I got there.

PLUME   In what respect?

KITE   Early this morning, a butler in green livery brought her a basket of baby clothes.

PLUME   Who in the world could have done that?

KITE   It was Simpkins, Miss Victoria's butler.

PLUME   Victoria?

WORTHY   Victoria Balance? Impossible!

PLUME   Who is Victoria Balance?

WORTHY   Don't you remember Miss Pritchett's boarding school on Walnut Road?

PLUME   Ah, yes! The little sixteen-year-old!

WORTHY   Who almost fell out the window when you waved to her.

PLUME   Yes, she was very funny. She sent me a note at the Raven but there was no time. But why should she make Molly presents? A grown woman might do that, not a schoolgirl. And only one woman in a thousand, one who's above jealousy, so to speak.

WORTHY   At that age a year makes all the difference. She's almost grown-up.

PLUME   What a noble gesture! I should say she deserves to be remembered. Worthy, who serves the best wine? That's the place to discuss our business.

WORTHY   Yes, that's what I've come for. Where do you propose to buy boots for your grenadiers? From Worthy and Co., I trust?

PLUME   First I must find grenadiers for your boots, Worthy. I shall pay my respects to Mr. Balance at once. Kite, have the drummer proclaim my arrival. Starting tomorrow, I order you to stir up such a commotion that Shrewsbury will stand on its head and salute with its feet.

(Plume and Worthy depart to the Raven. Kite salutes)

2

At the home of Mr. Balance.

Mr. Balance is reading a school notebook. Drumming and shouts are heard from the street.

DRUMMER   Latest news from the Raven! The hero of Bunker Hill has arrived from overseas! His Majesty's Captain William G. Plume presents his greetings to the glorious city of Shrewsbury.
(Mr. Balance hides the notebook behind his back as his daughter Victoria enters)

VICTORIA   Father, a Sergeant Kite was here. He says Captain Plume has arrived from London and wishes to pay you his respects.

BALANCE *(sarcastically)*   To *me?*—Victoria—

VICTORIA   Sir—

BALANCE   What was in that basket you had Simpkins take to a certain Molly Fastspittle?

VICTORIA   A few cakes, sir.

BALANCE   Indeed! Baby clothes were in it.

VICTORIA   How horrid of Simpkins.

BALANCE   Of course you had no idea that Captain Plume was the father of Miss Fastspittle's illegitimate child? *(She is silent)* What are Captain Plume's illegitimate children to you, will you tell me that?
(A trumpet sounds)

VICTORIA   Not children, there's only one child.

BALANCE   What is it to you?

VICTORIA   Father, when lovers are separated by this war in the colonies . . .

BALANCE   Lovers!—Victoria, how old were you when your mother died?

VICTORIA   Four.

BALANCE   Have I ever denied you anything? Haven't I always treated you with indulgence and loving care?—Well. Your brother's death has made you sole heir to my estate. That means an income of twelve hundred pounds for you. Get that captain out of your head!

VICTORIA   Sir, Captain Plume has never been in my head . . . And he would never offend a man in your high position by . . .

BALANCE   . . . seducing you? He would, though. I know the thoughts and feelings of young officers because I remember my own thoughts and feelings when I was a young officer. I'd have given my right arm to seduce the daughter of a worthy old squire on whom I was billeted . . .

VICTORIA   I'm surprised at you, sir.

BALANCE   I should hope so.

VICTORIA   You may be justified in your opinion of English officers; but perhaps you have more confidence in English girls, father.

BALANCE   None whatever! Any English girl with any spirit—your case, I hope—will let herself be seduced by an English officer. I suspect the two of you have . . .

VICTORIA   Father, you're beastly. *(Icily, as Balance produces the notebook)* Sir, have you been reading my diary?

BALANCE   Not yet, but don't oblige me to. Tell me the truth.

VICTORIA   There's nothing to tell, father. *(As her father is about to open the notebook)* Next to nothing. Last Whit Sunday Captain Plume was here for dinner. He didn't even speak to me. Except to say: "Little girl, a blue ribbon would be even more becoming," as he was passing me the pudding. That same evening I went back to school and I haven't seen him since. *(Balance again makes a motion to open the notebook)* Except once. He came strolling by with Mr. Worthy as I was standing at the window with some friends, and he waved to me. There's really nothing else. *(Balance threatens again to open the diary)* Only the note I sent him, wishing him a pleasant journey. It would have been rude not to.

BALANCE   Very well. *(Hands her the diary)*

VICTORIA   Only last Sunday you said the recruiting wouldn't get off the ground until Plume arrived. You praised him to the skies.

BALANCE   And I still think highly of him as a recruiter of soldiers, not of my daughter. In short: put Captain Plume out of your mind. Or any captain, for that matter. Sit down, Victoria. *(Victoria sits down)* Captains are paupers. You own forests. Captains are notorious for turning everything they can lay hands on into cash. They have an inborn aversion to anything green; they can't bear to leave trees standing. Old Hambleton down in Cheshire showed me a patch of land two miles square that had been stripped bare of trees. A captain of the Wimbleford Dragoons had acquired it by marriage. Two weeks after the wedding, a builder appeared on the scene; and every oak and elm, even the hundred-year-old beeches, were turned into sills, portals and sashes, or auctioned off to provide the noble captain with money for one of those fancy houseboats that have come into fashion on the Thames. *(He walks to the door and shouts at the top of his lungs)* Simpkins. The coach-and-four! *(To Victoria)* Victoria, I speak to you not as a father, but as a friend. I would rather advise than command. Your Uncle Harry has invited me to a pheasant shoot. Be sensible; go on ahead of me.

(Simpkins comes in)

SIMPKINS   The coach will be ready in ten minutes, sir, and Captain Plume is here to pay his respects.

BALANCE   Show him into the library. *(Simpkins goes out)* Pack your bag, Victoria.

VICTORIA   Are you speaking as a father or as a friend?

BALANCE   Whichever you prefer . . .

VICTORIA   Is that your last word?

BALANCE   Yes.

VICTORIA   Thank you. *(She goes out)*

BALANCE   *(shouting)* Victoria!—Simpkins!—Show the gentleman in.

(Plume comes in)

BALANCE   *(with outstretched arms)* Captain Plume!

PLUME   Mr. Balance.

BALANCE   Welcome to Shrewsbury! The gates of our city are open wide to you.

PLUME   Thank you, Mr. Balance.

BALANCE   You must again regard this house as yours.

PLUME   You are very kind. And how is your charming daughter, Mr. Balance?

BALANCE   Let me wish you every success in your efforts to carry off . . .

PLUME   *(startled)*   Sir? . . .

BALANCE   . . . a splendid company of grenadiers.

PLUME   Quite so, sir. Quite so.

BALANCE *(sits down)*   You must give me a detailed account of our military situation over there, captain.

PLUME   Our situation over there is a situation . . . how shall I put it? . . . an unusual situation. From a military point of view. From a military standpoint.—May I inquire whether your daughter . . .

BALANCE   I have to admit that six months ago I trembled for England. Bunker Hill has restored my confidence.

PLUME   I have something to show you. As a lawyer you may be interested in this rubbish they're handing out all over America.

(Simpkins comes in with whiskey)

BALANCE *(reading)*   "Draft of a Declaration of Independence." The gall! "When in the course of human events it becomes necessary for one people to dissolve the political bonds which have connected them with another hitherto . . ." High treason!

SIMPKINS   Scoundrels.

BALANCE *(reading)*   "All men are created equal . . ." Where does the Bible say that?—"Liberty and the pursuit of happiness . . ." So here it is in black and white; these new ideas we've heard so much about. It's base greed, that's what it is!

(Simpkins shakes his head sadly)

BALANCE   Do these rebels—these Franklins, Jeffersons, and Washingtons—really think the English crown will stand for such ideas?

SIMPKINS   Pah!

BALANCE   On the pretext that it costs too much, they refuse to import our tea. More than ten thousand cases of unsold tea are rotting in Liverpool docks at this very moment. At the same time, these lawyers and backwoods generals, reared in equality, want to sell their cotton, which we need here, to God knows who, merely because they get better prices. Imagine a colony presuming to trade with the whole world. Whoever heard of such a thing!

SIMPKINS   Tsk, tsk.

BALANCE   Is something wrong, Simpkins?

SIMPKINS   I beg your pardon, sir.

BALANCE   Imagine, sir, if your tenants suddenly proclaimed their independence and, instead of sending you their eggs, decided to send them to town and let you perish for want of albumen?

PLUME   I have no tenants, sir, but of course you're right.

BALANCE   What's more, these "new ideas" are contagious—they spread like the plague. The whole civilized world must join forces against these rebels. The Germans, I hear, have already come forward, with thirty thousand Hessians.—Have our losses been considerable?

PLUME   Considerable. You could make my work here a good deal easier, Mr. Balance, by taking the example of most other counties. Instead of sending the shiftless riffraff to jail, send them off to war.

BALANCE   I don't hold with such practices. There's no need for them in Shrewsbury. Our people know what they owe our king.

SIMPKINS   Thank God!

(Balance stamps his foot. Simpkins goes out)

PLUME   I hope you're right, sir. So far I must admit . . .

BALANCE   Your presence will change all that, Plume. A bit of martial music in the square, a captured flag or two, a patriotic speech, not too high-flown for our good country folk, and, of course, you can always count on the ardent support of our fair sex. Shrewsbury will give you everything you need, captain, everything!

(Victoria, in traveling attire, comes in, followed by a servant carrying her bags. She nods briefly and goes out)

PLUME   Your daughter, Mr. Balance?

BALANCE   Yes. On her way to visit her uncle in the country, Captain Plume.

PLUME   Oh.

3

At Melinda Moorhill's house.

Melinda sings, accompanying herself on the harp.

MELINDA

Chloe in the forest glade.
Achilles from behind a tree
Stepped, "Oh could you, pretty maid
Favor me?"
   Fearfully the maiden gazed
   Hid her features in the meadow grass.
   Said the hero, mournful and amazed
   "Don't you care then for my gold cuirass?"

As Achilles turned to go
Birds fell silent in the brake.
Listening to the brook's bright flow
Chloe spake.
   Said the maid: "It's easy to resist
   Lion, stag, and strutting peacock, too.
   Golden armor leaves me unimpressed
   But I have noticed that your eyes are blue."

(Victoria rushes in followed by her servant with her bags. The servant puts the bags down and leaves)

VICTORIA   Can I stay with you, Melinda? For a week. Father wanted me to go to Uncle Harry's in the country. But I can't leave Shrewsbury at the moment.

MELINDA   Of course. You know you are always welcome here.
   (They embrace)

VICTORIA   I'm so unhappy!

MELINDA   I'm so miserable!
   (They both burst into tears)

VICTORIA   Dearest Melinda!

MELINDA   Dearest Victoria! *(Calling)* Lucy, bring the tea! *(To Victoria)* Is it your captain? I hear he's back.

VICTORIA   This time I shall make sure he doesn't go off again. How are things between you and Worthy?

MELINDA   Oh, Worthy! I must have made some mistake. Now he wants to marry me.

VICTORIA   Well?

MELINDA   I don't know.

VICTORIA   But you love him.

MELINDA   Yes, but . . .

VICTORIA   And he loves you. To be sure, he's not a hero . . .

MELINDA   What do you mean? Everyone can't go dashing around the world like your Captain Plume. What have you got against Worthy?

VICTORIA   Against Worthy? Nothing. On the contrary, I fail to see why you treat the poor man so cruelly. He's a gentleman of rank and fortune. Besides, he is friends with my Plume, and if you're not nicer to him . . .

MELINDA   Heavens, Victoria! Must we talk about Worthy and me? I only said that he was getting rather stodgy.

VICTORIA   Small wonder when you've trained him like a dog.

MELINDA   Worthy is not a dog, Victoria. And now let me tell you what I think of your Captain Plume! He's a depraved, lazy, importunate fop!

VICTORIA   My dear Melinda, your opinion only proves how well suited you are to your stodgy Worthy now that you've inherited twenty thousand pounds. You treated him like a man as long as you were trying to extract five hundred pounds a year from him. Without success, of course.

MELINDA   What do you mean by that?

VICTORIA   My meaning is perfectly clear.
(Pause)

MELINDA   Without success! I don't envy you your success. Such success is easily come by.

VICTORIA   You think so?

MELINDA   Besides, you don't stand a chance.

VICTORIA   Really?

MELINDA   You poor deluded goose! Do you think a dashing young officer, who in the past six months has had half the world at his feet and has a girl in every town, is going to settle down in a God-forsaken hole like Shrewsbury for the sake of the insignificant daughter of a justice of the peace?

VICTORIA   What do I care how many girls he's got waiting for him! I wouldn't want a man with nothing on his mind but me!

MELINDA   Victoria, have you lost all pride, throwing yourself at the first rowdy rake of an officer . . . ?

VICTORIA   There you go again! Unfortunately, this is your house, Melinda . . .

MELINDA   I wouldn't have taken it amiss if you had stayed in yours, Victoria . . .

VICTORIA   Don't worry, Melinda, I'll take your gentle hint.

MELINDA   The sooner the better.

VICTORIA   I am always quick to follow my inclinations. Your humble servant, madam. *(Flounces out)*
(Her servant picks up her bags and follows. Lucy brings in the tea)

MELINDA   Impudent hussy.

4

Market place.

The recruiting officers have arranged a band concert. A platform has been set up in front of Mr. Balance's house. The recruiting booth is decorated with captured flags. A broad-shouldered man is sitting at a table outside the Raven. The band strikes up a military march. Kite steps out of the inn and stops in front of the broad-shouldered man, eyeing him admiringly. Pearmain and Appletree are looking at the pictures on the wall of the booth.

KITE *(to the broad-shouldered man)*   Oh! Allow me to congratulate you on your chest development.—Mike!—Money's no object to our good King George. *(Mike the potboy has come out of the inn)* Mike! Ale for the gentleman. *(He catches sight of the farm boys and walks toward the recruiting booth)* Gentlemen, may I invite you to drink a pint of ale with me this evening?

APPLETREE   When it comes to that, we'll take on the best of them.

(Plume, Balance, Melinda, and Worthy come out of Mr. Balance's house. They step up to the platform to a flourish of trumpets)

KITE   Shrewsbury salutes the hero of Bunker Hill!

(Plume waves to the crowd in all directions)

KITE   Three cheers for Captain Plume! Hip, hip, hurrah!

(The farm boys join in)

KITE   Let's have a cheer for the king and the honor of Micklesbury! *(He goes into the inn with the laughing farm boys)*

(The guests of honor take their places on the platform. Simpkins serves them whiskey)

BALANCE   Ladies and gentlemen! You have just seen one of the men who are making it possible for England to pursue her policy of strength throughout the world.

WORTHY   A herculean task! *(He listens to the music)*

BALANCE *(points to the square)*   The ice is beginning to melt; Shrewsbury is yielding to the martial strains of Höchstedt and Blafontaine. The blare of brass is injecting a little heroism into the anemic souls of our citizens. Plume! I insist on an account of the battle of Bunker Hill.

PLUME   This is rather embarrassing, Mr. Balance. One battle is very much like another.

SIMPKINS   Ahem!

BALANCE   Did you say something, Simpkins?

SIMPKINS   Begging your pardon, sir, but we know all about Bunker Hill here in Shrewsbury, sir. Indeed we do, captain.

BALANCE   What do you know?

SIMPKINS   The river is called the Hudson, Mr. Balance. Upstream there's a dam and a mill pond, sir; downstream, barley fields. The rebels had managed to cross the Hudson but under cover of night, Captain Plume—begging your pardon, sir—maneuvered eighty grenadiers and a field-piece through their lines. A single well-aimed shot—am I right, captain?—sweeps the dam away and the water starts flooding their barley fields. To be sure, our brave soldiers were decimated by murderous musket volleys, but then it happened as Captain Plume had anticipated. Those rebels are no soldiers, they're common dirt-farmers who've forced themselves into uniform. At the sight of a good-sized flood, such people soon revert to being dirt-farmers, he he he! That night a whole corps of dirt-farmers ran off to repair the dam and save the drowning livestock on their flooded farms. At eight o'clock in the morning we attacked. The outcome is common knowledge. Pardon, sir. Pardon, captain.

BALANCE   Thank you, Simpkins.

(Simpkins goes out)

BALANCE *(to Plume)*   What would you say was our main base of operations at present?

PLUME   Boston.

BALANCE   Boston? You'll have to explain that.

PLUME *(using whiskey glasses to illustrate)*   Boston, Howe, Washington. *(He makes a sign to Worthy and during the following explains the battle to Balance)*

WORTHY *(to Melinda)*   Madam, I am obliged to express my astonishment at your coldness to my friend Plume. You know how highly I regard him.

MELINDA   Is that a reprimand? Are you finding fault with my manners?

WORTHY *(meekly)*   Not at all. I am merely making an observation.

MELINDA   Whatever has been the matter with you these last few days? The day before yesterday, no sign of you. Where were you? Yesterday you sent your servant for the novels you had lent me, which I hadn't even read! Today . . .

WORTHY   Today?

MELINDA   You seem to have fallen under some bad influence. Have you come here for the sole purpose of insulting me?

WORTHY   I had no intention of either insulting you or seeing you. I came, I must admit, in the hope of meeting someone else.

MELINDA   Oh!

(Brazen comes in)

BALANCE   Who is that overdressed fellow with the sash? Never saw him before! What regiment is that anyway?

WORTHY   I'll wager he knows you, though. He knows every-body and his brother. It's Captain Brazen. He's a Caesar with the ladies; veni, vidi, vici, and there you have it. No sooner has he talked to the maid than he's slept with the mistress.

BRAZEN   *(approaching with outstretched arms)*   Mr. Worthy, your humble servant, and so forth. Listen, my dear fellow . . . *(He whispers in Worthy's ear)*

WORTHY   Don't whisper. When company's present . . .

BRAZEN   Mort de ma vie! I beg the lady's pardon. Do introduce me, my dear fellow.

WORTHY   Captain Brazen—Miss Moorhill.

BRAZEN   Moorhill! *(Strikes himself on the forehead)* The Sussex Moorhills or the Welsh Moorhills? Lovely lady, your servant, and so forth. And who might that be?

WORTHY   Ask him.

BRAZEN   So I will. Your name, sir.

BALANCE   Most laconic, sir.

BRAZEN   Laconic! A very fine name, indeed. I've known several Laconics abroad, splendid chaps. Poor Jack Laconic. Killed in the battle of Peshawar. On the Ganges. Well I remember that fateful day, he was wearing a blue ribbon on his cap and all we found in his pocket afterwards was a piece of dried ox tongue. Malaventura! I have good reason to remember: on that very day, twenty-two horses were killed under me.

BALANCE   You must have ridden mighty hard, sir.

BRAZEN   Torn to pieces by cannon balls, they were, all but six that were gored to death on the enemy's chevaux-de-frise.

BALANCE   Do you know Plume? Captain Plume?

BRAZEN   Plume? No. Is he related to Dick Plume, who was with the East India Company? He married the daughter of old Tonguepad, chairman of the Lord Raleigh shipyards. An exceptionally pretty girl, apart from a slight squint in her left eye. She died giving birth to her first child. The child survived. A little girl, it was. But whether she was called Margaret or Margery, upon my honor, my dear fellow, I can't remember.

MELINDA   Mr. Worthy, would you see me home? It's rather noisy here.

WORTHY   Not at all. The band plays these marches beautifully, Mr. Balance.

MELINDA   I asked you to see me home, Mr. Worthy.

WORTHY   I should be delighted to, madam, if, as I mentioned before, I hadn't arranged to meet someone here.

MELINDA   I do hope there's one gentleman here who will be good enough to see me home.

BRAZEN *(putting his arm around her waist)*   Dear child, here is my hand, my life-blood, and so forth. Your servant, Worthy. Ditto, Laconic.

(Brazen and Melinda leave)

KITE *(from the taproom)*   Ladies and gentlemen: long live our good King George! Hip, hip, hurrah!

BALANCE *(laughing)*   Veni, vidi, vici!—What's come over you, Worthy? *(Goes into the house)*

WORTHY   Plume!

(Kite comes out of the taproom. The broad-shouldered man lifts his glass; it is empty)

KITE   Mike! Another pint for the gentleman. *(He goes out)*

WORTHY   Plume! She's thrown herself into the arms of another man!

PLUME   She's all yours, man. *(Follows Balance into the house. Worthy in consternation follows them)*

KITE *(back in the taproom)*   Long live our good King George! Hip, hip, hurrah!

(The light changes. More shouts of "hip, hip, hurrah" are heard from the darkened taproom. The stage is dark and empty. Pearmain and Appletree, slightly tipsy, and Kite emerge from the Raven. The broad-shouldered man is still sitting outside the taproom.

KITE   Hey, boys. That's the soldier's life! Plenty of grub and plenty of ale. We live, as the saying goes—we live—how can I describe it? . . . we live like lords. *(To the broad-shouldered man)* May I ask, sir, how you enjoyed the king's ale, sir?

BROAD-SHOULDERED MAN   Couldn't be better, sir.

KITE   You'd enjoy the king's service even more, sir.

BROAD-SHOULDERED MAN *(drains his glass)*   Don't make me laugh, sir. I've been sitting here all day at your expense. *(Gets up to leave)*

KITE   One moment, sir. You know the Severn, but do you know the Mississippi? *(The man clumps off. We see that he has a wooden leg)* What's this! *(Calling after him)* Where's your leg?

BROAD-SHOULDERED MAN   Bunker Hill.

APPLETREE   He's lost a leg.

KITE   For the king, though. Hats off, boys!—All right; he's lost a leg. But so has some damned rebel over there.

BROAD-SHOULDERED MAN   For himself, though. *(Goes out)*

PEARMAIN   For himself, though. *(Laughs)*

KITE   *(stares after the broad-shouldered man)*   This is a case for the constabulary.—Now listen to me!—The swine!—Have you ever seen a picture of the king?

BOTH   No.

KITE   I'm surprised at you. I happen to have two of them with me, set in gold; the spitting image of His Majesty, God bless him. Here, both of them set in pure gold. *(He takes two gold coins from his pocket and holds them up)*

APPLETREE   *(looks at the coin)*   A miracle of nature! *(He looks at it earnestly)*

PEARMAIN   Pretty!

KITE   I'll make you a present of them, one each. *(Hands them the coins)* Think nothing of it. One good turn deserves another. *(Laughing, they pocket the coins. Plume and Worthy come out of the judge's house)*

PLUME   Chin up, Worthy!

(Worthy takes his leave and goes out)

KITE   Atten-shun! Off with your hats! Damn your souls to hell! Off with hats! It's the captain, your captain!

APPLETREE   *(laughing)*   We've seen the captain before. I'll keep my cap on.

PEARMAIN   There ain't a captain in all England I'd take my hat off to, sir. My father owns five acres of land.

PLUME   Who are these jolly lads, sergeant?

KITE   A couple of farm lads from Micklesbury. I've just enlisted 'em as volunteers in your command, captain.

PEARMAIN   Tummas? Art tha' enlisted?

APPLETREE   Not I, damn me. Art tha', Costar?

PEARMAIN   By Jesus, no! Not I! *(They both laugh)*

KITE   What! Not enlisted!—Ha ha ha! That's a good one, by God, very good.

PEARMAIN   Come on, Tummas, let's go home.

APPLETREE   Aye, come on. *(They start to leave)*

KITE   Gentlemen, watch your manners in the presence of your captain!—Dear Tummas!—Honest Costar!

APPLETREE   No, no; we must be going.

KITE   I command you to stay! You're in the army now. I'm putting you both on sentry duty here for the next two hours. And the first one who dares to leave his post before he's relieved gets this sword in his guts! There.

PLUME   What's the trouble, sergeant? Aren't you being a little harsh on these two gentlemen?

KITE   Too soft, sir, much too soft. These fellows are refusing to obey orders, sir; one of 'em ought to be shot as an example to the other.

PEARMAIN   Shot, Tummas?

PLUME   Gentlemen, what's this all about?

PEARMAIN   We don't know. The sergeant has talked himself into a proper rage, sir. But . . .

KITE   They refuse to obey orders and they deny that they're soldiers.

APPLETREE   No, no, sergeant, we don't deny it outright; we wouldn't dare, for fear of being shot. But as humbly and respectfully as you please, we'd like to go home now.

PLUME   That's easily settled. Has either of you received any of the king's money?

PEARMAIN   No, sir.

KITE   Turn out your pockets.

PEARMAIN   Nothing there, sir; only the king's picture. *(Produces the coin)*

KITE   You see? A gold piece, and what a gold piece; three and twenty shillings and sixpence. The other one's got the king's money in his left trouser pocket.

PLUME   Gentlemen, you are enlisted.

(Kite goes to the recruiting booth and gets the muster roll)

APPLETREE   We're enlisted, Costar!

PEARMAIN   Damnation, that we ain't, Tummas! I want to be brought before the justice of the peace. It was a present, captain!

PLUME   A present! *(Aside to Kite)* You and your damned tricks! *(Pretending to hit him)* I won't stand for it. You scoundrel, you whoreson, I'll teach you to trick an honest man! Cutthroat! Villain!

PEARMAIN   There's a captain for you!

PLUME   *(turning to them)*   What a shabby way to treat two lads like you.—I come to you as an officer to enlist soldiers, not as a kidnapper to carry off slaves.

APPLETREE   Hear that, Costar? Ain't that nice?

PLUME   It's true, gentlemen, I could take advantage of you; the king's money was in your pocket and my sergeant is ready to swear you've enlisted. But I don't believe in using force. Gentlemen, you are free to go.

PEARMAIN   Thankee, captain. You're a real gentleman.
(They turn to leave)

PLUME   Wait, boys, just one more thing. You're first-rate chaps, both of you, and—believe it or not—the army is the one place to make real men of you. The world is a lottery; every man has his ticket and you've got yours. Look at me: a little while ago I carried a musket; today, I'm commanding a company.

PEARMAIN   I'd follow him to the ends of the earth!

APPLETREE   Better not, Costar.

PEARMAIN   Captain, I'd follow you to the ends of the earth!

APPLETREE   Costar, don't be daft!

PLUME   Here, my young hero, here are two real English guineas. That's only a taste of what I'll do for you later on.

PEARMAIN   Gimme!

APPLETREE   Don't take it, don't take it, Costar. *(He begins to cry and tries to pull Pearmain back by the arm)*

PEARMAIN   I will, I will!—Damn ye, don't hold me back when something tells me I'll be a captain yet.—I'll take *your* money, sir.

PLUME   There. And now you and I will go marching across the world, and wherever we set foot, we shall be the masters.

PEARMAIN   To the end of the world!

PLUME   *(aside)*   Bring your friend with you, if you can.

PEARMAIN   Yes, sir. Tummas, must we part?
(Appletree undergoes an inner struggle)

APPLETREE   No, Costar! I can't leave 'ee—I'd rather come along, captain.

PLUME   Here, my boy. *(Gives Appletree the money)* There. Now: your name?

APPLETREE   Thomas Appletree.

PLUME   And yours?

PEARMAIN   Costar Pearmain.

PLUME   Look after them, Kite. *(Goes into the Raven)*

KITE *(beckons them to come over)*   A fine pair you turned out to be. I bet you've tried to talk the captain into giving me the boot and making one of you sergeant. Which one of you wants my sergeant's pike?

BOTH   Me.

KITE   Here.—In your guts!—Get a move on, you bastards! *(Drives them off)*

5

Market place.

Plume and Kite are sitting in the recruiting booth. They are bored. Workless, an unemployed laborer, passes by.

KITE   Sir, you know the Severn, but do you know the Mississippi?

WORKLESS   Nope. *(Goes out)*

KITE   We're getting no place fast!

ROSE'S VOICE   Pullets! Young and tender! Fresh Picklewood pullets! Get your pullets!

PLUME   Look what's coming!

KITE   Look at the strapping farm boy with her.

PLUME   That concert cleaned out the company's funds and only bagged us two recruits. Both yokels. Perhaps we ought to pay more attention to the rural population.

KITE   We'll give another concert next Sunday.

PLUME   What will we use for money?

(Rose and her brother, Bullock, approach. Rose is carrying a basket of pullets)

PLUME   Here, chick, chick! Here, pretty child!

ROSE   Buy a chicken, sir?

KITE   Show the captain all you have!

PLUME   You tend to your own knitting, Mr. Kite.
    (Rose laughs)

KITE   *(leads Bullock to the recruiting booth)*   Sir, you know the Severn, but do you know the Mississippi?

PLUME   Come, child; I'll take all you have.

ROSE   All I have is at your service, sir. *(She laughs)*

PLUME   Let me see. Young and tender, you say. *(Chucks her under the chin)* What is your name, pretty creature?

ROSE   Rose, sir. My father's a tenant farmer. We're always here on market day. I sell chickens, eggs, and butter; my brother Bullock sells the corn.

PLUME   May I touch, my pretty?

ROSE   Touching is buying, sir.

BULLOCK   Hurry up, Rose!

ROSE   Twelve shillings, sir, and it's all yours.

PLUME   Here's a pound, my dear.

ROSE   I can't make change, sir.

PLUME   Oh, but you can. My lodgings are two steps from here. You can make change there, my pretty. Tell me, have you many admirers in Picklewood?

ROSE   Yes, six admirers, and one intended.

PLUME   Wouldn't any of them want to join the army?

ROSE   No.

PLUME   We'll have to talk that over too. Come along.
    (Plume and Rose disappear into the Raven. Bullock is looking at the pictures on the recruiting booth)

BULLOCK   Would you be needing a drum major, for instance?

KITE   No, only grenadiers.
    (Bullock looks at the display again)

BULLOCK   What's that?

KITE   It's the Sultan of Okk's harem.

BULLOCK   Okk? Is that in America?

KITE   Where else?

BULLOCK   And you pay money for it?

KITE   Of course.

BULLOCK   I'd get seasick.

KITE   Where are you from?

BULLOCK   Picklewood.

KITE   Picklewooders don't get seasick.

BULLOCK   *(looking again at the display)*   There isn't even a shop in all Picklewood. I'm yer man, sergeant.

KITE   And here's your money. Your name?

BULLOCK   Bullock.

KITE   Bullock, you're in the army now.

BULLOCK   Rose! Where did Rose get to? Rose! Rose!

KITE   Stop that noise. She's probably gone off with your captain.

BULLOCK   To hell with you and your harem! *(Runs off)*

KITE   Wait till you see those harems—you're in for a big surprise.

(Victoria enters, disguised as a young squire)

VICTORIA   I must see Captain Plume at once.

KITE   Hmmm.

VICTORIA   Where is he?

(Kite doesn't answer. Victoria hands him some money)

KITE   He's at the Raven. But you can't see him now. He'll be back.

VICTORIA   Is Captain Plume busy?

KITE   I should say so. He's working himself to a frazzle.

VICTORIA   May I ask what he's busy with?

KITE   The rural population, sir. The rural population. Right now we've got our eye on the rural population.

VICTORIA   Quite so. The rural population is a breed apart. How long do you think your captain will be busy?

KITE   A good fifteen minutes.

VICTORIA   Then I'll wait.

(Brazen approaches the booth)

BRAZEN   Sergeant, where's your captain? I've got to shake his hand. What's his name again?

KITE   *(standing at attention)*   Captain Plume, Captain.

BRAZEN   *(catching sight of Victoria)*   Stop! Let me look at you. *(Victoria shrinks back)* Would you believe it! Mort de ma vie! But that's . . . Like two bullets from the same barrel! The spit and image of Charles! Charles! *(He embraces Victoria and whirls her around)*

VICTORIA   Sir, what's the meaning of this?

BRAZEN   The very image of Charles! Even the voice! Except for a slight modulation to minor, E–G sharp–A, don't you know.

VICTORIA   My name's Wilful, sir, Victor Wilful.

BRAZEN   The Kentish Wilfuls or the Devonshire Wilfuls?

VICTORIA   Both, sir, both. I am related to all the Wilfuls in Europe. At present I am head of the whole Wilful family.

BRAZEN   Splendid. *(To Kite)* Where's Frank?

KITE   Captain Plume is engaged in business . . .

BRAZEN   I see. Business and so forth . . . *(Looks at his watch)* A scoundrel, that's what I am! See you later, gentlemen. Wilful, your servant and so forth. *(Goes out)*

VICTORIA   *(mopping her forehead; subdued)*   My name *is* Wilful.

KITE   Of course, sir.

(Enter Lady Prude with Bullock)

PRUDE   Where is your captain, sergeant? This young man, the son of my tenant, tells my Captain Plume has abducted his sister. What do you know about this?

KITE   Nothing, madam.

BULLOCK   But he was there. He showed me the pi . . . *(Lady Prude looks at him sternly)* . . . pictures. And meantime the captain disappeared with the slut!

KITE   Atten-shun! Why don't you take better care of your sister?

PRUDE   Are you Turks? Where is the girl?

BULLOCK   He told me himself that she went off with the captain.

KITE   Shut up!

PRUDE   Where *is* the captain? By your mother's immortal soul, where is he?

KITE   Madam, by that same immortal soul, I swear I don't know.

PRUDE   Turks!

VICTORIA   *(to Kite)*   Busy! With the rural population! *(Crosses the square and goes into the Raven)*

PRUDE   Who was that young man? *(To Bullock)* Fetch the justice! *(Bullock leaves)*

KITE   You're wasting your time, madam.

PRUDE   *(looks at the pictures)*   Disgusting! You are an evil man.

KITE   Why?

PRUDE   Because you lie like Caiaphas. You may think you're doing it for your captain, but it's lying all the same. Where's the girl?

KITE   *(reproachfully)*   Madam!
       (Loud voices are heard from the inn)

LANDLADY'S VOICE   You know very well you're not allowed into the officers' quarters.

ROSE'S VOICE   I was only selling my chickens.

LANDLADY'S VOICE   Chickens indeed! I know that kind of chickens. This isn't a bawdyhouse. Get out!
       (Rose runs out of the inn. She is met by Lady Prude)

PRUDE   Rose!

ROSE   Oh, Lady Prude! I've sold the lot. At two shillings a piece! Begging Your Grace's pardon, what would this lace be worth a yard? *(Shows her a piece of genuine lace)*

PRUDE   Mercy me! Creole lace! Where did you get it, child?

ROSE   I came by it honestly, my lady.

PRUDE   I doubt it very much. What did you give in return? Look me in the eye!

ROSE   Why? I'm giving my brother for a soldier. And Cartwheel, my intended, as well. And two or three of my admirers from the village. That's what the captain wanted. Would you believe it, my lady; he took me into his own quarters, and he made me a garter out of a band off his sleeve, and put it on with his own hands. He was dreadfully sorry, he told me so, when the landlady knocked at the door and said she had to speak to him. But we're going to see each other again.

PRUDE   Turks!
       (Balance enters with Bullock)

BALANCE   Lady Prude . . .

PRUDE   Mr. Balance, you are the justice of the peace in this town, but what has become of the peace in this town?

BALANCE   Are you, perchance, referring to the officer who is honoring Shrewsbury with his presence?

PRUDE   He's a scoundrel—that's what he is!

BALANCE   *(grandly)*   Lady Prude, you cannot stop England's daughters from giving England's fighting men their proper due.

PRUDE *(dryly)*   Perhaps you ought to think of your own daughter when you say that, Mr. Balance.

BALANCE *(dryly)*   I have thought of her, Lady Prude.

6

Billiard room at the Raven.

Victoria is waiting for Plume. After a short while Plume appears.

VICTORIA   I hope I haven't disturbed you in a delicate situation, captain. The landlady seemed upset when she learned that you were not alone in your room. I'm so sorry.

PLUME   What brings you here, Mr. . . .

VICTORIA   Wilful.—I have a letter for you. *(Hands him a letter. Plume sits down)* You may be wondering how I come to have this letter. Well, the other day, as I was returning from a morning canter extra muros, a carriage suddenly came thundering in my direction. My horse shied. The coachman tried to rein in his horses, but they reared. A cry of fright from inside the carriage, the sound of a wheel splintering against the curbstone. I leapt from my horse to offer my assistance. You will appreciate my relief at finding that the beautiful young person gazing wanly at me from the cushions was unharmed. While the driver changed the wheel I kept the fair stranger company. I learned that she was the daughter of Balance, the justice of the peace, who, for some whim, had sent her off to the country. She soon confided that this had separated her from someone she loved dearly, of whom she then spoke at some length. Sitting on the very curbstone that had brought about this happy encounter, she hastily penned a note. "For Captain Plume," she said simply, got back into the carriage, and drove off.

(Plume, who has been sipping his whiskey all through Victoria's account, opens the letter and reads it. He bursts into loud laughter)

VICTORIA   Why are you laughing?

PLUME *(laughing)* Read it yourself, young man.

VICTORIA *(reads)* "A young friend will reveal the true reason for my departure. With the fervent hope that you will remain in Shrewsbury forever this time, Yours, Victoria Balance." Captain, you're a lucky man!

PLUME   Priceless! She expects me to resign my commission for her!

VICTORIA *(with a forced laugh)* How perfectly naive!

PLUME   I could die laughing.—How about a game?

(They go over to the billiard table)

VICTORIA   On the other hand, captain, the young lady's sentiments seem to be of a serious nature. Of course your profession stands in the way of serious commitments and I can see you would never want to give up your noble calling. Though there are men who would, if the reasons were important enough.

PLUME   Quite so.

VICTORIA   And there are such reasons, captain. There are men who, for one reason or another, would not take up this profession in the first place. I suppose you would advise them to put a bullet through their heads.

PLUME   Not at all.

VICTORIA   Why not?

PLUME   After all, there *are* other professions.

VICTORIA   Indeed? For instance?

PLUME   Well, all sorts.

VICTORIA   Yes, of course. But which would you choose? Justice of the peace?

PLUME   Justice of the peace? Never!

VICTORIA   Trade perhaps?

PLUME   No, not trade.

VICTORIA *(whose eyes are filling with tears)* Artist?

PLUME   You can't be serious, Mr. Wilful!

VICTORIA   In short—no other profession.

PLUME   It must be admitted that civilian professions have certain disadvantages.

VICTORIA   And the military profession has none?

PLUME   No, I wouldn't say that.

VICTORIA   What disadvantages? *(Plume seeks vainly for an answer)* Do you mean that an officer can't marry?

PLUME   Not if he's a man of principle. Of course there are compensations.

VICTORIA   I see.

PLUME   Incidentally, when will you be seeing Miss Balance?

VICTORIA   You mean that an affair with Miss Balance is *your* compensation for not being able to marry?

PLUME   Why not?

VICTORIA   Indeed. Why not? *(Victoria viciously jabs the cue into the table, tearing the cloth)*

PLUME   Anything wrong, Mr. Wilful?
(Mike the potboy comes in)

MIKE   Bull's-eye. *(He examines the damaged table)*

VICTORIA   Surely you can mend that.

MIKE   Mend it! The table's ruined. That will be two pounds.

PLUME   Charge it!

MIKE   How are you going to pay for it when you still owe for last Sunday's ale?

PLUME   Don't make a fuss, Mike! Put it on the slate!

MIKE   And the room where you receive your ladies? You haven't paid for that either! Put it on the slate! No more of that!

VICTORIA   Idiot! Is that a way to talk to one of England's heroes? Here are five pounds for last Sunday's ale and for the room. Where do you expect the captain to receive his ladies? Now get out!

MIKE   A brand new billiard table. *(Goes out)*

PLUME   Young man, I hope you haven't over-extended your-self.

VICTORIA   A mere trifle. By the way, Miss Balance hopes her little attention to a certain Molly at the Raven didn't strike you as presumptuous.

PLUME   By no means. I admire her generosity; a rare display of worldly wisdom in one so young.

VICTORIA   In any event mother and child are well provided for.

PLUME   I hope she didn't give her any money?

VICTORIA   I wouldn't know.

PLUME   *(calling out)* Kite! *(To Victoria)* The mother, my dear Wilful, happens to be my sergeant's wife. The poor creature spread the tale that I was the father in the hope that my friends would come to her assistance. She succeeded. *(Kite comes in)* Mr. Kite, I hope there wasn't any cash in the basket that was sent to Molly—I mean Mrs. Kite?

KITE   Yes, captain, there was. I only heard about it this morning. Those greedy people . . .

PLUME   How much?

KITE   Twenty pounds. Old Mrs. Fastspittle goes right out and buys a hat shop. What can I do with a hat shop, tell me that?

VICTORIA   You'd rather she'd bought a helmet shop, I suppose.

PLUME   Kite, you are to return the money to Miss Balance at once.

KITE   Me? You want me to pay out money on top of everything else?

PLUME   All right, you haven't got it. Very well, I shall pay your debts. I admire Miss Balance's solicitude, but money, no— that I can't permit. Wilful, lend me thirty pounds.

VICTORIA   I'll be glad to. *(Takes out her wallet and hands him thirty pounds)*

PLUME   I'll give you my note payable in three days. We'll have plenty of cash after the inspection.

VICTORIA   That's not necessary.

PLUME   Ah, but it is. Excuse me now. *(Goes out)*

VICTORIA   Three days? *(To Kite)* Will you be leaving in three days?

KITE   Three days and we're off to the New World. How would a little trip to America strike you? You know the Severn, but do you know the Mississippi? *(He produces some pictures)* Boston—Philadelphia—Baltimore.

VICTORIA   I don't believe, Mr. Kite, that the Bunker Hill area is quite the thing for tourists.

KITE   For soldiers, though!

VICTORIA   You think I ought to join the army?

KITE   You've got money to burn. Why not buy an ensign's commission?

VICTORIA   Where?

KITE   In our company.

VICTORIA   How much would it be?

KITE   About twenty pounds, I'd say.

VICTORIA   I could afford that, but . . .

KITE   Twenty pounds and a few more for extras—and you can come along with us!

VICTORIA   I must admit, one little chat with your captain has convinced me that a military career offers unparalleled pleasures, deeper satisfactions than love.

KITE   Than what?

VICTORIA   Than love.

KITE   I should think so. Uniform, boots, sword belt, cocked hat, —you'll get the lowest prices if you buy them through me. You're sure to get nicked if you don't. Say twenty-five pounds —no, twenty-four—no, better make it twenty-five. *(Since Victoria, who has been listening in amusement, seems to hesitate)* Cold feet? Balderdash. People die in bed, too, you know. True, Bunker Hill cost us eleven thousand men, but . . .

MIKE   *(busy tearing the torn cloth off the billiard table)* Eleven thousand? Did you say eleven thousand, sergeant?

KITE   What are you hanging around for? What have you heard?

MIKE   Nothing, sergeant, by St. Patrick.

KITE   You were listening when I was talking about Bunker Hill, weren't you? What exactly was said?

MIKE   Something about eleven thousand men—that's all.

KITE   And what did I say about them?

MIKE   *(after a pause)* That they were lost *(as Kite threatens him)* and found again.

KITE   Get out! Scoundrel! *(Mike goes out in a panic)* In round numbers, ensign, twenty-five pounds, everything included. But for that you'll find out what a man is.

VICTORIA   Of course, I'd be glad of that.

KITE   Take me, for instance: born in the gutter, grew up with the dregs to the age of ten. That's where I learned that the main thing in life is filling your belly. It's not the whole story, mind you, but it's the first step. My mother, Cleopatra, sold me for three gold florins to a gentleman who'd taken a fancy to my beauty. That's where I learned that a man's got to obey his master, body and soul. I was sacked because I took a liking to the master's fine linen and my lady's liqueurs. Then I worked as a bailiff. That's where I learned how to bully and hold out my palm. It was only after learning all that that I was found fit for military service. I had nothing more to learn but boozing and whoring. And marrying, of course.

VICTORIA   What do you mean by that?

KITE   Marrying in soldier fashion without benefit of parson or license. Our sword is our honor. We lay it on the ground. First the young hero jumps over it, then the girl. The buck leaps and the whore jumps. A roll of drums and off to bed. That's how we get married.

VICTORIA   What about the captain—can he do all that?

KITE   He hasn't an equal.

VICTORIA   I must own that I felt a certain liking for your captain even before I heard that. Perhaps he could do with a guardian angel while performing his strenuous duties in the New World. Sergeant Kite, I'm at your service. *(They shake hands) (Plume comes in)*

PLUME   My note, Wilful.

KITE   Ensign Wilful, sir. *(Plume looks at her with astonishment. She makes a hesitant gesture)* It's all settled, captain. Mr. Wilful wants to see the New World.

VICTORIA   What do you say, Captain Plume? Would you be willing to take me with you to the New World?

PLUME   I'm afraid I must decline to have a gentleman in my company.

VICTORIA   Oh.

KITE   Ensign Wilful will be glad to contribute five pounds to the next recruiting concert, captain.

PLUME   Learned to fence?

VICTORIA   Yes, sir.

PLUME   Whist?

VICTORIA   A little.

PLUME   I suppose half a bottle of port puts you under the table.

VICTORIA   No, sir.

PLUME   Make it ten pounds.—If there wasn't a certain je-ne-sais-quoi about you that appeals to me . . . Your treatment will depend on your conduct. Here's your note, Wilful, and kindly pass this letter on to your pretty friend. *(Hands her a letter)*

KITE That makes it forty pounds.

VICTORIA That's enough now, Mr. Kite. Thirty-five, and get out.

PLUME Let's get some breakfast, ensign.

VICTORIA *(hesitates)* Captain Plume, I have a confession to make. I hope it won't throw you into a rage. That country lass has made quite an impression on me. Are you very much involved?

PLUME Ah, ensign. In such matters we can easily come to terms. I'll exchange a woman for an able-bodied man any time. Suppose we discuss it over breakfast. *(Both go out)*

Interlude before the Curtain

VICTORIA *(with her uniform under her arm)* Ladies and gentlemen, your Victoria is faced with a hard decision. She has joined the army to be near the man she loves! Can she really mean to cross the ocean? Be that as it may, I cannot bear to leave his side during his last days in England, no matter how foolhardy this may be. How does the song go? *(She sings)*

At certain times in life we're driven
Head over heels to make a painful choice:
Whether to fate and passion we should give in
Or let ourselves be guided by reason's prudent voice.
  But the bosom swells with emotion
  And the mind hasn't got much to say
  The sail fills with wind on the ocean
  And the ship doesn't ask long: Which way?

Sister, what metal are you made of?
Where is your modesty and where your pride?
There's hardly any plight or peril you're afraid of
Once love has caught you up in its tumultuous tide.

The doe runs after the stag
And the lioness follows her lord
And to be with her lover a maid
Will go to the ends of the world.

7

Market place.

Plume and Kite are sitting in the recruiting booth. Jenny Mason and old Mrs. Cobb are standing outside.

MRS. COBB   Well, I've come for his things.

JENNY   That's old Mrs. Cobb. They say her son Bert was killed at Bunker Hill.

PLUME   I see.

KITE   *(rummages about and finds a watch)* The captain has brought this for you: his watch.

MRS. COBB   Thank-ee.

JENNY   It's been a blow to her. But now that I have the good fortune to see the captain, could I inquire about my husband, Jimmy Mason?

KITE   Jimmy Mason. He's even picked out the farm he's going to buy when it's all over. He's doing fine or I'm a worthless rogue.

JENNY   It's only that I've had no news of him for almost six months.

KITE   The bloody post, it's always the same thing. Don't you worry, Mrs. Mason, he's all right. Good evening to you!

MRS. COBB   *(to Jenny)*   Did Bert have a watch?
   (Both women go out. Kite mops his forehead)

PLUME   The devil take them!

KITE   She'll be all over Shrewsbury, driving everybody crazy.

PLUME   How many have we recruited so far?

KITE   Nine, captain.

PLUME   We had that many three days ago. Then there's the two Picklewooders that girl—what's her name again?—dragged in. Eleven in all. It's terrible! What's wrong with this place?

KITE   Recruiting's been slow in the last few days, captain.

PLUME   Why?

KITE   It's the rumors about the losses at Bunker Hill.

(Captain Brazen comes in)

BRAZEN   We meet again! How are you, my dear old boy? What's your name, dear fellow?

KITE   This is Captain Plume, Captain Brazen.

BRAZEN   Right. Plume, you're just the man I was going to ask for five pounds.

PLUME   *(laughs and makes a gesture of regret)*   Me? *(They sit down)*

PLUME   How's your recruiting, old boy?

BRAZEN   I beg your pardon?

PLUME   How many have you recruited?

BRAZEN   Shh!

PLUME   What's that?

BRAZEN   Shh! That's my last word.

PLUME   What's that you're holding?

BRAZEN   Two plans—for getting rid of twenty thousand pounds.

PLUME   Mightn't it be better to find a way of raising twenty thousand pounds?

BRAZEN   My dear fellow, you may find it hard to understand why a man like me should want to get rid of twenty thousand pounds. In the army I spend twenty times that much every day. But now, I want your advice. The building fit is on me. Which would you advise: a pirate ship or a theater?

PLUME   Pirate ship or theater—that's an odd question. Takes a bit of thinking. Brazen, I'm for the pirate ship.

BRAZEN   I don't agree with you, my dear fellow. A pirate ship can be badly built.

PLUME   So can a theater.

BRAZEN   But a pirate ship can also be badly manned.

PLUME   So can a theater.

BRAZEN   A pirate ship can founder without a trace.

PLUME   A theater is even more likely to.—Consequently my advice to you is still the same—stick to the pirate ship.

BRAZEN   Very well!—But what if I don't get the twenty thousand pounds?

PLUME   Where do you propose to get these twenty thousand pounds?

BRAZEN   It's a secret, my dear fellow. A lady I've ferreted out lately. At first I hung back. But now I really think I'll marry her. Twenty thousand pounds . . . She's to meet me next Sunday on the river bank half a mile out of town, and so forth. I must be off this minute.—Mum's the word, my dear fellow. *(Is about to leave. Turns back once more)* Twelve shillings?

(Plume repeats the gesture of regret)

(Brazen goes out)

KITE   We're pretty well cleaned out ourselves, sir.

PLUME   You don't say so?

KITE   We haven't raised a company. We've still got the ensign's ten pounds for next Sunday, but no ideas. I think I'll have to fall back on my old household remedy. Boots off, door bolted, six large beers, a bit of bread to munch in between. I remember in Bengal, when I'd been trying for three whole weeks to make the colonel's wife's maid and not getting anywhere, my favorite remedy gave me the answer.

PLUME   What was it?

KITE   To settle for the colonel's wife! Never fear, sir, right here by the Severn I'll come through again. Your company will be up to strength.

PLUME   Kite, what do you make of that little Balance girl who writes those letters? Doesn't she strike you as the sort who goes the limit on paper but calls for the preacher and wedding bells before she'll let you kiss her on the forehead? Not for us, eh? I don't remember her very well, damn it! Somehow she reminds me of our ensign—what do you think? Has she got a brother? *(Kite shrugs his shoulders sullenly)* What a bore Shrewsbury is this year. Admit it. Wilful may be stinking with money but I'll have to tell him it's not my way to give up a woman without getting something in return. He'll just have to produce the Balance girl. I'm not going to turn monk for his sake. Lord, is this Shrewsbury tedious!

KITE   Will you be by the Severn on Sunday, captain?

PLUME For the concert? Yes, I think so. But I don't know if I'll have any time for you.

KITE We may need you, sir. The inspecting officer from London will be here any day.

(Victoria comes in wearing the king's uniform)

VICTORIA Ensign Wilful reporting for duty.

PLUME Speaking of duty, what have you done with that wench from Picklewood, Wilful? Rose.

VICTORIA I've arranged to meet her, sir.

PLUME Where?

VICTORIA By the Severn.

PLUME When?

VICTORIA Sunday. Sunday afternoon.

PLUME Afternoon! To feed the swans? Hold hands? It may be none of my business, but if I find out that you lack enterprise in these matters, I'm through with you. You come around whining, I hand you a juicy morsel and you lock it up in the pantry. Furthermore, I'd have expected a man of your breeding to return the favor. What about the Balance girl?

(Victoria hurriedly produces a letter from her back pocket)

PLUME *(angrily)* No more letters! I want something tangible! And not next week but tomorrow, Sunday. Is that clear?

VICTORIA Yes, captain.

PLUME Dismiss!

(Victoria salutes)

8

By the Severn.

Plume is sitting on a bench, waiting. In the distance the strains of a military band.

KITE *(disguising himself behind the bushes. To Plume)* You're in for a surprise, captain. This may turn out to be the biggest idea

I've ever had. If this doesn't bring Shrewsbury around, my name is mud. *(Steps out of the bushes, disguised as a flower seller)* How do I look, captain?

PLUME   Terrible.

KITE   *(shuffles off, his feelings hurt)*   Lilacs! Fresh lilacs!
(Victoria comes in dressed in the uniform of an ensign)

PLUME   All alone?

VICTORIA   Captain Plume, I don't quite know how to explain it. Yesterday she was all set to come. Today she just couldn't make up her mind. Are you dreadfully disappointed?

PLUME   Nothing can disappoint me any more in Shrewsbury.

VICTORIA   She's not like Shrewsbury.

PLUME   But why wouldn't she come?

VICTORIA   Perhaps it's because she doesn't trust herself. She's a woman of spirit, you know.

PLUME   She's obviously well able to control that spirit of hers.

VICTORIA   That's not fair.

PLUME   I beg your pardon?

VICTORIA   Perhaps if you gave her more time . . .

PLUME   A soldier lives at a fast pace, Wilful. He's got to take his meals on the run. He must dispense with certain dishes. A chunk of bread and into the saddle. Have you arranged to meet with—what's her name again—Rose? This is an order: tell her to come to my quarters at the Raven tonight. And keep your proper distance, two paces, ensign. Is that clear?

VICTORIA   Yes, captain. *(Angrily)* Then you shouldn't write such letters.

PLUME   So you've been reading letters entrusted to you by your superior officer?

VICTORIA   Not at all. But when they're being read, I can tell if they were dictated by true sentiments or if they ring false.

PLUME   I'll thank you to keep your opinion of my technique to yourself, ensign.

VICTORIA   You've got no heart and you can count me out. *(She steps aside)*
(Worthy comes in)

WORTHY   Lost! Irrevocably lost! Plume, your stratagem has been my ruin. To hell with all strategists! Melinda and Brazen are to meet here by the river and they're rowing out to that notorious island.

PLUME Who told you that?

WORTHY Her maid.

PLUME So you called on her again. In spite of my warning. And were shown the door.

WORTHY Nothing of the sort, worse luck. Her maid came to me.

PLUME Then she was sent. To arouse your jealousy. And you want to throw up the game? Worthy, if you give in now—you'll lose everything. Melinda's maneuvers, clearly born of desperation, must be thwarted! She is only meeting Brazen because of you. I admit it may be unpleasant for you to watch them disappear into the bushes . . .

WORTHY Unpleasant? Unbearable!

PLUME Unbearable! Nonsense! We sacrifice a town in order to win a country. You accept a setback to ensure final victory. Worthy, your faint-heartedness will make you miss the greatest chance of your life.

WORTHY What! Am I to look on while the woman I love and that scoundrel . . .

PLUME By all means. And with perfect composure. You must give her an opportunity to find out for herself what a worthless rascal your rival is.

WORTHY But . . . in my presence?

PLUME How else?

WORTHY Plume, it's more than I can bear.

PLUME Nonsense. Come along to my quarters and have a toddy with plenty of rum. I'll have one myself.—Stop looking like a sick calf. You've never been closer to victory. (To Victoria, who is still standing about) What are you waiting for?

VICTORIA On my honor, captain, I don't understand you. Isn't Victoria worthier of you than all these Mollys and Roses and whatever their names may be in all the taverns of England and the New World?

PLUME Undoubtedly. But she's not here. And Rose will be. You'll see to that. (Goes out with Worthy)

VICTORIA Never, never, never. (Goes out)

(Mike and Lucy come in. Lucy carries a picnic basket. She curtsies to Worthy)

MIKE   Why that big smile for the shoe business?

LUCY   He gave me a pound.

MIKE   He gave you a pound?

LUCY   I was nice to him, so he gave me a pound.

MIKE   What's the story?

LUCY   Miss Moorhill sent me to tell Mr. Worthy that she was going to the Severn with a dashing captain and that if nobody stopped her something dreadful would happen. Mr. Worthy went white as a sheet and gave me a pound.

MIKE   Is she really up to something with that captain?

LUCY   Naw. She only wants to make Mr. Shoe Business jealous.

(They move toward the river. Mike spies a swan in the distance)

MIKE   *(pointing)* There's Felix.

LUCY   Kitchie-kitchie. Ten more errands like that one and we'll have the money for the fare. "America, here we come."

MIKE   But not the way they want us to be going, me as a grenadier and you as a you-know-what. Oh no, we're going into the hotel business. *(The swan swims close; they feed it)*

LUCY   I'll write to Aunt Emmy in New York tonight.

MIKE   What for? That hole! We're going to Boston.

LUCY   Hole, you say! It may be a small town now, but it's got a future.

MIKE   Too small for another hotel. Shh!

(Appletree in uniform comes in with his girl Maggie, William, a young blacksmith, and his girl Sally)

MAGGIE   Let's sit here—there's somebody here already.

SALLY   And here's the swan. I've got bread for him. Do you mind, Tummas?

WILLIAM   Who cares if he minds?

SALLY   He eats out of my hand.

MIKE   *(furious)* He does that.

(Mike and Lucy go out. The others look after them with surprise)

WILLIAM   *(to Sally)* You're making eyes at him because of his uniform.

APPLETREE   I only wish I could get rid of it.

MAGGIE   William is staying on in Micklesbury. What'll you have, William, an egg or some sausage?

APPLETREE   An egg. *(takes one)*

MAGGIE   William!

APPLETREE   You haven't said a word about the shoes and the pretty furs I'm going to bring back to you.

MAGGIE   It's easy to know who's going, but you can never tell who's coming back.
(Music)

SALLY   They're playing "When I Leave You." Sing it for me, Tummas.

APPLETREE   *(sings with the music)*

When I leave you for the war, dear
Leave you standing on the shore, dear
On the queen's great ship as out of port we sail
Find another sweetheart, Minny
For this ship goes to Virginny
And when I'm gone, my love, my love for you will pale . . .

MAGGIE   *(sings)*

I'll be cheering with the others
For our husbands, sweethearts, brothers
When the queen's great ship goes sailing with the tide.
Jimmy dear, you must believe me
Memories of you will grieve me
When I'm walking with another at my side.

(Kite comes in disguised as a flower girl)

KITE   Lilacs, fresh lilacs! Forget-me-nots, violets! Buy some violets for your sweetheart before he leaves for America. *(To Sally)* I can see your friend is a real fighting man. I've got seven of my own, all in the army where they belong.

MAGGIE   He's staying right here. He's a blacksmith.

KITE   Go on with you. *(To William)* Here, let's look at your hand. Blacksmith. A violent man by profession. You were born under Biceps.

MAGGIE   Biceps? What's that?

KITE   One of the signs of the zodiac. There's Leo, Sagittarius,

Biceps, Anvil, Boston, Massachusetts, Kentucky, Philadelphia, Mumps, and so on. Twelve in all.—Let's see. Have you
ever made bombs or cannon balls?

WILLIAM   Not I.

KITE   Either you've made them or you're going to make them.
It's scientific. What's more, it's in the stars—Oh! What a
future! In exactly two years, three months, and two hours you
will become a captain.

SALLY   A captain!
(The farmers listen in, some attentively, some skeptically)

KITE   In the artillery. You'll have two batmen and ten shillings
a day. It's written in the stars, the fixed stars.

WILLIAM   What do the stars say about my smithy?

KITE   What's that?

WILLIAM   What'll happen to my smithy?

KITE   Where would the fixed stars be if they started worrying
about every filthy village smithy?

WILLIAM   In that case, shit on your fixed stars.

KITE   You'll pay for that once we're away from home. *(Aside, in
leaving)* I'll get that man or I'm not a . . .
(Victoria comes in)

KITE   *(salutes)*   The trumpeter won't play his solo. He wants
another pound. Scum.
(Victoria hands him money)

SALLY   She's a funny one.

WILLIAM   Did you see her salute?
(Kite goes out. Victoria walks toward a boat. Appletree salutes)

SALLY   How smartly he does it!

WILLIAM   He's got to.

APPLETREE   *(eager to go)*   Come, let's go.
(The farmers leave. Victoria has sat down on the side of the boat)

MAGGIE   But I've still got bread for Felix! *(She gathers her things
and runs after the others. Victoria remains sitting on the boat. Suddenly Rose's voice is heard)*

ROSE'S VOICE   Chickens! Fresh Picklewood chickens!

VICTORIA   *(jumps to her feet)*   Damn it. Here come the chickens!
*(Rose and her brother Bullock emerge from the grove. Bullock is in
uniform)*

ROSE   *(to Bullock)*   Who's that officer over there?

BULLOCK   That's our new ensign.

ROSE   Go and ask him where the captain is.

VICTORIA *(to herself)*   Up and at 'em, Victoria. You're wearing breeches now.

(Bullock approaches her)

BULLOCK   Where's the captain, sir?

VICTORIA   Attention! Didn't they teach you to salute an officer? About turn! Right leg, raise! Left leg, raise! About turn! At the double, march! Double mark time! Left, right, left, right! Halt! On the face, down! Up, down, up, down! How do you recognize an ensign?

BULLOCK *(still lying on the ground)*   By his uniform and bearing, sir.

VICTORIA   Up, man!—Do you know the difference between a horse cart and a cart horse, you old dungfork?

BULLOCK   Yessir!

VICTORIA   About her, now. Who's she?

BULLOCK   My sister Rose. She's got to see the captain.

VICTORIA   Come here, child, and give me a kiss.

ROSE   But I don't know you, sir.

VICTORIA   What's that got to do with it? We soldiers have to eat on the run.

(Rose is kissed)

VICTORIA   I am Captain Plume's ensign, Rose. It's my job to look after you, the captain is busy today.

ROSE   But I was to see him personally.

VICTORIA   What for? You can see me instead.

ROSE   He wanted to give me something, sir.

VICTORIA   I'll give it to you all right.

ROSE   Please, sir, tell him I'll come tonight.

VICTORIA   Where?

ROSE   Why, to the Raven.

VICTORIA   You'd go to the Raven? At night? How can you make yourself so cheap?

ROSE   He'll get what he wants from me, and I'll get what I want from him.

BULLOCK   On the up and up, sir. Have a care what you say, Rose, don't shame your parents.

ROSE   I'm doing it for Charles too, you know.

VICTORIA   Charles?

BULLOCK   Charles Cartwheel, her intended.

ROSE   He's to be a drum major!

VICTORIA   Doesn't he mind your going to see the captain?

ROSE   Why should he? "If the captain's good to you," says Charles, "he's sure to be good to me when I'm his soldier." Whatever I do, I'm doing it for the village and for Charles.

VICTORIA   *(takes Rose aside)*   Look here, child, the captain isn't going to be at the Raven at all tonight.

ROSE   *(stubbornly)*   Then I'll wait in the hall.

VICTORIA   You will not wait in the hall. You will wait in my room. Aren't I a handsome fellow? A kiss, this minute.

ROSE   Yours to command. *(Kisses her; to Bullock)*   If the ensign wants . . .

VICTORIA   Here's a pound for your chickens, child. Now let's be off to the dance. And you, there, carry the chickens. *(Victoria pulls Rose away. Bullock follows. Melinda comes in)*

MELINDA   *(looking around)*   Heaven help me! A hazardous enterprise; if I'm found out the whole town will condemn me. Ah, Worthy, there is nothing I wouldn't do to make you mine! Worthy!

(Brazen comes in)

BRAZEN   *(catches sight of Melinda and looks at his watch)*   As punctual as the bugler! Madam, I am your humble servant and so forth.—Nice little river, the old Severn.—Do you like fishing, madam?

MELINDA   A pleasant, melancholy pastime.

BRAZEN   I'll fetch the fishing rods at once.

MELINDA   *(aside)*   Where can Worthy be?

BRAZEN   You must know, madam, that I have fought in Flanders against the French, in Hungary against the Turks, in Tangiers against the Moors, but I have never been so much in love before. Slit my belly, madam, if you will; in all my campaigns I have never met so fine a woman as your ladyship.

MELINDA   And of all the men I have known, none has ever paid me so fine a compliment. You soldiers are the best-mannered of men, that we must allow.

BRAZEN   Some of us, madam, not all! There are brutes among us too, sad brutes, ah yes, madam. As for me, I've always had the good fortune to prove agreeable. I have had splendid offers, madam. I might have married a German princess, worth some fifty thousand pounds a year. But her bathroom disgusted me. Shall we repair to the woods? *(Melinda makes a negative gesture)* The daughter of a Turkish pasha fell in love with me when I was a prisoner among the infidels. She offered to steal her father's treasure and run away with me. But I don't know why, my time had not yet come. Hanging and marriage, you know, are governed by fate. Fate has preserved me for one of the most seductive ladies in all Shrewsbury. And, so I am told, one of the wealthiest as well. What would you say to a stroll in these delightful woods, my little nymph? *(Melinda tries to run away, but Brazen catches up with her and pulls her into the wood)*

(The swan swims closer to the shore as Lucy and Mike reappear)

LUCY   The one thing I'll miss when I'm over there is Felix.

MIKE   He'll miss us too on Sunday afternoons. *(Takes out a slip of paper)*

LUCY   What's that?

MIKE   From the New World. It was given to me by a coachman who got it from a Liverpool sailor. Listen! Run along, Felix! Down with the king. Down with the archbishop, down with the lords. We in the New World need no more kings and no more lords, who grew fat on our sweat. We in the State of America wish to be an English colony no longer. Signed: Franklin.

LUCY   When did you learn to read, Mike? *(She takes the paper from him)*

MIKE   Oh, Fred showed me yesterday how it's done.

LUCY   It says something entirely different.

MIKE   What does it say?

LUCY   "Declaration of Independence."

MIKE   Sounds good too. Read it.

LUCY   "That all men are created equal, that they are endowed by their . . ." I can't make out that word . . . "with certain . . . rights: Life, Liberty and the Pursuit of Happiness . . ."

MIKE   Lucy, that's the place for us.

LUCY   *(as if announcing)*   At the Sign of the Swan, Proprietors

Mr. and Mrs. Mike W. Laughton. *(Play-acting)* Don't take in any more guests, Mike W. Laughton. All I've left on the spit is two sides of beef.

MIKE   Right, Mrs. Mike W. Laughton. I'll just have to turn away the lord mayor of Philadelphia. But first, let's have a little dance, in the kitchen. After all, we've paid the musicians. *(They dance)*

LUCY   Bolt the doors, Mike W. Laughton, the redcoats are coming!

MIKE   Load my musket, woman! Those god-damned English! Bang—bang! These muskets aren't oiled properly, Mrs. Mike W. Laughton!

LUCY   My best salad oil!

MIKE   Bang. Bull's-eye. *(He stretches out on the ground)*
(Enter the farm boys, followed by Kite disguised as a preacher)

THE FARM BOYS *(walking up to the swan)*   Kitchie-kitchie.

KITE *(who has followed them)*   Kitchie-kitchie.
(The swan swims away hurriedly)

KITE *(preaching)*   Brothers and sisters in Christ! My visits to the sick have chanced to bring me to your lovely Severn on this fine day. And I feel I should say a few words to you. I said to myself: What do my dear sisters and brothers in the villages know about the great recruiting campaign for our good King George's army, which has been going on these past few weeks in town and country? In these weeks when England's glory and prestige in the world are at stake. In these weeks His eye is upon us. It is written in Deuteronomy, Book 2, Chapter 27, Verse 14: The Lord sees the black ant on the black stone in the black night. Dearly beloved, are there any questions that torment you? Speak up, my son.

WILLIAM   Your Reverence, is it not true that a man may do his duty by staying home as well?

KITE   A most intelligent question, a question that deserves an answer. Dearly beloved, it has come to the attention of the church that there are some in these parts who shrink back from defending English liberty in America because their flesh is weak and afraid. Nonsense, say I. Flesh is dust and shall return to dust, but England is England and will be England for all eternity. Not only here, but in that godforsaken America as well, ye shining lights of Micklesbury!

MIKE   But isn't it true, Your Reverence, that the people over there are people just like us?

KITE   *(thundering)*   What about geographology, you snotnose? What about the Ninth Commandment, you slopjar? Is it not written: "Thou shalt not covet thy neighbor's wife and house"? And hasn't America belonged to our good King George of England ever since the Lord created it? And now it is being coveted by those Americans, the devil take every last one of them, begging the ladies' pardon.

MIKE   Isn't it true, Your Reverence, that there are no lords or kings in America?

KITE   Whoever put that into your head, you whiskey thief? According to the latest census, there are 44,302 lords in America and no less than seven kings, and not a one of them is any good.

APPLETREE   That's a fact.

MIKE   And isn't it true, Your Reverence, that you aren't a reverend gent at all and that you're Mr. Kite, son of Cleopatra the Gypsy, jailbird and lifelong sergeant?

(Maggie cries out; the farm boys look at Kite)

KITE   What a bunch of creeps you turned out to be. *(To Appletree who salutes him)* Deserters will be shot on the spot. *(Kite departs amid loud laughter)*

WILLIAM   I'll be damned.

SALLY   *(rising)*   Who'll come to the woods with me? I know where to find raspberries!

(Appletree, slightly embarrassed, follows her)

MIKE   *(getting up)*   Let's go. *(He and Lucy go into the woods)*

MAGGIE   *(in tears)*   William, take me home. *(William leads Maggie into the woods)*

(Melinda comes out of the woods, followed by Brazen who is playing a panpipe)

MELINDA   Oh, Worthy, my dear Worthy, save me from this madman!

BRAZEN   As you see, madam, the king's service has preserved my vigor, enabling me to serve the most ardent of English women with undiminished powers of body and soul. Confidentially, madam, you see before you a warrior who longs to lay

his laurel-crowned head on a loving bosom. Which explains
why I am offering you the opportunity of accepting my hand.
(Pearmain, wearing a uniform, comes in)

PEARMAIN   Stand by, captain!

BRAZEN   On Sunday?

PEARMAIN   Yessir, captain. The inspecting officer from London, sir!

BRAZEN   I'm busy!

PEARMAIN   Yessir, captain! *(Goes out)*

BRAZEN   Melinda!

MELINDA   Captain Brazen, how can I accept your tempting
offer? Surrender myself to a soldier whom the king may take
away from me at any time? I've sworn not to. And I shall keep
my oath. I shall never marry a soldier.

BRAZEN   Never marry a soldier?

MELINDA   Never, captain. Your uniform will always be a barrier between us.

(Worthy storms in with pistols)

MELINDA *(overjoyed)*   Worthy!

WORTHY   Fickle woman! And all for this gaudy fly-by-night
. . . who has the audacity . . . Here, take your choice! *(Holds
out the pistols to Brazen)*

BRAZEN   Pistols? Are they loaded?

WORTHY   Each with its charge of death.

MELINDA   What has this to do with you, Mr. Worthy? I didn't
know you took the slightest interest in my affairs.

(Drumroll)

BRAZEN   Harkee. Stand by. Besides, I'm a foot soldier. I don't
favor pistols.

WORTHY   I am here to fight for the honor of Shrewsbury. We
men of Shrewsbury will not stand idly by while our women
throw themselves at men who tomorrow will be gone over
the hills and over the sea.

BRAZEN   Fire and brimstone! Sir, I've tasted the smoke from the
cannon's iron mouth. *(He picks a pistol and takes a dueling stance)*

MELINDA *(to Worthy)*   Monster! *(She sobs)* How can you! It's all
over between us. *(Runs out)*

WORTHY   That's it! Run away! Leave me here to die alone.
(Takes his place and counts paces) One, two, three . . .

BRAZEN   Stop! Where's the lady?

WORTHY   *(darkly)*   Gone.

BRAZEN   In that case, why fight? Embrace me, my dear fellow, life is short enough as it is. *(Drops the pistol and walks over to the bench. Worthy sits down beside him.)*

WORTHY   Turning tail! And in the king's uniform!

BRAZEN   Come, come, Worthy, the uniform doesn't make the man.

WORTHY   How can you say that? You who owe your despicable triumphs entirely to your uniform?

BRAZEN   On the contrary, Mr. Worthy. I've learned different. My uniform stands in my way. Excuse me, my dear fellow. *(Goes out)*

(Kite drives all the soldiers out of the woods. The girls are trying to hold them, calling out their names piteously)

KITE   Inspection! All in uniform back to town! Get going, you sons of bitches! *(Turning to the girls)* Civilians can stay. *(To Sally, sobbing and clutching at Appletree)* Stop bawling!

GIRL   *(calling after the drummer)*   Jonathan!

WORTHY   *(who has remained sitting on the bench)*   Bandits!

9

At the house of Mr. Balance.

Same evening. Balance is reading a letter; he is very upset. Simpkins is holding a candle.

SIMPKINS   Bad news, sir?

BALANCE   Frightful.

SIMPKINS   I'm sorry, sir.

BALANCE   The sun is setting on the British Empire.
    (Worthy comes in)

BALANCE   How is the inspection coming along, Worthy?

WORTHY   *(shrugs his shoulders)*   I'm afraid that lot of recruits in the market place won't empty my warehouse for me. It's not enough to have boots for the soldiers; we must have soldiers for the boots. Here comes Plume.

BALANCE   Dreadful! *(Plume comes in)* How are things, Plume? I hope the inspecting officer from London found your company up to strength.

PLUME   The inspecting officer from London found exactly eleven recruits.

BALANCE   Terrible.

WORTHY   If it will do you any good, Plume, I'll join your company. There is nothing to keep me here any longer.

BALANCE   What's got into you, Worthy? You're a shoe manufacturer, not a soldier. You might as well ask me to shoulder a musket.

PLUME   Mr. Balance, my mind is made up. I'm asking for a transfer to East India. Give your daughter my respectful regards.

BALANCE   Captain Plume!

PLUME   Mr. Balance?

BALANCE   Be seated.

PLUME   I am seated.

SIMPKINS   He is seated.

BALANCE   Captain Plume, you can't go to the East Indies, your place is in America. I shall not be divulging military secrets if I tell you the bad news that has precipitated the inspector general's visit. Boston has fallen to the rebels.

SIMPKINS   Impossible!

BALANCE   I beg your pardon? *(He motions Simpkins to leave the room)*

PLUME   All right. We've lost Boston. Do you expect me to retake Boston with my bare hands?

BALANCE   Plume, you can't let England down in this fateful hour, and neither can Shrewsbury. Until now I did not think it necessary to resort to compulsory recruitment. Now I see that it is necessary. *(Takes a law book from the bookcase)* Recruitment Act, 1704.

WORTHY   But this is 1776. There was a scandal when they tried to enforce these laws in Welshpool.

BALANCE   But they yielded two full companies of able-bodied convicts. Are we to allow undesirable elements to grow fat in our prisons or defile our streets? Put them in the army! In a way you could even call it cruelty to leave these people in jail, or let the unemployed vegetate in the streets, when they could be dying a hero's death for English liberty in the New World. It is in every respect our patriotic duty to give them this opportunity. Come with me to the prison, Captain Plume.

(Melinda comes in)

MELINDA   Uncle! Will you permit me to speak to Mr. Worthy in private?

BALANCE   Gladly, my child. Do speak to him, he's got a bee in his bonnet. Make yourselves at home, Simpkins will bring you tea. Come along, captain. *(Goes out with Plume)*

MELINDA   Surely you understand, Mr. Worthy, that after what has happened I find it intolerable that my letters should be in your possession.

WORTHY   I shall return them to you before I embark, madam. Permit me to bid you farewell, Miss Moorhill.

MELINDA   How long have you been in this traveling humor?

WORTHY   It is only natural, madam, for us to avoid what disturbs our peace of mind.

MELINDA   I should interpret it rather as a desire for change, which is even more natural in men.

WORTHY   Change would seem to have a special attraction for women as well, madam; why, otherwise, would you be so fond of it?

MELINDA   You are mistaken, Mr. Worthy! I am not so fond of change as to leave home. Nor do I think it wise of you to fling yourself into danger and expense in the slender expectation of questionable pleasures.

WORTHY   The pleasures awaiting me abroad are indeed questionable, madam, but one thing I am sure of: I shall meet with less cruelty on the battlefields of the New World, amongst the barbarous cowboys and fur trappers, than I have found here, in my own country.

MELINDA   Mr. Worthy, you and I have wasted enough words. I believe we would come to an agreement sooner if each of us were to tender his accounts.

WORTHY   Indeed, madam. If we do, you will find yourself very
much in my debt. My fears, sighs, vows, promises, assiduities,
and anxieties have accrued for a whole year without eliciting
the slightest return.

MELINDA   A whole year! Oh, Mr. Worthy! What you owe me
cannot be repaid by less than seven years of servitude. How
did you treat me last year when, taking advantage of my innocence and poverty, you tried to make me your mistress, that
is, your slave? Add to that your shameless behavior, your loose
language, the familiar tone of your letters, your ill-man-
nered visits—do you remember all that, Mr. Worthy? *(Sobs)*

WORTHY   I remember well. Too bad nothing came of it.—But
you for your part must take into account . . .

MELINDA   Sir, I'll take nothing into account. It's to your interest
that I should forget. You have treated me barbarously; I have
only been cruel to you. Weigh the one against the other. And
now, if you wish to turn a new leaf, stop acting like an
adventurer and behave like a gentleman. How could you
leave me standing in the market place the other day like a
leftover sack of wool?

WORTHY   I only did that to test you, and, believe me, I regret
it more than anything I have ever done. But you and that
captain, before my very eyes . . . *(His voice breaks)*

MELINDA   I was only trying to arouse your jealousy. That was
the only reason; can't you believe me?

WORTHY   Melinda.

MELINDA   Worthy. *(They go toward each other, arms outstretched)*
(Simpkins comes in)

SIMPKINS   Captain Brazen!

BRAZEN *(pushes him aside)*   Mister Brazen! *(He stands there beaming
in a shabby civilian frock coat)*
(Melinda looks at him in consternation)

BRAZEN   Melinda! Your wish is fulfilled. For you I did what I've
never done before. One word from you and I laid down my
weapons. Darling, come to my arms! *(He puts his arm around
her waist)*

MELINDA   How dare you? Can't you see Mr. Worthy? *(Slaps his
face)*

BRAZEN   No, no. I'm blinded. Worthy! 'Sbodkins! My lady has

wit in her very fingertips. Deplorable blunder. I beg your
pardon, madam, the ways of an old warrior, don't you know.
Worthy! So you're the lucky man! Have I got it straight?

WORTHY   Heaven forbid! Rather say unlucky. I've got more
than enough proof of that now.

MELINDA   Worthy!

WORTHY   Your letters will be returned to you, madam. If you
care to read them over, you will see what you have done to
me.

MELINDA   Albert!

WORTHY   No, it's all clear to me now, only too clear.

MELINDA   No!

WORTHY   No? Yes. Can your fickleness go so far as to deceive
this man who has sacrificed his career to you at your bidding?
If you do that, there's no gentleman on earth who will have
anything to do with you.

MELINDA   This is too much. Mr. Worthy . . .

WORTHY   This is too much. What's too much? Stick to this
dubious chameleon, since you obviously prefer outward glit-
ter to a true heart. No, I'm not the lucky one, Mr. Brazen. But
I don't envy you your luck if your great sacrifice earns you
such striking favors.

MELINDA   My favors were bestowed on the wrong man, Mr.
Worthy. From now on you can expect nothing better, if you
should ever cross my path again. I beg your forgiveness, Mr.
Brazen.

BRAZEN   Granted.

MELINDA   Would you see me home and . . .

BRAZEN   And so forth, madam.—Courage, my dear fellow. The
fortunes of war, you know. (Goes out with Melinda)

SIMPKINS   (entering)   Tea, Mr. Worthy?

WORTHY   (bellows)   Whiskey!

SIMPKINS   Sir, I must beg your pardon for these little over-
sights. (His voice breaking) Boston has fallen to the rebels.
(Simpkins goes out)
(Balance and Plume enter in a dejected mood. They sit down without
a word)

BALANCE   (calling)   Simpkins!

SIMPKINS   (entering)   Mr. Balance!

BALANCE *(shouts)* Whiskey!

SIMPKINS   You must forgive me today. *(Goes out)*

BALANCE   What's the matter with him?

WORTHY *(over his shoulder)* Boston.

(Pause)

BALANCE   Why are you looking out the window so gloomily, Worthy?

WORTHY   You don't seem too cheerful yourself, sir.

BALANCE   Worthy, we've been too lenient in Shrewsbury these last few years. The jail is empty. One solitary prisoner. A sex maniac, and that's all. A drop in the bucket.

SIMPKINS *(comes in)* Lady Prude. Mr. Smuggler.

BALANCE   Lady Prude? I have an idea. Show them in.

(Lady Prude and Mr. Smuggler come in)

PRUDE   Balance, one more Sunday like this and I shall leave Shrewsbury forever. The behavior of those soldiers on the banks of our fair Severn would have put Sodom and Gomorrah to shame. Mr. Smuggler, the banker from London, was here for lunch. His hair stood on end.

SMUGGLER   Your servant, Mr. Balance.

BALANCE   Your servant, Mr. Smuggler.

PRUDE   I see one of the main culprits right here in your parlor. Molly Fastspittle can tell you all about him. And so can Rose, my tenant's daughter.

PLUME   Sir, since this town has showered me with insults instead of soldiers, I beg to take my leave. *(Goes out)*

BALANCE   Captain Plume!—*(To Lady Prude)* I do wish you would learn to control your unfortunate prejudice against the only people who can hope to give England a certain measure of order and discipline.

PRUDE   For the last ten days I have been battling the military rabble; to no avail.

BALANCE   Do you call the heroic sons of England military rabble? They are risking their lives for you, my lady.

PRUDE   I'm paying them for it. A fifth of my income goes toward their upkeep. But I'm not paying them to sing bawdy songs and sin in the bushes on the Sabbath.

BALANCE   My lady, it is not my habit to scrutinize the bushes on the Sabbath.

SMUGGLER   In London we have special houses for such things.

PRUDE   We have them here too, Mr. Smuggler. I could tell you a thing or two. Chicken Street!

SMUGGLER   *(to himself)*   Chicken Street!

PRUDE   And not only in Chicken Street. In the taverns and inns! This town is overrun with disreputable elements of all ages, drunkards, pickpockets, and unemployed, who flaunt their sins with impunity. Will the authorities never . . .

BALANCE   *(who has been listening with growing interest, now raises his hand)*   You're perfectly right, my lady, and the authorities *will.* We shall teach the rabble patriotism. We shall give justice and morality free rein, even if it means filling Shrewsbury's prison to the bursting point!

PRUDE   You are contemplating a cleanup?

BALANCE   A most thorough cleanup, Lady Prude.

10

At the Raven.

Victoria is asleep on a chair. She has taken off her sword, boots, and coat. Commotion in the inn. Loud knocking and shouts of "Open up," "The constables."

VICTORIA   What's going on?

ROSE   *(from behind a screen)*   There's a rumpus down in the hall.

VICTORIA   Five in the morning. The night has passed without trouble; I've slept soundly, but I'm afraid my companion is less pleased. Poor Rose! *(To Rose)* Good morning, my pet. And how are you this fine morning? *(Starts to pull on her boots)*

ROSE   Same as yesterday. You've made me neither better nor worse.

VICTORIA   Didn't you like your bed-fellow?

ROSE   I don't know if I had one or not. Ruining a poor girl's reputation for nothing!

VICTORIA   I saved your reputation. You didn't get your lace frock, but don't fret. I shall give you much nicer things than the captain.

ROSE   You can't. Now I know.

(*Knocking at the door*)

VOICE   Open up! The constables!

VICTORIA   Good God, I'm half naked.

VOICE (*outside*)   Open the door or we'll break it down!

VICTORIA   Just a minute!—Rose, my hat, give me my hat.

(*Constable Bridewell forces his way in*)

VICTORIA   What's the meaning of this?

BRIDEWELL   Two more lovebirds! (*To Victoria*) This is a raid. You're under arrest.

VICTORIA   Get back, fellow! If you come any closer you're a dead duck.

BRIDEWELL   Put away that sword, pipsqueak, or I'll knock out your milk teeth, in the name of the king!

VICTORIA   Just try it, flatfoot!

BRIDEWELL   That's an insult to His Majesty! Insult me and you insult the king. You're under arrest, pipsqueak.

(*Sergeant Kite comes in*)

BRIDEWELL   Another haul, Mr. Kite. Goose and gander, both in the trap.

KITE   Blarney!

(*Lady Prude comes in*)

PRUDE (*sees Rose*)   Rose! Rose! My poor child! Did he . . .

VICTORIA   I protected her, Lady Prude. Captain Plume was going to . . .

BRIDEWELL   And you did instead.

ROSE   He hasn't done a thing.

KITE   That's our ensign, Mr. Wilful. Our job is to jail civilians, my lady.

PRUDE   Our job is to jail monsters and he's a monster! Constable, take him away.

KITE   Hands off. You can't arrest an officer without the consent of his superior. Just a minute. (*Goes out and is heard calling out "captain"*)

VICTORIA   My lady, I don't think there's any need to get Captain Plume . . .

(*Plume comes in without coat or sword, followed by Kite*)

PLUME   Ensign Wilful . . .

ROSE *(runs over to Plume)* I've been wanting to talk to you, captain. I was waiting for you here.

BRIDEWELL In the ensign's room. Caught in flagrante.

PRUDE Rose, come here!

PLUME *(going toward Victoria)* So this is how you carry out my orders, ensign? Boston has fallen and you amuse yourself— like this. There's never been anything like it in all military history. Why do the likes of you join the army, that's what I'd like to know. For no other reason than to f . . . fulfill your desires. Man, I don't know what to think of you.

ROSE Man! Ha! I wouldn't be too hard on him, captain. He's quite harmless.

PLUME Harmless? Hmm. An uncontrolled satyr. *(Rose giggles)* This is no laughing matter.

ROSE It is, though!

PLUME What are you anyway? No ensign would behave like that, only a . . . Harmless? *(A light dawns on him)* I'll speak to you later. *(To the audience)* Victoria Balance! Well, I'll be jiggered! She herself never shows up, but she keeps every other girl away from me. I'll show her! *(To Lady Prude)* My lady, I cannot but agree with you. Constable, take the ensign to jail!

KITE Captain, sir, what's the good of this idiotic raid? We were looking for grenadiers, and now we're even losing our officers.

PRUDE You don't understand, sergeant. Your captain intends to clean up not only Shrewsbury but the king's army as well. Constable, do your duty.

PLUME *(virtuously)* Exactly, Lady Prude. The law makes no distinction between civilians and soldiers.

PRUDE Well said!

PLUME *(to Victoria)* You have defiled the king's uniform; off to prison with you!

BRIDEWELL Come on, pipsqueak. *(Grabs her)*

VICTORIA Captain!

PLUME One more thing. Rose, my child, come here. *(He puts his arms around her)* I swear, before these witnesses, to make up for all the wrong this scoundrel has done you. And now, take him away.

PRUDE   Stop! Just a word. It seems to me that we've caught the
   pike, but what about the shark? Sir, behind that cloak of
   moral indignation I detect your own lust, naked and una-
   bashed.

VICTORIA   How discerning of you, Lady Prude. You libertine!
   But I'll put a spoke in your wheel. This note bears your
   signature, Captain Plume. It fell due at midnight. Can you
   meet it? I demand immediate payment!

PLUME   Wilful!

VICTORIA   You can't pay? Very well! Constable, take this man
   to debtors' prison at once. I demand it.

PRUDE   Quite so! Gets them with child, and won't marry; bor-
   rows money, and won't pay it back! Take him away too!

KITE   'Sblood!

BRIDEWELL   But I can't arrest a man for debt without a warrant.
   I'm sorry, my lady. Besides, he's an officer.

KITE   Exactly!

VICTORIA   I thought the law made no distinction between officers and civilians.

PRUDE   Take him away!

KITE   Hands off! I'll bite off my leg before I let you arrest my
   captain.

PRUDE   Sergeant, you have shown the most commendable zeal
   all night. Don't weaken now, let virtue be your captain.

PLUME   Dismiss, Mr. Kite. Farewell, Rose, we must part.
   Never accept money from strangers. (Plume goes out, followed
   by Bridewell and Victoria)

KITE   Now we've got a company and no captain. (Goes out)

ROSE   What's going to happen now?

PRUDE   Nothing, my child. You will go back to Picklewood.

ROSE   But there's not a man left there.

PRUDE   Thanks to you, my poor misguided lamb!

11

Jailhouse.

Plume is busy with his toilet. Victoria is sitting on a bench.

PLUME   We wouldn't want to waste our time here, Wilful. Let
me teach you the favorite song of our glorious company. Two
—three! *(Sings)*

Seventeen reservists from Z Battery
Stand eyeing the women of Gaa.
Then each reservist pushes
One of them into the bushes
Where they take a close look at the evening star.
    And that will be the only star
    She'll see in Gaa
    It stays there for an hour or two, then au revoir.
    Aha.
*(Plume motions to Victoria. Under Plume's direction she sings the
stanza over)*

PLUME   Second verse!   *(Sings)*

In the morning you won't find Z Battery
They ride off at first light.
But on leaving each reservist
Has a fig to give his dearest
—Which makes a pound of figs, if I am right.
    That fig will be the only thi-
    ng she'll get to see
    A fig is all she ever gets, apparently.
    Dear me.

(Victoria repeats the stanza)

VICTORIA   Dear me . . .
(Through the bars of the door one sees the prisoners being driven by)

BRIDEWELL *(outside)*   Eleven shillings and I'll turn you loose.

PICKPOCKET *(outside)*   Eleven shillings? That's highway robbery.

BRIDEWELL *(outside)*   Lock him up!

MINER *(outside)*   I've got at least fifteen shillings in the house. Send for my wife.

BRIDEWELL *(outside)*   Lock him up!

PLUME   Filthy scum!

VICTORIA   You may find it hard to understand, but having you arrested was an act of real friendship, Plume. You are better off here than falling into the snares of the Mollys and Roses who pursue you without appreciating a man of your fine qualities. *(Plume remains silent)* The money doesn't matter to me. I've proved that I'm not petty in these matters. But why should I always be the one to finance your debaucheries? *(Bridewell comes in with fresh water for Victoria)*

BRIDEWELL *(gleeful)*   Come on, pipsqueak. Time to wash! You're appearing in court.

VICTORIA   I don't want to wash.

BRIDEWELL   What?

VICTORIA   I have a cold.

PLUME   He has a cold.

VICTORIA   Yes, I have a cold. *(She sneezes)*

PLUME   Whatever made you join the army? I mean, if you're so delicate and inclined to colds.
(Bridewell pours the water into the pail)

VICTORIA *(shouting at the constable)*   I told you I have a cold!

BRIDEWELL   I can't make out why these people never want to wash.

PLUME *(cruelly)*   I suppose you just sprinkle powder on it. Cleanliness is the hallmark of a good soldier. Before washing, a soldier removes his clothes. With soap, and, if necessary after field drill, with pumice, he cleanses all parts of his body.

BRIDEWELL   Take off your coat and wash!

VICTORIA   No.

PLUME   He likes dirt, that's what it is.

BRIDEWELL   In the name of the king, off with your coat and wash!

VICTORIA   Not as long as I live. *(She eludes Bridewell and he chases her)*

VICTORIA   Captain!

PLUME   No rough stuff, constable. *(Motions him to stop)*

BRIDEWELL   Fusses like a blooming woman.

PLUME   Doesn't he, though? *(Bridewell goes out)* It's not just a question of physical cleanliness, Wilful; you're a deplorable character in every respect. You malinger, you squirm out of things, and you try to deceive your superiors. You are neither honest nor straightforward. Your motives for joining the army are obscure. How do I know you're not a common spy?

VICTORIA   That's not fair, captain.

PLUME   How dare you! And where's your soldierly bearing? I'll teach you discipline. On duty and off, I set the tone around here, understand? Altogether, your behavior is an offense to the moral standards of our profession. No back talk! Let one example suffice: an ensign keeps his fingers out of his captain's love affairs, even if it kills him. Now I shall have to see how I can make it up to that poor girl. To top it all, you seem to have disappointed her. She didn't seem very enthusiastic about you this morning, Wilful. But in spite of all that, because I still feel an inexplicable liking for you, I'll make you a fair proposition. Tear up that note. For two pounds the constable will let you go.

VICTORIA   No. Besides, you haven't left me two pounds.

PLUME   Then you'll stop at nothing?

VICTORIA   That's right. You must pay your debts.

(In the background more prisoners are led past)

UNEMPLOYED MAN *(outside)*   You've no right to lock me up just because I can't find work.

ANOTHER PRISONER *(outside)*   The mills have shut down.

BRIDEWELL *(outside)*   But the barracks are open. Get in there!

UNEMPLOYED MAN *(outside)*   It's a bloody shame!

BRIDEWELL *(outside)*   Halt! Who said that? You've insulted the constabulary. I'm turning you over to the dragoons.

(Kite brings in another prisoner, the banker Smuggler, wearing a lady's dressing gown over his fine underwear)

SMUGGLER   For the last time I'm asking you to return my

clothes. *(He smiles and bows to Plume and Victoria)* A mistake, gentlemen.

KITE   Were you or were you not in Chicken Street? *(Goes out)*

(Smuggler offers cigars. Victoria declines. Plume takes two)

SMUGGLER   Gentlemen! Boston has fallen, and with it the stock-market. Obviously firm measures are in order. The decimated ranks of our regiments must be replenished—but not with bankers! If you start putting *us* in the army, we may decide to let the New World go. What would that do to your profession, young man?

(Worthy bursts in)

WORTHY   *(to Bridewell)*   Open up, you blockhead! *(Bridewell unlocks the door)* Mr. Smuggler. Some subordinate has blundered. Come with me. A thousand pardons. Hello, Plume.

SMUGGLER   Captain Plume, your servant.

(Leaves with Worthy and Kite)

(Plume offers Victoria a cigar. They smoke in silence for a while)

PLUME   Wilful, I find it hard to understand how Victoria could choose a messenger of your stamp.

VICTORIA   Perhaps she couldn't get any other. ("Loch Lomond" *is heard from backstage)*

PLUME   It's the same old story, Wilful. Miss Balance and I have failed to make contact again.

(Tears well up in Victoria's eyes, she steps aside with dignity)

PLUME   Since it's "marriage or nothing" in these latitudes, as it should be, I suppose nothing will come of it, except that I'll go wandering through the foggy forests of Massachusetts, the corn fields of Virginia, the swamps of Delaware, and the burning prairies of Maryland with the image of a wonderful girl in my heart.

VICTORIA   *(angrily)*   I should have thought Miss Balance deserved a better fate than to have her image carried through burning cities along with the drunkards, thieves and desperadoes of all sorts that you will be in command of from now on. Aren't you ashamed of such a company? I shall discard my uniform without delay, and I urge you to do the same.

PLUME   *(wearily)*   Go right ahead. *(Victoria takes fright)* Let me tell you something; a cheese on the shelf wants to be paid for before it's eaten. But one thing it doesn't do—it doesn't bite the customer in the leg.

(Enter Bridewell with Plume's hat and sword)

BRIDEWELL   The justice of the peace wants you in court right away, captain. He is furious about your being arrested.

VICTORIA   What about the note?

PLUME   Look here! I'm riding off in the morning and embarking the day after, note or no note. Our brief acquaintance has now come to an end. When I come back in a year or two, if I do come back, I hope I find you less designing.—Your servant, Miss Victoria Balance. *(Goes out)*

VICTORIA   Go to the devil, you beast! *(Starts bawling)*

Interlude before the Curtain

Worthy leads Mr. Smuggler past quickly, covering him with his coat. They are followed by Bridewell, who is pulling a number of prisoners along on a rope. The last prisoner is the miner, who sings loudly.

MINER *(sings)*

> Everybody paid—more or less
> When the king was in distress
> Armies cost a lot each day
> All paid up without delay
> All except for E.N. Smith

BRIDEWELL   Quiet!

MINER

> But the king got very tough
> Didn't think they gave enough
> Plucked them out of bed and alehouse
> Packed them all off to the jailhouse
> All except for E.N. Smith.

12

In the house of Mr. Balance.

The library, where Simpkins is waiting with the judicial robes. Balance receives Plume in the adjoining hall, which has been converted into a courtroom.

BALANCE   Captain Plume! Excuse this unfortunate incident. Do permit me to advance you the thirty pounds. Bridewell! *(Bridewell comes in and Balance gives him the money)* Give this to the ensign—what's his name again?—in return for the note. *(Bridewell goes out)*

PLUME   Thank you, Mr. Balance.

BALANCE   Your ensign seems to be a rather peculiar fellow. The impudence of the man!

PLUME   Yes, indeed. Just between you and me, sir, a most unusual person, obstinate and totally unfit for military service. I've had to discharge him.

BALANCE   Aren't you being a bit too hard on him? My dear captain. You will sit beside me on the bench. Captain Brazen ought to be here before long. *(He goes into the library)*

PLUME   Thank you, Mr. Balance. *(He glances through the list of names)*

SIMPKINS *(in the library, helping Balance on with his robe)*   I understand the raid last night was rather productive, sir.

BALANCE   Yes. There are always plenty of rogues.

SIMPKINS   I presume that not a few of them will be put to the sword.

BALANCE   Don't be so bloodthirsty, Simpkins.

SIMPKINS   Yes, sir. Shrewsbury expects a good deal of today's trial.

(Melinda and Lucy come in)

MELINDA   My life is shattered, sir. Captain Brazen, whom an incomprehensible caprice led me to encourage, has resigned from the army, and I feel obligated to him.

BALANCE   What about Worthy?

MELINDA   That's just it!

BALANCE   What's this about quitting the service in the midst of a war? Just when Boston has fallen! I won't stand for it. What would become of England?

SIMPKINS   Monstrous!

BALANCE   I beg your pardon?

MELINDA   But uncle, how can you make him stay in the service?

BALANCE   Leave that to me, my child. (*Ponders for a moment*) Civil law—false representations concerning non-existent dowry.

MELINDA   Uncle, you *must* send him off to America!

BALANCE   Don't worry. Lucy, what do you know of your mistress's intimate affairs?

LUCY   Nothing, sir.

BALANCE   In other words, everything. Lucy, go and find Captain Brazen. Tell him you've been sent by your mistress, who is at home, choking with tears. Tell him her entire fortune was invested in a cargo of tea, which the rebels have wantonly dumped into Boston harbor.

LUCY   My wages!

BALANCE   Tell him that in view of her misfortune Miss Moorhill feels she can no longer expect the captain to abandon his glorious military career. If Captain Brazen shows any signs of chivalry, self-sacrifice or sincere devotion, which seems unlikely, you must ask him for two pounds for the household. That should bring him to his senses.

LUCY   Is the money really gone, sir?

BALANCE   Run along now, Lucy, and trust your masters.

LUCY   Very well, sir. But in money matters, I like to know where I stand. (*Goes out*)

MELINDA   Uncle, I don't know how I shall ever repay you.

SIMPKINS   (*to the departing Balance*) God be with you, sir.

(*Kite and Pearmain, the latter carrying bundles of uniforms, come into the adjoining courtroom. Bridewell brings in the pickpocket and puts him under the measuring rod; Pearmain takes his measure. The public enters from the other side of the hall*)

UNEMPLOYED MAN'S WIFE   They got my husband. Did they get yours?

MINER'S WIFE   Yes, they got mine too.

THE BROAD-SHOULDERED MAN   They want to put them all in the army.

JENNY   They've gone through all the taverns.

MRS. COBB   And certain other houses as well.

UNEMPLOYED MAN'S WIFE   I hear they've nabbed a banker and an officer.

THE BROAD-SHOULDERED MAN   You won't see them here, you can lay to that.

BRIDEWELL   Silence!

(Balance has come into the courtroom in the meantime, and has walked up to the table)

BALANCE   The court is in session.

PLUME   Name?

PICKPOCKET   Billy Pickpocket.

KITE   If it please the court, I would like to testify in this case as king's counsel.

BALANCE   You have the floor, sergeant.

KITE   Bridewell, where's the watch? *(Turning to the pimp)* Freddy, this individual stole a gold watch from you, am I right?

PIMP   It's the gospel truth, mister.

PICKPOCKET   Beg your pardon, Your Worship. It's my watch.

KITE   Can you prove to the court that this is your watch, Freddy?

PIMP   Tell 'em, Kitty.

KITTY   Your Worship, I gave Freddy a watch for his birthday. It's got a scratch on the back.

KITE   That's the one!

KITTY   "Kitty," he says to me, he says: "Kitty, if I ever have to wallop you, just say: 'Freddy, the watch!'"

PIMP   She's too free with her money, Your Worship. And don't talk so much.

BALANCE   *(to the pickpocket)*   A clear case of pickpocketing. That man is fit for military service.

KITE   Absolutely.

PLUME   Take him away.

(The pickpocket is led away; Freddy starts to leave too)

JENNY   They're picking up everybody they can lay their hands on.

KITE *(calls out)* Just a minute, Freddy. *(Addressing the bench)* Name: Freddy Big. *(To Kitty)* Kitty, is this wretched watch the only thing you ever gave your protector?

KITTY   You don't know my Freddy, Mr. Kite. Whatever I takes in, he takes offa me. Ouch!

(The pimp has slapped her face)

KITE   Your Worship, I believe that does it. I can't save you after that, Freddy, that's pimping.

PIMP   Bartholomy, that ain't fair.

KITE   In the name of the king, I declare this man to be a brutal, lazy and greedy element, and consequently fit for the army.

BALANCE   Take him away.

(The pimp falls down in a faint. He is measured and dragged off)

KITTY *(as the court attendant leads her out)* Freddy, I didn't do it on purpose.

THE BROAD-SHOULDERED MAN   Fine grenadiers they're getting.

MINER'S WIFE   Good enough for over there.

UNEMPLOYED MAN'S WIFE   It's only the scum that's going over now.

(Brazen comes in wearing civilian clothes)

BALANCE   There's Brazen!

BRAZEN   You'll have to excuse me, Mr. Laconic, I'm retiring into private life. I'm getting married.

BALANCE   You don't say! In spite of everything? Amazing! Permit me to prepare Melinda.—Bridewell, who's next?

BRAZEN   Is she here? *(Runs after Balance)*

BALANCE *(goes into the library; to Melinda)* I'm so sorry, my dear, I was mistaken.

BRAZEN *(has followed Balance into the library)* Melinda!

(In the courtroom the miner is brought in and measured)

MINER'S WIFE   Bob!

BRAZEN *(in the library)* My nymph! The parson is waiting, we must leave this instant, my love.

(Melinda faints)

BRAZEN *(to Balance)* Happiness, my dear fellow.

UNEMPLOYED MAN'S WIFE *(in the courtroom)*   Where did they nab him?

MINER'S WIFE   At the Blue Bear; peacefully drinking his ale. Be sensible, don't make a fuss.

(Lucy hurries through the courtroom into the library)

LUCY   I've looked all over for you, Mr. Brazen—at the inn, at the hat shop . . .

BRAZEN   Hahaha! I was at the flower shop.

BALANCE   Ah, you missed him, he knows nothing. The world's beginning to make sense again. Tell him.

LUCY   Mr. Brazen, Miss Moorhill is beside herself. We have to ask you for two pounds for household expenses. All Miss Moorhill's money was invested in a cargo of tea. The rebels have dumped it in Boston harbor.

BRAZEN   All of it?

LUCY   All of it.

BRAZEN   Damnation! The scoundrels! It goes without saying that this relieves you of any obligation to me. Your servant, madam. *(Goes out)*

BALANCE   Simpkins! *(Simpkins comes in)* Take Miss Moorhill to the parlor.

(Balance returns to the courtroom. Simpkins and Lucy leave the library with the unconscious Melinda)

(In the courtroom Bridewell steps forward with the miner)

THE BROAD-SHOULDERED MAN   *(to the miner's wife)*   Your husband has visible means of support. Which means they can't put him in the army. That's the law.

PLUME   Name?

MINER   Bob Miner, sir.

BALANCE   What have you got on him, Bridewell?

BRIDEWELL   Nothing, Your Worship, except that he's a very decent fellow.

BALANCE   Then why have you brought him here?

PLUME   Mr. Balance, let me at least have *one* decent fellow in my company.

BALANCE   Trade?

MINER   Miner. I work in the colliery.

MINER'S WIFE   See! My husband has visible means of support. *(Pause)*

THE BROAD-SHOULDERED MAN   See?

KITE   If it please the court, this man's means of support is not visible; he works underground.

MINER'S WIFE   It's work, though.

BALANCE   You can't be a miner any more, you shall be a grenadier. Thanks to you, other miners will be able to remain miners.

MINER   But I'm a married man.

BALANCE   Don't you know that we've lost Boston?

MINER   No, Your Worship. I don't know the gentleman.

BALANCE   You mean you don't even know what Boston is? Is that all the fate of England means to you? Into the army with you!

PLUME   Take him away.

MINER   Pack of skunks! (*He is led away*)

MINER'S WIFE (*as she is being dragged off*)   You can't do this! Bob! I'm going to have a child!

UNEMPLOYED MAN'S WIFE   What's Boston got to do with him!

JENNY   The whole thing is illegal.

THE BROAD-SHOULDERED MAN   It's legal, but . . .

WIFE OF UNEMPLOYED MAN   They make the laws to suit themselves.

THE BROAD-SHOULDERED MAN   That's it!

BRIDEWELL   Silence!

MRS. COBB (*to Bridewell*)   Stop shouting.
    (*Enter Victoria in the uniform of an ensign*)

VICTORIA (*to Balance*)   My name is Wilful, sir. Captain Plume, the gentleman sitting beside you, must not be permitted to leave England under any circumstances. The wrong he has done is so appalling that I can speak of it only if you clear the court, sir.

BALANCE (*under his breath*)   Victoria, have you lost your mind?

VICTORIA   Oh, you've recognized me?

BALANCE   What is the meaning of this ridiculous masquerade? Go into the library at once! (*Victoria goes out*) Next!

MRS. COBB   They're bringing one in.

UNEMPLOYED MAN'S WIFE   John!

BRIDEWELL   Silence in the court!

JENNY   You're worse than wolves.

BALANCE *(to Victoria in the library)*   So you ran after him.

VICTORIA   You must stop him leaving England.

BALANCE   Is that all?

VICTORIA   You must marry us at once.

BALANCE   Are you out of your mind?

VICTORIA   Do you want your daughter to become a camp follower, creeping after an officer, abandoning herself to him in
some ditch? She has done everything in her power to resist
her emotions. All in vain. She can't go on much longer; not
another minute!

BALANCE   Great God! That damned Plume. *(Calls into the courtroom)* Plume!—Bridewell, send for Captain Brazen.

JENNY   What's up with the ensign?

(Plume goes into the library)

THE BROAD-SHOULDERED MAN *(referring to Plume who walks into the
library)*   Looks like the captain's nose isn't quite clean either.

BALANCE *(to Victoria in the library)*   So you've been pulling the
wool over my eyes. Hiding a criminal love affair under the
king's uniform. Captain Plume, I know all. What have you
got to say for yourself?

PLUME   Well, Mr. Wilful . . .

BALANCE   Mr. Wilful! You persist in speaking of a Mr. Wilful
to me?

PLUME   Yes, sir. Mr. Wilful.

BALANCE   Mr. Wilful?

PLUME   Yes, Mr. Wilful and . . . *(To Victoria)* I'm surprised to
see you in this uniform. Haven't I told you explicitly that I
forgo the pleasure of having you in my company?

VICTORIA   William, we mustn't deceive father any longer. Forgive your Victoria; at this juncture she must tell the truth.
Father, we are married.

BALANCE   Ah!

VICTORIA   We are married in soldier fashion. We soldiers need
no preacher, marriage bells, or license. Our sword is our
honor. We lay it down on the ground. First the young hero
jumps over it, then the amazon. The buck leaps and the whore
jumps. A roll of drums and off to bed. That's how we get
married. The ceremony is brief and dignified. And now your
daughter is bearing twins.

BALANCE   This is too much!

PLUME   On my honor, sir . . .

VICTORIA   Yes, yes, William, defend your honor and deny everything, dishonor me a second time and deal me the finishing blow by saying "There has been nothing between us."

PLUME   I'm surprised at you, Victoria.

BALANCE   Is that all you have to say?

PLUME   Surely you don't believe all this?

BALANCE   I believe it. I know my daughter.

PLUME   There has been nothing between us, sir.

VICTORIA   Nothing! Do you call this nothing! You induce me to put on a uniform and charge me forty pounds for it; you lure me to America to keep me near you! Nothing?!

BALANCE   Nothing indeed! You'll have to get married at once!

VICTORIA   Marry a soldier? Never! Captains are notorious for turning everything they can lay their hands on into cash. They have an inborn aversion to anything green. Sir, I own forests!

BALANCE   Quite right. Plume, you will have to quit the service at once.

PLUME   That's ridiculous.

BALANCE   What's ridiculous?

PLUME   It's my profession, sir!

BALANCE   Your profession! And my reputation?

PLUME   And my duty to England?

BALANCE   And your duty to my daughter?
    (*The loud voices in the library have caught the attention of the people in the courtroom*)

THE BROAD-SHOULDERED MAN   What's going on in there?

KITE   Shh!

BALANCE   You have unlawfully pressed a female into service with the object of abducting her to America. I'll give you five minutes to think it over. It's a father's blessing: my daughter plus twelve hundred pounds a year—hm, let's say one thousand pounds—or the full force of the law: bread and water in a dungeon. (*To Victoria*) Take off those rags.
    (*Victoria goes out*)
    (*Balance returns to the courtroom*)

BALANCE   (*calling through the window*)   Mike!

THE BROAD-SHOULDERED MAN *(to the unemployed man's wife)* Your husband had better not say he's out of work or they'll nab him for sure.

UNEMPLOYED MAN'S WIFE They'll be in for a big surprise.

BALANCE *(at the window)* Mike! A jug of ale! *(To Bridewell)* Where *is* Captain Brazen? Next! *(Sits down)* Name?

UNEMPLOYED MAN John Workless. Unemployed.

BALANCE Well, constable, what are the charges against this man?

BRIDEWELL With your permission, sir, there are no charges against this man.

UNEMPLOYED MAN'S WIFE That's right.

BALANCE What did you bring him here for?

BRIDEWELL Please, Your Worship, I don't know.

THE BROAD-SHOULDERED MAN What does it say in the warrant?

BRIDEWELL I can't read.

KITE May it please the court. The country can spare this man, the army needs him. Besides, he's cut out by nature to be a grenadier.

THE BROAD-SHOULDERED MAN He's chicken-breasted.

UNEMPLOYED MAN Do you want a punch on the nose?

BRIDEWELL Silence!

KITE In wrestling and boxing he'll take on all comers. He's the quickest man with a knife in the whole county. Every Saturday night he gets drunk and beats up his wife.

UNEMPLOYED MAN'S WIFE That's a bloody lie. He's the kindest, most considerate man in the parish. My five young ones will bear me out.

MRS. COBB There's one with five kids!

BALANCE Tell me, my friend, how do you provide for your wife and five children?

UNEMPLOYED MAN I don't.

UNEMPLOYED MAN'S WIFE That's the truth.

KITE Poaching, sir. The man has picked off every hare and partridge for five miles around. He's got a gun.

BALANCE A gun! If he likes to shoot, he ought to be picking off rebels.

MRS. COBB A woman with five children!

UNEMPLOYED MAN'S WIFE Yes. That's why they want to send

my husband away. They know I get one every year and they're afraid they'll be a burden to the parish.

KITE   Mr. Balance, this honest woman has hit the nail on the head. Won't the township be better off taking five children under its wing now than six or seven next year? With his nutritious, stimulating diet, this man is capable of saddling you with two or three little poachers at a go.

UNEMPLOYED MAN'S WIFE   Look here, sergeant. The parish won't get on any better by sending my John away. As long as there's a man left in this town, I'll saddle you with kids.

BALANCE   Put that woman in the workhouse! Take her away! *(Bridewell leads her off)* As for the husband . . .

KITE   I'll take care of him, Mr. Balance.

MRS. COBB   What about the children?

BALANCE   Clear the court! *(Bridewell and the court attendant clear the court)*

MRS. COBB   There must be somebody we can complain to.

THE BROAD-SHOULDERED MAN   There is—the justice of the peace.

JENNY   But he's the one who's sending them to the army.

THE BROAD-SHOULDERED MAN   That's just it.

BALANCE   Bridewell, call the next. *(Goes off into the library)*

BALANCE   Your answer, sir?

PLUME   All this is unlawful, sir. You can't do a thing to me.

BALANCE   I've asked you for your answer.

PLUME   Now that my company is up to strength.

BALANCE   Your answer, sir?

PLUME   So far I have never seen your daughter dressed in a manner that would make marriage conceivable.

BALANCE   It's either my daughter, or debtors' prison.

PLUME   Did you say twelve hundred pounds?

BALANCE   One thousand.

PLUME   Twenty-four hundred.

BALANCE   Never.

(Returning to the courtroom, he sees Mike bringing in a jug of ale and gives him a strange look)

BALANCE   Look here, Mike, why aren't you in the army?

MIKE   I can't go, Your Worship, I'm under eighteen.

BALANCE   You never knew your father or mother; you grew up in the orphanage. How would you know how old you are? I decide on your age, you oaf! That's the law. Eighteen and a half. Take his measure.

(Mike is measured and led away)

BALANCE   All orphans are in my care. Bridewell, next!

BRIDEWELL   There aren't any more.

BALANCE   No more? There were twelve a minute ago.

BRIDEWELL   They're all gone now.

BALANCE   Usher!

ATTENDANT   Mr. Balance?

BALANCE   I understand they're all gone?

ATTENDANT   Please, Your Worship, Bridewell let them go after they'd each paid him eleven shillings. As usual.

BALANCE   *(to Bridewell)*   You're discharged! No, you're not discharged, you're being handed over to Mr. Kite. Take his measure.

BRIDEWELL   *(reaches in his pocket)*   Just a minute, Mr. Balance. I intend to buy my discharge. I'll go as high as two pounds.

BALANCE   Two pounds? All you've got.

BRIDEWELL   All?

BALANCE   All. On the table!—All! Including what you took from the ensign. *(Bridewell pays)* Excellent. Take his measure.

BRIDEWELL   But I've paid up, sir!

(Pearmain puts him under the measuring rod)

BRIDEWELL   *(waves him aside)*   Five foot. *(He is led away)*

BALANCE   Mr. Kite, Shrewsbury wishes to provide your new company with a flag. *(Kite pockets Bridewell's money)* Now let us compare your roll with my record. *(They sit down and compare lists)*

(Victoria comes into the library dressed as a woman. Plume, smoking his cigar, looks at her silently)

VICTORIA   Are you angry with me?

(Plume does not answer)

VICTORIA   Is that all you have to say?—Since you hate me that much . . . I shall withdraw my charges. I don't want to force you . . .

PLUME   *(grinning)*   I understand.

VICTORIA William.

BALANCE *(in the courtroom)* Correct.—Read the Articles of War!

KITE Captain Plume will have to do that.

BALANCE You won't be seeing him again. *(Goes into the library)*

VICTORIA What is it you don't like about me, William? Is it my hair style? Is it my dress? All that can be changed.

BALANCE So it can.

PLUME I've made my decision.

VICTORIA AND BALANCE Yes?

(Brazen comes in, still in civilian clothes)

BRAZEN Mr. Laconic.

BALANCE Still in civilian dress?

BRAZEN I'm dreadfully upset. The tailor has made a child's coat out of my uniform.

PLUME *(takes off his coat)* Take mine, old boy.

BRAZEN You're quitting?

VICTORIA William!

BRAZEN Eureka!

BALANCE The solution!

BRAZEN Is she the one? Congratulations! Hold on, I've seen that face before. *(They toss each other their coats)*

(Victoria helps Plume and Balance helps Brazen put them on)

PLUME Mr. Balance, I've decided in favor of the twenty-four hundred pounds.

BALANCE Never!—Captain Brazen, read the Articles of War.

BRAZEN At once, sir! Who to?

PLUME Haven't you any recruits at all, man?

BRAZEN Not a one.

PLUME Take my company.

BRAZEN Plume, brother, do you mean that? Where is it?

PLUME In my left-hand pocket.

BRAZEN *(pulls out a document)* I'm your man forever!

(Brazen rushes into the courtroom and bellows at Kite, who in the meantime has lined up the recruits)

BRAZEN I shall now read the Articles of War!

BALANCE *(in the library)* And herewith I empower you as her husband to punish her as you see fit.

VICTORIA William!

BRAZEN *(in the courtroom, begins to read the Articles of War)*
  Whosoever . . . *(Mumbles)*

PLUME *(in the library)*   Sir, a town besieged by a regiment may
  defend itself.

BRAZEN *(in the courtroom)*   . . . will be shot! Whosoever . . .
  (mumbles)

PLUME *(in the library)*   Faced with an army, it hands over the
  keys.

BRAZEN *(in the courtroom)*   . . . will be shot! Whosoever . . .
  (mumbles)

PLUME *(in the library)*   Safe from battlefield injuries, I look reso-
  lutely forward to the prospect of gout.

BRAZEN *(in the courtroom)*   . . . will be shot! Whosoever . . .
  (mumbles)

PLUME *(in the library)*   To your love, Victoria, I sacrifice my
  ambition.

BRAZEN *(in the courtroom)*   . . . will be shot!

PLUME *(in the library)*   More glorious to be defeated by your
  charms than to conquer all America.

VICTORIA   William!

BRAZEN *(in the courtroom)*   In short: all will be shot. Everybody
  about turn—quick march! *(Led by Brazen, the recruits leave)*
  (Outside, the sound of drums and marching feet)
  (Simpkins enters the library)

SIMPKINS   That's the recruits from Welshpool. Shrewsbury is
  trailing behind!

BALANCE *(shouts at him)*   Pull yourself together, Simpkins. And
  fetch the champagne.
  (Simpkins goes out)

LUCY *(who has meanwhile rushed into the library through the courtroom)*   Mr. Balance! *(She pulls him back into the courtroom)*
  They're taking my Mike.

BALANCE   England needs him.

LUCY   What about me?

BALANCE   What about you?

LUCY   I need him too.

BALANCE   Get the boy out of your head, he's going to be a
  grenadier.

LUCY   Mike W. Laughton has other plans, sir, and if you don't
  set him free . . .

BALANCE   What then?

LUCY   Then everybody is going to find out who gets to be an ensign around here.

BALANCE   Lucy!

LUCY   Mr. Balance . . .

BALANCE   Usher, bring back the potboy. *(Court attendant brings back Mike. Kite follows)*

KITE   What about this man, Mr. Balance?

BALANCE   For the last time: how old are you, Mike?

MIKE   I think I'm seventeen, Your Worship.

BALANCE   Do you think you can drag off children to America, sergeant? The boy is only seventeen. This is an outrage! Discharge him at once.

LUCY   The uniform will be handed in. *(She helps Mike take off the coat. Assisted by Lucy, Mike totters over to the bench. Lucy hands Kite the coat)*

KITE   Please, Mr. Balance! Now we're short *another* man!

BALANCE   We almost forgot this one. *(To the attendant)* How much did you get from that rogue Bridewell? Shut your mouth! Enlist him in the company!

KITE   Thank you, Mr. Balance. *(He hands the uniform to the court attendant; both leave)*
   (Worthy comes in)

WORTHY   Thank you, Mr. Balance. Where's Melinda?

MELINDA   *(rushes into the library)*   Here!

WORTHY   *(also rushing into the library)*   Melinda!

MELINDA   Albert! *(They embrace)*
   (Lady Prude arrives with Mr. Smuggler, the banker)

PRUDE   My respects, Mr. Balance. A historical day for Shrewsbury!

SMUGGLER   England's on the march again. I take my hat off to you, Mr. Balance.
   (All have gathered in the courtroom. Simpkins has brought in champagne and glasses. From outside the departing recruits are heard singing a soldier's song)

RECRUITS
   Come on Johnny, take your gear
   In Virginia you won't hear
   Children's screams or woman's plea
   Over the hills and over the sea.

BALANCE *(lifts his glass)* To good old England!

MIKE *(to Lucy, aside)* To a *new* one, a better one!

SMUGGLER Long live English liberty, at home and overseas.

LUCY *(aside to Mike)* To us.

PRUDE Prosperity to our colonies over the sea!

MIKE *(aside to Lucy)* May they be free!

SIMPKINS Let God prevail!
  (A cork pops)

RECRUITS
  Our King George is older now
  Care and worry crease his brow
  His empire's gone for a cup of tea
  Over the hills and over the sea.

BRAZEN *(calls up from the street)* Mr. Laconic, your servant and so forth.—Good day, Mr. Smuggler. *(To Plume)* Congratulations on a fine catch, Plume.

PLUME *(at the window)* Kite!

KITE *(from the street, coldly)* A pleasant evening to you, *Mister* Plume.

RECRUITS
  Sweetheart, if I'm left to die
  Happiness will have passed us by
  While good King George reigns immovably
  Over the hills and over the sea.
  (The song fades away)

SIMPKINS *(sobbing)* England, England, first and always!

BALANCE And now: off to the pheasant shoot!

ALL TOGETHER Ah!

BALANCE Simpkins! The coach and four!

Notes

THE TUTOR

Texts by Brecht

Notes to *The Tutor*

RESULT OF THE REHEARSALS

The Berliner Ensemble's production of *The Tutor* was directed by a collective consisting of Brecht, Neher, Monk, and Besson. Neher's episodic sketches served as a basis for the arrangements, while most of the suggestions put forward by the collective and by the actors were tested out, usually in accordance with intructions shouted from the stalls, even at the most delicate moments. This testing meant that the usual psychological discussion could be dispensed with, while the shouts hampered the (equally usual) establishment of a "creative climate," in which consciousness comes off second best. The rehearsals lasted for nine weeks, and for at least five hours each day. Under R. Berlau's direction photographs and descriptions of the production were prepared for a "Model Book," from which the following extracts come.

Prologue

The prologue in front of the curtain was spoken to the delicate sound of a music box. As the speaker was being made to stand for the entire historical species known as Hofmeister [or household tutor to a noble family], he was given something of the mechanical quality of a figure on a performing clock; the movements of his head and limbs were jerky and his speech clipped. The impression given was by no means dainty, more on the sinister side, not least because of the cynical grin accompanying the words "Those nobles made me only too willing," together with the cynically discreet shielding of the mouth at "the sorry state of Germany." Despite a certain snapping of the jaw, and a double jerk at every bow, as is usual with automata, the whole thing was not pressed too far but remained in the realm of suggestion, never obscuring the fact that the actor was alive. In later performances, however, he developed the same doll-like quality further, and we had a high enough regard for his virtuosity to allow this.

1. Bowing and scraping

The scene is the street outside the privy councillor's garden gate. It shows Läuffer* working his beat, as it were. He lies in wait for the major as the latter takes his customary walk accompanying the privy councillor home after their morning glass. The two brothers pause in conversation while still a few paces from the gate, and only move on when Läuffer approaches, pretends to be surprised at the encounter, and begins while still at a distance to execute his first long-drawn, careful bow. They walk past him without acknowledgment; none the less he hurriedly makes two further bows, likewise while walking. Chilled by his reception, he gives the brothers a nasty look over his shoulder, then turns round and performs a fourth bow to their backs, cursing the while under his breath. (It took us five rehearsals to realize that he must utter his curses during the bow and not after it, which shows how easy it is at the outset to overlook the most obvious and essential points.) Meanwhile the brothers speak of Läuffer in the most indifferent manner, as the

*[In these notes the characters are referred to by the names given them by Brecht, which are generally the same as in Lenz's original. As these are in many cases fabricated word portraits (cf. Sir Toby Belch, Captain Brazen, Lady Dumbello, etc.), in our English version of the text they have been translated as follows:

Läuffer (from *laufen*, to run, and *läufig*, in heat)—Hasty
Pätus (from Latin *paetus*, cross-eyed)—Squint
Bollwerk (bulwark)—Buttress
Jungfer Rehhaar—Miss Swandown
Jungfer Watten—Miss Cotton
Jungfer Rabenjung—Miss Gosling
Gustchen (Lenz's diminutive of Augusta) has been anglicized into Gussie.]

privy councillor fishes out one of his many keys and opens the gate. Laughingly saying "He may be good enough for that," he gives the major a pat on the shoulder and lets him into the garden, where the major pauses and studies a plant at the foot of the wall. The fern in question interests him only mildly, but it is enough to overshadow whatever interest he has in Läuffer; he is far more deeply concerned by its history than by that of the man who is to be in charge of his children's education. This scene will not work properly unless the privy councillor puts his question "But tell me, brother, do you know . . ." with sudden concern, to be answered by the major with a great vague shrug of the shoulders.

2. The lovers' parting

The privy councillor, who, being better off than his brother "wouldn't want anything cheap," is not prepared to make do with a tutor for his son Fritz but sends him to Halle university instead—which of course allows a tutor to have undisputed access to his girl Gustchen. Their parting scene must show delicately how the young von Berg fends off his cousin; she wants him to take her into the summer-house, but he takes her through Klopstock instead, until he finds the latter filling him with irrepressible feelings and flings her on the bed as he swears his oath: a literary detour. The lovers are separated by his olympian father, with the result that, having been parted in the name of reason, they end up just as remote from one another as at the beginning. He goes off in order to become worthy of her, and by so doing makes certain that she will become unworthy of him.

3. Engaging a tutor

The trail has been laid. The daughter of the house has been sensually aroused, and this has been further aggravated by the fact that her lover's departure deprives her of him. The family is vulnerable, the tutor can be taken on. As he performs one or two minuet steps to the major's wife the poor devil is fighting for his life, the eye which she keeps on his feet is no sharper than his own. He wipes the sweat from his forehead ("My son will not require any other dancing master for the time being"), while she calls for one more *pas*. Meanwhile Leopold, the son he is applying to educate, is catching flies against the wall; he has seen so many employees engaged. Läuffer grunts with pleasure as the major's wife sings her minuet; he has hurried over to turn the pages for her. Then some Prussian provincial French. When, after chiding him for kissing her hand—it's not done in France—she none the less grins graciously and stretches out her paw for a further kiss, Läuffer's success so goes to his head that a faux-pas is bound to follow. He comes forward, between the major's wife at the keyboard and the count on the sofa, and lets the latter know his opinion of the dancer. (Incidentally, this scene failed to work until Läuffer made a distinctive movement to express his "daring to step forward." He had to move down to the center of the stage; the words alone were not nearly enough.) The gentry freeze; deadly lorgnettes are leveled at him. He stammers out some excuse—the man had been booed off the stage at Koch's theater—and is dismissed from the room. In his nervousness he nonetheless turns round once more in the doorway on hearing himself talked about, thereby inviting another swipe. After his departure there is a moment's pause. The major's wife sails over to the sofa, the count gets up, walks past her in counter-motion; they approach one another with constrained smiles, then let the smile drop, hurriedly reassuming it as they once more turn towards each other. As he mulls over the scandalous incident, already planning how to present it to further houses, he mechanically pinches the cheek of the maid who serves him his chocolate, before going on to pinch the handle of the cup. The major's wife's final remark answers the question why Läuffer is not sacked: he is cheap.

4. Insterburg rebuffs

Once Läuffer has been put in his place indoors we turn to him again and show that his position also prevents him from finding pasture outside. If necessary this scene can be cut, but it does present Läuffer's situation in a good exteriorized way. It calls for a refined virtuosity (special figure-skating skills on Läuffer's part, an enchanting but simple stage set and so on). We showed Läuffer severely handicapped by his obligation to look after the half-witted Leopold, who at once tumbles over and as soon as the young ladies appear is parked by Läuffer against one of the posts for the lights. When Läuffer runs over to the rear after his vain attempt to establish contact he bares his teeth as evidence of the savage feelings which he is finally to turn against himself. Immediately thereafter he becomes an object of utter ridicule; on getting him back his pupil clumsily pulls himself up, bringing Läuffer to the ground.

5. A new pupil

Now Läuffer can be thrown the bait; we have isolated him both inside and out; he is starved and kept short, and we are now about to lock him in with the eatables and make them tasty and ripe. He must not realize his "good fortune" at once; let us give it to him as an additional exploitation, as overtime work. First we shall reinforce the foundations, thicken the atmosphere of hostility and boredom. Mime can be used to develop the relationship between Läuffer and his pupil Leopold: the very sight of the latter makes Läuffer yawn; by infection Leopold follows suit. There is no chalk for the blackboard; Leopold has it and pushes it over to Läuffer with his foot. The tutor reciprocates with uncontrolled hatred, then starts copying the word "agricola" from the book, but he is so badly prepared that he has to check the spelling after the first two syllables. The major is in a bad mood because he wants the fellow to perform a service which he himself cannot pay for. His efforts to educate his son are a miserable failure. He charges at him like Zieten's hussars charging the Austrians, renewing the attack in silent desperation when the first effort fails to make Leopold sit up as straight as he wants. Eventually it turns out that he only launched this offensive because he wished to get Leopold out of the room. He then spends some time going round the awkward subject, and his sense of having made a tactical error in arguing about Läuffer's salary is apparently such that when the latter asks for a horse he promises to look into the matter. This is too much for Läuffer. Having resentfully lain down under all the haggling and the imposition of new tasks, he had put his request with every expectation of being refused. Now he outdoes himself in bows, and hastens to display his drawings. The major merely looks at the first of them and shoves the second aside. Standing in the doorway, he warns Läuffer that he must "be gentle with" his daughter.

6. Philosophy and physiology

Now let us have a look at the new pupil's far-away lover, and let us wheel in Halle on our revolving stage. It is here, at the university, that the young store up experiences both on the intellectual and on the physical plane. We see our man Fritz von Berg poised between sacred and profane lovers, between Pätus and Bollwerk. Pätus is scared of his landlady but not of his professor; Bollwerk favors crawling to the professor but has the landlady under his thumb. Fritz opts for philosophy, but goes off to look at girls with Bollwerk. Fritz needs to be presented as the observant guest.

7. Catechism lesson

The daughter of the house is not disinclined to play with fire, and we have seen to it that such playing is made easy for her. Thus Läuffer must not be made to fall in love; he is lost from the outset ("he loves because he wants to go to bed"). Accordingly he seems all the more rigid, a cat among the pigeons, though a cat who is his own trainer. Nonetheless, this scene provides a chance to display Gustchen's social superiority. She combines the resources of her body and of her social position to get him dancing. At the beginning of the scene the teacher is gazing at a smiling pupil, and the story goes on in such a way as to make us believe that this is her attitude to Läuffer's teaching. He successfully stares her down. Guiltily she begins reciting the Creed. "I believe that God created me." When she gets stuck, Läuffer starts moving towards her with loud, measured, deliberate steps which seem to tick off the seconds of the silence between them. As he circles round her, looking down at her derisively, she restarts the sentence in a kind of panic and then, with the man behind her, gets stuck again. Then suddenly she smiles and looks up at him, repeating the last words "created me" with a shift of emphasis from "created" to "me": the graceful and unashamed triumph of the female. From this instant his advance proves to have been an error which leads straight to defeat. The examination conducted by him quickly turns into an examination conducted by her; it is no longer he who helps her out with the right word, but she him. (She openly mocks the schoolmasterly pedantry of his diction [. . .], delivering her "From all perils, and guards and defends me" with her head on one side in such a way as to suggest that it is he who has lost the thread and needs a helping hand. His "protects" is spoken with hopelessness, and his "Without any merit or worthiness in me" contains a childish reproach.) Then comes the row over her drawing lesson. Her haughty assurance that she had no time calls for the utmost self-control on his part. He paces restlessly and painfully to and fro, twists round like a top as on the skating rink, stops abruptly with his ruler tightly gripped between his elbows behind him as if to fetter himself. She looks him over as though he were some intriguing insect and for a moment is almost touched; she goes up to him and apologizes for having disappointed him. He lets this opportunity slip and looks stubbornly away. At once she resumes the employer's mantle and imitates her mother, ("It was quite impossible,") in order to put him in his place. What makes him finally lose control is her teasing remark that drawing is the one thing she enjoys doing. She is genuinely frightened by the savagery of his outburst. Once he has rushed out she stretches self-indulgently: he is a plebeian, with a plebeian's strength.

8. My kingdom for a horse!

Wanted: an outlet. Society's imperious finger points to the brothel. But the unhappy victim of the conflagration cannot get at the sole permissible cooling draught unless his employer first hands him the ladle. Läuffer, abandoned, armed only with a promise (i.e., unarmed), has to choose a mediator, his father, who must in turn address himself to a mediator, the employer's brother.

The eighth scene takes place in the privy councillor's garden, which we already know (from outside) from scene 1. In his shirtsleeves, wearing a rustic gardener's apron and broad-brimmed straw hat, the privy councillor, after refusing the pastor's request, bends his knees in order to clip a box tree. Greatly to the disadvantage of Läuffer, who gets no chance to state his practical demand, an ideological argument develops between the two elderly gentlemen, conducted on the pastor's side with irascibility, on the privy councillor's with the infuriating self-control of a man of the world. The latter too on one occasion gives a look typical of his class ("interesting to see how people like this behave") as the pastor bellows out the words "a shepherd of souls" in a vain attempt to make the authority of the church tell on his side. When Läuffer cannot contain himself his father intervenes, out of concern for his son's dignity. Thus he has to wrestle with his father to get his request for mediation across. His father's presence prevents him from letting the privy councillor have it straight; he feels forced to deny the real objective of the proposed visits. Brutally, the privy councillor states it. Läuffer, a broken man, follows his agitated father to the garden gate, only to turn round once more, stare at the privy councillor with a snort and warn him darkly that something terrible may happen. Then father and son go off in haste, gesticulating angrily as they pass along the garden wall. The privy councillor has raised his voice for just one sentence: "Been feeling your oats?" He carefully now and again clips an overgrown shoot from the box tree with his big shears.

9. The abandoned vacation

While in Insterburg his Gustchen finds herself abandoned to a sex-starved tutor who has been deprived of any outlet, far away in Halle Fritz von Berg undergoes an experience which prevents him from hastening to her rescue, while at the same time giving him the intellectual equipment finally to understand her situation and to forgive it. He sacrifices his holiday money for Mistress Rehhaar, who had slept with the student

Bollwerk while thinking allegedly of the student Pätus. What needs to be lightly and comically shown here is the peculiar form of self-castration adopted by German intellectuals of middle-class background, who are capable of experiencing not only other people's revolutions but also their own private life on an exclusively "intellectual plane."

Details

The transition to Pätus' big outburst (from "There are times when I feel almost weary" to "Bollwerk, Bollwerk") needs to be abrupt and utterly unexpected.

Fritz von Berg's attitude in this scene is freer, and he has also begun wearing a Schiller-style shirt. When he thumps his fist on the table after remarking "I too have developed in this Halle of yours" it is out of a sense of having become "one of the boys." With a gesture of freedom he announces his intention not to sleep with his girl. It is the moment of his self-castration, and it bears the same heroic stamp as will the unfortunate Läuffer's.

A good gesture by Fritz: at "Your duty is my duty," his hand is on his heart in true romantic style. A little hesitantly, it creeps down to his waistcoat pocket: "Command my purse."

Pätus counts the twenty thalers out on the table, coin by coin, lending the operation a symbolic significance.

10. Sooner or later it had to happen

Lenz had Läuffer sitting by the bed. We thought it would help the development of the story if we showed him and Gustchen in bed together. This needs to be the next thing one sees after seeing how he was denied a horse for his excursions to Königsberg. First and foremost it is the solution to a problem; only then do scruples begin to appear, together with the shadows of difficulties to come. The scene is a difficult one for the actor playing Läuffer. He must never let himself be harsh, merely lost in other thoughts. On top of that he is physically relaxed, sated, even though he finds, poor devil, that reflecting on the possibility of unpleasant consequences sours the long-awaited sensual pleasure. His occasional cynicism (as in the sentence about his over-nourishment, with which he bears out the privy councillor's "Been feeling your oats?") has something helpless about it. He has got up to help himself to Gustchen's morning chocolate on the table. On his return to the bedside his broody mood deepens. Every minute the chasm between the two of them grows wider. Quickly it becomes evident that they have simply been using one another.

So far as Gustchen is concerned the subject of "love by proxy" has already been introduced in the previous scene. At first she is relaxed, stretches out comfortably and speaks with a lazy frivolousness, as if from another planet. She takes his hand briskly as if picking up a prop, puts it on the edge of the bed before her and ponders over it, stroking the air above it as if contact might destroy the illusion that it is Fritz's. Nonetheless there is an underlying sexual satisfaction to the frivolous tone of the first sentences, and when she makes up to Läuffer using the *Romeo and Juliet* monologue she had been saving for Fritz, it is because she is at the same time nervous that he may draw away as soon as he begins thinking. Läuffer's departure is hurried and undignified, and not on his part alone. Reproaching him for having stayed too long, she hands him his vest, which has been lying on the bed, a witness of their union. There is one touching moment for Gustchen in this scene, where she reacts to his "I'm not Romeo, I'm Läuffer" by sitting up, staring at him as if she were seeing an unknown man in her bed, then falling back and weeping. But whatever element of tragedy enters into this must be on Läuffer's side. Where she for him still stands proxy for an anonymous Nature, he for her has to stand proxy for a quite specific man: Fritz.

11. The discovery

Frau von Berg's passion for singing is evidence that ugly and beautiful sentiments are entirely compatible; after all, didn't that Gestapo butcher Heydrich adore his Bach? What makes her performance ugly is not so much her voice as her unbridled energy. When she upbraids her husband the major, meanwhile playing the "Largo," she does so because he is coming from work; he for his part sees music as a source of slovenly conduct, and sweeps the music off the spinet with his hoe. The major's wife's angry lamentations over the family disgrace are made all the more piquant by the audience's knowledge that this is a family where the mother is trying to steal her daughter's suitor (though that is as far as the comic aspect must go). The parts of the major and his wife should be given to actors with vitality; Europe has had two hundred years in which to learn how horribly vital their class is.

12. *Läuffer finds a refuge*

Läuffer's dark premonitions have been fulfilled. We see him seeking refuge in a village school, hunted like a criminal. Here, in the gutter, everything will be repeated—his aggression, his reduction to impotence, his persecution—except that this time the persecutor is himself. The refuge turns into a rat-trap. The schoolmaster Wenzeslaus' mistrust yields to a recognition that he has found a cheap slave in this victim of persecution who is ready to do anything in exchange for shelter. Soon he has him sitting down at the table correcting exercise books, and is able himself to lean back in his chair and take things easy. The victim has to eat, work, smoke, and listen to self-satisfied homilies all at the same time, and he does all this with crawling humility. The element of exploitation here is so naive and so coated with morality that Läuffer still calls the schoolmaster his benefactor a year later—something that needs to be brought out by the actor. We must combine Wenzelaus' worst features—his appalling sense of humor, his thirst for freedom that can be slaked by beer and cheap gin, his combination of pedantry and high-flying base thoughts, etc.—with as much approach at humanity as can be managed. At the same time the model in whose image he brings up children must be such as to inspire terror.

When the feudal mob bursts in it is a good idea to have the wounded Läuffer lying as long as possible uncared-for: the injustices inflicted on and by him get debated across his bleeding body. The major charges into the room in search of his daughter, then goes on marching to and fro, so as to carry on the search for her by this movement. The privy councillor merely demonstrates fear of scandal. Dramaturgically speaking, the twelfth scene is a seesaw, a plank laid across a beam. The tutor steps on to the plank in the most profound distress, prior to walking further and further up it until his weight makes it tip over and drop him into the bottommost depths.

13. Gustchen at the lake

Leaving Läuffer to a confused fate (which still has one or two things up its sleeve for him) we observe his employers setting their affairs in order. The life-saving scene by the lake will bear a certain amount of comedy; it may be a disaster, but there are servants at one's call. However, true though it may be that tragedy leads a precarious existence wherever the standard of living is high, it would be wrong to strip Gustchen and the major of any kind of seriousness. It should of course be shown how Gustchen waits for her rescuers before wading into the lake, how she takes off her shoes in order to leave them a clue, how she turns round once more in order to add her carefully folded shawl, then steps into the water with her face averted; all this, however, is really because she knows that in their circles anything can be arranged and straightened out, given a little good will. There is more comedy in the count, who has forgotten his status as a suitor and has simply come along to glean impressions for his chronique scandaleuse, likewise in the privy councillor who, being in no position to lift a finger himself, makes do with "organizing" the rescue operation and putting forward observations of an appropriately general kind. The major's accents are entirely serious, as are his wild cursing of the domestics who fail to hand him the pole quickly enough, and the sermon which he reads his daughter. At the end of the scene, when she is in her father's arms, we allowed her to give a contented little waggle of the feet.

14. The self-castration

The fourth act is one of the most subtle ever written, and the whole of it needs to be clearly lifted out of the rest of the play and to have its poetry underlined in such a way that the audience can transfer the self-mutilation from the sexual to the wider intellectual sphere. For it we changed the lighting; by omitting the projections normally used to indicate locality we made a very dark and unfamiliar background without otherwise altering the harsh lighting of the set. In addition we enclosed the three scenes in a musical framework, using Mozart's "Turkish March" scored for harpsichord, cymbals, and piccolos. For the rest we took particular pains to bring out the realistic element in the acting. After all, if this episode is left uninterpreted, presented in its own terms, i.e., signifying nothing more than the dilemma of a poor devil forced to opt for a sexual life or a professional one, it will still be typical enough of the social order in question.

14 a.

This scene shows Läuffer undergoing a nightmare. Once more his sex rises up against him. The arrangement accordingly needs to hark back to scene 7, the catechism lesson. The same way of stalking the victim, of trying to get behind it. The escape to the window. The unsteady walk thence to the wall, as if an invisible storm were blowing a leaf to perdition. The slaps he gives himself with a ruler.

One or two further details: when Lise comes back with the coffee pot and knocks, Läuffer has his pen poised to make a correction. Still holding it thus poised he walks over to the door as in a dream, opens it, takes the pot from Lise, pushes her away, closes the door, comes back to the table, puts the pot down, then finally makes the correction. Lise, as her guardian is dragging her off at the end of the scene, breaks away from him, goes back to the table with averted face and fetches her lamp.

14 b.

Läuffer delivered his soliloquy standing in front of the blackness of the open window. In it the element of speculation predominated, but there was something like an explosion with the phrase "in the presence of her creation," while the decision seemed to be reached with "Shall I pluck out the eye that offends me?" When he ripped off his coat at the end one saw the wildness that marks counter-revolution.

14 c.

For this scene we created total silence; the stormy night of its predecessors was intended purely to let us achieve a silence that should be almost audible. Overturned furniture, scattered clothing provided evidence of the wildness that had gone before. At the end of the scene the snow which was to fall throughout the fifth act became visible for the first time on the cyclorama. Some such mixture of realistic and poetic elements seemed to us absolutely necessary at this point. The big problem for the actors is the breathtakingly swift transition from Läuffer's tragic admission that he has castrated himself to the schoolmaster's hymn of praise. The audience hardly has time to feel sorry for the wretched man before it is once again being asked to feel contempt for him. No sooner has the poor tutor's persecution achieved its goal than the playwright attacks him too. This rapid transition, which is necessary for the development of the comedy since it is only in this way that we can erase the individual, surgical element, works if the actor playing the schoolmaster gives full effect to his emotional shock and likewise to his natural fright, then allows this fright to tinge his "Say no more. You shouldn't have done it!" and calls him a "second Origen" as if he were announcing a discovery.

An alternative solution was suggested by the Swiss playwright Frisch: to start with "You shouldn't have done it!" leaving the audience to wonder nervously what had happened, and in the reading of the letter insert after "by my own decision —a cruel one, I can assure you—" the words "to castrate myself."

In any case it is essential for the actor playing the schoolmaster to remain as realistic as possible, as did Friedrich Maurer in the Berlin production. He said "What, regret it?" with the mild incredulity of someone who observes a hero at a moment of weakness and smilingly recalls him to himself. At the end of the scene, however, he slightly overstressed the note of hearty, optimistic encouragement, as if he still had some faint private doubts.

15. End of an Italian journey

Everything has now been prepared for the ending. The abnormal has been recognized as such; normality once again comes into "its own." The sacrificial rites have been performed; the survivors can get married off.

Now that all is open and above-board we change the set for this last act, without drawing the curtain, against a sky still full of gently falling snow.

The philosopher pats his discreet little tummy and slyly narrates his treachery: that accounts for the first couple. Fritz von Berg remains uneasy. Pacing the room with great strides he describes an Italian journey whose artistic experiences have become increasingly clouded by concern about his Gustchen. Fritz dare not open his letter from home, and when Pätus reads it out to him he collapses in a faint near the stove. Pätus runs for some cold water. Back in his easy chair he offers his "realistic" opinion of women. Karoline Pätus, entering at this point, knows no misfortune whose memory cannot be blotted out by a good cup of coffee. Staggering, Fritz hastens away from the wreckage of his friend to seek the tomb of his beloved.

16. Engagement in the snow

From the outset the second of the closing scenes dispels any fears on the part of the audience and of Fritz von Berg. The von Berg family is tragedy-proof. There is only one brush with the play's more disturbing events: when the young lover, after intellectually reconciling himself to his beloved's unfaithfulness, is led up to the cradle and sees the flesh and blood result. He hesitates for a second or two.

17. Lise gets Läuffer

Finally the most difficult of the endings: that for Läuffer. The scene is set on a Sunday morning and has many festive features. Lise is spreading a snowy-white tablecloth, while the two men concentrate on a dignified subject, the sermon. Läuffer sits and

speaks with new-found authority, also with the false modesty
that goes with it. None the less he has been robbed of his force.
He absorbs the schoolmaster's suggestions that the old Adam is
still active in him with nothing more than distaste, Lise's readiness to marry him without particular surprise.

> [GW *Schriften zum Theater*, pp. 1221–39, also in *Versuche 11* (1951);
> scenes 13–15 in *Theaterarbeit*. These and the following scene-
> by-scene notes were written during rehearsals with the Ber-
> liner Ensemble in 1950. It was Brecht's intention to make a
> "model book" (or permanent photographic record) of this
> production. Insterburg, now called Chernyakhovsk, is near
> Königsberg (Kaliningrad) in the part of East Prussia an-
> nexed by the USSR at the end of the Second World War.
> The University of Halle near Leipzig was founded in 1694;
> it is now the Martin Luther Universität Halle-Wittenberg.
> The Swiss novelist-playwright-architect Max Frisch had
> seen much of Brecht during the year and a half which he
> spent based in Zurich.]

On poetry and virtuosity

For some time to come we shall need to talk about the poetry
of a play and the virtuosity of its production, something that
seemed of little urgency in the recent past. It seemed not merely
to lack urgency but to be a positive distraction, and this less
because the poetic element had been inadequately developed
and appreciated than because it had been used as a pretext for
maltreating reality, in that people imagined they would find
poetry wherever reality was made to take a back seat. Lies
masqueraded as inventiveness, imprecision as lavishness, slavery to prevailing forms as mastery of form, and so on. This
made it necessary to test images of reality in the arts for their
truth to reality, and to examine the artists' intentions towards
it. As a result we were forced to make a distinction between
truth and poetry. More recently we have almost given up examining works of art from their poetic (artistic) aspect and made
do with works lacking any appeal as poetry and productions
from which virtuosity is absent. Such works and such produc-

tions may be effective on some level or other, but it cannot be a deep one, nor take a political direction. For it is a peculiarity of the means employed by the theater that they communicate insights and impulses in the form of pleasures, and that the depth of the latter corresponds to the depth of the former.

What follows is a description of some elements of virtuosity in the performance of *The Tutor* which accompany poetic factors in the play. The fact that the latter in turn accompany social factors is herewith to be noted, but should not hinder anybody from dwelling on those making for poetry and virtuosity.

1

The four bows executed by Läuffer, the first on seeing the two brothers, then a hurried pair of twin bows as he passes them, and a final one, spiced by a curse, to their backs, are, if precisely executed, a piece of virtuosity that gives rhythmical and plastic expression to Läuffer's social subservience, choreographic training, and under-nourishment, not to mention the awkwardness peculiar to him. Setting the scene outside the garden gate of the privy councillor's town residence is poetic, for it helps the spectator to become aware of the brothers' morning glass, of their well-entrenched habits and their comfortable standard of living. With Shakespeare this might have been a bit too much; not so however with Lenz's intimate, small-scale, comedy of manners. None the less the setting is not designed to achieve illusion, this being impeded from the outset by the projecting of a hand-colored steel engraving in the taste of that time.

2

The realization that people can be drawn together by poetry is itself poetic. A masterly description of the seductiveness that arises from the reading of a love poem can be found in the fifth canto of Dante's *Inferno*. A touch of this poetry, mildly alienated by comic allusions, should enter into the reading of Klopstock by the two lovers. A further factor is the way in which the couple's position at the outset of the scene matches that at the end: both times they are seen in profile, at the same correct distance, except that the second time they have her father sitting between them; it is thanks to him that this distance has been restored. You may ask if such subtleties are noticed by the audience, but it is an unworthy question. Another subtle point is that the audience's attention is drawn to Gustchen's bed when her young lover leads her over to it to swear eternal devotion; in due course we shall see her lying in it with the tutor. At a first seeing of the play, the effect may simply be to suggest that they are only drawn to the bed by the thought of eventual unfaithfulness, but the ensuing tenth scene will become all the more effective, and when the play is seen a second time the former will also gain added significance—one should always reckon with a second visit.

3

For this scene we arranged the lighting effects in a way that can be called poetic. Generally speaking we were not using effects but full lighting. In this case, however, the projections prevented us from making full use of the lighting equipment, while a particular consideration led us to keep the walls at the back noticeably in the dark. The actor playing Leopold caught flies so well and so amusingly as to distract attention from the simultaneous cross-examining of Läuffer. Not having the heart to cramp the young actor's style, we felt forced to take the light off him. This had the poetic advantage that for the rest of the scene only the people of rank, the count and the major's wife, stood out plastically, while Leopold and the maid provided the background, and Läuffer only came into the full light on making his faux-pas, after which he was thrust into the half-darkness again. The little mime in which major's wife, count, and maid change position after the tutor has been thrown out, so that the two persons of rank can be on their own, is a virtuoso element which is described in the notes [p. 332]. Läuffer's examination, where the sweat gathers on his brow as he has to give evidence of his gracefulness, was of course likewise carefully performed as a virtuoso "turn."

4

Scene 4 shows Läuffer in all the loneliness which makes a normal love life impossible for him. He is the cock of the walk being treated as a cat among the pigeons. He shows off his arts, performing the most hazardous leaps. (Läuffer, of course, must under no circumstances be made to appear vain. He is far too busy trying to impress the girls to be carried away by his own impressiveness.) He is brought down by the clumsiness of his pupil, with whom he is already fed up, and this puts the lid on his failure, for which he himself is in no way responsible. For the group of girls we took on a new actress who knew how to giggle. In the event this giggling in itself was evidence of the girls' sexual awareness and inhibitions.

5

It is a poetic factor when Läuffer, having been forced in his loneliness to take on Gustchen as an extra pupil, in return tries bargaining for permission to use a horse to go into Königsberg for "study." This deal is evidence of his initially innocent attitude with regard to Gustchen, but also of the famine from which he suffers.

6

Our demonstration that the freedom in question was thoroughly limited must not be allowed to detract from the account given of the freedom-loving atmosphere in university towns at that time. Even Bollwerk's dirty jokes tend to represent extreme daring. The light needs to be shown here, as well as the bushel that hides it. The costumes were particularly beautiful, with their black breeches and white linen shirts, and there was rhythm and grandeur in the gestures and the movements. It was not so much that the portrayal of the students was romantic as that their romanticism was portrayed.

7

The flame kindled in the sixth scene spread to the seventh in the person of the ex-student Läuffer. Prior to his outburst, admittedly, Läuffer keeps a tight rein on himself. His fate is settled as soon as the audience sees his new pupil sitting there with a smile on her face. The twisting movement by which he at one point recovers himself, and which Gustchen greets with a "I never saw you so deep in thought," recalls the skating figures of scene 4. It is a first-rate poetic invention. So is his use of his schoolmaster's ruler, as he pins himself to it as to a cross-beam, jamming it under his armpits, or raps himself with it to punish his sexual longings. The same rapping process in the fourteenth scene will tell the audience that his sex has once more risen against him.

8

The privy councillor praises freedom's sweetness and necessity, while at the same time clipping back his box trees.—His argument with the pastor about intellectual principles not only blocks Läuffer's request but develops into an agitated dispute between the pastor, who is now full of all kinds of forebodings, and his son; they are seen gesticulating as they walk off behind the garden wall.—And Läuffer's frantic demands (his desperate "my kingdom for a horse!") allow the audience to infer the danger now menacing Läuffer's pupil. (Meanwhile the privy councillor has no idea that his strict stand for morality has delivered his son's fiancée into the tutor's hands.)

9

The second of the Halle scenes once again calls for a certain fire, which must of course be felt to be that of the characters, not of the actors. Though the emotional extravagances of their "intellectual adventures"—a veritable Catalaunian battle whose fallen victims go on fighting in the air—need to appear comic, neither Pätus' despair nor von Berg's spirit of self-sacrifice should be made to seem anything but genuine (e. g., by exaggeration). Nor should Bollwerk and Rehhaar cease to be likable just because Bollwerk has deceived Pätus while Mistress Rehhaar's predicament forces her to flirt. Young people's problems carry an element of helplessness which makes them touching.

Both Halle scenes were brought round on the revolving stage as the half-curtain opened, so as to allow the happenings in "far-away Halle" to be visibly adduced.

10

The question, what in the narrative should come after what, is a poetic one. We debated whether the second Halle scene should be played between the catechism lesson and the request for a horse, or between the request for a horse and the love scene. We opted for the second, but others may take a different view. It is fine if Läuffer can be seen in Gustchen's bed directly after being refused the horse. On the other hand it is also a good thing if the love scene can be immediately preceded by the second Halle scene with its posing of the problem of love by proxy.

This scene needs to be very much like a real love scene, even though the only yearnings which it satisfies are Gustchen's for Fritz, and Läuffer's which could equally well be satisfied in Königsberg. The union has induced proximity; such distances as remain are due to the disparity of the couple's social positions.

11

We are once again in the realm of beautiful feelings when disaster suddenly irrupts. The major's wife's attempt to woo Count Wermuth—that contrived approach on wings of song—is a grotesque counterpart to the reading of Klopstock in scene 2. Poetic parallels are Tolstoy's *Kreutzer Sonata* and Dante's *Inferno*. The poetic element will be destroyed if the major's wife's performance is so caricatured as to lose *all* charm. It is an act of virtuosity designed to achieve a poetic effect when she plays Handel's "Largo" during her bickering with the major. A certain aesthetic and social-critical piquancy is added if the actor performing the latter can give a superficial flavor to the outraged father's outburst, so that it becomes the banal expression of a social convention. The audience must presume that it will fail. The background to this scene is furnished by the maid's infatuated attentions to the count.

12

One or two anticipated effects: the fact that it is entirely by the power of the human spirit that the schoolmaster succeeds in beating off the first attack of the feudal gang, before naked force bursts in and the shot is fired; the way his initial suspicion of having to deal with a criminal is transformed into confidence in a serf who can be made use of because he has committed a crime and needs a refuge; the way Läuffer's complaint that his victim was forced on him is directed to his next victim.

It also seems legitimate to let the spectator take a certain pleasure in understanding the construction of this pivotal scene which links the two halves of the play. Expelled from the feudal world, Läuffer takes refuge in that of the petty bourgeoisie. He swaps tyrants, his examination is repeated, as is his faux-pas too: having aired his views of the arts in the one, he now raises the question of pay in the other. His trade will be even more lowly than before, his calling definitely nobler.

13

The confused sounding of the tocsin from the village tells the audience that the search operation has begun. We quickly realize that it is going to succeed.—While the girl is being fished for, privy councillor and count indulge in some profound reflections. The former prepares consoling remarks in case she is dead, the latter, being unable to swim, washes his hands of all responsibility.—For an instant or two at the beginning of the scene, however, what was said above about young people's problems still needs to apply.

14

Before a stage of largely bare boards one has the impression of a terrible station on the road to Calvary. The gentle movements to and fro of the confused child, the cup that will not pass. The horse-blanket round Läuffer's shoulders, showing how cold the room is, with a coldness that stimulates the need which it cannot subdue. The teacher raps himself again. Then the victim of seduction turns into a violator.—The violator turns into an avenger. The soliloquy remains a total revolt, the action to which it leads is a blind suppression of revolt of any kind, the action to end all actions.—The grayness of the next morning brings utter weakness, along with its canonization.

Interlude

Letting the stage revolve visibly, bringing on the different settings in such a way as to fix the existing state of everything and show the developments of the next twelve months, is a device that also allows the play's three conclusions to be brought together by having the stage rotate once more, this time with fully performed scenes.

15

The philosopher has arrived, not on Parnassus but beside a warm stove; his drink is thin red wine, not the hemlock. It is true that we are dealing with mediocrities for whom the tragedy has involved no personal loss, but that makes the sight all the more depressing. Pätus' dream world may be comic, but his awareness of reality is pathetic. One wonders with indifference whether he will leave his whip behind when he goes to the rector's daughter; he certainly doesn't fail to conceal his Kant. —Fritz's mild disappointment, buried among his other worries, is a key point of the part. Another poetic factor is the way in which his account of the interruption of his Italian journey (the classic educational operation of that time) betrays that it was in fact an escape.—As for Karoline, both by her speech and by her appearance she should prompt the reflection that it may well be better to be deceived by someone like Mistress Rehhaar than married by someone like Karoline.

16

It is tempting to sacrifice the opening of this scene, the little family ceremony with the privy councillor's short speech about the snow, to the instinct to speed up the three concluding scenes (three endings) in order to polish them off. To permit this is to lose a poetic element. The snow whose beauty (purity) is thus praised is the same snow as had such a ghastly significance at the end of scene 14, in the gray morning light following the tutor's act of self-castration. Their mockery of the self-mutilator concludes logically enough with a great roar of laughter at his letter of request.—The maid's story and Fritz von Berg's speech must be performed as bravura pieces; both characters are glad to abandon themselves to the general atmosphere of cosiness.

17

The castrated man's little tummy is of course a piece of poetic license; like his red cheeks it represents a distortion of the character in the direction of cosy contentment. On top of that we have the fairy-tale note in the answers given by the admirable Lise, which recall Grimm's Hans in Luck. Nor is this all that can be done to create an atmosphere of calm. The whole picture must be beautiful. In our production the black of the men's and Lise's clothes, together with the white of the tablecloth, gave an impression of purity, while the grouping round the table was agreeable to the eye.

> [GW *Schriften zum Theater*, pp. 1239–49, also in *Versuche 11* (1951). Introduction and descriptions of scenes 15–17 included in *Theaterarbeit*. Leopold was acted by Joseph Noerden; photographs of his fly-catching performance are on p. 103 of the latter volume.]

Details of the Production

THE REBELLIOUS MINUET

The major's wife is examining the candidate Läuffer to see if he is a suitable tutor for her son Leopold. She is sitting at the spinet, Leopold in the background catching flies against the paneling. Läuffer downstage left by the footlights bows greedily in response to the rapidly intoned demands which have presumably already been put by the major's wife to a whole host of tutors. He claims a little hoarsely to have had "at least five" dancing masters in his life. She calls for a *compliment* from the minuet. Instantly she starts pounding the delicate keys. Läuffer is unprepared; for an instant it looks as if he cannot dance at all, then we see that it is his confusion, and he just needs a few seconds to collect his thoughts. Holding himself very upright, with his fists supported on his hips, he executes a few finished steps across the front of the stage, raising his legs very high and carefully apportioning the space available to him for this dance figure. His head looks rather twisted, screwed round on his shoulders. It is as if he were skirting thin ice; at the same time the way he carries his shoulders is a bit challenging, he strides like a caged tiger, as it were, with savage grace. Halfway across he turns towards the major's wife and executes a *compliment* so elaborate in conception that it would call for an entire corps de ballet. She appears satisfied. ("Well, well, not bad.") The young master, before whose eyes the examination is being conducted, boredly goes back to catching flies. Läuffer pulls out his handkerchief and mops the nervous sweat from his brow; he thinks he has made it. But the major's wife is thirsty for more sweat. "Now, if you please, a *pas*." Making a face, which the audience can see since Gaugler turns his head round again, he goes on to perform a *pas*, after which he stands there completely exhausted. In her excitement the major's wife graciously plays him a minuet, letting the spinet as it were feel the weight of her fists. Läuffer briefly pulls himself together, then goes over to the spinet with long gliding steps, continually wiping the sweat from his face, there to deliver a deep, animal-like noise of pleasure and bend greedily over the major's wife's meaty hand. What gave the scene its meaning was Gaugler's ability to reveal the low-born Läuffer's brutal and rebellious vitality strapped into the corset of feudal etiquette. The rudiments of the tragicomedy have herewith been hinted at.

[GW *Schriften zum Theater*, pp. 1249–50. This additional note on scene 3 was written for *Theaterarbeit*, 1952. Gaugler is the Swiss actor Hans Gaugler, who had acted in Brecht's *Antigone* in Chur in 1948 and came to Berlin to play Läuffer.]

END OF AN ITALIAN JOURNEY (SCENE 15)

1

The beginning of the scene shows how Pätus, now that he is a married man, can only read his Kant in secret. The little book, once so openly and provocatively displayed on his table, now has to be fished out from behind a barricade of other, more officially acceptable writings. Kant has gone underground. Though Pätus still reads him on occasion he will no longer be seen with him in public.

2

The Latin word "matrimonium" needs to be rolled appreciatively round the tongue in just the same way as the privy councillor's "farra communis" or Wenzeslaus' "nervi corrupti" (in scene 12). But whereas the privy councillor perceptibly acts the educated man in the presence of his more uncouth brother, and Wenzeslaus produces his diagnosis with philistine pomposity, Pätus dwells only slightly on his "matrimonium." He is the least anxious of the three to show off his knowledge.

3

Once again the Kant quotation is rapidly reeled off. The only passages to be specially brought out are those calculated philosophically to underline Kant's restrictive influence on Pätus. (". . . no arbitrary contract, but one made *necessary* by the laws of mankind," "they *must* of necessity marry, and this necessity follows from the laws proscribed by *pure reason.*")

356 The Tutor: Notes

4

"Only in public. How else could I . . ." is brought out hurriedly and with more emphasis than necessary. Pätus is entrenching himself. He knows that Kant is a black spot on his career. There is a chance here for the actor to display bad conscience.

5

Pätus has put his Kant on the footstool before him. At the words "and as you see right here, I had to" he points down at it.

6

Fritz's "So your favorite philosopher has proved to you" is not merely an answer to what Pätus has been saying but also his first faint realization of the inadequacy of all human endeavor. On the one hand Pätus' desertion shows that even the gnarled oak may be riddled with worm, while ceaseless dripping will wear down stone; on the other hand it confirms his own sudden exasperation with the world and its ways. Fritz is maturing, and the process has reached the stage of a gloomy recognition of what our world is like.

His hurried, absent-minded nodding at Pätus' big speeches, together with his nervous way of playing with the letter at the start of the scene, have already combined to show that Fritz is not entirely with us. It is only his politeness that prevents him from coming out with his fears then and there. He is just waiting for the right moment to unload his worries.

7

The brief "What was the subject of your thesis?" momentarily paralyzes Pätus. This innocent question touches him on a very sensitive spot. A point has been reached when no further philosophical explanation is possible, and when not even Kant can offer anything to justify his betrayal. His feeble answer, with its self-revealing cleverness, needs to be spoken as such. It has to be made clear that Pätus himself is not entirely easy at his carefree reply. He can laugh in places where there is nothing to laugh at, be over-emphatic where it would really be better to speak in an undertone, and so on.

8

Pätus may make a large gesture to accompany his exclamation, "Karoline is very different," but the sour face he pulls at the ensuing "made for marriage" suggests that marriage with the well-upholstered Karoline has its drawbacks. His "Incidentally, she's the rector's daughter" really is remarked incidentally. Pätus no longer has inhibitions about specifying the amount of his bribe.

9

Fritz's "So the two of you live here beside the stove" is a mixture of contrasting thoughts and feelings. This final balance-sheet of Pätus' "roaring youth" is somewhat depressing. It strikes Fritz as peculiar that the sum total of so many heroic actions can equal nought. None the less there is something to be said for the warm stove.

Back from his Italian journey, the traveler is not entirely unmarked by self-pity either. The sight of Pätus' placidity relentlessly reminds him of the enormous billows and tempests he must still survive on the oceans of life.

10

"I find that I've rather cooled toward him" is most haughtily spoken. Pätus leans back in his chair with his whole weight, blows a thick blue cloud of smoke up at the ceiling, then starts to speak with the slightly grating voice of a budding lecturer.

11

After Pätus' "How was Italy?" Fritz jumps into the fray. He deals summarily with the obligatory part ("Divine. It's made a man of me.") His speech shows that he too has changed. His gait has become smooth and dignified, his voice has developed a steely edge. The actual situation may not be quite like that, but the words themselves emerge nicely turned. Like a connoisseur he negligently drops in the titbits (such as "olives," "Pompeii," and "headlong journey"), thereby adding to their effectiveness.

12

We tried two alternative approaches to Fritz's collapse. First we made him fall by the door-jamb in the center of the stage, but abandoned this because here Fritz's slow crumpling attracted too much attention. So we settled for a faint by the window.

13

When Pätus pauses in his reading of the letter after the words "uncle's house" Fritz impatiently says "Go on!" and stamps his foot. The criminal refuses to be blindfolded and begs the judge to deal with his case according to the rule-book.

14

At this point Pätus makes his voice hard as steel. This is supposed to encourage Fritz to take what is coming to him like a man.

15

Fritz's furious self-criticism must be performed with the utmost Sturm und Drang. The two men have swapped parts. Where in Scene 9 it was Pätus who beat his breast in despair it is now Fritz. But now that Pätus is compromising more and more with the establishment, the friends' lofty sentiments no longer coincide. Fritz alone survives as an idealist relic.

16

Pätus' advice is thoroughly realistic. His vocabulary suggests that he already has his own beer-drinking circle. Such phrases as "women have got to be kept in hand" and "Women! we know what they are" show that he has progressed a good way along the road from Kant to Nietzsche. These middle-class platitudes need to be delivered in a voice redolent of beer.

17

The sound of Karoline's footsteps takes Pätus by surprise. He quickly pops Kant into a tobacco jar. Not even the conjugal bedroom is immune from the long arm of the social hierarchy. One sees the drawbacks of a rational marriage.

18

Karoline Pätus is a very important character. When she enters the room, Rococo, Biedermeier and Art Nouveau all appear together. A paralyzing atmosphere of coffee-cups seeps in. There's nothing else for it: it's farewell to rebellious youth.

19

The scene originally ended with Fritz staggering off, leaving the tableau of Pätus and Karoline. The spuriousness of their idyll was underlined by the subsequent addition of "Sad, but it's no concern of ours." The ensuing "Come and warm yourself by the stove" is just the final nail in the coffin of the Sturm und Drang with which Pätus' career began. The quondam moral giant and subsequent traitor withdraws to a life of bourgeois heroism.

20

As the lights dim and the stage begins to revolve, Karoline goes over to the stove and sits down.

> [From *Theaterarbeit*, pp. 90–92, headed "Examples from the production notes." These notes would appear to be Brecht's, though they are not signed. Brecht's term for the "a life of bourgeois heroism" is "das bürgerliche Heldenleben," an allusion at once to Richard Strauss's tone-poem and to Carl Sternheim's cycle of plays.]

The choice of play

In order to provide plays for the German theater (its classical repertoire having shrunk alarmingly in these troubled times) and at the same time to create a link with Shakespeare, without whom a national theater is hardly feasible, it seemed a good idea to go back to the beginnings of classicism, to the point where it is both poetic and realistic. Plays like Lenz's *The Tutor* allow us to find out how Shakespeare might be staged here, for they represent his initial impact on Germany. In them substance has not yet been raped by ideology but develops handsomely in every direction, in natural disorder. The audience is still involved in the great debate; the playwright is putting forward ideas and provoking them, rather than offering the whole work as their embodiment. This forces (or enables) us to play the incidents that take place between his characters and keep their remarks separate; no need to make them our own. In this way the characters, instead of being either serious *or* comic, are sometimes serious, sometimes comic. The tutor himself claims our sympathy for being so utterly crushed, together with our contempt for letting this happen.

[GW *Schriften zum Theater*, p. 1221. Written for *Theaterarbeit*, 1952.]

Aspects of taste in the production

Lenz's play, with its crude subject matter, calls for unusually elegant treatment. Moreover the view given of the German Misère could not be allowed to depress the spectator, but must inspire him to help overcome it. Everything depended on the gracefulness of the movements and the musicality of the words. Color and cut of the costumes had to be first rate, as had the furniture and any architectural elements shown. The Ensemble looked to tasteful old engravings, etc., for ideas. What emerged was by no means an idealization of the period. Its standard of taste was in fact relatively high. The maggot had not yet grown up into a dragon. Students' rooms, village schools, and country houses still looked very different from what they do now.

The sets and costumes for *The Tutor* were by Caspar Neher, the projections by Hainer Hill.

[From *Theaterarbeit*, p. 113.]

Is *The Tutor* a "negative" play?

The Tutor has been criticized in some quarters for being a "negative," or unconstructive, play. In the opinion of the Berliner Ensemble this play, containing as it does three portraits of schoolmasters (privy councillor, Wenzeslaus, and Läuffer) and three of students who intend to become schoolmasters (von Berg, Pätus, Bollwerk), and being set in the period when the German bourgeoisie was evolving its educational system, offers a stimulating satirical view of this aspect of the German Misère. The production was a perfectly valid contribution to the great process of educational reform which is currently being undertaken in our republic. As can be seen from such works as *Tartuffe*, *Don Quixote*, *Candide*, and *The Inspector General*, satire is not normally concerned to set up exemplary characters as a contrast to those which it mocks; in the concave mirrors which it uses to exaggerate and emphasize its targets the "positive" character would not escape distortion. The positive element in *The Tutor* is its bitter anger against inhuman conditions of unjustified privilege and twisted thinking.

[From GW *Schriften zum Theater*, pp. 1250–51. Written for *Theaterarbeit*. The fact that the privy councillor also belongs in the educational system—at its top—emerges more clearly from the original than from Brecht's adaptation.]

Editorial Note

Adapting Lenz

To judge from the surviving typescripts, Brecht seems to have begun with a first adaptation "by the Berliner Ensemble" which bears no marks of his own hand and could well have been prepared by his collaborators. This was very much closer to Lenz's original than is our text, and took in large tracts of it uncut. The main differences came in the second half of the play, and were concerned above all with clearing away unnecessary characters and entanglements. Lenz, for instance, made Gustchen go away for a whole year after being caught in bed with Läuffer (which occurred in Act III, scene 1), have her child, leave it to be brought up by an old blind woman, then come back and stage her suicide in the lake. The old woman brought the child first to Läuffer, then to the Bergs, who found that by a strange chance she was Pätus' grandmother; old Pätus, another Insterburg dignitary, had quarreled with her (as also with his son), but in the end the family were reconciled all round. As a further complication Lenz introduced a Herr von Seiffenblase and *his* tutor, who visited the three students in Leipzig, carried home discreditable reports about them, and seem to have had nebulous designs on Gustchen and Miss Rehhaar alike.

All these extra characters are eliminated in the first adaptation, as is also Miss Rehhaar's father, who in Lenz had given Fritz lute lessons and fought a ridiculous duel with Pätus over his daughter: she herself first appearing in Königsberg, where Seiffenblase had taken her and made her pregnant. The events too are tightened up. Gustchen goes into the lake immediately after being caught with Läuffer, while the three scenes in the village school—Lenz's III, 2, where Läuffer seeks refuge and

Count Wermuth looks for him, his III, 4 with Wenzeslaus tedi-
ously expounding his rules of life, and his IV, 3 with the shooting of Läuffer a year later—are strung together into one
enormous scene preceding Gustchen's wetting, finishing with
a new reference by Läuffer to the horse problem and his sex life.
Then where Lenz had made Läuffer reveal his self-mutilation
to Wenzeslaus before ever seeing Lise (servant, not ward, to
Wenzeslaus in the original), the adaptation moved the dialogue
with Lise about her suitors, etc., from the beginning of V, 10 to
before the castration, adding the monologue for Läuffer virtually as in the final scene 14 b.

The other principal new passages, apart from the prologue,
were the major's remarks about Läuffer's view of the "Hero-
King" (added to I, 4); the catechism lesson at the beginning of
Gustchen's first scene with Läuffer (II, 2); the major's wife's
singing at the start of her scene with the count (II, 6, now moved
forward to follow II, 2); the introduction of Bollwerk at the
beginning of the first student scene (in Lenz's II, 3 he only
appears at the end) and his references to Kant; further reference
to Kant early in the second student scene (V, 6, now shifted to
the beginning of Act V); a new ending to the scene where
Läuffer reveals his self-castration (V, 3), which cites his letter to
the major and shows his anxiety about his job; and the new
festive beginning and ending to the last scene, in which Fritz
and Gustchen reunite over the baby (V, 11 and 12 after the elimination of old Pätus), so that the play finishes on the song "Oh
silent winter snow." Besides the castration monologue there is
also one other entirely new scene, which replaces the original
II, 4. Here Lenz had two girls, Jungfer Hamster and Jungfer
Knicks, reporting to Frau Hamster on the absurd sight of Pätus
rushing off to the theater in a wolf-skin with three dogs after
him. Instead the adaptation introduces Miss Rehhaar, and
shows Pätus being made ridiculous in her eyes by Bollwerk's
cruel exploitation of his limp.

This first (or at any rate first surviving) version was heavily
reworked by Brecht in a second adaptation using about one-
third of its pages as they stood, and otherwise making many
changes, cuts, and transpositions. Dated "22. 12. 49" on its last
page, the new typescript established the text very much as we

now have it. Apart from making some massive (and necessary) cuts, what Brecht did here was partly to get the episodes into a more logical narrative sequence, incidentally scrapping the new scene just described, together with the original II, 7 (Fritz going to jail for Pätus' debts), and throwing II, 6 and III, 1 into a single scene; partly to bring out certain elements in the situation which he had found hints of in Lenz—for instance, the notion of Fritz as philosopher and the major as would-be rustic, the sexual basis of Läuffer's plea for a horse, Gustchen's use of Läuffer as a surrogate for Fritz, and Pätus' ultimate choice of the cosy life. He also introduced further quotations from Kant and, for the first time, Klopstock, and devised some good openings for the actors: e.g., the skating scene, first conceived as an episode on the Insterburg promenade, and the maid's speech in the last festive scene.

To start with Act I, he rewrote scene 1 in more or less its final form, moved the lovers' parting (Lenz's scenes 5 and 6, which had been telescoped to make scene 4 of the first adaptation) forward to become scene 3, then added a note:

> *Position of scenes 2 and 3*
> With this kind of construction everything depends on the sequence, on what precedes what in the story. So the LOVERS' PARTING needs to come before TAKING ON A TUTOR; the lover has left before the educator moves in. Another reason for putting the departure scene at the beginning is that it does not carry the story further but merely sets out a situation which is decisive for what follows (daughter of the house ready for a man). Gustchen's erotic inclination towards Fritz, aggravated by their parting, is interpreted as awakening her erotically rather than as tying her hands.

So the two were switched, after Count Wermuth's inquiry about Gustchen, and the major's wife's answer, had been added to the end of the earlier scene. Most of the major's closing speech in scene 4 (the present scene 5) was new, and the skating scene followed as the first of the second act. Then came the catechism scene and the first student scene, much as we now have it, with its new references to girls, to the unfortunate effect of Kant on university examiners, and its invocations of "Pätus, the just," etc., building up the philosopher's figure; the first mention of Miss Rehhaar was also inserted here. The garden scene followed virtually in its final form, with Läuffer's two new interruptions about the horse and the privy councillor's "Been feeling your oats?" inserted in Brecht's writing. The act finished with the bedroom scene, more or less in its final form, and Gustchen's exclamation "My Romeo!"

The second student scene, which introduced the third act, was new, though still lacking its opening Klopstock quotation (see our scene 9); Miss Rehhaar now appeared for the first time, together with the quite new notion that she had been made pregnant by Bollwerk as a kind of stand-in for Pätus. In the telescoped II, 6 and III, 1, which now followed (scene 11, the discovery scene), the references to farming and the major's talk about Berlin banks and ballets were likewise new. The long composite scene with Wenzeslaus (12) was severely cut, eliminating inter alia the appearance of the village barber to dress Läuffer's wound. Lise, now more clearly identified as Wenzeslaus' "daughter," made her appearance with the beer—an afterthought of Brecht's—flung herself in front of Läuffer and repeated Gustchen's message about the pond as in the final text, leaving the von Berg party to rush out. After the pond scene itself (13), which has Gustchen "throwing herself into the pond" with no hesitation and no backward glances, and omits the Berg servants, there is the interlude much as in the final version, but with no mention of Karoline, merely of Pätus "*skating with a new girl.*"

For his fourth act Brecht made a new scene 14 by taking the three consecutive village school scenes of the previous version and treating them as (a), (b), and (c), though almost without changes apart from the addition of Wenzeslaus' encouraging remarks about Läuffer's qualifications just before his letter. The fifth act then began with scene 15, third and last of the student scenes, with its new references to Fritz's Italian journey (an allusion to Goethe's book of that name) and to Pätus' marriage and heating arrangements; Karoline initially being described as "née Rehhaar," a detail which was changed in a further version which also introduced her offer of coffee. The present final scene came next, very much as now and extensively cut by comparison with the previous version, and was followed by the festive finale at the Bergs', in which the central section was new with its speech for the maid and its long speech for Fritz; an incidental point later dropped is that the latter announced his intention of becoming a schoolmaster. The play still ended on the song, and there was no epilogue.

This second adaptation was completed some four months before the première. Leaving aside those changes which were made in rehearsal (described in Egon Monk's notes which follow) there were few further developments. Leopold was brought into the skating scene, which was moved forward into the first act, and Pätus' remarks on "German servility" were added to scene 6. In the bedroom scene (10) Läuffer, who had hitherto sat on the bed, was shown lying in it, while the confusion with Fritz was further underlined (e.g., by Läuffer's "I'm not Romeo, I'm Läuffer" and the final "Oh Fritz, my love!"). The von Berg servants were brought into the shooting and pond scenes (12, 13), as were the count's and the privy councillor's reactions to them in the latter. In 15, the last student scene, Pätus was shown dismissing Miss Rehhaar in his pride at having married the rector's daughter; his final invitation to sit by the stove was also new. So we can briefly summarize what survived of Lenz's play in the final text, scene by scene as follows:

Act One

1. The bows come from Lenz's I, 1 and 2, and the suggestion that Läuffer's father was too poor to complete his son's education.
2. The middle of the scene (after the Klopstock quotations) and the gist of the privy councillor's intervention are from I, 5 and 6.
3. Nearly all from Lenz's I, 3.
4. Nothing.
5. Well over half from I, 4, including the argument over pay.

Act Two

6. Pätus and Bollwerk, and the episode of Frau Blitzer and the coffee are in II, 3, as is the lure of the theater.
7. The second half from Lenz's II, 2.
8. More than half from II, 1, including the lines "I was promised a horse to ride to Königsberg every three months."

Act Three

9. Nothing, apart from the figure of Miss Rehhaar.
10. About half from II, 5, including the *Romeo and Juliet* quotation and Gustchen's remark "Your father forbade you to write to me," which shows the identification with Fritz.
11. About half is from the combined II, 6 and III, 1, notably almost the whole of the ending after the major's wife irrupts.
12. The greater part comes from the fusion of III, 2 and 4 and IV, 3, including all Wenzeslaus' pedantry.
13. About half is from the combined IV, 4 and 5.

Interlude

Nothing.

Act Four

14. (b) is new, but about half each of (a) and (c) come from V, 3 and 10, including Wenzeslaus' applause for Läuffer's action

Act Five

15. Less than half is from V, 6. The reference to Seiffenblase (Soapbubble) is a loose end.

16. V, 11 and 12 provide the major's appeal to Fritz's philosophical disposition, and Fritz's ensuing acceptance of the child.
17. Nearly all is from a fusion of V, 9 with the second half of V, 10, notably Lise's love for Läuffer and Wenzeslaus' reaction to it.

Changes during rehearsal

NOTES BY EGON MONK

During rehearsals the order of the scenes was quite often changed, shortened or added to. In most cases these alterations were not the result of any theoretical considerations but arose from the continual growth of the arrangement, the increasing elegance of the narration, the noting of social inaccuracies, the attempt to give lightness to the performance, and so on. Where the rehearsals revealed new and unsuspected potentialities in such characters as Pätus we tried to follow them up. [. . .]

1. In scene 1 the audience learns from the privy councillor that Läuffer cannot get a job at the local school because he is not educated enough. In the privy councillor's view he is just about adequate to "drum a little knowledge and good manners" into the major's son, so that he may become a soldier like his father. This judgement is subsequently confirmed when scene 5 (the school scene) shows Läuffer stumbling pathetically over the simple Latin word "agricola." It took one or two rehearsals for us to realize that it wasn't enough just to establish that Läuffer was unqualified. If we wanted to explain his behavior in terms of his situation in society we must give some indication of his origins. So we made the privy councillor follow up his remark "but he's not trained for it" by adding "his father's purse gave out before his finals."

The reason why the production of *The Tutor* made so complete an overall impression was its accumulation of a large number of details, some of them very small.

2. So as to show how much more interested the major was in the origins of his fern than in those of his son's prospective tutor (an idea that only evolved during the rehearsals) we had him add " 'Sblood! Enough about that lout, we were talking about your fern here."

3. Changes in the scene order usually led to changes in the text. In the first version of *The Tutor* Fritz von Berg in Halle renounced his holidays *after* Gustchen at Insterburg had allowed herself to be seduced. During rehearsal we realized what the right order of events had to be: it is because Fritz in Halle high-mindedly gives up spending the holidays at Insterburg with his Gustchen that she feels herself abandoned by him and so lets the tutor seduce her (she is taking a substitute). But since the play had contained no previous reference to Fritz's wanting to come to Insterburg in the holidays we made Gustchen add, when plighting her troth to her Fritz by the bed in scene 2: "That you'll always fly to the arms of your Gussie at holiday time and come back from the university in three years." Fritz breaks his promise and Gustchen turns to the tutor. However, his experiences in Halle, where he sacrifices his holiday money for Miss Rehhaar, put him in a position to understand his Gustchen and forgive her.

4. We also wanted to show that Läuffer's bodily needs arose from a lack of understanding on society's part. [. . .] He has to ensure that he can now and again get away from Insterburg. During the rehearsing of scene 5 we accordingly added the dialogue from "Major, would it be too bold of me" to "for two or three days?" Having put his request in the most obsequious possible way, Läuffer acknowledges the major's half-assent with lavish motions of gratitude. He executes several marked bows in rapid succession, and in exchange for the faint prospect of a horse is prepared to shoulder any other burden the major puts on him. That is to say, not only the reduction which has just

been effected in his salary but also the doubling of his responsibilities as tutor. The major fails to keep his promise and Läuffer, after a most desperate attempt to get the privy councillor to understand, allows his pampered body to commit a sin.

5. During rehearsal the student Pätus emerged as the most interesting character in the play after Läuffer. Where Läuffer castrates himself physically—which of course at the same time stands for a spiritual castration: the abjuring of rebellion—the self-castration practised by Pätus can only be understood in a spiritual sense. Pätus in *The Tutor* goes the opposite road to Schiller's: his Misère declines from extravagance to banality in the course of the play. To make this development clear we had first to lead Pätus to the highest summits before letting him fall headlong into the pit of philistine self-satisfaction. An opportunity was provided by the Kant quotation in the first student scene. Initially we chose a passage about apodictic and assertive sentences [. . .] with the result that Pätus, whom we meant to play a considerable part in our play, seemed not merely to Bollwerk but also to such spectators as occasionally came to rehearsals to be a muddleheaded clown whom nobody could possibly take seriously. We replaced it with an extract about the Ding an sich, but this made matters no better. Stage and auditorium alike confirmed that Bollwerk was right to ridicule Pätus' Kant-worship; which was not at all what we had intended. Finally we picked a passage from Kant's work "Zum ewigen Frieden," which had the desired effect. Pätus had to attain a genuine ethical high point before writing his thesis on war as the father of all things. He achieves something like greatness by his stubborn loyalty to Kant's truly progressive views. He is tellingly subversive, even if only in his ideas. He explains his stubbornness in another sentence added later: "And my 'No' . . . to some supreme leader." Bollwerk doubts whether such views are useful, but nobody supports him, Fritz too having said "It doesn't seem so wrong to me."

So we had the high point from which the fall could take place. [. . .]

6. In scene 12 we tried to show how Wenzeslaus the schoolmas-

ter, once he has been so generous as to open his house to the fugitive Läuffer, realizes his protégé's potential as cheap labor and, after overcoming his initial mistrust, decides to exploit Läuffer's predicament for his own advantage. At rehearsal it became clear that miming alone was not enough to make his intention evident. So we introduced an extra sentence after Wenzeslaus' big speech on the obligations of a German schoolmaster, to be spoken when he had sunk back in his armchair, exhausted by this effort: "I assume, young man . . . yes, that's how it is." Wenzeslaus has shielded Läuffer as one shields the ox that is due to pull one's cart.

7. We found in the course of rehearsal that in scene 14, where Lise says that her guardian would not give her to an officer because of the unsettled life and lack of possessions, we had to make Läuffer exclaim "And me? What have I got?" Subsequently, when Wenzeslaus asks him how he means to support her, Läuffer is telling the truth when he says he has told her already. As long as he remains capable of embarking on marriage he is hampered by his bad social position, and only his incapacity for marriage, after once castrating himself, puts him in a position to support his wife. [. . .]

8. Castration of the body is followed by castration of the mind. When Läuffer writes his letter to Major von Berg, begging him for God's sake not to deprive him of an existence for which he has made certain sacrifices, we added a postscript in which he promises "always to teach the martyrdom of our Hero-King without omissions."

9. Right up to the dress rehearsal we were uncertain whether the play ought to end with Fritz's return to Insterburg after the Pätus sub-plot has been rounded off, and his reconciliation with Gustchen, or with the castrated Läuffer's engagement to the schoolmaster's daughter. Till then the ending had been the phony idyll of the von Berg family reunion, complete with punchbowl and tears of joy over the happy turn of events as brought about by God. It was only after the dress rehearsal that we decided to end the play with Läuffer. For the tutor's splen-

dors and miseries are the subject of the story, and it was he who had been the pretext for an evening spent probing the causes of the German Misère.

[From the previously unpublished "Hofmeister. Textänderungen während der Probe" written up by Egon Monk from his rehearsal notes after discussion with Brecht in the summer holidays of 1950. These and Herr Monk's other unpublished notes on the production appear to have been destined for a "model book" which was never published. For Brecht's conception of the German Misère see p. xix.]

CORIOLANUS

Texts by Brecht

Enjoying the hero

As for enjoying the hero and the tragic element, we have to get beyond a mere sense of empathy with the hero Marcius in order to achieve a richer form of enjoyment. We must at least be able to "experience" the tragedy not only of Coriolanus himself but also of Rome, and specifically of the plebs.

There is no need to ignore the "tragedy of pride," or for that matter to play it down; nor, given Shakespeare's genius, would this be possible. We can accept the fact that Coriolanus finds it worthwhile to give his pride so much rein that death and collapse "just don't count." But ultimately society pays, Rome pays also, and it too comes close to collapsing as a result. While as for the hero, society is interested in another aspect of the question, and one that directly concerns it, to wit the hero's belief that he is indispensable. This is a belief to which it cannot succumb without running the risk of collapse. Thereby it is brought into irreconcilable conflict with this hero, and the kind of acting must be such as not only to permit this but to compel it.

[GW *Schriften zum Theater*, pp. 1252–53. Written in 1951 or 1952.]

Plan of the play

I

1 ROME caius marcius is prepared to quell a revolt of the starving plebs, but the threat of war with the volsces leads the senate to make the plebs concessions: they are given tribunes.

2 ANTIUM aufidius is advancing on rome at the head of the volsces.

3 ROME mother and wife see caius marcius off to the war.

4 CORIOLI caius marcius takes corioli, a volscian city. caius marcius is dissatisfied with his troops because they fight less well when taking it than when defending their own city.

II

1 ROME the city welcomes caius marcius as a conqueror. the tribunes are worried that he will put up for consul.

2 ROME the senate asks coriolanus to solicit the citizens' votes according to custom.

3 ROME coriolanus goes begging and is elected. the tribunes expose his plans for the plebs.

III

1 ROME coriolanus rejects the plebeians' demand for grain and attacks the tribunes.

2 ROME coriolanus is persuaded by his mother volumnia that it is worth apologizing to the people for the sake of power.

3 ROME instead of apologizing coriolanus loses control, insults the people, and is banished.

4 ROME volumnia and some senators accompany coriolanus to the city gate.

5 ROME volumnia curses the tribunes.

IV

1 CORIOLI a roman and a volscian discuss the situation.

2 ANTIUM coriolanus hires himself out to aufidius as leader of an army against rome.

3 ROME rome is seized by panic when it is learnt that coriolanus is moving on rome at the head of the volsces.

4 CORIOLI aufidius is merely waiting for rome to surrender before taking action against coriolanus.

V

1 ROME the senate sends menenius out to negotiate with coriolanus. it is not going to risk arming the plebs.

2 CORIOLI coriolanus packs menenius off without listening to his reasoned arguments.

3 ROME the tribunes call on the people to arm itself.

4 CORIOLI volumnia moves her son to turn back.

5 ROME rome receives volumnia without thanks on her return.

6 ANTIUM CORIOLANUS IS KILLED BY THE VOLSCES.

7 ROME ROME GIVES CERTAIN PATRICIAN LADIES LEAVE TO WEAR MOURN-ING FOR CORIOLANUS.

> [BBA 1769/02–3. This characteristic dissection of the story, emphasizing and at times adjusting what Brecht regarded as the points of interest, exists in at least three versions in the Brecht Archive, all identical except that one of them is amended so as to cut III, 1. The plan presumably dates from an early stage of the work on the play.]

Four short notes

(1) General

I don't believe the new approach to the problem would have prevented Shakespeare from writing a *Coriolanus*.

I believe he would have taken the spirit of our time into account much as we have done, with less conviction no doubt, but with more talent.

(2) The first scene

It is only by studying *the unity of opposites* that a proper disposition of the opening scene of Coriolanus becomes feasible; and this is the foundation on which the entire play rests. How else is the director to bring out the difference between Menenius Agrippa's phony *ideological* attempt to unify patricians and plebeians, and their real unification as a result of the war?

(3) A question arising from the first scene

What is the relationship between Marcius and the Senate? The patricians flatter Marcius (" 'tis true that you have lately told us, /The Volsces are in arms."). Marcius stifles his unease at the concession of the tribunate, as he is anxious to get a command in the war. But Marcius is made subordinate to Cominius, and the fact that Cominius has to remind him of his former promise suggests that he is at first none too pleased at this.

(4) Act IV, scene 4

In Act IV, scene 4 the citizens shouldn't change their opinions (as in Shakespeare) so as to regret Coriolanus' banishment; the nobility, however, should be clearly shown to be afraid (not for Rome, but for their own lives).

This can be brought out

(i) by having the citizens remark that it is better to have a vulture like Coriolanus *against* them than fighting in their ranks;

(ii) by letting the nobility fall into a panic, like a lot of flustered hens whose cock has flown off to a neighboring farmyard. They tremble to such an extent before their social equal that the weapons they are collecting fall from their hands.

> [The first and second of these passages are to be found, in reverse order, in GW *Schriften zum Theater*, p. 1253, and are attributed to 1951–52. The third is also to be found there, as part of a set of five such questions, the other four of which were embodied in the "Study" that now follows. The last is an unpublished note (BBA 1769/06) headed "Suggestions by Brecht." The result will be seen in the adaptation, where only one of the suggestions was carried out, and that in modified form.]

Study of the first scene of Shakespeare's *Coriolanus*

B.   How does the play begin?

R.   A group of plebeians has armed itself with a view to killing the patrician Caius Marcius, an enemy to the people, who is opposed to lowering the price of corn. They say that the plebeians' sufferance is the patricians' gain.

B.   ?

R.   Have I left something out?

B. Are Marcius' services mentioned?

R. And disputed.

P. So you think the plebeians aren't all that united? Yet they loudly proclaim their determination.

W. Too loudly. If you proclaim your determination as loudly as that it means that you are or were undetermined, and highly so.

P. In the normal theater this determination always has something comic about it: it makes the plebeians seem ridiculous, particularly as their weapons are inadequate: clubs, staves. Then they collapse right away, just because the patrician Agrippa makes a fine speech.

B. Not in Shakespeare.

P. But in the bourgeois theater.

B. Indeed yes.

R. This is awkward. You cast doubt on the plebeians' determination, yet you bar the comic element. Does that mean that you think after all that they won't let themselves be taken in by the patricians' demagogy? So as not to seem more comic still?

B. If they let themselves be taken in I wouldn't find them comic but tragic. That would be a possible scene, *for such things happen*, but a horrifying one. I don't think you realize how hard it is for the oppressed to become united. Their misery unites them—once they recognize who has caused it. "Our sufferance is a gain to them." But otherwise their misery is liable to cut them off from one another, for they are forced to snatch the wretched crumbs from each other's mouths. Think how reluctantly men decide to revolt! It's an adventure for them: new paths have to be marked out and followed; moreover the rule of the rulers is always accompanied by that of their ideas. To the masses revolt is the unnatural rather than the natural thing, and however bad the situation from which only revolt can free them they find the idea of it as exhausting as the scientist finds a new view of the universe. This being so it is often the more intelligent people who are opposed to unity and only the most intelligent of all who are also for it.

R. So really the plebeians have not become united at all?

B. On the contrary. Even the second citizen joins in. Only
    neither we nor the audience must be allowed to overlook
    the contradictions that are bridged over, suppressed, ruled
    out, now that sheer hunger makes a conflict with the patri-
    cians unavoidable.

R. I don't think you can find that in the text, just like
    that.

B. Quite right. You have got to have read the whole play. You
    can't begin without having looked at the end. Later in the
    play this unity of the plebeians will be broken up, so it is
    best not to take it for granted at the start, but to show it
    as having come about.

W. How?

B. We'll discuss that. I don't know. For the moment we are
    making an analysis. Go on.

R. The next thing that happens is that the patrician Agrippa
    enters, and proves by a parable that the plebeians cannot
    do without the rule of the patricians.

B. You say "proves" as if it were in quotes.

R. The parable doesn't convince me.

B. It's a world-famous parable. Oughtn't you to be objective?

R. Yes.

B. Right.

W. The man starts off by suggesting that the dearth has been
    made by the gods, not the patricians.

P. That was a valid argument in those days, in Rome I mean.
    Don't the interests of a given work demand that we re-
    spect the ideology of a given period?

B. You needn't go into that here. Shakespeare gives the
    plebeians good arguments to answer back with. And they
    strongly reject the parable, for that matter.

R. The plebeians complain about the price of corn, the rate
    of usury, and are against the burden of the war, or at any
    rate its unjust division.

B. You're reading that into it.

R. I can't find anything against war.

B. There isn't.

R. Marcius comes on and slangs the armed plebeians, whom
    he would like to see handled with the sword, not with

speeches. Agrippa plays the diplomat and says that the plebeians want corn at their own rates. Marcius jeers at them. They don't know what they are talking about, having no access to the Capitol and therefore no insight into the state's affairs. He gets angry at the suggestion that there's grain enough.

P. Speaking as a military man, presumably.

W. In any case as soon as war breaks out he points to the Volsces' corn.

R. During his outburst Marcius announces that the Senate has now granted the plebeians people's tribunes, and Agrippa finds this strange. Enter senators, with the incumbent consul Cominius at their head. Marcius is delighted at the idea of fighting the Volscian leader Aufidius. He is put under Cominius' command.

B. Is he agreeable to that?

R. Yes. But it seems to take the senators slightly by surprise.

B. Differences of opinion between Marcius and the senate?

R. Not important ones.

B. We've read the play to the end, though. Marcius is an awkward man.

W. It's interesting, this contempt for the plebeians combined with high regard for a national enemy, the patrician Aufidius. He's very class-conscious.

B. Forgotten something?

R. Yes. Sicinius and Brutus, the new people's tribunes, came on with the senators.

B. No doubt you forgot them because they got no welcome or greeting.

R. Altogether the plebeians get very little further attention. A senator tells them sharply to go home. Marcius "humorously" suggests that they should rather follow him to the Capitol. He treats them as rats, and that is when he refers them to the corn of the Volsces. Then it just says, "Citizens steal away."

P. The play makes their revolt come at an unfortunate moment. In the crisis following the enemy's approach the patricians can seize the reins once more.

B. And the granting of people's tribunes?

P. Was not really necessary.

R. Left alone, the tribunes hope that the war, instead of leading to Marcius' promotion, will devour him, or make him
fall out with the senate.

P. The end of the scene is a little unsatisfactory.

B. In Shakespeare, you mean?

R. Possibly.

B. We'll note that sense of discomfort. But Shakespeare presumably thinks that war weakens the plebeians' position,
and that seems to me splendidly realistic.

B. Beautiful things.

R. The wealth of events in a single short scene. Compare
today's plays, with their poverty of content!

P. The way in which the exposition at the same time gives
a rousing send-off to the plot!

R. The language in which the parable is told! The humor!

P. And the fact that it has no effect on the plebeians!

W. The plebeians' native wit! Exchanges like "Agrippa: Will
you undo yourselves? Citizen: We cannot, sir, we are un-
done already!"

R. The crystal clarity of Marcius' harangue! What an outsize
character! And one who emerges as admirable while
behaving in a way that I find beneath contempt!

B. And great and small conflicts all thrown on the scene at
once: the unrest of the starving plebeians plus the war
against their neighbors the Volsces; the plebeians' hatred
for Marcius, the people's enemy—plus his patriotism; the
creation of the post of people's tribune—plus Marcius'
appointment to a leading role in the war. Well—how
much of that do we see in the bourgeois theater?

W. They usually use the whole scene for an exposition of
Marcius' character: the hero. He's shown as a patriot,
handicapped by selfish plebeians and a cowardly and
weak-kneed senate. Shakespeare, following Livy rather
than Plutarch, has good reason for showing the senate
"sad and confused by a double fear—fear of the people and
fear of the enemy." The bourgeois stage identifies itself
with the patricians' cause, not the plebeians'. The plebei-

ans are shown as comic and pathetic types (rather than types who bear misfortune with humor), and Agrippa's remark labeling the senate's granting of people's tribunes as strange is used for the light it casts on Agrippa's character rather than to establish a preliminary link between the advance of the Volsces and the concessions made to the plebeians. The plebeians' unrest is of course settled at once by the parable of the belly and the members, which is just right for the bourgeoisie's taste, as shown in its relations with the modern proletariat. . . .

R. Although Shakespeare never allows Agrippa to mention that his parable has managed to convince the plebeians, only to say that though they lack discretion (to understand his speech) they are passing cowardly—an accusation, incidentally, that's impossible to understand.

B. We'll note that.

R. Why?

B. It gives rise to discomfort.

R. I must say, the way in which Shakespeare treats the plebeians and their tribunes rather encourages our theater's habit of letting the hero's hardships be aggravated as far as possible by the "foolish" behavior of the people, and so paving the way in anticipatory forgiveness for the later excesses of his "pride."

B. All the same Shakespeare does make a factor of the patricians' corn profiteering and their inclination at least to conscript the plebeians for war—Livy makes the patricians say something to the effect that the base plebs always goes astray in peacetime—and of the plebeians' unjust indebtedness to the nobles. In such ways Shakespeare refrains from presenting the revolt as a piece of pure folly.

W. But nor does he do much to bring out Plutarch's interesting phrase: "Once order had been restored in the city by these means, even the lower classes immediately flocked to the colors and showed the greatest willingness to let the ruling authorities employ them for the war."

B. All right; if that's so we'll read the phrase with all the more interest: we want to find out as much about the plebeians as we can.

P.   "For it may be a question of characteristics
     Of famous ancestors."

R.   There's another point where Shakespeare refrains from
     coming down on the aristocratic side. Marcius isn't al-
     lowed to make anything of Plutarch's remark that "The
     turbulent attitude of the base plebs did not go unobserved
     by the enemy. He launched an attack and put the country
     to fire and sword."

B.   Let's close our first analysis at this point. Here is roughly
     what takes place and what we must bring out in the thea-
     ter. The conflict between patricians and plebeians is (at
     least provisionally) set aside, and that between the Romans
     and the Volsces becomes all-predominant. The Romans,
     seeing their city in danger, legalize their differences by
     appointing plebeian commissars (people's tribunes). The
     plebeians have got the tribunate, but the people's enemy
     Marcius emerges, qua specialist, as leader in war.

B.   The brief analysis we made yesterday raises one or two
     very suggestive problems of production.

W.   How can one show that there has been opposition to the
     plebeians uniting, for instance? Just by that questionable
     emphasis on determination?

R.   When I told the story I didn't mention their lack of unity
     because I took the second citizen's remarks as a provoca-
     tion. He struck me as simply checking on the first citizen's
     firmness. But I don't suppose it can be played in this way.
     It's more that he's still hesitating.

W.   He could be given some reason for his lack of warlike
     spirit. He could be better dressed, more prosperous. When
     Agrippa makes his speech he could smile at the jokes, and
     so on. He could be disabled.

R.   Weakness?

W.   Morally speaking. The burnt child returns to its fire.

B.   What about their weapons?

R.   They've got to be poorly armed, or they could have got the
     tribunate without the Volsces' attacking; but they mustn't
     be weak, or they could never win the war for Marcius and
     the war against him.

B. Do they win their war against Marcius?

R. In our theater, certainly.

P. They can go in rags, but does that mean they have to go raggedly?

B. What's the situation?

R. A sudden popular rising.

B. So presumably their weapons are improvised ones, but they can be good improvisers. It's they who make the army's weapons; who else? They can have got themselves bayonets, butchers' knives on broom-handles, converted fire-irons, etc. Their inventiveness can arouse respect, and their arrival can immediately seem threatening.

P. We're talking about the people all the time. What about the hero? He wasn't even the center of R.'s summary of the content.

R. The first thing shown is a civil war. That's something too interesting to be mere background preparation for the entrance of the hero. Am I supposed to start off: "One fine morning Caius Marcius went for a stroll in his garden, went to the market place, met the people and quarreled," and so on? What bothers me at the moment is how to show Agrippa's speech as ineffective and having an effect.

W. I'm still bothered by P.'s question whether we oughtn't to examine the events with the hero in mind. I certainly think that before the hero's appearance one is entitled to show the field of forces within which he operates.

B. Shakespeare permits that. But haven't we perhaps over-loaded it with particular tensions, so that it acquires a weight of its own?

P. And *Coriolanus* is written for us to enjoy the hero!

R. The play is written realistically, and includes sufficient material of a contradictory sort. Marcius fighting the people: that isn't just a plinth for his monument.

B. Judging from the way you've treated the story it seems to me that you've insisted all of you from the first on smacking your lips over the tragedy of a people that has a hero against it. Why not follow this inclination?

P. There may not be much pretext for that in Shakespeare.

B. I doubt it. But we don't have to do the play if we don't enjoy it.

P. Anyway, if we want to keep the hero as the center of interest we can also play Agrippa's speech as ineffective.

W. As Shakespeare makes it. The plebeians receive it with jeers, pityingly even.

R. Why does Agrippa mention their cowardice—the point I was supposed to note?

P. No evidence for it in Shakespeare.

B. Let me emphasize that no edition of Shakespeare has stage directions, apart from those presumed to have been added later.

P. What's the producer to do?

B. We've got to show Agrippa's (vain) attempt to use ideology, in a purely demagogic way, in order to bring about that union between plebeians and patricians which in reality is effected a little—not very much—later by the outbreak of war. Their real union is due to force majeure, thanks to the military power of the Volsces. I've been considering one possibility: I'd suggest having Marcius and his armed men enter rather earlier than is indicated by Agrippa's "Hail, noble Marcius!" and the stage direction which was probably inserted because of this remark. The plebeians would then see the armed men looming up behind the speaker, and it would be perfectly reasonable for them to show signs of indecision. Agrippa's sudden aggressiveness would also be explained by his own sight of Marcius and the armed men.

W. But you've gone and armed the plebeians better than ever before in theatrical history, and here they are retreating before Marcius' legionaries. . . .

B. The legionaries are better armed still. Anyway they don't retreat. We can strengthen Shakespeare's text here still further. Their few moments' hesitation during the final arguments of the speech is now due to the changed situation arising from the appearance of armed men behind the speaker. And in these few moments we observe that Agrippa's ideology is based on force, on armed force, wielded by Romans.

W. But now there's unrest, and for them to unite there must be something more: war must break out.

R. Marcius can't let fly as he'd like to either. He turns up with armed men, but his hands are tied by the senate's "ruth." They have just granted the mob senatorial representation in the form of the tribunes. It was a marvelous stroke of Shakespeare's to make it Marcius who announces the setting-up of the tribunate. How do the plebeians react to that? What is their attitude to their success?

W. Can we amend Shakespeare?

B. I think we can amend Shakespeare if we can amend him. But we agreed to begin only by discussing changes of interpretation so as to prove the usefulness of our analytical method even without adding new text.

W. Could the first citizen be Sicinius, the man the senate has just appointed tribune? He would then have been at the head of the revolt, and would hear of his appointment from Marcius' mouth.

B. That's a major intervention.

W. There wouldn't have to be any change in the text.

B. All the same. A character has a kind of specific weight in the story. Altering it might mean stimulating interest that would be impossible to satisfy later, and so on.

R. The advantage would be that it would allow a playable connection to be established between the revolt and the granting of the tribunate. And the plebeians could congratulate their tribune and themselves.

B. But there must be no playing down of the contribution which the Volscian attack makes to the establishment of the tribunate; it's the main reason. Now you must start building and take everything into account.

W. The plebeians ought to share Agrippa's astonishment at this concession.

B. I don't want to come to any firm decision. And I'm not sure that that can be acted by pure miming, without any text. Again, if our group of plebeians includes a specific character, it wouldn't any longer be taken to stand for half of plebeian Rome, i.e., as a part standing for the whole. But I note your astonishment and inquisitiveness as you move around within this play and within these complex events on a particular morning in Rome, where there is much that a sharp eye can pick out. And certainly if you can find clues to these events, then all power to the audience!

W. One can try.

B. Most certainly.

R. And we ought to go through the whole play before deciding anything. You look a bit doubtful, B.

B. Look the other way.—How do they take the news that war has broken out?

W. Marcius welcomes it, like Hindenburg did, as a bath of steel.

B. Careful.

R. You mean, this is a war of self-defence.

P. That doesn't necessarily mean the same thing here as usually in our discussions and judgments. These wars led to the unification of Italy.

R. Under Rome.

B. Under democratic Rome.

W. That had got rid of its Coriolanuses.

B. Rome of the people's tribunes.

P. Here is what Plutarch says about what happened after Marcius' death: "First the Volsces began to quarrel with the Aequi, their friends and allies, over the question of the supreme command, and violence and death resulted. They had marched out to meet the advancing Romans, but almost completely destroyed one another. As a result the Romans defeated them in battle . . . ."

R. I.e., Rome without Marcius was not weaker, but stronger.

B. Yes, it's just as well not only to have read the play right through before starting to study the beginning, but also to have read the factual accounts of Plutarch and Livy, who were the dramatist's sources. But what I meant by "careful" was: one can't just condemn wars without going into them any further, and it won't even do to divide them into wars of aggression and wars of defence. The two kinds merge into one another, for one thing. And only a classless society on a high level of production can get along without wars. Anyhow this much seems clear to me: Marcius has got to be shown as a patriot. It takes the most tremendous events—as in the play—to turn him into a deadly enemy of his country.

R.   How do the plebeians react to the news of the war?

P.   We've got to decide that ourselves; the text gives no clue.

B.   And unhappily our own generation is particularly well qualified to judge. The choice is between letting the news come like a thunderbolt that smashes through everyone's defences, or else making something of the fact that it leaves them relatively unmoved. We couldn't possibly leave them unmoved without underlining how strange and perhaps terrible that is.

P.   We must make it have tremendous effects, because it so completely alters the situation, if for no other reason.

W.   Let's assume then that at first the news is a blow to them all.

R.   Even Marcius? His immediate reaction is to say he's delighted.

B.   All the same we needn't make him an exception. He can say his famous sentence "I'm glad on't; then we shall ha' means to vent/Our musty superfluity," once he has recovered.

W.   And the plebeians? It won't be easy to exploit Shakespeare's lacuna so as to make them seem speechless. Then there are still other questions. Are they to greet their new tribunes? Do they get any advice from them? Does their attitude towards Marcius change at all?

B.   We shall have to base our solution on the fact that there is no answer to these points; in other words, they have got to be raised. The plebeians must gather round the tibunes to greet them, but stop short of doing so. The tribunes must want to lay down a line, but stop short of it. The plebeians must stop short of adopting a new attitude to Marcius. It must all be swallowed up by the new situation. The stage direction that so irritates us, "Citizens steal away," simply represents the change that has taken place since they came on stage ("Enter a company of mutinous citizens with clubs, staves and other weapons"). The wind has changed, it's no longer a favorable wind for mutinies; a powerful threat affects all alike, and as far as the people goes this threat is simply noted in a purely negative way.

R. You advised us in our analysis to make a note to record our discomfort.

B. And our admiration of Shakespeare's realism. We have no real excuse to lag behind Plutarch, who writes of the base people's "utmost readiness" for the war. It is a new union of the classes, which has come about in no good way, and we must examine it and reconstitute it on the stage.

W. To start with, the people's tribunes are included in the new union; they are left hanging useless in mid-air, and they stick out like sore thumbs. How are we to create this visible unity of two classes which have just been fighting one another out of these men and their irreconcilable opponent Marcius, who has suddenly become so vitally needed, needed for Rome as a whole?

B. I don't think we'll get any further by going about it naïvely and waiting for bright ideas. We shall have to go back to the classic method of mastering such complex events. I marked a passage in Mao Tse-tung's essay "On Contradiction." What does he say?

R. That in any given process which involves many contradictions there is always a main contradiction that plays the leading, decisive part; the rest are of secondary, subordinate significance.—One example he gives is the Chinese Communists' willingness, once the Japanese attacked, to break off their struggle against Chiang Kai-shek's reactionary régime. Another possible example is that when Hitler attacked the USSR even the émigré white Russian generals and bankers were quick to oppose him.

W. Isn't that a bit different?

B. A bit different but also a bit the same thing. But we must push on. We've got a contradictory union of plebeians and patricians, which has got involved in a contradiction with the Volsces next door. The second is the main contradiction. The contradiction between plebeians and patricians, the class struggle, has been put into cold storage by the emergence of the new contradiction, the national war against the Volsces. It hasn't disappeared though. (The people's tribunes "stick out like sore thumbs.") The tribunate came about as a result of the outbreak of war.

W. But in that case how are we to show the *plebeian-patrician* contradiction being overshadowed by the main *Roman-Volscian* contradiction, and how can we do it in such a way as to bring out the disappearance of the new plebeian leadership beneath that of the patricians?

B.   That's not the sort of problem that can be solved in cold blood. What's the position? Starving men on one side, armed men on the other. Faces flushed with anger now changing color once more. New lamentations will drown the old. The two opposed parties take stock of the weapons they are brandishing against one another. Will these be strong enough to ward off the common danger? It's poetic, what's taking place. How are we going to put it across?

W.   We'll mix up the two groups: there must be a general loosening-up, with people going from one side to the other. Perhaps we can use the incident when Marcius knocks into the patrician Lartius on his crutches and says: "What, art thou stiff? stand'st out?" Plutarch says in connection with the plebeians' revolt: "Those without any means were taken bodily away and locked up, even though covered with scars from the battles and ordeals suffered in campaigns for the fatherland. They had conquered the enemy, but their creditors had not the least pity for them." We suggested before that there might be a disabled man of this sort among the plebeians. Under the influence of the naïve patriotism that's so common among ordinary people, and so often shockingly abused, he could come up to Lartius, in spite of his being a member of the class that has so maltreated him. The two war victims could recall their common share in the last war; they could embrace, applauded by all, and hobble off together.

B.   At the same time that would be a good way of establishing that it is generally a period of wars.

W.   Incidentally, do you feel a disabled man like this could perhaps prevent our group from standing as pars pro toto?

B.   Not really. He would represent the ex-soldiers.—For the rest, I think we could follow up our idea about the weapons. Cominius as consul and commander-in-chief could grin as he tested those homemade weapons designed for civil war and then gave them back to their owners for use in the patriotic one.

P. And what about Marcius and the tribunes?

B. That's an important point to settle. There mustn't be any kind of fraternization between them. The new-found union isn't complete. It's liable to break at the junction points.

W. Marcius can invite the plebeians condescendingly, and with a certain contempt, to follow him to the Capitol, and the tribunes can encourage the disabled man to accost Titus Lartius, but Marcius and the tribunes don't look at each other, they turn their backs on one another.

R. In other words both sides are shown as patriots, but the conflict between them remains plain.

B. And it must also be made clear that Marcius is in charge. War is still his business—especially his—much more than the plebeians'.

R. Looking at the play's development and being alert to contradictions and their exact nature has certainly helped us in this section of the story. What about the character of the hero, which is also something that must be sketched out, and in precisely this section of the story?

B. It's one of those parts which should not be built up from his first appearance but from a later one. I would say a battle-scene for Coriolanus, if it hadn't become so hard for us Germans to represent great wartime achievements after two idiotic wars.

P. You want Marcius to be Busch, the great people's actor who is a fighter himself. Is that because you need someone who won't make the hero too likable?

B. Not too likable, and likable enough. If we want to generate appreciation of his tragedy we must put Busch's mind and personality at the hero's disposal. He'll lend his own value to the hero, and he'll be able to understand him, both the greatness and the cost of him.

P. You know what Busch feels. He says he's no bruiser, nor an aristocratic figure.

B. He's wrong about aristocratic figures, I think. And he doesn't need physical force to inspire fear in his enemies. We mustn't forget a "superficial" point: if we are going to represent half the Roman plebs with five to seven men and the entire Roman army with something like nine—and not just for lack of actors—we can't very well use a sixteen-stone Coriolanus.

W.   Usually you're for developing characters step by step. Why not this one?

B.   It may be because he doesn't have a proper development. His switch from being the most Roman of the Romans to becoming their deadliest enemy is due precisely to the fact that he stays the same.

P.   *Coriolanus* has been called the tragedy of pride.

R.   Our first examination made us feel the tragedy lay, both for Coriolanus and for Rome, in his belief that he was irreplaceable.

P.   Isn't that because the play only comes to life for us when interpreted like this, since we find the same kind of thing here and feel the tragedy of the conflicts that result from it?

B.   Undoubtedly.

W.   A lot will depend on whether we can show Coriolanus, and what happens to and around him, in such a light that he can hold this belief. His usefulness has got to be beyond all doubt.

B.   A typical detail: as there's so much question of his pride, let's try to find out where he displays modesty, following Stanislavsky's example, who asked the man playing the miser to show him the point at which he was generous.

W.   Are you thinking of when he takes over command?

B.   Something like. Let's leave it at that for a start.

P.   Well, what does the scene teach us, if we set it out in such a form?

B.   That the position of the oppressed classes can be strengthened by the threat of war and weakened by its outbreak.

R.   That lack of a solution can unite the oppressed class and arriving at a solution can divide it, and that such a solution may be seen in a war.

P.   That differences in income can divide the oppressed class.

R.   That soldiers, and war victims even, can romanticize the war they survived and be easy game for new ones.

W.   That the finest speeches cannot wipe away realities, but can hide them for a time.

R.   That "proud" gentlemen are not too proud to kowtow to their own sort.

P.   That the oppressors' class isn't wholly united either.

B.   And so on.

R.   Do you think that all this and the rest of it can be read in the play?

B.   Read in it and read into it.

P.   Is it for the sake of these perceptions that we are going to do the play?

B.   Not only. We want to have and to communicate the fun of dealing with a slice of illuminated history. And to have firsthand experience of dialectics.

P.   Isn't the second point a considerable refinement, reserved for a handful of connoisseurs?

B.   No. Even with popular ballads or the peepshows at fairs the simple people (who are so far from simple) love stories of the rise and fall of great men, of eternal change, of the ingenuity of the oppressed, of the potentialities of mankind. And they hunt for the truth that is "behind it all."

[From *Versuche 15*, 1957; reprinted in GW *Schriften zum Theater*, pp. 869–888, and translated in *Brecht on Theatre*, 1964. This essay in dialogue form was written in 1954, after the project had apparently been put into mothballs, then used by Brecht as the opening (and most substantial) item of the mimeographed collection of new theoretical writings which he made in 1956 under the title *Dialectics in the Theater*. Of the four participants B. is of course Brecht himself, while P. is Peter Palitzsch, R. Käthe Rülicke, and W. Manfred Wekwerth, the eventual director of the Berliner Ensemble production and also of the 1971 National Theatre production in London, which showed that virtually the same interpretation of the play could be based on the original text.

P.'s mention of "famous ancestors" refers to Brecht's poem, "Literature will be scrutinized." Ernst Busch, whom Brecht expected to cast as Coriolanus, played Galileo and other leading parts (see Volume 5, p. xix) for the Ensemble, but Coriolanus was finally played by Brecht's son-in-law Ekkehard Schall.]

Editorial Note

Adapting Shakespeare

Brecht seems to have used *Coriolanus* as something of a training-ground for the younger dramaturgs and assistant directors, some of whose names appear in the note to the study of the first scene. They were divided into groups of two or three, says Peter Palitzsch, and set to analyze the story, check the translation, and suggest cuts and changes. It was in answer to the very radical nature of some of their proposals that Brecht made his dictum about amending Shakespeare, the emphasis in his answer being of course on the word "can." A great deal of his concept of the dispensability of the hero and the role to be given the plebeians was in fact already there in Shakespeare's text, so that gradually more modest ideas prevailed and the original play began to re-emerge. However, he felt that the play could not be left entirely unamended so long as the masses lacked self-awareness and their sense of history remained undeveloped, with the result that there are still some major alterations in the early outline plan printed above (pp. 375–377): notably Coriolanus' criticism of his troops in I, 4; the fact that the demand for grain in III, 1 is not just past history but something to be dealt with now; the whole business of arming the people in Act V (though Shakespeare's Sicinius provides a peg for this by his allusion in V, 1 to "the instant army we can make"); finally the *un*enthusiastic reception of Volumnia in V, 5 and the addition of the last scene.

The other notes which we print underline his intentions with regard to I, 1 and to IV, 4 (his eventual IV, 3), and most of the proposed alterations were in fact carried out. They would certainly have been more extensive if he had not preferred to leave it open what he would do to the battle scenes in Act I; thus Elisabeth Hauptmann's note when the play was finally published three years after his death in 1956:

> It was Brecht's intention to combine scenes 4 to 10 of Shakespeare's play to make one big battle scene, which would have formed his Act I, scene 3 [or scene 4 in the outline plan for the Berliner Ensemble acting version]. Brecht wanted to write this scene during the rehearsals, since he felt it essential to work out the text simultaneously with the positionings and movements.

Indeed Manfred Wekwerth and Joachim Tenschert did just this when they eventually staged the play for the Berliner Ensemble in September 1964; (they also restored a shortened version of I, 2). In the published text, however, which our translation necessarily follows, the original seven scenes have been merely renumbered 3a, 3b, etc., but are otherwise left as they stood in the old standard Schlegel-Tieck translation, here rendered in a modified version of Shakespeare's English.

This translation by Dorothea Tieck was the one from which the adaptors worked, and to some extent it survives in Brecht's final text even apart from the scenes in question. His was, in fact, not so much a new translation as a radical reworking of the old one, which underwent much the same roughening-up process as did A. W. Heymel's version of Marlowe's *Edward II* some thirty years earlier. Many of the Tieck lines and phrases have been taken over unchanged or still remain recognizable; some passages have been paraphrased and condensed; others have been entirely rewritten, sometimes for dramaturgical reasons, sometimes to bring them closer to the English. Thus Cominius' report in II, 2, which Tieck for some reason made finish up "and strikes with sudden reinforcement/The city like divine might" returns to something very near the original "And with a sudden re-enforcement struck/Corioli like a planet," while the "heart-hardening spectacles" of Coriolanus' speech on leaving Rome have become, not Tieck's "herzhärtend Schauspiel" but "herz-härtende Spektakel." It could also be more "gestic" (in Brecht's sense) to restore something like Shakespeare's word order and rhythms, as in Coriolanus' raging speech after his banishment in III, 3 (Brecht's III, 2), starting "You common cry of curs! whose breath I hate," where Brecht's version is altogether more forceful, rendering the final "There is a world elsewhere" not by Tieck's lilting "Noch anderswo gibt's eine Welt" but by an abrupt, challenging "s'gibt/Noch eine Welt woanders."

Brecht's cuts, which include the whole of Shakespeare's II, 2 and V, 5, are no more drastic than in any other modern production of this long play. Nor are his additions and interpolations all that lavish, the only heavily affected scenes being II, 3, where Coriolanus solicits the plebeians' votes, IV, 3 (the highway) and V, 4. Their extent and direction can be judged from the following scene-by-scene summary (Shakespeare's scene numbers being given each time in parentheses):

Act One

1. (I, 1) The man with the child is new, also the appearance of the armed men accompanying Marcius, whose entry has been brought forward by some sixteen lines. The messenger's entry has likewise been advanced. The citizens' applause for their tribunes is new, as is Marcius' expression of contempt for them ("And the newly baked/Tribunes"). The last twelve lines of the scene are new, and replace all Shakespeare's ending after Marcius' exit: Brutus now finds Marcius essential on military grounds, and the citizens, provided with a reason for leaving, no longer "steal away."

2. (I, 3. I, 2 is cut) Shakespeare's scene with some cuts.

3. (I, 4–10) Shakespeare's seven scenes in the old Tieck translation.

Act Two

1. (II, 1) The opening exchanges between Sicinius and Brutus are new, as far as Menenius' entry. His speeches have been cut to bare essentials, as far as the tribunes' exit, eliminating all discussion of Marcius' pride. At the end of the scene, when the tribunes are left alone, their exchanges are mainly new up to the point where Brutus says "I heard him swear,/Were he to stand for consul, never would he/Appear i' the marketplace." Their

ensuing proposal (just before the messenger's appearance) to tell the plebeians how Marcius hates them is cut.

2. (II, 2) Shakespeare with a few cuts.

3. (II, 3 followed by III, 1) The allusion to Marcius' indispensability is new at the end of the first citizen's second speech, together with the exchanges immediately following, as far as "Here he comes." So is everything from the entry of the man with the child up to that of three more citizens—Shakespeare's "two other citizens." So is Coriolanus' very Brechtian song. Then once Coriolanus has asked if he can change his clothes the rest of II, 3 is cut, so that the plebeians are no longer induced by the tribunes to revoke their votes ("almost all/Repent in their election"), and a new bridge passage inserted leading into III, 1 after the tribunes' entrance, where Menenius says "Be calm, be calm." This passage, from "Yes, that you may" to "Noble Marcius, what/Will you do with this grain if chosen consul," confronts Coriolanus with the question of whether to distribute the new grain, and it is his refusal to do this that now makes the plebeians change their minds, on plain materialistic grounds (the fourth citizen's "Where, Coriolanus, are the spoils /Of Corioli?"—another interpolated speech).

The attempt to arrest him follows, as in III, 1, but more violently and on different grounds, his offence in Shakespeare having been that he was a threat to the people's liberties. It is now all much more quickly over; almost as soon as the tribunes have called for his arrest he draws his sword, then is protected by the patricians and hustled out before worse can happen. Tribunes and people are accordingly not "beat in," as in Shakespeare, while all else that follows—the tribunes' threat to kill Coriolanus, their argument with Menenius and his offer to intercede—is cut.

Act Three

1. (III, 2) Virtually as in Shakespeare.

2. (III, 3) Ditto, except that Brecht adds the interpolated comments by the citizens, cuts Sicinius' suggestion that the people should vote "For death, for fine or banishment," and instead of Shakespeare's "Have you collected them by tribes?" substitutes

the more modern concept of "chairmen of the electoral districts."

3. (IV, 1) Close to Shakespeare, with cuts.

4. (IV, 2) Ditto.

Act Four

1. (IV, 3) In Shakespeare's scene too "a Roman and a Volsce" meet on the highway and discuss Coriolanus' banishment, but Brecht has rewritten it entirely in his own way, reminiscent in its mundane details of some of the dialogue in *Lucullus*.

2. (IV, 4 leading to IV, 5) Close to Shakespeare, with the one scene prefacing the other as there. The comic ending with the three servants, after Coriolanus' and Aufidius' exit, is cut, though Brecht must surely have regretted losing their Schweykian comments on war and peace.

3. (IV, 6) This is the IV, 4 of Brecht's plan, though in the event the changes are less radical than proposed there. In Sicinius' opening speech "without the hero" is a gloss. The citizens' remark at the end about Coriolanus' scorched-earth policy is new, while the second citizen's final question and Sicinius' curt "Yes" take the place of the original first citizen's "I ever said we were i' the wrong when we banished him" and the second citizen's reply "So did we all. . . ."

4. (IV, 7) Aufidius' closing speech is a paraphrase of the original, and the reference to the smoke signal is new (as are those in succeeding scenes); otherwise the scene is as in Shakespeare.

Act Five

1. (V, 1) Brutus' speech is new, with its order to distribute arms to the people. Otherwise Shakespeare's scene differs in having the tribunes on stage throughout, and its opening and closing speeches have been cut.

2. (V, 2) Shakespeare with cuts, notably of the closing exchanges.

3. (part of V, 4) The first half of the scene is new, with its evidence that a minority of the patricians are ready to join the plebs in defending the city. The ensuing exchanges between

Cominius and Sicinius are a shortened form of the Menenius-Sicinius dialogue at the beginning of the original V, 4. But Brecht's conclusion, again, is new, with its important statement by Brutus in lieu of Shakespeare's "the ladies have prevailed" and the jubilations that follow.

4. (V, 3) Two speeches by Coriolanus and one by Volumnia have been cut, during which Shakespeare makes him kneel to her, then refuse to let her kneel to him. Volumnia's first long speech ("If silence were possible") has had its beginning paraphrased, while her second, which shows her making use of every possible ground of appeal, has been entirely rewritten apart from its last three lines, so as to bring out (a) Coriolanus' dispensability, (b) the people's armed resistance, and (c) the patricians' dilemma whether to use the Volsces to defeat this resistance or vice versa. In Shakespeare Coriolanus' exclamation "O mother, mother" is followed by

> Behold the heavens do ope,
> The gods look down, and this unnatural scene
> They laugh at. O my mother, mother! O!
> You've won a happy victory for Rome . . .

Aufidius admits to being moved, and the scene ends, in flat contradiction to Brecht, with the lines "all the swords/In Italy, and her confederate arms,/Could not have made this peace."

5. (V, 5, showing Volumnia's triumphal return to Rome, has been cut) New scene, in which Brutus' couplet recalls the inter-scene verses in *Galileo*. It takes the place of the altered V, 5 proposed in Brecht's plan.

6. (V, 6) The scene has been simplified by eliminating Aufidius' "three or four conspirators" (who incidentally provided Christopher Isherwood with the title of his first novel) and instead having his officers kill Coriolanus with no preliminary instructions. The senators, a little confusingly, replace Shakespeare's lords of the city (of Antium, that is), and then everything after Coriolanus' death is cut: Aufidius helping to bear away the body, while the lords resolve "Let's make the best of it."

7. Entirely new. The suggestion in Brecht's plan is here reversed, and the ladies are *not* allowed to wear mourning.

THE TRIAL OF JOAN OF ARC AT ROUEN, 1431

Texts by Brecht

Dialectical factors in the adaptation and production of *The Trial of Joan of Arc at Rouen, 1431*

(B)   Interest common to occupying power and collaborationist clergy: destroy Joan. Clash of interests: the English wish to destroy her quâ rebel, the clergy quâ heretic.

(A)   When Joan calls for the expulsion of the English her spiritual judges sheepishly lower their heads. They know what they do.

(A)   In the second scene (opening of the trial) the clergy are all battling against Joan, but at the same time they are battling against one another for the honor of being the one to win the battle. They interrupt each other; one of them will contemptuously read the documents while another is examining the accused; Manchon, having been sent back to his place after a foolish question of his has given Joan an opening to launch an attack, thereafter sits and sulks, without taking any interest in the progress of the case.

(B)   Cut off from the people, Joan *suddenly* breaks down (in the eighth scene). But it can be observed (in the sixth) how her isolation keeps undermining her resistance.

(B)   The fourth scene (market day in Rouen) shows how the people are divided and confused by the clergy's ingenious solution of libeling the great patriot as a heretic; but also how this causes the clergy to lose ground.

(A)   Fear (at the sight of the executioner) stimulates Joan to make particularly bold answers. The more the church needs and uses such people, the less inclined she is to submit to its authority.—It is not the church's threats but her own mistaken assumption as to the people's passivity that temporarily breaks down Joan's resistance.

(A) (B)   Once she hears of the popular unrest in Rouen of which she is the center, her anger is directed against the Bishop of Beauvais, and it is anger at herself. For having lost faith in the people.

[GW *Schriften zum Theater*, pp. 1255–56.]

The last crowd scene

We took an astonishingly long time to work out the right attitude for the English soldiers; in fact we had quite a few performances behind us. They need to be brutal and on edge. When they turn their backs on the crowd they feel their backs and necks threatened even though the crowd is held off by a rope. Then when they thrust the crowd back (the rope having been coiled up) there is a characteristic instant. The crowd has collected in front of the peasant's son, the loose woman is hysterically screaming "Henry, go home!" One of the soldiers has given ground; he lowers the point of his pike. Will he run the wine merchant through? For three seconds everything stops. Then the soldier holds it level across his body once more, and growling "Back, back" continues to push back the crowd.

It is important to have fifteen seconds' pause as the burning starts, after the loose woman has softly remarked "Now!" and the prayers of the kneeling nuns have come to a stop in the middle of the Hail Mary. And it is likewise important that everyone should stare towards the stake (assumed to be on the apron), even right through the episode with the executioner and the peasant's son.

[GW *Schriften zum Theater*, p. 1256. The last-mentioned episode is not in our text.]

Editorial Note

Adapting Anna Seghers

Anna Seghers' radio play, which provided eleven of the seventeen scenes, together with the bulk of their dialogue, was first broadcast by the Belgian (Flemish-language) radio in 1935 and subsequently published in the Moscow *Internationale Literatur*. In 1950 it was broadcast by the East German radio. By using crowd noises and shouts, together with anonymous voices, it provided a feeling of the popular presence all through. The effect of this on Joan is much more lightly suggested than in the adaptation; the key which Brecht seized on is Joan's "Why are the people so gay" after her interrogation by La Fontaine (in Brecht's Scene 4), which the adaptation shifts to follow the threat of torture (two scenes later). Joan hears the crowd's shouts when she recants, and "draws in her breath"; nothing else is said to explain why she puts on men's clothes again during the ensuing popular riots. Altogether Seghers' court proceedings take up a far larger proportion of the play than those in the adaptation, while her crowd is more of a collective force and less differentiated, with none of Brecht's genre scenes.

The problem, then, for Brecht and Besson was (a) to make a full length play of this, (b) to bring out Seghers' implication that Joan's mystical voices somehow became the voice of the tangible people, and (c) to establish those people not as radio sound effects but as a group of individuals on the stage. This was done by taking the eleven sections into which the radio play falls—they are separated by clearly marked pauses or breaks—making separate scenes of them, and adding three entirely new crowd scenes (8, 10, and 11); which means that the second half of the cast list (i.e., all the characters after "English soldiers") are likewise new. At a later stage the opening and closing scenes in the Touraine countryside were added, with Jacques Legrain as a symbol of the French wine-growing peasantry recurring right through the play. The girls' song in these scenes was new, as was the mocking verse about Bishop Cauchon in the crowd scenes, the former being very freely derived from Christine de Pisan's poem of 1429: the first stanza from verse 35 and the third from verse 46. A second key remark was introduced in Cauchon's last interview with Joan (13) after she has put on a man's clothes once again; discussing her recantation she confesses "But then I doubted the people; I thought they wouldn't care if I died, and just go on drinking their wine. But they knew all about me the whole time!"

To take the scenes briefly:

1. New, not in Seghers.
2. Developed from anonymous crowd remarks at the opening of the radio play, which provide about half the dialogue.
3. Far the greater part comes from the radio play, with some rearrangement. The new passages tend to stress the role of the English as occupiers—e.g., the opening exchanges, and other use of the English language in Brecht's original play —together with the subservience of the French authorities towards them.
4. The middle section is new, including the exchanges about Catherine of La Rochelle and her visions.
5. Built round the exchanges between several (anonymous) assessors a little later in the radio play about Gerson's affidavit. Here the remarks are shared among identifiable characters. The market setting and whole first half of the scene (with the fishwife and company) are new, as are the closing speculations about Joan's virginity.
6. Almost entirely from the radio play.
7. From the radio play, but shifted back to come between the sight of the torture instruments and Joan's recantation.
8. New. The phrase of the scene title "Joan thinks the people have forgotten her" (penned by Brecht on one of his lists of scenes) can only refer back to the previous scene.
9. In the radio play Joan's recantation takes place in the audi-

ble presence of the crowd, and while the bishop begins reading the sentence and the executioner holds a burning torch ready to light the pyre. Maître Érard and his role are new. The condemnation read here by the bishop is that read by Chation in Seghers; virtually all the rest of the dialogue is new apart from the sentry's final remark. The English anger at Joan's escape is less labored in the radio play.

10. New.

11. New.

12. Apart from the first two remarks about collaboration with the English and the final hand-washing, this is virtually as in the radio play.

13. Like all the other scene titles and locations, this, with its "Joan has heard the voice of the people" is Brecht's. The scene is from the radio play, except the allusions to the people between the Bishop's "But you have publicly recanted" and his "In other words you are obstinate and guilty of a relapse." Here Anna Seghers simply had Joan say "Because I didn't know what a recantation meant."

14. Mainly from the radio play.

15. The crowd remarks here are partly from the end of the radio play, partly from the recantation scene (when the pyre was about to be lit). Brecht has shuffled them and distributed them to his individual characters. In the radio play the man who lit the flames is seized with remorse, and dominates the ending with his cries.

16. New.

DON JUAN

Texts by Brecht

On the adaptation

NOTES ON THE PRODUCTION

1

As setting, preferably Molière's original stage with its splendid perspectives, chandeliers, bare indications: the world as the grandees' ornamental fishpond.

2

The acting to be utterly serious, i.e., this is a society which takes itself very seriously indeed.

3

The great seducer never demeans himself by using specific erotic tricks. He seduces by means of his costume (and his way of wearing it), his position (and his barefaced abuse of it), his wealth (or his credit), and his reputation (or the self-assurance given him by his fame). He appears as a sexual Great Power.

4

Certain incidents can be accompanied by Lully's music. The conversations with Donna Elvira in the first and last acts are thereby made to lose their tragic character and become more suitably melodramatic. A flourish (*mort*) on the horns goes very well with the avenging brother's (Don Alonso's) appearance in the third act.

DON JUAN AS A CHARACTER

Don Juan is not an atheist in any progressive sense. His unbelief is not a militant one, calling for people to act. It is just a lack of belief—Don Juan may even believe in God, he would merely rather He was not mentioned, since this might disturb his own life of pleasure.—He will make use of any argument that gets a lady on her back, and equally any that gets her off his.

We are not on Molière's side here. His vote goes to Don Juan —the Epicurean (and follower of Gassendi) supporting the Epicurean. Molière ridicules heavenly justice, he feels this dubious arrangement for repressing joie de vivre is right up heaven's street. The only opponents he allows Don Juan are cuckolded spouses and so on.—We are against parasitic joie de vivre. Unfortunately the only bon vivant we can point to is the tiger.

BESSON'S PRODUCTION OF *DON JUAN* WITH THE BERLINER ENSEMBLE

When seventeenth-century German companies played Shakespeare, it was a vulgarized, bowdlerized Shakespeare in fancy dress. It was not till the classical revival that the texts were again straightened out and the significance of his works discovered. (Though it would be a mistake to assume that this led to a genuine Shakespearean tradition which could still be drawn on, since this splendid stream in turn rapidly stagnated, degenerating into routine banalities.) The bourgeois German theater disposed of Molière without wrecking the text; he was broken in by being "interpreted in depth," "humanized," "supernaturally charged." The miser became a "virtually" tragic figure, the "victim" of superhuman greed. Dandin, whom snobbery made a cuckold, became a kind of Woyzeck, whose wife is stolen by an aristocrat. Don Juan became the "perhaps positively tragic rake," "ever insatiably seeking and yearning."

The text before us offers no justification for such an interpretation, which betrays a total ignorance of the age Molière lived in and of his attitude towards it. We suffer today from a peculiar notion of progress which greatly hampers the theater in its efforts to resuscitate great works from the past. According to this view, progress consisted in artistic creation becoming less and less naïve and primitive as time progressed. It is a view which is also extremely popular in the bourgeois camp, which is where it properly belongs. When the English actor Olivier made his film of Shakespeare's *Henry V* he started off with a portrayal of the play's première in the Globe Theater. The acting was represented as emotional, stilted, primitive, virtually half-witted. Then "modern" acting took over. The crude old days were put behind us, the acting became elegant, superior, full of subtleties. I have hardly ever seen a film that irritated me so much. Fancy thinking Shakespeare could have been so much cruder and stupider a director than Mr. Olivier! Of course, I do not hold that the last century, or for that matter our own, has contributed nothing new to the portrayal of human social life or to the depiction of individuals. But there is not the least justification for giving older works "the benefit" of this, if they happen to be masterpieces. We mustn't impose features of Goethe's Faust on Marlowe's; it would not make him Goethean, nor would it help him to be more Marlovian. Old works have their own values, their own subtleties, their own scale of beauties and truths. Our job is to find these out. This doesn't mean that Molière has to be performed as he was in seventeen-something, only that he must not be performed as he was in 1850 (and for that matter in 1950). The variety of perceptions and beauties in his works is just what allows us to derive effects from them that are in tune with our own time. The old interpretations of Molière's *Dom Juan* are more use to us than the new (which are likewise old). We get more from the satire (closer to Molière) than from the semi-tragic psychological study. We find the glamor of this parasite less interesting than the parasitic aspects of his glamor. Leipzig philosophy students discussing Besson's production found the satirical presentation of the feudal concept of love as a hunt so topical that they burst out laughing and told us of present-day ladykillers. I hope and believe that they wouldn't have been nearly so interested by supernatural destroyers of souls.

There is in fact a double significance to Benno Besson's production of *Don Juan*. He restored the comic aspect of the character of Don Juan—justified, incidentally, by the original casting in Molière's theater of the actor who usually played the comic marquis—by restoring the play's social message. In the famous begging scene, which had hitherto served to present Don Juan as a free-thinker and progressive, Besson simply showed a libertine, too arrogant to admit any obligations, thus revealing how offhandedly the ruling clique treated the beliefs licensed and enforced by the state. He took a slight formal liberty by abandoning the play's division into five acts, a piece of period formalism, undoubtedly adding to the audience's entertainment by this simple measure, without at all detracting from the sense of the play. Another point of significance for the German stage was the extremely happy use Besson was able to make of the unique traditions of the French theater. The audience was delighted to observe the broadly universal quality of Molière's comic sense, that hazardous mixture of the finest chamber-music comedy with extreme farce, interrupted by those short, exquisitely serious passages which are unequaled elsewhere.

Our theater is at a lovely stage of learning. That is why its experiments matter and its errors can perhaps be forgiven.

[From *Stücke XII*, pp. 189–194. Also, with small typographical differences, in GW *Schriften zum Theater*, pp. 1257–61. The last section is dated 1954, and appeared that year in nos. 5–6 of the monthly *Sinn und Form*.]

Editorial Note

Adapting Molière

Don Juan is one of the less radical adaptations made by the Berliner Ensemble, and seems to be one of those with which Brecht himself had least to do; indeed there is less material in the Brecht Archive relating to it than even to some of the adaptations not normally credited to him, such as Gerhart Hauptmann's *Biberpelz* and Johannes R. Becher's *Winterschlacht*. Since he was relatively unfamiliar with French writing, the initiative and the bulk of the work on this play are almost certainly due to his bilingual collaborator Benno Besson, who directed its first production in November 1953. Besson had been co-translator of the French version of *Mother Courage* performed by the Théâtre National Populaire under Jean Vilar two years earlier, and they also staged *Dom Juan* (in its original version) at Avignon in 1953. That was the summer when Brecht was concentrating largely on his own last play *Turandot* and also wrote the cycle of poems called the "Buckow Elegies."

A note in GW *Schriften zum Theater* says that "the translation of the adaptation of the stage version was due to Bertolt Brecht, Benno Besson and Elisabeth Hauptmann," which would suggest that the adaptation itself may first have been made in French. A considerable number of its scenes are more or less straight translations from Molière, though there are also some dramaturgical changes, while the anti-aristocratic satire is strengthened (evidence of the Don's cowardice, extra references to his debts, etc.), and there is a new love adventure with the commander's daughter Angelica, who does not figure in the original at all (though there are other versions of the legend where Donna Elvira is his daughter, as in Da Ponte's libretto).

To resume the principal differences, in their order of occur-rence:

TITLE

Molière's play is called *Dom Juan* while its non-hero is Don Juan. Its sub-title "le Festin de Pierre" has been dropped.

ACT ONE

Scenes 1–3 are virtually I, 1–3 of the original, but 4 is a new scene, made from the conclusion of I, 2 (which deals with the proposed abduction at sea) and introducing the three boatmen, who are not in Molière at all. Hence scene 5 is entirely new. Scenes 6 and 7 are then made by bringing forward Don Luis' first appearance from IV, 4–5 together with parts of the dialogue, and adding the references to Donna Elvira and to the creditors.

ACT TWO

Scenes 1–6 are virtually Molière's II, 1–4, though 2 is an extra scene introduced to make the encounter with Mathurine more explicit, while in Molière Pieter (Pierrot) and the girls are peas-ants rather than fisherfolk. The dispute between the two girls is made more violent; in Molière they neither take off their sabots nor strike one another. Seven however is a new scene, replacing Molière's brief concluding scene 5, in which a bravo called La Ramée arrives to warn the Don that twelve horsemen are on his track. It omits La Ramée but introduces the comic doctor Marphurius, with the evident function of showing Don Juan to be a good deal more frightened of a beating from the infuriated boatmen than of any aristocratic duel.

ACT THREE

In his scene 1 Molière had Sganarelle disguised as a doctor, which allowed him to make some characteristic jibes at that profession, leading into the discussion of Don Juan's own scepticism about medicine: "Don't you believe in senna leaves?" and so on as in the adaptation. Scene 2 with the beggar is close to Molière's, except that the repeated indication that his remarks are addressed *"to Sganarelle"* have all been inserted; in the original there was a direct relationship between Don Juan and the beggar, with the former giving his own money. Scene 3 with Angelica's appearance and scene 4 with Sganarelle rather than Don Juan putting Don Carlos' attackers to flight (they being here identified with the boatmen) are both new, as is Don Juan's change of clothes at the beginning of the following scene, which introduces new references to the boatmen and their grudge against the aristocracy but is otherwise close to the original III, 3. Then 6, with Don Alonso's entry, is much shortened from III, 4, while 7 and 8 are carved out of III, 5, with additional references to Angelica as the commander's daughter.

ACT FOUR

This combines acts IV and V of the original, apart from the shifting forward of Don Luis' first entry (as above). Scenes 1–3 here are new, Seraphine not figuring in Molière's play at all, while Ragotin has only one line in it. Then 4–6 are IV, 1–3, the main difference being that the closing episode between the tailor and Sganarelle, who also owes him money, is cut. Scene 7 with Donna Elvira is IV, 6; scene 8 is entirely new; while in 9 the references to Elvira's effect on Don Juan come from IV, 7. The farcical meal here has however been cut, where Molière had Sganarelle stealing the Don's dishes while the lower servants stole his; and so has IV, 8, where the statue makes its brief second appearance.

Scene 10, Don Luis' second entrance, ends with a shortened version of V, 1, in which Molière had Don Juan "faisant l'hypocrite" to his father, an instruction that provides one of the clues to his play. Some of Don Luis' opening remarks derive from IV, 4, though Don Juan's account of the boat episode and the appearance of Angelica are of course new. Then scene 11 starts with part of V, 2, Don Juan's speech on hypocrisy being drastically shortened, but the preparations for the meal are new, together with the Don's rehearsal of his speech to the expected lady guest. V, 3 is cut, where his new-found hypocrisy is shown failing to work on Elvira's brother Don Carlos, who thus virtually drops out of the adaptation after the third act. The meal having been held back till now, the ghosts in V, 4 and 5 are eliminated and the commander's appearances in IV, 8 and V, 6 rolled together to make scene 12, whose conclusion with the Don dropping down the flaming hole is from the original.

After that, however, instead of Sganarelle's brief musings there is the new scene 13, with its parade of characters, including the tardy Angelica. Molière provides Sganarelle's concluding cry.

As for the actual translation, Molière's style has been largely allowed to go by the board. E.g., Sganarelle's "Je trouve fort vilain d'aimer de tous les côtés comme vous faites" becomes "Dieses Herumgeliebe ist was furchtbares" ("This indiscriminate loving is abominable," p. 194); Donna Elvira's "Vous plaît-il, Don Juan, nous éclaircir ces beaux mystères?" becomes "Don Juan, dürfte ich Sie um eine Erklärung dieser rätselhaften Erklärung [sic] bitten?" ("Don Juan, may I ask you to explain your puzzling explanation?" p. 197); while Charlotte's "Que veux-tu que j'y fasse? C'est mon himeur, et je ne me pis refondre" becomes "Ich bin nun mal so" ("That's the way I am," p. 206). It is not clear how far this kind of verbal clumsiness is deliberate, intended perhaps to be anti-aristocratic. In addition, of course, many speeches have been condensed in translation, rather than cut.

TRUMPETS AND DRUMS

Texts by Brecht

Plan of the play

1. *Headquarters*

Plume, the recruiting officer who has arrived from London, is informed by his sergeant Kite about the state of the market for recruits and love. Recruiting is going badly, but Victoria, the justice's daughter, who a year earlier had been in pigtails, has been visiting a girl put in the family way by Plume. Plume gives his friend the shoe manufacturer Worthy a word of advice in matters of the heart. In return Worthy offers him a handsome commission on boots, which Worthy needs soldiers to fill.

2. *The justice's house*

To shield her from Plume, Balance sends his daughter Victoria away to the country. A true patriot, he then receives Plume with open arms.

3. *Melinda's house*

Victoria finds no asylum at Melinda's.

4. *Market place*

Band concert and promenade. Shrewsbury salutes England's heroes. Worthy follows the strategy recommended by Plume, and gives Melinda the cold shoulder. She instantly consoles herself with one of the heroes, the fiery Captain Brazen. With Plume's assistance Kite manages to gaff two young fellows.

5. Headquarters

A young gentleman called Victor is looking for Captain Plume, who has just gone inside the inn with Rose, a country girl, for a business discussion. Her brother calls in the land-owner Lady Prude. She cross-examines Rose, who emerges from the inn with some lace.

6. Billiard room at the inn

Victor hands Plume a letter from Victoria. The young gentle-man has pots of money, and stands treat to Plume and Brazen. In a conversation with Plume he establishes the fact that the former cannot live without the excitements of the battlefield. He resolves to be recruited, and chooses Plume. The casualty lists for the victory at Höchstätt are made public.

7. Room at the inn

The recruiting drive has come to a standstill. Kite does his pathetic best, disguised as a fortune-teller. Worthy makes it up with Melinda. She agrees to leave Brazen.

8. Picnic by the Severn

Victor steals the country girl Rose away from Plume. Melinda tells Brazen that she is going to marry a civilian. The alarm is sounded. Couples emerge from the bushes. Kite drives them all to headquarters.

9. The justice's house

Lady Prude denounces Plume and Victor for immorality. Balance's attitude, as he opens the post from London, is "Thou shalt not muzzle the ox that treadeth out the corn": i.e., the town's defenders are entitled to the town's daughters. The post contains the Act of Impressment. But the prisons prove to be empty. How are they to be filled? A meeting of notables decides on a grand moral clean-up. Brazen presents himself to Melinda in civilian clothes.

10. Room at the inn

During the cleaning-up operation Victor and Rose are arrested as lovers. Victor demands Plume's arrest, which is effected, much to the delight of Lady Prude, by a weeping Kite. [. . .]

11. The justice's house

Among Plume's fellow prisoners is a business man who speaks enthusiastically to him of the excitements of the city. Victor refuses to wash in public and is led away. Then Balance starts forcing the malefactors into the army. On Plume's appearing before him he becomes enraged at Kite's lack of patriotism, and invites Plume to join him on the bench. Summoned out of the courtroom, however, he encounters Victoria. In his anger he cashiers Plume. At this Victoria, who is determined to fight for her beloved man, pretends to commit suicide. She announces that she is pregnant and forces her father to order Plume's release from the army. The latter now sees Victoria for the first time and is thrown into confusion. Buzzing round Melinda are Brazen (in civilian clothes) and Worthy (in uniform). But a bugler recognizes in Brazen a detested sergeant, and so Balance is able to make him take over Plume's battalion. Plume will become a stockbroker in the city and multiply Melinda's twenty thousand pounds for her. While a battalion from the neighboring town is marching past on its way to embark, that great patriot Balance shoves into the army whatever he has no personal need for at home.

> [BBA 651/01–2. This scheme, which follows the eventual division into scenes, apart from the subsequent insertion of the prison scene (11), dates from after the decision to call Farquhar's Silvia Victoria, but before the transposition of the whole play to the period of the War of Independence. The last scene in particular is very different.]

The love story

Victoria was sixteen and a pupil at a boarding school, when she had a brief "love affair" with Captain Plume lasting barely three days: letters (in which she insisted on marriage), a hasty rendezvous, a painful leavetaking. When Plume comes back he hardly remembers anything about it, but is told that she has stood by a girl whom he had put in the family way. Her father, the justice of the peace, is told so too; he sends her away to the country as Plume arrives.

Then a young man appears in Plume's quarters with a letter from Victoria. Plume is absent on business (with Rose). The young man, whose name is Victor, witnesses the scandal over Rose. Victor/Victoria finds the wartime climate unhealthy. At the same time a conversation informs her that Plume is entirely committed to his profession because it satisfies his love of excitement. Victor/Victoria agrees to enlist as an ensign [. . .] in order to be able to remain by Plume's side as his guardian angel. She asks Plume to abandon Rose to her. She does not, however, trust him when he wants to finish off his business with Rose. She herself arranges a rendezvous—with Rose—at Haughton's Hotel. The rendezvous [. . . proves] a failure. Rose asks for Plume. Victor meanwhile is arrested during the police raid and brought before her own father. Luckily Plume is arrested too. Victoria asks her father to reduce him to the ranks (I am carrying his twins). Plume now sees her for the first time, as she offers herself, her money, and the excitement of London.

> [BBA 983/71–72. The typescript is torn and partly illegible. "Haughton" for the hotel proprietor is presumably Farquhar's Horton, but may have helped suggest the name Laughton for the potboy in the final version. Charles Laughton's family were of course also in the hotel business.]

Three notes

a) Contradictions

The field within which characters and plot move displays, inter alia, the following contradictions:

An officer's profession and vocation.

An officer does his best to defend his own country, wherever he happens to be fighting, and to live off the country wherever he happens to be stationed; it too may be his own.

He provides himself with local girls, irrespective whether he is in his own country or abroad.

The conqueror gets himself conquered.

The ruling class find that patriotism and egotism coincide.

b) First scene

War as a universal concern and as a private one. On arriving Captain Plume is told how Shrewsbury is reacting to its "military suitors." Not many recruits have applied, but a girl has applied for the captain.

The war however is distasteful to the captain, whose job it is to get recruits for it. He is throwing soldiers into a battle with civilians.

Reluctant to fight as a soldier for civilian interests, the captain will transfer to civil life in the course of the story (thereafter to do his exploiting in England rather than America). Sergeant Kite's report indicates a conflict of interests between the young people of Shrewsbury and the Crown.

What sort of alienations are going to bring out these contradictions apart from an alienating style of acting?

c) Captain Plume

There is no reason why an English recruiting officer in a restoration comedy should be given any higher social status than, say, a traveler in wines in early twentieth-century Prussia. It was not what you might call a profession for the aristocracy, whose sons had regiments of their own by the age of eight. Plume is a farmer's boy who has worked his way up by his native wit, possibly combined with courage, and has no need of fine manners. The story of the play requires him to be reasonably well-built, and no one in the audience need share Victoria's feelings for him. Nor on the other hand does his rank have to be held against him. A subordinate, he is at the same time a plebeian.—As for his outward appearance: smartness or elegance of bearing should be avoided. Plume may wear a pretty uniform, but he neither poses as an aristocrat nor moves about like a flamingo.

> [GW *Schriften zum Theater*, pp. 1263–64. Ribbentrop, Hitler's foreign minister, was once a traveler in wines.]

Editorial Note

Adapting Farquhar

The main work on the adaptation seems to have been done in March and April, 1955, though the play was not produced till the following September. The first complete script in the Brecht Archive is marked "1955 brecht besson" in Brecht's hand, which suggests that Elisabeth Hauptmann's contribution came later. Initially the period of the play was to have been that of the Marlborough Wars, as with the original, while the heroine's name Silvia was also to be retained. However, a number of major dramaturgical changes seem to have been decided on from the outset, to judge from Brecht's early plans noting what he regarded as the main points of the story, some being Farquhar's and some new ideas of his own. Thus, to take the original scene by scene, the following is a rough summary of how Brecht proposed to use it:

I, 1 (Brecht's scene 1.) Worthy was from the first made into a shoe manufacturer with a vested interest in recruiting, summarized in the phrase "soldiers for boots." Plume's previous knowledge of Silvia was more extensive in Farquhar; Brecht reduced it to a minimal recollection.

I, 2. Melinda's apartment. (Originally 2, shifted to 3.) Brazen's letter is cut. Brecht's first idea seems to have been to bring on Brazen himself here, but this was abandoned.

II, 1 and 2. An apartment in Justice Balance's house and *Another apartment.* (Run together to make scene 3, shifted to 2.) All reference to the death of Silvia's brother—the occasion for a fine display of family indifference in the original—was omitted, also the exchanges between Plume and Silvia indicating a certain degree of previous devotion. At an early stage Brecht switched round the two halves of the composite scene so as to make Plume appear *after* Silvia's exit.

II, 3. The street. Included more or less intact in Brecht's scene 4, though there seems to have been an original intention to make Pearmain the potboy and allow him, before his recruitment, to overhear Balance discussing the war casualties, possibly however in a new scene.

III, 1. The market place. (Scene 5.) In the event, Brazen's first appearance was brought forward merely by one scene. (Brecht originally thought of making him a sergeant who masquerades as an officer and is recognized by Balance, but this was dropped). The episode between Plume and Rose was observed by Silvia, who is not in Farquhar's scene at all, and also by a new character, Lady Prude, in lieu of Balance. Prude, says a note, was to "complain to Balance about the decline of morality in Shrewsbury," and later to take part in a "meeting of Shrewsbury notables" where she would denounce Plume and call for police action; this was effected in Brecht's scene 9.

III, 2 and IV, 1. The walk by the Severn side. (Scene 8.) There seems to have been no intention to follow Farquhar in letting the two recruiting officers compete for Silvia's military services. Brecht's notes say: "Disguised as a young man, Silvia lets herself be recruited so as to be near Plume"; "Brazen confesses his war-weariness to Melinda" (not in Farquhar); and "Silvius [i.e., Silvia in male attire] steals the farmer's daughter Rose away from Plume." In the original the actual recruiting of Silvia only occurs when the justices order her into the army in the last act.

IV, 2. It looks as if nothing from this scene was ever meant to be kept, since Lucy has no role in the adaptation quâ maid to Melinda (whereas Farquhar here has her trying to blackmail her mistress), while the advancing of the duel eliminates the Worthy-Brazen quarrel.

IV, 3. A chamber. Kite's fortune-telling act played no part in Brecht's plans, though part of the scene was in fact taken into scene 8.

V, 1. An anteroom adjoining Silvia's bedchamber. (Scene 10.) "A raid on the inn leads to the arrest of Silvius and Rose as lovers," says an early note. In Farquhar the only other characters to appear here are Bridewell and Bullock; Plume, still ignorant of "Wilful's" identity, is not present.

V, 2. Justice Balance's house. Once again, nothing in this scene, which brings the freshly arrested Silvia (still unrecognized) before her father, seems to figure in Brecht's schemes, though there is a very approximate equivalent in Lady Prude's reactions in the second half of scene 10, which also includes Rose's reference to her bedfellow as "the most harmless man in the world."

V, 3. Melinda's apartment. Brecht's notes suggest that he has no interest in Worthy except as a shoe manufacturer. However, a good part of the exchanges between Worthy and Melinda in his otherwise new scene 9 come from here.

V, 4. The market place. Another scene of no dramaturgical use to Brecht, though Plume's and Brazen's discussion about how best to lay out twenty thousand pounds was taken into the otherwise new scene 7.

V, 5. A court of justice. Incorporated in scene 12, as described below.

V, 6. The fields. The mock-duel has been taken into Brecht's scene 8. As for Lucy's weakness for Brazen, like her whole role in the intrigue around Melinda it has gone.

V, 7. Justice Balance's house. Fused with V, 5 to make scene 12. Brecht's interpretation of justice here follows the early note which says "Having just received the Pressing Act from London, Balance imagines he can go to work in a big way. The prisons being relatively empty, it is decided to fill them. This means going along with Lady Prude, Plume's old enemy," the ground for this now being prepared in the new scene 9, which makes the play's relation to the Mutiny and Impressment Acts (promulgated when Farquhar himself was a recruiting officer in Shrewsbury) that much more explicit. The prisoners Workless and Miner are drawn from Farquhar (though he gives them no names), likewise the arrest of Bridewell. Silvia, however, is tried too in Farquhar's V, 5, and sent into the army to the accompaniment of Plume's reading of the Articles of War. She is only recognized and released in V, 7, after which, as one of Brecht's notes puts it, "Brazen condemns Plume to civilian life."

In the "1955 brecht besson" script the references were originally to the battles of Marlborough's time—Plume, for instance, was "the hero of Schellenberg" (i.e., Donauwörth, 1704)—but they have been amended, often in Brecht's own hand, and remarks about America, the colonies, Boston harbor and so forth worked in (though by an evident oversight Kite's list of heavenly bodies in scene 8 was left with "Dixmude, Namur, Brussels, Charleroy," as in Farquhar, instead of the "Boston, Massachusetts, Kentucky, Philadelphia" of the final script). This version contains the twelve scenes in their final order, also the prologue and three of the songs: "When I leave you for the war, dear" from scene 8, "E.N. Smith" from the interlude after scene 11, and "Over the hills and over the sea," though instead of concluding the play this was sung by Kite in scene 4, and in a version much closer to Farquhar's original in the corresponding II, 3.

Besides Lady Prude, it introduced another new "notable" in the shape of Mr. Smuggler, the London banker, who was given rather more to do than in the final version. Thus in scene 11 he had to tell Plume and Kite of a city coup in wool which he claimed was as exciting as any military encounter, after which he gave Plume his card, saying, "If I can be useful to you at any time . . ." while in the last scene he recognized Brazen as his absconding cashier Jack. The butler Simpkins, however, figured on many pages of this version as "a servant," with virtually nothing to say, though there are additions which build the part up slightly, and retyped pages which give him his name. The Mike-Lucy sub-plot too is barely started (Mike being called George and Maggie Minnie, which explains the use of that name in the scene 8 song); while the other two justices, Scale and Scruple, still make their unnecessary appearance as in Farquhar. As for Silvia, she has become (anachronistically) Victoria, but is still not recognized by Plume in the prison scene. Apparently it comes as a complete surprise to him when, as he starts to sign her release (as in Farquhar), she exclaims "Father, I can no longer deceive you. William, pardon your Victoria if she now tells the truth," then goes on very much as on p. 318.

The Worthy-Melinda relationship is left unresolved at the end of the play (Worthy in this version having actually enlisted under Plume in scene 9), and the two lovers only come together as the company takes its bow. The two scenes that differ most from the final text, however, are scenes 8, *By the Severn*, and 12, the concluding court scene. The first of these was evidently conceived as consisting of two settings "wooden bench by the copse" and "punt in the reeds," which would have alternated on a revolving stage; also the blacksmith was an extra character called Flock, later to be merged with William. In scene 12, which showed the court and an antechamber, the sequence of episodes was as follows (showing their present order in parentheses):

Balance with Melinda and Lucy (2)

Plume invited to join the justices (1)

Trial of Workless (9)

Trial of Miner (5)

Victoria pleads for Plume's arrest and is recognized by Balance (6)

Victoria with Balance and Plume in the antechamber (7)

Lucy's report to Brazen (4)

Question of Plume's and Victoria's marriage (8)

Balance instantly sentences five anonymous prisoners for having no visible means of support (—)

Trial of prostitute, pimp, and pickpocket (3)

George (Mike) and Bridewell sentenced (10)

Plume accepts Victoria, hands his uniform to Brazen who reads the Articles of War (11)

Balance sentences three unemployed men (—)

Lucy gets George (Mike) discharged (12)

Brazen marches off with recruits. Balance, Victoria, and Plume leave for the pheasant shoot (13)

This left considerable changes to be made in the play before the present text was arrived at, notably the further development of the references to the American War of Independence and the repeated insertion of Kite's catch-phrase about the Mississippi. The broad-shouldered man was introduced in scene 4 and the court scene, where it was decided to give more prominence to the crowd; hence the former's comments, together with those of the wives, Jenny, Mrs. Cobb, etc. Simpkins the butler was further built up, possibly using elements from Charles Laughton's *Ruggles of Red Gap* and a few Wodehouse recollections, to fill in the new American background (as by his account of the battle of Bunker Hill in scene 4) and at the same time perhaps to give a good if anachronistic role to the actor Wolf von Beneckendorff. Scene 6 in the billiard room was amended to start with yet another account of Bunker Hill, this time from the potboy, but this was then dropped. In scene 8 by the Severn the swan was introduced and the Mike/Lucy passages built up so as to show their sympathy for the colonists. Scene 10 (the bedroom scene) was likewise lengthened, showing inter alia that

Plume recognizes Victoria. The songs were added to, initially
by Melinda's song (scene 3) and the second and third verses of
"Over the hills and over the sea" in the last scene. Victoria's
song at the end of scene 6 came later, as did the Kiplingesque
"Women of Gaa" (? Goa. Scene 11) and the first verse of "Over
the hills." Other late additions were the exchanges between
Lucy and Mike (now surnamed Laughton) about their hotel in
New York and its defence against the redcoats, and a number
of Simpkins' patriotic comments and interjections.

Thus Brecht's new scenes additional to Farquhar are: 6, the
billiard room, which may derive from Brecht's early note that
"Silvius tries to find out how strongly Plume is committed to
the military profession. Plume can't imagine either himself or
Silvius having any other"; 7 on the market place; most of 9,
culminating in the meeting of notables; and 11 in prison. Significant points taken from the original include the personalities of
Kite and Brazen together with much of the latter's dialogue—
for instance such expressions as "my dear" and "Mr. Laconic"
—and his interest in Melinda's twenty thousand pounds; likewise Balance's warning against predatory captains [p. 257], the
episodes with Rose (and her chickens) and Appletree and Pearmain, the cases of Workless and Miner in the last scene and,
above all, the whole central notion of magistrates sending men
into the army.

BERTOLT

Bertolt Brecht: Plays, Poetry, & Prose

Edited by

Ralph Manheim and John Willett

Wolfgang Sauerlander, Associate Editor

BRECHT

COLLECTED PLAYS

VOLUME 5

Life of Galileo

The Trial of Lucullus

Mother Courage and Her Children

VINTAGE BOOKS, *A Division of Random House, New York*

Contents

Introduction

The crisis years 1938–39 and their aftermath

1

The three works in this volume were of particular importance in Brecht's development, and they occupied him longer and more intensively than anything else he wrote. Dating from just after he turned forty, they are in every sense crucial, for not only did they originate in a crisis of human history but their later evolution spanned much the same years as that crisis took to work itself out. In Brecht's own life they cover three very different periods: his Scandinavian exile, his years on the fringe of Hollywood, then his return after the Second World War to an honored position in the Communist half of Germany. Two of them, *Galileo* and *Mother Courage*, were in 1947 and 1949 given productions which struck him, quite rightly, as among the chief events in his theatrical career; all three were subjected to textual changes which have drawn much critical comment and attention, notably those made to *Lucullus* in 1951; finally it has become common, if questionable, practice to take the figure of Galileo as in every way a spokesman for the author's own opinions. Hence the wealth of notes and variant material relating to these plays. Hence also the inclusion of so much of it in the present edition.

For Brecht 1938 seems to have been a general turning-point, marking a new detachment from immediate political tasks, whether anti-Nazi like the sketches making up *Fear and Misery of the Third Reich* (whose wartime version was called *The Private Life of the Master Race*) or pro-Soviet like the "Lenin Cantata" which he wrote with Hanns Eisler the previous year. The

change affected his esthetic outlook, not only his willingness to tackle contemporary themes, and it came at a time when Brecht on his Danish island was finding himself in sharp disagreement with the concept of Socialist Realism advocated by Georg Lukács and the more influential Moscow-based exiled intellectuals. What made this extra painful was that Lukács's views were being set out in *Das Wort*, a Moscow monthly magazine of which Brecht was an editor and in which his anti-Nazi sketches and his short poems for the German Freedom Radio were then appearing. When in June, a month after a group of the *Fear and Misery* sketches had been performed in Paris under the title *99%*, Lukács wrote approvingly about one of them, Brecht commented in his diary that "Lukács has welcomed 'The Informer' as if I were a sinner who had entered the bosom of the Salvation Army." Evidently this was something that he was by no means keen to do.

There was something much more serious at stake here than a mere literary debate, and Brecht was made fully aware of this fact by his knowledge of the Soviet scene. Of the three Russian friends whom he had approached in March 1937 with a view to forming an international "Diderot Society" of like-minded theater people, within a matter of weeks Eisenstein had been denounced in *Pravda* and stopped working on *Bezhin Meadow*, Okhlopkhov had lost his theater, and Tretiakov had been arrested and shot. This was only part of a much more widespread cultural reaction which also involved measures against Meyerhold and Tairov, the other two Soviet theater directors of that time who can be linked with Brecht, and which coincided unmistakeably with the political terror under Stalin's notorious Commissar for Internal Affairs, Yezhov. By the middle of 1937 Kun and Knorin, the two Comintern members who had shown themselves friendly to him in Moscow in 1935, had been arrested and tortured, while one of his leading actresses, Carola Neher, had been arrested with her Russian husband and sentenced to ten years' hard labor on an espionage charge; all three were later killed. Such horrifying developments within Brecht's own camp combined with the unchecked progress of the Nazi enemy (e.g., the swallowing of Austria in the spring of 1938), to bring a new element of sadness and solitude into his work. Thus

Walter Benjamin, who arrived in Brecht's village at the end of June 1938 when Tretiakov's probable fate had become clear, and stayed till after the Munich Agreement, found that his friend seemed to have got much less prickly and provocative, and interpreted this in a letter to Theodor Adorno as a sign of his growing isolation.

It was what Brecht in his verse of 1938–39 calls "the dark times," a "bad time for poetry": a kind of paralyzed horror fills the poems which he then wrote about Neher and Tretiakov and which remained unpublished until after his death. Though the émigré press continued to publish his earlier and more topical writings, the satires, songs, and playlets now fell off, nor after 1937 did he make any further public statements or speeches in the anti-Fascist cause. He did however write a number of essays in refutation of the "arbiter of art" Lukács, all of which likewise remained unpublished even though the two best known were clearly intended for *Das Wort;* after March 1939 that magazine itself ceased to appear. Also during 1938 Brecht began writing the still more private *Me-Ti* aphorisms (or *Book of Changes*), with their half-camouflaged criticisms of Stalin and evident doubts about the Soviet show trials. Elsewhere he had begun to turn increasingly to remoter peoples and periods: to Roman history in his unfinished Julius Caesar novel, to the Chinese poets in a group of translations from Arthur Waley, to the German classics in the literary sonnets of that summer. At the same time he was bringing out a new selection of his poems, originally as part of the Malik-Verlag edition of his work, whose first two volumes had appeared in the spring, then when the Nazis seized the sheets at the binders' in the Sudetenland, as a new book of *Svendborger Gedichte* to be printed in Copenhagen.

He wrote *Galileo* during the first three weeks of November 1938, though he must have carried the idea around in his head much longer than that and got through a good deal of preliminary reading. It was his first big play for four years, and from the outset it was a statement of faith in the "new age," irrespective of setbacks, and also in the power of the human reason in face of authoritarian systems of thought. The principal figure had long interested him, for Galileo's had been one of the cases considered for the series of trial scenes which he had planned

to write before 1933, and (as Professor Schumacher has suggested in his valuable book on the play; see p. 265) it could indeed have been brought to mind again by the tricentenary in that year. Among the books which he used in his researches, according to Schumacher, were the standard German biography by Emil Wohlwill, nineteenth-century translations of the *Discorsi* and of Bacon's *Novum Organum*, and German versions of Jeans's *The Mysterious Universe* and Eddington's *The Nature of the Physical World*; he also had discussions with the Danish physicist Professor C. Møller, then one of Niels Bohr's assistants. He stuck quite closely to the historical facts, apart from altering Galileo's family circumstances (he actually had three children, of whom Virginia disappeared into a convent at the age of sixteen); the smuggling out of the *Discorsi* in 1636 did indeed take place. Since other left-wing German novelists and playwrights had already begun using comparable historical settings—Feuchtwanger and Heinrich Mann for instance, and Friedrich Wolf in his Beaumarchais play—Brecht was far from being unorthodox in this (for him) new venture. And, satisfactory as it must have been to have Aristotle as the ideological villain of the piece, he almost at once began worrying about the conventionality of its form.

Early in 1939 he revised it, but without making any drastic changes; inspired by the *Dialogues Concerning the Two Chief World Systems*, he also began working on *The Messingkauf Dialogues*, which were to set out his theoretical ideas of theater. In March he looked out his old project for *The Good Woman of Szechwan*, then on April 23 he left Denmark for Lindingo in Sweden, where he was to stay a bare year. It was here that he wrote the other two plays in this volume, both of which were finished by early November and seem to have been written more rapidly and with greater ease than *Szechwan*, on which he worked inconclusively during the summer. *Lucullus* was commissioned by Stockholm radio and completed in a fortnight; Hilding Rosenberg was due to write the music, but it never got done and the broadcast did not take place. The play itself can be seen as a by-product of the Caesar novel, or at least of Brecht's reading for it, which had included Plutarch, Dio Cassius, Suetonius and Sallust, now reviewed in the light of the Nazi invasion of Po-

land and the Anglo-French mobilization. *Mother Courage*, with its theme of the devastating effects of a European war and the blindness of anyone hoping to profit by it, is said to have been written in a month; judging by the almost complete absence of drafts or any other evidence of preliminary studies it must have been an exceptionally direct piece of inspiration. The obvious precedents here, though we do not know how Brecht actually used them, were Schiller's *Wallensteins Lager*, with its mongrel army milling round the canteen tents and Grimmelshausen's picaresque seventeenth-century novel *Die Landstörzerin Courasche*, which must have given him the name. But if Grimmelshausen's Amazonian adventuress shared certain turns of speech with Brecht's canteen woman, she none the less sprang from a higher social class and followed a career more like that of his Yvette. Nor, contrary to what some critics have suggested, can he have been much influenced by the sutler Lotte Svård of Johan Ludvig Runeberg's early nineteenth-century ballads about the Russian-Swedish war, for she (in C. B. Shaw's translation) was "a pearl on the pathway of war," always up with the troops; "And the dear young soldiers' heroic mood/ She loved in its full display." Brecht's Courage was more like a blend of Widow Begbick in his *A Man's a Man* with that favourite military character, Jaroslav Hašek's Good Soldier Schweyk.

The first of the three plays to be performed was *Lucullus*, which was broadcast by the Bern studio of the Swiss-German radio on May 12, 1940, while Norway and Holland were falling to Hitler and the blitzkrieg on France was impending; alas, no recording has survived. Brecht himself at that time had just arrived in Finland, where he now began work with the opera conductor Simon Parmet on the setting of the *Courage* songs. According to Parmet's recollections of some seventeen years after, Brecht was hoping for a counterpart to the *Threepenny Opera*, in which the songs would play a similar role and lead to a comparable success. Though he appeared satisfied with the result, the music for the first production at the Zurich Schauspielhaus a year later was written by the Swiss composer Paul Burkhard, seemingly without the benefit of any personal contact with Brecht. *Galileo* too was under consideration by the

same theater, which by then must have been the one professional German-language theater left outside the Nazi orbit; but unfortunately the swift Nazi victory in the west seems to have made it too dangerous to stage any successor to *Mother Courage* until the whole tide of the war had turned. Not that the timing of these three Swiss productions can in fact have been all that important from Brecht's point of view, since under wartime conditions he could neither attend them nor have any effective say. Nor indeed were they what he had originally planned to do with the plays, for *Galileo* had been meant for production in New York, while part of the object of putting a dumb character in *Mother Courage* is said to have been to give his wife Helene Weigel a role which she could act in any non-German theatre (e.g., in the first place, Stockholm). As for their results, he could only judge them by such hearsay as he could pick up, which was to the effect that despite fine settings by Teo Otto and a magnificent performance by Therese Giehse as Courage the point of both plays had somehow been missed, Courage impressing the audience above all as the irrepressible mother, Galileo three and a half years later as the cunning intellectual who shows that in the end reason must prevail and the truth get out.

2

Within a month of the *Courage* première—hence before he could take the play up again—Brecht left Finland and traveled via Moscow and the Trans-Siberian railway to California, where he found a house in Santa Monica. Living in what the actor Fritz Kortner called "a kind of penurious comfort," he seems at first to have been quite disorientated and unable to work, then in the course of 1942 to have embarked on various more or less mediocre film projects, of which the most important and lucrative was a script for Fritz Lang's *Hangmen Also Die*. Though he himself moved almost entirely among the exiled German community who had sponsored his entry into the United States, even then the first steps were being taken to introduce his work to American readers, for in 1941 New Directions published a

translation of *Mother Courage* by H. R. Hays, to whom Eisler had
given a script, while two years later a translation of *Lucullus*
followed. Brecht's own first serious return to these two plays
dates from his meeting with Paul Dessau in New York early in
1943, in connection with a Brecht recital at the New School in
which Peter Lorre and Elisabeth Bergner were to take part.
Dessau, who was then working on a New Jersey chicken farm,
had written the music for the Paris *99%*, and a song of his was
on the program; when the lady soloist dropped out Brecht made
Dessau sing it himself. Pleased with the result, Brecht gave him
a number of texts with a view to possible setting, then invited
him to Hollywood, where at some undefined date he handed
him the *Mother Courage* songs, specifying the melody for the
opening song as he had previously done with Parmet; these
were actually completed in 1946. He also gave him the script of
Lucullus, leading Dessau to conclude that he "wanted to see
Lucullus turned into an opera." However, by asking Dessau if
he could not interest Stravinsky in writing the music for this
work he seems to have effectively discouraged the one composer
without getting any response from the other, who in the event
told Dessau that he was booked up for the next two years. Later,
after the end of the war, the director Henry Schnitzler got
Brecht's agreement to let Roger Sessions make an opera, which
was performed at Los Angeles on April 18, 1947, but has remained surprisingly little known. It does not seem that Brecht
took any very close interest in this undertaking, which was of
course based on Hays's translation rather than on his own text.

It was otherwise with the American *Galileo*, which for Brecht
was certainly the most important achievement of his whole
six-year stay in the United States, and of all productions of his
plays the one to which he devoted the most thought. He had
looked at the play briefly in the winter of 1941–42, when Oskar
Homolka was thinking of a production, but when nothing came
of this he put it aside first for film work, then to concentrate on
the writing of *Simone Machard*, *Schweyk*, and *The Duchess of Malfi*
adaptation (his first venture into English). In the winter of
1943–44—that is, after the Zurich première had at last taken
place—he spent some four months in New York, where he
managed to interest the producer Jed Harris, who had put on

Wilder's *Our Town* in 1938. When he got back to Santa Monica (and to concentrated work on *The Caucasian Chalk Circle*) he began thinking how to amend *Galileo* so as to make the smuggling of the *Discorsi* seem less heroic and more in tune with the real fate of the truth in Nazi Germany and the conformist attitude of scientists at war. The Harris project somehow fizzled out, but he was now seeing a certain amount of Charles Laughton, who invited him to one-man readings of *Measure for Measure* and *The Tempest*, and for whom he wrote the long poem "Garden in Progress" that summer. Stimulated possibly by Orson Welles, at some point Laughton got and read a translation of Brecht's play.

Two factors seem to have influenced Laughton in his preoccupation with *Galileo*, which lasted on and off for the next three years. The first was his discontent with the kind of supporting parts and second-rate scripts which he had been getting after his brilliant start in such films as Korda's *Rembrandt* (for which Brecht's old colleague Carl Zuckmayer had written the script). As his biographer Kurt Singer put it,

> How could he escape this treadmill? He thought he saw his great opportunity in a play by the German dramatist Berthold Brecht.

The second, also according to Singer, was his organization of a small Shakespeare reading group with a discharged GI called Bill Cottrell who heard one of his solo readings in Californian army hospitals and became the inquisitor in the Hollywood production. That autumn he agreed with Brecht that they would set aside the existing translations (which included one by Desmond Vesey and one by Welles's nominees Brainerd Duffield and Emerson Crocker) in order to adapt the play into English together. Brecht's diary shows that they had started by December 10, 1944, but in the first half of the new year there were long interruptions, first between February and April, (when Laughton was acting in the pirate film *Captain Kidd* and Brecht consoled himself by starting to put the Communist Manifesto into hexameters), then in June and July when Brecht was in New York for the production of Eric Bentley's translation of *The Private Life of the Master Race* and further work on

The Duchess of Malfi. During this year he also wrote some more film treatments. Otherwise the collaboration seems to have gone much as he describes it in "Building up a part," (see p. 230) with Laughton proposing the elimination of Doppone, the "positive appearance" of the iron founder in scene 2, the argument between Ludovico and Galileo in the sunspot scene, and the transposition of the handing-over of the *Discorsi* in scene 14, while Brecht worked to make the latter more of a piece with Galileo's concern for his own comforts, of which thinking now became one. In this, as in the new emphasis on Galileo's sensuality, he was aided by Laughton's character, of which Professor Bentley has said that

> It is unlikely that anyone again will combine as he did every appearance of intellectual brilliance with every appearance of physical self-indulgence.

An added topicality was given by the dropping of the first atomic bomb on August 6, but about the only significant change to which this led was the addition of the passage about a "universal cry of fear" in that same scene. The concept of a Hippocratic oath for scientists was not yet included, though Brecht drafted the relevant passage, (the idea itself having already been put forward by Lancelot Law Whyte in *Nature* in 1938 and discussed in an editorial in the *New York Times*).

With the exception of the ballad-singer's song the American version of the play was finished by December 1, 1945, when Laughton read the result to the Brechts, Eisler, Berthold Viertel, Feuchtwanger, and friends. A little later he read it also to Orson Welles, who agreed to direct it in the following spring, when the impresario Paul Czinner hoped to finance a production. Laughton thought this too early, while a subsequent discussion between Brecht, Mike Todd, and Joseph Losey (whom Brecht had met in Moscow in 1935) broke down, according to Losey, when Todd offered to "dress the production in Renaissance furniture from the Hollywood warehouses." This occurred some time in the middle of 1946, and left Laughton himself holding the baby, with Losey as director. Abe Burrows, part author of *Guys and Dolls*, was brought in to translate the missing songs, but his work was not accepted, so that in the end

the job was done by Brecht himself and Laughton, with some help from Losey and from Hanns Eisler who composed the music; (Albert Brush was named in the New York program as adaptor of the "lyrics"). The production finally materialized on July 30, 1947, in the little Coronet Theater in Beverly Hills, with simple sets by Robert Davison. A New York production was then to follow, presented by T. Edward Hambleton with an entirely different cast apart from Laughton himself, but by the time this opened on December 7 Brecht and Eisler had been heard before the Un-American Activities Committee and had left the country. A week later it closed abruptly, for the reasons given thus in Laughton's biography:

> At first it seemed destined for success. The New York drama critics hailed Laughton's performance and admired the skill with which he had adapted the original text, which was rather ponderous and wordy, into a fast-moving and stirring drama. However, the production soon ran into snags.
>
> The trouble lay in the political affiliations of the playwright. Berthold Brecht was a dyed-in-the-wool Communist. On the point of being deported from the United States for his Communist activities, he escaped and turned up in East Germany, where he became the Soviet's pet author, supervising the literary life of the Soviet-controlled zone and turning out odes to Stalin on the various state holidays. The musical score for the play on Galileo had been composed by Hanns Eisler, another convinced Communist who had composed many propaganda songs, including *The Comintern March*. Several actors in the cast turned out to be Communists, too. [. . .]
>
> When the facts of the matter were put before Laughton by his manager, Charles saw that he was playing into Communists' hands. He had fallen into bad company. There was nothing left for him to do but withdraw from the production . . .

3

None the less on arriving in Zurich Brecht set down his experiences of the collaboration in what was in effect the first of the "Model" books, "Building up a part," with its accompanying photographs of the two performances by Ruth Berlau; it also forms the subject of section 63 of the *Short Organum for the Theater*, which he was writing about the same time. A year later, on October 22, 1948, he went to East Berlin to join Erich Engel, the original director of *In the Jungle* in 1923, in staging *Mother Courage* at Max Reinhardt's old Deutsches Theater, now being managed by Wolfgang Langhoff, the Eilif of the Zurich première. This production too, with Helene Weigel in the title part, was decisive for him not only in leading to the formation of the Berliner Ensemble but, at the Paris International Theater Festival six years later, in securing his long-delayed recognition as the greatest theater man of our day. In the changes which he made to its text he was certainly influenced by what he understood to be the faults of the Zurich production, but, as our notes show, they were not in fact very extensive and they were supplemented by further small amendments before his Munich production with Therese Giehse in 1950. These alterations have been much discussed by Brecht's interpreters, as evidence that he was unable to make his characters as inhuman as his ideology required them to be, but they seem slight by comparison with his wholesale rewriting of his earlier plays, and more like safeguards against any misunderstanding by actors and director than revisions of the original conception.

The fact perhaps is that in this case Brecht's relentless itch to alter his own work was transferred to the (alas unrealized) film version, whose making was decided on as early as September 1949. Quite apart from the introduction of a love interest for dumb Kattrin and the changes (of nationality and prominence) resulting from the choice of Simone Signoret as Yvette and Bernard Blier as the cook, the basic conception of the play was in some measure altered to reflect the problems of occupied Germany after the war. With his old collaborator Emil Burri he now stressed the division of the country, the "Babylonian con-

fusion of languages," and the role of the camp prostitutes, of whom Yvette was just the most socially successful. As in his adaptation of *Coriolanus* in the same years, the defenders of the sleeping city in the drum scene became armed peasants, driving off the attacking Croats, with whom Courage finally decided her best interests lay. He also however included a devastating blow at those whom many German audiences liked to see as the play's true heroes, the "little people." "Nonsense," says a peasant in the take after Eilif's death. "The little people are the worst of the lot. Why? The big shots plan it, and the little people carry it out."

During the play's rehearsals he and Dessau met a Hamburg director who asked if *Lucullus* could be made into a radio opera for the North-West German Radio. No contract followed, but the suggestion again stimulated Dessau, who set to work on an opera version in the course of 1949 and to that end persuaded Brecht to make many of the textual changes described in our editorial note. It was he who insisted that this should be described as an opera, whereas Hermann Scherchen, the designated conductor, wanted it rather to be a "musical play." Unfortunately in February 1948 the Soviet Central Committee, with Zhdanov as its chief spokesman, had strongly condemned the "formalism" of such composers as Prokofieff and Shostakovitch, and in all the arts the old standards of Socialist Realism were now being reinforced, in East Germany no less dutifully than elsewhere. Thus the discordant score and the undifferentiating pacifism of the new work disturbed the cultural politicians, who only agreed to let it be performed at first to a closed audience of party people and Free German Youth on the very day (March 17, 1951) when the Central Committee passed a resolution "Against Formalism in Art and Literature." The ensuing reviews were predictably hostile, objecting alike to the Stravinskian flavor of the music and to the cool detachment of Brecht's text, which in the current state of international tension failed to come down explicitly on the Russian side. As a result the directors of the State Opera proposed to drop the planned production, and were threatened with legal action by Brecht, who had a contract and was not subject to any party discipline. This situation was only resolved by a meeting be-

tween Brecht and Dessau and members of the government led
by the prime minister, who persuaded them to add the passages
exempting a defensive war (which many intelligent East Germans then feared they might have to fight) from the general
condemnation. A good deal of outside criticism of Brecht followed, much of it coming from the western propaganda services
and the organs of the Congress for Cultural Freedom. Brecht
himself however was not at all averse to telling the story or, as
in his notes, spelling out the additions (though not the quite
equally drastic changes involved in making an opera of the play
in the first place). And certainly *Lucullus* as subsequently
played, starting with the public première on October 12 and
continuing through further productions and more revisions by
the composer, remains a serious work of art and very remote
from the kind of tuneful party-line optimism which its critics
would have best liked to see.

In 1953 Brecht also had a new version made of *Galileo*, which
kept the changed gist of the American version while re-intro-
ducing a number of passages, and even entire scenes or sub-
scenes, from the prewar version, of which the most vital was the
long opening speech about the "new times." This had its première at Cologne on April 15, 1955, after which Brecht began
preparing to stage it himself with the Berliner Ensemble. As
Galileo he now cast Ernst Busch, who was playing Azdak in
The Caucasian Chalk Circle and the cook in the revival of *Mother
Courage*, an old Communist friend who had sung to the troops
in Spain, been interned in 1939 by the French, then handed over
to the Gestapo and wounded in the bombing of Berlin: in short
a somewhat different proposition from Laughton. From mid-
December to the end of March 1956 he conducted rehearsals,
which were recorded on tape and have been extensively
analyzed by his assistant Käthe Rülicke (in *Materialien zu Brecht's
"Leben des Galilei,"* Suhrkamp-Verlag, 1963). They were brought
to an end by his illness, so that the production was only completed under Engel's direction and after Brecht's death, when
Busch, who had all along disagreed with him about the need
to "condemn" Galileo in scene 14, was unable to make the
handing-over of the *Discorsi* seem anything but a piece of justified foxiness. The best clue to Brecht's own intentions lies

perhaps in his repeated insistence to the actors that Galileo's "My aim is not to prove that I've been right but to find out whether or not I have been" was the most important sentence in the play.

The marks of all these vicissitudes lie buried in the texts as we now have them; they will, we hope, become visible from a study of the notes. Their background is what gives Brecht's works their particular depth, as well as those elements of inconsistency which were so characteristic of him. Yet these three plays' surface seems firm enough, and it has not really altered all that much since their origins at the beginning of the war. *Lucullus* may have been more economical in its original form, but it is still an antimilitarist work, not an apology for the People's Army and the People's Police. *Mother Courage* still argues that war is a continuation of business by other means and that those who make it so are being fatally short-sighted, often against their own better instincts. *Galileo* is still a hymn to reason and a stubborn proclamation of faith in the "new age," however delayed it may be, besides being an attack on rigid official dogmas—of which there is only one in Eastern Europe today, as its East German audiences cannot but know. The two latter plays overlap significantly in their coverage of the first third of the seventeenth century, a period which specially interested Brecht because it led to scientific humanism as he understood it (as well as to the late Shakespeare plays), yet at the same time did such lasting damage to his own country. The Thirty Years' War, he told Parmet, should really be known as the Three Hundred Years' War.

The most obvious thing about these works is that they mark the start of a new stage in Brecht's writing, the period (in most critics' opinion) of his greatest plays. They represent a decisive break from the more short-term and (on the whole) short-winded political works which preceded them, whether it be interpreted as a development away from propagandist Communism to a more broadly human outlook or, as nowadays in Eastern Europe, as a reaction against such sectarian methods as montage and agit-prop and a reconciliation with the spirit of the Popular Front against Fascism and with Socialist Realism as it

is now conceived to be. Which of these views one in fact favors scarcely matters so long as nothing is done to falsify the attitudes of mind adopted by Brecht himself and others at the time. Either way it is clear that these are critical plays, arising from a critical situation, and that for Brecht, as for the wider world, the crisis lay not only in the policies of the Nazis and their helpers but also inside Stalin's USSR. Here, as so often, he proved to be a writer geared to his age, which was at once a new one and a dark one. As that crisis erupted in war, with all its consequences, many of the old polarities which had stimulated him were blurred or altered. The world itself was changing, as well as his own sometimes precarious circumstances, and in these three plays, for the rest of his life, he was working the implications out.

THE EDITORS

Life of Galileo

Play

Collaborator: M. Steffin

Translators: Wolfgang Sauerlander and Ralph Manheim

CHARACTERS

GALILEO GALILEI

ANDREA SARTI

MRS. SARTI, Galileo's housekeeper, Andrea's mother

LUDOVICO MARSILI, a rich young man

MR. PRIULI, procurator of the university of Padua

SAGREDO, Galileo's friend

VIRGINIA, Galileo's daughter

FEDERZONI, a lens grinder, Galileo's collaborator

THE DOGE

SENATORS

COSMO DE' MEDICI, Grand Duke of Florence

THE LORD CHAMBERLAIN

THE THEOLOGIAN

THE PHILOSOPHER

THE MATHEMATICIAN

THE OLDER LADY-IN-WAITING

THE YOUNGER LADY-IN-WAITING

A LACKEY at the Grand Duke's court

TWO NUNS

TWO SOLDIERS

THE OLD WOMAN

A FAT PRELATE

TWO SCHOLARS

TWO MONKS

TWO ASTRONOMERS

A VERY THIN MONK

THE VERY OLD CARDINAL

FATHER CHRISTOPHER CLAVIUS, an astronomer

THE LITTLE MONK

THE CARDINAL INQUISITOR

CARDINAL BARBERINI, later Pope Urban VIII

CARDINAL BELLARMINE

TWO ECCLESIASTICAL SECRETARIES

TWO YOUNG LADIES

FILIPPO MUCIUS, a scholar

MR. GAFFONE, rector of the university of Pisa

THE BALLAD SINGER

HIS WIFE

VANNI, an iron founder

AN ATTENDANT

A HIGH OFFICIAL

A SHADY INDIVIDUAL

A MONK

A PEASANT

A BORDER GUARD

A CLERK

MEN, WOMEN, CHILDREN

1

Galileo Galilei, teacher of mathematics in Padua, sets out to demonstrate the new Copernican system.

> In the year sixteen hundred and nine
> Science' light began to shine.
> At Padua city, in a modest house
> Galileo Galilei set out to prove
> The sun is still, the earth is on the move.

Galileo's modest study in Padua. It is morning. A boy, Andrea, the housekeeper's son, brings in a glass of milk and a roll.

GALILEO (*washing his torso, puffing and happy*)   Put the milk on the table, but don't shut any books.

ANDREA   Mother says we've got to pay the milkman. Or he'll make a circle around our house, Mr. Galilei.

GALILEO   You must say, "describe a circle," Andrea.

ANDREA   Of course. If we don't pay he'll describe a circle around us, Mr. Galilei.

GALILEO   And Mr. Cambione, the bailiff, will head for us in a straight line, covering what sort of distance between two points?

ANDREA (*grinning*)   The shortest.

GALILEO   Good. I've got something for you. Look behind the star charts.

(Andrea fishes a large wooden model of the Ptolemaic system from behind the star charts)

ANDREA   What is it?

GALILEO   An armillary sphere. It shows how the stars move around the earth, in the opinion of the ancients.

ANDREA   How?

GALILEO   Let's examine it. First of all: description.

ANDREA   There's a little stone in the middle.

GALILEO   That's the earth.

ANDREA   There are rings around it, one inside another.

GALILEO   How many?

ANDREA   Eight.

GALILEO   Those are the crystal spheres.

ANDREA   There are balls fastened to the rings . . .

GALILEO   The stars.

ANDREA   There are tags with words painted on them.

GALILEO   What kind of words?

ANDREA   Names of stars.

GALILEO   Such as?

ANDREA   The bottommost ball is the moon, it says. The one above it is the sun.

GALILEO   Now spin the sun around.

ANDREA (*sets the rings in motion*)   That's pretty. But we're so shut in.

GALILEO (*drying himself*)   Yes, that's just what I felt when I saw the thing for the first time. Some people feel that way. (*Throws Andrea the towel, meaning that he should rub his back*) Walls and rings and immobility. For two thousand years men believed that the sun and all the stars of heaven were circling around them. The pope, the cardinals, princes and scholars, the captains, merchants, fishwives and schoolchildren, all thought they were sitting motionless inside this crystal sphere. But now we'll get out of it, Andrea, we're in full sail. Because the old times are gone, and this is a new age. For the last hundred years mankind has seemed to be expecting something.

Cities are narrow, and so are minds. Superstition and plague. But now we say: Since things are thus and so, they will not remain thus and so. Because, my friend, everything is in motion.

I like to think that it all started with ships. From time immemorial ships had hugged the shores, but suddenly they abandoned the shores, and sailed out upon the oceans.

A rumor has sprung up on our old continent—that there are new continents. And now that our ships have been going

there, people on all the laughing continents are saying that
the big dreaded ocean is nothing but a small lake. And a great
desire has arisen to find the causes of all things: Why a stone
falls when it's released and how it goes up when it's thrown
into the air. Every day something new is being discovered.
Even men a hundred years old let youngsters shout in their
ears to tell them about the latest discoveries.

A great deal has been discovered, but there's much more to
be discovered. Plenty of work for future generations.

When I was a young man in Siena I saw some masons, after
arguing for five minutes, discard an age-old method of moving granite blocks in favor of a new and more practical arrangement of the ropes. Then and there I realized that the old
times are over and that this is a new day. Some men will know
all about their habitat, this heavenly body they live on.
They're no longer satisfied with what it says in the ancient
books.

Because where faith had ruled for a thousand years, doubt
has now set in. Today everybody is saying: Yes, that's what
the books tell us, but we want to see for ourselves. The most
sacred truths are being looked into. Things that were never
held in doubt are being doubted now.

All this has stirred up a breeze that lifts even the gold-
braided coats of princes and prelates, revealing stout or
spindly legs, legs just the same as ours. The heavens, we know
now, are empty. And that has given rise to joyous laughter.

The waters of the earth supply power to the new spinning
wheels, and in shipyards and the workshops of ropers and
sailmakers new methods enable five hundred hands to work
together.

I foresee that in our lifetime people will talk astronomy in
the market place. Even the sons of fishwives will go to school.
The people of our cities are always eager for novelty, they
will be glad to hear that in our new astronomy the earth
moves too. It has always been taught that the stars are pinned
to a crystal vault, which prevents them from falling down.
Now we've mustered the courage to let them float free, with
nothing to hold them; they're in full sail, just as our ships are
in full sail.

And the earth rolls merrily around the sun, and all the fishwives, merchants, princes and cardinals, and even the pope, roll with it.

Overnight, the universe has lost its center and now in the morning it has any number of centers. Now any point in the universe may be taken as a center. Because, suddenly, there's plenty of room.

Our ships sail far out into the ocean, our planets revolve far out in space, and even in chess nowadays the rooks range over many fields.

What does the poet say? "Oh, early morning . . ."

ANDREA
"Oh, early morning of beginning!
Oh, breath of wind that
Comes from new-found shores!"
And you'd better drink your milk. There'll be people coming in a minute.

GALILEO   Did you figure out what I told you yesterday?

ANDREA   What? You mean Kippernick and all that turning business?

GALILEO   Yes.

ANDREA   No. Why do you want me to figure it out? It's too hard for me, I'll only be eleven in October.

GALILEO   I want you to understand it, you in particular. To make everybody understand, that's why I work and buy expensive books instead of paying the milkman.

ANDREA   But I can see that the sun's not in the same place in the evening and morning. So it can't stand still. It just can't.

GALILEO   You "see"! What do you see? You see nothing at all. You're just gaping. Gaping isn't seeing. (*He places the iron washstand in the center of the room*) Now, that's the sun. Sit down. (*Andrea sits down in the only chair. Galileo stands behind him*) Where is the sun, right or left?

ANDREA   Left.

GALILEO   And how does it get to the right?

ANDREA   When you carry it over to the right. Naturally.

GALILEO   Only then? (*He picks up the chair with him in it and turns it halfway around*) Where's the sun now?

ANDREA   On the right.

GALILEO Has it moved?

ANDREA I guess it hasn't.

GALILEO What moved?

ANDREA Me.

GALILEO (*roars*) Wrong! Stupid! the chair!

ANDREA But me with it!

GALILEO Obviously. The chair is the earth. You're sitting on it.

MRS. SARTI (*has come in to make the bed. She has watched the scene*) Mr. Galileo, what on earth are you doing with my boy?

GALILEO I'm teaching him how to see, Mrs. Sarti.

MRS. SARTI By carrying him around the room?

ANDREA Never mind, mother. You don't understand.

MRS. SARTI Is that so? But of course you understand. A young gentleman is here, he wants to take lessons. Very well dressed, and he has a letter of recommendation. (*Hands over the letter*) When you get through with my Andrea, he'll be saying that two times two make five. You've got him all mixed up. Last night he tried to prove to me that the earth moves around the sun. He says some fellow by the name of Kippernick figured it out.

ANDREA Didn't that Kippernick figure it out, Mr. Galilei? You tell her.

MRS. SARTI Do you really tell him such nonsense? He blabs it out in school and the priests come running to me because of all the sinful stuff he says. You should be ashamed of yourself, Mr. Galilei.

GALILEO (*eating his breakfast*) Mrs. Sarti, as a result of our investigations, and after heated arguments, Andrea and I have made discoveries which we can no longer keep secret from the world. A new age has dawned, a great age, and it's a joy to be alive.

MRS. SARTI I see. I hope we'll be able to pay the milkman in the new age, Mr. Galilei. (*Pointing at the letter*) Just do me a favor and don't turn this one away. I'm thinking of the milk bill. (*Out*)

GALILEO (*laughing*) Just give me time to finish my milk!—(*To Andrea*) Well, you seem to have understood something yesterday after all.

ANDREA   I only told her to get a rise out of her. But it's not true. You only turned the chair with me in it around sideways, but not like this. (*He moves his arm in a circle to the front*) Because I'd have fallen off the chair, and that's a fact. Why didn't you turn the chair over? Because that would prove I'd fall off the earth if it moved that way. There.

GALILEO   But I proved to you . . .

ANDREA   But last night I figured out that if the earth turned that way I'd hang down head first at night, and that's a fact.

GALILEO (*takes an apple from the table*)   Look here. This is the earth.

ANDREA   Don't always use that kind of example, Mr. Galilei. That way you can prove anything.

GALILEO (*putting the apple back*)   Very well.

ANDREA   You can do anything with examples if you're clever. But I can't carry my mother around in a chair like that. So you see, it was a bad example. And what would happen if the apple were the earth? Nothing would happen.

GALILEO (*laughs*)   I thought you weren't interested.

ANDREA   All right, take the apple. What would keep me from hanging head down at night?

GALILEO   Well, here's the earth, and you're standing here. (*He sticks a splinter from a log into the apple*) And now the earth turns.

ANDREA   And now I'm hanging head down.

GALILEO   What do you mean? Look closely! Where's the head?

ANDREA   (*shows on the apple*)   There. Below.

GALILEO   Sure? (*Turns the apple back*) Isn't the head still in the same place? Aren't the feet still below it? When I turn it, do you stand like this? (*He takes the splinter out and turns it upside down*)

ANDREA   No. Then, why don't I notice the turning?

GALILEO   Because you're turning too. You and the air above you and everything else on the globe.

ANDREA   But why does it look as if the sun were moving?

GALILEO (*again turns the apple with the splinter*)   Look, you see the earth underneath, it stays that way, it's always underneath and as far as you're concerned it doesn't move. Now look up. The lamp is over your head. But now that I've turned it,

what's over your head, in other words, above?

ANDREA (*making the same turn*)   The stove.

GALILEO   And where's the lamp?

ANDREA   Below.

GALILEO   Aha!

ANDREA   That's great. That'll get a rise out of her.

(*Ludovico Marsili, a rich young man, enters*)

GALILEO   This place is as busy as a pigeon house.

LUDOVICO   Good morning, sir. My name is Ludovico Marsili.

GALILEO (*examining his letter of recommendation*)   You've been in Holland?

LUDOVICO   Where I heard a great deal about you, Mr. Galilei.

GALILEO   Your family owns property in the Campagna?

LUDOVICO   My mother wanted me to look around and see what's going on in the world. That kind of thing.

GALILEO   And in Holland they told you that in Italy, for instance, I was going on?

LUDOVICO   And since mother also wanted me to take a look at the sciences . . .

GALILEO   Private lessons: Ten scudi a month.

LUDOVICO   Very well, sir.

GALILEO   What are your interests?

LUDOVICO   Horses.

GALILEO   I see.

LUDOVICO   I have no head for science, Mr. Galilei.

GALILEO   I see. In that case it'll be fifteen scudi a month.

LUDIVICO   Very well, Mr. Galilei.

GALILEO   I'll have to take you first thing in the morning. You'll be the loser, Andrea. Naturally I'll have to drop you. You understand, you don't pay.

ANDREA   All right, I'm going. Can I take the apple?

GALILEO   Yes.

(*Andrea leaves*)

LUDOVICO   You'll have to be patient with me. Mostly because in science everything's the opposite of common sense. Take that crazy tube they're selling in Amsterdam. I've examined it carefully. A green leather casing and two lenses, one like this (*he indicates a concave lens*) and one like this (*indicates a convex lens*). As far as I know, one magnifies and the other reduces.

Any sensible person would expect them to cancel each other out. But they don't. When you look through the thing everything's five times as big. That's science for you.

GALILEO   What do you see five times as big?

LUDOVICO   Steeples, pigeons, anything far away.

GALILEO   Have you seen these magnified steeples?

LUDOVICO   Certainly, sir.

GALILEO   You say the tube has two lenses? (*He makes a sketch on a sheet of paper*) Like this? (*Ludovico nods*) How old is this invention?

LUDOVICO   I believe it wasn't much more than a few days old when I left Holland, at least it hadn't been on the market any longer than that.

GALILEO (*almost friendly*)   Why do you insist on physics? Why not horse breeding?

(*Enter Mrs. Sarti, unnoticed by Galileo*)

LUDOVICO   Mother thinks a little science won't hurt me. Everybody's eating and drinking science nowadays, you know.

GALILEO   Why not try a dead language or theology? They're easier. (*Sees Mrs. Sarti*) All right, come Tuesday morning.

(*Ludovico leaves*)

GALILEO   Don't look at me like that. I've accepted him.

MRS. SARTI   Because you saw me in the nick of time. The procurator of the university is here.

GALILEO   Bring him in. He's important. It might mean five hundred scudi. Then I wouldn't have to take pupils.

(*Mrs. Sarti shows the procurator in. Galileo has completed dressing while scribbling figures on a slip of paper*)

GALILEO   Good morning, lend me half a scudo. (*Gives the coin the procurator has fished out of his purse to Mrs. Sarti*) Sarti, would you send Andrea to the spectacle maker for some lenses? Here are the measurements.

(*Mrs. Sarti goes out with the slip of paper*)

THE PROCURATOR   I've come in regard to your request for a raise of salary. You have asked for a thousand scudi. Unfortunately I cannot recommend such an increase to the university. You are aware, I am sure, that courses in mathematics don't attract students to the university. Mathematics doesn't pay. Not that

the republic doesn't value it highly. It may not be as important as philosophy or as useful as theology; still, it gives endless pleasure to the connoisseur.

GALILEO (*immersed in his papers*) My dear man, I can't get along on five hundred scudi.

THE PROCURATOR But, Mr. Galilei, all you do is give a two-hour lecture twice a week. Surely your extraordinary reputation must attract any number of students who can afford private lessons. Haven't you got private pupils?

GALILEO Sir, I have too many! I'm teaching all the time. When am I to learn? Good God, man, I'm not as clever as the gentlemen of the philosophical faculty. I'm stupid. I don't understand a thing. I've got to plug the holes in my knowledge. And where am I to find time for that? When am I to study and experiment? My knowledge, sir, is thirsty for more knowledge. In all the biggest problems we still have nothing but hypotheses to go by. What we need is proofs. How can I get anywhere if, to keep my household going, I have to drum it into the head of every idiot who can pay that parallel lines meet in infinity?

THE PROCURATOR The republic may not pay as much as certain princes, but don't forget, it guarantees freedom of inquiry. We in Padua even admit Protestants as students. And we grant them doctor's degrees. Did we hand Mr. Cremonini over to the Inquisition when we had proof—proof, Mr. Galilei!—that he had made sacrilegious statements? No, we even granted him an increase in salary. As far away as Holland Venice is known as the republic where the Inquisition has nothing to say. That ought to be worth something to an astronomer like you, working in a field where the doctrines of the church have not been held in due respect of late.

GALILEO You handed Giordano Bruno over to Rome. Because he professed the teachings of Copernicus.

THE PROCURATOR Not because he professed the teachings of Mr. Copernicus which, incidentally, are wrong, but because he was not a citizen of Venice and was not employed here. You can leave him out of it, even if they did burn him. And by the by, for all our liberties I shouldn't advise you to make too free with a name that has been expressly anathematized

by the church, not even here, no, not even here.

GALILEO   Your protection of freedom of thought is rather good business, isn't it? You get good teachers for low pay by pointing out that other towns are run by the Inquisition, which burns people. In return for protection from the Inquisition, your professors work for next to nothing.

THE PROCURATOR   You're being unfair. What good would it do you to have all the time you want for research if any witless monk of the Inquisition could simply suppress your ideas? No rose without thorns, Mr. Galilei, no prince without monks!

GALILEO   And what's the use of free investigation without free time to investigate? What happens to the results? Why don't you submit my work on the laws of falling bodies (*He points at a sheaf of manuscript*) to the gentlemen of the signoria and ask them if it's not worth a few scudi more.

THE PROCURATOR   It's worth infinitely more, Mr. Galilei.

GALILEO   Not infinitely more, sir, but five hundred scudi more.

THE PROCURATOR   Only what brings in scudi is worth scudi. If you want money, you'll have to come up with something different. If you have knowledge to sell, you can ask only as much as it earns the purchaser. For instance, the philosophy Mr. Colombe is selling in Florence brings the prince at least ten thousand scudi a year. Granted, your laws of falling bodies raised some dust. They're applauding you in Paris and Prague. But the gentlemen who applaud don't pay the university of Padua what you cost it. Your misfortune, Mr. Galilei, is your field.

GALILEO   I get it: free trade, free research. Free trade in research, is that it?

THE PROCURATOR   But Mr. Galilei! How can you say such a thing? Permit me to observe that I don't fully appreciate your witticism. The flourishing trade of the republic is hardly to be sneered at. Much less can I, as long-time procurator of the university, countenance the, I must say, frivolous tone in which you speak of research. (*While Galileo sends longing glances toward his worktable*) Think of the world around us! The whip of slavery under which science is groaning at certain universities—where old leather-bound tomes have been cut into

whips. Where no one cares how the pebble falls, but only what Aristotle writes about it. The eyes have only one purpose: reading. What use are the new laws of gravity when the law of suavity is all that matters? And then think of the immense joy with which our republic accepts your ideas. Here you can do research! Here you can work! Nobody spies on you, nobody oppresses you. Our merchants, who know the importance of better linen in their competition with Florence, listen with interest to your cry for "Better physics!" And don't forget how much physics owes to the campaign for better looms! Our most eminent citizens—men for whom time is money—take an interest in your work, they come to see you and watch demonstrations of your discoveries. Don't despise trade, Mr. Galilei! None of us here would ever allow your work to be interfered with or permit outsiders to create difficulties for you. You've got to admit, Mr. Galilei, that this is the ideal place for your work!

GALILEO (*in despair*)   Yes.

THE PROCURATOR   Then the financial aspect: All you have to do is come up with another invention as clever as that splendid proportional compass of yours which a person ignorant of mathematics can use to (*He counts on his fingers*) trace a line, compute compound interest, reproduce a land survey in enlarged or reduced scale, and determine the weight of cannon balls.

GALILEO   Flimflam.

THE PROCURATOR   An invention that delighted and amazed our leading citizens and brought in money—you call that flimflam. I'm told that even General Stefano Gritti can do square roots with it.

GALILEO   Quite a gadget—all the same, Priuli, you've given me an idea. Priuli, I may have something along those lines for you. (*He picks up the sheet with his sketch*)

THE PROCURATOR   Really? That would be the solution. (*Gets up*) Mr. Galilei, we know you are a great man. A great but dissatisfied man, if I may say so.

GALILEO   Yes, I am dissatisfied and that's what you should be paying me for if you had any sense. Because I'm dissatisfied with myself. But you do everything to make me dissatisfied

with you. I admit it amuses me to do my bit for my Venetian friends, working in your great arsenal with its shipyards and armories. But you leave me no time to follow up the speculations which result from this work. You muzzle the ox that does your threshing. I'm forty-six years old and I've accomplished nothing that satisfies me.

THE PROCURATOR   In that case I won't disturb you any longer.

GALILEO   Thank you.

(*The procurator leaves. Galileo remains alone for a few moments and begins to work. Then Andrea comes running in*)

GALILEO (*at work*)   Why didn't you eat the apple?

ANDREA   I need it to show her that the earth turns.

GALILEO   I must tell you something, Andrea. Don't mention our ideas to other people.

ANDREA   Why not?

GALILEO   Our rulers have forbidden it.

ANDREA   But it's the truth.

GALILEO   Even so, they forbid it.—And there's another reason. We still have no proofs for what we know to be right. Even the doctrine of the great Copernicus is not yet proven. It's only a hypothesis. Give me the lenses.

ANDREA   Half a scudo wasn't enough. I had to leave him my jacket. As a pledge.

GALILEO   How will you get through the winter without a jacket?

(*Pause. Galileo arranges the lenses on the sheet with the sketch*)

ANDREA   What's a hypothesis?

GALILEO   It's when we consider something probable but have no facts. We assume that Felice, nursing her baby down there outside the basket weaver's shop, is giving milk to the baby and not getting milk from it. That's a hypothesis as long as we can't go and see for ourselves and prove it. In the face of the heavenly bodies we're like worms with dim eyes that see very little. The ancient doctrines that have been accepted for a thousand years are rickety. There's less solid timber in those immense edifices than in the props needed to keep them from collapsing. Too many laws that explain too little, whereas our new hypothesis has few laws that explain a great deal.

ANDREA   But you've proved it all to me.

GALILEO   Only that it's possible. You see, the hypothesis is a very elegant one and there's no evidence to the contrary.

ANDREA   I want to be a physicist too, Mr. Galilei.

GALILEO   Very sensible in view of all the problems remaining to be solved in our field. (*He has gone to the window and looked through the lenses. Mildly interested*) Take a look, Andrea.

ANDREA   Holy Mary! Everything comes close. The bells of the campanile are right here. I can even read the copper letters: GRACIA DEI.

GALILEO   It'll get us five hundred scudi.

2

Galileo presents a new invention to the republic of Venice.

> No one's virtue is complete:
> Great Galileo liked to eat.
> You will not resent, we hope
> The truth about his telescope.

The great arsenal of Venice near the harbor. Senators, headed by the doge. On one side Galileo's friend Sagredo and Virginia Galilei, fifteen; she is holding a velvet cushion on which lies a telescope about two feet long, encased in red leather. Galileo is standing on a dais. Behind him the tripod for the telescope; the lens grinder Federzoni is in charge of it.

GALILEO   Your Excellency, august signoria! As professor of mathematics at your university in Padua and director of the great arsenal here in Venice, I have always felt it incumbent upon me not only to fulfill my duties as a teacher but also to procure special advantages to the republic of Venice by means of useful inventions. With great satisfaction and in all

due humility, I shall demonstrate and present to you today an entirely new instrument, my spyglass or telescope, manufactured in your world-famous great arsenal in accordance with the highest scientific and Christian principles, the fruit of seventeen years of your obedient servant's patient labors. (*Galileo leaves the dais and stands next to Sagredo*)

(*Applause, Galileo takes a bow*)

GALILEO (*softly to Sagredo*) What a waste of time!

SAGREDO (*softly*) You'll be able to pay the butcher, old friend.

GALILEO Yes, they'll make money on it. (*Makes another bow*)

THE PROCURATOR (*steps up on the dais*) Your Excellency, august signoria! Once again a glorious page in the great book of human accomplishments is being written in Venetian characters. (*Polite applause*) A scholar of world renown is presenting to you, and to you alone, a highly salable tube for you to manufacture and market at your pleasure. (*Stronger applause*) Has it occurred to you that in the event of war this instrument will enable us to recognize the nature and number of the enemy's ships at least two hours before they have a clear view of ours and, in full cognizance of his strength, decide whether to pursue, engage or withdraw? (*Loud applause*) And now, Your Excellency, august signoria, Mr. Galilei bids you accept this instrument of his invention, this evidence of his genius, from the hands of his charming daughter.

(*Music. Virginia steps forward, bows, hands the telescope to the procurator who passes it on to Federzoni. Federzoni places it on the tripod and adjusts it. The doge and the senators mount the dais and look through the tube*)

GALILEO (*softly*) I can't promise to go through with this farce. They think they're getting a profitable gadget, but it's much more than that. Last night I turned the tube on the moon.

SAGREDO What did you see?

GALILEO It has no light of its own.

SAGREDO What?

SENATORS Mr. Galilei, I can see the fortifications of Santa Rosita.—Over there on that boat they're having lunch. Fried fish. I'm getting hungry.

GALILEO I tell you, astronomy has been marking time for a thousand years for lack of a telescope.

SENATOR   Mr. Galilei!

SAGREDO   You're wanted.

SENATOR   One sees too well with that thing. I'll have to warn
my ladies to stop bathing on the roof.

GALILEO   Do you know what the Milky Way consists of?

SAGREDO   No.

GALILEO   I do.

SENATOR   A thing like that is worth its ten scudi, Mr. Galilei.
(*Galileo bows*)

VIRGINIA (*takes Ludovico to her father*)   Ludovico wants to congratulate you, father.

LUDOVICO (*embarrassed*)   Congratulations, sir.

GALILEO   I've improved on it.

LUDOVICO   So I see, sir. You made the casing red. In Holland it
was green.

GALILEO (*turns to Sagredo*)   I wonder if I couldn't prove a certain
doctrine with that thing.

SAGREDO   Watch your step!

THE PROCURATOR   Your five hundred scudi are in the bag, Mr.
Galilei.

GALILEO (*paying no attention to him*)   Of course, I'm always wary
of rash conclusions.
(*The doge, a fat, modest man, has approached Galileo and is attempting, with clumsy dignity, to address him*)

THE PROCURATOR   Mr. Galilei, His Excellency the doge.
(*The doge shakes Galileo's hand*)

GALILEO   Oh yes, the five hundred! Are you satisfied, Your Excellency?

DOGE   Unfortunately our city fathers always need some sort of
pretext before they can do anything for our scholars.

THE PROCURATOR   Otherwise, where would the incentive be,
Mr. Galilei?

DOGE (*smiling*)   This is our pretext.
(*The doge and the procurator lead Galileo to the senators, who surround him. Virginia and Ludovico slowly go away*)

VIRGINIA   Did I do it all right?

LUDOVICO   It seemed all right to me.

VIRGINIA   What's the matter?

LUDOVICO   Oh, nothing. A green casing might have done just as
well.

VIRGINIA   I think they're all very pleased with father.
LUDOVICO   And I think I'm beginning to understand something
about science.

3

January 10, 1610: By means of the telescope Galileo
discovers celestial phenomena which prove the
Copernican system. Warned by his friend of the possible consequences of his investigations, Galileo
affirms his faith in reason.

> January ten, sixteen ten:
> Galileo Galilei abolishes heaven.

*Galileo's study in Padua. Night. Galileo and Sagredo, both in heavy
overcoats, at the telescope.*

SAGREDO (*looking through the telescope, in an undertone*)   The edge
of the crescent is quite irregular, rough and serrated. In the
dark part near the luminous edge there are luminous points.
They are emerging, one after another. From these points the
light spreads out over wider and wider areas and finally
merges with the larger luminous part.
GALILEO   How do you account for those luminous points?
SAGREDO   It can't be.
GALILEO   But it is. They're mountains.
SAGREDO   On a star?
GALILEO   Gigantic mountains. Their peaks are gilded by the
rising sun while the surrounding slopes are still deep in darkness. You can see the light descending from the highest peaks
into the valleys.

SAGREDO   But that contradicts all the astronomy of two thousand years.

GALILEO   True. No mortal has ever seen what you are seeing, except me. You're the second.

SAGREDO   But the moon can't be another earth with mountains and valleys, any more than the earth can be a planet.

GALILEO   The moon can be an earth with mountains and valleys, and the earth can be a planet. Simply another heavenly body, one among thousands. Take another look. Is the dark part of the moon entirely dark?

SAGREDO   No. When I look closely, I see a feeble gray light on it.

GALILEO   What can that light be?

SACREDO   ?

GALILEO   It's from the earth.

SAGREDO   Nonsense. How can the earth with its mountains and forests and oceans—a cold body—give light?

GALILEO   The same way the moon sheds light. Because both bodies are illuminated by the sun, that's why they shed light. What the moon is to us we are to the moon. The moon sees us by turns as a crescent, as a half-circle, as full, and then not at all.

SAGREDO   Then there's no difference between moon and earth?

GALILEO   Apparently not.

SAGREDO   Less than ten years ago a man was burned in Rome. His name was Giordano Bruno and he had said the same thing.

GALILEO   I know. But we can see it. Keep your eyes to the tube. What you see is that there's no difference between heaven and earth. This is the tenth of January, 1610. Humanity notes in its diary: Heaven abolished.

SAGREDO   It's terrifying.

GALILEO   I've discovered something else. Perhaps something even more amazing.

MRS. SARTI (*comes in*)   The procurator.

(*The procurator rushes in*)

THE PROCURATOR   I apologize for the late hour. I'd be much obliged if we could talk privately.

GALILEO   Mr. Sagredo can hear anything I can hear, Mr. Priuli.

THE PROCURATOR   It might embarrass you to have the gentle-man hear what has happened. Unfortunately, it's something quite incredible.

GALILEO   Mr. Sagredo is used to hearing incredible things in my presence.

THE PROCURATOR   I wonder. (*Pointing at the telescope*) There it is, your splendid gadget. You might as well throw it away. It's worthless, absolutely worthless.

SAGREDO (*who has been restlessly pacing the floor*)   What do you mean?

THE PROCURATOR   Do you realize that this invention of yours, "the fruit of seventeen years of patient labor," is for sale on every street corner in Italy for a couple of scudi? Made in Holland, I might add. At this very moment a Dutch freighter is unloading five hundred telescopes in the harbor.

GALILEO   You don't say.

THE PROCURATOR   Your equanimity, sir, is beyond me.

SAGREDO   I fail to see what's troubling you. Let me tell you that just in these last few days Mr. Galilei—with this very instru-ment—has made the most revolutionary discoveries concern-ing heavenly bodies.

GALILEO (*laughing*)   Have a look for yourself, Priuli.

THE PROCURATOR   Let me tell you that after having Mr. Galilei's salary doubled on the strength of this worthless gadget I'm quite satisfied with the discovery I've already made. It's sheer accident that when the gentlemen of the signoria first looked through your tube, confident of having acquired something for the republic that could be manufactured only here, they failed to see—seven times magnified—a common peddler on the next corner hawking that same tube for a song.

(*Galileo roars with laughter*)

SAGREDO   Dear Mr. Priuli, I may not be able to judge the in-strument's value to the economy, but its value to philosophy is so enormous that . . .

THE PROCURATOR   To philosophy! What business has Mr. Gali-lei, a mathematician, meddling with philosophy? Mr. Galilei, you once invented a very respectable pump for the city; your irrigation system functions. The weavers, too, are very pleased with your machine. How on earth could I have an-ticipated anything like this?

GALILEO   Not so fast, Priuli. Sea routes are still long, unsafe and expensive. We lack a dependable clock in the sky. A guide to navigation. I have reason to believe that with the telescope we can very clearly perceive certain stars with very regular motions. New star charts, Mr. Priuli, could save the shipping interests millions of scudi.

THE PROCURATOR   Forget it. I've heard more than enough. In return for my kindness you've made me the laughingstock of the city. I'll be remembered as the procurator who fell for a worthless telescope. You have every reason to laugh. You've got your five hundred scudi. But I'm telling you, and I speak as an honest man: This world makes me sick! (*He leaves, banging the door behind him*)

GALILEO   He's rather likable when he gets angry. Did you hear what he said: A world where you can't do business makes him sick.

SAGREDO   Did you know about the Dutch instruments?

GALILEO   Of course. From hearsay. But the one I made for those skinflints in the signoria is twice as good. How can I do my work with the bailiff at the door? And Virginia will need her trousseau soon, she's not bright. Besides, I like to buy books, and not only about physics, and I like to eat well. I get my best ideas over a good meal. A rotten time to live in! They weren't paying me as much as the teamster who carts their wine barrels. Four cords of firewood for two courses in mathematics. I've wormed five hundred scudi out of them, but I've got debts, some of them twenty years old. Give me five years of leisure and I'll prove everything. Let me show you something else.

SAGREDO (*hesitates to go to the telescope*)   I almost think I'm afraid, Galileo.

GALILEO   I want to show you a milky-white patch of luminous mist in the galaxy. Tell me what it's made of.

SAGREDO   Why, stars, countless stars.

GALILEO   In the constellation of Orion alone there are five hundred fixed stars. Those are the many worlds, the countless other worlds, the stars beyond stars that the man they burned talked about. He didn't see them, but he knew they would be there.

SAGREDO   Even if our earth is a star, it's still a long way to

Copernicus' contention that the earth revolves around the sun. There isn't any star in the heavens with another revolving around it. And the earth, you'll have to admit, has the moon revolving around it.

GALILEO   Sagredo, I wonder. I've been wondering for two days. There's Jupiter. (*He adjusts the telescope*) Now, near it there are four smaller stars that you can only make out through the tube. I saw them on Monday but I didn't pay too much attention to their positions. Yesterday I looked again. I could have sworn that all four had moved. I recorded their positions. Now they're different again. What's that now? There were four of them. (*Getting excited*) You look!

SAGREDO   I see three.

GALILEO   Where's the fourth? Here are the tables. We must compute the movements they can have made.

(*Agitated, they sit down to work. The stage turns dark, but on a cyclorama Jupiter and its satellites remain visible. When it grows light again, they are still sitting there in their winter coats*)

GALILEO   Now we have proof. The fourth must have moved behind Jupiter where we can't see it. There you have a star with another revolving around it.

SAGREDO   But the crystal sphere that Jupiter is fastened to?

GALILEO   Where is it indeed? How can Jupiter be fastened to anything if other stars revolve around it? There is no scaffolding in the sky, there's nothing holding the universe up! There you have another sun!

SAGREDO   Calm down. You're thinking too fast.

GALILEO   Fast, hell! Man, get excited! You're seeing something that nobody ever saw before. They were right!

SAGREDO   Who? The Copernicans?

GALILEO   Yes, and you know who. The whole world was against them, and yet they were right. That's something for Andrea! (*Beside himself, he runs to the door and shouts*) Mrs. Sarti! Mrs. Sarti!

SAGREDO   Galileo, please calm yourself!

GALILEO   Sagredo, please get excited! Mrs. Sarti!

SAGREDO (*turning the telescope aside*)   Will you stop yelling like a fool?

GALILEO Will you stop standing there like a stockfish when we've discovered the truth?

SAGREDO I'm not standing here like a stockfish, I'm trembling for fear it's the truth.

GALILEO What?

SAGREDO Have you taken leave of your senses? Don't you realize what you're getting into if what you see is really true? And if you go shouting all over town that the earth is a planet and not the center of the universe?

GALILEO Yes, and that the whole enormous cosmos with all its stars doesn't revolve around our tiny earth, as anyone could have guessed anyway.

SAGREDO So that there's nothing but stars!—But where does that put God?

GALILEO What do you mean?

SAGREDO God! Where's God?

GALILEO (*furious*) Not out there! Any more than He'd be on earth if somebody out there started looking for Him here.

SAGREDO Where is God then?

GALILEO Am I a theologian? I'm a mathematician.

SAGREDO First of all you're a human being. And I ask you: Where is God in your world system?

GALILEO Inside us or nowhere!

SAGREDO (*shouting*) As the man who was burned said?

GALILEO As the man who was burned said!

SAGREDO That's why he was burned! Less than ten years ago!

GALILEO Because he couldn't prove it! Because all he could do was say so! Mrs. Sarti!

SAGREDO Galileo, I know you're a clever man. For three years in Pisa and seventeen here in Padua you've patiently instructed hundreds of students in the Ptolemaic system as advocated by the church and confirmed by the scriptures on which the church is grounded. Like Copernicus you thought it was wrong, but you taught it.

GALILEO Because I couldn't prove anything.

SAGREDO (*incredulous*) You think that makes a difference?

GALILEO All the difference in the world! Look here, Sagredo! I believe in man and that means I believe in reason. Without

that belief I wouldn't have the strength to get out of bed in the morning.

SAGREDO   Then let me tell you this: I don't believe in reason. Forty years' experience has taught me that human beings are not accessible to reason. Show them a comet with a red tail, put dark fear into them, and they'll rush out of their houses and break their legs. But make a reasonable statement, prove it with seven good reasons, and they'll just laugh at you.

GALILEO   That's all wrong and it's slander. I don't see how you can love science if you believe that. Only the dead are impervious to argument.

SAGREDO   How can you mistake their contemptible cunning for reason?

GALILEO   I'm not talking about their cunning. I know they call a donkey a horse when they're selling and a horse a donkey when they're buying. That's their cunning. But the old woman with calloused hands who gives her mule an extra bunch of hay the night before setting out on a trip; the sea captain who allows for storms and doldrums when he lays in his stores; the child who puts on his cap when he realizes that it may rain—these people are my hope, they accept the law of cause and effect. Yes, I believe in the gentle force of reason, in the long run no one can resist it. Nobody can watch me drop (*He lets a pebble fall from his hand to the floor*) a pebble and say: It doesn't fall. Nobody can do that. The seduction of proof is too strong. Most people will succumb to it and in time they all will. Thinking is one of the greatest pleasures of the human race.

MRS. SARTI (*comes in*)   Did you want something, Mr. Galilei?

GALILEO (*back at the telescope, scribbling notes, very kindly*)   Yes, I want Andrea.

MRS. SARTI   Andrea? But he's in bed, he's sound asleep.

GALILEO   Can't you wake him?

MRS. SARTI   What do you want him for, may I ask?

GALILEO   I want to show him something that'll please him. He's going to see something that no one but us has ever seen since the earth began.

MRS. SARTI   Something through your tube?

GALILEO   Something through my tube, Mrs. Sarti.

MRS. SARTI   And for that you want me to wake him in the middle of the night? Are you out of your mind? He needs his sleep. I wouldn't think of waking him.

GALILEO   Not a chance?

MRS. SARTI   Not a chance.

GALILEO   Mrs. Sarti, in that case maybe you can help me. You see, a question has come up that we can't agree on, perhaps because we've read too many books. It's a question about the sky, involving the stars. Here it is: Which seems more likely, that large bodies turn around small bodies or small bodies around large ones?

MRS. SARTI (*suspiciously*)   I never know what you're up to, Mr. Galilei. Is this a serious question or are you pulling my leg again?

GALILEO   A serious question.

MRS. SARTI   Then I can give you a quick answer. Do I serve your dinner or do you serve mine?

GALILEO   You serve mine. Yesterday it was burned.

MRS. SARTI   And why was it burned? Because you made me get your shoes while I was cooking it. Didn't I bring you your shoes?

GALILEO   I presume you did.

MRS. SARTI   Because it's you who went to school and can pay.

GALILEO   I see. I see there's no difficulty. Good morning, Mrs. Sarti.

(*Mrs. Sarti, amused, goes out*)

GALILEO   And such people are supposed not to be able to grasp the truth? They snatch at it.

(*The matins bell has begun to peal. In comes Virginia in a cloak, carrying a shaded candle*)

VIRGINIA   Good morning, father.

GALILEO   Up so early?

VIRGINIA   I'm going to matins with Mrs. Sarti. Ludovico will be there too. How was the night, father?

GALILEO   Clear.

VIRGINIA   May I look through it?

GALILEO   What for? (*Virginia has no answer*) It's not a toy.

VIRGINIA   I know, father.

GALILEO   By the way, the tube's a big flop. You'll hear all about

it soon. It's being sold on the street for three scudi, it was invented in Holland.

VIRGINIA   Didn't you find anything new in the sky with it?

GALILEO   Nothing for you. Only a few dim specks on the left side of a big star, I'll have to find a way of calling attention to them. (*Speaking to Sagredo over his daughter's head*) Maybe I'll call them the "Medicean Stars" to please the grand duke of Florence. (*Again to Virginia*) It may interest you, Virginia, to know that we'll probably move to Florence. I've written to ask if the grand duke can use me as court mathematician.

VIRGINIA (*radiant*)   At court?

SAGREDO   Galileo!

GALILEO   I need leisure, old friend. I need proofs. And I want the fleshpots. With a position like that I won't have to ram the Ptolemaic system down the throats of private students, I'll have time—time, time, time, time!—to work out my proofs. What I've got now isn't enough. It's nothing, it's just bits and pieces. I can't stand up to the whole world with that. There's still no proof that any heavenly body revolves around the sun. But I'm going to find the proofs, proofs for everybody from Mrs. Sarti to the pope. The only thing that worries me is that the court may not want me.

VIRGINIA   Oh, I'm sure they'll take you, father, with your new stars and all.

GALILEO   Go to your mass.

(*Virginia leaves*)

GALILEO   I'm not used to writing letters to important people. (*He hands Sagredo a letter*) Do you think this will do?

SAGREDO (*reading aloud the end of the letter which Galileo has handed him*)   "Withal I am yearning for nothing so much as to be nearer to Your Highness, the rising sun which will illuminate this age." The grand duke of Florence is nine years old.

GALILEO   I know. I see, you think my letter is too servile. I wonder if it's servile enough, not too formal, as if I were lacking in genuine devotion. A more restrained letter might be all right for someone with the distinction of having proved the truth of Aristotle; not for me. A man like me can only get a halfway decent position by crawling on his belly. And you know I despise men whose brains are incapable of filling their stomachs.

(*Mrs. Sarti and Virginia walk past the two men on their way to mass*)

SAGREDO   Don't go to Florence, Galileo.

GALILEO   Why not?

SAGREDO   Because it's ruled by monks.

GALILEO   There are distinguished scholars at the Florentine court.

SAGREDO   Toadies.

GALILEO   I'll take them by the scruff of their necks and drag them to my tube. Even monks are human beings, Sagredo. Even monks can be seduced by proofs. Copernicus—don't forget that—wanted them to trust his figures, I'm only asking them to trust the evidence of their eyes. When truth is too weak to defend itself, it has to attack. I'll take them by the scruff of their necks and make them look through the tube.

SAGREDO   Galileo, you're on a dangerous path. It's bad luck when a man sees the truth. And delusion when he believes in the rationality of the human race. Who do we say walks with open eyes? The man who's headed for perdition. How can the mighty leave a man at large who knows the truth, even if it's only about the remotest stars? Do you think the pope will hear your truth when you tell him he's wrong? No, he'll hear only one thing, that you've said he's wrong. Do you think he will calmly write in his diary: January 10, 1610, Heaven abolished? How can you want to leave the republic with the truth in your pocket and walk straight into the trap of the monks and princes with your tube in your hands? You may be very skeptical in your science, but you're as gullible as a child about anything that looks like a help in pursuing it. You may not believe in Aristotle, but you believe in the grand duke of Florence. A moment ago when I saw you at your tube looking at the new stars I thought I saw you on a flaming pyre and when you said you believed in proofs I smelled burnt flesh. I love science, but I love you more, my friend. Galileo, don't go to Florence!

GALILEO   If they'll have me I'll go.

(*On a curtain appears the last page of the letter*)

In assigning the sublime name of the Medicean line to these stars newly discovered by me I am fully aware that

when gods and heroes were elevated to the starry skies they were thereby glorified, but that in the present case it is the stars that will be glorified by receiving the name of the Medici. With this I recommend myself as one among the number of your most faithful and obedient servants, who holds it the highest honor to have been born your subject.

Withal I yearn for nothing so much as to be nearer to Your Highness, the rising sun which will illuminate this age.

Galileo Galilei

4

Galileo has exchanged the Venetian republic for the court of Florence. The discoveries he has made with the help of the telescope are met with disbelief by the court scholars.

> The old says: What I've always done I'll always do.
> The new says: If you're useless you must go.

Galileo's house in Florence. Mrs. Sarti is getting Galileo's study ready to receive guests. Her son Andrea is seated, putting celestial charts away.

MRS. SARTI   Ever since we arrived in this marvelous Florence I've seen nothing but bowing and scraping. The whole town files past this tube and I can scrub the floor afterwards. But it won't do us a bit of good. If these discoveries amounted to anything, the reverend fathers would know it, wouldn't they? For four years I was in service with Monsignor Filippo, I never managed to dust the whole of his library. Leather-

bound volumes up to the ceiling and no love poems either. And the good monsignor had two pounds of boils on his behind from poring over all that learning. Wouldn't a man like that know what's what? The big demonstration today will be another flop and tomorrow I won't be able to look the milkman in the face. I knew what I was saying when I told him to give the gentlemen a good dinner first, a nice piece of lamb, before they start in on his tube. Oh no! (*She imitates Galileo*) "I've got something better for them."
(*Knocking downstairs*)

MRS. SARTI (*looks in the window-mirror*) Goodness, there's the grand duke already. And Galileo still at the university! (*She runs downstairs and admits Cosmo de' Medici, grand duke of Tuscany, accompanied by the lord chamberlain and two ladies-in-waiting*)

COSMO I want to see the tube.

THE LORD CHAMBERLAIN Perhaps Your Highness would prefer to wait until Mr. Galilei and the other gentlemen have returned from the university. (*To Mrs. Sarti*) Mr. Galilei wanted the professors of astronomy to examine the newly discovered stars which he calls the Medicean stars.

COSMO They don't believe in the tube, far from it. Where is it?

MRS. SARTI Upstairs, in his workroom.
(*The boy nods, points to the staircase, and upon a nod from Mrs. Sarti dashes up the stairs*)

THE LORD CHAMBERLAIN (*a very old man*) Your Highness! (*To Mrs. Sarti*) Must we go up there? I only came because the tutor is ill.

MRS. SARTI Nothing can happen to the young gentleman. My boy's upstairs.

COSMO (*entering above*) Good evening.
(*The two boys ceremoniously bow to each other. Pause. Then Andrea goes back to his work*)

ANDREA (*much like his teacher*) This place is as busy as a pigeon house.

COSMO Lots of visitors?

ANDREA Stumble about and gape and don't know beans.

COSMO I see. Is that . . . ? (*Points at the tube*)

ANDREA Yes, that's it. But don't touch it. It's not allowed.

COSMO   And what's that? (*He indicates the wooden model of the Ptolemaic system*)

ANDREA   That's the Ptolemaic system.

COSMO   It shows how the sun moves, doesn't it?

ANDREA   Yes, so they say.

COSMO (*sitting down in a chair, he takes the model on his knees*) My tutor has a cold. So I was able to get away early. It's nice here.

ANDREA (*is restless, ambles about irresolutely, throwing suspicious glances at the strange boy, and at last, unable to resist the temptation any longer, takes from behind the star charts another wooden model representing the Copernican system*) But of course it's really like this.

COSMO   What's like this?

ANDREA (*pointing at the model on Cosmo's knees*) That's the way people think it is and that's (*Pointing at his model*) the way it really is. The earth turns around the sun. See?

COSMO   You really think so?

ANDREA   Of course. It's been proven.

COSMO   You don't say!—I wish I knew why they didn't let me go in to see the old man. Last night he was at dinner as usual.

ANDREA   You don't seem to believe it, or do you?

COSMO   Why certainly, I do.

ANDREA (*pointing at the model on Cosmo's knees*) Give it back, you don't even understand that one!

COSMO   But you don't need two.

ANDREA   Give it back this minute. It's not a toy for little boys.

COSMO   I don't mind giving it back but you ought to be a little more polite, you know.

ANDREA   You're stupid and I don't care about being polite. Give it back or you'll see.

COSMO   Hands off, do you hear.

(*They start fighting and are soon rolling on the floor*)

ANDREA   I'll show you how to treat a model. Give up!

COSMO   You've broken it. You're twisting my hand.

ANDREA   We'll see who's right and who isn't. Say it turns or I'll box your ears.

COSMO   I won't. Ouch, you redhead. I'll teach you good manners.

ANDREA   Redhead? Am I a redhead?

(*They continue to fight in silence. Below, Galileo and several university professors enter. Behind them Federzoni*)

THE LORD CHAMBERLAIN   Gentlemen, a slight illness has prevented Mr. Suri, His Highness' tutor, from accompanying His Highness.

THE THEOLOGIAN   Nothing serious, I hope.

THE LORD CHAMBERLAIN   No, no, by no means.

GALILEO (*disappointed*)   Isn't His Highness here?

THE LORD CHAMBERLAIN   His Highness is upstairs. May I ask you gentlemen to proceed. The court is so very anxious to hear the opinion of our illustrious university about Mr. Galilei's extraordinary instrument and those marvelous new stars.

(*They go upstairs*)

(*The boys lie still. They have heard sounds downstairs*)

COSMO   Here they come. Let me up.

(*They quickly get up*)

THE GENTLEMEN (*as they file upstairs*)   No. No, there's nothing to worry about.—The faculty of medicine has declared that the cases in the inner city can't possibly be plague. The miasma would freeze at the present temperature.—The worst danger in these situations is panic.—We can always expect an epidemic of colds at this time of year.—No ground for suspicion. —Nothing to worry about.

(*Salutations upstairs*)

GALILEO   Your Highness, I am extremely pleased that you should be present while I communicate our new discoveries to the gentlemen of your university.

(*Cosmo makes formal bows to all, including Andrea*)

THE THEOLOGIAN (*seeing the broken Ptolemaic model on the floor*)   There seems to have been some breakage here.

(*Cosmo stoops quickly and hands the model politely to Andrea. At the same time Galileo slyly puts away the other model*)

GALILEO (*at the telescope*)   As Your Highness no doubt knows, we astronomers have for some time been encountering great difficulties in our calculations. We are using a very old system which seems to be in agreement with philosophy but unfortu-

nately not with the facts. According to this old system, the Ptolemaic system, the movements of the planets are extremely complicated. Venus, for instance, is supposed to move something like this. (*He sketches on a blackboard the epicyclic course of Venus according to Ptolemy*) But if we predicate these complicated movements, we are unable to calculate the position of any star accurately in advance. We do not find it in the place where it should be. Furthermore there are stellar motions for which the Ptolemaic system has no explanation at all. According to my observations, certain small stars I have discovered describe motions of this kind around the planet Jupiter. If you gentlemen are agreeable, we shall begin with the inspection of the satellites of Jupiter, the Medicean stars.

ANDREA (*pointing to the stool in front of the telescope*)   Kindly sit here.

THE PHILOSOPHER   Thank you, my child. I'm afraid it will not be so simple. Mr. Galilei, before we apply ourselves to your famous tube, we should like to request the pleasure of a disputation: Can such planets exist?

THE MATHEMATICIAN   A formal disputation.

GALILEO   I thought you'd just look through the telescope and see for yourselves.

ANDREA   Here, if you please.

THE MATHEMATICIAN   Yes, yes.—You are aware, of course, that in the view of the ancients no star can revolve around any center other than the earth and that there can be no stars without firm support in the sky.

GALILEO   Yes.

THE PHILOSOPHER   And, regardless of whether such stars are possible, a proposition which the mathematician (*He bows to the mathematician*) seems to doubt, I as a philosopher should like with all due modesty to raise this question: Are such stars necessary? Aristotelis divini universum . . .

GALILEO   Oughtn't we to continue in the vernacular? My colleague, Mr. Federzoni, doesn't understand Latin.

THE PHILOSOPHER   Does it matter whether he understands us?

GALILEO   Yes.

THE PHILOSOPHER   I beg your pardon. I thought he was your lens grinder.

ANDREA   Mr. Federzoni is a lens grinder and a scholar.

THE PHILOSOPHER   Thank you, my child. If Mr. Federzoni insists . . .

GALILEO   I insist.

THE PHILOSOPHER   The debate will lose in brilliance, but this is your house.—The cosmos of the divine Aristotle with its spheres and their mystical music, with its crystal vaults and the circular courses of its heavenly bodies, with the oblique angle of the sun's course and the mysteries of its tables of satellites and the wealth of stars in the catalog of the southern hemisphere and the inspired construction of the celestial globe is an edifice of such order and beauty that we shall be well advised not to disturb its harmony.

GALILEO   Your Highness, would you care to observe those impossible and unnecessary stars through the telescope?

THE MATHEMATICIAN   One might be tempted to reply that if your tube shows something that cannot exist it must be a rather unreliable tube.

GALILEO   What do you mean by that?

THE MATHEMATICIAN   It certainly would be much more to the point, Mr. Galilei, if you were to tell us your reasons for supposing that there can be free-floating stars moving about in the highest sphere of the immutable heavens.

THE PHILOSOPHER   Reasons, Mr. Galilei, reasons!

GALILEO   My reasons? When a look at these stars and my calculations demonstrate the phenomenon? This debate is getting absurd, sir.

THE MATHEMATICIAN   If it were not to be feared that you would get even more excited than you are, one might suggest that what is in your tube and what is in the sky might be two different things.

THE PHILOSOPHER   It would be difficult to put it more politely.

FEDERZONI   They think we painted the Medicean stars on the lens!

GALILEO   You accuse me of fraud?

THE PHILOSOPHER   We wouldn't dream of it! In the presence of His Highness!

THE MATHEMATICIAN   Your instrument, whether we call it your own or your adoptive child, has doubtless been very cleverly constructed.

THE PHILOSOPHER   And we are convinced, Mr. Galilei, that neither you nor anyone else would ever dare to grace stars with
the illustrious name of the ruling house if there were the
slightest doubt of their existence.

(*All bow deeply to the grand duke*)

COSMO (*turning to the ladies-in-waiting*)   Is there something
wrong with my stars?

THE OLDER LADY-IN-WAITING (*to the grand duke*)   Your Highness'
stars are fine. The gentlemen are only wondering whether
they really and truly exist.

(*Pause*)

THE YOUNGER LADY-IN-WAITING   They say you can see the scales
of the Dragon with this instrument.

FEDERZONI   Yes, and you can see all sorts of things on the Bull.

GALILEO   Are you gentlemen going to look through it, or not?

THE PHILOSOPHER   Certainly, certainly.

THE MATHEMATICIAN   Certainly.

(*Pause. Suddenly Andrea turns around and walks stiffly out through
the length of the room. His mother intercepts him*)

MRS. SARTI   What's got into you?

ANDREA   They're stupid. (*Tears himself loose and runs away*)

THE PHILOSOPHER   A deplorable child.

THE LORD CHAMBERLAIN   Your Highness, gentlemen, may I remind you that the state ball is due to start in forty-five minutes?

THE MATHEMATICIAN   Why beat about the bush? Sooner or later
Mr. Galilei will have to face up to the facts. His moons of
Jupiter would pierce the crystal sphere. That's all there is to
it.

FEDERZONI   You'll be surprised, but there is no crystal sphere.

THE PHILOSOPHER   Any textbook will tell you there is, my good
man.

FEDERZONI   Then we need new textbooks.

THE PHILOSOPHER   Your Highness, my esteemed colleague and
I are supported by no less an authority than the divine Aristotle.

GALILEO (*almost abjectly*)   Gentlemen, belief in the authority of
Aristotle is one thing, observable facts are another. You say
that according to Aristotle there are crystal spheres up there

and that certain motions are impossible because the stars would have to pierce the spheres. But what if you observed these motions? Wouldn't that suggest to you that the spheres do not exist? Gentlemen, I humbly beseech you to trust your own eyes.

THE MATHEMATICIAN   My dear Galilei, though it may seem dreadfully old-fashioned to you, I'm in the habit of reading Aristotle now and then, and I can assure you that when I read Aristotle I do trust my eyes.

GALILEO   I'm used to seeing the gentlemen of all faculties close their eyes to all facts and act as if nothing had happened. I show them my calculations, and they smile; I make my telescope available to help them see for themselves, and they quote Aristotle.

FEDERZONI   The man had no telescope!

THE MATHEMATICIAN   Exactly!

THE PHILOSOPHER (*grandly*)   If Aristotle, an authority acknowledged not only by all the scientists of antiquity but by the church fathers themselves, is to be dragged through the mire, a continuation of this discussion seems superfluous, at least to me. I refuse to take part in irrelevant arguments. Basta.

GALILEO   Truth is the child of time, not of authority. Our ignorance is infinite, let's whittle away just one cubic millimeter. Why should we still want to be so clever when at long last we have a chance of being a little less stupid? I've had the good fortune to lay hands on a new instrument with which we can observe a tiny corner of the universe a little more closely, not much though. Make use of it.

THE PHILOSOPHER   Your Highness, ladies and gentlemen, I can only wonder what all this will lead to.

GALILEO   I submit that as scientists we have no business asking what the truth may lead to.

THE PHILOSOPHER (*in wild alarm*)   Mr. Galilei, the truth can lead to all sorts of things!

GALILEO   Your Highness. In these nights telescopes are being directed at the sky all over Italy. The moons of Jupiter don't lower the price of milk. But they have never been seen before, and yet they exist. The man in the street will conclude that a good many things may exist if only he opens his eyes. And

you ought to back him up. It's not the motions of some remote stars that make Italy sit up and take notice, but the news that doctrines believed to be unshakeable are beginning to totter, and we all know that of these there are far too many. Gentlemen, we oughtn't to be defending shaky doctrines!

FEDERZONI   You are teachers, you ought to be doing the shaking.

THE PHILOSOPHER   I wish your man there would keep out of a scientific debate.

GALILEO   Your Highness! My work in the great arsenal of Venice brought me into daily contact with draftsmen, architects and instrument makers. Those people taught me many new ways of doing things. They don't read books but they trust the testimony of their five senses, most of them without fear as to where it will lead them . . .

THE PHILOSOPHER   Fancy that!

GALILEO   Very much like our seamen who left our shores a hundred years ago, without the slightest idea of what other shores, if any, they might reach. It looks as if we had to go to the shipyards nowadays to find the high curiosity that was the glory of ancient Greece.

THE PHILOSOPHER   After what we have heard here today, I have no doubt that Mr. Galilei will find admirers in the shipyards.

THE LORD CHAMBERLAIN   Your Highness, I note to my great dismay that this exceedingly instructive conversation has taken a little longer than foreseen. Your Highness must rest a while before the court ball.

(*At a signal, the grand duke bows to Galileo. The court quickly prepares to leave*)

MRS. SARTI (*stepping in the way of the grand duke and offering him a plate of pastry*)   A bun, Your Highness?

(*The older lady-in-waiting leads the grand duke away*)

GALILEO (*running after them*)   But all you gentlemen need do is look through the instrument.

THE LORD CHAMBERLAIN   His Highness will not fail to obtain an expert opinion on your statements by consulting our greatest living astronomer, Father Christopher Clavius, astronomer-in-chief at the papal college in Rome.

5

Undaunted even by the plague, Galileo continues his
investigations.

a)

Early morning. Galileo bending over his notes at the telescope. Virginia
comes in with a traveling bag.

GALILEO   Virginia! Is anything wrong?

VIRGINIA   The convent is closed. They sent us home. There are
five cases of plague in Arcetri.

GALILEO (*calls out*)   Sarti!

VIRGINIA   And last night our market was roped off. They say
two people have died in the old city, and there are three more
dying in the hospital.

GALILEO   As usual, they've hushed it up until the last minute.

MRS. SARTI (*comes in*)   What are you doing here?

VIRGINIA   The plague.

MRS. SARTI   My God! I'd better pack. (*Sits down*)

GALILEO   No need to pack. Take Virginia and Andrea. I'll go
get my notes.
(*He hurries back to the table and gathers his papers in great haste.*
Mrs. Sarti puts a coat on Andrea as he runs in, and goes to get some
food and bedding. One of the grand duke's lackeys enters)

LACKEY   His Highness has left the city for Bologna because of
the raging disease. Before leaving he insisted that Mr. Galilei
should be given an opportunity to escape. The coach will be
here in two minutes.

MRS. SARTI (*to Virginia and Andrea*)   Go right outside, you two.
Here, take this.

ANDREA   Why? If you don't tell me why, I won't go.

MRS. SARTI   It's the plague, my child.

VIRGINIA   We'll wait for father.

MRS. SARTI   Mr. Galilei, are you ready?

GALILEO (*wrapping the telescope in a tablecloth*)   Put Virginia and Andrea in the coach. I'll join you in a minute.

VIRGINIA   No, we won't leave without you. You'll never be ready if you start packing your books.

MRS. SARTI   The carriage is here.

GALILEO   Be reasonable, Virginia. If no one gets in, the coachman will just drive away. The plague is no joke.

VIRGINIA (*protesting as Mrs. Sarti leads her and Andrea out*)   Help him with his books or he won't come.

MRS. SARTI (*calls out from the house door*)   Mr. Galilei! The coachman says he won't wait.

GALILEO   Mrs. Sarti, I don't think I should leave. Everything is in such a muddle here, you know, all my notes of the last three months, I might as well throw them away if I don't go on with them for a night or two. And anyway the plague is everywhere.

MRS. SARTI   Mr. Galilei! Come this minute! You're out of your mind.

GALILEO   You go with Virginia and Andrea. I'll come later.

MRS. SARTI   In another hour they won't let anyone leave the city. You must come! (*Listens*) He's driving off! I've got to stop him. (*Out*)
    (*Galileo walks back and forth. Mrs. Sarti returns, very pale, without her bundle*)

GALILEO   Don't stand around like that! The coach with the children will leave without you.

MRS. SARTI   They've left. They had to hold Virginia down. The children will be taken care of in Bologna. But who'd get you your meals?

GALILEO   You're crazy. Staying in the city to cook! . . . (*Takes up his papers*) You mustn't take me for a fool, Mrs. Sarti. I can't interrupt my observations. I have powerful enemies, I've got to supply proofs for certain propositions.

MRS. SARTI   You needn't apologize. But it's not reasonable.

b)

Outside Galileo's house in Florence. Galileo comes out of the door and looks down the street. Two nuns are passing by.

GALILEO (*addresses them*)   Sisters, could you tell me where I can buy milk? This morning the milk woman didn't come, and my housekeeper is away.

THE FIRST NUN   Only the shops in the lower city are open.

THE OTHER NUN   Did you come out of this house? (*Galileo nods*) This is the street!

(*The two nuns cross themselves, mumble an Ave Maria and run. A man passes*)

GALILEO (*addresses him*)   Aren't you the baker who brings us our bread? (*The man nods*) Have you seen my housekeeper? She must have gone out last night. She hasn't been here all morning.

(*The man shakes his head. A window across the street is opened and a woman looks out*)

THE WOMAN (*screams*)   Run! Quick! They've got the plague!

(*Frightened, the man runs away*)

GALILEO   Do you know anything about my housekeeper?

THE WOMAN   Your housekeeper collapsed in the street. Up there. She must have known. That's why she left you. How can people be so inconsiderate? (*She bangs the window shut*)

(*Children come down the street. When they see Galileo they run away screaming. As Galileo turns around, two soldiers in full armor come rushing in*)

THE SOLDIERS   Get back in that house! (*With their long lances they push Galileo back into his house. They bolt the door behind him*)

GALILEO (*at a window*)   Can you tell me what's happened to the woman?

THE SOLDIERS   They take 'em to potter's field.

THE WOMAN (*appears at her window again*)   The whole street back there's infected. Why don't you close it off?

(*The soldiers stretch a rope across the street*)

THE WOMAN   But now nobody can get into our house! Don't put your rope there. We're all well here. Stop! Stop! Can't you hear? My husband's gone to the city, he won't be able

to get back. You beasts! You beasts!
(*Her sobbing and screaming are heard from inside. The soldiers leave.
An old woman appears at another window*)

GALILEO   There seems to be a fire back there.

THE OLD WOMAN   The firemen won't touch it if there's any suspicion of plague. All they can think about is the plague.

GALILEO   Just like them! Their whole system of government is like that. They cut us off like a withered fig branch that's stopped bearing fruit.

THE OLD WOMAN   You mustn't say that. They're helpless, that's all.

GALILEO   Are you alone in your house?

THE OLD WOMAN   Yes. My son sent me a note. Thank God he heard last night that someone had died around here, so he didn't come home. There've been eleven cases in the neighborhood during the night.

GALILEO   I can't forgive myself for not sending my housekeeper away in time. I had urgent work to finish, but she had no reason to stay.

THE OLD WOMAN   We can't go away either. Who would take us in? You mustn't reproach yourself. I saw her. She left this morning, at about seven o'clock. She was sick, because when she saw me step out to bring in the bread she circled around me. I suppose she didn't want your house to be sealed off. But they get wise to everything.
(*A rattling sound is heard*)

GALILEO   What's that?

THE OLD WOMAN   They're making noise to drive away the clouds that carry the seeds of the plague.
(*Galileo roars with laughter*)

THE OLD WOMAN   How can you laugh?
(*A man comes down the street and finds it roped off*)

GALILEO   Hey, you! The street's closed and there's nothing to eat in the house.
(*The man has already run away*)

GALILEO   You can't just let us starve here! Hey! Hey!

THE OLD WOMAN   Maybe they'll bring us something. If they don't, I can put a pitcher of milk on your doorstep, if you're not afraid, but not until after dark.

GALILEO   Hey! Hey! Somebody ought to hear us.

(*Suddenly Andrea stands at the rope. His face is stained with tears*)

GALILEO   Andrea! How did you get here?

ANDREA   I was here this morning. I knocked, but you didn't open. People told me . . .

GALILEO   Didn't you go away?

ANDREA   I did. But I managed to jump out. Virginia went on. Can I come in?

THE OLD WOMAN   No, you can not. You must go to the Ursulines. Maybe your mother is there too.

ANDREA   I've been there. But they wouldn't let me see her. She's too sick.

GALILEO   Did you walk the whole way back? You've been gone for three days.

ANDREA   That's how long it took, don't be angry. And once they caught me.

GALILEO (*helplessly*)   Don't cry, Andrea. You know, I've found out a few things in the meantime. Shall I tell you? (*Andrea nods, sobbing*) But listen carefully, or you won't understand. Remember when I showed you the planet Venus? Don't listen to that noise, it's nothing. Remember? You know what I saw? It's like the moon. I saw it as a half-circle and I saw it as a crescent. What do you think of that? I can show you the whole thing with a little ball and a lamp. It proves that Venus has no light of its own either. And it describes a simple circle around the sun, isn't that marvelous?

ANDREA (*sobbing*)   Yes, and that's a fact.

GALILEO (*softly*)   I didn't stop her from leaving.

(*Andrea is silent*)

GALILEO   But of course if I hadn't stayed it wouldn't have happened.

ANDREA   Will they have to believe you now?

GALILEO   I've got all the proofs I need. You know what? When all this is over, I'll go to Rome and show them.

(*Two muffled men with long poles and buckets come down the street. With the poles they hold out bread to Galileo and the old woman in their windows*)

THE OLD WOMAN   There's a woman with three children over there. Give her some too.

GALILEO I've nothing to drink. There's no water in the house. (*The two shrug their shoulders*) Will you be back tomorrow?

THE MAN (*with muffled voice, his mouth covered by a cloth*) Who knows what tomorrow will bring?

GALILEO If you do come, could you reach up to me a little book that I need for my work?

THE MAN (*with a muffled laugh*) A book won't do you any good now. Lucky if you get bread.

GALILEO This boy, my pupil, will be here to give it to you. It's a table showing the period of Mercury, Andrea. I've mislaid mine. Will you find me one at school?

(*The men have already moved on*)

ANDREA Sure. I'll get it for you, Mr. Galilei. (*Out*)

(*Galileo retires. The old woman steps out of the house opposite and places a pitcher at Galileo's door*)

6

1616: The Collegium Romanum, the research institute of the Vatican, confirms Galileo's discoveries.

> Things take indeed a wondrous turn
> When learned men do stoop to learn.
> Clavius, we are pleased to say
> Upheld Galileo Galilei.

Large hall in the Collegium Romanum, Rome. It is night. High ecclesiastics, monks, scholars, in groups. Galileo on one side, alone. Great merriment. Before the scene opens, boisterous laughter is heard.

A FAT PRELATE (*holds his belly for laughter*) Oh stupidity! Oh stupidity! Can anyone tell me of a proposition that has *not* been believed?

A SCHOLAR What about the proposition that you have an incon-

querable aversion to food, monsignor!

THE FAT PRELATE   Will be believed, never fear. Only reasonable statements are not believed. The existence of the devil is being doubted. But that the earth spins around like a marble in a gutter, that's being believed. Sancta simplicitas!

A MONK (*acting out a comedy*)   I'm dizzy. The earth is turning too fast. Permit me to hold on to you, professor. (*He pretends to stagger and holds on to a scholar*)

THE SCHOLAR (*joining in the fun*)   Yes, she's dead drunk again, the old hag.

THE MONK   Stop, stop! We're sliding off! Stop, I say!

ANOTHER SCHOLAR   Venus is listing badly. I can only see half of her behind. Help!

(*A cluster of monks is forming who with much laughter pretend to be on a storm-tossed ship, struggling to avoid being thrown overboard*)

ANOTHER MONK   If only we don't get thrown on the moon. Brothers, they say it bristles with sharp mountain peaks!

THE FIRST SCHOLAR   Plant your foot against it.

THE FIRST MONK   And don't look down. I feel as sick as a monkey.

THE FAT PRELATE (*pointedly loud in Galileo's direction*)   What! Monkey business in the Collegium Romanum?

(*Loud laughter. Two astronomers of the Collegium come out of a door. Quiet sets in*)

A MONK   Still investigating? That's a scandal!

THE FIRST ASTRONOMER (*angrily*)   Not us!

THE SECOND ASTRONOMER   Where's this going to end? I can't understand Clavius . . . Are all the claims made in the last fifty years to be taken at face value? In 1572 a new star appeared in the highest sphere, the eighth, the sphere of the fixed stars. It was rather larger and brighter than its neighbors and a year and a half later it was gone, overtaken by perdition. Is that any reason to question the eternal immutability of the heavens?

THE PHILOSOPHER   If we let them, they'd smash up the whole universe.

THE FIRST ASTRONOMER   Yes, what's the world coming to! Five years later, Tycho Brahe, a Dane, determined the trajectory of a comet. It started above the moon and broke through all

the spheres, the material carriers of all movable celestial bodies. It met with no resistance, its light was not deflected. Is that any reason to doubt the existence of the spheres?

THE PHILOSOPHER   Out of the question! How can Christopher Clavius, the greatest astronomer of Italy and of the church, lower himself to investigating such stuff!

THE FAT PRELATE   Scandalous!

THE FIRST ASTRONOMER   But there he is, investigating. There he sits, gaping through that devil's tube.

THE SECOND ASTRONOMER   Principiis obsta! The whole trouble began years ago when we started using the tables of Copernicus—a heretic—for calculating such things as the length of the solar year, the dates of solar and lunar eclipses, the positions of the celestial bodies.

A MONK   I ask you: What is better, to get a lunar eclipse three days behind schedule or to miss out on eternal salvation altogether?

A VERY THIN MONK (steps forward with an open Bible, fanatically stabbing his finger at a passage)   What does the Book say? "Sun, stand thou still upon Gibeon; and thou, moon, in the valley of Ajalon." How can the sun stand still if it never moves as these heretics claim? Does the Book lie?

THE FIRST ASTRONOMER   No, and that's why we're leaving.

THE SECOND ASTRONOMER   Yes, there are phenomena that perplex us astronomers, but must man understand everything? (Both go out)

THE VERY THIN MONK   They degrade the home of mankind, a planet they call it. They load man, animal, plant and soil on a cart and chase it in circles through the empty sky. Heaven and earth, they claim, have ceased to exist. The earth because it's a star in the sky, and the sky because it consists of many earths. There's no longer any difference between above and below, between eternal and transient. That we are transient, that we know. But now they tell us that heaven itself is transient. There are sun, moon and stars, but we live on this earth, that's what we've learned and what the Book says; but now, according to them, the earth is just another star. One day they'll be saying there's no difference between man and beast, that man himself is an animal and only animals exist.

THE FIRST SCHOLAR (*to Galileo*) Mr. Galilei, you've dropped something.

GALILEO (*who had taken his pebble out of his pocket during the preceding speech and dropped it on the floor, as he stoops to pick it up*) It didn't drop, monsignor, it rose.

THE FAT PRELATE (*turns his back on him*) The insolence of the man!

(*A very old cardinal comes in, supported by a monk. The others reverentially make room for him*)

THE VERY OLD CARDINAL Are they still in there? Can't they get this foolishness over with? Surely Clavius knows his astronomy. I hear this Mr. Galilei has moved man from the center of the universe to somewhere on the edge. Obviously he's an enemy of mankind. And ought to be treated as such. Man is the crown of creation, every child knows that, he's God's highest and most beloved creature. Would God have put his most marvelous work, his supreme effort on a little far-away star that's constantly on the move? Would he have sent His Son to such a place? How can there be men so perverse as to believe these slaves of their mathematical tables? How can one of God's creatures put up with such a thing?

THE FAT PRELATE (*in an undertone*) The gentleman is present.

THE VERY OLD CARDINAL (*to Galileo*) Oh, you're the man? You know, I don't see too well any more, but I can see that you look remarkably like the man—what was his name again?—whom we burned a few years ago.

THE MONK Your Eminence, you mustn't excite yourself. The doctor . . .

THE VERY OLD CARDINAL (*brushing him off, to Galileo*) You want to degrade our earth, though you live on it and receive everything from it. You're fouling your own nest! But I for one will not stand for it. (*He pushes the monk out of the way and struts proudly back and forth*) I'm not some nondescript being on some little star that briefly circles around somewhere. I walk with assurance on a firm earth, it stands still, it is the center of the universe, I am in the center, and the Creator's eye rests on me, on me alone. Around me, fixed to eight crystal spheres, revolve the fixed stars and the mighty sun, which was created

to illumine my surroundings. And myself as well, in order that God may see me. Hence obviously and irrefutably, everything depends on me, man, the supreme work of God, the creature in the center, the image of God, imperishable and . . . (*He collapses*)

THE MONK   Your Eminence, you have overtaxed yourself!

(*At this moment the door in the rear is opened and the great Clavius comes in at the head of his astronomers. Quickly, without a word or a glance aside, he traverses the hall and, near the exit, says to a monk*)

CLAVIUS   He's right.

(*He goes out, followed by the astronomers. The door in the rear remains open. Deadly silence. The very old cardinal revives*)

THE VERY OLD CARDINAL   What happened? Has there been a decision?

(*No one dares to tell him*)

THE MONK   Your Eminence, you must let them take you home.

(*The old man is helped out. All leave the hall, perturbed. A little monk, a member of Clavius' investigating commission, stops at Galileo's side*)

THE LITTLE MONK (*furtively*)   Mr. Galilei, before he left Father Clavius said: Now the theologians can see about setting the heavenly spheres right again. You have prevailed. (*Out*)

GALILEO (*trying to hold him back*)   It has prevailed. Not I, reason has prevailed!

(*The little monk has gone. Galileo is leaving too. In the doorway he meets a tall cleric, the cardinal inquisitor, accompanied by an astronomer. Galileo bows. Before going out, he whispers a question to a doorkeeper*)

DOORKEEPER (*whispering back*)   His Eminence the cardinal inquisitor.

(*The astronomer leads the cardinal inquisitor to the telescope*)

7

But the Inquisition places the Copernican doctrine on the Index (March 5, 1616).

> When Galileo was in Rome
> A cardinal asked him to his home.
> He wined and dined him as his guest
> And only made one small request.

The house of Cardinal Bellarmine in Rome. A ball is in progress. In the vestibule, where two ecclesiastical secretaries are playing chess and exchanging observations about the guests, Galileo is received by an applauding group of masked ladies and gentlemen. He is accompanied by his daughter Virginia and her fiancé Ludovico Marsili.

VIRGINIA   I won't dance with anyone else, Ludovico.

LUDOVICO   Your shoulder clasp is loose.

GALILEO

"Your tucker, Thaïs, is askew. Don't
Set it straight, for preciously it shows me
And others too some deeper disorder.
In the candlelight of the swirling ballroom
It makes them dream of
Darker coigns in the expectant park."

VIRGINIA   Feel my heart.

GALILEO (*places his hand on her heart*)   It's beating.

VIRGINIA   I want to look beautiful.

GALILEO   You'd better, or else they'll start doubting again that the earth revolves.

LUDOVICO   It doesn't revolve at all. (*Galileo laughs*) All Rome is talking of nothing but you, sir. After tonight Rome will be talking about your daughter.

GALILEO   Everybody agrees that it's easy to look beautiful in the Roman spring. I myself probably look like a paunchy Adonis.

(*To the secretaries*) I'm to wait here for the cardinal. (*To the couple*) Run along and enjoy yourselves!
(*Before they reach the ballroom in the rear Virginia skips back once more*)

VIRGINIA   Father, the hairdresser on Via del Trionfo took me first and made four ladies wait. He knew your name right away. (*Out*)

GALILEO (*to the secretaries playing chess*)   How can you go on playing chess the old way? Too confined. As it's played now, the larger pieces can range over many fields. The rook goes like this (*He demonstrates it*) and the bishop like this, and the queen like this and this. That gives you plenty of room and you can plan ahead.

THE FIRST SECRETARY   It doesn't fit in with our small salaries. We can only afford to move like this. (*He makes a short move*)

GALILEO   It's the other way round, my friend. If you live grandly, you can get away with anything. You must go with the times, gentlemen. You mustn't keep hugging the shore, one fine day you must venture out on the high seas.
(*The very old cardinal of the previous scene crosses the stage, steered by his monk. He notices Galileo, passes him by, then turns uncertainly and greets him. Galileo sits down. The beginning of Lorenzo de' Medici's famous poem about the transience of the world is heard from the ballroom, sung by boys*)

"I who have seen the summer's roses die
And all their petals pale and shriveled lie
Upon the chilly ground, I know the truth:
How evanescent is the flower of youth."

GALILEO   Rome.—Big party?

THE FIRST SECRETARY   The first carnival after the years of plague. All the great families of Italy are represented here tonight. The Orsinis, the Villanis, the Nuccolis, the Soldanieris, the Canes, the Lecchis, the Estensis, the Colombinis . . .

THE SECOND SECRETARY (*interrupts*)   Their Eminences, Cardinals Bellarmine and Barberini.
(*Enter Cardinal Bellarmine and Cardinal Barberini. They hold,*

respectively, a lamb's and a dove's mask mounted on sticks before their faces)

BARBERINI (*pointing his index finger at Galileo*) "The sun also ariseth, and the sun goeth down, and hasteth to his place where he arose." So says Solomon, and what does Galileo say?

GALILEO When I was this big (*He shows with his hand*), Your Eminence, I was on a ship, and I cried out: The shore's moving away.—Today I know that the shore stood still and the ship was moving.

BARBERINI Clever, clever. What we see, Bellarmine, to wit, that the stars in heaven are turning, need not be so, witness ship and shore. And what is true, to wit, that the earth turns, cannot be observed! Very clever. On the other hand, his satellites of Jupiter are hard nuts for our astronomers. Unfortunately, I too once read a little astronomy, Bellarmine. It clings to you like the itch.

BELLARMINE We must go with the times, Barberini. If star charts based on a new hypothesis make navigation easier for our seamen, let's use them. We disapprove only of doctrines that put scripture in the wrong. (*He waves a greeting to the ballroom*)

GALILEO Scripture.—"He that withholdeth corn, the people shall curse him." Proverbs of Solomon.

BARBERINI "A prudent man concealeth knowledge." Proverbs of Solomon.

GALILEO "Where no oxen are, the crib is clean: but much increase is by the strength of the ox."

BARBERINI "He that ruleth his spirit is better than he that taketh a city."

GALILEO "But a broken spirit drieth the bones." (*Pause*) "Doth not wisdom cry?"

BARBERINI "Can one go upon hot coals, and his feet not be burned?"—Welcome to Rome, my dear Galileo. You remember the founding of Rome? Two little boys, the story goes, received milk and shelter from a she-wolf. Ever since then all the she-wolf's children have had to pay for their milk. In return, the she-wolf provides all manner of pleasures, spiritual and worldly, from conversations with my learned

friend Bellarmine to three or four ladies of international repute, would you like to see them? (*He leads Galileo toward the
rear to show him the ballroom. Galileo follows reluctantly*) No? He
prefers a serious discussion. Very well. Are you sure, friend
Galilei, that you astronomers aren't just trying to make astronomy a little easier for yourselves? (*He leads him back to the
front*) You like to think in circles or ellipses and in uniform
velocities, in simple motions commensurate with your minds.
But what if God had been pleased to make His stars move like
this? (*He moves his finger through the air in a very complicated course
with varying velocity in the air*) What would become of your
calculations?

GALILEO   Your Eminence, if God had created the world like this
(*He retraces Barberini's course*) He would have constructed our
minds like this too (*He repeats the same course*) to enable them
to recognize these courses as the simplest. I believe in reason.

BARBERINI   I consider reason inadequate. No answer. He's too
polite to say he considers mine inadequate. (*Laughs and returns
to the balustrade*)

BELLARMINE   Reason, my friend, doesn't go very far. All around
us we see nothing but falsehood, crime and weakness. Where
is the truth?

GALILEO (*angrily*)   I believe in reason.

BARBERINI (*to the secretaries*)   Don't take anything down. This is
a scientific discussion among friends.

BELLARMINE   Consider for a moment the intellectual effort it
cost the church fathers and many after them to make some
sense out of this world (abominable, isn't it?). Consider the
cruelty of those who have their peasants whipped half-naked
around their estates in the Campagna and the stupidity of the
wretches who kiss their feet in return.

GALILEO   Shameful! On my way here I saw . . .

BELLARMINE   We've transferred the responsibility for such conditions (the very stuff of life) which we cannot understand to
a higher being, we say that certain purposes are served
thereby, that a master plan is being followed. Not that our
minds are set entirely at ease. But now you come along and
accuse this supreme being of not knowing how the planets
move, when it's perfectly clear to you. Is that wise?

GALILEO (*launching into an explanation*) I'm a faithful son of the church . . .

BARBERINI He's really dreadful. In all innocence he accuses God of the juiciest boners in astronomy! I suppose God didn't work hard enough at His astronomy before He wrote Holy Scripture? My *dear* friend!

BELLARMINE Don't you think it likely that the Creator knows more about His creation than any of His creatures?

GALILEO But, gentlemen, after all we can misinterpret not only the movements of the heavenly bodies, but the Bible as well.

BELLARMINE But wouldn't you say that after all the interpretation of the Bible is the business of the Holy Church?
(*Galileo is silent*)

BELLARMINE You see, you don't answer. (*He makes a sign to the secretaries*) Mr. Galilei, the Holy Office has decided tonight that the doctrine of Copernicus, according to which the sun is the center of the cosmos and motionless, whereas the earth moves and is not the center of the cosmos, is inane, absurd, and heretical. I have been charged to admonish you to relinquish this opinion. (*To the first secretary*) Please repeat.

FIRST SECRETARY His Eminence, Cardinal Bellarmine, to the aforementioned Galileo Galilei: The Holy Office has decided that the doctrine of Copernicus, according to which the sun is the center of the cosmos and motionless, whereas the earth moves and is not the center of the cosmos, is inane, absurd and heretical. I have been charged to admonish you to relinquish this opinion.

GALILEO What does this mean?
(*From the ballroom another verse of the poem is heard, sung by boys*)

"I said, the seasons do not stay
Pluck the roses while it's May."

(*Barberini motions Galileo to keep quiet while the singing continues. They all listen*)

GALILEO What about the facts? I understand that the astronomers of the Collegium Romanum have confirmed my observations.

BELLARMINE And expressed their profound satisfaction, in a manner most complimentary to you.

GALILEO   But the satellites of Jupiter, the phases of Venus . . .

BELLARMINE   The Holy Congregation has arrived at its decision without taking these particulars into account.

GALILEO   In other words, all further scientific research . . .

BELLARMINE   Is guaranteed, Mr. Galilei. In keeping with the church tenet that we cannot know but may investigate. (*Again he salutes a guest in the ballroom*) You are at liberty to deal with this doctrine as a mathematical hypothesis. Science is the legitimate and most beloved daughter of the church, Mr. Galilei. None of us seriously believes that you wish to undermine man's trust in the church.

GALILEO   (*angrily*)   To invoke trust is to exhaust it.

BARBERINI   Really? (*Laughing heartily, he slaps his shoulder. Then with a sharp look he says, not unkindly*) Don't throw the baby out with the bath water, my friend. Nor shall we. We need you more than you need us.

BELLARMINE   I can't wait to introduce Italy's greatest mathematician to the commissioner of the Holy Office who has the highest regard for you.

BARBERINI   (*taking Galileo's other arm*)   Whereupon he changes back into a lamb. You too, my friend, should have come here in disguise—as a respectable doctor of scholastic philosophy. It's my mask that allows me a little freedom tonight. When I wear it, you may even hear me murmuring: If God did not exist, we should have to invent Him. Well, let's put our masks on again. Poor Galilei hasn't got one.

(*They take Galileo between them and lead him into the ballroom*)

FIRST SECRETARY   Have you got the last sentence?

SECOND SECRETARY   Putting it down. (*They write eagerly*) What was that about his believing in reason?

(*Enter the cardinal inquisitor*)

THE INQUISITOR   Has the interview taken place?

FIRST SECRETARY   (*mechanically*)   First Mr. Galilei arrived with his daughter. She was betrothed today to Mr. . . . . (*The inquisitor motions him to skip it*) Mr. Galilei went on to tell us about the new method of playing chess in which, contrary to the rules, the pieces are moved over many squares.

THE INQUISITOR   (*again beckons "no"*)   The minutes.

(*A secretary hands him the minutes and the cardinal sits down to skim*

*through them. Two young ladies in masks cross the stage and curtsy
to the cardinal)*

THE FIRST LADY   Who's that?

THE SECOND LADY   The cardinal inquisitor.

(They giggle and leave. Enter Virginia, looking around for someone)

THE INQUISITOR *(from his corner)*   Well, my daughter?

VIRGINIA *(with a little start as she has not seen him)*   Oh, Your
Eminence!

*(The inquisitor, without looking up, tenders his right hand. She ap-
proaches, kneels down, and kisses his ring)*

THE INQUISITOR   Glorious night! Allow me to congratulate you
on your engagement. Your fiancé comes of a distinguished
family. Will you stay in Rome?

VIRGINIA   Not for the present, Your Eminence. There's so
much to be done for a wedding.

THE INQUISITOR   Then you'll go back to Florence with your
father. I'm glad to hear it. I imagine your father needs you.
Mathematics is a cold housewife, I should say. A woman of
flesh and blood in such surroundings makes all the difference.
It's so easy to lose oneself in the universe which is so very
immense if one happens to be a great man.

VIRGINIA *(breathless)*   You're very kind, Your Eminence. I really
know practically nothing about these things.

THE INQUISITOR   Indeed? *(He laughs)* Well, I suppose they don't
eat fish in the fisherman's house. It will amuse your father
to hear that, come right down to it, you learned what you
know about the heavenly bodies from me. *(Leafing through the
minutes)* I read here that our innovators, whose acknowledged
leader is your father—a great man, one of the greatest—regard our present ideas about the importance of our good earth
as somewhat exaggerated. Well then, from the age of
Ptolemy, a sage of antiquity, to the present day, the whole of
creation, that is, the entire crystal globe with the earth at its
center, has been computed to measure approximately two
thousand earth diameters. Quite a lot of space, but not
enough, not nearly enough, for the innovators. They maintain, so I hear, that the universe extends further than we can
imagine, that the distance between earth and sun—a rather
considerable distance, we always thought—is so negligibly

small when compared with the distance between our poor earth and the fixed stars on the outermost crystal sphere, that there is no need whatever to consider it in our calculations. Yes, our innovators live on a very grand scale.

(*Virginia laughs. The inquisitor, too, laughs*)

THE INQUISITOR   And indeed, certain gentlemen of the Holy Office, not so long ago, came very close to taking offence at such a picture of the world, compared to which our old picture is a mere miniature that might well be hanging from the charming neck of a certain young lady. The gentlemen of the Holy Office are worried that a prelate or even a cardinal might get lost in such enormous spaces. The Almighty might even lose sight of the pope himself. Yes, it's all very amusing. But even so, my dear child, I'm glad that you'll be staying with your eminent father, whom we all hold in the highest esteem. I wonder if I know your father confessor . . .

VIRGINIA   Father Christopher of St. Ursula.

THE INQUISITOR   Well then, I'm glad you'll be going with your father. He will need you, perhaps you can't conceive of such a thing, but the time will come. You're very young and very much alive and greatness is not always an easy thing to bear for those to whom God has given it, no, not always. No mortal is too great to be included in a prayer. But I'm keeping you, dear child, and I'm making your fiancé jealous and perhaps your father too by telling you something about the heavenly bodies—which may, to be sure, be quite obsolete. Hurry back to the ball, but don't forget to give Father Christopher my regards.

(*Virginia, after a deep curtsy, leaves quickly*)

8

A Conversation

> Galileo, feeling grim
> A young monk came to visit him.
> The monk was born of common folk.
> It was of science that they spoke.

In the palace of the Florentine ambassador to Rome, Galileo listens to the little monk, who after the session of the Collegium Romanum repeated Father Clavius' remark to him in a whisper.

GALILEO Speak up, speak up! The cloth you wear entitles you to say what you please.

THE LITTLE MONK I've studied mathematics, Mr. Galilei.

GALILEO That might be a good thing if it led you to admit that two times two is sometimes four.

THE LITTLE MONK For three nights I haven't been able to sleep, Mr. Galilei. I can't figure out how to reconcile the decree which I've read with the satellites of Jupiter which I've seen. So I decided to read mass this morning and come and see you.

GALILEO To tell me that Jupiter has no satellites?

THE LITTLE MONK No. I recognized the wisdom of the decree. It showed me how dangerous unrestricted inquiry can be to mankind, and I've decided to give up astronomy. Still, I felt I had to acquaint you with the motives which compel me, even though I'm an astronomer, to desist from pursuing a certain doctrine.

GALILEO I can assure you that such motives are well known to me.

THE LITTLE MONK I understand your bitterness. You're thinking of certain exceptional means of pressure exerted by the church.

GALILEO Don't beat about the bush: instruments of torture.

THE LITTLE MONK   Yes, but I'd like to speak of other motives. Forgive me if I talk about myself. I grew up in the Campagna. My parents are peasants, simple folk. They know all about olive trees, but very little else. As I observe the phases of Venus, I can see my parents sitting by the stove with my sister, eating lasagna. I see the beams over their heads, blackened by the smoke of centuries, I see distinctly their work-worn old hands and the little spoons they hold in them. They're very poor, but even in their misery there is a certain order. There are cyclic rhythms, scrubbing the floor, tending the olive trees in their seasons, paying taxes. There's a regularity in the calamities that descend on them. My father's back wasn't bowed all at once, no, a little more with every spring in the olive grove, just as the child-bearing that has made my mother more and more sexless occurred at regular intervals. What gives them the strength to sweat their way up stony paths with heavy baskets, to bear children, even to eat, is the feeling of stability and necessity they get from the sight of the soil, of the trees turning green every year, of their little church standing there, and from hearing Bible verses read every Sunday. They have been assured that the eye of God is upon them, searching and almost anxious, that the whole world-wide stage is built around them in order that they, the players, may prove themselves in their great or small roles. What would my people say if I were to tell them they were living on a small chunk of stone that moves around another star, turning incessantly in empty space, one among many and more or less significant? What would be the good or necessity of their patience, of their acquiescence in their misery? What would be the good of the Holy Scripture which explains everything and demonstrates the necessity of all their sweat, patience, hunger and submission, if it turns out to be full of errors? No, I can see their eyes waver, I can see them rest their spoons on the table, I can see how cheated and betrayed they feel. In that case, they will say, no one is watching over us. Must we, untaught, old and exhausted as we are, look out for ourselves? No one has given us a part to play, only this wretched role on a tiny star which is wholly dependent, around which nothing turns? There is no sense in our

misery, hunger means no more than going without food, it is
no longer a test of strength; effort means no more than bending and carrying, there is no virtue in it. Can you understand
now that in the decree of the Holy Congregation I discern a
noble motherly compassion, a great goodness of soul?

GALILEO Goodness of soul! Don't you simply mean that there's
nothing left, the wine's been drunk, their lips are parched, so
let them kiss the cassock. But why is nothing left? Why is
there no order in this country but the order in an empty
drawer, and no necessity but the necessity of working oneself
to death? Amid overflowing vineyards and wheat fields? Your
peasants in the Campagna are paying for the wars which the
vicar of gentle Jesus is waging in Spain and Germany. Why
does he put the earth at the center of the universe? Because
he wants the See of St. Peter to be in the center of the world!
That's the crux of the matter. You're right; the question is not
the planets, but the peasants of the Campagna. And don't talk
to me about the beauty of phenomena in the golden glow of
old age. Do you know how the Margaritifera oyster produces
pearls? By contracting a near-fatal disease, by enveloping an
unassimilable foreign body, a grain of sand, for instance, in
a ball of mucus. It almost dies in the process. To hell with the
pearl, give me the healthy oyster. Virtue is not bound up with
misery, my friend. If your people were prosperous and
happy, they could develop the virtues of prosperity and happiness. But today the virtues of exhausted people derive from
exhausted fields, and I reject those virtues. Yes, sir, my new
water pumps can work more miracles than your preposterous
superhuman toil.—"Be fruitful and multiply," because your
fields are barren and you are decimated by wars. You want
me to lie to your people?

THE LITTLE MONK (*in great agitation*) The very highest motives
bid us keep silent: the peace of mind of the wretched and
lowly!

GALILEO Would you care to see a Cellini clock that Cardinal
Bellarmine's coachman left here this morning? You see, my
friend, as a reward for my letting your good parents have
their peace of mind, the government offers me the wine
which they press in the sweat of their countenance, which as

P 50

you know was fashioned in the image of God. If I agreed to keep silent, my motives would undoubtedly be rather sordid: an easy life, no persecution, and so on.

THE LITTLE MONK   Mr. Galilei, I'm a priest.

GALILEO   You're also a physicist. And you can see that Venus has phases. Look out there. (*He points out the window*) Can you see the little Priapus by the laurel tree at the well? The god of gardens, birds, and thieves, rustic, obscene, two thousand years old. He wasn't so much of a liar. All right, we'll skip that, I too am a son of the church. But do you know the *Eighth Satire* of Horace? I've been rereading him lately, he gives me a certain balance. (*He reaches for a small book*) He puts words in the mouth of this same Priapus, a little statue that used to stand in the Esquiline Gardens. Here's how it starts:

"I was a figtree stump, wood of little use
When once a carpenter, pondering whether
To fashion a Priapus or a footstool
Decided on the god . . ."

Do you think Horace would have let anyone forbid him the footstool and put a table in the poem instead? Sir, a cosmology in which Venus has no phases violates my esthetic sense! We can't invent machines for pumping river water if we're forbidden to study the greatest machine before our eyes, the mechanism of the heavenly bodies. The sum total of the angles in a triangle can't be changed to suit the requirements of the curia. Nor can I calculate the courses of flying bodies in such a way as to account for witches riding on broomsticks.

THE LITTLE MONK   Don't you think the truth will prevail, even without us, if it is the truth?

GALILEO   No, no, no. Truth prevails only when we make it prevail. The triumph of reason can only be the triumph of reasoning men. You describe your peasants in the Campagna as if they were moss on their huts. How can anyone imagine that the sum of the angles of a triangle runs counter to *their* needs! But if they don't rouse themselves and learn how to think, the best irrigation systems in the world won't do them any good. Damn it, I see the divine patience of your people, but where is their divine wrath?

THE LITTLE MONK   They're tired.

GALILEO (*throws a bundle of manuscripts in front of him*)   Are you a physicist, my son? Here you'll find the reasons for the ocean's tides. But don't read it, do you hear. Ah, reading already? I see you're a physicist.

(*The little monk has immersed himself in the papers*)

GALILEO   An apple from the tree of knowledge. He gobbles it up. He'll be damned for all eternity, but he's got to bolt it down, the hapless glutton. Sometimes I think I'd gladly be locked up in a dungeon ten fathoms below ground, if in return I could find out one thing: What is light? And the worst of it is: What I know I must tell others. Like a lover, a drunkard, a traitor. It's a vice, I know, and leads to ruin. But how long can I go on shouting into empty air—that is the question.

THE LITTLE MONK (*points at a passage in the papers*)   I don't understand this sentence.

GALILEO   I'll explain it to you, I'll explain it to you.

9

After a silence of eight years Galileo feels encouraged by the enthronement of a new pope, himself a scientist, to resume his research in the forbidden field. The sunspots.

> Eight long years with tongue in cheek
> Of what he knew he did not speak.
> The temptations grew too great
> And Galileo challenged fate.

Galileo's house in Florence. Galileo's pupils, Federzoni, the little monk and Andrea Sarti, now a young man, are gathered for an experiment. Galileo, standing, is reading a book.—Virginia and Mrs. Sarti are sewing bridal linen.

VIRGINIA   Sewing a trousseau is fun. This is for the long dining table, Ludovico loves to have company. But it has got to be right, his mother notices every stitch. She isn't happy about father's books. Any more than Father Christopher.

MRS. SARTI   He hasn't written a book in years.

VIRGINIA   I think he saw he was mistaken. In Rome, a very high ecclesiastic told me a lot of things about astronomy. The distances are too great.

ANDREA (*writes the program for the day on a blackboard and reads aloud*)   "Thursday afternoon: Floating bodies."—That means ice again; bucket of water; scales; iron needle; Aristotle. (*He fetches the objects*)
(*The others are looking up things in books. Enter Filippo Mucius, a scholar in his middle years. He appears to be upset*)

MUCIUS   Would you tell Mr. Galilei he must see me? He has condemned me without a hearing.

MRS. SARTI   I've told you he doesn't wish to see you.

MUCIUS   God will reward you if you ask him again. I must speak to him.

VIRGINIA (*goes to the staircase*)   Father!

GALILEO   What is it?

VIRGINIA   Mr. Mucius!

GALILEO (*looks up brusquely, goes to the head of the stairs, his pupils trailing behind him*)   What do you want?

MUCIUS   Mr. Galilei, I request permission to explain the passages in my book which seem to indicate a condemnation of the Copernican doctrine that the earth revolves. I've . . .

GALILEO   What is there to explain? You are in full agreement with the Holy Congregation's decree of 1616. You are perfectly within your rights. It's true, you studied mathematics with us, but we have no authority to make you say that two times two is four. You have every right to say that this stone (*He takes the pebble from his pocket and throws it down to the ground floor*) has just flown up to the ceiling.

MUCIUS   Mr. Galilei, I . . .

GALILEO   Don't talk about difficulties! The plague didn't prevent me from going on with my observations.

MUCIUS   Mr. Galilei, the plague is not the worst.

GALILEO   Let me tell you this: Not to know the truth is just

stupid. To know the truth and call it a lie is criminal! Leave my house at once!

MUCIUS (*tonelessly*)   You are right. (*He goes out*)

(*Galileo returns to his study*)

FEDERZONI   That's how it is, I'm afraid. He doesn't amount to much and no one could pay any attention to him if he hadn't been your pupil. But now of course they all say: He's heard everything Galileo had to say and is forced to admit that it's all wrong.

MRS. SARTI   I feel sorry for the gentleman.

VIRGINIA   Father was very fond of him.

MRS. SARTI   I wanted to talk to you about your marriage, Virginia. You're such a young thing, and you have no mother, and your father just puts little pieces of ice in water. Anyway, I wouldn't ask him questions about your marriage if I were you. He would say the most dreadful things for a week, naturally at meals when the young people are there, because he hasn't half a scudo's worth of shame in him, never did have. That's not what I had in mind, I'm thinking of what the future has in store. Not that I know anything, I'm only an ignorant woman. But this is a very serious thing, you mustn't go into it blindly. I do think you should go to a real astronomer at the university and consult him about your horoscope. Then you'll know what to expect. Why are you laughing?

VIRGINIA   Because I've been.

MRS. SARTI (*very curious*)   What did he say?

VIRGINIA   For three months I must be careful because the sun will be in Aries, but then I get a very good ascendant and the clouds will part. As long as I don't lose sight of Jupiter, I can go on any journey I please, because I'm an Aries.

MRS. SARTI   And Ludovico?

VIRGINIA   He's a Leo. (*After a little pause*) That means sensual, I think.

(*Pause*)

VIRGINIA   I know that step. It's Mr. Gaffone, the rector.

(*Enter Mr. Gaffone, the rector of the university*)

GAFFONE   Just thought I'd bring you a book that might be of interest to your father. For heaven's sake don't disturb Mr. Galilei. I can't help feeling that every minute taken from that

great man is a minute taken from Italy. I'll just put the book in your little hands, and disappear, on tiptoe.

(*He goes out. Virginia hands the book to Federzoni*)

GALILEO What's it about?

FEDERZONI I don't know. (*Spelling it out*) "De maculis in sole."

ANDREA On the sunspots. Another one!

(*Federzoni angrily hands it to him*)

ANDREA Listen to this dedication! "To the greatest living authority on physics, Galileo Galilei."

(*Galileo has immersed himself once more in his book*)

ANDREA I've read the treatise by Fabricius in Holland. He believes the spots are clusters of stars passing between the earth and the sun.

THE LITTLE MONK Isn't that doubtful, Mr. Galilei?

(*Galileo does not answer*)

ANDREA In Paris and Prague they think they're vapors from the sun.

FEDERZONI Hm.

ANDREA Federzoni has his doubts.

FEDERZONI Kindly leave me out of it. I said "Hm," that's all. I'm the lens grinder, I grind lenses, you people look through them and observe the sky, and what you see is not spots, but "maculis." How can I doubt anything? How many times do I have to tell you I can't read these books, they're in Latin.

(*In his anger he gesticulates with the scales. A pan falls to the floor. Galileo walks over and silently picks it up*)

THE LITTLE MONK It's blissful to doubt; I wonder why.

ANDREA Every sunny day in the last two weeks I've climbed up to the attic, right under the roof. A thin beam of light comes down through a tiny crack in the tiles. With that beam you can catch the reverse image of the sun on a sheet of paper. I saw a spot as big as a fly and blurred like a small cloud. It moved. Why don't we investigate those spots, Mr. Galilei?

GALILEO Because we're working on floating bodies.

ANDREA Mother has whole baskets full of letters. All Europe wants your opinion. With the reputation you've built up, you can't be silent.

GALILEO Rome has allowed me to build up a reputation because I've kept silent.

FEDERZONI   But you can't afford to be silent any more.

GALILEO   Nor can I afford to be roasted over a wood fire like a ham.

ANDREA   Do you think the spots come into it?
(*Galileo does not answer*)

ANDREA   All right, let's stick to our little pieces of ice. They can't hurt you.

GALILEO   Exactly.—Our proposition, Andrea!

ANDREA   We assume that whether a body floats or not depends essentially not on its shape, but on whether it is lighter or heavier than water.

GALILEO   What does Aristotle say?

THE LITTLE MONK   "Discus latus platique . . ."

GALILEO   Translate, translate!

THE LITTLE MONK   "A broad, flat disk of ice floats in water, whereas an iron needle sinks."

GALILEO   Why then, according to Aristotle, doesn't ice sink?

THE LITTLE MONK   Because, being broad and flat, it cannot divide the water.

GALILEO   Very well. (*A piece of ice is handed to him and he puts it into the bucket*) Now I press the ice firmly down to the bottom of the bucket. I remove the pressure of my hands. What happens?

THE LITTLE MONK   It rises to the surface.

GALILEO   Correct. In rising it seems to be able to divide the water. Fulganzio!

THE LITTLE MONK   But why then does it float at all? Ice is heavier than water, because it is condensed water.

GALILEO   What if it were diluted water?

ANDREA   It must be lighter than water, or it wouldn't float.

GALILEO   Aha!

ANDREA   Just as an iron needle can't float. Everything lighter than water floats, everything heavier sinks. Which was to be proved.

GALILEO   Andrea, you must learn to think carefully. Give me the iron needle. A sheet of paper. Is iron heavier than water?

ANDREA   Yes.

(*Galileo places the needle on a sheet of paper and floats it in the water. Pause*)

GALILEO   What happens?

FEDERZONI   The needle floats! Holy Aristotle, they never checked up on him!

(*They laugh*)

GALILEO   One of the main reasons for the poverty of science is that it is supposed to be so rich. The aim of science is not to open the door to everlasting wisdom, but to set a limit to everlasting error. Take that down.

VIRGINIA   What's the matter?

MRS. SARTI   Every time they laugh, a fright comes over me. I wonder what they're laughing about.

VIRGINIA   Father says theologians have their church bells and physicists have their laughter.

MRS. SARTI   At least I'm glad he doesn't look through his tube so much any more. That was much worse.

VIRGINIA   No, he only puts pieces of ice in water. No harm can come of that.

MRS. SARTI   Who knows?

(*Enter Ludovico Marsili in traveling garb, followed by a manservant with luggage. Virginia runs toward him and embraces him*)

VIRGINIA   Why didn't you let us know you were coming?

LUDOVICO   I was near here inspecting our vineyards, and I just couldn't stay away.

GALILEO (*as though nearsighted*)   Who's that?

VIRGINIA   Ludovico.

THE LITTLE MONK   Can't you see him?

GALILEO   Oh yes, Ludovico. (*Goes toward him*) How are the horses?

LUDOVICO   They're fine, sir.

GALILEO   Sarti, let's celebrate. Bring us a jug of that old Sicilian wine!

(*Mrs. Sarti goes out with Andrea*)

LUDOVICO (*to Virginia*)   You look pale. Country life will do you good. Mother is expecting you in September.

VIRGINIA   Wait, I want to show you my wedding dress. (*Runs out*)

GALILEO   Sit down.

LUDOVICO   I hear you have more than a thousand students in

your lectures at the university, sir. What are you working on at the moment?

GALILEO   Routine stuff. Did you come through Rome?

LUDOVICO   Yes.—Before I forget, mother congratulates you on your admirable tact in connection with all that fuss over the sunspots in Holland.

GALILEO (*dryly*)   That's kind of her.

(*Mrs. Sarti and Andrea bring wine and glasses. All gather around the table*)

LUDOVICO   Rome has found a topic of conversation for February. Christopher Clavius said he was afraid the whole earth-around-the-sun circus would flare up again because of those sunspots.

ANDREA   Don't let it worry you.

GALILEO   Any other news from the Holy City, apart from hopes for new sins on my part?

LUDOVICO   You heard, of course, that the Holy Father is dying?

THE LITTLE MONK   Oh.

GALILEO   Who's mentioned as successor?

LUDOVICO   Mostly Barberini.

GALILEO   Barberini.

ANDREA   Mr. Galilei knows Barberini personally.

THE LITTLE MONK   Cardinal Barberini is a mathematician.

FEDERZONI   A scientist in the chair of St. Peter!

(*Pause*)

GALILEO   I see, now they need men like Barberini who've read a little mathematics. Things will start moving, Federzoni, we may live to see the day when we won't have to glance over our shoulders like criminals every time we say that two times two is four. (*To Ludovico*) I like this wine, Ludovico. What do you think of it?

LUDOVICO   It's good.

GALILEO   I know the vineyard. The slope is steep and stony, the grapes are almost blue. I love this wine.

LUDOVICO   Yes, sir.

GALILEO   There are little shadows in it. And it's almost sweet, but stops at the "almost."—Andrea, put the stuff away, the ice and bucket and needle.—I value the consolations of the flesh.

I have no patience with cowardly souls who speak of weakness. I say: To enjoy yourself is an achievement.

THE LITTLE MONK   What are you taking up next?

FEDERZONI   We're starting in again on the earth-around-the-sun circus.

ANDREA (*singing in an undertone*)
The Book says it stands still. And so
Each learned doctor proves.
The Holy Father takes it by the ears
And holds it fast. And yet it moves.
(*Andrea, Federzoni and the little monk hurry to the workbench and clear it*)

ANDREA   We might even find out that the sun revolves too. How would you like that, Marsili?

LUDOVICO   What's the excitement about?

MRS. SARTI   You're not going back to those abominations, Mr. Galilei?

GALILEO   Now I know why your mother sent you here. Barberini is on the rise. Knowledge will be a passion and research a delight. Clavius is right, these sunspots do interest me. You like my wine, Ludovico?

LUDOVICO   I said I did, sir.

GALILEO   You really like it?

LUDOVICO (*stiffly*)   I like it.

GALILEO   Would you go so far as to accept a man's wine or his daughter without asking him to give up his profession? What has my astronomy got to do with my daughter? The phases of Venus don't affect my daughter's rear end.

MRS. SARTI   Don't be vulgar. I'll go get Virginia.

LUDOVICO (*holds her back*)   In families like mine marriages are not decided by sexual considerations alone.

GALILEO   Did they prevent you from marrying my daughter for the last eight years because I was on probation?

LUDOVICO   My wife will also have to cut a figure in our village church.

GALILEO   You mean, your peasants won't pay their rent if the lady of the manor is insufficiently saintly?

LUDOVICO   In a way.

GALILEO   Andrea, Fulganzio, get the brass mirror and the

screen! We'll project the sun's image on it to protect our eyes. That's your method, Andrea.

(*Andrea and the little monk get mirror and screen*)

LUDOVICO   Years ago in Rome, sir, you signed a pledge to stay away from this earth-around-the-sun business.

GALILEO   Oh well. We had a reactionary pope in those days.

MRS. SARTI   Had! His Holiness isn't even dead yet!

GALILEO   Pretty near, pretty near!—Put a grid over the screen. We'll proceed methodically. And we'll be able to answer all those letters, won't we, Andrea?

MRS. SARTI   "Pretty near!" Fifty times that man weighs his pieces of ice, but when something happens that suits his purposes he believes it blindly!

(*The screen is put up*)

LUDOVICO   Mr. Galilei, if His Holiness should die, the next pope—no matter who he is or how much he loves science—will have to take account of how much the country's leading families love him.

THE LITTLE MONK   God made the physical world, Ludovico; God made the human brain; God will allow physics.

MRS. SARTI   Galileo, let me tell you something. I've watched my son fall into sin for the sake of these "experiments" and "theories" and "observations," and I haven't been able to do anything about it. You set yourself against the authorities and they gave you a warning. The greatest cardinals spoke to you the way you'd speak to a sick horse. It worked for a while, but two months ago, right after the Immaculate Conception, I caught you sneaking back to your "observations." In the attic! I didn't say anything, but I knew. I ran out and lit a candle for St. Joseph. It's more than I can bear. When we're alone you show some sense, you say you've got to behave because it's dangerous, but two days of "experiments" and you're as bad as ever. If I lose my eternal salvation because I stand by a heretic, that's my business, but you have no right to trample your daughter's happiness with your big feet!

GALILEO (*gruffly*)   Get the telescope!

LUDOVICO   Giuseppe, put the luggage back in the coach.

(*The manservant goes out*)

MRS. SARTI   She'll never get over this. You can tell her yourself.

(*She runs out, still holding the pitcher*)   ◆

LUDOVICO   I see you've made up your mind. Mr. Galilei, three quarters of the year mother and I live on our estate in the Campagna and I can assure you that our peasants lose no sleep over your treatises on the moons of Jupiter. They work too hard in the fields. It might upset them, though, if they heard that attacks on the holy doctrine of the church were going unpunished. Don't forget that those poor brutalized wretches get everything mixed up. They really are brutes, you have no idea. A rumor that somebody's seen a pear growing on an apple tree makes them run away from their work to gab about it.

GALILEO (*with interest*)   Really?

LUDOVICO   Animals. When they come to the manor with a trifling complaint, mother has to have a dog whipped in front of them to remind them of discipline and order and good manners. You, Mr. Galilei, you may occasionally see flowering corn fields from your traveling coach, or absent-mindedly eat our olives and our cheese, but you have no idea how much effort it takes to raise all these things—all the supervision!

GALILEO   Young man, I never eat my olives absent-mindedly. (*Rudely*) You're wasting my time. (*Calls toward outside*) Is the screen ready?

ANDREA   Yes. Are you coming?

GALILEO   You whip more than dogs to keep discipline, don't you, Marsili?

LUDOVICO   Mr. Galilei, you have a marvelous brain. Too bad.

THE LITTLE MONK (*amazed*)   He's threatening you.

GALILEO   Yes, I might stir up his peasants to think new thoughts. And his servants and his overseers.

FEDERZONI   How? They don't know Latin.

GALILEO   I could write in the vernacular for the many instead of in Latin for the few. For our new ideas we need people who work with their hands. Who else wants to know the causes of everything? People who never see bread except on their tables have no desire to know how it's baked; those bastards would rather thank God than the baker. But the men who make the bread will understand that nothing can move unless something moves it. Fulganzio, your sister at the olive press won't be much surprised—she'll probably laugh—when she

hears that the sun is not a gold escutcheon, but a lever: The earth moves because the sun moves it.

LUDOVICO   You'll always be a slave to your passions. Convey my apologies to Virginia. It's better, I think, if I don't see her now.

GALILEO   The dowry is at your disposal. At any time.

LUDOVICO   Good day. (*He goes*)

ANDREA   Our regards to all the Marsilis!

FEDERZONI   Who tell the earth to stand still so their castles won't fall off.

ANDREA   And to the Cencis and Villanis!

FEDERZONI   The Cervillis!

ANDREA   The Lecchis!

FEDERZONI   The Pierleonis!

ANDREA   Who'll only kiss the pope's foot as long as he tramples the people with it.

THE LITTLE MONK (*also at the instruments*)   The new pope will be an enlightened man.

GALILEO   And now let's start observing these spots in the sun which interest us—at our own risk, not counting too much on the protection of a new pope . . .

ANDREA (*interrupting*)   But fully confident of dispelling Mr. Fabricius' star shadows and the solar vapors of Prague and Paris, and proving that the sun rotates.

GALILEO   Reasonably confident that the sun rotates. My aim is not to prove that I've been right, but to find out whether or not I have been. I say: Abandon hope, all ye who enter upon observation. Maybe it's vapors, maybe it's spots, but before we assume that they're spots, though it would suit us if they were, we'd do better to assume they're fishtails. Yes, we shall start all over again from scratch. And we won't rush ahead with seven-league boots, but crawl at a snail's pace. And what we find today we'll wipe from the blackboard tomorrow, and not write it down again until we find it a second time. And if there's something we hope to find, we'll regard it with particular distrust when we do find it. Accordingly let us approach our observation of the sun with the inexorable resolve to prove that the earth *stands still!* Only after we have failed, after we have been totally and hopelessly defeated and are licking our wounds in utter dejection, only then shall we

begin to ask whether the earth does not indeed move! (*With a twinkle*) But then, when every other hypothesis has gone up in smoke, then no mercy for those who have never observed anything, yet go on talking. Take the cloth off the tube and focus it on the sun! (*He adjusts the brass mirror*)

THE LITTLE MONK   I knew you had taken up your work again. I knew it when you didn't recognize Mr. Marsili.
(*In silence they begin their examinations. When the flaming image of the sun appears on the screen Virginia in her bridal gown runs in*)

VIRGINIA   You've sent him away! (*She faints. Andrea and the little monk rush to her aid*)

GALILEO   I've got to know.

10

In the course of the next ten years Galileo's doctrine is disseminated among the common people. Pamphleteers and ballad singers everywhere seize upon the new ideas. In the carnival of 1632 the guilds in many Italian cities take astronomy as the theme for their carnival processions.

A half-starved couple of show people with a five-year-old girl and an infant enter a market place where many people, some with masks, are awaiting the carnival procession. They carry bundles, a drum and other props.

THE BALLAD SINGER (*drumming*)   Citizens, ladies and gentlemen! Before the great carnival procession of the guilds arrives we bring you the latest Florentine song which is being sung all over northern Italy. We've imported it at great expense. The title is: The horrendous doctrine and teaching of Mr. Galileo Galilei, court physicist, or, A Foretaste of the Future. (*He sings*)

When the Almighty made the universe
He made the earth and then he made the sun.
Then round the earth he bade the sun to turn—
That's in the Bible, Genesis, Chapter One.
And from that time all beings here below
Were in obedient circles meant to go.

They all began to turn around
The little fellows round the big shots
And the hindmost round the foremost
On earth as it is in heaven.
Around the popes the cardinals
Around the cardinals the bishops
Around the bishops the secretaries
Around the secretaries the aldermen
Around the aldermen the craftsmen
Around the craftsmen the servants
Around the servants the dogs, the chickens and the
   beggars.

That, my friends, is the great order, ordo ordinum, as the
theologians call it, regula aeternis, the rule of rules. And then,
my friends, what happened then? (*He sings*)

   Up stood the learned Galileo
   (Chucked the Bible, pulled out his telescope, and took a
      look at the universe)
   And told the sun: Stand still!
   From this time on, the wheels
   Shall turn the other way.
   Henceforth the mistress, ho!
   Shall turn around the maid.
Now that was rash, my friends, it is no matter small:
For heresy will spread today like foul diseases.
Change Holy Writ, forsooth? What will be left at all?
Why: each of us would say and do just what he pleases!

Esteemed citizens, such doctrines are utterly impossible. (*He
sings*)

Good people, what will come to pass
If Galileo's teachings spread?
The server will not serve at mass
No servant girl will make the bed.
Now that is grave, my friends, it is no matter small:
For independent spirit spreads like foul diseases!
Yet life is sweet and man is weak and after all—
How nice it is, for once, to do just as one pleases!

Now, my good friends, here, look to the future and see what
the most learned doctor Galileo Galilei predicts. (*He sings*)

Two ladies at a fishwife's stall
Are in for quite a shock
The fishwife takes a loaf of bread
And gobbles up all her stock.
The carpenters take wood and build
Houses for themselves, not pews
And members of the cobblers' guild
Now walk around in shoes!
Is this permitted? No, it is no matter small:
For independent spirit spreads like foul diseases!
Yet life is sweet and man is weak and after all—
How nice it is, for once, to do just as one pleases!

The tenant kicks his noble master
Smack in the ass like that
The tenant's wife now gives her children
Milk that made the parson fat.
No, no my friends, for the Bible is no matter small:
For independent spirit spreads like foul diseases!
Yet life is sweet and man is weak and after all—
How nice it is for once to do just as one pleases!

THE SINGER'S WIFE

The other day I tried it too
And did my husband frankly tell
Let's see now if what you can do
Other stars can do as well.

BALLAD SINGER

No, no, no, no, no, no, stop, Galileo, stop!
For independent spirit spreads like foul diseases.
People must keep their place, some down and some on top!
Though it is nice for once to do just as one pleases.

BOTH

Good people who have trouble here below
In serving cruel lords and gentle Jesus
Who bids you turn the other cheek just so
While they prepare to strike the second blow:
Obedience will never cure your woe
So each of you wake up and do just as he pleases!

THE BALLAD SINGER   Esteemed citizens, behold Galileo Galilei's phenomenal discovery: The earth revolving around the sun! (*He belabors the drum violently. His wife and child step forward. The wife holds a crude replica of the sun, and the child, holding a gourd, image of the earth, over her head, circles around the woman. The singer excitedly points at the little girl as if she were performing a dangerous acrobatic feat in jerkily taking step after step in rhythm with the drumbeats. Then drumming from the rear*)

A DEEP VOICE (*calls out*)   The procession!
(*Enter two men in rags drawing a little cart. The "Grand Duke of Florence," a figure in sackcloth with a cardboard crown, sits on a ridiculous throne and peers through a telescope. Over the throne a painted sign "Looking for trouble." Next, four masked men march in carrying a huge tarpaulin. They stop and bounce a large doll representing a cardinal. A dwarf has posted himself to one side with a sign "The New Age." Among the crowd a beggar raises himself by his crutches and stomps the ground in a dance until he collapses. Enter a stuffed figure, more than life-size, Galileo Galilei, which bows to the audience. In front of it a child displays a giant open Bible with crossed-out pages.*)

THE BALLAD SINGER   Galileo Galilei, the Bible-smasher!
(*An outburst of laughter among the crowd*)

11

1633. The inquisition summons the world-famous scholar to Rome.

> The depths are hot, the heights are chill
> The streets are loud, the court is still.

Antechamber and staircase of the Medici Palace, Florence. Galileo and his daughter are waiting to be admitted to the grand duke.

VIRGINIA   It's been a long wait.

GALILEO   Yes.

VIRGINIA   There's that man again who's been following us. (*She points at a shady individual who passes by without paying attention to them*)

GALILEO (*whose eyesight is impaired*)   I don't know him.

VIRGINIA   I've seen him several times lately. He gives me the shivers.

GALILEO   Nonsense. We're in Florence, not among Corsican robbers.

VIRGINIA   There's Rector Gaffone.

GALILEO   *He* frightens *me*. The blockhead will draw me into another interminable conversation.
(*Mr. Gaffone, the rector of the university, descends the stairs. He is visibly startled when he sees Galileo and walks stiffly past the two, with rigidly averted head and barely nodding.*)

GALILEO   What's got into him? My eyes are bad again. Did he greet us at all?

VIRGINIA   Just barely.—What have you said in your book? Can they think it's heretical?

GALILEO   You hang around church too much. Getting up before dawn and running to mass is ruining your complexion. You pray for me, don't you?

VIRGINIA   There's Mr. Vanni, the iron founder. The one you

designed the smelting furnace for. Don't forget to thank him
for the quails.

(*A man has come down the stairs*)

VANNI How did you like the quails I sent you, Mr. Galileo?

GALILEO Maestro Vanni, the quails were excellent. Again
many thanks.

VANNI They're talking about you upstairs. They claim you're
responsible for those pamphlets against the Bible that are
being sold all over.

GALILEO I know nothing about pamphlets. My favorite books
are the Bible and Homer.

VANNI Even if that were not the case: Let me take this opportunity of assuring you that we manufacturers are on your
side. I don't know much about the movement of stars, but the
way I look at it, you're the man who is fighting for the freedom to teach new knowledge. Just take that mechanical cultivator from Germany that you described to me. Last year
alone five works on agriculture were published in London.
Here we'd be grateful for one book about the Dutch canals.
It's the same people who are making trouble for you and
preventing the physicians in Bologna from dissecting corpses
for research.

GALILEO Your vote counts, Vanni.

VANNI I hope so. Do you know that in Amsterdam and London
they have money markets? And trade schools too. And news-
papers that appear regularly. Here we're not even free to
make money. They're against iron foundries because they
claim too many workers in one place promote immorality. I
swim or sink with men like you, Mr. Galilei! If ever they try
to harm you, please remember that you have friends in every
branch of industry. The cities of northern Italy are behind
you, sir.

GALILEO As far as I know no one has any intention of harming
me.

VANNI Really?

GALILEO Really.

VANNI I believe you'd be better off in Venice. Not so many
cassocks. You'd be free to carry on the fight. I have a coach
and horses, Mr. Galilei.

GALILEO   I can't see myself as a refugee. I love comfort.

VANNI   I understand. But to judge by what I heard up there, there's no time to be lost. I got the impression that right now they'd prefer not to have you in Florence.

GALILEO   Nonsense. The grand duke is a pupil of mine, not to mention the fact that if anyone tries to trip me up the pope himself will tell him where to get off.

VANNI   You don't seem able to distinguish your friends from your enemies, Mr. Galilei.

GALILEO   I'm able to distinguish power from lack of power. (*He brusquely steps away*)

VANNI   Well, I wish you luck. (*Goes out*)

GALILEO (*back at Virginia's side*)   Every Tom, Dick and Harry with a grievance picks me as his spokesman, especially in places where it doesn't exactly help me. I've written a book on the mechanism of the universe, that's all. What people make or don't make of it is no concern of mine.

VIRGINIA (*in a loud voice*)   If people only knew how you condemned the goings-on at last year's carnival.

GALILEO   Yes. Give a bear honey if it's hungry and you'll lose your arm.

VIRGINIA (*in an undertone*)   Did the grand duke send for you today?

GALILEO   No, but I've sent in my name. He wants the book, he's paid for it. Ask somebody, complain about the long wait.

VIRGINIA (*goes to talk to an attendant, followed by the individual*)   Mr. Mincio, has His Highness been informed that my father wishes to speak to him?

THE ATTENDANT   How should I know?

VIRGINIA   That's no answer.

THE ATTENDANT   Really?

VIRGINIA   You ought to be polite.

(*The attendant half turns his back on her and yawns while looking at the shady individual*)

VIRGINIA (*has come back*)   He says the grand duke is still busy.

GALILEO   I heard you say something about "polite." What was it?

VIRGINIA   I thanked him for his polite answer, that's all. Can't you just leave the book for him? You're wasting your time.

GALILEO I'm beginning to wonder what my time is worth. Maybe I should accept Sagredo's invitation to go to Padua for a few weeks. My health hasn't been up to snuff.

VIRGINIA You couldn't live without your books.

GALILEO We could take some of the Sicilian wine, one, two cases.

VIRGINIA You always say it doesn't travel. And the court owes you three months' salary. They won't forward it.

GALILEO That's true.

VIRGINIA (*whispers*) The cardinal inquisitor!

(*The cardinal inquisitor descends the stairs. Passing them, he bows low to Galileo*)

VIRGINIA What's the cardinal inquisitor doing in Florence, father?

GALILEO I don't know. His attitude was respectful, I think. I knew what I was doing when I came to Florence and held my peace all these years. Their praises have raised me so high that they have to take me as I am.

THE ATTENDANT (*announces*) His Highness, the grand duke!

(*Cosmo de' Medici comes down the stairs. Galileo approaches him. Cosmo, slightly embarrassed, stops*)

GALILEO May I present Your Highness with my *Dialogues on the Two Chief Syst* . . .

COSMO I see, I see. How are your eyes?

GALILEO Not too good, Your Highness. With Your Highness' permission, I should like to present my . . .

COSMO The state of your eyes alarms me. Yes, it alarms me a good deal. Haven't you been using your splendid tube a little too much? (*He walks off without accepting the book*)

GALILEO He didn't take the book, did he?

VIRGINIA Father, I'm afraid.

GALILEO (*subdued, but firmly*) Don't show your feelings. We are not going home, but to Volpi, the glass cutter's. I've arranged with him to have a cart with empty wine casks ready in the tavern yard next door, to take me away at any time.

VIRGINIA Then you knew . . .

GALILEO Don't look back.

(*They start to leave*)

A HIGH OFFICIAL (*descending the stairs*) Mr. Galilei, I have orders

to inform you that the court of Florence is no longer in a position to oppose the request of the Holy Inquisition for your interrogation in Rome. Mr. Galilei, the coach of the Holy Inquisition is waiting for you.

multiplication
2×2 = or 4

12

The pope.

A room in the Vatican. Pope Urban VIII (formerly Cardinal Barberini) has received the cardinal inquisitor. During the audience the pope is being dressed. From outside the shuffling of many feet is heard.

THE POPE (*very loud*)   No! No! No!

THE INQUISITOR   Then Your Holiness really means to tell the doctors of all the faculties, the representatives of all the religious orders and of the entire clergy, who have come here guided by their childlike faith in the word of God as recorded in scripture to hear Your Holiness confirm them in their faith —you mean to inform them that scripture can no longer be considered true?

THE POPE   I won't permit the multiplication tables to be broken. No!

THE INQUISITOR   Yes, these people say it is only a matter of the multiplication tables, not of the spirit of rebellion and doubt. But it is not the multiplication tables. It is an alarming unrest that has come over the world. It is the unrest of their own minds, which they transfer to the immovable earth. They cry out: The figures force our hands! But where do these figures come from? Everyone knows they come from doubt. These people doubt everything. Is our human community to be built on doubt and no longer on faith? "You are my master, but I doubt whether that is a good arrangement." "This is your house and your wife, but I doubt whether they should

not be mine." On the other hand, as we can read on the house walls of Rome, disgraceful interpretations are being put on Your Holiness' great love for art, to which we owe such marvelous collections: "The Barberinis are stripping Rome of what the barbarians failed to take." And abroad? It has pleased God to visit heavy tribulation upon the Holy See. Your Holiness' policy in Spain is misunderstood by persons lacking in insight, your rift with the emperor is deplored. For fifteen years Germany has been a shambles, people have been slaughtering one another with Bible quotations on their lips. And at a time when under the onslaught of plague, war and reformation, Christianity is being reduced to a few disorganized bands, a rumor is spreading through Europe that you are in secret league with Lutheran Sweden to weaken the Catholic emperor. This is the moment these mathematicians, these worms, choose to turn their tubes to the sky and inform the world that even here, the one place where your authority is not yet contested, Your Holiness is on shaky ground. Why, one is tempted to ask, this sudden interest in so recondite a science as astronomy? Does it make any difference how these bodies move? Yet, thanks to the bad example of that Florentine, all Italy, down to the last stableboy, is prattling about the phases of Venus and thinking at the same time of many irksome things which are held in our schools and elsewhere to be immutable. Where will it end, if all these people, weak in the flesh and inclined to excess, come to rely exclusively on their own reason, which this madman declares to be the ultimate authority? They begin by doubting whether the sun stood still at Gibeon and end up directing their unclean doubts at the church collections. Since they began sailing the high seas—to which I have no objection—they have been putting their trust in a brass sphere that they call a compass, and no longer in God. Even as a young man this Galileo wrote about machines. With machines they expect to work miracles. What kind of miracles? Of course they have no more use for God, but what is to be the nature of these miracles? For one thing, they expect to do away with Above and Below. They don't need it any more. Aristotle, whom in other respects they regard as a dead dog, said—and this they

quote—: If the shuttle were to weave by itself and the plectron to pluck by itself, masters would no longer need apprentices nor lords servants. They believe that this time has come. This evil man knows what he is doing when he writes his astronomical works not in Latin but in the idiom of fishwives and wool merchants.

THE POPE   It's certainly in bad taste. I'll tell him.

THE INQUISITOR   Some he incites, others he bribes. The north Italian ship owners keep clamoring for Mr. Galilei's star charts. We shall have to yield to them, since material interests are involved.

THE POPE   But these star charts are based on his heretical statements, on the movements of certain heavenly bodies which become impossible if his doctrine is rejected. You can't reject the doctrine and accept the star charts.

THE INQUISITOR   Why not? It's the only solution.

THE POPE   This shuffling makes me nervous. Forgive me if I seem distracted.

THE INQUISITOR   Perhaps it speaks to you more clearly than I can, Your Holiness. Are all these people to go home with doubts in their hearts?

THE POPE   After all the man is the greatest physicist of our time, a beacon for Italy, and not some good-for-nothing crank. He has friends. There's Versailles. There's the court in Vienna. They will call the church a cesspool of rotten prejudices. Hands off!

THE INQUISITOR   Actually, we wouldn't have to go very far in his case. He is a man of the flesh. He would cave in very quickly.

THE POPE   He gets pleasure out of more things than any man I ever met. Even his thinking is sensual. He can never say no to an old wine or a new idea. I will not stand for any condemning of physical facts, any battle cry of "church" against "reason." I gave him leave to write his book provided it ended with a statement that the last word is not with science but with faith. He has complied.

THE INQUISITOR   But how did he comply? His book is an argument between a simpleton who—naturally—propounds the opinions of Aristotle, and an intelligent man, just as naturally voicing Mr. Galilei's opinions; and the concluding remark, Your Holiness, is made by whom?

THE POPE   What was that again? Who states our opinion?

THE INQUISITOR   Not the intelligent one.

THE POPE   That is impudence. This stamping in the halls is insufferable. Is the whole world coming here?

THE INQUISITOR   Not the whole world, but the best part of it. (*Pause. The pope is now fully robed*)

THE POPE   At the very most the instruments may be shown to him.

THE INQUISITOR   That will suffice, Your Holiness. Mr. Galilei is well versed in instruments.

13

On June 22, 1633, Galileo Galilei abjures his doctrine of the motion of the earth before the Inquisition.

> June twenty-second, sixteen thirty-three
> A momentous day for you and me.
> Of all the days that was the one
> An age of reason could have begun.

Palace of the Florentine ambassador in Rome. Galileo's pupils are waiting for news. The little monk and Federzoni are playing the new chess with its sweeping movements. Virginia kneels in a corner saying an Ave Maria.

THE LITTLE MONK   The pope refused to see him. No more scientific debates.

FEDERZONI   The pope was his last hope. I guess Cardinal Barberini was right when he said to him years ago: We need you. Now they've got him.

ANDREA   They'll kill him. The *Discorsi* will never be finished.

FEDERZONI (*with a furtive glance at him*)   You think so?

ANDREA   Because he'll never recant.

(*Pause*)

THE LITTLE MONK   When you lie awake at night you chew on the most useless ideas. Last night I couldn't get rid of the thought that he should never have left the republic of Venice.

ANDREA   He couldn't write his book there.

FEDERZONI   And in Florence he couldn't publish it.

(*Pause*)

THE LITTLE MONK   I also kept wondering whether they'd let him keep the stone he always carries in his pocket. His touchstone.

FEDERZONI   Where they're taking him people don't wear pockets.

ANDREA (*screaming*)   They won't dare! And even if they do, he'll never recant. "Not to know the truth is just stupid. To know the truth and call it a lie is criminal."

FEDERZONI   I don't think so either, and I wouldn't want to go on living if he did, but they have the power.

ANDREA   Power isn't everything.

FEDERZONI   Maybe not.

THE LITTLE MONK (*softly*)   He's been in prison for twenty-three days. Yesterday was the great interrogation. Today the judges are in session. (*As Andrea is listening, he raises his voice*) When I came to see him here two days after the decree, we were sitting over there; he showed me the little Priapus by the sundial in the garden—you can see it from here—and compared his own work with a poem by Horace, in which it is also impossible to change anything. He spoke of his esthetic sense, which compels him to look for the truth. And he told me his motto: Hieme et aestate, et prope et procul, usque dum vivam et ultra. He was referring to the truth.

ANDREA (*to the little monk*)   Did you tell him what he did in the Collegium Romanum while they were examining his tube? Tell him! (*The little monk shakes his head*) He acted the same as always. He put his hands on his hams, stuck out his belly and said: Gentlemen, I beg for reason! (*Laughingly he imitates Galileo*)

(*Pause*)

ANDREA (*referring to Virginia*)   She's praying for him to recant.

FEDERZONI   Let her pray. She's all mixed up since they talked to her. They brought her confessor down from Florence.

(*Enter the shady individual from the grand ducal palace in Florence*)

THE SHADY INDIVIDUAL   Mr. Galilei will be here soon. He may want a bed.

FEDERZONI   Has he been released?

THE SHADY INDIVIDUAL   Mr. Galilei is expected to recant at five o'clock before the plenary session of the Inquisition. The big bell of St. Mark's will be rung and the wording of the abjuration will be proclaimed publicly.

ANDREA   I don't believe it.

THE SHADY INDIVIDUAL   Because of the crowds in the streets, Mr Galilei will be conducted to the postern on this side of the palace. (*Out*)

ANDREA (*suddenly in a loud voice*)   The moon is an earth and has no light of its own. And Venus has no light of its own either and is like the earth and moves around the sun. And four moons revolve around the planet Jupiter which is as far away as the fixed stars and not fastened to any sphere. And the sun is the center of the universe and immovable in its place, and the earth is not the center and not immovable. And he was the man who proved it.

THE LITTLE MONK   No force can make what has been seen unseen.

(*Silence*)

FEDERZONI (*looks at the sundial in the garden*)   Five o'clock.

(*Virginia prays louder*)

ANDREA   I can't stand it! They're beheading the truth! (*He holds his hands to his ears, so does the little monk. The bell is not rung. After a pause filled with Virginia's murmured prayers Federzoni shakes his head in the negative. The others drop their hands*)

FEDERZONI (*hoarsely*)   Nothing. It's three minutes past five.

ANDREA   He's resisting.

THE LITTLE MONK   He hasn't recanted!

FEDERZONI   No. Oh, my friends!

(*They embrace. They are wildly happy*)

ANDREA   You see: They can't do it with force! Force isn't everything! Hence: Stupidity is defeated, it's not invulnerable! Hence: Man is not afraid of death!

FEDERZONI   Now the age of knowledge will begin in earnest. This is the hour of its birth. Just think! If he had recanted!

THE LITTLE MONK   I didn't say anything but I was very worried.

I was faint of heart.

ANDREA   I knew it.

FEDERZONI   It would have been as if morning had turned back to night.

ANDREA   As if the mountain said: I'm water.

THE LITTLE MONK (*kneels down in tears*)   Lord, I thank Thee.

ANDREA   But now everything has changed. Man is lifting his head, tormented man, and saying: I can live. All this is accomplished when one man gets up and says No!

(*At this moment the big bell of St. Mark's begins to boom. All stand transfixed*)

VIRGINIA (*getting up*)   The bell of St. Mark's. He hasn't been condemned!

(*From the street the announcer is heard reciting Galileo's recantation*)

ANNOUNCER'S VOICE   "I, Galileo Galilei, professor of mathematics and physics in Florence, hereby abjure what I have taught, to wit, that the sun is the center of the world and motionless in its place, and the earth is not the center and not motionless. Out of a sincere heart and unfeigned faith, I abjure, condemn and execrate all these errors and heresies as I do all other errors and all other opinions in opposition to the Holy Church."

(*Darkness*)

(*When it grows light again, the bell is still booming, then it stops. Virginia has left. Galileo's pupils are still there*)

FEDERZONI   He never paid you properly for your work. You couldn't buy a pair of pants or publish anything. You had to put up with all that because you were "working for science"!

ANDREA (*loudly*)   Unhappy the land that has no heroes!

(*Galileo has come in, completely, almost unrecognizably, changed by the trial. He has heard Andrea's exclamation. For a few moments he hesitates at the door, expecting a greeting. As none is forthcoming and his pupils shrink back from him, he goes slowly and because of his bad eyesight uncertainly to the front where he finds a footstool and sits down*)

ANDREA   I can't look at him. I wish he'd go away.

FEDERZONI   Calm yourself.

ANDREA (*screams at Galileo*)   Wine barrel! Snail eater! Have you

saved your precious skin? (*Sits down*) I feel sick.

GALILEO (*calmly*)   Get him a glass of water.

(*The little monk goes out to get Andrea a glass of water. The others pay no attention to Galileo who sits on his footstool, listening. From far off the announcer's voice is heard again*)

ANDREA   I can walk now if you'll help me.

(*They lead him to the door. When they reach it, Galileo begins to speak*)

GALILEO   No. Unhappy the land that needs a hero.

A reading in front of the curtain:

Is it not obvious that a horse falling from a height of three or four ells will break its legs, whereas a dog would not suffer any damage, nor would a cat from a height of eight or nine ells, or a cricket from a tower, or an ant even if it were to fall from the moon? And just as smaller animals are comparatively stronger than larger ones, so small plants too stand up better: an oak tree two hundred ells high cannot sustain its branches in the same proportion as a small oak tree, nor can nature let a horse grow as large as twenty horses or produce a giant ten times the size of man unless it changes all the proportions of the limbs and especially of the bones, which would have to be strengthened far beyond the size demanded by mere proportion.—The common assumption that large and small machines are equally durable is apparently erroneous.

Galileo, *Discorsi*

14

1633–1642. Galileo Galilei spends the rest of his life in a villa near Florence, as a prisoner of the Inquisition. The *Discorsi*.

> Sixteen hundred thirty-three to
> sixteen hundred forty-two
> Galileo Galilei remains a prisoner
> of the church until his death.

A large room with a table, a leather chair and a globe. Galileo, now old and almost blind, is experimenting carefully with a small wooden ball rolling on a curved wooden rail. In the anteroom a monk is sitting on guard. A knock at the door. The monk opens and a peasant comes in carrying two plucked geese. Virginia emerges from the kitchen. She is now about forty years old.

THE PEASANT   I'm supposed to deliver these.

VIRGINIA   Who from? I didn't order any geese.

THE PEASANT   I was told to say from someone that's passing through. (*Out*)

(*Virginia looks at the geese in astonishment. The monk takes them from her and examines them suspiciously. Satisfied, he gives them back and she carries them by the necks to Galileo in the large room*)

VIRGINIA   A present, dropped off by someone who's passing through.

GALILEO   What is it?

VIRGINIA   Can't you see?

GALILEO   No. (*He goes closer*) Geese. Was there any name?

VIRGINIA   No.

GALILEO (*taking one goose from her*)   Heavy. Maybe I'll have some.

VIRGINIA   You can't be hungry again. You just finished dinner. And what's wrong with your eyes today? You ought to be able to see them from where you are.

GALILEO   You're standing in the shadow.

VIRGINIA   I'm not in the shadow. (*She carries the geese out*)

GALILEO   Put in thyme and apples.

VIRGINIA (*to the monk*)   We must send for the eye doctor. Father couldn't see the geese.

THE MONK   I'll need permission from Monsignor Carpula.— Has he been writing again?

VIRGINIA   No. He's dictating his book to me, you know that. You have pages 131 and 132, they were the last.

THE MONK   He's an old fox.

VIRGINIA   He doesn't do anything against the rules. His repentance is real. I keep an eye on him. (*She gives him the geese*) Tell them in the kitchen to fry the liver with an apple and an onion. (*She comes back into the large room*) And now we're going to think of our eyes and stop playing with that ball and dictate a little more of our weekly letter to the archbishop.

GALILEO   I don't feel up to it. Read me some Horace.

VIRGINIA   Only last week Monsignor Carpula, to whom we owe so much—those vegetables the other day—told me the archbishop keeps asking him what you think of the questions and quotations he's been sending you. (*She has sat down ready for dictation*)

GALILEO   Where was I?

VIRGINIA   Section four: Concerning the reaction of the church to the unrest in the arsenal in Venice, I agree with Cardinal Spoletti's attitude concerning the rebellious rope makers . .

GALILEO   Yes. (*Dictates*) . . . agree with Cardinal Spoletti's attitude concerning the rebellious rope makers, to wit, that it is better to dispense soup to them in the name of Christian charity than to pay them more for their ship's cables and bell ropes. All the more so, since it seems wiser to strengthen their faith than their greed. The Apostle Paul says: Charity never faileth.—How does that sound?

VIRGINIA   It's wonderful, father.

GALILEO   You don't think it could be mistaken for irony?

VIRGINIA   No, the archbishop will be very pleased. He's a practical man.

GALILEO   I rely on your judgment. What's the next point?

VIRGINIA   A very beautiful saying: "When I am weak then I am strong."

GALILEO   No comment.

VIRGINIA   Why not?

GALILEO   What's next?

VIRGINIA   "And to know the love of Christ, which passeth knowledge." Paul to the Ephesians three nineteen.

GALILEO   I must especially thank Your Eminence for the magnificent quotation from the epistle to the Ephesians. Inspired by it, I found the following in our incomparable "Imitation": (*He quotes from memory*) "He to whom speaketh the eternal word is free from much questioning." May I seize this opportunity to say something on my own behalf? To this day I am being reproached for once having written a book on celestial bodies in the language of the market place. In so doing, I did not mean to suggest, or to express my approval of the writing of books on such important subjects as theology in the jargon of spaghetti vendors. The argument in favor of the service in Latin—that the universality of this language enables all nations to hear mass in exactly the same way—seems less than fortunate since the scoffers, who are never at a loss, may well argue that the use of this language prevents all nations from understanding the text. I for my part prefer to forego the cheap intelligibility of things holy. The Latin tongue, which protects the eternal verities of the church from the prying of the ignorant, inspires confidence when recited by priests, sons of the lower classes, in the pronunciation of their local dialects.—No, strike that out.

VIRGINIA   The whole thing?

GALILEO   Everything after the spaghetti vendors.

(*A knocking at the door. Virginia goes into the anteroom. The monk opens the door. Andrea Sarti appears. He is a man in his middle years*)

ANDREA   Good evening. I am leaving Italy. To do scientific work in Holland. I was asked to see him on my way through and bring the latest news of him.

VIRGINIA   I don't know if he'll want to see you. You never came to visit us.

ANDREA   Ask him.

(*Galileo has recognized the voice. He sits motionless. Virginia goes in to him*)

GALILEO   Is it Andrea?

VIRGINIA   Yes. Should I send him away?

GALILEO (*after a pause*)   Bring him in.

(*Virginia leads Andrea inside*)

VIRGINIA (*to the monk*)   He's harmless. He was his pupil. So now he's his enemy.

GALILEO   Leave us alone, Virginia.

VIRGINIA   I want to hear what he says. (*She sits down*)

ANDREA (*cool*)   How are you?

GALILEO   Come closer. What are you doing? Tell me about your work. I hear you're on hydraulics.

ANDREA   Fabricius in Amsterdam has asked me to inquire about your health.

(*Pause*)

GALILEO   I'm well. I receive every attention.

ANDREA   I shall be glad to report that you are well.

GALILEO   Fabricius will be glad to hear it. And you may add that I am living in reasonable comfort. The depth of my repentance has moved my superiors to allow me limited scientific pursuits under clerical control.

ANDREA   Oh yes. We too have heard that the church is pleased with you. Your total submission has borne fruit. The authorities, I am told, are most gratified to note that since your submission no work containing any new hypothesis has been published in Italy.

GALILEO (*listening in the direction of the anteroom*)   Unfortunately there are countries which elude the protection of the church. I fear the condemned doctrines are being perpetuated in those countries.

ANDREA   There too your recantation has resulted in a setback most gratifying to the church.

GALILEO   You don't say. (*Pause*) Nothing from Descartes? No news from Paris?

ANDREA   Oh yes. When he heard you had recanted he stuffed his treatise on the nature of light in his desk drawer.

(*Long pause*)

GALILEO   I keep worrying about some of my scientific friends whom I led down the path of error. Has my recantation helped them to mend their ways?

ANDREA   I am going to Holland to carry on my work. The ox is not allowed to do what Jupiter denies himself.

GALILEO   I understand.

ANDREA   Federzoni is back at his lens grinding, in some shop in Milan.

GALILEO (*laughs*)   He doesn't know Latin.
(*Pause*)

ANDREA   Fulganzio, our little monk, has given up science and returned to the fold.

GALILEO   Yes. (*Pause*) My superiors are looking forward to my complete spiritual recovery. I'm making better progress than expected.

ANDREA   I see.

VIRGINIA   The Lord be praised.

GALILEO (*gruffly*)   Attend to the geese, Virginia.
(*Virginia leaves angrily. In passing she is addressed by the monk*)

THE MONK   I don't like that man.

VIRGINIA   He's harmless. You heard what he said. (*On her way out*) We've got fresh goat cheese.
(*The monk follows her out*)

ANDREA   I'm going to travel through the night so as to cross the border by morning. May I go now?

GALILEO   I can't see why you've come, Sarti. To stir me up? I've been living prudently and thinking prudently since I came here. I have my relapses even so.

ANDREA   I have no desire to upset you, Mr. Galilei.

GALILEO   Barberini called it the itch. He wasn't entirely free from it himself. I've been writing again.

ANDREA   You have?

GALILEO   I've finished the *Discorsi*.

ANDREA   What? The *Discourses Concerning Two New Sciences: Mechanics and Local Motion?* Here?

GALILEO   Oh, they let me have paper and pen. My superiors aren't stupid. They know that ingrained vices can't be uprooted overnight. They protect me from unpleasant consequences by locking up page after page.

ANDREA   Oh God!

GALILEO   Did you say something?

ANDREA   They let you plow water! They give you pen and

paper to quiet you! How could you ever write under such conditions?

GALILEO   Oh, I'm a slave of habit.

ANDREA   The *Discorsi* in the hands of monks! When Amsterdam and London and Prague are clamoring for them!

GALILEO   I can just hear Fabricius wailing, demanding his pound of flesh, while he himself sits safely in Amsterdam.

ANDREA   Two new branches of science as good as lost!

GALILEO   No doubt he and some others will feel uplifted when they hear that I jeopardized the last pitiful remnants of my comfort to make a copy, behind my own back so to speak, for six months using up the last ounces of light on the clearer nights.

ANDREA   You have a copy?

GALILEO   So far my vanity has prevented me from destroying it.

ANDREA   Where is it?

GALILEO   "If thine eye offend thee, pluck it out." Whoever wrote that knew more about comfort than I do. I'm sure it's the height of folly to let it out of my hands. But since I've been unable to leave science alone, you may just as well have it. The copy is in the globe. Should you consider taking it to Holland, you would of course have to bear full responsibility. You'd say you bought it from someone with access to the Holy Office.

(*Andrea has gone to the globe. He takes out the copy*)

ANDREA   The *Discorsi*! (*He leafs through the manuscript. He reads*) "It is my purpose to establish an entirely new science in regard to a very old problem, namely, motion. By means of experiments I have discovered some of its properties, which are worth knowing."

GALILEO   I had to do something with my time.

ANDREA   This will be the foundation of a new physics.

GALILEO   Put it under your coat.

ANDREA   And we thought you had deserted us! My voice was the loudest against you!

GALILEO   You were absolutely right. I taught you science and I denied the truth.

ANDREA   That changes everything. Everything.

GALILEO   You think so?

ANDREA   You were hiding the truth. From the enemy. Even in ethics you were centuries ahead of us.

GALILEO   Explain that to me, Andrea.

ANDREA   With the man on the street we said: He'll die, but he'll never recant.—You came back and said: I've recanted but I shall live.—Your hands are stained, we said.—You said: Better stained than empty.

GALILEO   Better stained than empty. Sounds realistic. Sounds like me. A new science, a new ethics.

ANDREA   I should have known—better than anyone else. I was eleven when you sold another man's telescope to the senate in Venice. And I watched you make immortal use of that instrument. Your friends shook their heads when you humbled yourself to that child in Florence: But science found an audience. You've always laughed at heroes. "People who suffer bore me," you said. "Bad luck comes from faulty calculations," and "If there are obstacles the shortest line between two points may well be a crooked line."

GALILEO   I remember.

ANDREA   And in thirty-three when you decided to abjure a popular item of your doctrine, I should have known that you were merely withdrawing from a hopeless political brawl in order to further the true interests of science.

GALILEO   Which consist in . . .

ANDREA   . . . the study of the properties of motion, the mother of machines, which alone will make the earth so good to live on that we shall be able to do without heaven.

GALILEO   Hm.

ANDREA   You won the leisure to write a scientific work which you alone could write. Had you perished in the fiery halo of the stake, the others would have been the victors.

GALILEO   They are the victors. Besides, there is no scientific work that one man alone can write.

ANDREA   Then why did you recant?

GALILEO   I recanted because I was afraid of physical pain.

ANDREA   No!

GALILEO   They showed me the instruments.

ANDREA   Then it was not premeditated?

GALILEO It was not.

(*Pause*)

ANDREA (*loud*) In science only one thing counts: contribution to knowledge.

GALILEO And that I have supplied. Welcome to the gutter, brother in science and cousin in treason! You like fish? I have fish. What stinks is not my fish, it's me. I'm selling out, you are the buyer. Oh, irresistible sight of a book, that hallowed commodity. The mouth waters, the curses are drowned. The great Babylonian whore, the murderous beast, the scarlet woman, opens her thighs, and everything is different! Hallowed be our haggling, whitewashing, death-shunning community!

ANDREA To shun death is human. Human weaknesses are no concern of science.

GALILEO No?!—My dear Sarti, even in my present condition I believe I can give you a few hints about the science you are devoting yourself to.

(*A short pause*)

GALILEO (*in lecture style, hands folded over his paunch*) In my free time, and I've got plenty of that, I have reviewed my case and asked myself how the world of science, of which I no longer consider myself a member, will judge it. Even a wool merchant, in addition to buying cheap and selling dear, has to worry about the obstacles that may be put in the way of the wool trade itself. In this sense, the pursuit of science seems to call for special courage. Science trades in knowledge distilled from doubt. Providing everybody with knowledge of everything, science aims at making doubters of everybody. But princes, landlords and priests keep the majority of the people in a pearly haze of superstition and outworn words to cover up their own machinations. The misery of the many is as old as the hills and is proclaimed in church and lecture hall to be as indestructible as the hills. Our new art of doubting delighted the common people. They grabbed the telescope out of our hands and focused it on their tormentors—princes, landlords, priests. Those self-seeking violent men greedily exploited the fruits of science for their own ends but at the same time they felt the cold stare of science focused upon the

millennial, yet artificial miseries which mankind could obviously get rid of by getting rid of them. They showered us with threats and bribes, which weak souls cannot resist. But can we turn our backs on the people and still remain scientists? The movements of the heavenly bodies have become more comprehensible; but the movements of their rulers remain unpredictable to the people. The battle to measure the sky was won by doubt; but credulity still prevents the Roman housewife from winning her battle for milk. Science, Sarti, is involved in both battles. If mankind goes on stumbling in a pearly haze of superstition and outworn words and remains too ignorant to make full use of its own strength, it will never be able to use the forces of nature which science has discovered. What end are you scientists working for? To my mind, the only purpose of science is to lighten the toil of human existence. If scientists, browbeaten by selfish rulers, confine themselves to the accumulation of knowledge for the sake of knowledge, science will be crippled and your new machines will only mean new hardships. Given time, you may well discover everything there is to discover, but your progress will be a progression away from humanity. The gulf between you and humanity may one day be so wide that the response to your exultation about some new achievement will be a universal outcry of horror.—As a scientist, I had a unique opportunity. In my time astronomy reached the market place. Under these very special circumstances, one man's steadfastness might have had tremendous repercussions. If I had held out, scientists might have developed something like the physicians' Hippocratic oath, the vow to use their knowledge only for the good of mankind. As things stand now, the best we can hope for is a generation of inventive dwarfs who can be hired for any purpose. Furthermore, I have come to the conclusion, Sarti, that I was never in any real danger. For a few years I was as strong as the authorities. And yet I handed the powerful my knowledge to use, or not to use, or to misuse as served their purposes.

(*Virginia has come in with a dish and stops now*)

I have betrayed my calling. A man who does what I have done, cannot be tolerated in the ranks of science.

VIRGINIA   You have been received in the ranks of the faithful. (*She walks on and sets the dish on the table*)

GALILEO   Yes.—I must eat now.

(*Andrea offers him his hand. Galileo sees it but does not take it*)

GALILEO   You are teaching now yourself. Can you afford to shake a hand such as mine? (*He goes to the table*) Somebody on the way through has sent me two geese. I still like to eat.

ANDREA   Then you no longer believe that a new era has dawned?

GALILEO   I do.—Take good care of yourself when you pass through Germany with the truth under your coat.

ANDREA (*unable to leave*)   Regarding your opinion of the author we discussed I cannot answer you. But I refuse to believe that your devastating analysis can be the last word.

GALILEO   Thank you, sir. (*He begins to eat*)

VIRGINIA (*seeing Andrea out*)   We don't like visitors from the past. They upset him.

(*Andrea leaves. Virginia comes back*)

GALILEO   Any idea who could have sent the geese?

VIRGINIA   Not Andrea.

GALILEO   Maybe not. How is the night?

VIRGINIA (*at the window*)   Clear.

15

1637. Galileo's book *Discorsi* crosses the Italian border.

> The great book o'er the border went
> And, good folk, that was the end.
> But we hope you'll keep in mind
> You and I were left behind.
> May you now guard science' light
> Keep it up and use it right
> Lest it be a flame to fall
> One day to consume us all.

A small Italian border town. Early morning. Children are playing by the turnpike near the guard house. Andrea, beside a coachman, is waiting for his papers to be examined by the guards. He is sitting on a small box reading in Galileo's manuscript. The coach is on the far side of the turnpike.

THE CHILDREN (*sing*)

> Mary sat upon a stone
> Had a pink shift of her own
> The shift was full of shit.
> But when cold weather came along
> Mary put her shift back on
> Shitty is better than split.

THE BORDER GUARD   Why are you leaving Italy?

ANDREA   I'm a scholar.

THE BORDER GUARD (*to the clerk*)   Write under "Reason for Leaving": Scholar.

(*The clerk does so*)

THE FIRST BOY (*to Andrea*)   Don't sit there. (*He points at the hut in front of which Andrea is sitting*) A witch lives there.

THE SECOND BOY   Old Marina isn't a witch.

THE FIRST BOY   Want me to twist your arm?

THE THIRD BOY   She is too. She flies through the air at night.

THE FIRST BOY   If she's not a witch, why can't she get any milk anywhere in town?

THE SECOND BOY   How can she fly through the air? Nobody can do that. (*To Andrea*) Or can they?

THE FIRST BOY (*referring to the second boy*)   That's Giuseppe. He doesn't know anything, because he doesn't go to school, because his pants are torn.

THE BORDER GUARD   What's that book?

ANDREA (*without looking up*)   It's by Aristotle, the great philosopher.

THE BORDER GUARD (*suspiciously*)   What's he up to?

ANDREA   He's dead.

(*To tease Andrea, the boys walk around him in a way indicating that they too are reading books*)

THE BORDER GUARD (*to the clerk*)   See if there's anything about religion in it.

THE CLERK (*turning leaves*)   Can't see anything.

THE BORDER GUARD   Anyway there's no point in looking. Nobody'd be so open about anything he wanted to hide. (*To Andrea*) You'll have to sign a paper saying we examined everything.

(*Andrea hesitantly gets up and reading all the time goes into the house with the guards*)

THE THIRD BOY (*to the clerk, pointing at the box*)   Look, there's something else.

THE CLERK   Wasn't it here before?

THE THIRD BOY   The devil's put it there. It's a box.

THE SECOND BOY   No, it belongs to the traveler.

THE THIRD BOY   I wouldn't go near it. She's bewitched Passi the coachman's horses. I looked through the hole in the roof that the snowstorm made, and I heard them coughing.

THE CLERK (*almost at the box hesitates and goes back*)   Witchery, ha? Well, we can't examine everything. We'd never get through.

(*Andrea returns with a pitcher of milk. He sits down on the box again and continues to read*)

THE BORDER GUARD (*following him with papers*)   Close the boxes. Is that all?

THE CLERK   Yes.

THE SECOND BOY (*to Andrea*)   You say you're a scholar. Then tell me: Can people fly through the air?

ANDREA   Just a moment.

THE BORDER GUARD   You may proceed.

   (*The luggage has been picked up by the coachman. Andrea takes his box and prepares to go*)

THE BORDER GUARD   Wait! What's in that box?

ANDREA (*taking up his book again*)   Books.

THE FIRST BOY   It's the witch's box.

THE BORDER GUARD   Nonsense. How could she hex a box?

THE THIRD BOY   If the devil's helping her!

THE BORDER GUARD (*laughs*)   Not in our rule book. (*To the clerk*) Open it.

   (*The box is opened*)

THE BORDER GUARD (*listlessly*)   How many?

ANDREA   Thirty-four.

THE BORDER GUARD (*to the clerk*)   How long will it take you?

THE CLERK (*who has started rummaging superficially through the box*)   All printed stuff. You'd have no time for breakfast, and when do you expect me to collect the overdue toll from Passi the coachman when his house is auctioned off, if I go through all these books?

THE BORDER GUARD   You're right, we've got to get that money. (*He kicks at the books*) What could be in them anyway? (*To the coachman*) Pfftt!

   (*Andrea and the coachman who carries the box cross the border. Beyond it Andrea puts Galileo's manuscript in his bag*)

THE THIRD BOY (*points at the pitcher which Andrea had left behind*)   Look!

THE FIRST BOY   And the box is gone! Now do you see it was the devil?

ANDREA (*turning around*)   No, it was me. You must learn to use your eyes. The milk and the pitcher are paid for. Give them to the old woman. Oh yes, Giuseppe, I haven't answered your question. No one can fly through the air on a stick. Unless it has some sort of machine attached to it. Such machines don't exist yet. Maybe they never will because man is too heavy. But of course, we don't know. We don't know nearly enough, Giuseppe. We've hardly begun.

The Trial
of Lucullus

A Play for Radio

Collaborator: M. Steffin

Translator: Frank Jones

CHARACTERS

LUCULLUS, a Roman general

THE SPEAKER OF THE COURT OF THE DEAD

THE JUDGE OF THE DEAD

JURORS OF THE DEAD: THE TEACHER, THE COURTESAN, THE BAKER, THE FISHWIFE, THE FARMER

FIGURES ON A FRIEZE: THE KING, THE QUEEN, TWO VIRGINS WITH A TABLET, TWO SLAVES WITH A GOLDEN GOD, TWO LEGIONARIES, LUCULLUS' COOK, THE BEARER OF THE CHERRY TREE

THE TONELESS VOICE

AN OLD WOMAN

THE THREEFOLD VOICE

TWO SHADES

THE CRIER

TWO YOUNG GIRLS

TWO MERCHANTS

TWO WOMEN

TWO PLEBEIANS

A CART DRIVER

CHORUS OF SOLDIERS

CHORUS OF SLAVES

CHORUS OF CHILDREN

VOICES

1

The Funeral Procession

Sounds of a great mass of people.

THE CRIER
5   Hear ye: great Lucullus is dead!
    The general who conquered the east
    Who overthrew seven kings
    Who filled Rome, our city, with riches.
    Before his catafalque
10 Which is borne by soldiers
    Walk the most respected men of mighty Rome
    Their faces veiled. Beside him
    Walk his philosopher, his lawyer, and his favorite horse.
    SONG OF THE SOLDIERS CARRYING THE CATAFALQUE
15 Hold it steady, hold it shoulder-high!
    Let it not sway before these thousand eyes
    Now that the lord of the eastern earth
    Is passing to the shades. Careful, men, don't stumble!
    The thing you bear of flesh and metal
20 Was master of the world.
    THE CRIER
    Behind him they are hauling a colossal frieze, which
    Shows his deeds and is destined for his tomb.
    Once again
25 All the people admire his glorious life
    Of victories and conquests

And remember the time of his triumph.

VOICES
Think of the invincible, the mighty one!
Think of the scourge of both Asias
5   The darling of Rome and the gods
When he rode through the city
In his golden chariot, bringing you
Foreign kings and foreign animals!
Elephant, camel, panther
10   And carriage loads of captured ladies
Baggage wagons rattling with utensils
Ships, images, fine vessels
All carved in ivory, a whole Corinthful
Of brazen statues, hauled
15   Through the roaring ocean of the people! Think of the sight!
Think of the coins for the children
And the wines and sausages!
When he rode through the city
In his golden chariot
20   He, the invincible, he, the mighty one
He, the scourge of both Asias
Darling of Rome and the Gods!

SONG OF THE SLAVES HAULING THE FRIEZE
Watch out, men, don't stumble!
25   You haulers of the frieze portraying the triumph
Never mind if sweat gets in your eyes
Keep a grip on the stone! Think, if you let it drop
It may shatter into dust.

YOUNG GIRL
30   Look at red-helmet! No, the tall one there!

ANOTHER GIRL
Cross-eyed.

FIRST MERCHANT
All the senators have come!

35 SECOND MERCHANT
And all the tailors too.

FIRST MERCHANT
He got as far as India! Let's be fair!

SECOND MERCHANT
> But he was finished long before he died.
> It's sad but true.

FIRST MERCHANT
5 > Greater than Pompey, I tell you!
> Without that man there'd be no Rome.
> The victories he won!

SECOND MERCHANT
> Flukes most of them and gory!

10 FIRST WOMAN
> My son
> Was killed in Asia. All this hullabaloo
> Won't bring him back.

FIRST MERCHANT
15 > I know of quite a few
> Who thanks to him have done extremely well.

SECOND WOMAN
> My brother's boy—one more that won't come home.

FIRST MERCHANT
20 > We know how well he served the city
> Just think of all that glory!

FIRST WOMAN
> If it wasn't for the lies they tell
> Not a man would fall into their sack.

25 FIRST MERCHANT
> Heroism—what a pity—
> Is on its way out.

FIRST PLEBEIAN
> Man
30 > That glory stuff grinds on and on.

SECOND PLEBEIAN
> In Cappadocia, three legions gone
> Up the spout.

A CART DRIVER
35 > Can
> I get through?

SECOND WOMAN
> No, it's barred.

FIRST PLEBEIAN

When we're laying our generals in the ground
Even oxcarts are bound
To bide their time.

SECOND WOMAN

They've dragged my Pulcher into court:
Owing taxes was his crime!

FIRST MERCHANT

But for him it's plain
We wouldn't have our Asian colonies.

FIRST WOMAN

Is tuna up again?

SECOND WOMAN

Yes, and so is cheese!
(*The shouting of the crowd swells*)

THE CRIER

Now
They are passing through the triumphal arch
Which the city has erected for its great son.
The women lift their children up. The horsemen
Push back the rows of onlookers.
The street behind the procession lies orphaned.
For the last time
Great Lucullus has passed this way.
(*The noise of the crowd dies away, as does the martial tread of the procession*)

2

Quick Fade-out, and the Daily Round Resumes

THE CRIER
    The procession has vanished, now
5   The street fills up again. The wagoners drive their oxcarts
    Out of the choked alleys. The garrulous
    Crowd takes up its occupations.
    Busy Rome
    Goes back to work.

10

3

In the Schoolbooks

CHORUS OF CHILDREN
    In the schoolbooks
    Are written the names of the great generals.
15   You learn their battles by heart
    You study their wonderful lives
    If you long to be like them.
    To aim for that
    To rise above the crowd
20   Is our appointed task. Our city
    Is eager to write our names one day
    On the tablets of the immortals.
    Sextus conquers Pontus.
    And you, Flaccus, conquer the three Gauls.
25   But you, Quintilian
    March across the Alps!

4

The Burial

THE CRIER
   Out on the Appian Way
   Stands a small edifice, built ten years ago
   Destined to shelter
   The great man in death.
   Ahead of him
   The group of slaves hauling the triumphal frieze
   Turns off the road. Then
   The small rotunda with the clump of boxwood
   Receives him too.

A TONELESS VOICE
   Halt, soldiers!

THE CRIER
   A voice comes from
   The other side of the wall.
   From now on, it commands.

THE TONELESS VOICE
   Tilt the bier! Beyond this wall
   No one is carried. Beyond this wall
   A man goes on his own feet.

THE CRIER
   The soldiers tilt the bier. The general
   Stands upright now, a bit shaky.
   His philosopher wants to join him
   A wise maxim on his lips. But . . .

THE TONELESS VOICE
   Stand back, philosopher! Behind this wall
   You can wheedle no one.

THE CRIER
   Says the voice that commands there, and
   Next the lawyer comes forward
   To raise an objection.

THE TONELESS VOICE
  Overruled.
THE CRIER
  Says the voice that commands there.
5 And it says to the general:
THE TONELESS VOICE
  Now step up to the gate!
THE CRIER
  And the general walks to the little gate
10 Stands still a moment to look around
  And solemnly beholds the soldiers
  Beholds the slaves hauling the frieze
  Beholds the boxwood, final green. He hesitates.
  As the hall is open, the wind gets in
15 From the road.
  (*A gust of wind is heard*)
THE TONELESS VOICE
  Take off your helmet. Our gate is low.
THE CRIER
20 And the general takes his splendid helmet off.
  And steps in, crouching. With signs of relief the soldiers
  Pour out of the tomb, talking cheerfully.

5

Farewell of the Living

25 CHORUS OF SOLDIERS
  So long, Lacallous!
  We're quits, old goat!
  Let's leave this cavern
  And find a tavern!
30 He's earned his palace
  He's in his glory

That's not the whole story
There's living to do.
We'll drink till we float!
You were out of step too.
I'll come with you.
Trust me, I will.
Who'll buy the wine?
They'll put it on the bill.
Now he looks fine!
As for me, I'll look around for meat.
The little dark one? We'll come too.
No, that wouldn't do.
When you go in threes, she's not so sweet.
The slut!
Then let's watch the greyhounds race.
But
There's a gate charge. Not if they know your face.
I'll come too.
All right! One, two . . .
Break step! Forward march!

6

The Reception

The toneless voice is the voice of the gatekeeper of the realm of shades.
It takes over the narration.

THE TONELESS VOICE
  Since the newcomer entered
  He has been standing by the door, motionless, his helmet
    under his arm

A statue of himself.
The other dead who are new arrivals
Sit on the bench and wait
As formerly they waited many a time
5   For happiness and for death
In the tavern, until they got their wine
And by the fountain, until the loved one came
And in the thicket, in battle, until the command was given.
But this new one
10 Seems not to have learned to wait.

LUCULLUS

By Jupiter, what
Does this mean? I stand here waiting!
The greatest city on the globe still rings
5   With laments for me, and here
There's no one to receive me!
Outside my battle tent
Seven kings waited for me!
Is there no order in this place?
10 What's become of Lasus, my cook, at least?
A man who can turn thin air
Into a nice little bite to eat!
Supposing, now, that he'd been sent to meet me
Since he's staying down here too
15 I'd feel more at home.—Oh, Lasus!
Your lamb with bay leaves and dill!
Cappadocian venison! Those lobsters from Pontus
And those Phrygian cakes with bitter berries!
(Silence)
Escort me from this place. That is an order.
(Silence)
Must I stand here among these people?
(Silence)
I protest. Two hundred
Iron-armored ships, five legions
Advanced when I raised my little finger.
I protest.
(Silence)

THE TONELESS VOICE
No answer, but on the bench where people wait
An old woman says:

VOICE OF AN OLD WOMAN WAITING
Sit down, newcomer.
All that metal you're lugging, that heavy helmet
And breastplate must surely make you tired.
So sit down.
(Lucullus is silent)
Don't be stubborn. You can't stand the whole time.
You're going to have a long wait. I'm ahead of you.
You can't tell how long a hearing in there will last.
It's understandable. After all, everyone must be
Strictly appraised before it is decided
Whether he shall enter gloomy Hades or
The fields of the blest. Sometimes
The proceedings are brief, a look is enough for the judges.
That man, they say
Led a guiltless life and managed
To be useful to his fellows, for
A person's usefulness
Is what they value most. Please, they say to him
Take your rest. Of course in other cases
The trial can last for days, especially in the case of one
Who sent another down here to the realm
Of shades before his apportioned span
Of life had passed. The man in there right now
Won't take very long. A harmless little baker. As for me
I'm a bit worried, but I find some hope
In what I hear: that some of the jurors in there
Are little people who fully understand
How hard life is for the likes of us in warring times.
Newcomer, I advise you . . .

THE THREEFOLD VOICE *(interrupting)*
Tertullia!

THE OLD WOMAN
I'm being called.
Well, newcomer, you'll have to see how you get along.
Take a seat.

THE TONELESS VOICE

    The newcomer has been standing obstinately by the gate
    But the burden of his medals
    His own bellowing
5   And the old woman's kind words have changed him.
    He looks around to see if he is really alone. Now
    He is moving over to the bench.
    But before he can sit down
    He will be called. In the old woman's case
10   A look was enough for the judges.

THE THREEFOLD VOICE

    Lacallous!

LUCULLUS

    Lucullus is my name. Don't you people know that?
15   I come of an illustrious line
    Of statesmen and generals. Only in slums
    Docks and soldiers' taverns, in the unwashed mouths
    Of uncouth persons and scum
    Am I called Lacallous.

20 THE THREEFOLD VOICE

    Lacallous!

THE TONELESS VOICE

    And so, summoned more than once
    In the scorned parlance of the slums
25   Lucullus, the general
    Who conquered the east
    Who overthrew seven kings
    Who filled the city of Rome with riches
    Reports at eventide, when Rome sits down above the graves
        to eat
30   To the highest court in the realm of shades.

7

Choosing a Sponsor

THE SPEAKER OF THE COURT OF THE DEAD
  Before the highest court in the realm of shades
  Appears General Lacallous, who calls himself Lucullus.
  The judge of the dead presiding
  Five jurors conduct the questioning.
  One formerly a farmer
  One a slave who had been a teacher
  One a fishwife
  One a baker
  One a courtesan.
  They sit on a high bench
  And have no hands for taking or mouths for eating
  Their long-extinguished eyes impervious to glamor.
  Incorruptible they are, the ancestors of posterity.
  The judge of the dead opens the trial.

THE JUDGE OF THE DEAD
  Shade, you shall now be questioned.
  You shall render an account of your life among men.
  Whether you have been of use or harm to them
  Whether the sight of your face will be welcome
  In the fields of the blest.
  You need a sponsor.
  Have you a sponsor in the fields of the blest?

LUCULLUS
  I request that the great Alexander of Macedon be called.
  That he speak to you as an expert
  On deeds like mine.

THE THREEFOLD VOICE (*calls out in the fields of the blest*)
  Alexander of Macedon!
  (*Silence*)

THE SPEAKER
The man does not answer.

THE THREEFOLD VOICE
5   There is no Alexander of Macedon
In the fields of the blest.

THE JUDGE
Shade, your expert
Is unknown in the fields of the well-remembered.

LUCULLUS
10   What? The man who conquered all Asia to the Indus
The unforgettable one
Who unmistakably imprinted his boot upon the globe
The mighty Alexander . . .

THE JUDGE
15   Is not known here.
(Silence)

THE JUDGE
Unfortunate man! The names of the great
Arouse no fear among us below.
20   Here
They can no longer threaten. Their utterances
Pass for lies. Their deeds
Are not recorded. And their glory
Is to us like smoke, a sign
25   That a fire has raged.
Shade, your bearing indicates
That enterprises of some scope
Are associated with your name.
Those enterprises
30   Are not known here.

LUCULLUS
Then I request
That the frieze for my tomb be brought —
On which my triumphal procession is shown.
35   But how can it
Be brought? It's hauled by slaves. No doubt
The living are
Denied admission here.

THE JUDGE
    Not slaves. So little
    Separates them from the dead.
    They can barely
    Be said to live. The step from the world above
    Down to the realm of shades
    Is for them but a short one.
    Let the frieze be brought.

8

Bringing in the Frieze

THE TONELESS VOICE
    His slaves still linger
    Uncertainly by the wall.
    Where is the frieze to go? Then suddenly
    A voice speaks through the wall.

THE SPEAKER
    Come in.

THE TONELESS VOICE
    And, changed to shades
    By these two words
    They haul their load
    Through the wall by the boxwood.

CHORUS OF SLAVES
    Out of life and into death
    We haul our load ungrudgingly
    For years our time was not our own
    Unknown to us our destination.
    So we follow the new voice
    As we did the old one. Why ask questions?
    We leave nothing behind, expect nothing.

THE SPEAKER

    And so they go through the wall
    For men held back by nothing
    Are not held back by this wall either.
5   And they set down their load
    Before the supreme court of the shades
    The frieze with the triumphal procession.
    You, jurors of the dead, behold it:
    A captured king with mournful gaze
10   A sloe-eyed queen with seductive thighs
    A man with a little cherry tree, eating a cherry
    A golden god, carried by two slaves, very fat
    Two virgins with a tablet bearing the names of 53 cities
    Two legionaries
15   One standing, one dying and saluting his general
    A cook with a fish.

THE JUDGE

    Are these your witnesses, shade?

LUCULLUS

20   They are. But how
    Shall they speak? They're stones, they're mute.

THE JUDGE

    Not for us. They will speak.
    Are you ready, stony shades
25   To testify?

CHORUS OF FIGURES

    We figures, fashioned to stay in the light
    Stony shades of long-vanished victims
    To speak on earth and be silent on earth
30   We figures, once fashioned to represent
    In the light, at the victor's command, those flung
    To the ground, robbed of breath, struck dumb and forgotten
    Are ready for silence and ready for speech.

THE JUDGE

35   Shade, the witnesses to your greatness
    Are ready to testify.

9

The Trial

THE SPEAKER
And the general steps forward and
Points at the king.

LUCULLUS
Here you see a man whom I defeated.
In the few days between new moon and full moon
I smashed his army with all its chariots and armored riders.
In those few days
His empire collapsed like a hut struck by lightning.
When I appeared on his border he took flight
And the few days of the war
Were barely enough for both of us
To reach the other border of his empire.
The campaign was of such brief duration that a ham
Which my cook hung up to smoke
Was not fully smoked when I got back
And of seven whom I smashed he was but one.

THE JUDGE
Is this true, king?

THE KING
It is true.

THE JUDGE
Your questions, jurors.

THE SPEAKER
And the slave shade who was once a teacher
Leans forward sternly and asks a question:

THE TEACHER
How did it happen?

THE KING
As he says, we were overrun.

The farmer loading his hay
Still stood with pitchfork lifted as
His wagon, just now fully loaded
Was driven away.
5   The baker's loaf was not yet baked
When foreign hands reached out for it.
Everything he tells you about the lightning
That struck a hut is true. The hut
Is wrecked. Here
10 Stands the lightning.

THE TEACHER
And of seven you were . . .

THE KING
But one.

15 THE SPEAKER
The jurors of the dead consider
The testimony of the king.
(Silence)

THE SPEAKER
20 And the shade who was once a courtesan
Asks a question:

COURTESAN
You there, queen
How did you get here?

25 THE QUEEN
As I went in Taurion to
Bathe one morning early
Fifty foreign soldiers came
Down the hill of olives
30 And I was defeated.

For defense I had a sponge
For a screen clear water
But this armor that I had
Could not long protect me.
35 I was soon defeated.

Terrified, I looked around
Cried out for my handmaids
And the maids cried out in fright

From behind the bushes.
They were all defeated.

THE COURTESAN

And why do you walk in this procession?

THE QUEEN

Oh! To show the victory.

THE COURTESAN

What victory? Over you?

THE QUEEN

Me and lovely Taurion.

THE COURTESAN

And what did he call a triumph?

THE QUEEN

That the king, my wedded lord
Could not save with all his might
His possessions and his country
From the all-devouring Rome.

THE COURTESAN

Sister, my fate equals yours
For the all-devouring Rome
Could in my day not protect me
From the all-devouring Rome.

THE SPEAKER

The jurors of the dead consider
The testimony of the queen.
(Silence)

THE SPEAKER

And the judge of the dead turns
To the general.

THE JUDGE

Shade, do you wish to continue?

LUCULLUS

Yes, I notice that the losers
Have sweet voices. Once
5   They were harsher, though. The king there
Who is prevailing on your pity was in his lifetime
Exceeding cruel. Of tithe and tax
He took no less than I did. The cities
I wrested from him never missed him, but through me
10   Rome gained 53 cities.

TWO VIRGINS WITH A TABLET
> With streets and people and houses
> With temples and waterworks
> We stood in the landscape, now
5   Only our names are left upon this tablet.

THE SPEAKER
> And the juror shade who was once a baker
> Leans forward sternly and asks a question:

THE BAKER
10   Why is that?

THE TWO VIRGINS
> One day at noon an uproar was heard
> A river surged into the street
> It had human waves and swept
15   All that was ours away. By evening
> Only a pillar of smoke showed
> That a city had once stood there.

THE BAKER
> And what
20   Did he carry off, this man who sent the river and says
> That he gave the Romans 53 cities?

THE SPEAKER
> And the slaves who are hauling the golden god
> Begin to tremble and cry out.

25 THE SLAVES
> Us.
> Happy once, now cheaper than oxen
> To haul the booty, ourselves booty.

THE TWO VIRGINS
30   Once the builders
> Of 53 cities, of which only
> Names and smoke remain.

LUCULLUS
> Yes, I carried them away. They were
35   Twice a hundred and fifty thousand.
> At one time foes, but foes no longer.

THE SLAVES
> At one time men, but men no longer.

LUCULLUS
40   And with them I carried away their god

So that the world might look upon our gods
As greater than all other gods

THE SLAVES

And the god was very welcome
5   Because he was of gold and weighed two hundredweight
And each of us is worth a piece of gold
The size of a knucklebone.

THE SPEAKER

And the juror shade who was once a baker
10   In Marsilia, the city by the sea
Makes a proposal:

THE BAKER

Then in your favor, shade, we shall write down
Simply this: brought gold to Rome.

15 THE SPEAKER

The jurors of the dead consider
The testimony of the cities.
(Silence)

THE JUDGE

20   The defendant seems tired.
I declare a recess.

10

Back in Rome

THE SPEAKER

25   The court withdraws.
The defendant sits down.
Head thrown back, he squats
By the doorpost.

He is exhausted, but he overhears
A conversation behind the door
Where new shades have appeared.

A SHADE

5   I came to grief because of an oxcart.

LUCULLUS (*softly*)

Oxcart.

THE SHADE

It was hauling yet another load of sand to a building-site.

10 LUCULLUS (*softly*)

Building-site. Sand.

ANOTHER SHADE

Isn't it time to eat?

FIRST SHADE

15 Time to eat? I had my bread and onions
With me. I've lost my room.
The mob of slaves they're driving in
From the four quarters of the earth
Have ruined the shoemaker's trade.

20 SECOND SHADE

I was a slave too. Let's say the unlucky
Bring bad luck to the lucky.

LUCULLUS (*a bit louder*)

You: does the wind still blow up there?

25 SECOND SHADE

Hear that? Somebody's asking something.

FIRST SHADE (*loudly*)

Does the wind still blow up there? Maybe.
Possibly in the gardens.

30 In the stifling alleys
It can't be noticed.

11

The Trial Continues

THE SPEAKER
   The jurors return.
   The trial resumes.
   And the shade, once a fishwife
   Speaks up:
THE FISHWIFE
   There was talk of gold just now.
   I lived in Rome myself.
   But I never noticed any gold where I lived.
   I'd be glad to know what became of it.
LUCULLUS
   What a question!
   Was I to set out
   With my legions to capture
   A stool for a fishwife?
THE FISHWIFE
   If you brought nothing to the fish market
   You certainly took something away from the fish market:
   Our sons.
THE SPEAKER
   And the juror
   Addresses the warriors on the frieze:
THE FISHWIFE
   Tell me, what did he do to you in both Asias?
FIRST LEGIONARY
   I ran away.
SECOND LEGIONARY
   I was wounded.
FIRST LEGIONARY
   I carried him.

SECOND LEGIONARY
　　So he got killed too.

THE FISHWIFE
　　Why did you leave Rome?

5　FIRST LEGIONARY
　　I was starving.

THE FISHWIFE
　　And what did you get out there?

SECOND LEGIONARY
10　I got nothing.

THE FISHWIFE
　　You're holding your hand out.
　　Was it to salute the general?

SECOND LEGIONARY
15　I wanted to show him
　　That it was still empty.

LUCULLUS
　　I protest.
　　I rewarded the legionaries
20　After each campaign.

THE FISHWIFE
　　But not the dead ones.

LUCULLUS
　　I protest.
25　How can people judge war
　　When they don't understand it?

THE FISHWIFE
　　I understand it. My
　　Son was killed in battle. I
30　Was a fishwife in the Forum market.
　　One day there was news: the galleys
　　With the men back from the war in Asia
　　Had come in. I ran out of the market
　　And stood many hours by the Tiber
35　While they disembarked; by nightfall
　　All the ships were empty. But my son had
　　Not come down the gangplank.
　　It was windy in the harbor. I took
　　Fever, and in my fever went on looking

For my son. The more I looked, the
Colder I felt, and then, in death, I came here
To the realm of shades and kept on looking.
Faber, I called, for that was his name.
Faber, my son Faber
Whom I bore and whom I reared
My son Faber!
And I ran and ran among the shades
Calling Faber, until a gatekeeper
At the camps for soldiers killed in action
Caught me by the sleeve and said to me:
There are many Fabers here, old lady.
Sons of many mothers, all much missed
But they've lost their names, forgot them.
They were useful only for the army
But are useless here. These men no longer
Wish to meet their mothers, not since the
Day they let them go to bloody war.
There I stood, caught by my sleeve
And my cry stuck in my throat.
Silent I turned back, for I had lost
All desire to see my son again.

THE SPEAKER
    And the judge of the dead seeks
    The eyes of the jurors and announces:

THE JUDGE
    The court's opinion: the fallen man's mother
    Understands war.

THE SPEAKER
    The jurors of the dead consider
    The testimony of the warriors.
    (Silence)

THE JUDGE
    But the lady juror is shaken.
    The scales may tremble in
    Her wavering hand. She requires
    A recess.

12

Rome—A Last Time

THE SPEAKER
And again
5 The defendant sits down and listens
To the talk of the shades behind the door.
Once more
From above, from the world
A breath comes down.
10 SECOND SHADE
Why were you running so?
FIRST SHADE
To make inquiries. I'd heard they're recruiting legionaries
In the taverns by the Tiber, for the war in the west
15 Which is to be conquered next.
The country's name is Gaul.
SECOND SHADE
Never heard of it.
FIRST SHADE
20 Those countries are known only to the high and mighty.

13

The Trial Continues

THE SPEAKER
    And the judge smiles at the lady juror
    Summons the defendant and contemplates him sadly.

THE JUDGE
    Time is running out. You're not making use of it.
    Better stop provoking us with your triumphs.
    Have you no witnesses
    To any weakness, man?
    Your case looks bad. Your virtues
    Don't seem very useful, maybe
    Your weaknesses would make gaps
    In the chain of your violent deeds?
5   Call your weaknesses to mind
    That's my advice to you, shade.

THE SPEAKER
    And the juror, once a baker
    Asks a question:

10 THE BAKER
    I see a cook there with a fish.
    He looks cheerful. Cook
    Tell us how you came to be in the procession.

THE COOK
25   Just to show
    That, busy as he was with war, he still found time
    To find a recipe for a fish.
    I was his cook. Even now
    I often think of the splendid meats
30   The fowl and dark venison
    That he had me roast.
    And he didn't just sit there eating
    He gave me a word of praise

Often stood beside me over the pan
And mixed a dish himself.
Lamb à la Lucullus
Made our kitchen famous.
From Syria to Pontus
People spoke of Lucullus' cook.

THE SPEAKER

Then spoke the juror
Who was once a teacher:

THE TEACHER

What's it to us that he liked to eat?

THE COOK

But he let me cook
To my heart's content. I thank him for it.

THE BAKER

I understand him, I, who was a baker.
How often I had to put bran in my dough
Because my customers were poor. That man
Had a chance to be an artist.

THE COOK

Thanks to him!
In the triumph
He paraded me behind the kings
And showed respect for my art.
Therefore I call him human.

THE SPEAKER

The jurors of the dead consider
The testimony of the cook.
(Silence)

THE SPEAKER

And the juror, once a farmer
Asks a question:

THE FARMER

There's a man carrying a fruit tree.

THE CHERRY TREE BEARER

It's a cherry tree.
We brought it from Asia. We carried it
In the triumph. And planted it
On the slopes of the Apennines.

THE FARMER
     Oh, so it's you who brought it, Lacallous?
     I planted it too, but I didn't know
     It came from you.

5 THE SPEAKER
     And, smiling amiably
     The juror who was once a farmer
     Chats with the shade
     Who was once a general
10   About the tree.

THE FARMER
     It doesn't need much soil.

LUCULLUS
     But it won't take much wind.

15 THE FARMER
     The red cherries are meatier.

LUCULLUS
     And the black ones are sweeter.

THE FARMER
20   My friends, of all that has been conquered
     In bloody war of hated memory
     I call this best. This little tree lives on.
     A friendly newcomer, it takes its place
     Beside the vine and the hard-working berry bush
25   And, growing with the growing generations
     Bears fruit for them. And therefore I commend you
     For bringing it to us. When all the plunder
     Of both Asias has long turned to rot
     This, the smallest of your trophies
30   Will stand upon the windy hills and wave
     Each spring its bloom-white branches to the living.

14

The Verdict

THE SPEAKER
5   And the juror, once a fishwife in the market, springs to her
feet.

THE FISHWIFE
So, after all
You've found a penny in those
Bloody hands? And the robber is bribing
10   The court with his spoils?

THE TEACHER
One cherry tree! He could have made
That conquest with
One man only! Instead he has sent
15   80,000 down here!

THE BAKER
How much
Do they have to pay up there
For a glass of wine and a roll?

20 THE COURTESAN
Will they always have to sell their skins
When they want to lie with a woman? Send him to nothing-
ness!

THE FISHWIFE
25   Yes, to nothingness!

THE TEACHER
Yes, to nothingness!

THE BAKER
Yes, to nothingness!

0 THE SPEAKER
And they look at the farmer
The praiser of the cherry tree.
What say you, farmer?
(Silence)

THE FARMER
    80,000 for a cherry tree!
    Yes, to nothingness!

THE JUDGE
    Yes, to nothingness! For
    With all the violence and conquest
    Only one realm increases:
    The realm of shades.

THE JURORS
    And our gray world below
    Is already full
    Of half-lived lives. Yet here
    We have no plows for sinewy arms, or
    Hungry mouths, of which up there
5   You have so many! What but dust
    Could we heap upon
    The 80,000 slaughtered ones! And you
    Up there need houses! How often
    Shall we meet them on our
10   Paths that lead nowhere and hear them asking their eager
    Terrible questions, what
    The summer of the years is like, and the autumn
    And the winter?

THE SPEAKER
25   And the legionaries on the frieze of the dead
    Move and cry out:

THE LEGIONARIES
    Yes, send him to nothingness! What province
    Tips the scales against
30   Our unlived years that held so much?

THE SPEAKER
    And the slaves, haulers of the frieze
    Move and cry out:

THE SLAVES
35   Yes, to nothingness! How long
    Will they sit, he and his
    Inhuman kind, over men and lift
    Lazy hands and hurl the peoples
    Into bloody wars against each other?

How long shall we
Endure them and our kind endure them?

ALL

Yes, to nothingness
With him and all his kind!

THE SPEAKER

And from the high bench rise
The spokesmen of a posterity
Many-handed for taking
Many-mouthed for eating
Eagerly reaping
Rejoicing in life.

Mother Courage
and Her Children

A Chronicle of the Thirty Years' War

Translator: Ralph Manheim

CHARACTERS

MOTHER COURAGE

KATTRIN, her mute daughter

EILIF, her elder son

SWISS CHEESE, her younger
    son

THE RECRUITER

THE SERGEANT

THE COOK

THE GENERAL

THE CHAPLAIN

THE ORDNANCE OFFICER

YVETTE POTTIER

THE MAN WITH THE PATCH
    OVER HIS EYE

THE OTHER SERGEANT

THE OLD COLONEL

A CLERK

A YOUNG SOLDIER

AN OLDER SOLDIER

A PEASANT

THE PEASANT'S WIFE

THE YOUNG MAN

THE OLD WOMAN

ANOTHER PEASANT

THE PEASANT WOMAN

A YOUNG PEASANT

THE LIEUTENANT

SOLDIERS

A VOICE

1

Spring, 1624. General Oxenstjerna recruits troops in Dalarna for the Polish campaign. The canteen woman, Anna Fierling, known as Mother Courage, loses a son.

Highway near a city.

A sergeant and a recruiter stand shivering.

THE RECRUITER How can anybody get a company together in a place like this? Sergeant, sometimes I feel like committing suicide. The general wants me to recruit four platoons by the twelfth, and the people around here are so depraved I can't sleep at night. I finally get hold of a man, I close my eyes and pretend not to see that he's chicken-breasted and he's got varicose veins, I get him good and drunk and he signs up. While I'm paying for the drinks, he steps out, I follow him to the door because I smell a rat: Sure enough, he's gone, like a fart out of a goose. A man's word doesn't mean a thing, there's no honor, no loyalty. This place has undermined my faith in humanity, sergeant.

THE SERGEANT It's easy to see these people have gone too long without a war. How can you have morality without a war, I ask you? Peace is a mess, it takes a war to put things in order. In peacetime the human race goes to the dogs. Man and beast are treated like so much dirt. Everybody eats what they like, a big piece of cheese on white bread, with a slice of meat on top of the cheese. Nobody knows how many young men or good horses there are in that town up ahead, they've never been counted. I've been in places where they hadn't had a war in as much as seventy years, the people had no names, they

didn't even know who they were. It takes a war before you get decent lists and records; then your boots are done up in bales and your grain in sacks, man and beast are properly counted and marched away, because people realize that without order they can't have a war.

THE RECRUITER   How right you are!

THE SERGEANT   Like all good things, a war is hard to get started. But once it takes root, it's vigorous; then people are as scared of peace as dice players are of laying off, because they'll have to reckon up their losses. But at first they're scared of war. It's the novelty.

THE RECRUITER   Say, there comes a wagon. Two women and two young fellows. Keep the old woman busy, sergeant. If this is another flop, you won't catch me standing out in this April wind any more.

(*A Jew's harp is heard. Drawn by two young men, a covered wagon approaches. In the wagon sit Mother Courage and her mute daughter Kattrin*)

MOTHER COURAGE   Good morning, sergeant.

SERGEANT (*barring the way*)   Good morning, friends. Who are you?

MOTHER COURAGE   Business people. (*Sings*)

Hey, Captains, make the drum stop drumming
And let your soldiers take a seat.
Here's Mother Courage, with boots she's coming
To help along their aching feet.
How can they march off to the slaughter
With baggage, cannon, lice and fleas
Across the rocks and through the water
Unless their boots are in one piece?
    The spring is come. Christian, revive!
    The snowdrifts melt. The dead lie dead.
    And if by chance you're still alive
    It's time to rise and shake a leg.

O Captains, don't expect to send them
To death with nothing in their crops.
First you must let Mother Courage mend them
In mind and body with her schnapps.

On empty bellies it's distressing
To stand up under shot and shell.
But once they're full, you have my blessing
To lead them to the jaws of hell.
 The spring is come. Christian, revive!
 The snowdrifts melt, the dead lie dead.
 And if by chance you're still alive
 It's time to rise and shake a leg.

THE SERGEANT Halt, you scum. Where do you belong?

THE ELDER SON Second Finnish Regiment.

THE SERGEANT Where are your papers?

MOTHER COURAGE Papers?

THE YOUNGER SON But she's Mother Courage!

THE SERGEANT Never heard of her. Why Courage?

MOTHER COURAGE They call me Courage, sergeant, because when I saw ruin staring me in the face I drove out of Riga through cannon fire with fifty loaves of bread in my wagon. They were getting moldy, it was high time, I had no choice.

THE SERGEANT No wisecracks. Where are your papers?

MOTHER COURAGE (*fishing a pile of papers out of a tin box and climbing down*) Here are my papers, sergeant. There's a whole missal, picked it up in Alt-Ötting to wrap cucumbers in, and a map of Moravia, God knows if I'll ever get there, if I don't it's a total loss. And this here certifies that my horse hasn't got foot-and-mouth disease, too bad, he croaked on us, he cost fifteen guilders, but not out of my pocket, glory be. Is that enough paper?

THE SERGEANT Are you trying to pull my leg? I'll teach you to get smart. You know you need a license.

MOTHER COURAGE You mind your manners and don't go telling my innocent children that I'd go anywhere near your leg, it's indecent. I want no truck with you. My license in the Second Regiment is my honest face, and if you can't read it, that's not my fault. I'm not letting anybody put his seal on it.

THE RECRUITER Sergeant, I detect a spirit of insubordination in this woman. In our camp we need respect for authority.

MOTHER COURAGE Wouldn't sausage be better?

THE SERGEANT Name.

MOTHER COURAGE Anna Fierling.

THE SERGEANT   Then you're all Fierlings?

MOTHER COURAGE   What do you mean? Fierling is my name. Not theirs.

THE SERGEANT   Aren't they all your children?

MOTHER COURAGE   That they are, but why should they all have the same name? (*Pointing at the elder son*) This one, for instance. His name is Eilif Nojocki. How come? Because his father always claimed to be called Kojocki or Mojocki. The boy remembers him well, except the one he remembers was somebody else, a Frenchman with a goatee. But aside from that, he inherited his father's intelligence; that man could strip the pants off a peasant's ass without his knowing it. So, you see, we've each got our own name.

THE SERGEANT   Each different, you mean?

MOTHER COURAGE   Don't act so innocent.

THE SERGEANT   I suppose that one's a Chinaman? (*Indicating the younger son*)

MOTHER COURAGE   Wrong. He's Swiss.

THE SERGEANT   After the Frenchman?

MOTHER COURAGE   What Frenchman? I never heard of any Frenchman. Don't get everything balled up or we'll be here all day. He's Swiss, but his name is Fejos, the name has nothing to do with his father. He had an entirely different name, he was an engineer, built fortifications, but he drank.

(*Swiss Cheese nods, beaming; the mute Kattrin is also tickled*)

THE SERGEANT   Then how can his name be Fejos?

MOTHER COURAGE   I wouldn't want to offend you, but you haven't got much imagination. Naturally his name is Fejos because when he came I was with a Hungarian, it was all the same to him, he was dying of kidney trouble though he never touched a drop, a very decent man. The boy takes after him.

THE SERGEANT   But you said he wasn't his father?

MOTHER COURAGE   He takes after him all the same. I call him Swiss Cheese, how come, because he's good at pulling the wagon. (*Pointing at her daughter*) Her name is Kattrin Haupt, she's half German.

THE SERGEANT   A fine family, I must say.

MOTHER COURAGE   Yes, I've been all over the world with my wagon.

THE SERGEANT   It's all being taken down. (*He takes it down*) You're from Bamberg, Bavaria. What brings you here?

MOTHER COURAGE   I couldn't wait for the war to kindly come to Bamberg.

THE RECRUITER   You wagon pullers ought to be called Jacob Ox and Esau Ox. Do you ever get out of harness?

EILIF   Mother, can I clout him one on the kisser? I'd like to.

MOTHER COURAGE   And I forbid you. You stay put. And now, gentlemen, wouldn't you need a nice pistol, or a belt buckle, yours is all worn out, sergeant.

THE SERGEANT   I need something else. I'm not blind. Those young fellows are built like tree trunks, big broad chests, sturdy legs. Why aren't they in the army? That's what I'd like to know.

MOTHER COURAGE (*quickly*)   Nothing doing, sergeant. My children aren't cut out for soldiers.

THE RECRUITER   Why not? There's profit in it, and glory. Peddling shoes is woman's work. (*To Eilif*) Step up; let's feel if you've got muscles or if you're a sissy.

MOTHER COURAGE   He's a sissy. Give him a mean look and he'll fall flat on his face.

THE RECRUITER   And kill a calf if it happens to be standing in the way. (*Tries to lead him away*)

MOTHER COURAGE   Leave him alone. He's not for you.

THE RECRUITER   He insulted me. He referred to my face as a kisser. Him and me will now step out in the field and discuss this thing as man to man.

EILIF   Don't worry, mother. I'll take care of him.

MOTHER COURAGE   You stay put. You no-good! I know you, always fighting. He's got a knife in his boot, he's a knifer.

THE RECRUITER   I'll pull it out of him like a milk tooth. Come on, boy.

MOTHER COURAGE   Sergeant, I'll report you to the colonel. He'll throw you in the lock-up. The lieutenant is courting my daughter.

THE SERGEANT   No rough stuff, brother. (*To Mother Courage*) What have you got against the army? Wasn't his father a soldier? Didn't he die fair and square? You said so yourself.

MOTHER COURAGE   He's only a child. You want to lead him off

to slaughter, I know you. You'll get five guilders for him.

THE RECRUITER   He'll get a beautiful cap and top boots.

EILIF   Not from you.

MOTHER COURAGE   Oh, won't you come fishing with me? said
the fisherman to the worm. (*To Swiss Cheese*) Run and yell that
they're trying to steal your brother. (*She pulls a knife*) Just try
and steal him. I'll cut you down, you dogs. I'll teach you to
put him in your war! We do an honest business in ham and
shirts, we're peaceful folk.

THE SERGEANT   I can see by the knife how peaceful you are. You
ought to be ashamed of yourself, put that knife away, you
bitch. A minute ago you admitted you lived off war, how else
would you live, on what? How can you have a war without
soldiers?

MOTHER COURAGE   It doesn't have to be my children.

THE SERGEANT   I see. You'd like the war to eat the core and spit
out the apple. You want your brood to batten on war, tax-
free. The war can look out for itself, is that it? You call
yourself Courage, eh? And you're afraid of the war that feeds
you. Your sons aren't afraid of it, I can see that.

EILIF   I'm not afraid of any war.

THE SERGEANT   Why should you be? Look at me: Has the soldier's life disagreed with me? I was seventeen when I joined
up.

MOTHER COURAGE   You're not seventy yet.

THE SERGEANT   I can wait.

MOTHER COURAGE   Sure. Under ground.

THE SERGEANT   Are you trying to insult me? Telling me I'm
going to die?

MOTHER COURAGE   But suppose it's the truth? I can see the mark
on you. You look like a corpse on leave.

SWISS CHEESE   She's got second sight. Everybody says so. She
can tell the future.

THE RECRUITER   Then tell the sergeant his future. It might
amuse him.

THE SERGEANT   I don't believe in that stuff.

MOTHER COURAGE   Give me your helmet. (*He gives it to her*)

THE SERGEANT   It doesn't mean any more than taking a shit in
the grass. But go ahead for the laugh.

MOTHER COURAGE (*takes a sheet of parchment and tears it in two*)
Eilif, Swiss Cheese, Kattrin: That's how we'd all be torn apart
if we got mixed up too deep in the war. (*To the sergeant*) Seeing
it's you, I'll do it for nothing. I make a black cross on this
piece. Black is death.

SWISS CHEESE   She leaves the other one blank. Get it?

MOTHER COURAGE   Now I fold them, and now I shake them up
together. Same as we're all mixed up together from the cradle
to the grave. And now you draw, and you'll know the answer.
(*The sergeant hesitates*)

THE RECRUITER (*to Eilif*)   I don't take everybody, I'm known to
be picky and choosy, but you've got spirit, I like that.

THE SERGEANT (*fishing in the helmet*)   Damn foolishness! Hocus-
pocus!

SWISS CHEESE   He's pulled a black cross. He's through.

THE RECRUITER   Don't let them scare you, there's not enough
bullets for everybody.

THE SERGEANT (*hoarsely*)   You've fouled me up.

MOTHER COURAGE   You fouled yourself up the day you joined
the army. And now we'll be going, there isn't a war every day,
I've got to take advantage.

THE SERGEANT   Hell and damnation! Don't try to hornswoggle
me. We're taking your bastard to be a soldier.

EILIF   I'd like to be a soldier, mother.

MOTHER COURAGE   You shut your trap, you Finnish devil.

EILIF   Swiss Cheese wants to be a soldier too.

MOTHER COURAGE   That's news to me. I'd better let you draw
too, all three of you. (*She goes to the rear to mark crosses on slips
of parchment*)

THE RECRUITER (*to Eilif*)   It's been said to our discredit that a lot
of religion goes on in the Swedish camp, but that's slander to
blacken our reputation. Hymn singing only on Sunday, one
verse! And only if you've got a voice.

MOTHER COURAGE (*comes back with the slips in the sergeant's helmet*)
Want to sneak away from their mother, the devils, and run
off to war like calves to a salt lick. But we'll draw lots on it,
then they'll see that the world is no vale of smiles with a
"Come along, son, we're short on generals." Sergeant, I'm
very much afraid they won't come through the war. They've

got terrible characters, all three of them. (*She holds out the helmet to Eilif*) There. Pick a slip. (*He picks one and unfolds it. She snatches it away from him*) There you have it. A cross! Oh, unhappy mother that I am, oh, mother of sorrows. Has he got to die? Doomed to perish in the springtime of his life? If he joins the army, he'll bite the dust, that's sure. He's too brave, just like his father. If he's not smart, he'll go the way of all flesh, the slip proves it. (*She roars at him*) Are you going to be smart?

EILIF   Why not?

MOTHER COURAGE   The smart thing to do is to stay with your mother, and if they make fun of you and call you a sissy, just laugh.

THE RECRUITER   If you're shitting in your pants, we'll take your brother.

MOTHER COURAGE   I told you to laugh. Laugh! And now you pick, Swiss Cheese. I'm not so worried about you, you're honest. (*He picks a slip*) Oh! Why, have you got that strange look? It's got to be blank. There can't be a cross on it. No, I can't lose you. (*She takes the slip*) A cross? Him too? Maybe it's because he's so stupid. Oh, Swiss Cheese, you'll die too, unless you're very honest the whole time, the way I've taught you since you were a baby, always bringing back the change when I sent you to buy bread. That's the only way you can save yourself. Look, sergeant, isn't that a black cross?

THE SERGEANT   It's a cross all right. I don't see how I could have pulled one. I always stay in the rear. (*To the recruiter*) It's on the up and up. Her own get it too.

SWISS CHEESE   I get it too. But I can take a hint.

MOTHER COURAGE (*to Kattrin*)   Now you're the only one I'm sure of, you're a cross yourself because you've got a good heart. (*She holds up the helmet to Kattrin in the wagon, but she herself takes out the slip*) It's driving me to despair. It can't be right, maybe I mixed them wrong. Don't be too good-natured, Kattrin, don't, there's a cross on your path too. Always keep very quiet, that ought to be easy seeing you're dumb. Well, now you know. Be careful, all of you, you'll need to be. And now we'll climb up and drive on. (*She returns the sergeant's helmet and climbs up into the wagon*)

THE RECRUITER (*to the sergeant*) Do something!

THER SERGEANT I'm not feeling so good.

THE RECRUITER Maybe you caught cold when you took your helmet off in the wind. Tell her you want to buy something. Keep her busy. (*Aloud*) You could at least take a look at that buckle, sergeant. After all, selling things is these good people's living. Hey, you, the sergeant wants to buy that belt buckle.

MOTHER COURAGE Half a guilder. A buckle like that is worth two guilders. (*She climbs down*)

THE SERGEANT It's not new. This wind! I can't examine it here. Let's go where it's quiet. (*He goes behind the wagon with the buckle*)

MOTHER COURAGE I haven't noticed any wind.

THE SERGEANT Maybe it is worth half a guilder. It's silver.

MOTHER COURAGE (*joins him behind the wagon*) Six solid ounces.

THE RECRUITER (*to Eilif*) And then we'll have a drink, just you and me. I've got your enlistment bonus right here. Come on. (*Eilif stands undecided*)

MOTHER COURAGE All right. Half a guilder.

THE SERGEANT I don't get it. I always stay in the rear. There's no safer place for a sergeant. You can send the men up forward to win glory. You've spoiled my dinner. It won't go down, I know it, not a bite.

MOTHER COURAGE Don't take it to heart. Don't let it spoil your appetite. Just keep behind the lines. Here, take a drink of schnapps, man. (*She hands him the bottle*)

THE RECRUITER (*has taken Eilif's arm and is pulling him away toward the rear*) A bonus of ten guilders, and you'll be a brave man and you'll fight for the king, and the women will tear each other's hair out over you. And you can clout me one on the kisser for insulting you. (*Both go out*)

(*Mute Kattrin jumps down from the wagon and emits raucous sounds*)

MOTHER COURAGE Just a minute, Kattrin, just a minute. The sergeant's paying up. (*Bites the half guilder*) I'm always suspicious of money. I'm a burnt child, sergeant. But your coin is good. And now we'll be going. Where's Eilif?

SWISS CHEESE He's gone with the recruiter.

MOTHER COURAGE (*stands motionless, then*)   You simple soul. (*To Kattrin*) I know. You can't talk, you couldn't help it.

THE SERGEANT   You could do with a drink yourself, mother. That's the way it goes. Soldiering isn't the worst thing in the world. You want to live off the war, but you want to keep you and yours out of it. Is that it?

MOTHER COURAGE   Now you'll have to pull with your brother, Kattrin.

(*Brother and sister harness themselves to the wagon and start pulling. Mother Courage walks beside them. The wagon rolls off*)

THE SERGEANT (*looking after them*)

If you want the war to work for you
You've got to give the war its due.

2

In 1625 and 1626 Mother Courage crosses Poland in the train of the Swedish armies. Outside the fortress of Wallhof she meets her son again.—A capon is successfully sold, the brave son's fortunes are at their zenith.

The general's tent.

Beside it the kitchen. The thunder of cannon. The cook is arguing with Mother Courage, who is trying to sell him a capon.

THE COOK   Sixty hellers for that pathetic bird?

MOTHER COURAGE   Pathetic bird? You mean this plump beauty? Are you trying to tell me that a general who's the biggest eater for miles around—God help you if you haven't got anything for his dinner—can't afford a measly sixty hellers?

THE COOK   I can get a dozen like it for ten hellers right around the corner.

MOTHER COURAGE   What, you'll find a capon like this right around the corner? With a siege on and everybody so starved you can see right through them. Maybe you'll scare up a rat, maybe, I say, 'cause they've all been eaten, I've seen five men chasing a starved rat for hours. Fifty hellers for a giant capon in the middle of a siege.

THE COOK   We're not besieged; they are. We're the besiegers, can't you get that through your head?

MOTHER COURAGE   But we haven't got anything to eat either, in fact we've got less than the people in the city. They've hauled it all inside. I hear their life is one big orgy. And look at us. I've been around to the peasants, they haven't got a thing.

THE COOK   They've got plenty. They hide it.

MOTHER COURAGE (triumphantly)   Oh, no! They're ruined, that's what they are. They're starving. I've seen them. They're so hungry they're digging up roots. They lick their fingers when they've eaten a boiled strap. That's the situation. And here I've got a capon and I'm supposed to let it go for forty hellers.

THE COOK   Thirty, not forty. Thirty, I said.

MOTHER COURAGE   It's no common capon. They tell me this bird was so talented that he wouldn't eat unless they played music, he had his own favorite march. He could add and subtract, that's how intelligent he was. And you're trying to tell me forty hellers is too much. The general will bite your head off if there's nothing to eat.

THE COOK   You know what I'm going to do? (He takes a piece of beef and sets his knife to it) Here I've got a piece of beef. I'll roast it. Think it over. This is your last chance.

MOTHER COURAGE   Roast and be damned. It's a year old.

THE COOK   A day old. That ox was running around only yesterday afternoon, I saw him with my own eyes.

MOTHER COURAGE   Then he must have stunk on the hoof.

THE COOK   I'll cook it five hours if I have to. We'll see if it's still tough. (He cuts into it)

MOTHER COURAGE   Use plenty of pepper, maybe the general won't notice the stink.

(The general, a chaplain and Eilif enter the tent)

THE GENERAL (*slapping Eilif on the back*)   All right, son, into your general's tent you go, you'll sit at my right hand. You've done a heroic deed and you're a pious trooper, because this is a war of religion and what you did was done for God, that's what counts with me. I'll reward you with a gold bracelet when I take the city. We come here to save their souls and what do those filthy, shameless peasants do? They drive their cattle away. And they stuff their priests with meat, front and back. But you taught them a lesson. Here's a tankard of red wine for you. (*He pours*) We'll down it in one gulp. (*They do so*) None for the chaplain, he's got his religion. What would you like for dinner, sweetheart?

EILIF   A scrap of meat. Why not?

THE GENERAL   Cook! Meat!

THE COOK   And now he brings company when there's nothing to eat.

(*Wanting to listen, Mother Courage makes him stop talking*)

EILIF   Cutting down peasants whets the appetite.

MOTHER COURAGE   God, it's my Eilif.

THE COOK   Who?

MOTHER COURAGE   My eldest. I haven't seen hide nor hair of him in two years, he was stolen from me on the highway. He must be in good if the general invites him to dinner, and what have you got to offer? Nothing. Did you hear what the general's guest wants for dinner? Meat! Take my advice, snap up this capon. The price is one guilder.

THE GENERAL (*has sat down with Eilif. Bellows*)   Food, Lamb, you lousy, no-good cook, or I'll kill you.

THE COOK   All right, hand it over. This is extortion.

MOTHER COURAGE   I thought it was a pathetic bird.

THE COOK   Pathetic is the word. Hand it over. Fifty hellers! It's highway robbery.

MOTHER COURAGE   One guilder, I say. For my eldest son, the general's honored guest, I spare no expense.

THE COOK (*gives her the money*)   Then pluck it at least while I make the fire.

MOTHER COURAGE (*sits down to pluck the capon*)   Won't he be glad to see me! He's my brave, intelligent son. I've got a stupid one too, but he's honest. The girl's a total loss. But at least she doesn't talk, that's something.

THE GENERAL   Take another drink, son, it's my best Falerno, I've only got another barrel or two at the most, but it's worth it to see that there's still some true faith in my army. The good shepherd here just looks on, all he knows how to do is preach. Can he do anything? No. And now, Eilif my son, tell us all about it, how cleverly you hoodwinked those peasants and captured those twenty head of cattle. I hope they'll be here soon.

EILIF   Tomorrow. Maybe the day after.

MOTHER COURAGE   Isn't my Eilif considerate, not bringing those oxen in until tomorrow, or you wouldn't have even said hello to my capon.

EILIF   Well, it was like this: I heard the peasants were secretly —mostly at night—rounding up the oxen they'd hidden in a certain forest. The city people had arranged to come and get them. I let them round the oxen up, I figured they'd find them easier than I would. I made my men ravenous for meat, put them on short rations for two days until their mouths watered if they even heard a word beginning with *me* . . . like measles.

THE GENERAL   That was clever of you.

EILIF   Maybe. The rest was a pushover. Except the peasants had clubs and there were three times more of them and they fell on us like bloody murder. Four of them drove me into a clump of bushes, they knocked my sword out of my hand and yelled: Surrender! Now what'll I do, I says to myself, they'll make hash out of me.

THE GENERAL   What did you do?

EILIF   I laughed.

THE GENERAL   You laughed?

EILIF   I laughed. Which led to a conversation. The first thing you know, I'm bargaining. Twenty guilders is too much for that ox, I say, how about fifteen? Like I'm meaning to pay. They're flummoxed, they scratch their heads. Quick, I reach for my sword and mow them down. Necessity knows no law. See what I mean?

THE GENERAL   What do you say to that, shepherd?

CHAPLAIN   Strictly speaking, that maxim is not in the Bible. But our Lord was able to turn five loaves into five hundred. So there was no question of poverty; he could tell people to love

their neighbors because their bellies were full. Nowadays it's different.

THE GENERAL (*laughs*)   Very different. All right, you Pharisee, take a swig. (*To Eilif*) You mowed them down, splendid, so my fine troops could have a decent bite to eat. Doesn't the Good Book say: "Whatsoever thou doest for the least of my brethren, thou doest for me"? And what have you done for them? You've got them a good chunk of beef for their dinner. They're not used to moldy crusts; in the old days they had a helmetful of white bread and wine before they went out to fight for God.

EILIF   Yes, I reached for my sword and I mowed them down.

THE GENERAL   You're a young Caesar. You deserve to see the king.

EILIF   I have, in the distance. He shines like a light. He's my ideal.

THE GENERAL   You're something like him already, Eilif. I know the worth of a brave soldier like you. When I find one, I treat him like my own son. (*He leads him to the map*) Take a look at the situation, Eilif; we've still got a long way to go.

MOTHER COURAGE (*who has been listening starts plucking her capon furiously*)   He must be a rotten general.

THE COOK   Eats like a pig, but why rotten?

MOTHER COURAGE   Because he needs brave soldiers, that's why. If he planned his campaigns right, what would he need brave soldiers for? The run-of-the-mill would do. Take it from me, whenever you find a lot of virtues, it shows that something's wrong.

THE COOK   I'd say it proves that something is all right.

MOTHER COURAGE   No, that something's wrong. See, when a general or a king is real stupid and leads his men up shit creek, his troops need courage, that's a virtue. If he's stingy and doesn't hire enough soldiers, they've all got to be Herculeses. And if he's a slob and lets everything go to pot, they've got to be as sly as serpents or they're done for. And if he's always expecting too much of them, they need an extra dose of loyalty. A country that's run right, or a good king or a good general, doesn't need any of these virtues. You don't need

virtues in a decent country, the people can all be perfectly ordinary, medium-bright, and cowards too for my money.

THE GENERAL   I bet your father was a soldier.

EILIF   A great soldier, I'm told. My mother warned me about it. Makes me think of a song.

THE GENERAL   Sing it! (*Bellowing*) Where's that food!

EILIF   It's called: The Song of the Old Wife and the Soldier. (*He sings, doing a war dance with his saber*)

A gun or a pike, they can kill who they like
And the torrent will swallow a wader
You had better think twice before battling with ice
Said the old wife to the soldier.
Cocking his rifle he leapt to his feet
Laughing for joy as he heard the drum beat
The wars cannot hurt me, he told her.
He shouldered his gun and he picked up his knife
To see the wide world. That's the soldier's life.
Those were the words of the soldier.

Ah, deep will they lie who wise counsel defy
Learn wisdom from those that are older
Oh, don't venture too high or you'll fall from the sky
Said the old wife to the soldier.
But the young soldier with knife and with gun
Only laughed a cold laugh and stepped into the run.
The water can't hurt me, he told her.
And when the moon on the rooftop shines white
We'll be coming back. You can pray for that night.
Those were the words of the soldier.

MOTHER COURAGE (*in the kitchen, continues the song, beating a pot with a spoon*)

Like the smoke you'll be gone and no warmth linger on
And your deeds only leave me the colder!
Oh, see the smoke race. Oh, dear God keep him safe!
That's what she said of the soldier.

EILIF   What's that?

MOTHER COURAGE (*goes on singing*)

And the young soldier with knife and with gun
Was swept from his feet till he sank in the run
And the torrent swallowed the waders.
Cold shone the moon on the rooftop white
But the soldier was carried away with the ice
And what was it she heard from the soldiers?

Like the smoke he was gone and no warmth lingered on
And his deeds only left her the colder.
Ah, deep will they lie who wise counsel defy!
That's what she said to the soldiers.

THE GENERAL   What do they think they're doing in my kitchen?

EILIF (*has gone into the kitchen. He embraces his mother*)   Mother! It's you! Where are the others?

MOTHER COURAGE (*in his arms*)   Snug as a bug in a rug. Swiss Cheese is paymaster of the Second Regiment; at least he won't be fighting, I couldn't keep him out altogether.

EILIE   And how about your feet?

MOTHER COURAGE   Well, it's hard getting my shoes on in the morning.

THE GENERAL (*has joined them*)   Ah, so you're his mother. I hope you've got more sons for me like this fellow here.

EILIF   Am I lucky! There you're sitting in the kitchen hearing your son being praised.

MOTHER COURAGE   I heard it all right! (*She gives him a slap in the face*)

EILIF (*holding his cheek*)   For capturing the oxen?

MOTHER COURAGE   No. For not surrendering when the four of them were threatening to make hash out of you! Didn't I teach you to take care of yourself? You Finnish devil!

(*The general and the chaplain laugh*)

3

Three years later Mother Courage and parts of a Finnish regiment are taken prisoner. She is able to save her daughter and her wagon, but her honest son dies.

Army camp.

Afternoon. On a pole the regimental flag. Mother Courage has stretched a clothesline between her wagon, on which all sorts of merchandise is hung in display, and a large cannon. She and Kattrin are folding washing and piling it on the cannon. At the same time she is negotiating with an ordnance officer over a sack of bullets. Swiss Cheese, now in the uniform of a paymaster, is looking on. A pretty woman, Yvette Pottier, is sitting with a glass of brandy in front of her, sewing a gaudy-colored hat. She is in her stocking feet, her red high-heeled shoes are on the ground beside her.

THE ORDNANCE OFFICER I'll let you have these bullets for two guilders. It's cheap, I need the money, because the colonel's been drinking with the officers for two days and we're out of liquor.

MOTHER COURAGE That's ammunition for the troops. If it's found here, I'll be court-martialed. You punks sell their bullets and the men have nothing to shoot at the enemy.

THE ORDNANCE OFFICER Don't be hard-hearted, you scratch my back, I'll scratch yours.

MOTHER COURAGE I'm not taking any army property. Not at that price.

THE ORDNANCE OFFICER You can sell it for five guilders, maybe eight, to the ordnance officer of the Fourth before the day is out, if you're quiet about it and give him a receipt for twelve. He hasn't an ounce of ammunition left.

MOTHER COURAGE Why don't you do it yourself?

THE ORDNANCE OFFICER   Because I don't trust him, he's a friend of mine.

MOTHER COURAGE (*takes the sack*)   Hand it over. (*To Kattrin*) Take it back there and pay him one and a half guilders. (*In response to the ordnance officer's protest*) One and a half guilders, I say. (*Kattrin drags the sack behind the wagon, the ordnance officer follows her. Mother Courage to Swiss Cheese*) Here's your underdrawers, take good care of them, this is October, might be coming on fall, I don't say it will be, because I've learned that nothing is sure to happen the way we think, not even the seasons. But whatever happens, your regimental funds have to be in order. Are your funds in order?

SWISS CHEESE   Yes, mother.

MOTHER COURAGE   Never forget that they made you paymaster because you're honest and not brave like your brother, and especially because you're too simple-minded to get the idea of making off with the money. That's a comfort to me. And don't go mislaying your drawers.

SWISS CHEESE   No, mother. I'll put them under my mattress. (*Starts to go*)

ORDNANCE OFFICER   I'll go with you, paymaster.

MOTHER COURAGE   Just don't teach him any of your tricks. (*Without saying good-bye the ordnance officer goes out with Swiss Cheese*)

YVETTE (*waves her hand after the ordnance officer*)   You might say good-bye, officer.

MOTHER COURAGE (*to Yvette*)   I don't like to see those two together. He's not the right kind of company for my Swiss Cheese. But the war's getting along pretty well. More countries are joining in all the time, it can go on for another four, five years, easy. With a little planning ahead, I can do good business if I'm careful. Don't you know you shouldn't drink in the morning with your sickness?

YVETTE   Who says I'm sick, it's slander.

MOTHER COURAGE   Everybody says so.

YVETTE   Because they're all liars. Mother Courage, I'm desperate. They all keep out of my way like I'm a rotten fish on account of those lies. What's the good of fixing my hat? (*She throws it down*) That's why I drink in the morning, I never used to, I'm getting crow's-feet, but it doesn't matter now. In

the Second Finnish Regiment they all know me. I should have stayed home when my first love walked out on me. Pride isn't for the likes of us. If we can't put up with shit, we're through.

MOTHER COURAGE Just don't start in on your Pieter and how it all happened in front of my innocent daughter.

YVETTE She's just the one to hear it, it'll harden her against love.

MOTHER COURAGE Nothing can harden them.

YVETTE Then I'll talk about it because it makes me feel better. It begins with my growing up in fair Flanders, because if I hadn't I'd never have laid eyes on him and I wouldn't be here in Poland now, because he was an army cook, blond, a Dutchman, but skinny. Kattrin, watch out for the skinny ones, but I didn't know that then, and another thing I didn't know is that he had another girl even then, and they all called him Pete the Pipe, because he didn't even take his pipe out of his mouth when he was doing it, that's all it meant to him. (*She sings the Song of Fraternization*)

When I was only sixteen
The foe came into our land.
He laid aside his sabre
And with a smile he took my hand.
   After the May parade
   The May light starts to fade.
   The regiment dressed by the right
   Then drums were beaten, that's the drill.
   The foe took us behind the hill
   And fraternized all night.

There were so many foes came
And mine worked in the mess.
I loathed him in the daytime.
At night I loved him none the less.
   After the May parade
   The May light starts to fade.
   The regiment dressed by the right
   Then drums were beaten, that's the drill.
   The foe took us behind the hill
   And fraternized all night.

The love which came upon me
Was wished on me by fate.
My friends could never grasp why
I found it hard to share their hate.
   The fields were wet with dew
   When sorrow first I knew.
   The regiment dressed by the right
   Then drums were beaten, that's the drill
   And then the foe, my lover still
   Went marching from our sight.

Well, I followed him, but I never found him. That was five years ago. (*She goes behind the wagon with an unsteady gait*)

MOTHER COURAGE   You've left your hat.

YVETTE   Anybody that wants it can have it.

MOTHER COURAGE   Let that be a lesson to you, Kattrin. Have no truck with soldiers. It's love that makes the world go round, so you'd better watch out. Even with a civilian it's no picnic. He says he'd kiss the ground you put your little feet on, talking of feet, did you wash yours yesterday, and then you're his slave. Be glad you're dumb, that way you'll never contradict yourself or want to bite your tongue off because you've told the truth, it's a gift of God to be dumb. Here comes the general's cook, I wonder what he wants.

(*The cook and the chaplain enter*)

THE CHAPLAIN   I've got a message for you from your son Eilif. The cook here thought he'd come along, he's taken a shine to you.

THE COOK   I only came to get a breath of air.

MOTHER COURAGE   You can always do that here if you behave, and if you don't, I can handle you. Well, what does he want? I've got no money to spare.

THE CHAPLAIN   Actually he wanted me to see his brother, the paymaster.

MOTHER COURAGE   He's not here any more, or anywhere else either. He's not his brother's paymaster. I don't want him leading him into temptation and being smart at his expense. (*Gives him money from the bag slung around her waist*) Give him

this, it's a sin, he's speculating on mother love and he ought to be ashamed.

THE COOK   He won't do it much longer, then he'll be marching off with his regiment, maybe to his death, you never can tell. Better make it a little more, you'll be sorry later. You women are hard-hearted, but afterwards you're sorry. A drop of brandy wouldn't have cost much when it was wanted, but it wasn't given, and later, for all you know, he'll be lying in the cold ground and you can't dig him up again.

THE CHAPLAIN   Don't be sentimental, cook. There's nothing wrong with dying in battle, it's a blessing, and I'll tell you why. This is a war of religion. Not a common war, but a war for the faith, and therefore pleasing to God.

THE COOK   That's a fact. In a way you could call it a war, because of the extortion and killing and looting, not to mention a bit of rape, but it's a war of religion, which makes it different from all other wars, that's obvious. But it makes a man thirsty all the same, you've got to admit that.

THE CHAPLAIN (to Mother Courage, pointing at the cook)   I tried to discourage him, but he says you've turned his head, he sees you in his dreams.

THE COOK (lights a short-stemmed pipe)   All I want is a glass of brandy from your fair hand, nothing more sinful. I'm already so shocked by the jokes the chaplain's been telling me, I bet I'm still red in the face.

MOTHER COURAGE   And him a clergyman! I'd better give you fellows something to drink or you'll be making me immoral propositions just to pass the time.

THE CHAPLAIN   This is temptation, said the deacon, and suc- cumbed to it. (Turning toward Kattrin as he leaves) And who is this delightful young lady?

MOTHER COURAGE   She's not delightful, she's a respectable young lady.

(The chaplain and the cook go behind the wagon with Mother Cour- age. Kattrin looks after them, then she walks away from the washing and approaches the hat. She picks it up, sits down and puts on the red shoes. From the rear Mother Courage is heard talking politics with the chaplain and the cook)

MOTHER COURAGE   The Poles here in Poland shouldn't have

butted in. All right, our king marched his army into their country. But instead of keeping the peace, the Poles start butting into their own affairs and attack the king while he's marching quietly through the landscape. That was a breach of the peace and the blood is on their head.

THE CHAPLAIN   Our king had only one thing in mind: freedom. The emperor had everybody under his yoke, the Poles as much as the Germans; the king had to set them free.

THE COOK   I see it this way, your brandy's first-rate, I can see why I liked your face, but we were talking about the king. This freedom he was trying to introduce into Germany cost him a fortune, he had to levy a salt tax in Sweden, which, as I said, cost the poor people a fortune. Then he had to put the Germans in jail and break them on the rack because they liked being the emperor's slaves. Oh yes, the king made short shrift of anybody that didn't want to be free. In the beginning he only wanted to protect Poland against wicked people, especially the emperor, but the more he ate the more he wanted, and pretty soon he was protecting all of Germany. But the Germans didn't take it lying down and the king got nothing but trouble for all his kindness and expense, which he naturally had to defray from taxes, which made for bad blood, but that didn't discourage him. He had one thing in his favor, the word of God, which was lucky, because otherwise people would have said he was doing it all for himself and what he hoped to get out of it. As it was, he always had a clear conscience and that was all he really cared about.

MOTHER COURAGE   It's easy to see you're not a Swede, or you wouldn't talk like that about the Hero-King.

THE CHAPLAIN   You're eating his bread, aren't you?

THE COOK   I don't eat his bread, I bake it.

MOTHER COURAGE   He can't be defeated because his men believe in him. (Earnestly) When you listen to the big wheels talk, they're making war for reasons of piety, in the name of everything that's fine and noble. But when you take another look, you see that they're not so dumb; they're making war for profit. If they weren't, the small fry like me wouldn't have anything to do with it.

THE COOK   That's a fact.

THE CHAPLAIN   And it wouldn't hurt you as a Dutchman to take a look at that flag up there before you express opinions in Poland.

MOTHER COURAGE   We're all good Protestants here! Prosit!
(*Kattrin has started strutting about with Yvette's hat on, imitating Yvette's gait.*)

(*Suddenly cannon fire and shots are heard. Drums. Mother Courage, the cook and the chaplain run out from behind the wagon, the two men still with glasses in hand. The ordnance officer and a soldier rush up to the cannon and try to push it away*)

MOTHER COURAGE   What's going on? Let me get my washing first, you lugs. (*She tries to rescue her washing*)

THE ORDNANCE OFFICER   The Catholics. They're attacking. I don't know as we'll get away. (*To the soldier*) Get rid of the gun! (*Runs off*)

THE COOK   Christ, I've got to find the general. Courage, I'll be back for a little chat in a day or two. (*Rushes out*)

MOTHER COURAGE   Stop, you've forgotten your pipe.

THE COOK (*from the distance*)   Keep it for me! I'll need it.

MOTHER COURAGE   Just when we were making a little money!

THE CHAPLAIN   Well, I guess I'll be going too. It might be dangerous though, with the enemy so close. Blessed are the peaceful is the best motto in wartime. If only I had a cloak to cover up with.

MOTHER COURAGE   I'm not lending any cloaks, not on your life. I've had bitter experience in that line.

THE CHAPLAIN   But my religion puts me in special danger.

MOTHER COURAGE (*bringing him a cloak*)   It's against my better conscience. And now run along.

THE CHAPLAIN   Thank you kindly, you've got a good heart. But maybe I'd better sit here a while. The enemy might get suspicious if they see me running.

MOTHER COURAGE (*to the soldier*)   Leave it lay, you fool, you won't get paid extra. I'll take care of it for you, you'd only get killed.

THE SOLDIER (*running away*)   I tried. You're my witness.

MOTHER COURAGE   I'll swear it on the Bible. (*Sees her daughter*

with the hat) What are you doing with that floozy hat? Take it off, have you gone out of your mind? Now of all times, with the enemy on top of us? *(She tears the hat off Kattrin's head)* You want them to find you and make a whore out of you? And those shoes! Take them off, you woman of Babylon! *(She tries to pull them off)* Jesus Christ, chaplain, make her take those shoes off! I'll be right back. *(She runs to the wagon)*

YVETTE *(enters, powdering her face)*   What's this I hear? The Catholics are coming? Where's my hat? Who's been stamping on it? I can't be seen like this if the Catholics are coming. What'll they think of me? I haven't even got a mirror. *(To the chaplain)* How do I look? Too much powder?

THE CHAPLAIN   Just right.

YVETTE   And where are my red shoes? *(She doesn't see them because Kattrin hides her feet under her skirt)* I left them here. I've got to get back to my tent. In my bare feet. It's disgraceful! *(Goes out)*

(Swiss Cheese runs in carrying a small box)

MOTHER COURAGE *(Comes out with her hands full of ashes. To Kattrin)*   Ashes. *(To Swiss Cheese)* What you got there?

SWISS CHEESE   The regimental funds.

MOTHER COURAGE   Throw it away! No more paymastering for you.

SWISS CHEESE   I'm responsible for it. *(He goes rear)*

MOTHER COURAGE *(to the chaplain)*   Take your clergyman's coat off, chaplain, or they'll recognize you, cloak or no cloak. *(She rubs Kattrin's face with ashes)* Hold still! There. With a little dirt you'll be safe. What a mess! The sentries were drunk. Hide your light under a bushel, as the Good Book says. When a soldier, especially a Catholic, sees a clean face, she's a whore before she knows it. Nobody feeds them for weeks. When they finally loot some provisions, the next thing they want is women. That'll do it. Let me look at you. Not bad. Like you'd been wallowing in a pigsty. Stop shaking. You're safe now. *(To Swiss Cheese)* What did you do with the cashbox?

SWISS CHEESE   I thought I'd put it in the wagon.

MOTHER COURAGE *(horrified)*   What! In my wagon? Of all the sinful stupidity! If my back is turned for half a second! They'll hang us all!

SWISS CHEESE   Then I'll put it somewhere else, or I'll run away with it.

MOTHER COURAGE   You'll stay right here. It's too late.

THE CHAPLAIN (*still changing, comes forward*)   Heavens, the flag!

MOTHER COURAGE (*takes down the regimental flag*)   Bozhe moi! I'm so used to it I don't see it. Twenty-five years I've had it. (*The cannon fire grows louder*)

(*Morning, three days later. The cannon is gone. Mother Courage, Kattrin, the chaplain and Swiss Cheese are sitting dejectedly over a meal*)

SWISS CHEESE   This is the third day I've been sitting here doing nothing; the sergeant has always been easy on me, but now he must be starting to wonder: where can Swiss Cheese be with the cashbox?

MOTHER COURAGE   Be glad they haven't tracked you down.

THE CHAPLAIN   What about me? I can't hold a service here either. The Good Book says: "Whosoever hath a full heart, his tongue runneth over." Heaven help me if mine runneth over.

MOTHER COURAGE   That's the way it is. Look what I've got on my hands: one with a religion and one with a cashbox. I don't know which is worse.

THE CHAPLAIN   Tell yourself that we're in the hands of God.

MOTHER COURAGE   I don't think we're that bad off, but all the same I can't sleep at night. If it weren't for you, Swiss Cheese, it'd be easier. I think I've put myself in the clear. I told them I was against the antichrist; he's a Swede with horns, I told them, and I'd noticed the left horn was kind of worn down. I interrupted the questioning to ask where I could buy holy candles cheap. I knew what to say because Swiss Cheese's father was a Catholic and he used to make jokes about it. They didn't really believe me, but their regiment had no provisioner, so they looked the other way. Maybe we stand to gain. We're prisoners, but so are lice on a dog.

THE CHAPLAIN   This milk is good. Though there's not very much of it or of anything else. Maybe we'll have to cut down on our Swedish appetites. But such is the lot of the vanquished.

MOTHER COURAGE   Who's vanquished? Victory and defeat don't always mean the same thing to the big wheels up top and the small fry underneath. Not by a long shot. In some cases defeat is a blessing to the small fry. Honor's lost, but nothing else. One time in Livonia our general got such a shellacking from the enemy that in the confusion I laid hands on a beautiful white horse from the baggage train. That horse pulled my wagon for seven months, until we had a victory and they checked up. On the whole, you can say that victory and defeat cost us plain people plenty. The best thing for us is when politics gets bogged down. (*To Swiss Cheese*) Eat!

SWISS CHEESE   I've lost my appetite. How's the sergeant going to pay the men?

MOTHER COURAGE   Troops never get paid when they're running away.

SWISS CHEESE   But they've got it coming to them. If they're not paid, they don't need to run. Not a step.

MOTHER COURAGE   Swiss Cheese, you're too conscientious, it almost frightens me. I brought you up to be honest, because you're not bright, but somewhere it's got to stop. And now me and the chaplain are going to buy a Catholic flag and some meat. Nobody can buy meat like the chaplain, he goes into a trance and heads straight for the best piece, I guess it makes his mouth water and that shows him the way. At least they let me carry on my business. Nobody cares about a shop-keeper's religion, all they want to know is the price. Protestant pants are as warm as any other kind.

THE CHAPLAIN   Like the friar said when somebody told him the Lutherans were going to stand the whole country on its head. They'll always need beggars, he says. (*Mother Courage disappears into the wagon*) But she's worried about that cashbox. They've taken no notice of us so far, they think we're all part of the wagon, but how long can that go on?

SWISS CHEESE   I can take it away.

THE CHAPLAIN   That would be almost more dangerous. What if somebody sees you? They've got spies. Yesterday morning, just as I'm relieving myself, one of them jumps out of the ditch. I was so scared I almost let out a prayer. That would have given me away. I suppose they think they can tell a

Protestant by the smell of his shit. He was a little runt with a patch over one eye.

MOTHER COURAGE (*climbing down from the wagon with a basket*) Look what I've found. You shameless slut! (*She holds up the red shoes triumphantly*) Yvette's red shoes! She's swiped them in cold blood. It's your fault. Who told her she was a delightful young lady? (*She puts them into the basket*) I'm giving them back. Stealing Yvette's shoes! She ruins herself for money, that I can understand. But you'd like to do it free of charge, for pleasure. I've told you, you'll have to wait for peace. No soldiers! Just wait for peace with your worldly ways.

THE CHAPLAIN   She doesn't seem very worldly to me.

MOTHER COURAGE   Too worldly for me. In Dalarna she was like a stone, which is all they've got around there. The people used to say: We don't see the cripple. That's the way I like it. That way she's safe. (*To Swiss Cheese*) You leave that box where it is, hear? And keep an eye on your sister, she needs it. The two of you will be the death of me. I'd sooner take care of a bag of fleas. (*She goes off with the chaplain. Kattrin starts clearing away the dishes*)

SWISS CHEESE   Won't be many more days when I can sit in the sun in my shirtsleeves. (*Kattrin points to a tree*) Yes, the leaves are all yellow. (*Kattrin asks him, by means of gestures, whether he wants a drink*) Not now. I'm thinking. (*Pause*) She says she can't sleep. I'd better get the cashbox out of here, I've found a hiding place. All right, get me a drink. (*Kattrin goes behind the wagon*) I'll hide it in the rabbit hole down by the river until I can take it away. Maybe late tonight. I'll go get it and take it to the regiment. I wonder how far they've run in three days? Won't the sergeant be surprised! Well, Swiss Cheese, this is a pleasant disappointment, that's what he'll say. I trust you with the regimental cashbox and you bring it back.

(*As Kattrin comes out from behind the wagon with a glass of brandy, she comes face to face with two men. One is a sergeant. The other removes his hat and swings it through the air in a ceremonious greeting. He has a patch over one eye*)

THE MAN WITH THE PATCH   Good morning, my dear. Have you by any chance seen a man from the headquarters of the Second Finnish Regiment?

(*Scared out of her wits, Kattrin runs front, spilling the brandy. The two exchange looks and withdraw after seeing Swiss Cheese sitting there*)

SWISS CHEESE (*starting up from his thoughts*)   You've spilled half of it. What's the fuss about? Poke yourself in the eye? I don't understand you. I'm getting out of here, I've made up my mind, it's best. (*He stands up. She does everything she can think of to call his attention to the danger. He only evades her*) I wish I could understand you. Poor thing, I know you're trying to tell me something, you just can't say it. Don't worry about spilling the brandy, I'll be drinking plenty more. What's one glass? (*He takes the cashbox out of the wagon and hides it under his jacket*) I'll be right back. Let me go, you're making me angry. I know you mean well. If only you could talk.

(*When she tries to hold him back, he kisses her and tears himself away. He goes out. She is desperate, she races back and forth, uttering short inarticulate sounds. The chaplain and Mother Courage come back. Kattrin gesticulates wildly at her mother*)

MOTHER COURAGE   What's the matter? You're all upset. Has somebody hurt you? Where's Swiss Cheese? Tell it to me in order, Kattrin. Your mother understands you. What, the no-good's taken the cashbox? I'll hit him over the head with it, the sneak. Take your time, don't talk nonsense, use your hands, I don't like it when you howl like a dog, what will the chaplain think? It gives him the creeps. A one-eyed man?

THE CHAPLAIN   The one-eyed man is a spy. Did they arrest Swiss Cheese? (*Kattrin shakes her head and shrugs her shoulders*) We're done for.

MOTHER COURAGE (*takes a Catholic flag out of her basket. The chaplain fastens it to the flagpole*)   Hoist the new flag!

THE CHAPLAIN (*bitterly*)   All good Catholics here.

(*Voices are heard from the rear. The two men bring in Swiss Cheese*)

SWISS CHEESE   Let me go, I haven't got anything. Stop twisting my shoulder, I'm innocent.

THE SERGEANT   He belongs here. You know each other.

MOTHER COURAGE   What makes you think that?

SWISS CHEESE   I don't know them. I don't even know who they are. I had a meal here, it cost me ten hellers. Maybe you saw me sitting here, it was too salty.

THE SERGEANT   Who are you anyway?

MOTHER COURAGE   We're respectable people. And it's true. He had a meal here. He said it was too salty.

THE SERGEANT   Are you trying to tell me you don't know each other?

MOTHER COURAGE   Why should I know him? I don't know everybody. I don't ask people what their name is or if they're heathens; if they pay, they're not heathens. Are you a heathen?

SWISS CHEESE   Of course not.

THE CHAPLAIN   He ate his meal and he behaved himself. He didn't open his mouth except when he was eating. Then you have to.

THE SERGEANT   And who are you?

MOTHER COURAGE   He's only my bartender. You gentlemen must be thirsty, I'll get you a drink of brandy, you must be hot and tired.

THE SERGEANT   We don't drink on duty. (*To Swiss Cheese*) You were carrying something. You must have hidden it by the river. You had something under your jacket when you left here.

MOTHER COURAGE   Was it really him?

SWISS CHEESE   I think you must have seen somebody else. I saw a man running with something under his jacket. You've got the wrong man.

MOTHER COURAGE   That's what I think too, it's a misunderstanding. These things happen. I'm a good judge of people, I'm Mother Courage, you've heard of me, everybody knows me. Take it from me, this man has an honest face.

THE SERGEANT   We're looking for the cashbox of the Second Finnish Regiment. We know what the man in charge of it looks like. We've been after him for two days. You're him.

SWISS CHEESE   I'm not.

THE SERGEANT   Hand it over. If you don't you're a goner, you know that. Where is it?

MOTHER COURAGE (*with urgency*)   He'd hand it over, wouldn't he, knowing he was a goner if he didn't? I've got it, he'd say, take it, you're stronger. He's not that stupid. Speak up, you stupid idiot, the sergeant's giving you a chance.

SWISS CHEESE   But I haven't got it.

THE SERGEANT   In that case come along. We'll get it out of you.
(*They lead him away*)

MOTHER COURAGE (*shouts after them*)   He'd tell you. He's not that
stupid. And don't twist his shoulder off! (*Runs after them*)

(*The same evening. The chaplain and mute Kattrin are washing
dishes and scouring knives*)

THE CHAPLAIN   That boy's in trouble. There are cases like that
in the Bible. Take the Passion of our Lord and Saviour.
There's an old song about it. (*He sings the Song of the Hours*)

In the first hour Jesus mild
Who had prayed since even
Was betrayed and led before
Pontius the heathen.

Pilate found him innocent
Free from fault and error.
Therefore, having washed his hands
Sent him to King Herod.

In the third hour he was scourged
Stripped and clad in scarlet
And a plaited crown of thorns
Set upon his forehead.

On the Son of Man they spat
Mocked him and made merry.
Then the cross of death was brought
Given him to carry.

At the sixth hour with two thieves
To the cross they nailed him
And the people and the thieves
Mocked him and reviled him.

This is Jesus King of Jews
Cried they in derision
Till the sun withdrew its light
From that awful vision.

At the ninth hour Jesus wailed
Why hast thou me forsaken?
Soldiers brought him vinegar
Which he left untaken.

Then he yielded up the ghost
And the earth was shaken.
Rended was the temple's veil
And the saints were wakened.

Soldiers broke the two thieves' legs
As the night descended
Thrust a spear in Jesus' side
When his life had ended.

Still they mocked, as from his wound
Flowed the blood and water
Thus blasphemed the Son of Man
With their cruel laughter.

MOTHER COURAGE (*enters in a state of agitation*)   His life's at stake.
But they say the sergeant will listen to reason. Only it mustn't
come out that he's our Swiss Cheese, or they'll say we've been
giving him aid and comfort. All they want is money. But
where will we get the money? Hasn't Yvette been here? I met
her just now, she's latched onto a colonel, he's thinking of
buying her a provisioner's business.

THE CHAPLAIN   Are you really thinking of selling?

MOTHER COURAGE   How else can I get the money for the sergeant?

THE CHAPLAIN   But what will you live on?

MOTHER COURAGE   That's the hitch.

(*Yvette Pottier comes in with a doddering colonel*)

YVETTE (*embracing Mother Courage*)   My dear Mother Courage.
Here we are again! (*Whispering*) He's willing. (*Aloud*) This is
my dear friend who advises me on business matters. I just
chanced to hear that you wish to sell your wagon, due to
circumstances. I might be interested.

MOTHER COURAGE   Mortgage it, not sell it, let's not be hasty. It's
not so easy to buy a wagon like this in wartime.

YVETTE (*disappointed*)   Only mortgage it? I thought you wanted

to sell it. In that case, I don't know if I'm interested. (*To the colonel*) What do you think?

THE COLONEL   Just as you say, my dear.

MOTHER COURAGE   It's only being mortgaged.

YVETTE   I thought you needed money.

MOTHER COURAGE (*firmly*)   I need the money, but I'd rather run myself ragged looking for an offer than sell now. The wagon is our livelihood. It's an opportunity for you, Yvette, God knows when you'll find another like it and have such a good friend to advise you. See what I mean?

YVETTE   My friend thinks I should snap it up, but I don't know. If it's only being mortgaged . . . Don't you agree that we ought to buy?

THE COLONEL   Yes, my dear.

MOTHER COURAGE   Then you'll have to look for something that's for sale, maybe you'll find something if you take your time and your friend goes around with you. Maybe in a week or two you'll find the right thing.

YVETTE   Then we'll go looking, I love to go looking for things, and I love to go around with you, Poldi, it's a real pleasure. Even if it takes two weeks. When would you pay the money back if you get it?

MOTHER COURAGE   I can pay it back in two weeks, maybe one.

YVETTE   I can't make up my mind, Poldi, chéri, tell me what to do. (*She takes the colonel aside*) I know she's got to sell, that's definite. The lieutenant, you know who I mean, the blond one, he'd be glad to lend me the money. He's mad about me, he says I remind him of somebody. What do you think?

THE COLONEL   Keep away from that lieutenant. He's no good. He'll take advantage. Haven't I told you I'd buy you something, pussykins?

YVETTE   I can't accept it from you. But then if you think the lieutenant might take advantage . . . Poldi, I'll accept it from you.

THE COLONEL   I hope so.

YVETTE   Your advice is to take it?

THE COLONEL   That's my advice.

YVETTE (*goes back to Mother Courage*)   My friend advises me to do

it. Write me out a receipt, say the wagon belongs to me complete with stock and furnishings when the two weeks are up. We'll take inventory right now, then I'll bring you the two hundred guilders. (*To the colonel*) You go back to camp, I'll join you in a little while, I've got to take inventory, I don't want anything missing from my wagon. (*She kisses him. He leaves. She climbs up in the wagon*) I don't see very many boots.

MOTHER COURAGE Yvette. This is no time to inspect your wagon if it is yours. You promised to see the sergeant about my Swiss Cheese, you've got to hurry. They say he's to be court-martialed in an hour.

YVETTE Just let me count the shirts.

MOTHER COURAGE (*pulls her down by the skirt*) You hyena, it's Swiss Cheese, his life's at stake. And don't tell anybody where the offer comes from, in heaven's name say it's your gentle-man friend, or we'll all get it, they'll say we helped him.

YVETTE I've arranged to meet One-Eye in the woods, he must be there already.

THE CHAPLAIN And there's no need to start out with the whole two hundred, offer a hundred and fifty, that's plenty.

MOTHER COURAGE Is it your money? You just keep out of this. Don't worry, you'll get your bread and soup. Go on now and don't haggle. It's his life. (*She gives Yvette a push to start her on her way*)

THE CHAPLAIN I didn't mean to butt in, but what are we going to live on? You've got an unemployable daughter on your hands.

MOTHER COURAGE You muddlehead, I'm counting on the regi-mental cashbox. They'll allow for his expenses, won't they?

THE CHAPLAIN But will she handle it right?

MOTHER COURAGE It's in her own interest. If I spend her two hundred, she gets the wagon. She's mighty keen on it, how long can she expect to hold on to her colonel? Kattrin, you scour the knives, use pumice. And you, don't stand around like Jesus on the Mount of Olives, bestir yourself, wash those glasses, we're expecting at least fifty for dinner, and then it'll be the same old story: "Oh my feet, I'm not used to running around, I don't run around in the pulpit." I think they'll set

him free. Thank God they're open to bribery. They're not wolves, they're human and out for money. Bribe-taking in humans is the same as mercy in God. It's our only hope. As long as people take bribes, you'll have mild sentences and even the innocent will get off once in a while.

YVETTE (*comes in panting*)   They want two hundred. And we've got to be quick. Or it'll be out of their hands. I'd better take One-Eye to see my colonel right away. He confessed that he'd had the cashbox, they put the thumb screws on him. But he threw it in the river when he saw they were after him. The box is gone. Should I run and get the money from my colonel?

MOTHER COURAGE   The box is gone? How will I get my two hundred back?

YVETTE   Ah, so you thought you could take it out of the cashbox? You thought you'd put one over on me. Forget it. If you want to save Swiss Cheese, you'll just have to pay, or maybe you'd like me to drop the whole thing and let you keep your wagon?

MOTHER COURAGE   This is something I hadn't reckoned with. But don't rush me, you'll get the wagon, I know it's down the drain, I've had it for seventeen years. Just let me think a second, it's all so sudden. What'll I do, I can't give them two hundred, I guess you should have bargained. If I haven't got a few guilders to fall back on, I'll be at the mercy of the first Tom, Dick, or Harry. Say I'll give them a hundred and twenty, I'll lose my wagon anyway.

YVETTE   They won't go along. One-Eye's in a hurry, he's so keyed-up he keeps looking behind him. Hadn't I better give them the whole two hundred?

MOTHER COURAGE (*in despair*)   I can't do it. Thirty years I've worked. She's twenty-five and no husband. I've got her to keep too. Don't needle me, I know what I'm doing. Say a hundred and twenty or nothing doing.

YVETTE   It's up to you. (*Goes out quickly*)
(*Mother Courage looks neither at the chaplain nor at her daughter. She sits down to help Kattrin scour the knives*)

MOTHER COURAGE   Don't break the glasses. They're not ours any more. Watch what you're doing, you'll cut yourself. Swiss Cheese will be back, I'll pay two hundred if I have to.

You'll have your brother. With eighty guilders we can buy a peddler's pack and start all over. Worse things have happened.

THE CHAPLAIN   The Lord will provide.

MOTHER COURAGE   Rub them dry. (*They scour the knives in silence. Suddenly Kattrin runs sobbing behind the wagon*)

YVETTE (*comes running*)   They won't go along. I warned you. One-Eye wanted to run out on me, he said it was no use. He said we'd hear the drums any minute, meaning he'd been sentenced. I offered a hundred and fifty. He didn't even bother to shrug his shoulders. When I begged and pleaded, he promised to wait till I'd spoken to you again.

MOTHER COURAGE   Say I'll give him the two hundred. Run. (*Yvette runs off. They sit in silence. The chaplain has stopped washing the glasses*) Maybe I bargained too long. (*Drums are heard in the distance. The chaplain stands up and goes to the rear. Mother Courage remains seated. It grows dark. The drums stop. It grows light again. Mother Courage has not moved*)

YVETTE (*enters, very pale*)   Now you've done it with your haggling and wanting to keep your wagon. Eleven bullets he got, that's all. I don't know why I bother with you any more, you don't deserve it. But I've picked up a little information. They don't believe the cashbox is really in the river. They suspect it's here and they think you were connected with him. They're going to bring him here, they think maybe you'll give yourself away when you see him. I'm warning you: You don't know him, or you're all dead ducks. I may as well tell you, they're right behind me. Should I keep Kattrin out of the way? (*Mother Courage shakes her head*) Does she know? Maybe she didn't hear the drums or maybe she didn't understand.

MOTHER COURAGE   She knows. Get her.

(*Yvette brings Kattrin, who goes to her mother and stands beside her. Mother Courage takes her by the hand. Two soldiers come in with a stretcher on which something is lying under a sheet. The sergeant walks beside them. They set the stretcher down*)

THE SERGEANT   We've got a man here and we don't know his name. We need it for the records. He had a meal with you. Take a look, see if you know him. (*He removes the sheet*) Do you know him? (*Mother Courage shakes her head*) What? You'd never

seen him before he came here for a meal? (*Mother Courage shakes her head*) Pick him up. Throw him on the dump. Nobody knows him. (*They carry him away*)

4

Mother Courage sings the Song of the Great Capitulation.

Outside an officer's tent.

Mother Courage is waiting. A clerk looks out of the tent.

THE CLERK   I know you. You had a Protestant paymaster at your place, he was hiding. I wouldn't put in any complaints if I were you.

MOTHER COURAGE   I'm putting in a complaint. I'm innocent. If I take this lying down, it'll look as if I had a guilty conscience. First they ripped up my whole wagon with their sabers, then they wanted me to pay a fine of five talers for no reason at all.

THE CLERK   I'm advising you for your own good: Keep your trap shut. We haven't got many provisioners and we'll let you keep on with your business, especially if you've got a guilty conscience and pay a fine now and then.

MOTHER COURAGE   I'm putting in a complaint.

THE CLERK   Have it your way. But you'll have to wait till the captain can see you. (*Disappears into the tent*)

A YOUNG SOLDIER (*enters in a rage*)   Bouque la Madonne! Where's that stinking captain? He embezzled my reward and now he's drinking it up with his whores. I'm going to get him!

AN OLDER SOLDIER (*comes running after him*)   Shut up. They'll put you in the stocks!

THE YOUNG SOLDIER   Come on out, you crook! I'll make chops

out of you. Embezzling my reward! Who jumps in the river? Not another man in the whole squad, only me. And I can't even buy myself a beer. I won't stand for it. Come on out and let me cut you to pieces!

THE OLDER SOLDIER   Holy Mary! He'll ruin himself.

MOTHER COURAGE   They didn't give him a reward?

THE YOUNG SOLDIER   Let me go. I'll run you through too, the more the merrier.

THE OLDER SOLDIER   He saved the colonel's horse and they didn't give him a reward. He's young, he hasn't been around long.

MOTHER COURAGE   Let him go, he's not a dog, you don't have to tie him up. Wanting a reward is perfectly reasonable. Why else would he distinguish himself?

THE YOUNG SOLDIER   And him drinking in there! You're all a lot of yellowbellies. I distinguished myself and I want my reward.

MOTHER COURAGE   Young man, don't shout at me. I've got my own worries and besides, go easy on your voice, you may need it. You'll be hoarse when the captain comes out, you won't be able to say boo and he won't be able to put you in the stocks till you're blue in the face. People that yell like that don't last long, maybe half an hour, then they're so exhausted you have to sing them to sleep.

THE YOUNG SOLDIER   I'm not exhausted and who wants to sleep? I'm hungry. They make our bread out of acorns and hemp seed, and they skimp on that. He's whoring away my reward and I'm hungry. I'll murder him.

MOTHER COURAGE   I see. You're hungry. Last year your general made you cut across the fields to trample down the grain. I could have sold a pair of boots for ten guilders if anybody'd had ten guilders and if I'd had any boots. He thought he'd be someplace else this year, but now he's still here and everybody's starving. I can see that you might be good and mad.

THE YOUNG SOLDIER   He can't do this to me, save your breath, I won't put up with injustice.

MOTHER COURAGE   You're right, but for how long? How long won't you put up with injustice? An hour? Two hours? You see, you never thought of that, though it's very important, because it's miserable in the stocks when it suddenly dawns

on you that you *can* put up with injustice.

THE YOUNG SOLDIER   I don't know why I listen to you. Bouque la Madonne! Where's the captain?

MOTHER COURAGE   You listen to me because I'm not telling you anything new. You know your temper has gone up in smoke, it was a short temper and you need a long one, but that's a hard thing to come by.

THE YOUNG SOLDIER   Are you trying to say I've no right to claim my reward?

MOTHER COURAGE   Not at all. I'm only saying your temper isn't long enough, it won't get you anywhere. Too bad. If you had a long temper, I'd even egg you on. Chop the bastard up, that's what I'd say, but suppose you don't chop him up, because your tail's drooping and you know it. I'm left standing there like a fool and the captain takes it out on me.

THE OLDER SOLDIER   You're right. He's only blowing off steam.

THE YOUNG SOLDIER   We'll see about that. I'll cut him to pieces. (*He draws his sword*) When he comes out, I'll cut him to pieces.

THE CLERK (*looks out*)   The captain will be here in a moment. Sit down.

(*The young soldier sits down*)

MOTHER COURAGE   There he sits. What did I tell you? Sitting, aren't you? Oh, they know us like a book, they know how to handle us. Sit down! And down we sit. You can't start a riot sitting down. Better not stand up again, you won't be able to stand the way you were standing before. Don't be embarrassed on my account, I'm no better, not a bit of it. We were full of piss and vinegar, but they've bought it off. Look at me. No back talk, it's bad for business. Let me tell you about the great capitulation. (*She sings the Song of the Great Capitulation*)

When I was young, no more than a spring chicken
I too thought that I was really quite the cheese
(No common peddler's daughter, not I with my looks and my
    talent and striving for higher things!)
One little hair in the soup would make me sicken
And at me no man would dare to sneeze.
(It's all or nothing, no second best for me. I've got what it
    takes, the rules are for somebody else!)

But a chickadee
Sang wait and see!
   And you go marching with the show
   In step, however fast or slow
   And rattle off your little song:
   It won't be long.
   And then the whole thing slides.
   You think God provides—
   But you've got it wrong.

And before one single year had wasted
I had learned to swallow down the bitter brew
(Two kids on my hands and the price of bread and who do
    they take me for anyway!)
Man, the double-edged shellacking that I tasted
On my ass and knees I was when they were through.
(You've got to get along with people, one good turn deserves
    another, no use trying to ram your head through the wall!)
And the chickadee
Sang wait and see!
   And she goes marching with the show
   In step, however fast or slow
   And rattles off her little song:
   It won't be long.
   And then the whole thing slides
   You think God provides—
   But you've got it wrong.

I've seen many fired by high ambition
No star's big or high enough to reach out for.
(It's ability that counts, where there's a will there's a way, one
    way or another we'll swing it!)
Then while moving mountains they get a suspicion
That to wear a straw hat is too big a chore.
(No use being too big for your britches!)
And the chickadee
Sings wait and see!
   And they go marching with the show
   In step, however fast or slow
   And rattle off their little song:
   It won't be long.

And then the whole thing slides!
You think God provides—
But you've got it wrong!

MOTHER COURAGE (*to the young soldier*)   So here's what I think:
Stay here with your sword if your anger's big enough, I know
you have good reason, but if it's a short quick anger, better
make tracks!

THE YOUNG SOLDIER   Kiss my ass! (*He staggers off, the older soldier
after him*)

THE CLERK (*sticking his head out*)   The captain is here. You can
put in your complaint now.

MOTHER COURAGE   I've changed my mind. No complaint. (*She
goes out*)

5

Two years have passed. The war has spread far and
wide. With scarcely a pause Mother Courage's little
wagon rolls through Poland, Moravia, Bavaria, Italy,
and back again to Bavaria. 1631. Tilly's victory at Mag-
deburg costs Mother Courage four officers' shirts.

Mother Courage's wagon has stopped in a devastated village.

*Thin military music is heard from the distance. Two soldiers at the bar
are being waited on by Kattrin and Mother Courage. One of them is
wearing a lady's fur coat over his shoulders.*

MOTHER COURAGE   What's that? You can't pay? No money, no
schnapps. Plenty of victory marches for the Lord but no pay
for the men.

THE SOLDIER   I want my schnapps. I came too late for the looting. The general skunked us: permission to loot the city for
exactly one hour. Says he's not a monster; the mayor must
have paid him.

THE CHAPLAIN (*staggers in*)   There's still some wounded in the
house. The peasant and his family. Help me, somebody, I
need linen.

(*The second soldier goes out with him. Kattrin gets very excited and
tries to persuade her mother to hand out linen*)

MOTHER COURAGE   I haven't got any. The regiment's bought up
all my bandages. You think I'm going to rip up my officers'
shirts for the likes of them?

THE CHAPLAIN (*calling back*)   I need linen, I tell you.

MOTHER COURAGE (*sitting down on the wagon steps to keep Kattrin
out*)   Nothing doing. They don't pay, they got nothing to
pay with.

THE CHAPLAIN (*bending over a woman whom he has carried out*)
Why did you stay here in all that gunfire?

THE PEASANT WOMAN (*feebly*)   Farm.

MOTHER COURAGE   You won't catch them leaving their property. And I'm expected to foot the bill. I won't do it.

THE FIRST SOLDIER   They're Protestants. Why do they have to be
Protestants?

MOTHER COURAGE   Religion is the least of their worries. They've
lost their farm.

THE SECOND SOLDIER   They're no Protestants. They're Catholics
like us.

THE FIRST SOLDIER   How do we know who we're shooting at?

A PEASANT (*whom the Chaplain brings in*)   They got my arm.

THE CHAPLAIN   Where's the linen?

(*All look at Mother Courage, who does not move*)

MOTHER COURAGE   I can't give you a thing. What with all my
taxes, duties, fees and bribes! (*Making guttural sounds, Kattrin
picks up a board and threatens her mother with it*) Are you crazy?
Put that board down, you slut, or I'll smack you. I'm not
giving anything, you can't make me, I've got to think of
myself. (*The chaplain picks her up from the step and puts her down
on the ground. Then he fishes out some shirts and tears them into
strips*)

My shirts! Half a guilder apiece! I'm ruined!
(The anguished cry of a baby is heard from the house)

THE PEASANT   The baby's still in there!

(Kattrin runs in)

THE CHAPLAIN *(to the woman)*   Don't move. They're bringing him out.

MOTHER COURAGE   Get her out of there. The roof'll cave in.

THE CHAPLAIN   I'm not going in there again.

MOTHER COURAGE *(torn)*   Don't run hog-wild with my expensive linen.

(Kattrin emerges from the ruins carrying an infant)

MOTHER COURAGE   Oh, so you've found another baby to carry around with you? Give that baby back to its mother this minute, or it'll take me all day to get it away from you. Do you hear me? *(To the second soldier)* Don't stand there gaping, go back and tell them to stop that music, I can see right here that they've won a victory. Your victory's costing me a pretty penny.

(Kattrin rocks the baby in her arms, humming a lullaby)

MOTHER COURAGE   There she sits, happy in all this misery; give it back this minute, the mother's coming to. *(She pounces on the first soldier who has been helping himself to the drinks and is now making off with the bottle)* Pshagreff! Beast! Haven't you had enough victories for today? Pay up.

FIRST SOLDIER   I'm broke.

MOTHER COURAGE *(tears the fur coat off him)*   Then leave the coat here, it's stolen anyway.

THE CHAPLAIN   There's still somebody in there.

6

Outside Ingolstadt in Bavaria Mother Courage attends the funeral of Tilly, the imperial field marshal. Conversations about heroes and the longevity of the war. The chaplain deplores the waste of his talents. Mute Kattrin gets the red shoes. 1632.

Inside Mother Courage's tent.

A bar open to the rear. Rain. In the distance drum rolls and funeral music. The chaplain and the regimental clerk are playing a board game. Mother Courage and her daughter are taking inventory.

THE CHAPLAIN   The procession's starting.

MOTHER COURAGE   It's a shame about the general—socks: twenty-two pairs—I hear he was killed by accident. On account of the fog in the fields. He's up front encouraging the troops. "Fight to the death, boys," he sings out. Then he rides back, but he gets lost in the fog and rides back forward. Before you know it he's in the middle of the battle and stops a bullet —lanterns: we're down to four. (*A whistle from the rear. She goes to the bar*) You men ought to be ashamed, running out on your late general's funeral! (*She pours drinks*)

THE CLERK   They shouldn't have been paid before the funeral. Now they're getting drunk instead.

THE CHAPLAIN (*to the clerk*)   Shouldn't you be at the funeral?

THE CLERK   In this rain?

MOTHER COURAGE   With you it's different, the rain might spoil your uniform. It seems they wanted to ring the bells, naturally, but it turned out the churches had all been shot to pieces by his orders, so the poor general won't hear any bells when they lower him into his grave. They're going to fire a three-gun salute instead, so it won't be too dull—seventeen sword belts.

CRIES (*from the bar*)   Hey! Brandy!

MOTHER COURAGE   Money first! No, you can't come into my tent with your muddy boots! You can drink outside, rain or no rain. (*To the clerk*) I'm only letting officers in. It seems the general had been having his troubles. Mutiny in the Second Regiment because he hadn't paid them. It's a war of religion, he says, should they profit by their faith?

(*Funeral march. All look to the rear*)

THE CHAPLAIN   Now they're marching past the body.

MOTHER COURAGE   I feel sorry when a general or an emperor passes away like this, maybe he thought he'd do something big, that posterity would still be talking about and maybe put up a statue in his honor, conquer the world, for instance, that's a nice ambition for a general, he doesn't know any better. So he knocks himself out, and then the common people 'come and spoil it all, because what do they care about greatness, all they care about is a mug of beer and maybe a little company. The most beautiful plans have been wrecked by the smallness of the people that are supposed to carry them out. Even an emperor can't do anything by himself, he needs the support of his soldiers and his people. Am I right?

THE CHAPLAIN (*laughing*)   Courage, you're right, except about the soldiers. They do their best. With those fellows out there, for instance, drinking their brandy in the rain, I'll undertake to carry on one war after another for a hundred years, two at once if I have to, and I'm not a general by trade.

MOTHER COURAGE   Then you don't think the war might stop?

THE CHAPLAIN   Because the general's dead? Don't be childish. They grow by the dozen, there'll always be plenty of heroes.

MOTHER COURAGE   Look here, I'm not asking you for the hell of it. I've been wondering whether to lay in supplies while they're cheap, but if the war stops, I can throw them out the window.

THE CHAPLAIN   I understand. You want a serious answer. There have always been people who say: "The war will be over some day." I say there's no guarantee the war will ever be over. Naturally a brief intermission is conceivable. Maybe the war needs a breather, a war can even break its neck, so to speak. There's always a chance of that, nothing is perfect here be-

low. Maybe there never will be a perfect war, one that lives up to all our expectations. Suddenly, for some unforeseen reason, a war can bog down, you can't think of everything. Some little oversight and your war's in trouble. And then you've got to pull it out of the mud. But the kings and emperors, not to mention the pope, will always come to its help in adversity. On the whole, I'd say this war has very little to worry about, it'll live to a ripe old age.

A SOLDIER (*sings at the bar*)

> A drink, and don't be slow!
> A soldier's got to go
> And fight for his religion.
>
> Make it double, this is a holiday.

MOTHER COURAGE   If I could only be sure . . .

THE CHAPLAIN   Figure it out for yourself. What's to stop the war?

THE SOLDIER (*sings*)

> Your breasts, girl, don't be slow!
> A soldier's got to go
> And ride away to Pilsen.

THE CLERK (*suddenly*)   But why can't we have peace? I'm from Bohemia, I'd like to go home when the time comes.

THE CHAPLAIN   Oh, you'd like to go home? Ah, peace! What becomes of the hole when the cheese has been eaten?

THE SOLDIER (*sings*)

> Play cards, friends, don't be slow!
> A soldier's got to go
> No matter if it's Sunday.
>
> A prayer, priest, don't be slow!
> A soldier's got to go
> And die for king and country.

THE CLERK   In the long run nobody can live without peace.

THE CHAPLAIN   The way I see it, war gives you plenty of peace. It has its peaceful moments. War meets every need, including the peaceful ones, everything's taken care of, or your war couldn't hold its own. In a war you can shit the same as in the dead of peace, you can stop for a beer between battles, and even on the march you can always lie down on your elbows and take a little nap by the roadside. You can't play cards when you're fighting; but then you can't when you're plowing in the dead of peace either, but after a victory the sky's the limit. Maybe you've had a leg shot off, at first you raise a howl, you make a big thing of it. But then you calm down or they give you schnapps, and in the end you're hopping around again and the war's no worse off than before. And what's to prevent you from multiplying in the thick of the slaughter, behind a barn or someplace, in the long run how can they stop you, and then the war has your progeny to help it along. Take it from me, the war will always find an answer. Why would it have to stop?

(Kattrin has stopped working and is staring at the chaplain)

MOTHER COURAGE   Then I'll buy the merchandise. You've convinced me. *(Kattrin suddenly throws down a basket full of bottles and runs out)* Kattrin! *(Laughs)* My goodness, the poor thing's been hoping for peace. I promised her she'd get a husband when peace comes. *(She runs after her)*

THE CLERK *(getting up)*   I win, you've been too busy talking. Pay up.

MOTHER COURAGE *(comes back with Kattrin)*   Be reasonable, the war'll go on a little longer and we'll make a little more money, then peace will be even better. Run along to town now, it won't take you ten minutes, and get the stuff from the Golden Lion, only the expensive things, we'll pick up the rest in the wagon later, it's all arranged, the regimental clerk here will go with you. They've almost all gone to the general's funeral, nothing can happen to you. Look sharp, don't let them take anything away from you, think of your dowry.

(Kattrin puts a kerchief over her head and goes with the clerk)

THE CHAPLAIN   Is it all right letting her go with the clerk?

MOTHER COURAGE   Who'd want to ruin her? She's not pretty enough.

THE CHAPLAIN I've come to admire the way you handle your business and pull through every time. I can see why they call you Mother Courage.

MOTHER COURAGE Poor people need courage. Why? Because they're sunk. In their situation it takes gumption just to get up in the morning. Or to plow a field in the middle of a war. They even show courage by bringing children into the world, because look at the prospects. The way they butcher and execute each other, think of the courage they need to look each other in the face. And putting up with an emperor and a pope takes a whale of a lot of courage, because those two are the death of the poor. (*She sits down, takes a small pipe from her pocket and smokes*) You could be making some kindling.

THE CHAPLAIN (*reluctantly takes his jacket off and prepares to chop*) Chopping wood isn't really my trade, you know, I'm a shepherd of souls.

MOTHER COURAGE Sure. But I have no soul and I need firewood.

THE CHAPLAIN What's that pipe?

MOTHER COURAGE Just a pipe.

THE CHAPLAIN No, it's not "just a pipe," it's a very particular pipe.

MOTHER COURAGE Really?

THE CHAPLAIN It's the cook's pipe from the Oxenstjerna regiment.

MOTHER COURAGE If you know it all, why the mealy-mouthed questions?

THE CHAPLAIN I didn't know if *you* knew. You could have been rummaging through your belongings and laid hands on some pipe and picked it up without thinking.

MOTHER COURAGE Yes. Maybe that's how it was.

THE CHAPLAIN Except it wasn't. You knew who that pipe belongs to.

MOTHER COURAGE What of it?

THE CHAPLAIN Courage, I'm warning you. It's my duty. I doubt if you ever lay eyes on the man again, but that's no calamity, in fact you're lucky. If you ask me, he wasn't steady. Not at all.

MOTHER COURAGE What makes you say that? He was a nice man.

THE CHAPLAIN   Oh, you think he was nice? I differ. Far be it from me to wish him any harm, but I can't say he was nice. I'd say he was a scheming Don Juan. If you don't believe me, take a look at his pipe. You'll have to admit that it shows up his character.

MOTHER COURAGE   I don't see anything. It's beat up.

THE CHAPLAIN   It's half bitten through. A violent man. That is the pipe of a ruthless, violent man, you must see that if you've still got an ounce of good sense.

MOTHER COURAGE   Don't wreck my chopping block.

THE CHAPLAIN   I've told you I wasn't trained to chop wood. I studied theology. My gifts and abilities are being wasted on muscular effort. The talents that God gave me are lying fallow. That's a sin. You've never heard me preach. With one sermon I can whip a regiment into such a state that they take the enemy for a flock of sheep. Then men care no more about their lives than they would about a smelly old sock that they're ready to throw away in hopes of final victory. God has made me eloquent. You'll swoon when you hear me preach.

MOTHER COURAGE   I don't want to swoon. What good would that do me?

THE CHAPLAIN   Courage, I've often wondered if maybe you didn't conceal a warm heart under that hard-bitten talk of yours. You too are human, you need warmth.

MOTHER COURAGE   The best way to keep this tent warm is with plenty of firewood.

THE CHAPLAIN   Don't try to put me off. Seriously, Courage, I sometimes wonder if we couldn't make our relationship a little closer. I mean, seeing that the whirlwind of war has whirled us so strangely together.

MOTHER COURAGE   Seems to me it's close enough. I cook your meals and you do chores, such as chopping wood, for instance.

THE CHAPLAIN (goes toward her)   You know what I mean by "closer"; it has nothing to do with meals and chopping wood and such mundane needs. Don't harden your heart, let it speak.

MOTHER COURAGE   Don't come at me with that ax. That's too close a relationship.

THE CHAPLAIN   Don't turn it to ridicule. I'm serious, I've given it careful thought.

MOTHER COURAGE   Chaplain, don't be silly. I like you, I don't want to have to scold you. My aim in life is to get through, me and my children and my wagon. I don't think of it as mine and besides I'm not in the mood for private affairs. Right now I'm taking a big risk, buying up merchandise with the general dead and everybody talking peace. What'll you do if I'm ruined? See? You don't know. Chop that wood, then we'll be warm in the evening, which is a good thing in times like these. Now what? (*She stands up*)

(*Enter Kattrin out of breath, with a wound across her forehead and over one eye. She is carrying all sorts of things, packages, leather goods, a drum, etc.*)

MOTHER COURAGE   What's that? Assaulted? On the way back? She was assaulted on the way back. Must have been that soldier that got drunk here! I shouldn't have let you go! Throw the stuff down! It's not bad, only a flesh wound. I'll bandage it, it'll heal in a week. They're worse than wild beasts. (*She bandages the wound*)

THE CHAPLAIN   I can't find fault with them. At home they never raped anybody. I blame the people that start wars, they're the ones that dredge up man's lowest instincts.

MOTHER COURAGE   Didn't the clerk bring you back? That's because you're respectable, they don't give a damn. It's not a deep wound, it won't leave a mark. There, all bandaged. Don't fret, I've got something for you. I've been keeping it for you on the sly, it'll be a surprise. (*She fishes Yvette's red shoes out of a sack*) See? You've always wanted them. Now you've got them. Put them on quick before I regret it. It won't leave a mark, though I wouldn't mind if it did. The girls that attract them get the worst of it. They drag them around till there's nothing left of them. If you don't appeal to them, they won't harm you. I've seen girls with pretty faces, a few years later they'd have given a wolf the creeps. They can't step behind a bush without fearing the worst. It's like trees. The straight tall ones get chopped down for ridgepoles, the crooked ones enjoy life. In other words, it's a lucky break. The shoes are still in good condition, I've kept them nicely polished.

(Kattrin leaves the shoes where they are and crawls into the wagon)

THE CHAPLAIN   I hope she won't be disfigured.

MOTHER COURAGE   There'll be a scar. She can stop waiting for peace.

THE CHAPLAIN   She didn't let them take anything.

MOTHER COURAGE   Maybe I shouldn't have drummed it into her. If I only knew what went on in her head. One night she stayed out, the only time in all these years. Afterwards she traipsed around as usual, except she worked harder. I never could find out what happened. I racked my brains for quite some time. *(She picks up the articles brought by Kattrin and sorts them angrily)* That's war for you! A fine way to make a living! *(Cannon salutes are heard)*

THE CHAPLAIN   Now they're burying the general. This is a historic moment.

MOTHER COURAGE   To me it's a historic moment when they hit my daughter over the eye. She's a wreck, she'll never get a husband now, and she's so crazy about children. It's the war that made her dumb too, a soldier stuffed something in her mouth when she was little. I'll never see Swiss Cheese again and where Eilif is, God knows. God damn the war.

7

Mother Courage at the height of her business career.

Highway.

The chaplain, Mother Courage and her daughter Kattrin are pulling the wagon. New wares are hanging on it. Mother Courage is wearing a necklace of silver talers.

MOTHER COURAGE   Stop running down the war. I won't have it.
I know it destroys the weak, but the weak haven't a chance
in peacetime either. And war is a better provider. (*Sings*)

> If you're not strong enough to take it
> The victory will find you dead.
> A war is only what you make it.
> It's business, not with cheese but lead.

And what good is it staying in one place? The stay-at-homes
are the first to get it. (*Sings*)

> Some people think they'd like to ride out
> The war, leave danger to the brave
> And dig themselves a cozy hideout—
> They'll dig themselves an early grave.
> I've seen them running from the thunder
> To find a refuge from the war
> But once they're resting six feet under
> They wonder what they hurried for.

(*They plod on*)

8

In the same year Gustavus Adolphus, King of Sweden, is killed at the battle of Lützen. Peace threatens to ruin Mother Courage's business. Her brave son performs one heroic deed too many and dies an ignominious death.

A camp.

A summer morning. An old woman and her son are standing by the wagon. The son is carrying a large sack of bedding.

MOTHER COURAGE'S VOICE (*from the wagon*)   Does it have to be at this unearthly hour?

THE YOUNG MAN   We've walked all night, twenty miles, and we've got to go back today.

MOTHER COURAGE'S voice   What can I do with bedding? The people haven't any houses.

THE YOUNG MAN   Wait till you've seen it.

THE OLD WOMAN   She won't take it either. Come on.

THE YOUNG MAN   They'll sell the roof from over our heads for taxes. Maybe she'll give us three guilders if you throw in the cross. (*Bells start ringing*) Listen, mother!

VOICES (*from the rear*)   Peace! The king of Sweden is dead!

MOTHER COURAGE (*sticks her head out of the wagon. She has not yet done her hair*)   Why are the bells ringing in the middle of the week?

THE CHAPLAIN (*crawls out from under the wagon*)   What are they shouting?

MOTHER COURAGE   Don't tell me peace has broken out when I've just taken in more supplies.

THE CHAPLAIN (*shouting toward the rear*)   Is it true? Peace?

VOICE   Three weeks ago, they say. But we just found out.

THE CHAPLAIN (*to Mother Courage*) What else would they ring the bells for?

VOICE There's a whole crowd of Lutherans, they've driven their carts into town. They brought the news.

THE YOUNG MAN Mother, it's peace. What's the matter?
(*The old woman has collapsed*)

MOTHER COURAGE (*going back into the wagon*) Heavenly saints! Kattrin, peace! Put your black dress on! We're going to church. We owe it to Swiss Cheese. Can it be true?

THE YOUNG MAN The people here say the same thing. They've made peace. Can you get up? (*The old woman stands up, still stunned*) I'll get the saddle shop started again. I promise. Everything will be all right. Father will get his bed back. Can you walk? (*To the chaplain*) She fainted. It was the news. She thought peace would never come again. Father said it would. We'll go straight home. (*Both go out*)

MOTHER COURAGE'S VOICE Give her some brandy.

THE CHAPLAIN They're gone.

MOTHER COURAGE'S VOICE What's going on in camp?

THE CHAPLAIN A big crowd. I'll go see. Shouldn't I put on my clericals?

MOTHER COURAGE'S VOICE Better make sure before you step out in your antichrist costume. I'm glad to see peace, even if I'm ruined. At least I've brought two of my children through the war. Now I'll see my Eilif again.

THE CHAPLAIN Look who's coming down the road. If it isn't the general's cook!

THE COOK (*rather bedraggled, carrying a bundle*) Can I believe my eyes? The chaplain!

THE CHAPLAIN Courage! A visitor!
(*Mother Courage climbs down*)

THE COOK Didn't I promise to come over for a little chat as soon as I had time? I've never forgotten your brandy, Mrs. Fierling.

MOTHER COURAGE Mercy, the general's cook! After all these years! Where's Eilif, my eldest?

THE COOK Isn't he here yet? He left ahead of me, he was coming to see you too.

THE CHAPLAIN I'll put on my clericals, wait for me. (*Goes out behind the wagon*)

MOTHER COURAGE   Then he'll be here any minute. (*Calls into the wagon*) Kattrin, Eilif's coming! Bring the cook a glass of brandy! (*Kattrin does not appear*) Put a lock of hair over it, and forget it! Mr. Lamb is no stranger. (*Gets the brandy herself*) She won't come out. Peace doesn't mean a thing to her, it's come too late. They hit her over the eye, there's hardly any mark, but she thinks people are staring at her.

THE COOK   Ech, war! (*He and Mother Courage sit down*)

MOTHER COURAGE   Cook, you find me in trouble. I'm ruined.

THE COOK   What? Say, that's a shame.

MOTHER COURAGE   Peace has done me in. Only the other day I stocked up. The chaplain's advice. And now they'll all demobilize and leave me sitting on my merchandise.

THE COOK   How could you listen to the chaplain? If I'd had time, I'd have warned you against him, but the Catholics came too soon. He's a fly-by-night. So now he's the boss here?

MOTHER COURAGE   He washed my dishes and helped me pull the wagon.

THE COOK   Him? Pulling? I guess he's told you a few of his jokes too, I wouldn't put it past him, he has an unsavory attitude toward women, I tried to reform him, it was hopeless. He's not steady.

MOTHER COURAGE   Are you steady?

THE COOK   If nothing else, I'm steady. Prosit!

MOTHER COURAGE   Steady is no good. I've only lived with one steady man, thank the Lord. I never had to work so hard, he sold the children's blankets when spring came, and he thought my harmonica was unchristian. In my opinion you're not doing yourself any good by admitting you're steady.

THE COOK   You've still got your old bite, but I respect you for it.

MOTHER COURAGE   Don't tell me you've been dreaming about my old bite.

THE COOK   Well, here we sit, with the bells of peace and your world-famous brandy, that hasn't its equal.

MOTHER COURAGE   The bells of peace don't strike my fancy right now. I don't see them paying the men, they're behindhand already. Where does that leave me with my famous brandy? Have you been paid?

THE COOK (*hesitantly*)   Not really. That's why we demobilized ourselves. Under the circumstances, I says to myself, why should I stay on? I'll go see my friends in the meantime. So here we are.

MOTHER COURAGE   You mean you're out of funds?

THE COOK   If only they'd stop those damn bells! I'd be glad to go into some kind of business. I'm sick of being a cook. They give me roots and shoe leather to work with, and then they throw the hot soup in my face. A cook's got a dog's life these days. I'd rather be in combat, but now we've got peace. (*The chaplain appears in his original dress*) We'll discuss it later.

THE CHAPLAIN   It's still in good condition. There were only a few moths in it.

THE COOK   I don't see why you bother. They won't take you back. Who are you going to inspire now to be an honest soldier and earn his pay at the risk of his life? Besides, I've got a bone to pick with you. Advising this lady to buy useless merchandise on the ground that the war would last forever.

THE CHAPLAIN (*heatedly*)   And why, I'd like to know, is it any of your business?

THE COOK   Because it's unscrupulous. How can you meddle in other people's business and give unsolicited advice?

THE CHAPLAIN   Who's meddling? (*To Mother Courage*) I didn't know you were accountable to this gentleman, I didn't know you were so intimate with him.

MOTHER COURAGE   Don't get excited, the cook is only giving his private opinion. And you can't deny that your war was a dud.

THE CHAPLAIN   Courage, don't blaspheme against peace. You're a battlefield hyena.

MOTHER COURAGE   What am I?

THE COOK   If you insult this lady, you'll hear from me.

THE CHAPLAIN   I'm not talking to you. Your intentions are too obvious. (*To Mother Courage*) But when I see you picking up peace with thumb and forefinger like a snotty handkerchief, it revolts my humanity; you don't want peace, you want war, because you profit by it, but don't forget the old saying: "He hath need of a long spoon that eateth with the devil."

MOTHER COURAGE   I've no use for war and war hasn't much use for me. Anyway, I'm not letting anybody call me a hyena, you and me are through.

THE CHAPLAIN   How can you complain about peace when it's such a relief to everybody else? On account of the old rags in your wagon?

MOTHER COURAGE   My merchandise isn't old rags, it's what I live off, and so did you.

THE CHAPLAIN   Off war, you mean. Aha!

THE COOK (*to the chaplain*)   You're a grown man, you ought to know there's no sense in giving advice. (*To Mother Courage*) The best thing you can do now is to sell off certain articles quick, before the prices hit the floor. Dress yourself and get started, there's no time to lose.

MOTHER COURAGE   That's very sensible advice. I think I'll do it.

THE CHAPLAIN   Because the cook says so!

MOTHER COURAGE   Why didn't *you* say so? He's right, I'd better run over to the market. (*She goes into the wagon*)

THE COOK   My round, chaplain. No presence of mind. Here's what you should have said: me give you advice? All I ever did was talk politics! Don't try to take me on. Cockfighting is undignified in a clergyman.

THE CHAPLAIN   If you don't shut up, I'll murder you, undignified or not.

THE COOK (*taking off his shoe and unwinding the wrappings from his feet*)   If the war hadn't made a godless bum out of you, you could easily come by a parsonage now that peace is here. They won't need cooks, there's nothing to cook, but people still do a lot of believing, that hasn't changed.

THE CHAPLAIN   See here, Mr. Lamb. Don't try to squeeze me out. Being a bum has made me a better man. I couldn't preach to them any more.

(*Yvette Pottier enters, elaborately dressed in black, with a cane. She is much older and fatter and heavily powdered. Behind her a servant*)

YVETTE   Hello there! Is this the residence of Mother Courage?

CHAPLAIN   Right you are. With whom have we the pleasure?

YVETTE   The Countess Starhemberg, my good people. Where is Mother Courage?

THE CHAPLAIN (*calls into the wagon*)   Countess Starhemberg wishes to speak to you!

MOTHER COURAGE   I'm coming.

YVETTE   It's Yvette!

MOTHER COURAGE'S VOICE   My goodness! It's Yvette!

YVETTE   Just dropped in to see how you're doing. (*The cook has turned around in horror*) Pieter!

THE COOK   Yvette!

YVETTE   Blow me down! How did you get here?

THE COOK   In a cart.

THE CHAPLAIN   Oh, you know each other? Intimately?

YVETTE   I should think so. (*She looks the cook over*) Fat!

THE COOK   You're not exactly willowy yourself.

YVETTE   All the same I'm glad I ran into you, you bum. Now I can tell you what I think of you.

THE CHAPLAIN   Go right ahead, spare no details, but wait until Courage comes out.

MOTHER COURAGE (*comes out with all sorts of merchandise*)   Yvette! (*They embrace*) But what are you in mourning for?

YVETTE   Isn't it becoming? My husband the colonel died a few years ago.

MOTHER COURAGE   The old geezer that almost bought my wagon?

YVETTE   His elder brother.

MOTHER COURAGE   You must be pretty well fixed. It's nice to find somebody that's made a good thing out of the war.

YVETTE   Oh well, it's been up and down and back up again.

MOTHER COURAGE   Let's not say anything bad about colonels. They make money by the bushel.

THE CHAPLAIN   If I were you, I'd put my shoes back on again. (*To Yvette*) Countess Starhemberg, you promised to tell us what you think of this gentleman.

THE COOK   Don't make a scene here.

MOTHER COURAGE   He's a friend of mine, Yvette.

YVETTE   He's Pete the Pipe, that's who he is.

THE COOK   Forget the nicknames, my name is Lamb.

MOTHER COURAGE (*laughs*)   Pete the Pipe! That drove the women crazy! Say, I've saved your pipe.

THE CHAPLAIN   And smoked it.

YVETTE   It's lucky I'm here to warn you. He's the worst rotter that ever infested the coast of Flanders. He ruined more girls than he's got fingers.

THE COOK   That was a long time ago. I've changed.

YVETTE   Stand up when a lady draws you into a conversation!

How I loved this man! And all the while he was seeing a little bandylegged brunette, ruined her too, naturally.

THE COOK   Seems to me I started you off on a prosperous career.

YVETTE   Shut up, you depressing wreck! Watch your step with him, his kind are dangerous even when they've gone to seed.

MOTHER COURAGE (to Yvette)   Come along, I've got to sell my stuff before the prices drop. Maybe you can help me, with your army connections. (Calls into the wagon) Kattrin, forget about church, I'm running over to the market. When Eilif comes, give him a drink. (Goes out with Yvette)

YVETTE (in leaving)   To think that such a man could lead me astray! I can thank my lucky stars that I was able to rise in the world after that. I've put a spoke in your wheel, Pete the Pipe, and they'll give me credit for it in heaven when my time comes.

THE CHAPLAIN   Our conversation seems to illustrate the old adage: The mills of God grind slowly. What do you think of my jokes now?

THE COOK   I'm just unlucky. I'll come clean: I was hoping for a hot meal. I'm starving. And now they're talking about me, and she'll get the wrong idea. I think I'll beat it before she comes back.

THE CHAPLAIN   I think so too.

THE COOK   Chaplain, I'm fed up on peace already. Men are sinners from the cradle, fire and sword are their natural lot. I wish I were cooking for the general again, God knows where he is, I'd roast a fine fat capon, with mustard sauce and a few carrots.

THE CHAPLAIN   Red cabbage. Red cabbage with capon.

THE COOK   That's right, but he wanted carrots.

THE CHAPLAIN   He was ignorant.

THE COOK   That didn't prevent you from gorging yourself.

THE CHAPLAIN   With repugnance.

THE COOK   Anyway you'll have to admit those were good times.

THE CHAPLAIN   I might admit that.

THE COOK   Now you've called her a hyena, your good times here are over. What are you staring at?

THE CHAPLAIN   Eilif! (Eilif enters, followed by soldiers with pikes. His hands are fettered. He is deathly pale) What's wrong?

EILIF   Where's mother?

THE CHAPLAIN   Gone to town.

EILIF   I heard she was here. They let me come and see her.

THE COOK (*to the soldiers*)   Where are you taking him?

A SOLDIER   No good place.

THE CHAPLAIN   What has he done?

THE SOLDIER   Broke into a farm. The peasant's wife is dead.

THE CHAPLAIN   How could you do such a thing?

EILIF   It's what I've been doing all along.

THE COOK   But in peacetime!

EILIF   Shut your trap. Can I sit down till she comes?

THE SOLDIER   We haven't time.

THE CHAPLAIN   During the war they honored him for it, he sat
at the general's right hand. Then it was bravery. Couldn't we
speak to the officer?

THE SOLDIER   No use. What's brave about taking a peasant's
cattle?

THE COOK   It was stupid.

EILIF   If I'd been stupid, I'd have starved, wise guy.

THE COOK   And for being smart your head comes off.

THE CHAPLAIN   Let's get Kattrin at least.

EILIF   Leave her be. Get me a drink of schnapps.

THE SOLDIER   No time. Let's go!

THE CHAPLAIN   And what should we tell your mother?

EILIF   Tell her it wasn't any different, tell her it was the same.
Or don't tell her anything.
(*The soldiers drive him away*)

THE CHAPLAIN   I'll go with you on your hard journey.

EILIF   I don't need any sky pilot.

THE CHAPLAIN   You don't know yet. (*He follows him*)

THE COOK (*calls after them*)   I'll have to tell her, she'll want to see
him.

THE CHAPLAIN   Better not tell her anything. Or say he was here
and he'll come again, maybe tomorrow. I'll break it to her
when I get back. (*Hurries out*)
(*The cook looks after them, shaking his head, then he walks anxiously
about. Finally he approaches the wagon*)

THE COOK   Hey! Come on out! I can see why you'd hide from
peace. I wish I could do it myself. I'm the general's cook,
remember? Wouldn't you have a bite to eat, to do me till your
mother gets back? A slice of ham or just a piece of bread while

I'm waiting. (*He looks in*) She's buried her head in a blanket. (*The sound of gunfire in the rear*)

MOTHER COURAGE (*runs in. She is out of breath and still has her merchandise*)   Cook, the peace is over, the war started up again three days ago. I hadn't sold my stuff yet when I found out. Heaven be praised! They're shooting each other up in town, the Catholics and Lutherans. We've got to get out of here. Kattrin, start packing. What have *you* got such a long face about? What's wrong?

THE COOK   Nothing.

MOTHER COURAGE   Something's wrong, I can tell by your expression.

THE COOK   Maybe it's the war starting up again. Now I probably won't get anything hot to eat before tomorrow night.

MOTHER COURAGE   That's a lie, cook.

THE COOK   Eilif was here. He couldn't stay.

MOTHER COURAGE   He was here? Then we'll see him on the march. I'm going with our troops this time. How does he look?

THE COOK   The same.

MOTHER COURAGE   He'll never change. The war couldn't take him away from me. He's smart. Could you help me pack? (*She starts packing*) Did he tell you anything? Is he in good with the general? Did he say anything about his heroic deeds?

THE COOK (*gloomily*)   They say he's been at one of them again.

MOTHER COURAGE   Tell me later, we've got to be going. (*Kattrin emerges*) Kattrin, peace is over. We're moving. (*To the cook*) What's the matter with you?

THE COOK   I'm going to enlist.

MOTHER COURAGE   I've got a suggestion. Why don't . . . ? Where's the chaplain?

THE COOK   Gone to town with Eilif.

MOTHER COURAGE   Then come a little way with me, Lamb. I need help.

THE COOK   That incident with Yvette . . .

MOTHER COURAGE   It hasn't lowered you in my estimation. Far from it. Where there's smoke there's fire. Coming?

THE COOK   I won't say no.

MOTHER COURAGE   The Twelfth Regiment has shoved off. Take the shaft. Here's a chunk of bread. We'll have to circle around

to meet the Lutherans. Maybe I'll see Eilif tonight. He's my favorite. It's been a short peace. And we're on the move again. (*She sings, while the cook and Kattrin harness themselves to the wagon*)

From Ulm to Metz, from Metz to Pilsen
Courage is right there in the van.
The war both in and out of season
With shot and shell will feed its man.
But lead alone is not sufficient
The war needs soldiers to subsist!
Its diet elseways is deficient.
The war is hungry! So enlist!

9

The great war of religion has been going on for sixteen years. Germany has lost more than half its population. Those whom the slaughter has spared have been laid low by epidemics. Once-flourishing countrysides are ravaged by famine. Wolves prowl through the charred ruins of the cities. In the fall of 1634 we find Mother Courage in Germany, in the Fichtelgebirge, at some distance from the road followed by the Swedish armies. Winter comes early and is exceptionally severe. Business is bad, begging is the only resort. The cook receives a letter from Utrecht and is dismissed.

Outside a half-demolished presbytery.

Gray morning in early winter. Gusts of wind. Mother Courage and the cook in shabby sheepskins by the wagon.

THE COOK   No light. Nobody's up yet.

MOTHER COURAGE   But it's a priest. He'll have to crawl out of bed to ring the bells. Then he'll get himself a nice bowl of hot soup.

THE COOK   Go on, you saw the village, everything's been burned to a crisp.

MOTHER COURAGE   But somebody's here, I heard a dog bark.

THE COOK   If the priest's got anything, he won't give it away.

MOTHER COURAGE   Maybe if we sing . . .

THE COOK   I've had it up to here. (*Suddenly*) I got a letter from Utrecht. My mother's died of cholera and the tavern belongs to me. Here's the letter if you don't believe me. It's no business of yours what my aunt says about my evil ways, but never mind, read it.

MOTHER COURAGE (*reads the letter*)   Lamb, I'm sick of roaming around, myself. I feel like a butcher's dog that pulls the meat cart but doesn't get any for himself. I've nothing left to sell and the people have no money to pay for it. In Saxony a man in rags tried to foist a cord of books on me for two eggs, and in Württemberg they'd have let their plow go for a little bag of salt. What's the good of plowing? Nothing grows but brambles. In Pomerania they say the villagers have eaten up all the babies, and that nuns have been caught at highway robbery.

THE COOK   It's the end of the world.

MOTHER COURAGE   Sometimes I have visions of myself driving through hell, selling sulphur and brimstone, or through heaven peddling refreshments to the roaming souls. If me and the children I've got left could find a place where there's no shooting, I wouldn't mind a few years of peace and quiet.

THE COOK   We could open up the tavern again. Think it over, Anna. I made up my mind last night; with or without you, I'm going back to Utrecht. In fact I'm leaving today.

MOTHER COURAGE   I'll have to talk to Kattrin. It's kind of sudden, and I don't like to make decisions in the cold with nothing in my stomach. Kattrin! (*Kattrin climbs out of the wagon*) Kattrin, I've got something to tell you. The cook and me are thinking of going to Utrecht. They've left him a tavern there. You'd be living in one place, you'd meet people. A lot of men would be glad to get a nice, well-behaved girl, looks aren't

everything. I'm all for it. I get along fine with the cook. I've got to hand it to him: He's got a head for business. We'd eat regular meals, wouldn't that be nice? And you'd have your own bed, wouldn't you like that? It's no life on the road, year in year out. You'll go to rack and ruin. You're crawling with lice already. We've got to decide, you see, we could go north with the Swedes, they must be over there. (*She points to the left*) I think we'll do it, Kattrin.

THE COOK   Anna, could I have a word with you alone?

MOTHER COURAGE   Get back in the wagon, Kattrin.

(*Kattrin climbs back in*)

THE COOK   I interrupted you because I see there's been a misunderstanding. I thought it was too obvious to need saying. But if it isn't, I'll just have to say it. You can't take her, it's out of the question. Is that plain enough for you?

(*Kattrin sticks her head out of the wagon and listens*)

MOTHER COURAGE   You want me to leave Kattrin?

THE COOK   Look at it this way. There's no room in the tavern. It's not one of those places with three taprooms. If the two of us put our shoulder to the wheel, we can make a living, but not three, it can't be done. Kattrin can keep the wagon.

MOTHER COURAGE   I'd been thinking she could find a husband in Utrecht.

THE COOK   Don't make me laugh! How's she going to find a husband? At her age? And dumb! And with that scar!

MOTHER COURAGE   Not so loud.

THE COOK   Shout or whisper, the truth's the truth. And that's another reason why I can't have her in the tavern. The customers won't want a sight like that staring them in the face. Can you blame them?

MOTHER COURAGE   Shut up. Not so loud, I say.

THE COOK   There's a light in the presbytery. Let's sing.

MOTHER COURAGE   How could she pull the wagon by herself? She's afraid of the war. She couldn't stand it. The dreams she must have! I hear her groaning at night. Especially after battles. What she sees in her dreams, God knows. It's pity that makes her suffer so. The other day the wagon hit a hedgehog, I found it hidden in her blanket.

THE COOK   The tavern's too small. (*He calls*) Worthy gentleman

and members of the household! We shall now sing the Song of Solomon, Julius Caesar, and other great men, whose greatness didn't help them any. Just to show you that we're God-fearing people ourselves, which makes it hard for us, especially in the winter. (*They sing*)

You saw the wise King Solomon
You know what came of him.
To him all hidden things were plain.
He cursed the hour gave birth to him
And saw that everything was vain.
How great and wise was Solomon!
Now think about his case. Alas
A useful lesson can be won.
It's wisdom that had brought him to that pass!
How happy is the man with none!

Our beautiful song proves that virtues are dangerous things, better steer clear of them, enjoy life, eat a good breakfast, a bowl of hot soup, for instance. Take me, I haven't got any soup and wish I had, I'm a soldier, but what has my bravery in all those battles got me, nothing, I'm starving, I'd be better off if I'd stayed home like a yellowbelly. And I'll tell you why.

You saw the daring Caesar next
You know what he became.
They deified him in his life
But then they killed him just the same.
And as they raised the fatal knife
How loud he cried: "You too, my son!"
Now think about his case. Alas
A useful lesson can be won.
It's daring that had brought him to that pass!
How happy is the man with none!

(*In an undertone*) They're not even looking out. Worthy gentleman and members of the household! Maybe you'll say, all right, if bravery won't keep body and soul together, try honesty. That may fill your belly or at least get you a drop to drink. Let's look into it.

You've heard of honest Socrates
Who never told a lie.
They weren't so grateful as you'd think
Instead they sentenced him to die
And handed him the poisoned drink.
How honest was the people's noble son!
Now think about his case. Alas
A useful lesson can be won.
His honesty had brought him to that pass.
How happy is the man with none!

Yes, they tell us to be charitable and to share what we have,
but what if we haven't got anything? Maybe philanthropists
have a rough time of it too, it stands to reason, they need a
little something for themselves. Yes, charity is a rare virtue,
because it doesn't pay.

St. Martin couldn't bear to see
His fellows in distress.
He saw a poor man in the snow.
"Take half my cloak!" He did, and lo!
They both of them froze none the less.
He thought his heavenly reward was won.
Now think about his case. Alas
A useful lesson can be won.
Unselfishness had brought him to that pass.
How happy is the man with none!

That's our situation. We're God-fearing folk, we stick together, we don't steal, we don't murder, we don't set fire to
anything! You could say that we set an example which bears
out the song, we sink lower and lower, we seldom see any
soup, but if we were different, if we were thieves and murder-
ers, maybe our bellies would be full. Because virtue isn't
rewarded, only wickedness, the world needn't be like this,
but it is.

And here you see God-fearing folk
Observing God's ten laws.
So far He hasn't taken heed.

You people sitting warm indoors
Help to relieve our bitter need!
Our virtue can be counted on.
Now think about our case. Alas
A useful lesson can be won.
The fear of God has brought us to this pass.
How happy is the man with none!

VOICE (*from above*)   Hey, down there! Come on up! We've got some good thick soup.

MOTHER COURAGE   Lamb, I couldn't get anything down. I know what you say makes sense, but is it your last word? We've always been good friends.

THE COOK   My last word. Think it over.

MOTHER COURAGE   I don't need to think it over. I won't leave her.

THE COOK   It wouldn't be wise, but there's nothing I can do. I'm not inhuman, but it's a small tavern. We'd better go in now, or there won't be anything left, we'll have been singing in the cold for nothing.

MOTHER COURAGE   I'll get Kattrin.

THE COOK   Better bring it down for her. They'll get a fright if the three of us barge in. (*They go out*)

(*Kattrin climbs out of the wagon. She is carrying a bundle. She looks around to make sure the others are gone. Then she spreads out an old pair of the cook's trousers and a skirt belonging to her mother side by side on a wheel of the wagon so they can easily be seen. She is about to leave with her bundle when Mother Courage comes out of the house*)

MOTHER COURAGE (*with a dish of soup*)   Kattrin! Stop! Kattrin! Where do you think you're going with that bundle? Have you taken leave of your wits? (*She examines the bundle*) She's packed her things. Were you listening? I've told him it's no go with Utrecht and his lousy tavern, what would we do there? A tavern's no place for you and me. The war still has a thing or two up its sleeve for us. (*She sees the trousers and skirt*) You're stupid. Suppose I'd seen that and you'd been gone? (*Kattrin tries to leave, Mother Courage holds her back*) And don't go thinking I've given him the gate on your account. It's the wagon.

I won't part with the wagon, I'm used to it, it's not you, it's the wagon. We'll go in the other direction, we'll put the cook's stuff out here where he'll find it, the fool. (*She climbs up and throws down a few odds and ends to join the trousers*) There. Now we're shut of him, you won't see me taking anyone else into the business. From now on it's you and me. This winter will go by like all the rest. Harness up, it looks like snow.
(*They harness themselves to the wagon, turn it around and pull it away. When the cook comes out he sees his things and stands dumbfounded*)

10

Throughout 1635 Mother Courage and her daughter Kattrin pull the wagon over the roads of central Germany in the wake of the increasingly bedraggled armies.

Highway.

Mother Courage and Kattrin are pulling the wagon. They come to a peasant's house. A voice is heard singing from within.

THE VOICE

> The rose bush in our garden
> Rejoiced our hearts in spring
> It bore such lovely flowers.
> We planted it last season
> Before the April showers.
> A garden is a blessèd thing
> It bore such lovely flowers.
>
> When winter comes a-stalking
> And gales great snow storms bring
> They trouble us but little.
> We've lately finished caulking
> The roof with moss and wattle.
> A sheltering roof's a blessèd thing
> When winter comes a-stalking.

(*Mother Courage and Kattrin have stopped to listen. Then they move on*)

11

January 1636. The imperial troops threaten the Protestant city of Halle. The stone speaks. Mother Courage loses her daughter and goes on alone. The end of
the war is not in sight.

*The wagon, much the worse for wear, is standing beside a peasant house
with an enormous thatch roof. The house is built against the side of a
stony hill. Night.*

A lieutenant and three soldiers in heavy armor step out of the woods.

THE LIEUTENANT   I don't want any noise. If anybody yells, run
him through with your pikes.

FIRST SOLDIER   But we need a guide. We'll have to knock if we
want them to come out.

THE LIEUTENANT   Knocking sounds natural. It could be a cow
bumping against the barn wall.
*(The soldiers knock on the door. A peasant woman opens. They hold
their hands over her mouth. Two soldiers go in)*

A MAN'S VOICE (*inside*)   Who's there?
(The soldiers bring out a peasant and his son)

THE LIEUTENANT (*points to the wagon, in which Kattrin has appeared*)   There's another one. (*A soldier pulls her out*) Anybody
else live here?

THE PEASANT COUPLE   This is our son.—That's a dumb girl.—
Her mother's gone into the town on business.—Buying up
people's belongings, they're selling cheap because they're getting out.—They're provisioners.

THE LIEUTENANT   I'm warning you to keep quiet, one squawk
and you'll get a pike over the head. All right. I need somebody
who can show us the path into the city. (*Points to the young
peasant*) You. Come here!

THE YOUNG PLEASANT   I don't know no path.

THE SECOND SOLDIER (*grinning*)   He don't know no path.

THE YOUNG PEASANT   I'm not helping the Catholics.

THE LIEUTENANT (*to the second soldier*)   Give him a feel of your pike!

THE YOUNG PEASANT (*forced down on his knees and threatened with the pike*)   You can kill me. I won't do it.

THE FIRST SOLDIER   I know what'll make him think twice. (*He goes over to the barn*) Two cows and an ox. Get this: If you don't help us, I'll cut them down.

THE YOUNG PEASANT   Not the animals!

THE PEASANT WOMAN (*in tears*)   Captain, spare our animals or we'll starve.

THE LIEUTENANT   If he insists on being stubborn, they're done for.

THE FIRST SOLDIER   I'll start with the ox.

THE YOUNG PEASANT (*to the old man*)   Do I have to? (*The old woman nods*) I'll do it.

THE PEASANT WOMAN   And thank you kindly for your forbearance, Captain, for ever and ever, amen.
(*The peasant stops her from giving further thanks*)

THE FIRST SOLDIER   Didn't I tell you? With them it's the animals that come first.
(*Led by the young peasant, the lieutenant and the soldiers continue on their way*)

THE PEASANT   I wish I knew what they're up to. Nothing good.

THE PEASANT WOMAN   Maybe they're only scouts.—What are you doing?

THE PEASANT (*putting a ladder against the roof and climbing up*)   See if they're alone. (*On the roof*) Men moving in the woods. All the way to the quarry. Armor in the clearing. And a cannon. It's more than a regiment. God have mercy on the city and everybody in it.

THE PEASANT WOMAN   See any light in the city?

THE PEASANT   No. They're all asleep. (*He climbs down*) If they get in, they'll kill everybody.

THE PEASANT WOMAN   The sentry will see them in time.

THE PEASANT   They must have killed the sentry in the tower on the hill, or he'd have blown his horn.

THE PEASANT WOMAN   If there were more of us . . .

THE PEASANT   All by ourselves up here with a cripple . . .

THE PEASANT WOMAN   We can't do a thing. Do you think . . .

THE PEASANT   Not a thing.

THE PEASANT WOMAN   We couldn't get down there in the dark.

THE PEASANT   The whole hillside is full of them. We can't even give a signal.

THE PEASANT WOMAN   They'd kill us.

THE PEASANT   No, we can't do a thing.

THE PEASANT WOMAN (*to Kattrin*)   Pray, poor thing, pray! We can't stop the bloodshed. If you can't talk, at least you can pray. He'll hear you if nobody else does. I'll help you. (*All kneel, Kattrin behind the peasants*) Our Father which art in heaven, hear our prayer. Don't let the town perish with everybody in it, all asleep and unsuspecting. Wake them, make them get up and climb the walls and see the enemy coming through the night with cannon and pikes, through the fields and down the hillside. (*Back to Kattrin*) Protect our mother and don't let the watchman sleep, wake him before it's too late. And succor our brother-in-law, he's in there with his four children, let them not perish, they're innocent and don't know a thing. (*To Kattrin, who groans*) The littlest is less than two, the oldest is seven. (*Horrified, Kattrin stands up*) Our Father, hear us, for Thou alone canst help, we'll all be killed, we're weak, we haven't any pikes or anything, we are powerless and in Thine hands, we and our animals and the whole farm, and the city too, it's in Thine hands, and the enemy is under the walls with great might.
(*Kattrin has crept unnoticed to the wagon, taken something out of it, put it under her apron and climbed up the ladder to the roof of the barn*)

THE PEASANT WOMAN   Think upon the children in peril, especially the babes in arms and the old people that can't help themselves and all God's creatures.

THE PEASANT   And forgive us our trespasses as we forgive them that trespass against us. Amen.
(*Kattrin, sitting on the roof, starts beating the drum that she has taken out from under her apron*)

THE PEASANT WOMAN   Jesus! What's she doing?

THE PEASANT   She's gone crazy.

THE PEASANT WOMAN   Get her down, quick!

(*The peasant runs toward the ladder, but Kattrin pulls it up on the roof*)

THE PEASANT WOMAN   She'll be the death of us all.

THE PEASANT   Stop that, you cripple!

THE PEASANT WOMAN   She'll have the Catholics down on us.

THE PEASANT (*looking around for stones*)   I'll throw rocks at you.

THE PEASANT WOMAN   Have you no pity? Have you no heart? We're dead if they find out it's us! They'll run us through!

(*Kattrin stares in the direction of the city, and goes on drumming*)

THE PEASANT WOMAN (*to the peasant*)   I told you not to let those tramps stop here. What do they care if the soldiers drive our last animals away?

THE LIEUTENANT (*rushes in with his soldiers and the young peasant*)   I'll cut you to pieces!

THE PEASANT WOMAN   We're innocent, captain. We couldn't help it. She sneaked up there. We don't know her.

THE LIEUTENANT   Where's the ladder?

THE PEASANT   Up top.

THE LIEUTENANT (*to Kattrin*)   Throw down that drum. It's an order!

(*Kattrin goes on drumming*)

THE LIEUTENANT   You're all in this together! This'll be the end of you!

THE PEASANT   They've felled some pine trees in the woods over there. We could get one and knock her down . . .

THE FIRST SOLDIER (*to the lieutenant*)   Request permission to make a suggestion. (*He whispers something in the lieutenant's ear. He nods*) Listen. We've got a friendly proposition. Come down, we'll take you into town with us. Show us your mother and we won't touch a hair of her head.

(*Kattrin goes on drumming*)

THE LIEUTENANT (*pushes him roughly aside*)   She doesn't trust you. No wonder with your mug. (*He calls up*) If I give you my word? I'm an officer, you can trust my word of honor.

(*She drums still louder*)

THE LIEUTENANT   Nothing is sacred to her.

THE YOUNG PEASANT   It's not just her mother, lieutenant!

THE FIRST SOLDIER   We can't let this go on. They'll hear it in the city.

THE LIEUTENANT   We'll have to make some kind of noise that's louder than the drums. What could we make noise with?

THE FIRST SOLDIER   But we're not supposed to make noise.

THE LIEUTENANT   An innocent noise, stupid. A peaceable noise.

THE PEASANT   I could chop wood.

THE LIEUTENANT   That's it, chop! (*The peasant gets an ax and chops at a log*) Harder! Harder! You're chopping for your life.
(*Listening, Kattrin has been drumming more softly. Now she looks anxiously around and goes on drumming as before*)

THE LIEUTENANT (*to the peasant*)   Not loud enough. (*To the first soldier*) You chop too.

THE PEASANT   There's only one ax. (*Stops chopping*)

THE LIEUTENANT   We'll have to set the house on fire. Smoke her out.

THE PEASANT   That won't do any good, captain. If the city people see fire up here, they'll know what's afoot.
(*Still drumming, Kattrin has been listening again. Now she laughs*)

THE LIEUTENANT   Look, she's laughing at us. I'll shoot her down, regardless. Get the musket!
(*Two soldiers run out. Kattrin goes on drumming*)

THE PEASANT WOMAN   I've got it, captain. That's their wagon over there. If we start smashing it up, she'll stop. The wagon's all they've got.

THE LIEUTENANT (*to the young peasant*)   Smash away. (*To Kattrin*) We'll smash your wagon if you don't stop.
(*The young peasant strikes a few feeble blows at the wagon*)

THE PEASANT WOMAN   Stop it, you beast!
(*Kattrin stares despairingly at the wagon and emits pitiful sounds. But she goes on drumming*)

THE LIEUTENANT   Where are those stinkers with the musket?

THE FIRST SOLDIER   They haven't heard anything in the city yet, or we'd hear their guns.

THE LIEUTENANT (*to Kattrin*)   They don't hear you. And now we're going to shoot you down. For the last time: Drop that drum!

THE YOUNG PEASANT (*suddenly throws the plank away*) Keep on drumming! Or they'll all be killed! Keep on drumming, keep on drumming . . .
(*The soldier throws him down and hits him with his pike. Kattrin starts crying, but goes on drumming*)

THE PEASANT WOMAN Don't hit him in the back! My God, you're killing him.
(*The soldiers run in with the musket*)

THE SECOND SOLDIER The colonel's foaming at the mouth. We'll be court-martialed.

THE LIEUTENANT Set it up! Set it up! (*To Kattrin, while the musket is being set up on its stand*) For the last time: Stop that drumming! (*Kattrin in tears drums as loud as she can*) Fire!
(*The soldiers fire. Kattrin is hit. She beats the drum a few times more and then slowly collapses*)

THE LIEUTENANT Now we'll have some quiet.
(*But Kattrin's last drumbeats are answered by the city's cannon. A confused hubbub of alarm bells and cannon is heard in the distance*)

FIRST SOLDIER She's done it.

12

Night, toward morning. The fifes and drums of troops marching away.

Outside the wagon Mother Courage sits huddled over her daughter. The peasant couple are standing beside them.

THE PEASANT (*hostile*)   You'll have to be going, woman. There's only one more regiment to come. You can't go alone.

MOTHER COURAGE   Maybe I can get her to sleep. (*She sings*)

> Lullaby baby
> What stirs in the hay?
> The neighbor brats whimper
> Mine are happy and gay.
> They go in tatters
> And you in silk down
> Cut from an angel's
> Best party gown.
>
> They've nothing to munch on
> And you will have pie
> Just tell your mother
> In case it's too dry.
> Lullaby baby
> What stirs in the hay?
> The one lies in Poland
> The other—who can say?

Now she's asleep. You shouldn't have told her about your brother-in-law's children.

THE PEASANT   Maybe it wouldn't have happened if you hadn't gone to town to swindle people.

MOTHER COURAGE   I'm glad she's sleeping now.

THE PEASANT WOMAN   She's not sleeping, you'll have to face it, she's dead.

THE PEASANT   And it's time you got started. There are wolves around here, and what's worse, marauders.

MOTHER COURAGE   Yes. (*She goes to the wagon and takes out a sheet of canvas to cover the body with*)

THE PEASANT WOMAN   Haven't you anybody else? Somebody you can go to?

MOTHER COURAGE   Yes, there's one of them left. Eilif.

THE PEASANT (*while Mother Courage covers the body*)   Go find him. We'll attend to this one, give her a decent burial. Set your mind at rest.

MOTHER COURAGE   Here's money for your expenses. (*She gives the peasant money*)
(*The peasant and his son shake hands with her and carry Kattrin away*)

THE PEASANT WOMAN (*on the way out*)   Hurry up!

MOTHER COURAGE (*harnesses herself to the wagon*)   I hope I can pull the wagon alone. I'll manage, there isn't much in it. I've got to get back in business.
(*Another regiment marches by with fifes and drums in the rear*)

MOTHER COURAGE   Hey, take me with you! (*She starts to pull*)
(*Singing is heard in the rear:*)

With all the killing and recruiting
The war will worry on a while.
In ninety years they'll still be shooting.
It's hardest on the rank-and-file.
Our food is swill, our pants all patches
The higher-ups steal half our pay
And still we dream of God-sent riches.
Tomorrow is another day!
    The spring is come! Christian, revive!
    The snowdrifts melt, the dead lie dead!
    And if by chance you're still alive
    It's time to rise and shake a leg.

Notes and Variants

LIFE OF GALILEO

Texts by Brecht

Foreword

It is well known how beneficially people can be influenced by the conviction that they are poised on the threshold of a new age. At such a moment their environment appears to be still entirely unfinished, capable of the happiest improvements, full of dreamt-of and undreamt-of possibilities, like malleable raw material in their hands. They themselves feel as if they have awakened to a new day, rested, strong, resourceful. Old beliefs are dismissed as superstitions, what yesterday seemed a matter of course is today subject to fresh examination. We have been ruled, says mankind, but now we shall be the rulers.

Around the turn of this century no other line from a song so powerfully inspired the workers as the line: "Now a new age is dawning"; old and young marched to it, the poorest, the down-and-outs and those who had already won something of civilization for themselves—all felt young. Under a house painter the unprecedented seductive power of these selfsame words was also tried and proved; for he too promised a new age. Here the words revealed their emptiness and vagueness. Their strength lay in their very indefiniteness, which was now being exploited in demoralizing the masses. The new age—that was something and is something that affects everything, leaves nothing unchanged, but is also still only unfolding its character gradually; something in which all imagination has scope to flower, and which is only restricted by too precise description. Glorious is the feeling of beginning, of pioneering; the fact of being a beginner inspires enthusiasm. Glorious is the feeling of

happiness in those who oil a new machine before it is to display its strength, in those who fill in a blank space on an old map, in those who dig the foundation of a new house, their house.

This feeling comes to the researcher who makes a discovery that will change everything, to the orator who prepares a speech that will create an entirely new situation. Terrible is the disappointment when men discover, or think they discover, that they have fallen victims to an illusion, that the old is stronger than the new, that the "facts" are against them and not for them, that their age—the new age—has not yet arrived. Then things are not merely as bad as before, but much worse because people have made immense sacrifices for their schemes and have lost everything; they have ventured and are now defeated; the old is taking its revenge on them. The researcher or the discoverer —an unknown but also unpersecuted man before he has published his discovery—when once his discovery has been disproved or discredited is a swindler and a charlatan, and all too well known; the victim of oppression and exploitation, when once his insurrection has been crushed, is a rebel who is subject to special repression and punishment. Exertion is followed by exhaustion, possibly exaggerated hope by possibly exaggerated hopelessness. Those who do not relapse into indifference and apathy fall into worse; those who have not sacrificed their energies for their ideals now turn those selfsame energies against those very ideals! There is no more remorseless reactionary than a frustrated innovator, no crueler enemy of the wild elephant than the tame elephant.

And yet these disappointed men may still go on existing in a new age, an age of great upheaval. Only, they know nothing of new ages.

In these days the conception of the new is itself falsified. The Old and the Very Old, now re-entering the arena, proclaim themselves as new, or else it is held to be new when the Old or the Very Old are put over in a new way. But the really New, having been deposed today, is declared old-fashioned, degraded to being a transitory phase whose day is done. The "new" for example is the system of waging wars, whereas "old," so they say, is a system of economy, proposed but never put into prac-

tice, which makes wars superfluous. In the new system, society is being entrenched in classes; and the old, so they say, is the desire to abolish classes. The hopes of mankind do not so much become discouraged in these times; rather, they become diverted. Men had hoped that one day there would be bread to eat. Now they may hope that one day there will be stones to eat.

Amid the darkness gathering fast over a fevered world, a world surrounded by bloody deeds and no less bloody thoughts, by increasing barbarism which seems to be leading irresistibly to perhaps the greatest and most terrible war of all time, it is difficult to adopt an attitude appropriate to people on the threshold of a new and happier age. Does not everything point to night's arrival and nothing to the dawning of a new age? So shouldn't one, therefore, assume an attitude appropriate to people heading towards the night?

What is this talk of a "new age"? Is not this expression itself obsolete? When it is shouted at us, it is bellowed from hoarse throats. Now indeed, it is mere barbarism which impersonates the new age. It says of itself that it hopes it will last a thousand years.

So should one hold fast to the old times? Should one discuss sunk Atlantis?

Am I already lying down for the night and thinking, when I think of the morning, of the one that has passed, so as to avoid thinking of the one to come? Is that why I occupy myself with that epoch of the flowering of the arts and sciences three hundred years ago? I hope not.

These images of the morning and the night are misleading. Happy times do not come in the same way as a morning follows a night's sleep.

[Dated 1939; not revised by Brecht. From Werner Hecht (ed.): *Materialien zu Brechts "Leben des Galilei,"* Frankfurt, Suhrkamp, 1968, pp. 7 ff.]

The *Life of Galileo* Is Not a Tragedy

So, from the point of view of the theater, the question will arise whether the *Life of Galileo* is to be presented as a tragedy or as an optimistic play. Is the keynote to be found in Galileo's "Salutation to the New Age" in scene 1 or in certain parts of scene 14? According to the prevailing rules of play-construction, the end of a drama must carry the greater weight. But this play is not constructed according to these rules. The play shows the dawn of a new age and tries to correct some of the prejudices about the dawn of a new age.

[Dated 1939. From Werner Hecht (ed.), *ibid.*, p. 13.]

Portrayal of the Church

For the theater it is important to understand that this play must lose a great part of its effect if its performance is directed chiefly against the Catholic Church.

Of the dramatis personae, many wear the church's garb. Actors who, because of that, try to portray these characters as odious would be doing wrong. But neither, on the other hand, has the church the right to have the human weaknesses of its members glossed over. It has all too often encouraged these weaknesses and suppressed their exposure. But in this play there is also no question of the church being admonished: "Hands off science!" Modern science is a legitimate daughter of the church, a daughter who has emancipated herself and turned against the mother.

In the present play the church functions, even when it opposes free investigation, simply as authority.

Since science was a branch of theology, the church is the intellectual authority, the ultimate scientific court of appeal. But it is also the temporal authority, the ultimate political court of appeal. The play shows the temporary victory of authority, not the victory of the priesthood. It corresponds to the historical

truth in that the Galileo of the play never turns directly against the church. There is not a sentence uttered by Galileo in that sense. If there had been, such a thorough commission of investigation as the Inquisition would undoubtedly have brought it to light. And it equally corresponds to the historical truth that the greatest astronomer of the Papal Roman College, Christopher Clavius, confirmed Galileo's discoveries (scene 6). It is also true that clerics were among his pupils (scenes 8, 9, and 13).

To take satirical aim at the worldly interests of high dignitaries seems to me cheap (it would be in scene 7). But the casual way in which these high officials treat the physicist is only meant to show that, by reason of their past experiences, they think they can count on ready complaisance from Galileo. They are not mistaken.

Considering our bourgeois politicians, one cannot but extol the spiritual (and scientific) interests of those politicians of old.

The play, therefore, ignores the falsifications made to the protocol of 1616 by the Inquisition of 1633, falsifications established by the recent historical studies under the direction of the German scholar Emil Wohlwill. Doubtless the judgment and sentence of 1633 were thereby made juridically possible. Anybody who understands the point of view outlined above will appreciate that the author was not concerned with this legal side of the trial.

There is no doubt that Urban VIII was personally incensed at Galileo and, in the most detestable manner, played a personal part in the proceedings against him. The play passes this over.

Anyone who understands the standpoint of the author will appreciate that this attitude implies no reverence for the church of the seventeenth, let alone of the twentieth century.

Casting the church as the embodiment of authority in this theatrical trial of the persecutors of the champions of free research certainly does not help to secure an acquittal for the church. But it would be highly dangerous, particularly nowadays, to treat a matter like Galileo's fight for freedom of research as a religious one; for thereby attention would be most unhappily deflected from present-day reactionary authorities of a totally unecclesiastical kind.

[Dated 1939. From Werner Hecht (ed.), *ibid.*, pp. 14 f.]

Three Notes on the Character of Galileo

1. [The new type of physicist]

[. . .] It's important that you shouldn't idealize Galileo: You know the kind of thing—the stargazer, the pallid intellectualized idealist. I know you wouldn't if left to yourself, but the pictures you'll see in the books are already idealized. My Galileo is a powerful physicist with a tummy on him, a face like Socrates, a vociferous, full-blooded man with a sense of humor, the new type of physicist, earthly, a great teacher. Favorite attitude: stomach thrust forward, both hands on the buttocks, head back, using one meaty hand all the time to gesticulate with, but with precision; comfortable trousers for working in, shirtsleeves or (particularly at the end) a long whitish-yellow robe with broad sleeves, tied with a cord round his stomach. You get the idea—preferably an etching of this figure or some kind of steel engraving or wood engraving to maintain its historical flavor: in other words, realistic. Or for that matter one could have pen drawings standing freely on the page. Don't be scared of a bit of humor. History without humor is a ghastly thing . . .

N.B. As far as I know, Galileo's telescope was about two-and-a-half feet long and the thickness of a man's arm. You can stand it on an ordinary tripod. The model of the Ptolemaic system (in scene 1) is of wood, some twenty inches in diameter. You could probably get a rough idea from the keeper of the planetarium.

2. The Sensual Element in Galileo

Galileo of course is not a Falstaff: He insists on his physical pleasures because of his materialist convictions. He wouldn't, for instance, drink at his work; the point is that he *works* in a sensual way. He gets pleasure from handling his instruments with elegance. A great part of his sensuality is of an intellectual kind: for instance, the "beauty" of an experiment, the little theatrical performance with which he gives shape to each of his lessons, the often abrupt way in which he will confront some-

body with the truth, not to mention those passages in his speeches (in 1, 7, 13) where he picks good words and tests them like a spice. (This has nothing to do with that bel canto of the actor who may produce his arias as if he enjoyed them, but fails to show the enjoyment of the character he is playing.)

3. About the Part of Galileo

What gives this new historical character his quality of strangeness, novelty, strikingness, is the fact that he, Galileo, looks at the world of 1600 around him as if he himself were a stranger. He studies this world and finds it remarkable, outdated, in need of explanation. He studies:

in scene 1, Ludovico Marsili and Priuli
in scene 2, the way in which the senators look through the telescope (When am I going to be able to buy one of these things?)
in scene 3, Sagredo (the prince being a child of nine)
in scene 4, the court scholars
in scene 5, the monks
in scene 7, the young monk
in scene 8, Federzoni and Ludovico
in scene [11], (for just one second) Virginia
in scene [13], his pupils
in scene [14], Andrea and Virginia.

> [From Werner Hecht (ed.), *ibid.* pp. 27 f. The first section comes from a letter from Brecht to the painter Hans Tombrock in March 1941, and refers to the first version of the play, which Tombrock illustrated for a proposed publication in the USSR which never materialized. The second and third are undated, but appear to refer to the second, American version.]

Drafts for a Foreword to *Life of Galileo*

The *Life of Galileo* was written in those last dark months of 1938, when many people felt fascism's advance to be irresistible and the final collapse of Western civilization to have arrived. And

ndeed we were approaching the end of that great age to which
he world owes the development of the natural sciences, together with such new arts as music and the theater. There was
a more or less general expectation of a barbaric age "outside
history." Only a minority saw the evolution of new forces and
sensed the vitality of the new ideas. Even the significance of
expressions like "old" and "new" had been obscured. The doctrines of the socialist classics had lost the appeal of novelty, and
seemed to belong to a vanished day.

The bourgeois single out science from the scientist's consciousness, setting it up as an island of independence so as to be
able in practice to interweave it with *their* politics, *their* economics, *their* ideology. The research scientist's object is "pure"
research; the product of that research is not so pure. The for-
mula $E = mc^2$ is conceived of as eternal, not tied to anything.
Hence other people can do the tying: Suddenly the city of
Hiroshima became very short-lived. The scientists are claiming
the irresponsibility of machines.

Let us think back to the founding father of experimental
science, Francis Bacon, whose phrase that one must obey nature
in order to command her was not written in vain. His contemporaries obeyed his nature by bribing him with money, and so
thoroughly commanded him when he was Lord Chief Justice
that in the end Parliament had to lock him up. Macaulay, the
puritan, drew a distinction between Bacon the scientist, whom
he admired, and Bacon the politician, of whom he disapproved.
Should we be doing the same thing with the German doctors
of Nazi times?

Among other things, war promotes the sciences. What an
opportunity! It creates discoverers as well as thieves. A higher
responsibility (that of the higher ranks) replaces the lower (that
for the lowly). Obedience is the midwife of arbitrariness. Disorder is perfectly in order. Those doctors who combatted yellow
fever had to use themselves as guinea pigs; the fascist doctors
had material supplied them. Justice played a part too; they had
to freeze only "criminals," in other words those who did not
share their opinions. For their experiments in using "animal

warmth" as a means of thawing they were given prostitutes, women who had transgressed the rule of chastity. They had served sin; now they were being allowed to serve science. It incidentally emerged that hot water restores life better than a woman's body; in its small way it can do more for the fatherland. (Ethics must never be overlooked in war.) Progress all round. At the beginning of this century the lower classes' politicians were forced to treat the prisons as their universities. Now the prisons became universities for the warders (and doctors). Their experiments would of course have been perfectly in order —"from a scientific point of view," that is—even if the state had been forced to exceed the ethical bounds. None the less the bourgeois world still has a certain right to be outraged. Even if it is only a matter of degrees it is a matter of degrees. When Generals von Mackensen and Mältzer were being tried in Rome for shooting hostages, the English prosecutor, a certain Colonel Halse, admitted that "reprisal killings" in war were not illegal so long as the victims were taken from the scene of the incident in question, an attempt was made to find the persons responsible for it, and there were not too many executions. The German generals however had gone too far. They took ten Italians for every German soldier killed (not twenty, though, as demanded by Hitler), and dispatched the whole lot too quickly, within some twenty-four hours. The Italian police, by an oversight, handed over several Italians too many, and by another oversight the Germans shot them too, out of a misplaced reliance on the Italians. But here again they had ransacked the prisons for hostages, taking criminals or suspects awaiting trial, and filling the gaps with Jews. So a certain humanity asserted itself, and not merely in the errors of arithmetic. All the same, bounds were exceeded in this case, and something had to be done to punish the excess.

It can none the less be shown that, in this period when the bourgeoisie has gone completely to pieces, those pieces are still made of the same stuff as the original polished article.

And so in the end the scientists get what they want: state resources, large-scale planning, authority over industry; their Golden Age has come. And their great production starts as the production of weapons of destruction; their planning leads to

extreme anarchy, for they are arming the state against other states. As soon as he represents such a threat to the world, the people's traditional contempt for the unworldly professor turns into naked fear. And just when he has wholly cut himself off from the people as the complete specialist, he is appalled to see himself once again as one of the people, because the threat applies to him too; he has reason to fear for his own life, and the best reason of anybody to know just how much. His protests, of which we have heard quite a number, refer not only to the attacks on his science, which is to be hampered, sterilized, and perverted, but also to the threat which his knowledge represents to the world, and also to the threat to himself.

The Germans have just undergone one of those experiences that are so difficult to convert into usable conclusions. The leadership of the state had fallen to an ignorant person who associated himself with a gang of violent and "uneducated" politicians to proclaim a vast war and utterly ruin the country. Shortly before the catastrophic end, and for some time after it, the blame was attributed to these people. They had conducted an almost total mobilization of the intellectuals, providing every branch with trained manpower, and although they made a number of clumsy attempts to interfere, the catastrophe cannot be ascribed to clumsy interference alone. Not even the military and political strategy appears to have been all that wrong, while the courage of the army and of the civil population is beyond dispute. What won in the end was the enemy's superiority in men and technology, something that had been brought into play by a series of almost unpredictable events.

Many of those who see, or at any rate suspect, capitalism's shortcomings are prepared to put up with them for the sake of the personal freedom which capitalism appears to guarantee. They believe in this freedom mainly because they scarcely ever make use of it. Under the scourge of Hitler they saw this freedom more or less abrogated; it was like a little nest-egg in the savings bank which could normally be drawn on at any time, though it was clearly more sensible not to touch it, but had now as it were been frozen—i.e., could not be drawn on, although

it was still there. They regarded the Hitler period as abnormal; it was a matter of some warts on capitalism, or even of an anticapitalist movement. The latter was something that one could only believe if one accepted the Nazis' own definition of capitalism, while as for the wart theory one was after all dealing with a system where warts flourished, and there was no question of the intellectuals being able to prevent them or make them go away. In either case freedom could only be restored by a catastrophe. And when the catastrophe came, not even it was able to restore freedom, not even it.

Among the various descriptions of the poverty prevailing in denazified Germany was that of spiritual poverty. "What they want, what they're waiting for is a message," people said. "Didn't they have one?" I asked. "Look at the poverty," they said, "and at the lack of leadership." "Didn't they have leadership enough?" I asked, pointing to the poverty. "But they must have something to look forward to," they said. "Aren't they tired of looking forward to such things?" I asked. "I understand they lived quite a while on looking forward either to getting rid of their leader or to having him lay the world at their feet for them to pillage."

The hardest time to get along without knowledge is the time when knowledge is hardest to get. It is the condition of bottommost poverty where it seems possible to get along without knowledge. Nothing is calculable any longer, the measures went up in the fire, short-range objectives hide those in the distance; at that point chance decides.

> [From Werner Hecht (ed.): *ibid.*, pp. 16 ff. These different items are given in the same order as there, though they appear to date from after the Second World War and not, as there suggested, mainly from 1938–1939.]

Unvarnished Picture of a New Age

PREAMBLE TO THE AMERICAN VERSION

When, during my first years in exile in Denmark, I wrote the play *Life of Galileo*, I was helped in the reconstruction of the Ptolemaic cosmology by assistants of Niels Bohr who were working on the problem of splitting the atom. My intention was, among others, to give an unvarnished picture of a new age —a strenuous undertaking since all those around me were convinced that our own era lacked every attribute of a new age. Nothing of this aspect had changed when, years later, I began together with Charles Laughton to prepare an American version of the play. The "atomic" age made its debut at Hiroshima in the middle of our work. Overnight the biography of the founder of the new system of physics read differently. The infernal effect of the great bomb placed the conflict between Galileo and the authorities of his day in a new, sharper light. We had to make only a few alterations—not a single one to the structure of the play. Already in the original version the church was portrayed as a secular authority, its ideology as, fundamentally, interchangeable with many others. From the first, the keystone of the gigantic figure of Galileo was his conception of a science for the people. For hundreds of years and throughout the whole of Europe people had paid him the honor, in the Galileo legend, of not believing in his recantation, just as they had for long derided scientists as biased, unpractical and eunuch-like old fogeys. [. . .]

> [Dated 1946. From Werner Hecht (ed.), *ibid.*, pp. 10 ff. The rest of the note, here omitted, was incorporated in the Model Book (see p. 238–239 below).]

Praise or Condemnation of Galileo?

It would be a great weakness in this work if those physicists were right who said to me—in a tone of approval—that Galileo's recantation of his teachings was, despite one or two "wa-

verings," portrayed as being sensible, with the argument that this recantation enabled him to carry on with his scientific work and to hand it down to posterity. The fact is that Galileo enriched astronomy and physics by simultaneously robbing these sciences of a greater part of their social importance. By discrediting the Bible and the church, these sciences stood for a while at the barricades on behalf of all progress. It is true that a forward movement took place in the following centuries, and these sciences were involved in it, but it was a slow movement, not a revolution; the scandal, so to speak, degenerated into a dispute between experts. The church, and with it all the forces of reaction, was able to bring off an organized retreat and more or less reassert its power. As far as these particular sciences are concerned, they never again regained their high position in society, neither did they ever again come into such close contact with the people.

Galileo's crime can be regarded as the "original sin" of modern natural sciences. From the new astronomy, which deeply interested a new class—the bourgeoisie—since it gave an impetus to the revolutionary social current of the time, he made a sharply defined special science which—admittedly through its very "purity," i.e., its indifference to modes of production—was able to develop comparatively undisturbed.

The atom bomb is, both as a technical and as a social phenomenon, the classical end-product of his contribution to science and his failure to contribute to society.

Thus, the "hero" of this work is not Galileo but the people, as Walter Benjamin has said. This seems to me to be rather too briefly expressed. I hope this work shows how society extorts from its individuals what it needs from them. The urge to research, a social phenomenon no less delightful or compulsive than the urge to reproduce, steers Galileo into that most dangerous territory, drives him into agonizing conflict with his violent desires for other pleasures. He raises his telescope to the stars and delivers himself to the rack. In the end he indulges his science like a vice, secretly and probably with pangs of conscience. Confronted with such a situation, one can scarcely wish only to praise or only to condemn Galileo.

[Dated 1947. From Werner Hecht (ed.), *ibid.*, pp. 12 f.]

Prologue to the American Production

Respected public of the way called Broad
Tonight we invite you to step on board
A world of curves and measurements, where you'll descry
The newborn physics in their infancy.
Here you will see the life of the great Galileo Galilei.
The law of falling bodies versus the GRATIAS DEI
Science's fight versus the rulers, put on stage
At the beginning of the modern age.
Here you'll see science in its blooming youth
Also its first compromises with the truth.
The Good, so far, has not been turned to goods
But already there's something nasty in the woods
Which stops that truth from reaching the majority
And won't relieve, but aggravate their poverty.
We think such sights are relevant today
The modern age is so quick to pass away
We hope you'll lend a charitable ear
To what we say, since otherwise we fear
If you won't learn from Galileo's experience
The Bomb will put in a personal appearance.

[From Werner Hecht (ed.), *ibid.*, p. 38.]

Epilogue of the Scientists

And the lamp his work ignited
We have tried to keep alight
Stooping low, and yet high-minded
Unrestrained, yet laced up tight.
Making moon and stars obey us
Groveling at our rulers' feet
We sell our brains for what they'll pay us
To satisfy our bodies' need.
So, despised by those above us

Ridiculed by those below
We've found out the laws that move us
Keep this planet on the go.
Knowledge grows too large for nitwits
Servitude expands as well
Truth becomes so many titbits
Liberators give us hell.
Riding in new railway coaches
To the new ships on the waves
Who is it that now approaches?
Only slave-owners and slaves.
Only slaves and slave-owners
Leave the trains
Taking the new aeroplanes
Through the heaven's age-old blueness.
Till the latest one arrives
Astronomic
White, atomic
Obliterating all our lives.

[From Werner Hecht (ed.), *ibid.*, pp. 38 f.]

Notes on Individual Scenes

[Scene 11]

Could Galileo have acted any differently?

This scene gives ample reasons for Galileo's hesitation about escaping from Florence and seeking asylum in the North Italian cities. None the less the audience can imagine him putting himself in the hands of Matti the iron founder, and discover various tendencies in his character and situation which would support this.

The actor Laughton showed Galileo in a state of great inner agitation during his talk with the iron founder. He played it as a moment of decision—the wrong one. (Connoisseurs of dialec-

tics will find Galileo's possibilities further clarified in the ensuing scene "The Pope," where the inquisitor insists that Galileo
must be forced to recant his theory because the Italian maritime
cities need his star charts, which derive from it and of which it
would not be possible to deprive them.)

An objectivist approach is not permissible here.*

[*Scene 14*]

Galileo after his recantation

His crime has made a criminal of him. When he reflects on
the *scale* of his crime he is pleased with himself. He defends
himself against the outside world's impertinent expectations of
its geniuses. What has Andrea done to oppose the Inquisition?
Galileo applies his intellect to solving the problems of the
clergy, which these blockheads have overlooked. His mind
functions automatically, like a motor in neutral. His appetite
for knowledge feels to him like the impetus that makes him
twitch. Scholarly activity, for him, is a sin: mortally dangerous,
but impossible to do without. He has a fanatical hatred for
humanity. Andrea's readiness to revise his damning verdict as
soon as he sees the book means that he has been corrupted. As
to a lame and starving wolf, Galileo tosses him a crust, the
logical scientific analysis of the Galileo phenomenon. Behind
this lies his rejection of the moral demands of a humanity which
does nothing to relieve the deadliness of that morality and those
demands.

[. . .]

Once Galileo knows that his book has set out on its journey
towards publication he changes his attitude again. He proposes
that the book should be prefaced by an introduction sharply
condemning the author's treachery. Andrea passionately
refuses to pass on such a request, pointing out that everything
is different now, that Galileo's recantation gave him the chance
to finish this immensely significant work. What needs to be

*Objectivists who prove the necessity of a given sequence of facts are always
in danger of slipping into the position of justifying those facts (Lenin).

altered is the popular concept of heroism, ethical precepts and so on. The one thing that counts is one's contribution to science, and so forth.

At first Galileo listens in silence to Andrea's speech, which builds a golden bridge for his return to the esteem of his fellow scientists, then contemptuously and cuttingly contradicts him, accusing Andrea of squalidly recanting every principle of science. Starting with a denunciation of "bad thinking" which seems designed as a brilliant demonstration of how the trained scientist ought to analyse a case like his own, he proves to Andrea that no achievement is valuable enough to make up for the damage caused by a betrayal of mankind.

Galileo's portrayal in scene 14

The fact that the author is known to all and sundry as an opponent of the church might lead a theater to give the play's performance a primarily anticlerical slant. The church, however, is mainly being treated here as a secular establishment. Its specific ideology is being looked at in the light of its function as a prop to practical rule. The old cardinal (in scene 6) can be turned into a Tory or a Louisiana Democrat without much adjustment. Galileo's illusions concerning a "scientist in the chair of St. Peter" have more than one parallel in contemporary history, and these are scarcely related to the church. In scene 13 Galileo is not returning "to the bosom of the church"; as we know, he never left it. He is simply trying to make his peace with those in power. One can judge his demoralization by his social attitude; he buys his comfort (even his scientific activity has degenerated to the status of a comfort) by means of hackwork, unashamedly prostituting his intellect. (His use of clerical quotations is thus sheer blasphemy.) On no account should the actor make use of his self-analysis to endear the hero to the audience by his self-reproaches. All it does is to show that his brain is unimpaired, never mind what area he directs it to. Andrea Sarti's final remark in no sense represents the playwright's own view of Galileo, merely his opinion of Andrea Sarti. The playwright was not out to have the last word.

Galileo is a measure of the standard of Italian intellectuals in

the first third of the seventeenth century, when they were defeated by the feudal nobility. Northern countries like Holland and England developed productive forces further by means of what is called the Industrial Revolution. In a sense Galileo was responsible both for its technical creation and for its social betrayal.

[*Crime and Cunning*]

The first version of the play ended differently. Galileo had written the *Discorsi* in the utmost secrecy. He uses the visit of his favorite pupil Andrea to get him to smuggle the book across the frontier. His recantation had given him the chance to create a seminal work. He had been wise.

In the Californian version [. . .] Galileo interrupts his pupil's hymns of praise to prove to him that his recantation had been a crime, and was not to be compensated by this work, important as it might be.

In case anybody is interested, this is also the opinion of the playwright.

[Shortened from Werner Hecht (ed.), *ibid.*, pp. 32–37. These notes were written at various times, those on scene 14 mainly during Brecht's work on the Berliner Ensemble production. The reference to a new critical introduction to the *Discorsi* must relate to a proposed change which Brecht never made; it is not to be found in our text.]

Building up a Part: Laughton's Galileo

PREFACE

In describing Laughton's Galileo Galilei the playwright is setting out not so much to try and give a little more permanence to one of those fleeting works of art that actors create, as to pay tribute to the pains a great actor is prepared to take over a fleeting work of this sort. This is no longer at all common. It is not just that the under-rehearsing in our hopelessly commer-

cialized theater is to blame for lifeless and stereotyped portraits
—give the average actor more time, and he would hardly do
better. Nor is it simply that this century has very few outstand-
ing individualists with rich characteristics and rounded con-
tours—if that were all, care could be devoted to the portrayal
of lesser figures. Above all it is that we seem to have lost any
understanding and appreciation of what we may call a *theatrical
conception:* what Garrick did when, as Hamlet, he met his father's ghost; Sorel when, as Phèdre, she knew that she was
going to die; Bassermann when, as Philip, he had finished listening to Posa. It is a question of inventiveness.

The spectator could isolate and detach such theatrical concep-
tions, but they combined to form a single rich texture. Odd
insights into men's nature, glimpses of their particular way of
living together, were brought about by the ingenious contriv-
ance of the actors.

With works of art, even more than with philosophical systems, it is impossible to find out how they are made. Those who
make them work hard to give the impression that everything
just happens, as it were of its own accord, as though an image
were forming in a clear mirror that is itself inert. Of course this
is a deception, and apparently the idea is that if it comes off it
will increase the spectator's pleasure. In fact it does not. What
the spectator, anyway the experienced spectator, enjoys about
art is the making of art, the active creative element. In art we
view nature herself as if she were an artist.

The ensuing account deals with this aspect, with the process
of manufacture rather than with the result. It is less a matter
of the artist's temperament than of the notions of reality which
he has *and communicates;* less a matter of his vitality than of the
observations which underlie his portraits and can be derived
from them. This means neglecting much that seemed to us to
be "inimitable" in Laughton's achievement, and going on
rather to what can be learned from it. For we cannot create
talent; we can only set it tasks.

It is unnecessary here to examine how the artists of the past
used to astonish their public. Asked why he acted, L. answered:
"Because people don't know what they are like, and I think I

can show them." His collaboration in the rewriting of the play showed that he had all sorts of ideas which were begging to be disseminated, about how people *really* live together, about the motive forces that need to be taken into account here. L.'s attitude seemed to the playwright to be that of a realistic artist of our time. For whereas in relatively stationary ("quiet") periods artists may find it possible to merge wholly with their public and to be a faithful "embodiment" of the general conception, our profoundly unsettled time forces them to take special measures to penetrate to the truth. Our society will not admit of its own accord what makes it move. It can even be said to exist purely through the secrecy with which it surrounds itself. What attracted L. about *Life of Galileo* was not only one or two formal points but also the subject matter; he thought this might become what he called a contribution. And so great was his anxiety to show things as they really are that despite all his indifference (indeed timidity) in political matters he suggested and even demanded that not a few of the play's points should be made sharper, on the simple ground that such passages seemed "somehow weak" to him, by which he meant that they did not do justice to things as they are.

We usually met in L.'s big house above the Pacific, as the dictionaries of synonyms were too bulky to lug about. He had continual and inexhaustibly patient recourse to these tomes, and used in addition to fish out the most varied literary texts in order to examine this or that gest, or some particular mode of speech: Aesop, the Bible, Molière, Shakespeare. In my house he gave readings of Shakespeare's works to which he would devote perhaps a fortnight's preparation. In this way he read *The Tempest* and *King Lear*, simply for me and one or two guests who happened to have dropped in. Afterward we would briefly discuss what seemed relevant, an "aria" perhaps or an effective scene opening. These were exercises and he would pursue them in various directions, assimilating them in the rest of his work. If he had to give a reading on the radio he would get me to hammer out the syncopated rhythms of Whitman's poems (which he found somewhat strange) on a table with my fists, and once he hired a studio where we recorded half a dozen ways of telling the story of the creation, in which he was an African

planter telling the Negroes how he had created the world, or an English butler ascribing it to His Lordship. We needed such broadly ramified studies, because he spoke no German whatever and we had to decide the gest of each piece of dialogue by my acting it all in bad English or even in German and his then acting it back in proper English in a variety of ways until I could say: That's it. The result he would write down sentence by sentence in longhand. Some sentences, indeed many, he carried around for days, changing them continually. This system of performance-and-repetition had one immense advantage in that psychological discussions were almost entirely avoided. Even the most fundamental gests, such as Galileo's way of observing, or his showmanship, or his craze for pleasure, were established in three dimensions by actual performance. Our first concern throughout was for the smallest fragments, for sentences, even for exclamations—each treated separately, each needing to be given the simplest, freshly fitted form, giving so much away, hiding so much or leaving it open. More radical changes in the structure of entire scenes or of the work itself were meant to help the story to move and to bring out fairly general conclusions about people's attitudes to the great physicist. But this reluctance to tinker with the psychological aspect remained with L. all through our long period of collaboration, even when a rough draft of the play was ready and he was giving various readings in order to test reactions, and even during the rehearsals.

The awkward circumstance that one translator knew no German and the other scarcely any English compelled us, as can be seen, from the outset to use acting as our means of translation. We were forced to do what better-equipped translators should do too: to translate gests. For language is theatrical in so far as it primarily expresses the mutual attitude of the speakers. (For the "arias," as has been described, we brought in the playwright's own gest, by observing the bel canto of Shakespeare or the writers of the Bible.)

In a most striking and occasionally brutal way L. showed his lack of interest in the "book," to an extent the playwright could not always share. What we were making was just a text; the performance was all that counted. Impossible to lure him to

translate passages which the playwright was willing to cut for the proposed performance but wanted to keep in the book. The theatrical occasion was what mattered, the text was only there to make it possible: It would be expended in the production, would be consumed in it like gunpowder in a firework. Although L.'s theatrical experience had been in London, which had become thoroughly indifferent to the theater, the old Elizabethan London still lived in him, the London where theater was such a passion that it could swallow immortal works of art greedily and barefacedly as so many "texts." These works which have survived the centuries were in fact like improvisations thrown off for an all-important moment. Printing them at all was a matter of little interest, and probably only took place so that the spectators, in other words, those who were present at the actual event, the performance, might have a souvenir of their enjoyment. And the theater seems in those days to have been so potent that the cuts and interpolations made at rehearsal can have done little harm to the text.

We used to work in L.'s small library, in the mornings. But often L. would come and meet me in the garden, running barefoot in shirt and trousers over the damp grass, and would show me some changes in his flowerbeds, for his garden always occupied him, providing many problems and subtleties. The gaiety and the beautiful proportions of this world of flowers overlapped in a most pleasant way into our work. For quite a while our work embraced everything we could lay our hands on. If we discussed gardening it was only a digression from one of the scenes in *Galileo;* if we combed a New York museum for technical drawings by Leonardo to use as background pictures in the performance we would digress to Hokusai's graphic work. L., I could see, would make only marginal use of such material. The parcels of books or photocopies from books, which he persistently ordered, never turned him into a bookworm. He obstinately sought for the external: not for physics but for the physicists' behavior. It was a matter of putting together a bit of theater, something slight and superficial. As the material piled up, L. became set on the idea of getting a good draftsman to produce entertaining sketches in the manner of

Caspar Neher, to expose the anatomy of the action. "Before you amuse others you have to amuse yourself," he said.

For this no trouble was too great. As soon as L. heard of Caspar Neher's delicate stage sketches, which allow the actors to group themselves according to a great artist's compositions and to take up attitudes that are both precise and realistic, he asked an excellent draftsman from the Walt Disney Studios to make similar sketches. They were a little malicious; L. used them, but with caution.

What pains he took over the costumes, not only his own, but those of all the actors! And how much time we spent on the casting of the many parts!

First we had to look through works on costume and old pictures in order to find costumes that were free of any element of fancy dress. We sighed with relief when we found a small sixteenth-century panel that showed long trousers. Then we had to distinguish the classes. There the elder Brueghel was of great service. Finally we had to work out the color scheme. Each scene had to have its basic tone: the first, e.g., a delicate morning one of white, yellow, and gray. But the entire sequence of scenes had to have its development in terms of color. In the first scene a deep and distinguished blue made its entrance with Ludovico Marsili, and this deep blue remained, set apart, in the second scene with the upper bourgeoisie in their blackish-green coats made of felt and leather. Galileo's social ascent could be followed by means of color. The silver and pearl-gray of the fourth (court) scene led into a nocturne in brown and black (where Galileo is jeered by the monks of the Collegium Romanum), then on to the seventh, the cardinals' ball, with delicate and fantastic individual masks (ladies and gentlemen) moving about the cardinals' crimson figures. That was a burst of color, but it still had to be fully unleashed, and this occurred in the tenth scene, the carnival. After the nobility and the cardinals the poor people too had their masquerade. Then came the descent into dull and somber colors. The difficulty of such a plan of course lies in the fact that the costumes and their wearers wander through several scenes; they have always to fit in and contribute to the color scheme of the new scene.

We filled the parts mainly with young actors. The speeches

presented certain problems. The American stage shuns speeches except in (maybe because of) its frightful Shakespearean productions. Speeches just mean a break in the story and, as commonly delivered, that is what they are. L. worked with the young actors in a masterly and conscientious manner, and the playwright was impressed by the freedom he allowed them, by the way in which he avoided anything Laughtonish and simply taught them the structure. To those actors who were too easily influenced by his own personality he read passages from Shakespeare, without rehearsing the actual text at all; to none did he read the text itself. The actors were incidentally asked on no account to prove their suitability for the part by putting something "impressive" into it.

We jointly agreed on the following points:

1. The decorations should not be of a kind to suggest to the spectators that they are in a medieval Italian room or the Vatican. The audience should be conscious of being in a theater.

2. The background should show more than the scene directly surrounding Galileo; in an imaginative and artistically pleasing way, it should show the historical setting, but still remain background. (This can be achieved when the decoration itself is not independently colorful, but helps the actors' costumes and enhances the roundedness of the figures by remaining two-dimensional even when it contains three-dimensional elements, etc.)

3. Furniture and props (including doors) should be realistic and above all be of social and historical interest. Costumes must be individualized and show signs of having been worn. Social differences were to be underlined since we find it difficult to distinguish them in ancient fashions. The colors of the various costumes should harmonize.

4. The characters' groupings must have the quality of historical paintings (but not to bring out the historical aspect as an esthetic attraction; this is a directive which is equally valid for contemporary plays). The director can achieve this by inventing historical titles for the episodes. (In the first scene such titles might be: *Galileo the physicist explains the new Copernican theory to his subsequent collaborator Andrea Sarti and predicts the great historical importance of astronomy—To make a living the great Galileo teaches rich pupils—Galileo who has requested support for his continued*

investigations is admonished by the university officials to invent profitable instruments—Galileo constructs his first telescope based on information from a traveler.)

5. The action must be presented calmly and in a large sweep. Frequent changes of position involving irrelevant movements of the characters must be avoided. The director must not for a moment forget that many of the actions and speeches are hard to understand and that it is therefore necessary to express the underlying idea of an episode by the positioning. The audience must be assured that when someone walks, or gets up, or makes a gesture it has meaning and deserves attention. But groupings and movements must always remain realistic.

6. In casting the ecclesiastical dignitaries realism is of more than ordinary importance. No caricature of the church is intended, but the refined manner of speech and the "breeding" of the seventeenth-century hierarchy must not mislead the director into picking spiritual types. In this play, the church mainly represents authority; as types the dignitaries should resemble our present-day bankers and senators.

7. The portrayal of Galileo should not aim at rousing the audience to sympathy or empathy; they should rather be encouraged to adopt a deliberate attitude of wonder and criticism. Galileo should be portrayed as a phenomenon of the order of Richard III; the audience's emotions will be engaged by the vitality of this strange figure.

8. The more profoundly the historical seriousness of a production is established, the more scope can be given to humor. The more sweeping the over-all plan, the more intimately individual scenes can be played.

9. There is no reason why *Life of Galileo* cannot be performed without drastically changing the present-day style of production, as a historical "war-horse," for instance, with a star part. Any conventional performance, however (which need not seem at all conventional to the actors, especially if it contained interesting inventions), would weaken the play's real strength considerably without making it any easier for the audience. The play's main effects will be missed unless the theater changes its attitude. The stock reply, "Won't work here," is familiar to the author; he heard it at home too. Most directors treat such plays

as a coachman would have treated an automobile when it was first invented. On the arrival of the machine, mistrusting the practical instructions accompanying it, this coachman would have harnessed horses in front—more horses, of course, than to a carriage, since the new car was heavier—and then, his attention being drawn to the engine, he would have said, "Won't work here."*

The performance took place in a small theater in Beverly Hills, and L.'s chief worry was the prevailing heat. He asked that trucks full of ice be parked against the theater walls and fans be set in motion "so that the audience can think."

NOTES ON INDIVIDUAL SCENES

1

The Scholar, a Human Being

The first thing L. did when he set to work was to rid the figure of Galileo of the pallid, spiritual, stargazing aura of the text books. Above all, the scholar must be made into a man. The very term "scholar" [Gelehrter] sounds somewhat ridiculous when used by simple people; there is an implication of having been prepared and fitted, of something passive. In Bavaria people used to speak of the Nuremberg Funnel by which simpletons were more or less forcibly fed undue quantities of knowledge, a kind of enema for the brain. When someone had "crammed himself with learning," that too was considered unnatural. The educated—again one of those hopelessly passive words—talked of the revenge of the "uneducated," of their innate hatred for the mind; and it is true that their contempt was often mixed with hatred; in villages and working-class districts, the mind was considered something alien, even hostile. The same contempt, however, could also be found among the "better

*[Brecht added Note 9 at a later date for inclusion in his Notes to the Play.]

classes." A scholar was an impotent, bloodless, quaint figure, conceited and barely fit to live. He was an easy prey for romantic treatment. L.'s Galileo never strayed far from the engineer at the great arsenal in Venice. His eyes were there to see with, not to flash, his hands to work with, not to gesticulate. Everything worth seeing or feeling L. derived from Galileo's profession, his pursuit of physics and his teaching, the teaching, that is, of something very concrete with its concomitant real difficulties. And he portrayed the external side not just for the sake of the inner man—that is to say, research and everything connected with it, not just for the sake of the resulting psychological reactions—these reactions, rather, were never separated from the everyday business and conflicts, they never became "universally human," even though they never lost their universal appeal. In the case of the Richard III of Shakespeare's theater, the spectator can easily change himself along with the actor, since the king's politics and warfare play only a very vague role; there is hardly more of it than a dreaming man would understand. But with Galileo it is a continual handicap to the spectator that he knows much less about science than does Galileo. It is a piquant fact that in representing the history of Galileo, both playwright and actor had to undo the notion which Galileo's betrayal had helped to create, the notion that schoolteachers and scientists are by nature absent-minded, hybrid, castrated. (Only in our own day when, in the shape of ruling-class hirelings remote from the people, they delivered the latest product of Galileo's laws of motion, did popular contempt change to fear.) As for Galileo himself, for many centuries, all over Europe, the people honored him for his belief in a popularly based science by refusing to believe in his recantation.

Subdivisions and Line

We divided the first scene into several parts:

We had the advantage that the beginning of the story was also a beginning for Galileo, that is, his encounter with the telescope, and since the significance of this encounter is hidden from him for the time being, our solution was to derive the joy of beginning from the early morning: having him wash with

cold water—L., with bare torso, lifted a copper pitcher with a quick sweeping motion to let the jet of water fall into the basin —find his open books on the high desk, have his first sip of milk, and give his first lesson, as it happens, to a young boy. As the scene unfolds, Galileo keeps coming back to his reading at the high desk, annoyed at being interrupted by the returning student with his shallow preference for new-fangled inventions such as this spyglass, and by the procurator of the university who denies him a grant; finally reaching the last obstacle that keeps him from his work, the testing of the lenses which, however, would not have been possible without the two prior interruptions and makes an entirely new field of work accessible.

Interest in Interest and Thinking as Expression of Physical Contentment

Two elements in the action with the child may be mentioned: Washing himself in the background, Galileo observes the boy's interest in the armillary sphere as little Andrea circles around the strange instrument. L. emphasized what was novel in G. at that time by letting him look at the world around him as if he were a stranger and as if it needed explanation. His chuckling observation made fossils out of the monks at the Collegium Romanum. In that scene he also showed amusement at their primitive method of proof.

Some people objected to L.'s delivering his speech about the new astronomy in the first scene with a bare torso, claiming that it would confuse the audience if it were to hear such intellectual utterances from a half-naked man. But it was just this mixture of the physical and the intellectual that attracted L. "Galileo's physical contentment" at having his back rubbed by the boy is transformed into intellectual production. Again, in the ninth scene, L. brought out the fact that Galileo recovers his taste for wine on hearing of the reactionary pope's expected demise. His sensual walking, the play of his hands in his pockets while he is planning new researches, came close to being offensive. Whenever Galileo is creative, L. displayed a mixture of aggressiveness and defenseless softness and vulnerability.

Rotation of the Earth and Rotation of the Brain

L. arranges the little demonstration of the earth's rotation to be quick and offhand, leaving his high desk where he has begun to read and returning to it. He avoids anything emphatic, seems to pay no attention to the child's intellectual capacity, and at the end leaves him sitting there alone with his thoughts.

This casual manner, in keeping with his limited time, simultaneously admits the boy to the community of scholars. Thus L. demonstrated how for Galileo learning and teaching are one and the same—which makes his subsequent betrayal all the more horrible.

Balanced Acting

During this demonstration of the earth's rotation Galileo is surprised by Andrea's mother. Questioned about the nonsensical notions he is teaching the child he answers: "Apparently we are on the threshold of a new era, Mrs. Sarti." The way in which L. caressingly emptied his glass of milk while he said it was enchanting.

Response to a Good Answer

A small detail: The housekeeper has gone to let the new student in. Galileo feels constrained to make a confession to Andrea. His science is in no very good state, its most important concerns must be concealed from the authorities, and for the moment they are only hypotheses. "I want to become an astronomer," Andrea says quickly. At this answer Galileo looks at him with an almost tender smile. Usually actors do not rehearse such details separately, or often, enough to render them quickly in the performance.

[Dismissal of Andrea]

The dismissal of Andrea during the conversation with Ludovico is a piece of stage business for which time must be allowed. Galileo now drinks his milk as if it were the only

pleasure to be had, and one which will not last very long. He is fully aware of Andrea's presence. Ill-humoredly he sends him away. One of those unavoidable everyday compromises!

Galileo Underestimates the New Invention

Ludovico Marsili describes a new spyglass which he has seen in Holland and cannot understand. Galileo asks for detailed information and makes a sketch which solves the problem. He holds the cardboard with the sketch without showing it to his pupil, who expected to have a look. (L. insisted that the actor playing Ludovico should expect this.) The sketch itself he drew casually, just to solve a problem that offered some relief from the conversation. Then, his way of asking the housekeeper to send Andrea for lenses and borrowing a scudo from the entering procurator—all that had an automatic and routine quality. The whole incident seemed only to demonstrate that Galileo too was capable of plowing water.

A New Commodity

The birth of the telescope as a commodity took a long time to emerge clearly in the rehearsals. We found out why: L. had reacted too quickly and arrogantly to the university's refusal of a grant. All was well as soon as he accepted the blow in hurt silence and then went on, almost sadly, to speak like a poor man. As a natural result, Galileo's "Mr. Priuli, I may have something for you," came out in a way to make Galileo's dismissal of the new spyglass as "bosh" perfectly clear.

[Interruption of Work]

When Andrea returns with the lenses he finds Galileo deep in his work. (L. has shown, during a by no means brief interval, how the scholar handles his books.) He has already forgotten the lenses, he lets the boy wait, then proceeds, almost guiltily because he has no desire to take up the lucrative bosh, to arrange the two lenses on a piece of cardboard. Finally he takes the "thing" away, not without a little demonstration of his showmanship.

2

Fraud and Representation

Lesser actors would have delivered Galileo's speech representing the telescope as his own invention in a comical manner, simply in order to provide a strong contrast to the few excited words in which he tells his friend Sagredo about the instrument's scientific importance. This would have robbed the handing-over ceremony of all significance and belittled the fraud as a moral trifle. L. delivered the speech seriously, in a businesslike way (what Goethe called "artig"), that is, as a matter of routine, the sort of way in which the chief engineer at the great arsenal of Venice behaves on official occasions. Only when he mentioned the "Christian principles" according to which the "optical tube or telescope" was constructed was there a hint of the great gainsayer's delight in provocation.

It was highly entertaining to see how shamelessly the colossus bowed to his betters when, after a glance through the telescope, they applauded him, and how, on the other hand, he warded off their jovial and somewhat too familiar jokes while at the same time telling his friend, with supreme authority and passion, that he has turned the thing on the night sky.

Patience Guarantees Tempo

During rehearsals L. completely freed himself of the fever of an evening performance, that feeling that nothing is going fast enough which so easily infects the rehearsals. In this case things cannot go slowly enough. One has to rehearse as if the play could go on for twelve hours. L. rigorously rejected any suggestion of makeshift "bridges" to avoid loss of tempo. There were effects everywhere; the smallest detail could reveal peculiarities or habits of people's living together. (Loss of tempo occurs most often when a point is muddled and bungled and has to be glossed over.) For instance, the relatively cursory ending of the second scene cannot be staged adequately without very patient and detailed rehearsing.

The senators surround and congratulate Galileo and draw him to the rear, but the tiny exchange with Ludovico Marsili, with its imputation of plagiarism, must as it were still hover in the air; for when the half-curtain closes behind them [Ludovico and Virginia] and in front of Galileo and the others, they continue and conclude the conversation while exiting along the footlights. And Ludovico's cynical remark, "I am beginning to understand science," serves as a springboard for the ensuing third scene—that of the great discoveries.

3

[Confidence in Objective Judgment]

Galileo lets his friend Sagredo look through the telescope at the moon and Jupiter. L. sat down, his back to the instrument, relaxed, as though his work were done and he only wanted his friend to pass impartial judgment on what he saw, and that this were all he needed to do since his friend was now seeing for himself. By this means he established that the new possibilities of observation must bring all controversy about the Copernican system to an end.

This attitude explains at the very beginning of the scene the boldness of his application for the lucrative position at the court of Florence.

The Historical Moment

L. conducted the exchange with his friend at the telescope without any emphasis. The more casually he acted, the more clearly one could sense the historic night; the more soberly he spoke, the more solemn the moment appeared.

An Embarrassment

When the procurator of the university comes in to complain about the fraud of the telescope, L.'s Galileo shows noticeable

embarrassment by studiously looking through the telescope obviously less to observe the sky than to avoid looking the procurator in the eye. Shamelessly he exploits the "higher" function of the instrument which the Venetians have found not to be very profitable.

It is true that he also shows his behind to the angry man who has trusted him. But, far from trying to put him off with the discoveries of "pure" science, he at once offers him another profitable item, the astronomical clock for ships. When the procurator has left, he sits glumly before the telescope, scratching his neck and telling Sagredo about his physical and intellectual needs which must be satisfied in one way or another. Science is a milch cow for all to milk, he himself of course included. While at this point in time Galileo's attitude is still helpful to science, later on, in his fight with Rome, it is going to push science to the brink of the abyss, in other words, deliver it into the hands of the rulers.

The Wish Is Father to the Thought

Looking up from their calculations of the movements of Jupiter's moons, Sagredo voices his concern for the man about to publish a discovery so embarrassing to the church. Galileo mentions the seductive power of evidence. He fishes a pebble from his pocket and lets it fall from palm to palm, following gravity: "Sooner or later everybody must succumb to it" [the evidence]. As he argued along these lines, L. never forgot for a moment to do it in such a way that the audience would remember it later when he announced his decision to hand over his dangerous discoveries to the Catholic court of Florence.

[Rejection of Virginia]

L.'s Galileo used the little scene with his daughter Virginia to indicate how far he might be blamed for Virginia's subsequent behavior as a spy for the Inquisition. He does not take her interest in the telescope seriously and sends her off to matins. L. scrutinized his daughter after her question, "May I look through it?" before replying, "What for? It's not a toy."

The Fun in Contradictions

Saying, "I am going to Florence," Galileo carefully signs his letter of application. In this hasty capitalization of his discoveries as well as in his discourse on the seductive power of evidence and the representative value of great discoveries, L. left the spectator completely at liberty to study, criticize, admire Galileo's contradictory personality.

4

The Acting of Anger

Vis-à-vis the court scholars who refuse to look through the telescope, because to do so would either confirm Aristotle's doctrine or show up Galileo as a swindler, what L. acted was not so much anger as the attempt to dominate anger.

Servility

After Galileo, erupting at last, has threatened to take his new science to the dockyards, he sees the court depart abruptly. Deeply alarmed and disturbed, he follows the departing prince in cringing servility, stumbling, all dignity gone. In such a case an actor's greatness can be seen in the degree to which he can make the character's behavior incomprehensible or at least objectionable.

4 and 6*

The Fight and the Particular Manner of Fighting

L. insisted that throughout the two following scenes, 4 and 6, the sketch of Jupiter's moons from Galileo's original report should remain projected on the backdrop screen. It was a re-

---

* Scene 5 was not played in this production.

minder of the fight. To show one of its aspects, the heel-cooling
for the sake of truth, L., at the end of scene 4, when the chamberlain stays behind after the hasty departure of the court to
inform him of the appeal to Rome, let himself be driven out of
the space that stood for his house and stood in front of the
half-curtain. He stood there between scenes 4 and 6 and again
between scenes 6 and 7, waiting, and occasionally verifying that
the pebble from his pocket continued to fall from one raised
hand to the other stretched out below.

6

[Observation of the Clergy]

Galileo is not entirely devoid of appreciation when he observes the jeering monks at the Collegium Romanum—after all,
by pretending to stand on a rolling globe they are trying to *prove*
the absurdity of his propositions. The very old cardinal fills him
with pity.

After the astronomer Clavius has confirmed Galileo's
findings, Galileo shows his pebble to the hostile cardinal who
retreats in dismay; L. did this by no means triumphantly, rather
as if he wanted to offer his adversary a last chance to convince
himself.

7

Fame

Invited to the masked ball of Cardinals Bellarmine and Barberini, Galileo lingers for a moment in the anteroom, alone
with the clerical secretaries who later turn out to be secret
agents. He has been greeted on his arrival by distinguished
masked guests with great respect: obviously he stands in high
favor. From the halls a boys' choir is heard, and Galileo listens
to one of these melancholic stanzas which are sung amid the joy
of life. L. needed no more than this brief listening and the word

"Rome!" to express the pride of the conqueror who has the capital of the world at his feet.

The Duel of Quotations

In the brief duel of Bible quotations with Cardinal Barberini, L.'s Galileo shows, beside the fun he has with such intellectual sport, that the possibility of an unfavorable outcome to his affairs is dawning on him. For the rest, the effectiveness of the scene depends on the elegance of its performance; L. made full use of his heavy body.

Two Things at Once

The brief argument about the capacity of the human brain (which the playwright was delighted to have heard formulated by Albert Einstein) furnished L. the opportunity to show two traits: 1) a certain arrogance of the professional when his field is invaded by laymen, and 2) an awareness of the difficulty of such a problem.

[Disarmed by Lack of Logic]

When the decree is read out forbidding the guest to teach a theory acknowledged to have been proven, L.'s Galileo reacts by twice turning abruptly from the reading secretaries to the liberal Barberini. Thunderstruck, he lets the two cardinals drag him to the ball as if he were a steer stunned by the ax. L. was able, in a manner the playwright cannot describe, to give the impression that what mainly disarmed Galileo was the lack of logic.

8

[Indomitable Urge to Research]

If in the seventh scene Galileo experiences the *No* of the church, in the eighth he is confronted with the *No* of the people. It comes from the lips of the little monk, himself a physicist.

Galileo is disturbed, then recognizes the situation: in the fight against science it is not the church that defends the peasant, but the peasant who defends the church. It was L.'s theatrical conception to let Galileo be so profoundly upset that he delivers his counter-arguments in a spirit of defense, even of angry self-defense, and makes the throwing down of the manuscript into a gesture of helplessness. He blamed his indomitable urge to research like a sex offender blaming his glands.

Laughton Does Not Forget to Tell the Story

In the eighth scene one of Galileo's lines contains a sentence which continues the story: "Should I condone this decree . . ." L. distilled this small but important detail with great care.

9

[The Impatience of Galileo the Scientist]

Whereas L. insisted he must be allowed to give Galileo's character a markedly criminal evolution after the recantation in scene 13, he did not feel a similar need at the beginning of scene 9. Here too, to oblige the church, Galileo has for many years abstained from publicizing his discoveries, but this cannot be considered a betrayal like the later one. At this point the people know very little about the new science, the cause of the new astronomy has not yet been taken up by the North Italian bourgeoisie, the battle fronts are not yet political. There may not be an open declaration on his part, but there is no recantation either. In this scene therefore it is still the scientist's personal impatience and dissatisfaction which must be portrayed.

When Does Galileo Become Antisocial?

The issue in Galileo's case is not that a man must stand up for his opinion as long as he holds it to be true; that would entitle him to be called a "character." The man who started it all, Copernicus, did not stand up for his opinion; it would be

truer to say that he lay down for it inasmuch as he had it published only after his death; and yet, quite rightly, no one has ever reproached him for this. Something had been laid down to be picked up by anybody.

The man who had laid it down had gone, out of range of blame or thanks. Here was a scientific achievement which allowed simpler, shorter and more elegant calculations of celestial motions—let humanity make use of it. Galileo's life work is on the whole of the same order, and humanity used it. But unlike Copernicus who had avoided a battle, Galileo fought it and betrayed it. If Giordano Bruno, of Nola, who did not avoid the battle and had been burned twenty years earlier, had recanted, no great harm might have come of it; it could even be argued that his martyrdom deterred scientists more than it aroused them. In Bruno's time the battle was still a feeble one. But time did not stand still: A new class, the bourgeoisie with its new industries, had assertively entered the scene; no longer was it only scientific achievements that were at stake, but battles for their large-scale general exploitation. This exploitation had many aspects because the new class, in order to pursue its interests, had to come to power and smash the prevailing ideology that obstructed it. The church, which defended the privileges of princes and landowners as God-given and therefore natural, did not rule by means of astronomy, but it ruled within astronomy, as in everything else. And in no field could it allow its rule to be smashed. The new class, clearly, could exploit a victory in any field including that of astronomy. But once it had singled out a particular field and concentrated the battle in it, the new class became broadly vulnerable there. The maxim, "A chain is as strong as its weakest link," applies to chains that bind (such as the ideology of the church) as well as to transmission chains (such as the new class's new ideas about property, law, science, etc.). Galileo became antisocial when he led his science into this battle and then abandoned the fight.

Teaching

Words cannot do justice to the lightness and elegance with which L. conducted the little experiment with the pieces of ice in the copper basin. A fairly long reading from books was fol-

lowed by the rapid demonstration. Galileo's relationship with his pupils is like a duel in which the fencing master uses all his feints—using them against the pupil to serve the pupil. Catching Andrea out in a hasty conclusion, Galileo crosses out his wrong entry in the record book with the same matter-of-fact patience as he displays in correcting the ice's position in the submersion experiment.

Silence

With his own pupils he uses his tricks mainly to quell their dissatisfaction with him. They are offended by his keeping silent in the European controversy about sunspots, when his views are constantly being solicited as those of the greatest authority in the field. He knows he owes his authority to the church, and hence owes the clamor for his views to his silence. His authority was given him on condition that he should not use it. L. shows how Galileo suffers by the episode of the book on sunspots, which has been brought along and is discussed by his pupils. He pretends complete indifference, but how badly he does it! He is not allowed to leaf through the book, probably full of errors and thus twice as attractive. In little things he supports their revolt, though not himself revolting: When the lens grinder Federzoni angrily drops the scales on the floor because he cannot read Latin, Galileo himself picks them up—casually, like a man who would pick up anything that fell down.

Resumption of Research—a Sensual Pleasure

L. used the arrival of Ludovico Marsili, Virginia's fiancé, to show his own disgust at the routine nature of his work. He organized the reception of his guest in such a way that it interrupted the work and made his pupils shake their heads. On being told that the reactionary pope was on his deathbed Galileo visibly began to enjoy his wine. His bearing changed completely. Sitting at the table, his back to the audience, he experienced a rebirth; he put his hands in his pockets, placed one leg on the bench in a delicious sprawl. Then he rose slowly and walked up and down, with his glass of wine. At the same

time he let it be seen how his future son-in-law, the landowner and reactionary, displeased him more with every sip. His instructions to the pupils for the new experiment were so many challenges to Ludovico. With all this, L. still took care to make it plain that he was seizing the opportunity for new research not by the forelock, but just by a single little hair.

The Gest of Work

The speech about the need for caution with which Galileo resumes a scientific activity that defies all caution shows L. in a rare gest of creative, very vulnerable softness.

Even Virginia's fainting spell upon finding her fiancé gone barely interests Galileo. As the pupils hover over her, he says painfully: "I've got to know." And in saying it he did not seem hard.

10

Political Attitude on Dramatic Grounds

L. took the greatest interest in the tenth (carnival) scene, where the Italian people are shown relating Galileo's revolutionary doctrine to their own revolutionary demands. He helped sharpen it by suggesting that representatives of the guilds, wearing masks, should toss a rag doll representing a cardinal in the air. It was so important to him to demonstrate that property relationships were being threatened by the doctrine of the earth's rotation that he declined a New York production where this scene was to be omitted.

11

Decomposition

The eleventh scene is the decomposition scene. L. begins it with the same authoritative attitude as in the ninth scene. He does not permit his increasing blindness to detract one iota

from his virility. (Throughout, L. strictly refused to exploit this ailment which Galileo had contracted in the pursuit of his profession, and which of course could easily have won him the sympathy of the audience. L. did not want Galileo's surrender to be ascribable to his age or physical defects. Even in his last scene he was a man who was spiritually, not physically, broken.)

The playwright would sooner have Galileo's recantation in this scene, rather than let it take place before the Inquisition. Galileo executes it when he rejects the offer of the progressive bourgeoisie, in the person of the iron founder Vanni, to support him in his fight against the church, and insists that what he has written is an apolitical scientific work. L. acted this rejection with the utmost abruptness and strength.

Two Versions

In the New York production L. changed his gest for the meeting with the cardinal inquisitor as he emerges from the inner chambers. In the California production he remained seated, not recognizing the cardinal, while his daughter bowed. This created the impression of something ominous passing through, unrecognizable, but bowing. In New York, L. rose and himself acknowledged the cardinal's bow. The playwright finds no merit in the change, since it establishes a relationship between Galileo and the cardinal inquisitor which is irrelevant, and turns Galileo's ensuing remark, "His attitude was respectful, I think," into a statement rather than a question.

The Arrest

As soon as the chamberlain appears at the head of the stairs, Galileo hastily puts the book under his arm and runs upstairs, passing the startled chamberlain. Stopped short by the chamberlain's words, he leafs through the book as though its quality was all that mattered. Left standing on the lower part of the staircase, he must now retrace his steps. He stumbles. Almost at the footlights—his daughter has run to meet him—he completely pulls himself together and gives his instructions firmly

and to the point. It becomes clear that he has taken certain precautions. Holding his daughter close and supporting her, he sets out to leave the hall at a rapid, energetic pace. When he reaches the wings the chamberlain calls him back. He receives the fateful decision with great composure. Acting thus, L. shows that this is neither a helpless nor an ignorant man who is being caught, but one who has made great mistakes.

13

A Difficulty for the Actor: Some Effects become Apparent only when the Play is seen a Second Time

In preparing for the recantation scene L. never neglected in the preceding scenes to exhibit in all their fine shades the compliance and non-compliance in Galileo's conduct vis-à-vis the authorities, even those instances which would only mean anything to a spectator who had already seen the entire play once. Both he and the playwright recognized that in this type of play certain details unavoidably depend on a knowledge of the whole.

The Traitor

In the book there is a stage direction for Galileo when he returns to his pupils after he recanted to the Inquisition: *"He is changed, almost unrecognizable."* The change in L. was not of a physical nature as the playwright had intended. There was something infantile, bed-wetting in his loose gait, his grin, indicating a self-release of the lowest order, as if restraints had been thrown off that had been very necessary.

This, like what follows, can best be seen on photographs of the California production.

Andrea Sarti is feeling sick; Galileo has asked for a glass of water for him, and now the little monk passes by him, his face averted. Galileo's gaze is answered by Federzoni, the artisan-

scholar, and for some time the two stare at each other until the monk returns with the water. This is Galileo's punishment: it will be the Federzonis of the future centuries who will have to pay for his betrayal at the very inception of their great career.

"Unhappy the Land"

The pupils have abandoned the fallen man. Sarti's last word had been: "Unhappy is the land that breeds no hero." Galileo has to think of an answer, then calls after them, too late for them to hear: "Unhappy is the land that needs a hero." L. says it soberly, as a statement by the physicist who wants to take away nature's privilege to ordain tragedies and mankind's need to produce heroes.

14

The Goose

Galileo spends the last years of his life on an estate near Florence as a prisoner of the Inquisition. His daughter Virginia, whom he has neglected to instruct, has become a spy for the Inquisition. He dictates his *Discorsi* to her, in which he lays down his main teachings. But to conceal the fact that he is making a copy of the book he exaggerates the extent of his failing eyesight. Now he pretends not to recognize a goose which she shows him, the gift of a traveler. His wisdom has been degraded to cunning. But his zest for food is undiminished: He instructs his daughter carefully how he wants the liver prepared. His daughter conceals neither her disbelief in his inability to see nor her contempt for his gluttony. And Galileo, aware that she defends him vis-à-vis the Inquisition's guards, sharpens the conflicts of her troubled conscience by hinting that he may be deceiving the Inquisition. Thus in the basest manner he experiments with her filial love and her devotion to the church. Nonetheless, L. succeeded brilliantly in

eliciting from the spectator not only a measure of contempt but also a measure of horror at degradations that debase. And for all this he had only a few sentences and pauses at his disposal.

Collaboration

Anxious to show that crime makes the criminal more criminal, L. insisted, during the adaptation of the original version, on a scene in which Galileo collaborates with the authorities in full view of the audience. There was another reason for this: During the scene Galileo makes the most dignified use of his well-preserved intellectual powers by analyzing his betrayal for the benefit of his former pupil. So he now dictates to his daughter, to whom he had for many weeks been dictating his main work, the *Discorsi*, an abject letter to the archbishop in which he advises him how the Bible may be used for the suppression of starving artisans. In this he quite frankly shows his daughter his cynicism without being entirely able to conceal the effort this ignominious exercise costs him. L. was fully aware of the recklessness with which he swam against the stream by thus throwing away his character—no audience can stand a thing like that.

The Voice of the Visitor

Virginia has laid down the manuscript of the letter to the archbishop and gone out to receive a belated visitor. Galileo hears the voice of Andrea Sarti, formerly his favorite pupil who had broken with him after the recantation. To those readers of the play who complained that it gave no description of the spiritual agonies to which our nuclear physicists were subjected by the authorities ordering the bombs, L. could show that no first-rate actor needs more than a fleeting moment to indicate such spiritual discomfort. It is of course right to compare Galileo's submissiveness towards his authorities with that of our physicists towards rulers whom they distrust, but it would be wrong to go all the way into their stomach pains. What would be gained by that? L. was simply making this the moment to display his bad conscience, which could not have been shown

later in the scene when his betrayal is analyzed, without getting in his way.

The Laughter

The laughter in the picture [in the Model Book] was not suggested by the text, and it was frightening. Sarti, the former favorite pupil, calls and Virginia overhears the strained conversation. When Galileo inquires about his former collaborators, Sarti answers with utter frankness calculated to hurt his master. They get to Federzoni, a lens grinder whom Galileo had made his scientific collaborator even though he had no Latin. When Sarti reports he is back in a shop grinding lenses Galileo answers: "He can't read the books": Then L. makes him laugh. The laugh however does not contain bitterness about a society that treats science as something secret reserved for the well-to-do, but a disgraceful mocking of Federzoni's inadequacies together with a brazen complicity in his degradation, though this is simply (and completely) explained by his being inadequate. L. thus intended to make the fallen man a provocateur. Sarti, naturally, responds with indignation and seizes the opportunity to inflict a blow on the shameless recanter when Galileo cautiously inquires about Descartes's further work. Sarti coldly reports that Descartes shelved his investigations into the nature of light when he heard that Galileo had recanted. And Galileo once had exclaimed that he would willingly be "imprisoned a thousand feet beneath the earth, if in exchange he could find out what light is." L. inserted a long pause after this unpleasant information.

The Right to Submit

During the first sentences of his exchange with Sarti he listens inconspicuously for the footsteps of the Inquisition's official in the anteroom, who stops every now and then, presumably in order to eavesdrop. Galileo's inconspicuous listening is difficult to act since it must remain concealed from Sarti but not from the audience; concealed from Sarti because otherwise he would not take the prisoner's repentant remarks

at face value. But Galileo must convey them to him at face value so that his visitor can change them when he reaches foreign parts; it would not do at all if it were rumored abroad that the prisoner was recalcitrant. Then the conversation reaches a point where Galileo abandons this way of speaking for the benefit of hostile ears, and proclaims, authoritatively and forcefully, that it is his right to submit. Society's command to its members to produce is but vague and accompanied by no manner of guarantee; a producer produces at his own risk, and Galileo can prove any time that being productive endangers his comfort.

Handing over the Book

L. made the disclosure about the existence of the *Discorsi* quickly and with exaggerated indifference; but in a way suggesting that the old man was only trying to get rid of the fruits of a regrettable lapse, with yet another implication beneath this: anxiety lest the visitor reject the imposition together with the risk involved in taking the book with him. As he was protesting ill-humoredly that he wrote the book only as a slave of habit— the thoroughly vicious habit of thinking—the spectator could see that he was also listening. (Having made his eyesight worse by secretly copying the book which is endangered by the Inquisition, when he wants to gauge Sarti's reaction, he is wholly dependent on his ears.) Toward the end of his appeal he virtually abandons his attitude of "condescending grandeur" and comes close to begging. The remark about having continued his scientific work simply to kill time, uttered when Sarti's exclamation "The *Discorsi!*" had made him aware of his visitor's enthusiasm, came so falsely from L.'s lips that it could deceive no one.

It is furthermore important to realize that when Galileo so strongly emphasizes his own condemnation of the teaching activities which are now forbidden to him he is mainly trying to deceive himself. Since working, let alone sharing the results with the outside world, would threaten whatever was left of his comfort, he himself is passionately against this "weakness" which makes him like a cat that cannot stop catching mice.

Indeed the audience is witnessing his defeat when it sees him yield so reluctantly yet helplessly to an urge fostered in him by society. He must consider the risks to be larger than ever because now he is wholly in the hands of the Inquisition; his punishment would no longer be a public one; and the body of people who formerly would have protested has dispersed—thanks to his own fault. And not only has the danger increased, but he would be too late now with any contribution anyway, since astronomy has become apolitical, the exclusive concern of scientists.

Watchfulness

After the young physicist has found the book for which the scientific community no longer dares to hope, he at once changes his opinion about his former teacher and launches, with great passion, into a rationalization of Galileo's motives for the betrayal; motives, he finds, which exonerate him completely. Galileo has recanted so that he can go on with his work and find more evidence for the truth. Galileo listens for a while, interjecting monosyllables. What he is hearing now may well be all that he can expect posterity to say in recognition of his difficult and dangerous endeavor. First, he seems to be testing his pupil's improvised theory, just in the same way as any other theory must be tested for its validity. But presently he discovers that it is not tenable. At this point, immersed in the world of his scientific concerns, he forgets his watchfulness vis-à-vis a possible eavesdropper: he stops listening for steps.

The Analysis

Galileo's great counterattack against the golden bridge opens with a scornful outburst that abandons all grandeur: "Welcome to my gutter, dear colleague in science and brother in treason! I sold out, you are a buyer." This is one of the few passages which gave L. trouble. He doubted whether the spectator would get the meaning of the words, apart from the fact that the words are not taken from Galileo's usual, purely logical vocabulary. L. could not accept the playwright's argument that

there must be some gest simply showing how the opportunist damns himself by damning all who accept the rewards of opportunism; what he understood even less was that the playwright would be quite satisfied with the exhibition of a state of mind that defies rational analysis. The omission of a spiteful and strained grin at this point robbed the opening of the great instructional speech of its malice. It was not fully brought out that deriding the ignorant is the lowest form of instruction and that it is an ugly light that is shed solely for the purpose of letting one's own light shine. Because the lowest starting point was missing some spectators were unable to gauge the full height which L. undoubtedly reached in the course of the great speech, nor was it entirely possible to see the collapse of Galileo's vain and violently authoritarian attitude that colored even his scientific statements. The theatrical content of the speech, in fact, is not directly concerned with the ruthless demonstration of bourgeois science's fall from grace at the beginning of its rise—its surrender of scientific knowledge to the rulers who are authorized "to use it, not use it, abuse it, as it suits their ends." The theatrical content derives from the whole course of the action, and the speech should show how well this perfect brain functions when it has to judge its owner. That man, the spectator should be able to conclude, is sitting in a hell, more terrible than Dante's, where the true function of intellect has been gambled away.

Background of the Performance

It is important to realize that our performance took place at the time and in the country of the atom bomb's recent production and military application and where nuclear physics was then shrouded in deepest secrecy. The day the bomb was dropped will not easily be forgotten by anyone who spent it in the U.S.

The Japanese war had cost the U.S. real sacrifices. The troop ships left from the west coast, and the wounded and the victims of tropical diseases returned there. When the news reached Los Angeles it was at once clear that this was the end of the hateful war, that sons and brothers would soon come home. But the

great city rose to an astonishing display of mourning. The playwright heard bus drivers and saleswomen in fruit markets express nothing but horror. It was victory, but it was the shame
of defeat. Next came the suppression of the tremendous energy
source by the military and politicians, and this upset the intellectuals. Freedom of investigation, the exchange of scientific
discoveries, the international community of scholars were jetti-
soned by authorities that were strongly distrusted. Great physicists left the service of their bellicose government in headlong
flight; one of the best known took an academic position where
he was forced to waste his working time in teaching rudimen-
tary essentials solely to escape working for the government. It
had become ignominious to make new discoveries.

[From *Aufbau einer Rolle/Laughtons
Galilei, East Berlin, Henschel, 1956.]

APPENDICES TO "BUILDING UP A PART"

Sense and sensuality

The demonstrative style of acting, which depicts life in such
a way that it is laid open to intervention by the human reason,
and which strikes Germans as thoroughly doctrinaire, presented no special difficulty to the Englishman L. What makes
the sense seem so striking and insistent once it is "lugged in"
is our particular lack of sensuality. To lack sensuality in art is
certainly senseless, nor can any sense remain healthy if it is not
sensual. Reason, for us, immediately implies something cold,
arbitrary, mechanical, presenting us with such pairs of alterna-
tives as ideas and life, passion and thinking, pleasure and utility.
Hence when we stage a performance of our *Faust*—a regular
occurrence for educational reasons—we strip it of all sensuality
and thus transport the audience into an indefinite atmosphere
where they feel themselves confronted with all sorts of
thoughts, no single one of which they can grasp clearly. L.
didn't even need any kind of theoretical information about the

required "style." He had enough taste not to make any distinction between the supposedly lofty and the supposedly base, and he detested preaching. And so he was able to unfold the great physicist's contradictory personality in a wholly corporeal form, without either suppressing his own thoughts about the subject or forcing them on us.

Beard or no beard

In the California production L. acted without a beard, in the New York with one. This order has no significance, nor were there any fundamental discussions about it. It is the sort of case where the desire for a change can be the deciding factor. At the same time it does of course lead to modifications in the character. People who had seen the New York production confirmed what can be seen from the pictures [in the Model Book], namely that L. acted rather differently. But everything essential was still there, and the experiment can be taken as evidence to show how much play is left for the "personal" element.

The leavetaking

Certainly nothing could have been more horrible than the moment when L. has finished his big speech and hastens to the table saying "I must eat now," as though in delivering his insights Galileo has done everything that can be expected of him. His leavetaking from Sarti is cold. Standing absorbed in the sight of the goose he is about to eat, he replies to Sarti's repeated attempt to express his regard for him with a formal "Thank you, sir." Then, relieved of all further responsibility, he sits down pleasurably to his food.

Concluding remark

Though it resulted from several years of preparation and was brought about by sacrifices on the part of all concerned, the production of *Galileo* was seen by a bare ten thousand people. It was put on in two small theaters, a dozen times in each: first in Beverly Hills, Los Angeles, and then with a competely new

cast in New York. Though all the performances were sold out the notices in the main papers were bad. Against that could be set the favorable remarks of such people as Charles Chaplin and Erwin Piscator, as well as the interest of the public, which looked like being enough to fill the theater for some considerable time. But the large cast meant that the potential earnings were low even if business was really good, and when an artistically interested producer made an offer it had to be rejected because L., having already turned down a number of film engagements and made considerable sacrifices, could not afford to turn down another. So the whole thing remained a private operation by a great artist who, while earning his keep outside the theater, indulged himself by displaying a splendid piece of work to a (not very large) number of interested parties. Though this is something that needed to be said, it does not however convey the complete picture. Given the way the American theater was organized in those years, it was impossible that such plays and such productions should reach their audience. Productions like this one, therefore, should be treated as examples of a kind of theater that might become possible under other political and economic conditions. Their achievements, like their mistakes, make them object lessons for anyone who is looking for a theater of great themes and rewarding acting.

[From Werner Hecht (ed.), *Materialien zu Brechts "Leben des Galilei*," pp. 78–80. In the last of these notes Brecht is perhaps being undeservedly kind to Laughton, since the actor's wariness of Communist associations, at a time when Brecht and Hanns Eisler were being heard by the Un-American Activities Committee, appears to have been another strong factor in deciding him to close the play.]

Note of two conversations with Caspar Neher about *Life of Galileo*

After the Italian fashion, a lightly built stage that is recognizable as having been lightly built. Nothing stony, weighty, massive. No interior decoration.

Color to emerge from the costumes, i.e. in movement.

The stage shows Galileo's background, making use of contemporary evidence (Leonardo's technical drawings, Romulus and Remus with the she-wolf, a man of war from the Venice arsenal, and so on).

No projections, since this would prevent the full illumination of the stage. Giant photographs, maybe, nobly suspended. A flagged floor.

[Dated October 3 and 5, 1955. From Werner Hecht (ed.), *ibid.*, p. 88. The eventual stage set for the Berliner Ensemble's production, completed by Erich Engel after Brecht's death and first performed on January 15, 1957, was somewhat different from this.]

Editorial Note

Much of the information that follows, including some of the quotations from Brecht, is derived from Ernst Schumacher's *Drama und Geschichte. Bertolt Brecht's "Leben des Galilei" und andere Stücke*, Henschel, East Berlin 1965, whose usefulness is gratefully acknowledged.

1. General

Judging by the proportion of Brecht's papers devoted to it in the Brecht Archive in Berlin, *Galileo* is much the most heavily worked-over of all his plays. None of the others went through such stages, for not only did *Galileo* occupy him during the last nineteen years of his life, but its linguistic, theatrical, and thematic bases all changed drastically during that period, as did the dramatist's own circumstances. Thus it was written in German, then entirely rewritten in English (with Brecht himself contributing in a mixture of English and German), then rewritten in German again largely on the basis of the English-language version. Again, it was first written with no clear prospect of production, then rewritten for a specific actor, Laughton, and a specific production before an American audience, then rewritten once more for Brecht's own Berliner Ensemble to play in East Berlin. During Brecht's work on the first version, it became known that Niels Bohr had split the uranium atom; while he and Laughton were preparing the second, the first atom bomb dropped on Hiroshima, on August 6, 1945. Finally, Brecht himself was at first living as an exile, close to Germany, on the eve of an impending war; he rewrote the play once in the aura

of Hollywood, when an allied victory was at last certain, then again after his own successful reestablishment in his country, within a bitterly divided world.

There are thus three principal versions of the play whose differences will be described in what follows. The first is the German version whose earliest typescript was entitled *The Earth Moves* and which was originally written in November 1938. What appear to be early sketches lay down a structure as follows:

Life of Galileo

1. PADUA/Welcoming the new age/Copernicus's hypothesis/ authoritarian economy in Italy.
2. SIGNORIA/Landscape.
3. RESEARCH/Danger of the truth/speech about reason and its seductions.
4. DEMONSTRATIONS/The addicts of authority exhorted to see.
5. PLAGUE.
6. COLLEGIUM ROMANUM/The Copernican system ridiculed.
7. THE DECREE/On the church's responsibilities/the ch. system too all-embracing.
7a. CONVERSATION/The monk's parents/Horace.
8. THE SUNSPOTS/On science/Keunos.
9. The new age without fear/strict research/hope in working people.
9a. BALLAD.
10. THE INQUISITION'S SUMMONS.
11. INQUISITION/Condemnation of doubt.
12. RECANTATION/Praise of steadfastness.
13. THE PRISONER/Passage from the *Discorsi*/On the scientist's duty/On expropriation/The new age, a harridan.
14. SMUGGLING.

It did not take long to complete. On November 17 his secretary-collaborator Margarete Steffin wrote to Walter Benjamin:

Ten days ago Brecht began getting *Galileo* down in dramatic

form, after it had been plaguing his mind for some time. He has already finished nine of the fourteen scenes, and very fine they are.

A mere six days after that, according to his diary, he had completed it, commenting that

The only scene to present difficulties was the last one. As in *St. Joan* [*of the Stockyards*] I needed some sort of twist at the end to make absolutely certain of the necessary detachment on the part of the audience. At any rate, now even a man subject to unthinking empathy must experience the A-effect in the course of identifying himself with Galileo. A legitimate degree of empathy occurs, given strictly epic presentation.

On January 6, 1939, the *Berlingske Tidende* published an interview in which he said that the play was "really written for New York"; though it is not clear just what he had in mind. A few weeks later he carefully revised it under the title *Life of Galileo* and had a number of duplicated copies run off, of which Walter Benjamin and Fritz Sternberg each appear to have been given one. This was also to all intents and purposes the version sent to Zurich and staged there in the middle of the war. But already Brecht was dissatisfied with it:

Technically, *Life of Galileo* is a great step backwards, far too opportunist, like *Señora Carrar's Rifles*. The play would need to be completely rewritten to convey that "breeze that comes from new shores," that rosy dawn of science. It would all have to be more direct, without the interiors, the atmospherics, the empathy. And all switched to planetary demonstration. The division into scenes can be kept, Galileo's characterization likewise, but work, the pleasures of work, would need to be realized in practical form, through contact with a theater. The first thing would be to study the *Fatzer* and *Breadshop* fragments. Technically those represent the highest standard.

So he noted on February 25. On the 27th he heard a Danish radio interview with three of Niels Bohr's assistants, one of whom, Professor C. Møller, knew Brecht and recalls discussing Galileo and the *Discorsi* with him early the previous year. This interview described the splitting of the uranium atom, which (so Ernst Schumacher suggests) may have prompted the passage in

the revised text about "the greatest discoveries . . . being made at one or two places." The revision, however, certainly did nothing to change the play "technically." Though an early but undated note speaks of a *Life of Galileo* version for workers, there appears to be no indication that a start was ever made on this.

The second or American version dates from April 1944, when Brecht took up the play again as a result of a meeting with Jed Harris, the producer of Thornton Wilder's *Our Town*. A translation of the first version had already been made by Desmond Vesey; in addition Brecht now got a rough interlinear translation made by one of his own collaborators, followed by a new acting version by two of Orson Welles's associates, Brainerd Duffield and Emerson Crocker. The two last-named had been recommended to him by Charles Laughton, who seems to have become interested in the play some time that autumn and to have used their version for his own work with Brecht on the adaptation. "Now working systematically with Laughton on the translation and stage version of *The Life of the Physicist Galileo*" said a diary note of December 10. In the course of this activity, which lasted off and on until December 1945, Brecht redrafted many passages in a remarkable mixture of German and English; thus his sketch for the beginning of scene 4 runs:

Rede des Mathematikers

Das Universum des göttlichen Aristoteles mit seinen

mystisch musizierenden Sphären und Kristallnen Gewöl-
circles   heavenly bodies
ben sowie den Kreisläufen seiner Himmelskörper,
obliquity of the eclyptic
seinem Schiefenwinkel der Sonnenbahn / den Geheimnissen
Sternen
der Table of Cords, dem / Reichtum des Catalogue
inspirierten
for the southern hemisphere / der / construction of a

celestial globe is ein Gebäude von grosser Ordnung

und Schönheit.

The Universe of the divine Classics.

For the New York production, which took place after Brecht's return to Europe, there were, according to its director Joseph Losey, "Different words, thanks in part to the collaboration of George Tabori in rewriting with Laughton and me from notes left behind in New York by Brecht."

The text as we reproduce it in the appendix (pp. 403–467) was published by Indiana University Press in 1952 in *From the Modern Repertoire, Series Two*, edited by Eric Bentley, then in *Seven Plays by Bertolt Brecht*, Grove Press, New York, 1961, and separately by Grove Press again in 1966. The play still struck Brecht himself as formally conventional, to judge from a note of January 1945 which found that

> with its interiors and atmospheric effects the construction of the scenes, derived from the epic theatre, makes a singularly theatrical impact.

He also told an interviewer somewhat apologetically that summer that "Galileo is anyway interesting as a contrast to my parables. Where they embody ideas, it extracts ideas from a subject."

In 1953, six years after the Hollywood and New York productions, he got Elisabeth Hauptmann and Benno Besson of the Berliner Ensemble, with some advice from Ruth Berlau (who had helped with, and photographed, the American version) to draft a third version in German, using the best parts of the previous texts. This he himself revised to form the play which was given its German première at Cologne in April 1955, published as *Versuche 14* and subsequently rehearsed by him for some three months with his own company. With minor amendments it is the text of the *Gesammelte Werke* on which our edition is based. It differs substantially from the second version.

2. The first version, 1938–1943

From Brecht's first completed typescript, dating presumably from November 1938, to the text used for the Zurich production of 1943, the play remained essentially the same, the only changes of real substance being those in the last scene but one which define the nature of Galileo's crime. The general structure of this first version was already very similar to that of the text which we have followed, and certain scenes, or large parts of them, were taken into the latter without drastic rewriting, for instance the first half of scene 1, scene 3, the start of scene 4, scene 5b (Plague), scene 6 (Collegium Romanum), much of scene 8, scene 11 (The Pope) and the last (Smuggling) scene. Even the carnival scene (10) had the same place, gist and purpose, though the ballad round which it centers was later rewritten. There were, however, some striking differences among the characters. To sum these up briefly:

Mrs. Sarti originally died of the plague in scene 5b. The character in 9 was "the housekeeper." This was altered after the first typescript.

Ludovico, Virginia's fiancé, did not appear till scene 7 (The Ball). He was then called Sitti, and was not a member of the landowning aristocracy; indeed in scene 9 (Sunspots) he lamented that he has no fortune of his own. His function of introducing Galileo to the principle of the telescope (scenes 1 and 2) was performed by a silly-ass character called Doppone, son of a wool merchant, whose only other appearance was, briefly, as a papal chamberlain in the ball scene.

Virginia was much less contemptuously treated by her father. Her relations with Andrea were friendlier, though her role in the penultimate scene was the same.

Federzoni the lens grinder did not figure in the play at all. Some of his lines were spoken by an "elderly scholar."

Vanni the iron founder did not figure in the play either. Stove-fitter and doctor appeared in the penultimate scene.

In the first typescript the play was called *The Earth Moves* (Die Erde bewegt sich) and the scenes bore no titles. The title *Life*

of Galileo, together with the individual scene titles, more or less in their final form, are to be found in the revised scripts of early 1939. The verses before each scene are absent from this version.

The following is a scene-by-scene account of it.

I

Galileo Galilei, teacher of mathematics in Padua, sets out to demonstrate the new Copernican system.

Galileo's long speech about the "new age" (pp. 4–6) is about ten lines shorter, omitting inter alia the passages about the ships previously hugging the shores and about the masons in Siena, but taking in the lines about "The ancient doctrines that have been accepted for a thousand years" which come at the close of the scene in the final text (p. 14). Andrea's age was not originally specified, but the revised versions make him thirteen (as opposed to eleven in the final text).

The whole episode with Ludovico is absent. Instead Galileo explains to Andrea the nature of a hypothesis. Copernicus, he says, knows that the earth rotates

> only because he has worked it out. Actually he doesn't know it at all. He's assuming it. It's simply what is called a hypothesis. No facts. No proofs. They're being looked for. A few people in Prague and in England are looking for the proofs. It's the greatest hypothesis there has ever been, but it's no more than that. Hence the great flaw in the new system is that nobody who isn't a mathematician *can* understand why it's like that and can't be any other way. All I've showed you is that it can be that way. There's no reason why not, if you see what I mean.

ANDREA   Can't I become a mathematician and find out the reason why it should?

GALILEO   And how am I going to pay the butcher and the milkman and the bookseller if I start giving you lessons for nothing? Off you go, now; I must get on with my work.

In the revised versions Andrea asks "What's a hypothesis?" and gets the answer which the final text puts at the end of the scene, down to "that see very little" (p. 14), concluding "Copernicus's

hypothesis is the greatest hypothesis there has ever been, but it's no more than that."

ANDREA   Then what about what the church is saying? What's that?

GALILEO   Oh, that's a hypothesis too, but not such a good one. Lots of laws that don't explain very much. But the great flaw of the new system . . .

—and so on, as above.

The episode with the procurator of the university, which follows, is close to the final text, though the reference to the scientific implications of "the campaign for better looms" is lacking. Doppone appears *after* this, and is taken on as a private pupil for thirty scudi a month; his father wants him to become a theologian, since he likes arguing. Before leaving, he tells Galileo about the telescope, which Galileo then constructs from two lenses bought for him by Andrea. The scene ends with them looking through it.

GALILEO   You didn't eat the apple—which shows you've got the makings of a mathematician. A taste for unrewarding art. I'll teach you. It won't break me. This flimflam is worth five hundred scudi.

ANDREA   (*after Galileo has allowed him another look*) How clearly one sees. Here's Signor Gambione the bailiff coming up to our house.

GAMBIONE   Quick, shove those forty-five scudi in your pocket!

2

Galileo presents a new invention to the Republic of Venice.

Federzoni and Ludovico do not figure in this scene, which is dated August 24, 1609. Nor does Virginia. The telescope is handed over by Andrea, who however has nothing to say. The scene starts with Galileo's telling Sagredo that he has used it to look at the moon. Then his presentation speech is read for him by the procurator, including as Galileo's own the emphasis on the instrument's military usefulness; he adds a comment that

Galileo hopes to continue serving the Venetians. During this speech Doppone appears and tries to catch the eye of Galileo, who is annoyed and embarrassed: "It's one of my pupils, an unbelievable idiot. I can't imagine what he wants." As the city fathers try the instrument Galileo goes on talking to Sagredo about its relevance to Copernican theory.

> GALILEO (*without looking at him*)   How about this? Flecks of light on the dark portion of the disk, dark patches on the bright sickle. It fits almost too well. Of course, I'm very skeptical, extremely skeptical.

The scene ends with Doppone breaking through the palace guards and saying breathlessly:

> Signor Galilei, why wouldn't you listen to me before the presentation? It's all wrong. The cover ought to be green. It was green; trust Doppone.

3

January 10, 1610: By means of the telescope Galileo discovers celestial phenomena which prove the Copernican system. Warned by his friend of the possible consequences of his investigations, Galileo affirms his faith in reason.

Up to Mrs. Sarti's exit two-thirds of the way through (p. 25) this scene is very close to the final text, the main differences being the omission of Galileo's six lines on the value of star charts for navigation (p. 21); the fact that Sarti appears "in night attire"; and the doubling of Galileo's eventual salary (one thousand scudi in this version, as against the final five hundred). The episode with Virginia is then shifted to the end of the scene, after Sagredo's second "Galileo, don't go to Florence!" (p. 27), which leads to a cross-fade, thus:

> GALILEO   You'd do better helping me write my letter to the Florentines.
> SAGREDO   You really mean to go there?
> GALILEO   Certainly. And with the tube. And with the truth. And with my belief in human reason.

SAGREDO   Then there's nothing more to say, is there? (*He leaves hurriedly without speaking*)

GALILEO (*laughs as he sits down at the telescope and starts making notes. It gets dark. When the lights come on again it is morning. Galileo is still sitting at this table writing by two candles. He has his coat on, as the fire has evidently gone out. A bell is ringing for early mass. Enter Galileo's very young daughter Virginia, warmly dressed*)

As in the final text she announces that she is going to matins, though without mention of Ludovico. In her dialogue with her father, which is rather differently phrased here, he does not snub her with such words as "It's not a toy" (p. 25) and "Nothing for you," though she complains of never being allowed to look through the telescope. He then tells her to read his letter to Duke Cosmo to see if it is humble enough, and she reads out the text which is now at the end of the scene. They discuss it, and in conclusion he sleepily comments:

The only way an unpopular and embarrassing man can get a job that gives him enough free time is by crawling on his belly.

VIRGINIA (*hugging him*)   Shall we have a big house there?

GALILEO   Time, that's the main thing, my dear, time!

Virginia expresses no particular joy about going to court.

4

Galileo has exchanged the Venetian republic for the court of Florence. The discoveries he has made with the help of the telescope are met with disbelief by the court scholars.

The first part, up to the quarrel between the two boys, is close to the final text, apart from the substitution of the court chamberlain for Cosmo's tutor and the fact that in the earliest typescript Mrs. Sarti's opening speech was about a third of its subsequent length. After that, however, the scene was, in the main, differently written (again, without Federzoni) and incorporated scene 5a, thus reducing the plague scene to 5b only. In this version the reason given for Cosmo's sudden departure was not

the court ball but "a particularly important message," leading the three representatives of orthodox physics to continue the speculations with which they made their original appearance.

> I wonder what sort of a message His Highness got? I don't like those cases of illness in the old town—The message couldn't possibly have anything to do with that! The medical faculty is quite certain that . . . (*There is a knock on the door downstairs. Mrs. Sarti opens it. Virginia comes in with a traveling bag*) (p. 37)

And so into 5a.

The preceding argument between Galileo and the three scholars (who in the typescript were simply Professors A, B, and C, before being distinguished in the revised versions as astronomer, mathematician and theologian) is the same in substance, but largely different in form. There is no formal dispute, no attempt to use Latin, no accompanying court ladies; the dialogue is slacker and more repetitive. Galileo's references to his work with the employees of the Venice arsenal and to the sailors are not yet included (p. 36). On the other hand, he begins his immediately preceding speech with:

> You must realize that it is up to you to set an example and trust your reason. That the meanest stableboy is waiting to be encouraged and challenged to trust your reason.

The next lines about "doctrines believed to be unshakeable are beginning to totter" were already there in the first typescript.

The cannibalized 5a is somewhat differently arranged, since Galileo appears at the top of the stairs, chuckling at the scholars' panicky departure, sees Virginia and asks what she is doing here (when she should be at her convent school). Virginia's presence in this scene was in fact an amendment to the first typescript, which originally gave her lines to the neighbor's wife. Sarti then announced that the neighbor had arranged a carriage to take them all away, but Brecht changed this to "The court is sending a carriage" and added the lackey's speech which in this version finished with a friendly message from Cosmo to Andrea.

After Mrs. Sarti's "But it's not reasonable" (p. 38) Galileo adds:

And I can tell you another reason. In times like these nobody can say how long he's going to remain alive. (*He smiles*) So let's go and paint more stars on the lens. (*Goes into his study*)

The first two of these sentences were added in pen to the original typescript.

5b [*5*]

Undaunted even by the plague, Galileo continues his investigations.

Originally, after the old woman's "Maybe your mother is there too," Andrea replied "No, she's dead." Brecht, however, amended this on the typescript to read as now. Otherwise the differences from the final text are insignificant. Conceivably this scene was a last-minute addition to the first typescript. The numbering and typing seem to suggest it.

6 [*5 on first typescript, 6 in revised versions*]

1616: The Collegium Romanum, the research institute of the Vatican, confirms Galileo's discoveries.

Virtually the same as the final text, apart from the ending, which in the first typescript (later reworded) read:

(*The astronomer escorts him in*)
THE ASTRONOMER   That was him, Your Eminence.
THE INQUISITOR (*very politely*)   May I look through the tube? I find this tube extremely interesting.

7 [*6 in first typescript only*]

But the Inquisition places the Copernican doctrine on the Index (March 5, 1616).

Though the structure and general gist of this, the ball scene, are the same as in the final version, there are considerable differ-

ences in the dialogue. Partly this is due to the fact that Ludovico, who makes his first appearance here, is not specifically identified with the aristocracy or even, in the first typescript, given a surname: hence the absence of the first secretary's reference to "All the great families of Italy," with their resounding names. Doppone also makes a last brief entry, speaking jerkily like Mr. Jingle:

GALILEO   I've concluded my business here.

DOPPONE   Yes, I know—known to one and all—brilliant triumph—sat at your feet myself—epicircle and all that.

Neither Galileo's verse ("Your tucker, Thaïs, is askew") nor the Lorenzo de' Medici madrigal are included. The old cardinal does not appear, and Bellarmine and Barberini are in different disguises, the former as a fox, the latter as a donkey.

In Galileo's argument with these two cardinals some of the key phrases are already there, such as Barberini's reference to astronomy as "the itch," Galileo's pronouncement "I believe in reason" (only uttered once however), Bellarmine's account of the Campagna peasants whose situation can only be justified by positing a Higher Being, and his objection that Galileo is accusing God of "the juiciest boners in astronomy" (p. 51). Bellarmine's reference to star charts and navigation, however, is once again missing, as is the subsequent bandying of Biblical texts and Barberini's "Welcome to Rome..." (p. 49) to which it leads. Instead the dialogue runs (after "the itch"):

BELLARMINE   Unfortunately not only have the new theories displaced our good earth, which the Almighty designated as our dwelling place, from the center of the cosmos, in an almost contemptuous way, but the assumption of utterly incredible distances in the cosmos makes the world seem so tiny that the interest which God evidently takes in the human race becomes almost impossible to understand.

GALILEO   As the Collegium Romanum has at last admitted . . .

BELLARMINE   What we feel is, that to say it's easier to explain phenomena by positing that the earth moves and the sun stands still, than by accepting the Ptolemaic cycles and epicycles, is a wholly admirable thing, risks nothing and is

all right for mathematicians. But suppose one tried to suggest that the sun is really at the center of our world and rotates only round itself without moving across from east to west while the earth circles round the sun at immense speed, then that would be a very risky affair, don't you think, because it would upset philosophy and the theologians, who are awkward customers and what's more it would make the scriptures untrue.

BARBERINI   But don't you see, Bellarmine, the scriptures don't satisfy his reason? Whereas Copernicus does . . .

After Barberini, leading Bellarmine aside, has asked Galileo about the possibility of God giving the stars irregular movements, Galileo makes much the same reply as in the final text, but forgets himself and calls the future pope "my dear man." Then the instruction to the secretaries not to take the discussion down comes some two dozen lines later than in the final text, just before Bellarmine formally tells Galileo of the Holy Office's decision. This is not repeated by the secretary, but in the revised versions Bellarmine on leaving instructs the secretaries to "Make a note of the fact that I have today informed Signor Galileo of the decree of the Holy Office concerning the Copernican doctrine."

The remainder of the scene, with the inquisitor, is almost as in the final text, except that he enters with two ladies, saying:

Oh, truly I don't know half what you do. You're so much crueller than I ever could be.

and in asking Virginia about her engagement omits the words "your fiancé comes of a distinguished family" (p. 53).

8 [*Transformation scene*]

This conversation with the little monk has no title, and is presumably intended to be played before the curtain. Its general direction, and much of its dialogue, have remained constant since the first typescript, though Brecht continually added to it. Notable differences in the first version are:

(1) The start:

THE LITTLE MONK   You're right.

GALILEO   Haven't you read the Index Congregation's decree?

THE LITTLE MONK   I have read it.

GALILEO   After that you can't go on saying I'm right, wearing the habit you wear.

THE LITTLE MONK   I haven't been able to sleep for four nights (etc.).

(2) In the first typescript Galileo's next speech ran:

See that man down there hiding behind the oleanders and peeping up now and again? Since the cardinal inquisitor looked through my tube I've never lacked for company. They're very interested in criminals in Rome. I'll give him one of my tubes to help him observe me better.

THE LITTLE MONK   Please believe me when I say that I have nothing to do with that man and the people who sent him. I'm a mathematician.

GALILEO   And I'm a criminal.

This was removed in revision. Then, after the little monk's long speech about his peasant family, ending "a great goodness of soul?" (p. 57), Galileo originally went straight to the speech about the Priapus (p. 58). The first part of his comment on the situation of the peasants was added on the first typescript, but not the passage about the oyster and the pearls. The important exchange about whether the truth will out ("Truth prevails only when we make it prevail," (p. 58) was added in the process of revision. The ensuing sentence about "divine patience" is not in this version.

9 [*8 or 7 in first typescript*]

After a silence of eight years Galileo feels encouraged by the enthronement of a new pope, himself a scientist, to resume his research in the forbidden field. The sunspots.

Apart from the penultimate scene, this is the most heavily

amended of them all. In place of Federzoni there is the "elderly scholar," while, in the first typescript only, "the housekeeper" figured instead of Mrs. Sarti. The exchanges with Ludovico are entirely different, as well as shorter; again Ludovico is no aristocrat, and his nervousness about his prospective father-in-law's theories seems to stem from hints dropped at the university where he is a student without private means. The order of events also underwent subsequent changes.

Thus the scene opens with Galileo demonstrating the behavior of floating bodies. He begins with an extended version of the remarks later put after the experiment with the needle (p. 64):

> GALILEO   The aim of science is not to open the door to ever-lasting wisdom, but to set a limit to everlasting error. Philosophy for the most part is limitless, wild and indefinite, but truth is restricted and contained in small examples. A main cause of poverty in the sciences is the illusion of wealth. We only conquer nature by obeying her. Whatever counts as a cause when we are observing counts as a rule when we are putting something into effect. By observing the small errors on which the great philosophies are erected we arrived in the course of the summer at all kinds of concepts which have been obstructing the advance of science ever since Aristotle's time. Such as cold and thinness, dampness and length, from which some people think they can construct a whole world if they put the words together the right way.

Andrea then puts the Aristotelian case, about the ice and the needle, going on to describe Galileo's disproof of it while Galileo demonstrates. When he succeeds they all laugh, leading the women to make their remarks about laughter (p. 64) up to Sarti's "Who knows?"

Mucius then appears, and is dealt with very much as in the final text. Then after Galileo has gone into his study Virginia and Mrs. Sarti have their chat about horoscopes (p. 61), in its final form—an episode which was not, however, in the first typescript—before Andrea starts asking Galileo about sunspots, saying he has read Fabricius' book. The dialogue here is largely

different. Thus when the elderly scholar asks Galileo "Is it really right to keep one's mouth shut?" Galileo replies with the Keuner story about the man who was asked if he would serve his enemy, served him for seven years till he died, and then bundled up his corpse, scrubbed out the room, breathed deeply and replied "No." Only Galileo tells it, in the first typescript, of "Mr. Sarrone, a philosopher in Modena," amended to "the Cretan philosopher Keunos, who was much loved by the Cretans for his libertarian views." As the others laugh Andrea shakes his head and (in the revised versions) says he doesn't care for the story.

Gaffone the rector makes his brief appearance, as on p. 61, followed by some twenty lines of dialogue between the two women, including Virginia's remark about "a very high ecclesiastic" (p. 60), some references to signs of official surveillance, and an inquiry to Andrea about his fiancée:

VIRGINIA   How's Jessica? Are you still quarreling?

ANDREA (*laughing*)   No, I've found out now why she didn't want to marry me. Pangs of conscience. Because astronomers are unholy people, you know. Of course that wasn't a very serious obstacle. We're together again. (*Goes upstairs*)

MRS. SARTI [in the revised versions]   She knows she's doing well for herself. Her father's just an ordinary artisan . . .

Ludovico enters in traveling clothes, followed by a servant, saying he has got to speak to Galileo, about a rumor. Is he writing a book on sunspots? Galileo says what nonsense; did Ludovico come all the way to ask that?

LUDOVICO   I hope you understand. They're all talking about Copernicus again in connection with these sunspots. And I was hoping you weren't getting involved. I've already had hints dropped at the university.

GALILEO   Oh, so you're frightened?

Like the final Ludovico, this one brings the news that Barberini may soon be pope. Much of Galileo's speech in the first typescript about what his election might mean for science—e.g.

This means nothing less than the start of a new century of the arts and sciences. No more fear. Knowledge will be a

passion and research a self-indulgence. What a dreadful age, where saying what is, is considered a crime. But now people will say, what a dreadful age it was. Who's scared of discoveries now, they'll ask. Who's got reason to be?

—was shifted to immediately in front of his "Put a grid over the screen" (p. 67), so that his order to focus the telescope on the sun follows instantly on the news, without any of the teasing of Ludovico which is found in the final text. Ludovico begs him not to join in the sunspot controversy, to which Galileo answers:

> . . . Are they to say Galileo hasn't got the courage to open his mouth? People are looking at me, man. The earth rotates—it's I who say that, do you get me? If I keep silent it'll stop!
>
> LUDOVICO   Virginia, I know I love you. But I can't marry you if this is how things are. I haven't any money of my own.

Andrea suggests Galileo should help them. "My Jessica has come to terms with her conscience, but after all she's only risking hell. I don't know what she'd do if the city clergy stopped getting their communion vessels from her father the silversmith. A threat of that sort is far worse." But Galileo turns away to his collaborators.

> LUDOVICO   Virginia, I love you, and I love your father the way he is. But his concerns are not mine; I don't understand them and I haven't got the courage.

And because Galileo remains silent, Virginia gives him back his ring.

Thus virtually everything in the final text from Mrs. Sarti's "Pretty near!" (p. 67) to Andrea's interruption (69) is missing in this version. Galileo goes straight on to his big speech (p. 69), including already such key phrases as "My aim is not to prove that I've been right, but to find out whether or not I have been," and "And if there's something we hope to find, we'll regard it with particular distrust when we do find it." As Ludovico embraces Virginia and leaves, Galileo continues (from "yet go on talking")

> Then we'll crush this stupidity underfoot, eh, my boy? We'll peel off its skin to carry as our banner. And we'll write on it in blood: Look out! Or, rather, in ink—which

is more dangerous. At last we're going to bang those nar-
row-minded heads together till they burst like eggshells.
Yes, we're going to make cruel use of our arguments. Perhaps it'll be the first time in history that cruelty has been
directed against ignorance. A historic date!

ANDREA   And are you going to write the book on the world
systems?

GALILEO   Yes, and not in Latin for the few but in Florentine
for the many. Because this book has got to be understood
by everybody. For that I need people who work with their
hands. Who else is going to want to know the causes of
everything? [Then, in the revised versions, as on p. 68 to
"she'll probably laugh".] And the peasants who force their
plough into the earth, and the weavers at their looms, the
people now stirring in every street, are all going to point
at the sun and say: It's not a golden coat of arms but a lever.
We move it, because it moves us.

Virginia repacks her trousseau, and Andrea closes the scene
with his four-line epigram from p. 66.

10 [9, or 8 in first typescript]

The Copernican doctrine circulates among the peo-
ple.

The setting is a street, with a street singer and his wife singing
to a hurdy-gurdy and the populace listening from windows.
The ballad differs, above all structurally, from that in the final
text, and is here translated for the first time:

Great Galileo told the sun
(Or so the story says)
To give up turning around the earth
On which it casts its rays.
What a to-do!
The sun has started turning around itself
Not around me and you.

And immediately the sun had ceased
Reserving all its light for us

The verger gave up following after the priest
The apprentice after his boss.
No doubt you've guessed:
They all want to turn around themselves
And do what suits them best.

The bricklayer who was building the house
Is now its occupier.
The woodcutter who chops down trees
Puts the wood on his own fire.
What a to-do!
The woodcutter was telling his wife
His feet were frozen through.

I saw two housewives shopping for fish
The clock was striking twelve.
The fishwife took out a piece of bread
And ate the fish herself.
What a to-do!
The fishwife thought she'd have fish for once
Very nutritious too.

The master appears, the maids don't get up
The footmen omit to bow.
The master observes to his great surprise
Nothing turns around him now.
No doubt you've guessed:
The footmen have their hands too full
The maids won't allow them to rest.

THE WOMAN

I too had been dancing out of line
And said to my husband, "My dear
Whatever you do for me might well be done
By any other star."

THE MAN

What a to-do!

My wife ought to turn around no one but me—
That's always been my view.

The princes clean their boots with their own hands.
The emperor bakes his own bread.
The soldiers no longer obey commands
But stroll in the streets instead.
No doubt you've guessed:
There was too much work for too many to do.
In the end they had to protest.

(*In a confidential undertone*)

The cardinals all stood in St. Peter's Square
When the pope showed himself to the crowd
The cardinals acted as if he weren't there.
And went on talking much too loud.
What a to-do!
Their eminences have taken to kissing their own feet—
You know who that's due to.

Three archangels came down to earth, to complain
It should praise God more audibly.
But the earth said; "There are so many worlds in space
Why do they have to pick on me?"
No doubt you've guessed:
If our earth is just one of a whole lot of worlds
It can share such chores with the rest.

At the end of the ballad "*a Jesuit crosses the square. He crouches when
he hears the song, and goes off like a drenched poodle. The people laugh
and throw down coins.*"

A note then says that the scene can develop into a ballet. "*A
popular carnival celebration can be shown in the style of Brueghel's* The
Battle Between Carnival and Lent. *Following the first verse of the
ballad a carnival procession can move across the square, including a man
dressed as a BIBLE with a hole in it, and a cart with a monk stretching
out, trying with both hands to hold back a collapsing ST. PETER'S
THRONE. Then after the last verse the MOON, SUN, EARTH and*

PLANETS can appear and demonstrate the new system of motion in a dance, to a severe musical setting."

11 [*10, or 9 in first typescript*]

1633. The Inquisition summons the world-famous scholar to Rome.

This short scene in the Medici palace is close to the final text, except that the episode with Vanni the iron founder from Virginia's "There's Mr. Vanni" on p. 74 to Galileo's "and you'll lose your arm" on p. 76 is not in this version. Instead a man passes to whom Galileo vainly calls out "Galliardo! Galliardo!," commenting:

> That was the director of artillery equipment. He must have seen me. He usually eats out of my hand. Today he's running away as if he thought I was infectious.

Then a student passes, who wants to stop and talk to Galileo but is called away by his tutor. Just before Cosmo's entrance Galileo comments:

> After all, we're not here to get polite attentions paid us. I crawled into this position years ago on all fours, since anybody wanting to introduce the truth—or even a morsel of it—into a place like this can only enter through the lowest hole of all, the one for dogs. But it was a good thing to do, as now they'll have to protect me. There's something in the air. If I hadn't got the pope's imprimatur for it I'd think it was the book. But they know the book has passed the censors. The pope would flatly reject any attempt to make a trap for me out of it. And after all the grand duke is my pupil. I shall complain to him.

The passage about Sagredo's invitation (p. 77) and the appearance of the cardinal inquisitor were added before this in revision. Galileo's resolve to escape in Volpi's wine cart is not in this version; nor is the last sentence of the final text.

12 [*11, or 10 in first typescript*]

The pope.

This scene is divided by a "transformation" into two halves, of which the second is not in the later versions and is given in full below. The first half, in the pope's own room, is a slightly shorter version of the final text. It excludes notably the reference to Galileo's star charts and the maritime cities' need for them, the mention of his powerful friends, leading to the pope's order "Hands off!" (p. 80) with the inquisitor's cynical reply and the pope's comment that "Even his thinking is sensual." This half accordingly ends with "Not the whole world, but the best part of it." Then, after the transformation:

Another room. At the window, Galileo, waiting. Here too the stamping and shuffling of many feet of the gathering congregation is heard. In the foreground two officials of the Inquisition.

OFFICIAL (*sotto voce to his companion*) He's got good nerves. He's having a look at all his enemies.

GALILEO I hope the interview with His Holiness will take place before the session. It's important for me, as I want to ask for my evidence and proofs to be investigated before any decision is come to. It is of course quite impossible for me to make any kind of statement in a matter of such importance for the world of science without my evidence and proofs first getting a most scrupulous hearing and examination. I'd be glad of a little water. (*The first official pours him some water from a carafe on the table. Galileo reaches for it uncertainly and spills some.*)

SECOND OFFICIAL (*when the first returns*) Having a look at his enemies, but at nothing else. Had you forgotten he's half blind?

GALILEO I suppose His Holiness really does want to see me?

FIRST OFFICIAL Definitely.

GALILEO Then I'd prefer to wait in another room if that's possible.

SECOND OFFICIAL It's not possible. You wouldn't like His Holiness to arrive and find you weren't here, because you couldn't stand the shuffling.

GALILEO (*looks at him blankly*)

SECOND OFFICIAL   Yes, you must be beginning to realize it isn't just a handful of people gathering there to testify against you. It's the most distinguished minds in Italy, the most learned scholars, the stars of all the universities, in short it's everybody.

GALILEO   Yes. (*He turns to his window again*)

FIRST OFFICIAL   He must feel rather like someone before the flood who was expecting a spring shower, then the real rain came, then came an endless downpour and that turned into the flood, don't you think?

(*A high official appears. Galileo turns to face him and makes a deep bow. He thinks it is the pope*)

THE HIGH OFFICIAL   Has this person eaten?

FIRST OFFICIAL   He was served a substantial meal.

THE HIGH OFFICIAL   The session later may go on a long time. (*Goes out*)

GALILEO (*has risen to his feet in confusion*)   Gentlemen, I know His Holiness personally, having met him once at Cardinal Bellarmine's. But my eyesight is not what it was, and I must beg you to tell me when he is coming.

FIRST OFFICIAL   Shall be done, even though you wouldn't oblige us by making a proper meal.

GALILEO   The fact that the gentleman who just left used the word "later" when speaking about the Inquisition's session today is surely a definite sign that His Holiness wants to speak to me first?

FIRST OFFICIAL (*shrugs his shoulders*)

GALILEO   Did you say something?

FIRST OFFICIAL   I shrugged my shoulders.

13 [*12 or 11 in first typescript*]

Apart from the fact that Federzoni's subsequent lines are given to the elderly scholar, that the end of the scene (after the blackout) was at first conceived as a short scene on its own, and that Andrea's insults ("Wine barrel!" etc., p. 84) are missing, this version is not much different from the final one. In the first

typescript a speech for the elderly scholar was written in; it appears to belong after Andrea's "He couldn't write his book there" (p. 82) but was omitted in revision.

Clearly he didn't pay enough attention to that part. It's true that he said: It's not enough to know something, you have to be able to prove it. And he held his tongue till he was forty-six years old, and only spoke when he was able to prove his knowledge. But then he talked about his proofs to people with bunged-up ears, not to those who were dissatisfied with what had been believed in up to then but to those who were content with it. His mistake was to think that the choice between speaking in a republic and speaking in a grand duchy wasn't an astronomical problem.

14 [*13, or 12 in first typescript*]

1633–1642. A prisoner of the Inquisition, Galileo continues his scientific studies up to his death. He manages to smuggle his principal work out of Italy.

Like 9, this is a heavily altered scene with substantial differences from the final text. To sum them up briefly: (a) Galileo has conspired with the stove-fitter to conceal and smuggle out his writings; (b) Virginia reads him aphorisms by Montaigne, not scribbled texts provided by the archbishop; (c) his big speech (pp. 93–94) is differently conceived, though containing one or two phrases that recur in its final form; it omits all but the most general references to science's social implications, accuses himself only of failure to speak up for reason, and includes neither the warning of a "universal outcry of horror," nor the proposal for a scientists' Hippocratic oath; (d) it is only *after* this speech that Virginia leaves the room and Galileo admits to having written the *Discorsi*; (e) Andrea's enthusiastic reaction in praise of the "new ethics" is missing, as also is Galileo's counter-speech of self-abasement ("Welcome to the gutter" p. 93); thus there are no dramatic reversals of feeling between the handing-over of the *Discorsi* and the end of the scene.

In the opening stage direction Galileo is described as "*old and*

ill, and moves like a blind man." Virginia solicitously serves him his supper ("Now let's eat up our good soup, and try not to spill a drop of it"). He then complains that the stove isn't working properly, and asks when the stove-fitter is coming. The official in the antechamber (the monk of the final text) complains to Virginia that manuscripts have been leaking out:

> Don't forget that the *Dialogue Concerning the Two Chief World Systems* was smuggled to Holland from here. And now they've intercepted a letter to Strasbourg, saying a manuscript will be coming. It must already have got out. Who took it? (*Enter a big, broad-shouldered man, the stove-fitter. He has his tools with him*)

The stove-fitter is indeed the agent responsible, but this time he has brought the manuscript back because "They are after us. Villagio has been arrested." The doctor then appears, to check on Galileo's eyesight.

THE OFFICIAL   Can he or can he not see?

THE DOCTOR (*shrugs his shoulders*)   I don't know; very little, I'd say. I'll be making my report.

Virginia then comes in again to read to her father. (The following passage was published in 1957 in *Versuche 15* as an addendum to the play.)

VIRGINIA   Shall I read to you?

GALILEO   Yes, those inscriptions on the beams of M. de Montaigne's library. But only the ones I've marked.

VIRGINIA (*gets the book and reads*)   54th Inscription: Without leaning .

GALILEO   Is that all?

VIRGINIA   Yes.

GALILEO   But that depends on at least three things: the force of the thrust applied to one, the visibility of the objective and the solidity of the base. Some advice! Go on.

VIRGINIA   52nd inscription: I do not understand.

GALILEO   That's good. It's a starting point.

VIRGINIA   13: It is possible and it is not possible.[1]

GALILEO   Good, so long as he gives reasons.

(1) Sextus Empiricus, *Hypotyposes*, 1, 21

VIRGINIA   5: It's no more like this than like that or like neither.[2]

GALILEO   Provided one goes on looking.

VIRGINIA   21: He who knows that he knows doesn't know how he knows.[3]

GALILEO   Again, that's very good. But it all tastes of defeatism.

VIRGINIA   10: What are heaven and earth and sea, with all they embrace, against the sum of sums of the immeasurable whole?[4]

GALILEO   One has to start, though. Make a note.

VIRGINIA   2: He gave them curiosity, that he might torment them.[5]

GALILEO   Rubbish.

VIRGINIA   15: Man is too fragile.[6]

GALILEO   Not fragile enough.

VIRGINIA   20: Be wise in moderation, that you may not grow stupid.[7]

GALILEO   Go on.

VIRGINIA   42: Men are not confused by things but by opinions about things.[8]

GALILEO   That could be wrong too. Who confuses the opinions?

VIRGINIA   Should I make a note of that?

GALILEO   No.

VIRGINIA   19: I am a human; nothing human is alien to me.[9]

GALILEO   Good.

(2) Ibid., 1, 19, cited Montaigne *Essays*, 2, 12.

(3) 1 Corinthians 8:2. The A. V. quotation is "And if any man think that he knoweth anything, he knoweth nothing yet as he ought to know."

(4) Lucretius, *De Rerum Natura*, 6, cited Montaigne *Essays* 2, 12.

(5) Ecclesiastes 1, of which verse 13 in A.V. reads "And I gave my heart to seek and search out by wisdom concerning all things that are done under heaven: this sore travail hath God given to the sons of man to be exercised therewith" (*Essays* 2, 17)

(6) Keramos anthropos. Wrongly attributed to Romans 9.

(7) Ecclesiastes 7: ". . . neither make thyself over wise: why shouldest thou destroy thyself?"

(8) Epictetus, cited by Stobaeus. (*Essays* 1, 14)

(9) Terence, *Heautontimoroumenos* Act 1 (*Essays*, 2, 2) This was Karl Marx's favorite saying.

VIRGINIA 37: God has created man like a shadow. Who can judge him once the sun has set?[10]

(*Galileo is silent*)

VIRGINIA 17: You should neither fear your last day nor yearn for it.[11]

GALILEO I used to find the first point difficult; now it's the second.

VIRGINIA 14: A wondrous thing is goodness.[12]

GALILEO Louder!

VIRGINIA (*louder*) A wondrous thing is goodness.

A much shorter alternative to the whole passage, which is also given in the first typescript, with Galileo and Virginia going over proofs, replaces it in the revised versions. In this Virginia reads Galileo the extract from the *Discorsi* which appears at the end of the previous scene in the final text.

At this point Andrea enters, and the dialogue is fairly close to the final text, up to where Galileo asks about his scientific friends: "Has my recantation helped them to mend their ways?" (p. 89). Andrea hardly answers the question; he says nothing about Fulganzio, or, of course, Federzoni; the immediately preceding exchange about Descartes is also missing. Instead the text continues:

ANDREA For a time there was a considerable difference of opinion about you. Some of your former friends insisted that you had recanted because of services you still hoped to render physics by remaining alive. Because of such works as only you could write.

GALILEO (*brusquely*) There are no such works.

ANDREA How do you mean? If you hadn't written the [*Dialogue*] . . .

GALILEO Then someone else would have written it.

ANDREA So that wasn't your motive?

(10) Ecclesiastes 7. Or more probably 6: 12, which reads "For who knoweth what is good for man in this life, all the days of his vain life which he spendeth as a shadow? For who can tell a man what shall be after him under the sun?" (*Essays* 2, 12)

(11) *Essays* 2, 37, after Martial, 10.

(12) Plato, *Cratylus*.

GALILEO Shortly after my trial various people who had
known me earlier were good enough to credit me with all
kinds of noble intentions. I wouldn't have this. To me it
simply signified a decline of the critical faculties, brought
about by the fact that they found drastic physical changes
in me.

After carefully considering all the circumstances, extenuating and otherwise, it is impossible to conclude that
a man could arrive at this state of—call it obedience, from
any other motive than an undue fear of death. (*Pause*) That
is not to deny (*Addressing Virginia*) the profound regret
which I, as a son of the church, felt when my superiors
induced me, by the most weighty of all arguments, to see
the error of my ways. As a rule nothing less than threatening a man with death will serve to dissuade him from something of which his reason, that most dangerous of all God's
gifts, has persuaded him. I fully understood that I could
now only expect that hell which, so the poet tells, is inhabited by people who have gambled away the gifts of the
mind and are accordingly without hope.

He tells Andrea that science should be able to get along without
authority (including his own). "Authority and absence of truth
doubtless go together, and so do truth and absence of authority." Andrea then sums up the case against him, as it emerges
in this version:

... a lot of people everywhere were hanging on your words
and actions because they felt what you stood for was not a
particular theory about the movements of the stars but the
freedom to theorize in any field. Not just for any particular
thoughts, in other words, but for the right to think in the
first place, which was now being threatened. So as soon as
these people heard you recanting all you had said they
concluded that it was not merely certain thoughts about
celestial motions that were being discredited but thinking
itself that was being regarded as unholy, since it operates
by means of causes and proofs.

Virginia replies that the church has not forbidden science, but
has even absorbed Galileo's main discoveries. "Only he mustn't
attack the opinions of theology, which is an entirely different

science." The big speech follows, starting very much as it does in the final text (p. 93):

GALILEO   In my free time, and I've got plenty of that, I have asked myself how the world of science, of which I no longer consider myself a member, even if I still know a thing or two about its pursuits, will judge my conduct. (*In lecture style, hands folded over his paunch*) It will have to take into account whether it is good enough for its members to provide it with a given number of sentences, for instance about the tendencies of falling bodies or the motions of certain stars. I have, as I said, excluded myself from the scientific way of thinking; however, I take it that when faced with the threat of destruction that world will be in no position to lay down more far-reaching duties for its members, e.g., that of collaborating in its own maintenance as science. Even a wool merchant, in addition to buying cheap and providing good wool, has to worry about his trade being permitted at all and without restriction. On that principle no member of the scientific world is logically entitled to point to his own possible contributions to research if he has failed to honor his profession as such and to defend it against any use of force. This, however, is a business of vast scope. For science consists, not in a license to subordinate facts to opinions, but in an obligation to subordinate opinions to facts. It is not in any position to permit restriction of these sentences or to establish them only for "certain views" and "those particular facts." In order to make sure that it can apply these sentences unrestrictedly at any one time, science has to fight to be respected in every sphere. For science and humanity as a whole happen to be in the same boat. So it can't say "What business is it of mine if the boat springs a leak at the other end?" [A passage cut from the original typescript here is repeated between two asterisks on p. 296 below.] Science has no use for people who fail to stick up for reason. It must expel them in ignominy, because, however many truths science knows, it could have no future in a world of lies. If the hand that feeds it occasionally seizes it unpredictably by the throat then humanity will have to chop it off. That is why science cannot tolerate a person like me in its ranks.

VIRGINIA (*with passion*) But you have been received in the ranks of the faithful. (cf. p. 95)

GALILEO That is the position. In my view I have wrecked every experiment that might have been injurious to blind faith. Only my ingrained habit of making allowances for improbabilities would lead me to say "nearly every experiment." Plainly nothing but the irresistible arguments put forward by the Inquisition could have convinced me of the harmfulness of my researches.

ANDREA (*in a strangled voice*) Yes.

Virginia leaves the room, and Galileo at once slyly admits that he has had relapses (p. 90). The dialogue then roughly anticipates that in the final text, up to where Andrea takes up the manuscript of the *Discorsi*, with the difference that Andrea never assumes that the work has been irrevocably handed over to "the monks" as occurs, with consequently heightened tension, in the final text. Nor does Galileo simply tell him to "Put it under your coat" (p. 91), but makes more elaborate and self-protective hints as to how he might take it away. Then as Andrea leaves, there is a significantly different exchange, to which the section in square brackets was added in the course of revision:

ANDREA (*who has concealed the manuscript on him*) Yes, I'm going now. [I realize it's as if a tower had collapsed which was enormously tall and thought to be unshakeable. The noise it made collapsing was louder than the noise of the builders and their machines during the whole period of its construction, and the column of dust which its collapse caused was even higher than it had been. But conceivably when the dust disperses it may turn out that although the top twelve stories fell down the bottom thirty are still standing. In which case the building could be developed further. Is that what you mean? It would be supported by the fact that the inconsistencies in our science are still all in evidence and have been sifted. The difficulty seems to have increased, but at the same time the necessity has become greater.] I'm glad I came. (*He holds out his hand to him*)

GALILEO (*does not take it; hesitantly*) My eyesight is bad, Andrea. I can't see any more, I only stare. You had better go. (*He walks slowly to [the globe and sees if it is shut*) I'm not

unresponsive to the kindnesses I'm always being shown. Travelers passing through remember me, and so on. I don't misinterpret such things.] I'm glad too to have talked to you, and to have found you as you are. You have had experiences which could have given you a quite wrong view of what we've always termed the future of reason. But of course, no single man could either bring it to pass or discredit it. *It is too big an affair ever to be contained inside a single head. Reason is something people can be divided into. It can be described as the egoism of all humanity. *Such egoism is not strong enough. But even a person like myself can still see that reason is not coming to an end but beginning. And I still believe that this is a new age. It may look like a bloodstained old harridan, but if so that must be the way new ages look. When light breaks in it does so in the uttermost darkness. While a few places are the scene of the most immense discoveries, which must contribute immeasurably to humanity's resources for happiness, great areas of this world still lie entirely in the dark. In fact the blackness has actually deepened there. Look out for yourself when you travel through Germany with the truth under your coat.

(*Andrea goes out*)

Andrea says nothing about a "devastating analysis" (p. 95). The scene quickly closes, somewhat as in the final text, though not on the word "Clear" but on Galileo's ensuing comment: "That's good. Then he'll be able to see his way."

15 [*14*]

1637. Galileo's book *Discorsi* crosses the Italian border.

Very close to the final text.

3. The American Version, 1944–1947

This English-language version, which Brecht and Laughton worked on from the end of 1944 up to the Hollywood production of July 1947, maintains the general structure of the play, but shortens and very largely rewrites it. The main structural changes are the omission of the first half of scene 4; the cutting of scene 5a off the end of scene 4 and the elimination of it and 5b (the plague scenes); also the cutting of the second half of scene 12 (pp. 287–288 above), with Galileo waiting for the pope. An element of social interest was introduced by making Ludovico an aristocrat and creating two new characters: Federzoni the lens grinder, who helps bring out the point of Galileo's use of the vernacular language, and the iron founder here called Matti, whose function is to appear in scenes 2 and 11 and show that the embryo bourgeoisie is on Galileo's side. Ludovico takes over Doppone's role in scenes 1 and 2; not surprisingly he becomes a little unconvincing. Federzoni too gets some of the elderly scholar's lines in scene 9. In this scene Mucius is cut, in scene 14 the stove-fitter and the doctor. According to Brecht it was Laughton who insisted on transposing the handing-over of the *Discorsi* in this scene so that Galileo's big self-accusatory speech should come after it.

The carnival scene (10) was rewritten entirely, with a new English-language ballad, though the gist of this remained much the same. The actions of the masqueraders and the crowd, while not exactly amounting to the "ballet" proposed in the first version, were described in some detail, finishing with the appearance of the enormous dummy figure of "Galileo, the Bible-killer."

Finally there are no scene titles in the text as published, but short English verses were put at the beginning of each scene,

and at the end of the play, which now finished with the warning:

> May you now guard science' light,
> Kindle it and use it right,
> Lest it be a flame to fall
> Downward to consume us all.

The full text of this version is given on pages 403–467. The following is a brief scene-by-scene commentary on the changes. Scene numbers are those of the final text, with the American version's numbering in square brackets.

1.

The scene begins with the arrival of the Ptolemaic model which was previously already there. Galileo's speech on the "new age" is shorter and simpler and more sloppily worded, ("A new age was coming. I was onto it years ago"), but includes the ships and the Sienese masons. His second demonstration to Andrea, with the apple (which is in both the first and the final versions), is cut from Andrea's "But it's not true" (p. 8) to Galileo's "Aha!" on p. 9. Ludovico then appears, the gist of the dialogue being much the same as in the final text, but very much shortened. Galileo's discussion with Andrea about hypotheses is cut. The procurator, who follows Ludovico's exit, is for some reason a museum curator; again the dialogue is shortened and simplified, even vulgarized:

> CURATOR   You've never let me down yet, Galilei.
>
> GALILEO   You are always an inspiration to me, Priuli.

The ending of the scene is likewise shorter.

2.

The form of the scene is as in the final text, except that Virginia makes the presentation, that Matti the (Florentine) iron founder appears, and that the doge has nothing to say. Note the curator's *"best chamber-of-commerce manner"* and the allusion to him as a businessman, also the new silliness of Virginia as exemplified in the closing exchanges.

3.

This is the same scene as in the final version, but shortened. It introduces Galileo's remarks about star charts, but cuts the episode with Mrs. Sarti (pp. 24–25) who does not appear at all. Virginia enters earlier—there is no cross-fade as before—and stays long enough to hear Sagredo read out the end of the letter to the grand duke. The scene now ends approximately as in the final text, though rather more abruptly.

4.

The first half of the scene has been cut: Mrs. Sarti's speech, the grand duke's arrival and the episode with the two boys, also Galileo's opening speech and the beginning of the scientific argument up to where Cosmo's three professors are invited to look through the telescope for themselves (p. 33 in the final version). Instead it begins with the philosopher talking Latin and the exchange (p. 32) about the need to use the vernacular for Federzoni's sake. The argument which follows, now interrupted by the court ladies with jarringly improbable comments, follows the same pattern as the final version, though again in shortened form. It introduces notably Galileo's remark, "Why defend shaken teachings? You should be doing the shaking," and the speech that follows about the arsenal workers and the sailors. The professors leave without speculating about Cosmo's hurried departure, now attributed to the state ball.

5.

[is cut]

6. [5]

Apart from the ending, this is a shortened form of the Collegium Romanum scene as we have it. The episode with the two astronomers is cut (from their entry p. 43 to their exit p. 44), apart from the very thin (or in this version infuriated) monk's first remark. His ensuing speech (starting "They degrade the

home of mankind") is likewise cut. The scene ends on the little
monk's remark about Galileo's having won. Galileo's answer
and the appearance of the cardinal inquisitor are omitted. The
inscription about astronomical charts which is lowered after
the curtain is not found in the other versions.

7. [6]

Again, this is a slightly shortened form of the final text. The
great families attending the ball are named, Doppone is omitted, the two cardinals are now lamb and dove, the reference to
star charts is new, Barberini swaps Biblical texts with Galileo
and welcomes him to Rome, Bellarmine's speech about the
Campagna peasants and the "master plan" is cut, the inquisitor
greets Virginia with the comment that her fiancé comes "from
a fine family." The Lorenzo de' Medici madrigal is still missing.

8. [7]

The scene with the little monk is virtually as in the final version.
Most of Galileo's speech about the Priapus is cut, but the beginning is as we now have it, and the phrases about the oyster and
the pearl, and the peasants' "divine patience" are included.

9. [8]

The order of events is as in the final text, though the episode
with Mucius has been cut. The scene thus starts with Virginia's
dialogue with Mrs. Sarti, including the talk about horoscopes.
The Keunos story has gone, as have all allusions to Andrea's
Jessica. Instead there is the dialogue between the collaborators
as the experiment is prepared, including the little monk's remark about "happiness in doubting" but omitting Andrea's
account of how he has been observing the sun's rays in the attic.
The whole episode with Ludovico corresponds closely to the
final text, from his entrance on p. 64 to his exit on p. 69, apart
from the omission of Mrs. Sarti's long speech (p. 67) and the
little monk's immediately preceding remark about God and

physics. The end of the scene too is the same, except that it stops at the end of Galileo's important speech.

10. [9]

The rewriting of this scene has already been mentioned (p. 297).

11. [10]

Close to the final text. Half the Vanni episode is here, though he is called Matti (as in scene 2) and it ends at the equivalent of "please remember that you have friends in every branch of industry" (p. 75). (The rest appears to have been written at the same time, but not included in the published text.) Galliardo and the student do not appear. The passages about Sagredo's invitation and the possibility of escape were not in the earlier version.

12. [11]

The inquisitor's long speech is shortened by half, notably by the references to papal politics and the abolition of top and bottom, with the ensuing quotation from Aristotle. The exchange about Galileo's self-indulgence is new. That about the conclusion of his book is omitted. The ending, after "but the best part of it" (p. 81) is new; the final stage instruction (which does not read like Brecht) being found only in this version. Otherwise this part of the scene is as we now have it. As already noted, the second part of the scene is cut.

13. [12]

From Andrea's cry "not to know the truth" (p. 82) to his imitation of Galileo is cut. The rest is as in the final version except for Federzoni's remark about Andrea not getting paid, and the shifting of Andrea's "Unhappy is the land that breeds no hero" to immediately before Galileo's answer.

14. [13]

The order of events has been shifted, and is the same as in the final text. There is now nothing about the Inquisition's suspicions that manuscripts are being smuggled out, and the episodes with the doctor and the stove-fitter are cut. The "weekly letter to the archbishop," whose discussion replaces that of the Montaigne inscriptions, is about half as long as in the final text. Andrea's ensuing dialogue with Galileo is as in the final text up to the point where Virginia leaves the room (which now comes very much earlier); that is to say it discusses what has happened to his former collaborators. The revelation of the *Discorsi* then comes before the analysis of Galileo's motives and conduct, which is now without the passages quoted on pp. 293 ff., but introduces Andrea's gradually waning praise of Galileo's behavior, from Andrea's "Two new branches of science" (p. 461) to Galileo's "It was not" (p. 462). The "welcome to the gutter" speech which follows is new, though shorter than its final version. The big speech is likewise about one-third shorter than in the final text, omitting notably the phrases "But can we turn our backs on the people and still remain scientists?" and "Science, Sarti, is involved in both battles," as well as the suggestion of a Hippocratic oath and the picture of scientists as "inventive dwarfs." The shift of emphasis from intellectual to social betrayal, the stressing of the liberating popular effects of the new science, finally the introduction of allusions to the horrors of the atom bomb, can all best be seen by comparing the actual text with that of the earlier version (pp. 462–463).

Galileo's view of "the new age," in the final exchanges, is expressed in the same terms as in the previous version. Again he ignores Andrea's hand, without comment. There is no mention of Andrea's journey through Germany, and the scene ends with Virginia's final remark.

15. [14]

The scene is broadly similar to its earlier version, but has been wholly rewritten, including the song. Among other things, the

witch's house is shown, and the children steal her milk jug and kick it over.

4. The Berlin Version, 1953–1956

We can now summarize what happened when Brecht decided to make a new German version of the play after his return to Berlin. Two principal texts are involved: that published in his *Versuche 14* in 1955, and the final revised text of the collected *Stücke* (1957), which incorporates minor changes made in the course of Brecht's rehearsals and as a result of the Cologne production in the former year. This version follows the general structure of the American version, giving more or less the same account of characters, incidents, motivations and social substructure. However, it brings back important stretches of dialogue from the first version, eliminating many of the crudities of the American text and giving more elbow-room to the arguments at the cost, of course, of making a considerably longer play.

The characters remain the same as in the American version, apart from the bringing back of Mucius at the beginning of scene 9, and the renaming of Vanni, who no longer figures in scene 2. So do their social roles. The plague scene is restored in a new form by running together 5a and 5b; this, presumably, being something that Brecht had wished to have "in the book" even though, like Laughton, he was excluding it from the acting version. Scene 4 is restored to its full length, scene 15 put back into its old form. The original German text of the ballad in scene 10 has not been restored; instead it has been (freely) re-translated from the English, so as to fit Eisler's setting, though with the addition of the singer's remarks to the crowd. The same applies to the between-scene verses, which were not done in time for the *Versuche* edition. The Lorenzo de' Medici madrigal in scene 7, (which appears to derive from the sixtieth and last stanzas of his Eclogue "La Ritrozia") now makes its appearance for the first time.

The play again begins as in the first version, though Galileo's speech on the "new age" has been slightly expanded; the second demonstration with Andrea and the full conversation with the procurator are restored. In scene 3 the episode with Mrs. Sarti is brought back, leading to the (shortened) conclusion, "They snatch at it" (p. 25), while immediately before her entry Galileo's speech is given a new last sentence: "Thinking is one of the greatest pleasures of the human race" (p. 24). Virginia is now made to leave before the reading of the letter to the grand duke. In scene 4 some of the fatuous remarks of the court ladies (e.g. "Perfect poise!" and "What diction!") are eliminated; the professors' proposal for a formal disputation is new, as is Federzoni's call for new textbooks.

In the plague scene the second half (b) is virtually as in the (revised) first version, but the first half has been revised, notably cutting Galileo's last remarks, with their reference to the uncertainty of remaining alive "in times like these." In the ball scene (7) Galileo's new poem, which could be a quasi-Horatian variant on Herrick's "Delight in Disorder," replaces the English one; while Bellarmine's remarks about the Campagna peasants and the (social) need to attribute all the world's horrors to a "master plan" are restored. In the sunspot scene (9) the episode with Mucius now comes near the start of the scene, which has been correspondingly rewritten; Mrs. Sarti's speech (p. 67) has also been restored, as has Galileo's call for "people who work with their hands" (p. 68), in lieu of the American version's too simple view that scientific work is not worth doing "for less than the population at large." The end of this scene ("I've got to know") is quite new.

In the carnival scene (10) the procession is now described briefly in a single stage direction at the end. In scene 11 the episode with Vanni is extended to emphasize Galileo's sense of security (and of his own comforts). Scene 12 restores the inquisitor's comments on papal politics and introduces the graffito about the Barberinis' love of art, as well as the exchange about condemning the doctrine and keeping its practical applications. For the slight changes in scenes 13 and 14 see pp. 301–302 above. There is in the Brecht-Archive a sketch for the notion of a Hippocratic oath for scientists which was evidently

noted down in America (in Brecht's homemade English) but for some reason not then worked into the play. It goes thus:

ingenious dwarfs
Hypocratic
hypocrades Oath
   Had I resisted, the natural sciences might have
      something like the   of the physicians.
   develloped their own Hypöcratic oath
     mankind
Now, the most we can hope for will be a race of ingenious dwarfs who can

be hired for any purpose who will, as on islands, produce whatever

their masters demand.

            means
   what's the use of progress, if it is a

   leaving behind of mankind? There even

   a state of things could develop, when our

   inventions

[Spelling and spacing as on Brecht's typescript, but not showing his corrections and deletions. From BBA 609/91, reproduced in Schumacher: *Drama und Geschichte*, 1965, p. 208.]

THE TRIAL
OF LUCULLUS

Texts by Brecht

Notes on the Opera *The Condemnation of Lucullus**

The radio play *The Trial of Lucullus* forms the basis of the opera *The Condemnation of Lucullus*. The earlier work concluded with the end of the trial and the lines:

> The court
> Withdraws to consider its verdict.

Scene 14 "The Verdict" has been added from the opera. The title, however, has been retained to help distinguish the play from the later work.

The opera does not include the testimony of the stone figures on the frieze. Instead, the shades of those represented on the frieze are summoned as witnesses. Here the new scene (cf. p. 114):

Bringing in the Frieze

THE SLAVES WITH THE FRIEZE
> Out of life and into death
> We haul our load ungrudgingly.
> For years our time was not our own
> Unknown to us our destination.
> So we follow the new voice

*Passages not in *Trial of Lucullus* translated by the Editors.

As we did the old one. Why ask questions?
We leave nothing behind, expect nothing.

LUCULLUS

You, jurors of the dead, behold my frieze.
A captured king, Tigranes of Pontus.
His sloe-eyed queen. Look at her lovely thighs.
A man with a little cherry tree, eating a cherry.
Two virgins with a tablet bearing the names of 53 cities.
Two legionaries
One standing, one dying and saluting his general.
My cook with a fish.

CHORUS

See how they've built themselves a monument
Of stony shades of long-vanished victims, fashioned
To speak on earth or to be silent on earth.
Helpless witnesses called to represent
In the light, at the victor's command, those flung
To the ground, robbed of breath, struck dumb and forgot-
    ten
Ready for silence and ready for speech.

THE SPEAKER

Shade, the jurors have taken
Note of your triumphal frieze.
They are eager to learn more about
Your triumph than the frieze relates.
They suggest that those
Depicted upon your frieze
Be summoned.

THE JUDGE

They shall be called.
For always
It is the victor who writes the history of the vanquished.
The slayer distorts
The features of the slain. The weaker
Vanishes from the world, the lies
Remain. Down here we
Have no need of your stones. There are
So many down here, general, of those
Who crossed your path. Rather than

Portraits we shall call the
Portrayed. We'd rather question
Shades than stones.

LUCULLUS
I object.
I do not wish to see them.

THE VOICES OF THREE WOMAN CRIERS
The victims of General Lacallous
On his campaigns in Asia!
(*From the background emerge the shades of those portrayed on the
triumphal frieze, and line up opposite the frieze*)

The beginning of the next scene had to be changed to correspond.

THE SPEAKER
Bow your head, shade.
These are your witnesses.

LUCULLUS
I protest.

THE SPEAKER
These are your witnesses.

LUCULLUS
But they are enemies!
There you see a man whom I defeated.
In the few days . . .

After the trial performance which the Ministry of Education
arranged at the Berlin State Opera, two interpolations were
made on the basis of prolonged discussions. The first shows why
it was possible for the defeated king, who in the opera appears
as a shade and not merely as a figure on the frieze, to be acquit-
ted in a trial similar to the one in which Lucullus will be condemned. The following interpolation was made in "The Trial"
(p. 118):

LUCULLUS
Yes, I notice that the losers
Have sweet voices. Once
They were different, though. The king there

Who is prevailing on your pity, was in his lifetime
No better than I. Of tithe and tax
He took no less than I did.
The silver that he mined
Never found its way to the people.

THE TEACHER (*to the king*)
Why then
Are you among us, king?

THE KING
Because I built cities.
Because I defended them when you
Romans demanded their surrender.

THE TEACHER
Not us. Him!

THE KING
Because, to defend the country, I proclaimed:
Man, woman and child
In hedgerow and water hole
With mattock, ax and plowshare
By day and night
By their speech, by their silence
Free or captive
In the face of the enemy
In the face of death.

THE TEACHER
I propose that we all
Rise to our feet before this witness
And in honor of those
Who defended their cities.
(*The jurors rise*)

LUCULLUS
What kind of Romans are you!
Applauding the enemy!
I didn't go on my own
It was an order
I was sent by
Rome.

THE TEACHER
Rome! Rome! Rome!

Who is Rome?
Were you sent by the masons who built her?
Were you sent by the bakers and fishermen
Or the peasants and ox drivers
And the gardeners who feed her?
Was it the tailors and furriers
Or the weavers and sheep shearers who clothe her?
Were you sent by the stone polishers
And wool dyers who adorn her?
Or were you sent by the tax farmers
And the silver merchants and the slave traders
And the bankers of the Forum, who plunder her?
(*Silence*)

LUCULLUS

Whoever sent me—
I won
53 cities for Rome.

THE TEACHER

And where are they?
Jurors, let us question the cities.

TWO VIRGINS WITH A TABLET

With streets and people and houses . . .

The second interpolation is at the end of the last scene, where
the legionaries who died on the Asian campaigns join in the
condemnation of Lucullus (p. 130). Instead of:

Yes, send him to nothingness! What province
Tips the scales against
Our unlived years that held so much?

it now reads:

THE LEGIONARIES

Serving the bandit
Committing arson and murder
We the sons of the
People met our death.
Yes, send him to nothingness!
Like the wolf
That breaks into the fold

And has to be killed
So we were killed
In his service.
Yes, send him to nothingness!
If only we
Had deserted the aggressor!
If only we
Had joined the defenders!
Send him to nothingness!

The insertion of the three new arias ("Summons to Defence,"
"Who is Rome?" "Song of the Fallen Legionaries") was also
intended to correct a certain disproportion arising from the fact
that less musical expression was given to the court than to the
defendant.

> [From GW *Stücke*, pp. 1479–1485. Signed "Brecht. Dessau."
> For a more exact account of the differences between the final
> text, as used for our translation, and the original radio
> play on the one hand and the opera text on the other, see
> pp. 316 ff. below.]

The Discussion about *The Condemnation of Lucullus*

The opera had already been accepted when the campaign
against formalism was launched. Objections were raised at the
Ministry of Education. The authors were asked to withdraw the
opera. But they were only willing to forego their contract, not
to withdraw the opera, because they did not regard it as formalistic. The arguments adduced did not convince them, in fact
those raised by the musical advisers struck them as themselves
formalistic. The authors stressed the importance of the message,
namely, a condemnation of predatory war, and proposed that
the rehearsals, which had already begun, should be continued
long enough to permit of a closed performance on the strength
of which an understanding might be reached between the au-

thors and an audience of government representatives. The proposal was accepted and everything was done to make such an understanding possible. When the performance took place, the theme had a powerful effect on the audience, for one thing because it corresponded to the peace-loving policy of the German Democratic Republic and its condemnation of predatory war. Nevertheless, grave objections were raised, and in the course of a three-hour discussion between the authors and leading members of the government under the chairmanship of the President of the German Democratic Republic, it was shown that in its present form the opera might introduce a certain element of confusion into the newly initiated campaign, which was extremely important because it was designed to bridge the gap which undeniably existed between the arts and their new public. The metaphoric character of the text made it hard to understand, the music was not sufficiently in keeping with the present state of musical education among the general public, and deviated from the classical line. Moreover, the somber, violent music portraying the aggressor dominated the score. Brecht and Dessau declared their willingness to make additions in the spirit of the discussion and to resubmit the work. When at a second discussion among the same persons new texts were submitted and the composer also held out the prospect of certain changes, the members of the government decided that the opera should be produced and thrown open to the criticism of the public.

[From GW *Schriften zum Theater*, pp. 1152–3.]

Changes in the Text of *Lucullus*

1

Question: Can the scene of the children in the mausoleum be so misunderstood as to suggest that we are opposed to the veneration of heroes?

Change: Though it transpires in the following that the hero being honored on this occasion is condemned as a war criminal by the court of posterity, a momentary misunderstanding can be avoided by having the *teacher* exhort the children to become conquerors, while the children merely repeat his words. (TEACHER Sextus conquers Pontus.—PUPIL Pontus.—And so on.)

2

Question: How can it be brought out that only wars of aggression are condemned, not defensive wars?

Change: A new scene is added to the questioning of the king and queen. The king of the invaded country is asked by the jurors how he managed to pass the test of posterity. He repeats the proclamation in which he called on the people to defend their country dauntlessly. (The proclamation is positive and rousing.) The jurors rise from their seats in honor of those who defended their country.

3

Question: How can it be brought out that the primary instigators of war are not the generals, but . . . ?

Change: Lucullus claims that he went out to conquer Asia by order of Rome. A juror asks: Who is Rome? He replies that he was sent to Asia not by the masons, bakers, weavers, and peasants, but by the silver merchants, slave traders, and bankers.

4

Question: In addition to condemning offensive war, would it be possible to say what can be done to combat it?

Change: Toward the end a song of Lucullus' legionaries who died in Asia is added. In it, they castigate themselves for having let themselves be misled and express their regret that they did not refuse to serve Lucullus and instead help his victims to defend their country.

5

The title is to be changed from *The Trial of Lucullus* to *The Condemnation of Lucullus.* And instead of being called *Opera*, it is to be called *A Musical Play*.

> [From GW *Schriften zum Theater,* pp. 1154–6. Paragraphs 1–4 deal with the main changes outlined in "Notes on the Opera *The Condemnation of Lucullus,*" as a result of the discussions held in 1951. Paragraph 5's proposal to change the category of the work to "musical play" was rejected by Dessau; according to Fritz Hennenberg it was originally Hermann Scherchen's suggestion.]

Three Short Notes

The action of the opera *The Trial of Lucullus*—the trial and conviction of predatory war by posterity—takes place in the nether world. This device was frequently used by classical authors (Prologue in Heaven in *Faust,* Classical Walpurgis Night in *Faust,* Gluck's *Orpheus and Euridice,* and so forth and so on). The main importance of this device is not that it serves to camouflage ideas for purposes of contraband—obviously such a work could not be performed in the west today if MacArthur were standing trial—but that art benefits when the spectator, by discovering its relevance for himself, is enabled to respond more deeply and intensely. In general, the enjoyment of art (and the enjoyment of insights and impulses through art) is enhanced

when the audience is stimulated to intellectual production, discovery and experience.

We are performing the opera *The Trial of Lucullus* by Paul Dessau. It is based on a radio play written by Brecht in 1939, a year marked by the outbreak of the wars of spoliation and conquest that culminated and ended in the Second World War. It deals with the trial of Lucullus, a Roman general who, in the last century before our era, invaded Asia with his legions and conquered vast territories for the Roman Empire.

The *Condemnation of Lucullus* is an opera based on a radio play. If any of the opera houses accept it, this will, I believe, mark the first appearance in that quarter of a work deriving from the collective effort of modern radio.

> [GW *Schriften zum Theater*, pp. 1151–2. These notes were written for different occasions. The last is signed "Dessau. Brecht."]

Editorial Note

Although Brecht's notes make it appear as if there were two versions of this play, the radio play and the opera libretto, there are basically three: (a) the radio play of 1939, (b) the revised text of 1949–50 as printed in the collected works, and (c) the opera libretto of 1951. The text which we have followed in this volume is in fact a hybrid, halfway between radio play and opera, and as far as we know it was not publicly performed in German in Brecht's lifetime.

The radio play (a) was performed by the Bern studio of the Swiss radio in 1940 and published in the German language Moscow monthly *Internationale Literatur* at the end of that year. Its text is very close to that set down in Brecht's first typescript, and, on paper at least, is much the most effective of the three versions, being shorter and leaving more to the imagination; this is especially the case with the last scene. Already Brecht seems to have had in mind a musical setting, for a page attached to the first script, (and likewise in his own typing) lists the musical numbers as follows:

1
song of the soldiers ("hold it steady")
song of the slaves ("watch out, men, don't stumble")

3
chorus of children ("in the schoolbooks")

4
duet of the crier and the gatekeeper ("out on the appian way")

5
conversation of the soldiers ("so long, lacallous")

6

lucullus' outburst ("by jupiter, what does this mean?")

quartet of lucullus and threefold voice ("lacallous" and
  "lucullus is my name")

7

recitative of the usher ("before the highest court")

trio of the threefold voice ("alexander of macedon")

8

chorus of slaves ("out of life and into death")

chorus of frieze figures ("we figures, fashioned to stay in the
  light")

9

triumphal song of lucullus ("here you see a man whom i
  defeated")

song of the king ("one morning")

song of the queen ("as i went in taurion to")

song of lucullus ("the losers have sweet voices")

song of the virgins ("with streets and people and houses")

10

recitative of the 2 new shades and lucullus ("i came to grief")

11

duet of the warriors ("i ran away")

report of the fishwife ("i was a fishwife in the forum market")

12

duet of the 2 new shades ("why were you running so?")

13

song of the cook ("i was his cook")

duet of the farmer and lucullus ("it doesn't need much soil")

14

recitative of the usher ("and from the high bench rise")

When Brecht and Dessau started work on the opera version
about 1949 they had (according to a note by Elisabeth Hauptmann) the radio play before them. The first version of the opera

libretto consisted essentially of this, with additions designed to give opportunities to the composer: the "voices" in scene 1 ("Think of the Invincible"), Lucullus' tribute to his cook in scene 6, the judge's aria in scene 7 ("Unfortunate Man!"), the third stanza of the queen's song in scene 9 and the invocations of "Faber, my son Faber" in the fishwife's aria in scene 11. In addition Brecht, at Dessau's suggestion, wrote a new, longer final scene, where the jurors, followed by the legionaries and the slaves, agree that Lucullus should be cast into nothingness.

This version is to all intents and purposes (b), that published in the collected works; in *Versuche 11* Brecht prefaced it a shade misleadingly as follows:

> *The Trial of Lucullus*, the 25th *Versuch*, is a radio play and was written in 1939 before the outbreak of the Second World War. It forms the basis of the opera *The Condemnation of Lucullus*, for which Paul Dessau wrote the music.

In the typescripts it is already headed "Opera in 2 x 7 scenes by Bertolt Brecht. Music by Paul Dessau," with a list of characters showing how unorthodox the operatic conception then was:

Singing parts

LUCULLUS	*Buffo tenor*, reminiscent of Julius Liebau
THE QUEEN	*Coloratura soprano*
THE COURTESAN	*Mezzo-soprano*
TWO VIRGINS	*Mezzo-sopranos*

Musically and vocally endowed actors

A TONELESS VOICE
THE OLD WOMAN
THE JUDGE OF THE DEAD
THE KING
THE TEACHER
THE BAKER
TWO SHADES
THE FISHWIFE
TWO WARRIORS
THE COOK
THE FARMER
THE MAN CARRYING THE CHERRY TREE

Speaking parts

THE ANNOUNCER

THE CRIER

TWO GIRLS

TWO MERCHANTS

TWO WOMEN

TWO PLEBEIANS

A CART DRIVER

SPOKESMAN FOR THE COURT OF THE DEAD

SINGING CHORUSES, SPEAKING CHORUSES, CHILDREN'S CHORUSES

From this first opera libretto was evolved the tightened-up second version headed (again in typescript) "Opera in 12 Scenes. By Paul Dessau. Text by Bertolt Brecht." This contains all the major dramaturgical switches and cuts of (c) the final opera text, but not the emendations described in Brecht's notes. Thus scene 2 is telescoped with scene 1, scene 3 is transposed, the courtesan's aria inserted in scene 8, scene 12 omitted, and so on; however, the middle of scene 8 and the end of the last scene (after the entry of the legionaries) are as in (b) the previous text. It was performed in this form in March 1951, on which occasion the East German government intervened and the crucial changes were made.

The published opera libretto (c) (Aufbau-Verlag, East Berlin, and Ars Viva Verlag, Zurich—Fritz Hennenberg has found the two printings to be identical—gives the text as amended, retitled and finally staged in October, 1951. Its list of characters reads:

LUCULLUS, a Roman general	*Tenor*
FIGURES ON THE FRIEZE:	
THE KING	*Bass*
THE QUEEN	*Soprano*
TWO CHILDREN	*Soprano and Mezzo*
TWO LEGIONARIES	*Basses*
LASUS, Lucullus' cook	*Tenor*
THE MAN CARRYING A CHERRY TREE	*Baritone*
JURORS OF THE DEAD:	
THE FISHWIFE	*Contralto*
THE COURTESAN	*Mezzo-soprano*

THE TEACHER	*Tenor*
THE BAKER	*Tenor*
THE FARMER	*Bass*
TERTULLIA, an old woman	*Mezzo-soprano*
THREE ROMAN WOMEN	*Sopranos*
VOICES OF THE THREE FEMALE CRIERS	
THE JUDGE OF THE DEAD	*High bass*
VOICE OF A WOMAN COMMENTATOR	

Speaking parts

THE SPEAKER OF THE COURT OF THE DEAD

THREE CRIERS

TWO GIRLS

TWO MERCHANTS

TWO WOMEN

TWO PLEBEIANS

A CART DRIVER

CHORUS OF THE CROWD: SOLDIERS, SLAVES, SHADES, CHILDREN

Shortly after approving this version Brecht suggested still further cuts and changes. Some, like the cutting of two stanzas of the queen's song and the beginning of the courtesan's aria, were rejected by Dessau; others however were made, and can be found in the Reclam edition of the text and in the piano score (1951 and 1961). The chorus became a single voice, the soldiers a quintet of officers, the speaker of the court of the dead was eliminated, his part being shared between the judge of the dead and the voice. The opera was staged in this form at its second East German production in Leipzig in 1957; Dessau in a program note confirmed that this was the fifth version of the text to date. After that (i.e., after Brecht's death) Dessau made one or two more dramaturgical changes for the State Opera production of 1960. These included the cutting of Lucullus' tribute to the cook, originally in scene 6, and the composition of a new chorus for the legionaries in the last scene. The composer, it seems, had never been satisfied with this scene and would have liked the work to end with a general chorus.

The two "radio plays" and the 1951 opera libretto

Accordingly, the following notes set out the differences between the text printed in the body of this volume, which calls itself a radio play but is in fact the first opera libretto of 1949–50, and the real radio play, published in *Internationale Literatur* in 1940, on the one hand and the amended opera libretto *Die Verurteilung des Lukullus* published by Aufbau-Verlag in 1951, on the other. By using these notes, both versions can be reconstituted completely, apart from one or two details of layout and punctuation.

CHANGES FROM 1940 RADIO PLAY

References are to page and line

101,	9	before = behind
	13	horse. = horse and before him
		They drag (. . . , continue with 101, 22 - 102, 1, followed by 101, 14–20)
102,	2–22	omitted
	27	after line, insert subhead
		THE CROWD
105,	23–26	omitted
106,	32	there = here
109,	5	death = death:
	11	LUCULLUS = LUCULLUS (*suddenly*)
	20–28	omitted
110,	36–39	omitted
113,	17–30	omitted

115, 24	Are you ready, stony shades = Are you ready, you figures You stony shades
116, 28	asks a question: = asks:
117, 36–118, 2	omitted
118, 18–22	omitted
23	after line, insert: And all fall silent.
119, 8	asks a question: = asks:
120, 11	Makes a proposal: = Leans negligently forward and says:
16	The jurors = And all fall silent. The jurors
23	Back in Rome = Rome
120, 25–121, 3	replace with: And the court withdraws. The defendant sits down. He squats by the doorpost, his head thrown back. He is exhausted, but he overhears a conversation behind the door Where new shades have appeared.
122, 4	The jurors = And the jurors
6–7	replace with: And the shade that was once a fishwife Says:
26	Tell me, what = And what
27	LEGIONARY = WARRIOR (throughout this scene)
30	I was = And I was
124, 5–7	omitted
15	were = are

124, 27	The fallen man's mother = The mother
30	The jurors = And all fell silent. The jurors
36–37	She requires A recess. = To restore Her composure she requires A recess.

Rome—A Last Time = Rome Once Again

125, 2	

126, 18	juror, once = juror who was once
127, 21	Thanks to him! = Thanks to him! Therefore I call him human.
25	Therefore I call him human. = And I also know That when the city of Amisus, daughter of magnificent Athens Full to the brim with books and art treasures was being looted He implored his soldiers with tears in his eyes not to set it on fire. Drenched in tears, he came to me for his supper. That too was human. Take account of it.
27	The jurors = And all fell silent. The jurors
31	juror, once = juror who was once
129, 2–131, 2	substitute original version of last scene:

Wheat and Chaff

THE JUDGE
  And so I conclude this trial.

Of your witnesses, shade
The most distinguished were not those who
said most in your favor. However
Lesser ones appeared in the end. Your bloody
hands
Were not found wholly empty. True enough
Even for your best gift, the cherry tree
The price was very high. That conquest
Could easily have been made with one man
only, but you
Sent 80,000 to Hades for it. As things stand
We must content ourselves with a few
Hours of happiness for a cook, tears
Wept for the destruction of books and other
such nonessentials.
Ah, with all the violence and conquest
Only one realm increases:
The realm of the shades.

THE JURORS
We, however, appointed to judge the dead
Take note when they leave the earth
Of what the earth has received from them.

THE SPEAKER
And from the high bench rise
The spokesmen of a posterity
Many-handed for taking
Many-mouthed for eating
Hard to deceive, eagerly reaping
Rejoicing in life.
The court
Withdraws to consider the verdict.

CHANGES MADE FOR 1951 OPERA TEXT

References are to page and line

101, 3   omitted

    4   THE CRIER = FIRST CRIER

101, 8	after line, insert: SECOND CRIER
21	THE CRIER = THIRD CRIER
102, 2	VOICES = SONG OF THE THREE ROMAN WOMEN
9–15	omitted
104, 16	THE CRIER = FIRST CRIER
25–26	omitted
105, 1–2	omitted
3	THE CRIER = SECOND CRIER
4	procession has vanished, now = ceremony is over. Now (This speech forms the conclusion of Scene I)
10–26	Scene 3 is transferred to after the present scene 5 and becomes scene IV
11	after line, insert: A SPEAKING VOICE From then on the teachers showed the schoolchildren The tomb of the great conqueror.
14	generals. = conquerors.
22	after line, insert: TEACHER (*sings last four lines*)
106, 1	4 = II
3	THE CRIER = CHORUS
106, 13–107, 22	replaced by stage direction: (*The catafalque and the frieze are carried in by soldiers and slaves. After the catafalque has been lowered into the tomb, the enormous frieze is set up in front of it. At the command: "Dismissed!" the soldiers go out*)
107, 23	5 = III
108, 21	6 = V
23–24	omitted
25	THE TONELESS VOICE = CHORUS (throughout this scene)

109, 28	with bitter berries! =
	with the bitter berries
	And all your innumerable spices:
	Sage and olive
	Thyme, nutmeg and crushed cinnamon
	What sauces, what salads, oh Lasus! .
110, 4	VOICE OF AN OLD WOMAN WAITING = TERTULLIA
34	THE THREEFOLD VOICE = VOICES OF THE THREE WOMEN CRIERS
	(throughout this scene)
112, 1	7 = VI
3	THE SPEAKER = SPEAKER (throughout entire text)
18	THE JUDGE = JUDGE (throughout entire text)
30	delete: (calls out in the fields of the blest)
113, 1–2	transposed to follow 113, 5
8	well-remembered = blest
16–17	delete: (Silence) THE JUDGE
114, 8	after line, add:
	VOICES OF THE THREE WOMEN CRIERS
	Let the frieze be brought!
9	8 = VII
	(The full text of the scene is as given in Brecht's notes, pp. 306–308)
116, 1	9 = VIII
3–7	replace with version in Brecht's notes (p. 308)
27–28	replace by:
	Here the slave
	Shade who was once a teacher, has a question:
117, 16	The jurors of the dead consider = Jurors of the dead, consider
21	Asks = Has

118, 22	after line insert new stanza: When my flesh was on the market Which began with sixteen summers I too bowed to blows and curses For a little oil and wormy pasta. So I know well what you suffered On the day of your disaster. Woman, I can feel for you.
24	The jurors of the dead consider = Jurors of the dead, consider
27–29	omitted
37–40	replace by the new interpolation from Brecht's notes (pp. 308–310)
119, 1	TWO VIRGINS = TWO CHILDREN
4	We = They
5	our = their
11	TWO VIRGINS = TWO CHILDREN
119, 19–40	replace with: Continue. TWO CHILDREN And in the cities were Two hundred and fifty thousand children. They are no more. The great Lucullus Descended on us with his iron chariots And defeated us all. LUCULLUS Yes, I shattered their insolent cities And took their gold and many kinds of treasure And I carried their people away to be our slaves. For they paid tribute to false gods. But I overthrew them
120, 3–7	omitted
9	juror shade = juror of the dead
16	The jurors of the dead consider = Jurors of the dead, consider

120, 22	10 = IX
23	Back in Rome = Rome

120, 24–121, 3	replace with:
	CHORUS
	  The defendant sits down.
	  He is exhausted, but he overhears
	  A conversation in the vestibule
	  Where new shades have appeared.

121, 4	A SHADE = FIRST SHADE
8	THE SHADE = FIRST SHADE
12	ANOTHER SHADE = SECOND SHADE
13	after line, insert: LUCULLUS Time to eat?
15	delete: Time to eat?
21	I was a slave too = I myself am a slave
22	to the lucky= to you lucky ones
23	delete: (*a bit louder*)
122, 1	11 = X
4–5	omitted
6–7	And the shade, once a fishwife Speaks up = Here the shade, once a fishwife Has a question
22–25	omitted

123, 37	after line, insert:
	  Faber, my son Faber
	  Whom I bore and whom I reared
	  My son Faber.

124, 23–25	omitted
30	The jurors of the dead consider = Jurors of the dead, consider
36–37	<blockquote>She requires A recess. = To restore Her composure she requires a recess</blockquote>
125, 1–20	omitted
126, 1	13 = XI
3–7	replace by: CHORUS The lady juror has recovered. SPEAKER Defendant, step forward! JUDGE Lacallous! Time is etc.
19	Asks = Has
22	delete: He looks cheerful.
127, 8	Then spoke the juror = Hear the juror
21	Thanks to him! = Thanks to him! Therefore I call him human.
22–25	omitted
27	The jurors of the dead consider = Jurors of the dead, consider
32	Asks = Has
34	fruit tree = cherry tree
128, 5	THE SPEAKER = CHORUS
129, 1	14 = XII
3	THE SPEAKER = CHORUS
4	And the juror = The juror
30	THE SPEAKER = CHORUS

129, 34   omitted

130, 4   omitted

11–14   replaced by:
                   Of half-lived lives.

                 FARMER
                   Yet here we have no plows for sinewy arms!

                 THE JURORS
                   Or hungry mouths, etc.

24–30   replaced by:

                 CHORUS
                   Here come the Asian
                   Legionaries fallen in battle.
                   (*Roman legionaries appear in formation*)
                 Then comes the legionaries' chorus as in Brecht's
                 notes (p. 310), except that the fifth line, ("Yes, send
                 him to nothingness!"), the tenth line ("In his ser-
                 vice!"), and the final "Send him to nothingness!"
                 are all cut.

MOTHER COURAGE AND HER CHILDREN

Texts by Brecht

The Story
CURVE OF THE DRAMATURGY

1

This scene emphasizes that things are at the beginning. Courage's canteen business and the new war as new undertakings of a familiar sort. (They begin and they continue; they begin by continuing.) Needed: energy, enterprise, the prospect of new times, arrival of new business, together with new dangers. She longs for war and at the same time fears it. She wants to join in, but as a peaceable business woman, not in a warlike way. She wants to maintain her family during the war and by means of it. She wants to serve the army and also to keep out of its clutches.

Her children: With her eldest son she is afraid of his bravery, but counts on his cleverness. With the second she is afraid of his stupidity but counts on his honesty. With her daughter she is afraid of her pity but counts on her dumbness. Only her fears prove to be justified.

She is anticipating business; she is going to go bankrupt.

The play begins with the entrance (i.e., hanging about) of the men of war. The vast disorder of war begins with order, the vast disorganization with organization.

The peaceful landscape and the men of iron. Courage arrives four strong, goes away three strong.

2

War as a business idyll. Courage swindles peasants out of a capon; her elder son robs peasants of their oxen. He wins fame and possessions; she profits. She pillages the army somewhat too. The danger for her son becomes more real.

3

Being taken prisoner need be no disadvantage to her business. It seems that she had nothing to say against her younger son's joining the army as a paymaster. All she thinks necessary in his case is honesty. This does him in. If he had not been connected with the army he would not have been killed. Her stubborn bargaining over her wagon costs her son his life. She stops her daughter from becoming a whore—the only career open to her in wartime, and one which brings good fortune to Yvette. In any case she is no Antigone.

4

Courage stifles her human reactions (any kind of outrage, rebellion or criticism) for the sake of her business. She thinks capitulation will do something for her.

5

All the same, human reactions sometimes overrun her business principles. The general's victory leads to financial losses.

6

Business, which is to earn her daughter's (peacetime) dowry, leads to her wartime disfigurement. Courage counts on the length of the war, which is helpful to her finances but means

spinsterhood for her daughter. Finally, for the first time she curses the war which, from a business standpoint, she must needs want.

7

Peacetime is pleasant, if also ruinous. As a result of the peace she does not get her son back, but loses him for good. In her daughter's case peace arrives too late. The son falls because he has applied the principles of war in peacetime. The former camp prostitute Yvette Pottier has prospered as a result of the war and married a colonel. The war starts up again. Is business going to start up again too?

8

Business is on the downgrade. The war is too long. Disorganization and disorder on every side. In a song Courage (qua beggar) curses all the human virtues as not only uncommercial but actually dangerous. For her daughter's sake she must give up the cook, who could have provided her with a roof over her head. She is bound to the war by pity for her daughter.

9

The daughter perishes because of her pity for other people's children. Courage goes on dragging her empty wagon, alone, in the wake of the tattered army.

[From Werner Hecht (ed.): *Materialien zu Brechts "Mutter Courage,"* Frankfurt, Suhrkamp, 1967, pp. 7–9.]

The Mother Courage Model

Now, after the great war, life goes on in our ruined cities, but it is a different life, the life of different or differently composed groups, guided or thwarted by new surroundings, new because so much has been destroyed. The great heaps of rubble are piled on the city's invaluable substructure, the water and drainage pipes, the gas mains and electric cables. Even the large building that has remained intact is affected by the damage and rubble around it, and may become an obstacle to planning. Temporary structures must be built and there is always a danger of their becoming permanent. All this is reflected in art, for our way of thinking is part of our way of living. In the theater we set up models to fill the gap. They immediately meet with strong opposition from all supporters of the old ways, of the routine that masquerades as experience and of the conventionality that calls itself creative freedom. And they are endangered by those who take them up without having learned to use them. Though meant to simplify matters, they are not simple to handle. They were designed not to make thought unnecessary, but to provoke it; not to replace but to compel artistic creation.

First of all we must imagine that the information which the printed text provides about certain events, here the adventures of Mother Courage and the losses she incurs, has to some extent been complemented; it has now been established that when the woman's dead son was brought to her she was sitting beside her mute daughter, and so on—the kind of information which an artist painting some historic incident can arrive at by questioning eye-witnesses. Later he can still change certain details as for one reason or another he may think advisable. Until one has learned to copy (and construct) models in a living and intelligent way, one had better not copy too much. Such things as the cook's makeup or Mother Courage's costume should not be imitated. The model should not be used to excess.

Pictures and descriptions of a performance are not enough. One does not learn much by reading that a character moves in

a particular direction after a given sentence, even if the tone of the sentence, the way of walking, and a convincing motive can be supplied—which is very difficult. The persons available for the imitation are not the same as those of the pattern; with them it would not have come into being. Anyone deserving of the name of artist is unique; he represents something universal, but in his own individual way. He can neither be perfectly imitated nor give a perfect imitation. Nor is it so important for artists to imitate art as to imitate life. The use of models is a particular kind of art, and there is a limit to what can be learned from it. The aim must be neither to copy the pattern exactly nor to break away from it too quickly.

In studying what follows—a number of explanations and discoveries emerging from the rehearsal of a play—one should, above all, be led by the solutions of certain problems to consider the problems themselves.

Music

Paul Dessau's music for *Mother Courage* is not meant to be particularly easy; like the stage set, it left something to be supplied by the audience; in the act of listening they had to link the voices with the melody. Art is not a land of Cockaigne. In order to make the transition to the musical parts, to let the music have its say, we lowered a musical emblem from the flies whenever there was a song which did not spring directly from the action, or which did spring from it but remained clearly apart. This consisted of a trumpet, a drum, a flag, and electric globes that lit up: a slight and delicate thing, pleasant to look at, even if scene 9 found it badly damaged. Some people regarded this as sheer playfulness, as an unrealistic element. But on the one hand playfulness in the theater should not be condemned out of hand as long as it is kept within bounds, and on the other hand it was not wholly unrealistic, for it served to set the music apart from the reality of the action. We made use of it as a visible sign of the shift to another artistic level—that of music—and in order to give the right impression, that these were musical insertions, rather than to lead people to think quite mistakenly

that the songs "sprang from the action." Those who object to this are quite simply opposed to anything intermittent, inorganic, pieced-together—this chiefly because they object to any shattering of illusion. What they ought to have objected to was not the tangible symbol of music, but the manner of fitting the musical numbers into the play: i.e., as insertions.

The musicians were placed so that they could be seen, in a box beside the stage—thus their performances became little concerts, independent contributions made at suitable points in the play. The box communicated with the stage, so that a musician or two could occasionally go backstage for trumpet calls or when music occurred as part of the action.

We began with the overture. It was a bit thin, for it was performed by only four musicians; still, it was a reasonably ceremonious preparation for the confusions of war.

Stage Design

For the production we are describing, at the Deutsches Theater in Berlin, we used the well-known model devised by Teo Otto during the war for the Zurich Schauspielhaus. There was a permanent framework of huge screens, making use of such materials as one would expect to find in the military encampments of the seventeenth century: tenting, wooden posts lashed together with ropes, etc. Three-dimensional structures, realistic both as to construction and as to material, were placed on the stage to represent such buildings as the presbytery and the peasants' house, but in artistic abbreviation, only so much being shown as was necessary for the action. Colored projections were thrown on the cyclorama, and the revolving stage was used to give the impression of travel—we varied the size and position of the screens and used them only for the camp scenes, so as to distinguish these from the scenes on the highway. The Berlin stage designer made his own versions of the buildings (in scenes 2, 4, 5, 9, 10, and 11), but on the same principle. We dispensed with the background projections used in Zurich and suspended the names of the various countries over the stage in large black letters. We used an even, white light, as much of it as our

equipment permitted. In this way we eliminated any vestige of "atmosphere" that could easily have given the incidents a romantic tinge. We retained almost everything else down to the smallest details (chopping block, hearth, etc.), particularly the admirable positionings of the wagon. This last was very important because it determined much of the grouping and movement from the outset.

Surprisingly little is lost by the sacrifice of complete freedom of "artistic creation." You have to start somewhere, with something, and it may as well be with something that has already been fully thought out. Freedom will be acquired through the principle of contradiction, which is continually active and vocal in all of us.

Realistic Theater and Illusion

Writing in 1826, Goethe spoke of the "inadequacy of the English wooden stage" of Shakespeare's day. He says: "There is no trace here of the aids to naturalness to which we have gradually become accustomed through the improvement in machinery, in the art of perspective and in costuming." "Who?" he asks, "would tolerate such a thing today? Under those conditions Shakespeare's plays would become highly interesting fairy tales, narrated by a number of persons who tried to increase their effectiveness somewhat by making up as the characters, by coming and going and carrying out the movements necessary to the story, but left it to the audience to imagine as many paradises and palaces as they pleased on the empty stage."

Since he wrote these words, the mechanical equipment of our theaters has been improving for a hundred years, and "aids to naturalness" have led to such emphasis on illusion that we latecomers would be more inclined to put up with Shakespeare on an empty stage than with a Shakespeare who had ceased to require or to provoke any use of the imagination.

In Goethe's day what improvement had been made in the mechanics of illusion was relatively harmless, since the machinery was so imperfect, so much "in the childhood of its beginnings," that theater itself was still a reality and both imagina-

tion and ingenuity could still be employed to turn nature into art. The sets were still theatrical displays, in which the stage designer gave an artistic and poetic interpretation of the places concerned.

The bourgeois classical theater occupied a happy halfway point on the road to naturalistic illusionism. Stage machinery provided enough elements of illusion to improve the representation of some aspects of reality, but not so much as to make the audience feel that they were no longer in a theater; art had not yet come to signify the obliteration of all indications that art is at work. Since there was no electricity, lighting effects were still primitive; where poor taste decreed sunset effects, poor equipment prevented total enchantment. The Meiningers' authentic costumes came later; they were usually magnificent, though not always beautiful, and they were after all compensated by an inauthentic manner of speaking. In short, the theater remained the theater, at least where it failed in its business of deception. Today the restoration of the theater's reality as theater is a precondition for any realistic representation of human relations. Too much heightening of the illusion in the setting, along with a "magnetic" manner of acting which gives the spectator the illusion of being present at a fleeting, fortuitous "real" event, create such an impression of naturalness that one can no longer interpose one's judgment, imagination or reactions, and must simply conform by sharing in the experience and becoming one of "nature's" objects. The illusion created by the theater must be a partial one, so that it can always be recognized as illusion. Reality, however completely represented, must be changed by art, in order that it may be seen to be subject to change and treated as such.

That is why we are demanding naturalness today—because we want to change the nature of our human relations.

Elements of Illusion?

No doubt the sight of the cyclorama behind a completely empty stage (in the prologue and in the seventh and last scenes)

creates the illusion of a flat landscape with the sky over it. There is no objection to this, because there must be some stirring of poetry in the soul of the spectator if such an illusion is to come about. Thanks to the ease with which it is created, the actors are able to suggest by their manner of playing, at the beginning that a wide horizon lies open to the business enterprise of the little family of provisioners, then at the end that the exhausted seeker after fortune is faced by boundless devastation. And we can always hope that this substantive impression of the play will combine with a formal one: that when the spectator sees the empty stage, soon to be inhabited, he will be able to share in the initial void from which everything arises. On this tabula rasa, he knows, the actors have been working for weeks, testing first one detail, then another, coming to know the incidents of the chronicle by portraying them, and portraying them by judging them. And now the play is starting and Mother Courage's wagon comes rolling onto the stage.

If in big matters such a thing as a beautiful approximation is possible, in matters of detail it is not. A realistic portrayal requires carefully worked-out detail in costumes and props, for here the imagination of the audience can add nothing. All implements connected with working and eating must have been most lovingly made. And the costumes, of course, cannot be as for a folklore festival; they must show signs of individuality and social class. They have been worn for a longer or shorter time, are made of cheaper or more expensive material, are well or not so well taken care of, etc.

The costumes for this production of *Mother Courage* were by [Kurt] Palm.

What is a performance of Mother Courage and Her Children *primarily meant to show?*

That in wartime the big profits are not made by little people. That war, which is a continuation of business by other means, makes the human virtues fatal even to their possessors. That no sacrifice is too great for the struggle against war.

Prologue

By way of a prologue, Mother Courage and her little family were shown on their way to the war zone. Mother Courage sang her business song from scene 1 (so that in scene 1 her answer "Business people" is followed immediately by the sergeant's question: "Halt, you scum. Where do you belong?"). After the overture, to spare the performer the exertion of singing against the rumbling of the revolving stage, the first stanza was played on a record, the house being darkened. Then the prologue begins.

The Long Road to War

The linen half-curtain, on which in the following the titles of the scenes are projected, opens and Mother Courage's wagon is rolled forward against the movement of the revolving stage.

The wagon is a cross between a military vehicle and a general store. A sign affixed to the side of it says: "Second Finnish Regiment" and another "Mother Courage, Groceries." On the canvas Swedish pork sausages are displayed next to a flag with a price tag indicating "Four Guilders." The wagon will undergo several changes in the course of the chronicle. There will be sometimes more, sometimes less merchandise hanging on it, the canvas will be dirtier or cleaner, the letters on the signs will be faded and then again freshly painted, depending on the state of business. Now at the start it is clean and richly covered with wares.

The wagon is pulled by the two sons. They sing the second stanza of Mother Courage's Business Song: "O Captains, don't expect to send them/ To death with nothing in their crops." On the box sit mute Kattrin, playing the Jew's harp, and Mother Courage. Courage is sitting in lazy comfort, swaying with the wagon and yawning. Everything, including her one backward

glance, indicates that the wagon has come a long way.

We had conceived of the song as a dramatic entrance, lusty and cocky—we had the last scene of the play in mind. But Weigel saw it as a realistic business song and suggested that it be used to picture the long journey to the war. Such are the ideas of great actors.

Once this was settled, it seemed to us that by showing the business woman's long journey to the war zone we would be showing clearly enough that she was an active and voluntary participant in the war. But certain reviews and many discussions with persons who had seen the play showed that a good many people regarded Mother Courage merely as a representative of the "little people" who "become involved in the war in spite of themselves," who are "helpless victims of the war," and so on. A deeply engrained habit leads the theater-goer to pick out the more emotional utterances of the characters and overlook everything else. Like descriptions of landscapes in novels, references to business are received with boredom. The "business atmosphere" is simply the air one breathes and as such requires no special mention. And so, regardless of all our efforts to represent the war as an aggregate of business deals, the discussions showed time and time again that people regarded it as a timeless abstraction.

Too Short can be Too Long

The two stanzas of the opening song plus the pause between them during which the wagon rolls silently along, take up a certain amount of time, too much time it seemed to us at first in rehearsal. But when we cut the second stanza, the prologue seemed longer, and when we prolonged the pause between the stanzas, it seemed shorter.

[. . .]

Scene 1

The business woman Anna Fierling, known as Mother Courage, encounters the Swedish army

Recruiters are going about the country looking for cannon fodder. Mother Courage introduces her mixed family, acquired in various theaters of war, to a sergeant. The canteen woman defends her sons against the recruiters with a knife. She sees that her sons are listening to the recruiters and predicts that the sergeant will meet an early death. To make her children afraid of the war, she has them too draw black crosses. Because of a small business deal, she nevertheless loses her brave son. And the sergeant leaves her with a prophecy:

> "If you want the war to work for you
> You've got to give the war its due."

Over-all arrangement

Recruiters are going about the country looking for cannon fodder. On the empty stage the sergeant and the recruiter are standing right front on the lookout, complaining in muffled voices of the difficulty of finding cannon fodder for their general. The city of which the sergeant speaks is assumed to be in the orchestra. Mother Courage's wagon appears and the recruiters' mouths water at the sight of the young men. The sergeant cries "Halt!" and the wagon stops.

Mother Courage introduces her mixed family, acquired in various theaters of war, to a sergeant. The professionals of commerce and of war meet, the war can start. At the sight of the military, the Fierlings may hesitate for a moment as though afraid: the soldiers on their own side are also enemies; the army gives, but it also takes. Mother Courage's "Good morning, sergeant" is spoken in the same curt, military monotone as his "Good morning, friends." Climbing down from her wagon, she makes it clear that she regards showing her papers as a formality, super-

fluous among professionals ("All right, we'll run through the whole routine"). She introduces her little family, acquired in various theaters of war, in a jocular tone: she puts on a bit of a "Mother Courage" act.

The wagon and the children are on the left, the recruiters on the right. Mother Courage crosses over with her tin box full of papers. She has been summoned, but she is also sallying forth to scout and do business. She describes her children from the other side of the stage, as though better able to take them in from a distance. The recruiter makes forays behind her back, stalking the sons, tempting them. The pivotal point is in the lines: "Wouldn't you need a nice pistol, or a belt buckle?" and "I need something else."

The canteen woman defends her sons against the recruiters with a knife. The sergeant leaves her standing there and goes over to the sons, followed by the recruiter. He thumps their chests, feels their calves. He goes back and stands before Mother Courage: "Why aren't they in the army?" The recruiter has stayed with the sons: "Let's see if you're a sissy." Mother Courage runs over, thrusts herself between the recruiter and her son: "He's a sissy." The recruiter goes over to the sergeant (on the right) and complains: "He insulted me"; Mother Courage snatches her Eilif away. The sergeant tries to reason, but Mother Courage pulls a knife and stands there in a rage, guarding her sons.

Mother Courage sees that her sons are listening to the recruiter and predicts that the sergeant will meet an early death. Again she goes over to the sergeant ("Give me your helmet"). Her children follow her and look on, gaping. The recruiter makes a flank movement, comes up to Eilif from behind and speaks to him.

When after some hesitation the sergeant has drawn his black cross, the children, satisfied, go back to the wagon, but the recruiter follows them. And when Mother Courage turns ("I've got to take advantage"), she sees the recruiter between her sons; he has his arms around their shoulders.

To make her children afraid of the war, Mother Courage has them too draw black crosses. The rebellion in her own ranks is in full swing. She runs angrily behind her wagon to paint black crosses for her children. When she returns to the wagon shaft with the helmet, the recruiter, grinning, leaves the children to her and

goes back (right) to the sergeant. When the somber ceremony is over, Mother Courage goes to the sergeant, returns his helmet, and with fluttering skirts climbs up on the seat of the wagon. The sons have harnessed themselves, the wagon starts moving. Mother Courage has mastered the situation.

Because of a small business deal, she nevertheless loses her brave son. But the sergeant has only been half defeated; on the recruiter's advice, he offers to make a purchase. Electrified, Mother Courage climbs down from the wagon and the sergeant draws her off left behind the wagon. While the deal is in progress, the recruiter takes the harness off Eilif and leads him away. Kattrin sees this, climbs down from the wagon and tries in vain to call her mother's attention to Eilif's disappearance. But Mother Courage is deep in her bargaining. Only after she has snapped her moneybag shut does she notice his absence. For a moment she has to sit down on the wagon shaft, still holding her buckles. Then she angrily flings them into the wagon, and the family, with one less member, moves gloomily off.

And the sergeant leaves her with a prophecy. Laughing, he predicts that if she wants to live off the war, she will also have to give the war its due.

[. . .]

The recruiters

The empty stage of the prologue was transformed into a concrete locality by means of a few clumps of wintry grass marking the edge of a highway. Here the military men stand waiting, freezing in their armor.

The great disorder of war begins with order, disorganization with organization. The troublemakers have troubles of their own. We hear complaints to the effect that it takes intelligence to get a war started. The military are businessmen. The sergeant has a little book that he consults, the recruiter has a map to help him fight with geography. The fusion of war and business cannot be established too soon.

Grouping

There will be some difficulty in persuading the actors playing the sergeant and the recruiter to stay together and in one place until Mother Courage's wagon appears. In our theater, groups always show a strong tendency to break up, partly because each actor believes he can heighten audience interest by moving about and changing his position, and partly because he wants to be alone, so as to divert the attention of the audience from the group to himself. But there is no reason not to leave the military men together; on the contrary, both the image and the argument would be impaired by a change of position.

Changes of position

Positions should be retained as long as there is no compelling reason for changing them; and a desire for variety is not a compelling reason. If one gives in to a desire for variety, the consequence is a devaluation of all movement on the stage; the spectator ceases to look for a specific meaning behind each movement, he stops taking movement seriously. But especially at the crucial points in the action, the full impact of a change of position must not be weakened. Legitimate variety is obtained by ascertaining the crucial points and planning the arrangement around them. For example, the recruiters have been listening to Mother Courage; she has succeeded in diverting and entertaining them with her tall talk and so putting them in a good humor; so far there has been only one ominous circumstance: the sergeant has asked for her papers; but he has not examined them—his only purpose was to prolong their stay. She takes the next step (also physically: she goes up to the sergeant, takes hold of his belt buckle, and says: "Wouldn't you need a belt buckle?"), she tries to sell them something, and that is when the recruiters spring into action. The sergeant says ominously: "I need something else" and along with the recruiter goes over to the sons at the wagon shaft. The recruiters look the sons over as they would horses. The crucial point is accented when the sergeant goes back to Mother Courage, comes to a standstill before her, and asks: "Why aren't they in

the army?" (The effect of such movements should not be weakened by having the actors speak during them.) If changes of position are needed to make certain developments clear to the audience, the movement must be utilized to express something significant for the action and for this particular moment; if nothing of the sort can be found, it is advisable to review the whole arrangement up to this point, it will probably be seen to be at fault, because the sole purpose of an arrangement is to express the action, and the action (it is to be hoped) involves a logical development of incidents, which the arrangement need only present.

On details

On the brightly lighted stage every detail, even the smallest, must of course be acted out to the full. This is especially true of actions which on our stage are glossed over almost as a matter of principle, such as paying on conclusion of a sale. Here Weigel devised (for the sale of the buckle in 1, the sale of the capon in 2, the sale of drinks in 5 and 6, the handing out of the burial money in 12, etc.) a little gesture of her own: she audibly snaps shut the leather moneybag that she wears slung from her neck. It is indeed difficult in rehearsals to resist the impatience of actors who are in the habit of trying to sweep an audience off its feet, and to work out the details painstakingly and inventively in accordance with the principle of epic theater: *one thing after another.* Even minute details are very revealing, e.g., the fact that when the recruiters step up to her sons and feel their muscles as if they were horses, Mother Courage displays maternal pride for a moment, until the sergeant's question ("Why aren't they in the army?") shows her the danger their qualities put them in: then she rushes between her sons and the recruiters. The pace at rehearsals should be slow, if only to make it possible to work out details; determining the pace of the performance is another matter and comes later.

A detail

In pulling a knife, Mother Courage shows no savagery. She is merely showing how far she will go in defending her chil-

dren. The performer must show that Mother Courage is familiar with such situations and knows how to handle them.

Mother Courage has her children draw lots. Only by a mild tirade and by eloquently averting her face when Swiss Cheese draws his slip from the helmet—in other words by a slightly exaggerated display of impartiality (see for yourself, no sleight-of-hand, no tricks) does the actress show that Mother Courage knows she has been tampering with fate—otherwise she fully believes what she says, namely, that in certain situations certain of her children's qualities and defects could be fatal.

Mother Courage predicts that the sergeant will meet an early death. We discovered that Mother Courage had to turn around toward Eilif before stepping up to the sergeant to let him draw his lot. Otherwise it would not have been understood that she does this in order to frighten her warlike son away from the war.

The belt-buckle deal. Mother Courage loses her son to the recruiter because she can't resist the temptation to sell a belt buckle. After climbing down from the wagon to bring the sergeant the buckle, she must at first show a certain amount of distrust by looking around anxiously for the recruiter. Once the sergeant seizing the string of buckles has drawn her behind the wagon, her distrust shifts to the area of business. When she goes to get schnapps for the sergeant, she takes the buckle, which has not yet been paid for, out of his hands; and she bites into the coin. The sergeant is dismayed at her distrust.

If the distrust at the beginning were omitted, we should have a stupid, utterly uninteresting woman, or a person with a passion for business but no experience. The distrust must not be absent, it must merely be too weak to do any good.

Pantomine

The recruiter must act out the scene where he removes the harness from Eilif ("the women will tear each other's hair out over you"). He is freeing him from his yoke.

He has forced a guilder on him; holding out his fist with the guilder in it in front of him, Eilif goes off as if in a trance.

Proportion

Weigel showed a masterful sense of proportion in playing Mother Courage's reaction to the abduction of her brave son. She showed dismay rather than horror. In becoming a soldier, her son has not been lost, he is merely in danger. And she will lose other children. To show that she knows very well why Eilif is no longer with her, Weigel let her string of belt buckles drag on the ground and threw it angrily into the wagon after holding it between her legs while sitting on the shaft for a few moments to rest. And she does not look her daughter in the face as she puts her into Eilif's harness.

Scene 2

Before the fortress of Wallhof Mother Courage meets her brave son again

Mother Courage sells provisions at exorbitant prices in the Swedish camp; while driving a hard bargain over a capon, she makes the acquaintance of an army cook who is to play an important part in her life. The Swedish general brings a young soldier into his tent and honors him for his bravery. Mother Courage recognizes her lost son in the young soldier; taking advantage of the meal in Eilif's honor, she gets a steep price for her capon. Eilif relates his heroic deed and Mother Courage, while plucking her capon in the kitchen adjoining the tent, expresses opinions about rotten generals. Eilif does a sword dance and his mother answers with a song. Eilif hugs his mother and gets a slap in the face for putting himself in danger with his heroism.

Over-all arrangement

Mother Courage sells provisions at exorbitant prices in the Swedish camp before the fortress of Wallhof; while driving a hard bargain over a capon she makes the acquaintance of an army cook who is to play an

important part in her life. In this scene the movement occurs at the pivotal point ("You know what I'm going to do?"). The cook stops peeling his carrots, fishes a piece of rotten meat out of the garbage barrel and takes it over to the butcher's block. Courage's attempt at blackmail has failed.

The Swedish general brings a young soldier into his tent and makes a short speech commending him for his bravery. A drumroll outside the tent announces the arrival of highly placed persons. It need not be clear whether the general drinks in order to honor the soldier or honors the soldier in order to drink. Meanwhile in the kitchen adjoining the tent the cook is preparing the meal. Courage stays right there with her capon.

Mother Courage recognizes her lost son in the young soldier; taking advantage of the meal in Eilif's honor, she gets a steep price for her capon. Mother Courage is overcome with joy at seeing her son, but not too overcome to turn Eilif's reappearance to her business advantage. Meanwhile, the general has the chaplain bring him a spill to light his clay pipe with.

Eilif relates his heroic deed and Mother Courage, while plucking her capon in the kitchen, expresses opinions about rotten generals. At first the mother beams as she listens to the story, then her face clouds over, and in the end she throws her capon angrily into the tub in front of her. Resuming her work, she lets it be known what she thinks of the general; at the same time the general in the tent shows her son on the map what new deeds of heroism he needs him for.

Eilif does a sword dance and his mother answers with a song. Eilif does his sword dance front stage near the partition between tent and kitchen. Mother Courage creeps up to the partition to finish the song. Then she goes back to her tub but she remains standing.

Eilif hugs his mother and gets a slap in the face for putting himself in danger with his heroism.

The capon deal

The bargaining over the capon between Courage and the cook served among other things to establish the beginning of

their tender relations. Both showed pleasure in the bargaining, and the cook expressed his admiration not only for her ready tongue but also for the shrewdness with which she exploited the honoring of her son for business purposes. Courage in turn was amused at the way the cook fished the chunk of rotten beef out of the garbage barrel with the tip of his long meat knife and carried it, carefully as though it were a precious object—though to be kept at a safe distance from one's nose—over to his kitchen table. The actor Bildt played the scene brilliantly, making the cook, a Don Juan fired by budding passion, prepare the capon with theatrical elegance. This dumb show, it should be observed, was performed with restraint, so that it did not distract attention from the scene in the tent.

Bildt even took the trouble to acquire a Dutch accent with the help of a Dutchman.

[. . .]

The general

The general was made into something of a cliché. Too much gruff bluster, and the performance showed too little about the ruling class. It would have been better to make him an effete Swedish aristocrat, who honors the brave soldier as a matter of routine action, almost absently. If this had been done, his very entrance—he is drunk, supports himself on the guest of honor, and heads straight for the wine jug—would have been more instructive. As it was, one saw little more than rowdy drunkenness.

[. . .]

The war of religion

The general's treatment of the chaplain is meant to show the role of religion in a war of religion. This was played rather crudely. The general has him bring the burning spill for his pipe and contemptuously pours wine over his coat; with his eyes on Eilif, the chaplain wipes the hem of his cassock, half protesting, half taking it as a joke. He is not invited to sit down

to table like the young murderer, nor is he given anything to drink. But what shows his position most clearly is the undignified way, resulting from the indignity of his position, with which he sits down at table and pours himself wine when the general leads the young soldier, in whose presence all this is enacted, to the map on the tent wall, so leaving the table unoccupied. This position is the source of the chaplain's cynicism.

Eilif's dance

The brave son's short sword dance must be executed with passion as well as ease. The young man is imitating a dance he has seen somewhere. It is not easy to make such things evident.

Costume: Eilif has a cheap, dented breast plate and is still wearing his frayed trousers. Not until scene 8 (the outbreak of peace) does he wear expensive clothing and gear; he dies rich.

A detail

During her angry speech about rotten generals Courage plucks her capon violently, giving the plucking a kind of symbolic significance. Brief bursts of laughter from the amused cook interrupt her blasphemies.

[. . .]

Scene 3

Mother Courage switches from the Lutheran to the Catholic camp and loses her honest son Swiss Cheese

Black marketing in ammunition. Mother Courage serves a camp whore and warns her daughter not to take up with soldiers. While Courage flirts with the cook and the chaplain, mute Kattrin tries on the whore's hat and shoes. The surprise attack. First meal in the Catholic camp. Conversation between brother and sister and arrest of Swiss Cheese.

Mother Courage mortgages her wagon to the camp whore in order to ransom Swiss Cheese. Courage haggles over the amount of the bribe. She haggles too long and hears the volley that lays Swiss Cheese low. Mute Kattrin stands beside her mother to wait for the dead Swiss Cheese. For fear of giving herself away, Courage denies her dead son.

Over-all arrangement

During the whole scene the wagon stands left with its shaft pointed toward the audience, so that those to the left of it are not seen by those on the right. Center rear there is a flagpole, right front a barrel serving as a dining table. The scene is divided into four parts: *The surprise attack, The arrest of the honest son, The bargaining, The denial.* After the first two parts the half-curtain is drawn; after the third part the stage is darkened.

Black marketing in ammunition. Mother Courage enters from the left, followed by an ordnance officer who is trying to talk her into something. For a moment she stands front stage with him; after "Not at that price," she turns away from him and sits down on a box near the wagon, where Swiss Cheese is already sitting. The business is conducted in an undertone. Kattrin is called away from taking down the washing and goes behind the wagon left with the ordnance officer. Courage has started mending Swiss Cheese's underdrawers; while working, she admonishes him to be honest. Returning from the other side of the wagon, the ordnance officer takes him away with him. This and the following scenes have the tone of an idyll.

Mother Courage serves a camp whore and warns her daughter not to take up with soldiers. Taking her sewing, Courage sits down with the Pottier woman. Kattrin listens to their conversation as she takes the washing off the line. After her song, Pottier, with a conspicuously whorish gait, goes behind the wagon.

While Courage flirts with the cook and the chaplain, mute Kattrin tries on the whore's hat and shoes. After some brief banter, Mother Courage leads her guests behind the wagon for a glass of wine and they strike up a political conversation. After the inserted sentence "And this war is a war of religion," the cook ironically

starts singing the hymn "A stronghold sure." This gives Kattrin time to try on Yvette's hat and shoes.

The surprise attack. The fixed point amid all the running and shouting of the surprise attack is the chaplain who stands still and gets in everybody's way. The rest of the arrangement follows from the printed text.

First meal in the Catholic camp. The chaplain, now Mother Courage's bartender, joins the little family around the cooking pot; Swiss Cheese keeps slightly to one side; he wants to get away.

Conversation between brother and sister and arrest of Swiss Cheese. The conversation between brother and sister takes place at the improvised dining table. When Kattrin sees the spy behind the wagon, she tries to stop her brother from climbing into it. When Courage comes back with the chaplain, Kattrin runs toward her as far as the center of the stage. Courage, the chaplain, and Kattrin group themselves around the table, waiting for the Catholics.

Mother Courage tries to mortgage her wagon to the camp whore in order to ransom Swiss Cheese. The chaplain runs to meet Courage; she is exhausted and he catches her in his arms in front of the wagon. She quickly frees herself from his embrace, which has restored her strength a little, and starts thinking. Her plan is all ready when Pottier comes along with the colonel. Pottier leaves the colonel standing there, runs over to Courage, gives her the kiss of Judas, runs back to her cavalier, and then crawls avidly into the wagon. Courage pulls her out, curses her, and sends her off with a push to negotiate over Swiss Cheese.

Mother Courage haggles over the amount of the bribe. Courage has set Kattrin and the chaplain to washing glasses and scouring knives, so creating a certain atmosphere of siege. Standing center stage between her family and the whore, she refuses to give up her wagon entirely—she has fought too hard for it. She sits down again to scour knives and does not stand up when Pottier comes back with the news that the soldiers are asking two hundred guilders. Now she is willing to pay.

Mother Courage hears the volley that lays Swiss Cheese low. No sooner has Courage sent Pottier away than she suddenly stands up and says: "Maybe I bargained too long." The volley rings

out, the chaplain leaves her and goes behind the wagon. It grows dark.

For fear of giving herself away, Courage denies her dead son. Yvette walks slowly out from behind the wagon. She scolds Courage, warns her not to give herself away, and brings Kattrin out from behind the wagon. Her face averted, Kattrin goes to her mother and stands beside her. Swiss Cheese is brought in. His mother goes over to him and denies him.

Movements and groupings

The arrangement of the movements and groupings must follow the rhythm of the story and give pictorial expression to the action.

In scene 3 a camp idyll is disrupted by the enemy's surprise attack. The idyll should be composed from the start in such a way as to make it possible to show a maximum of disruption. It must leave room for people to run back and forth in clearly laid-out confusion; the parts of the stage must be able to change their functions.

At the beginning of the scene Kattrin is hanging out washing on a clothesline stretched between the wagon and the cannon right rear so that Courage can hurriedly take it down at the end of the scene. In order to rescue her washing, Courage must go diagonally right across the stage. Kattrin sits huddled by the barrel right front, where at the beginning Yvette was being served as a customer; Courage takes soot from the wagon and brings it to the barrel to rub on her daughter's face. The same place which up until then had been devoted exclusively to business is now the scene of a private incident. Carrying the cashbox, Swiss Cheese enters diagonally from right rear to the wagon left front in such a way that his path crosses that of Courage hurrying to her daughter. First she runs a few steps past him, but she has seen the cashbox and turns around toward him just as he is about to enter the wagon. She stands for a moment like a hen between two endangered chicks, undecided which to save first. While she is smearing her daughter's face, her son hides the cash-box in the wagon; she cannot reprove

him until she has finished with her daughter and he comes back out of the wagon. She is still standing beside him when the chaplain rushes out from behind the wagon and points to the Swedish flag. Courage runs to it center rear and takes it down.

The camp idyll that is disrupted by the attack must be divided into distinct parts. After the shady little deal in black-market ammunition has been completed by the wagon steps, Swiss Cheese followed by the ordnance officer goes out right. The ordnance officer recognizes the camp whore who is sitting by the barrel, sewing her hat; he looks away in disgust. Yvette shouts something after him, and then, when the center of gravity has shifted to the right side of the stage, Courage also comes slowly over to the barrel. (A little later Kattrin follows, coming out from behind the wagon and starting once more to hang up the washing.) The two women talk and Kattrin listens as she hangs up the washing. Yvette sings her song. With a provocative gait, she goes out from right front to left rear. Kattrin watches her and is admonished by her mother. The cook and the chaplain come in from the right rear. After a brief bit of banter during which they attract the attention of the audience to Kattrin by the attention they pay to her, Mother Courage leads them behind the wagon. The political discussion and Kattrin's pantomine follow. She imitates Yvette, walking over the same ground. The alarm begins with the ordnance officer and soldiers running in from right rear. The cook goes out in that direction after Courage has run to the cannon to rescue her washing and Kattrin to the barrel to hide her feet.

Important

Courage's unflagging readiness to work is important. She is hardly ever seen not working. It is her energy and competence that make her lack of success so shattering.

A tiny scene

The tiny scene at the beginning of 3, in which army property is black-marketed, shows the general and matter-of-fact corrup-

tion in the army camps during the great war of religion. The honest son listens with half an ear, as to something quite usual; his mother does not conceal the crooked business from him, but admonishes him to be honest because he is not bright. His heeding of this advice is going to cost him his life.

Yvette Pottier

Kattrin has the example of Yvette before her. She herself must work hard, the whore drinks and lolls about. For Kattrin as well the only form of love available in the midst of the war would be prostitution. Yvette sings a song showing that other forms of love lead to grave trouble. At times the whore becomes powerful by selling herself at a high price. Mother Courage who only sells boots must struggle desperately to defend her wagon from her. Mother Courage of course makes no moral condemnation of Yvette and her special type of business.

The colonel

The colonel whom Yvette tows in to buy Courage's wagon for her is difficult to play, because he is a purely negative quantity. His only function is to show the price the whore must pay for her rise in life; consequently he must be repellent. [Georg-Peter] Pilz portrayed the aged colonel subtly, making him mime an ardent passion of which he was not for one moment capable. The old man's lechery erupted as though in response to a cue, and he seemed to forget his surroundings. An instant later he forgot his lechery and stared absently into the void. The actor produced a striking effect with his stick. In his passionate moments he pressed it to the ground so hard that it bent; an instant later it snapped straight—this suggested loathsome aggressive impotence and produced an irresistibly comic effect. Considerable elegance is required to keep such a performance within the limits of good taste.

A detail

Having finished hanging up the washing, Kattrin stares open-mouthed at the visitors from the general's tent. The cook honors her with special attention as he follows Courage behind the wagon. This is probably what gives her the idea of stealing Yvette's weapons.

The two sides

While on one side of the wagon the war is discussed with frank mockery, Kattrin is appropriating some of the tools of the whore's trade and practising Yvette's swaying gait, which she has just seen. Here [Angelika] Hurwicz's facial expression was strained and deeply serious.

"A stronghold sure"

The first part of Kattrin's pantomime occurs after "I can see why I liked your face." (The cook added: "And this is a war of religion.") At this point Courage, the cook and the chaplain placed themselves to one side of the wagon in such a way that they could not see Kattrin, and struck up "A stronghold sure." They sang it with feeling, casting anxious glances around them as though such a song were illegal in the Swedish camp.

The surprise attack

It must be brought out that Courage is used to such surprises and knows how to handle them. Before she thinks about saving the cannon, she rescues her washing. She helps the chaplain to disguise himself, she smears her daughter's face, she tells her son to throw the cashbox away, she takes down the Swedish flag. All this she does as a matter of routine, but by no means calmly.

[. . .]

The meal

Courage has prepared it. Enlarged by the new hired man who was a chaplain only that morning, the little family still seem somewhat flurried; in talking they look around like prisoners, but the mother is making jokes again; the Catholics, she says, need pants as much as the Protestants. They have not learned that honesty is just as mortally dangerous among Catholics as among Lutherans.

The chaplain

The chaplain has found a refuge. He has his own bowl to eat from and he makes himself awkwardly useful, hauls buckets of water, scours knives, and so on. Otherwise he is still an outsider; for this reason or because of his phlegmatic disposition he shows no exaggerated involvement in the tragedy of the honest son. While Courage is engaged in her too-long-drawn-out bargaining, he looks upon her simply as his source of support.

Swiss Cheese

It seems to be hard for an actor to repress his pity for the character he is playing and not to reveal his knowledge of his impending death. In speaking to his sister Swiss Cheese shows no forebodings; that is what makes him so moving when he is taken.

Brother and sister

The short conversation between mute Kattrin and Swiss Cheese is quiet and not without tenderness. Shortly before the destruction we are shown for the last time what is to be destroyed.

The scene goes back to an old Japanese play in which two boys conclude a friendship pact. Their way of doing this is that one shows the other a flying bird, while the second shows the first a cloud.

A detail

Kattrin gesticulates too wildly in telling her mother about the arrest of Swiss Cheese. Consequently Courage does not understand her and says: "Use your hands, I don't like it when you howl like a dog. What will the chaplain think? It gives him the creeps." Hurwicz made Kattrin pull herself together and nod. She understands this argument, it is a strong one.

A detail

While the sergeant was questioning her in the presence of Swiss Cheese, Courage rummaged in a basket—a busy business woman with no time for formalities. But after the sentence: "And don't twist his shoulder off!" she ran after the soldiers who were leading him away.

Yvette's three trips

Yvette runs back and forth three times for the sake of Courage's son and her wagon. Her anger changes from mere anger at Courage's attempt to swindle her by paying her out of the regimental cashbox to anger at Courage's betrayal of her son.

Kattrin and the bargaining over Swiss Cheese

The portrayal of mute Kattrin is not realistic if her goodness is stressed to the point of making her oppose her mother's attempt to get the amount of the bribe reduced. She runs off from scouring the knives when she begins to see that the bargaining has been going on too long. When after the execution Yvette sends her ahead and she goes to her mother with her face averted, there may be a reproach in this—but above all she cannot look her in the face.

The denial

Courage is sitting, holding the hand of her daughter who is standing. When the soldiers come in with the dead boy and she is asked to look at him, she stands up, goes over, looks at him, shakes her head, goes back and sits down. During all this she has an obstinate expression, her lower lip thrust forward. Here Weigel's recklessness in throwing away her character reaches its highest point.

(The actor playing the sergeant can command the spectator's astonishment by looking around at his men in astonishment at such hardness.)

Observation

Her look of extreme suffering after she has heard the shots, her unscreaming open mouth and backward-bent head probably derived from a press photograph of an Indian woman crouched over the body of her dead son during the shelling of Singapore. Weigel must have seen it years before, though when questioned she did not remember it. That is how observations are stored up by actors.—Actually it was only in the later performances that Weigel assumed this attitude.

[. . .]

Scene 4

The Song of the Great Capitulation

Mother Courage is sitting outside the captain's tent; she has come to put in a complaint about damage to her wagon; a clerk advises her in vain to let well enough alone. A young soldier appears, also to make a complaint; she dissuades him. The bitter "Song of the Great Capitula-

tion." Courage herself learns from the lesson she has given the young soldier and leaves without having put in her complaint.

Over-all arrangement

Mother Courage is sitting outside the captain's tent; she has come to put in a complaint about damage to her wagon; a clerk advises her in vain to let well enough alone. The clerk comes up to the bench where Courage is sitting and speaks to her kindly. She remains obstinate.

A young soldier appears, also to make a complaint; she dissuades him, arguing that his anger is too short. Two soldiers enter. The younger wants to rush into the captain's tent and the older is holding him back by main force. Courage intervenes and involves the young man in a conversation about the danger of short attacks of anger.

The bitter "Song of the Great Capitulation." The young soldier, whose anger has evaporated, goes off cursing.

Courage herself learns from the lesson she has given the young soldier, and leaves without putting in her complaint.

Courage's state of mind at the beginning of the scene

In the first rehearsals Weigel opened this scene in an attitude of dejection. This was not right.

Courage learns by teaching. She teaches capitulation and learns it.

The scene calls for bitterness at the start and dejection at the end.

Courage's depravity

In no other scene is Courage so depraved as in this one, where she instructs the young man in capitulation to the higher-ups and then puts her own teaching into effect. Nevertheless Weigel's face in this scene shows a glimmer of wisdom and even of nobility, and that is good. Because the depravity is not so much that of her person as that of her class, and because she herself

at least rises above it somewhat by showing that she understands this weakness and that it even makes her angry.
[. . .]

The scene played without alienation

Such a scene is socially disastrous if by hypnotic action the actress playing Mother Courage invites the audience to identify with her. This will only increase the spectator's own tendencies to resignation and capitulation—besides giving him the pleasure of being superior to himself. It will not put him in a position to feel the beauty and attraction of a social problem.

Scene 5

Mother Courage loses four officers' shirts and mute Kattrin finds a baby

After a battle. Courage refuses to give the chaplain her officers' shirts to bandage wounded peasants with. Kattrin threatens her mother. At the risk of her life Courage saves an infant. Courage laments the loss of her shirts and snatches a stolen coat away from a soldier who has stolen some schnapps, while Kattrin rocks the baby in her arms.

Over-all arrangement

After a battle. Courage is standing with two soldiers outside her wagon; its sideboard is lowered for use as a bar. Kattrin, sitting on the wagon steps, is uneasy. Courage gulps down two glasses of schnapps; she needs it to harden her to the sight of misery.

Courage refuses to give the chaplain her officers' shirts to bandage wounded peasants with. From inside a peasant's wrecked house the chaplain shouts for linen. Kattrin is prevented by her mother from taking officers' shirts from the wagon. Courage

obstinately blocks the wagon steps, letting no one in.

Kattrin threatens her mother. With the help of one soldier the chaplain has carried a wounded woman out of the house, then an old peasant whose arm is dangling. Again he calls for linen and all look at Courage who lapses into silence. Angrily Kattrin seizes a plank and threatens her mother. The chaplain has to take it away from her. He picks Courage up, sets her down on a chest, and takes some officers' shirts.

At the risk of her life Kattrin saves an infant. Still struggling with the chaplain, Courage sees her daughter rush into the house that is threatening to cave in, to save a baby. Tugged both ways, between Kattrin and the officers' shirts, she runs about until the shirts are torn into bandages and Kattrin comes out of the house with the infant. Now she runs after Kattrin to make her get rid of the baby. (Movements: Kattrin with the baby runs counter-clockwise around the wounded, then clockwise around the wagon.) Her mother stops in the middle of the stage because the chaplain is coming out of the wagon with the shirts. Kattrin sits down on the chest right.

Courage laments the loss of her shirts and snatches a stolen coat away from a soldier who has stolen some schnapps, while Kattrin rocks the baby in her arms. After springing like a tigress at the soldier who has failed to pay, Mother Courage stuffs his fur coat into the wagon.

A new Courage

A change has taken place in Courage. She has sacrificed her son to the wagon and now she defends the wagon like a tigress. She has been hardened by the hard bargains she drives.

A detail

At the beginning of the scene (after "Plenty of victory marches for the Lord but no pay for the men") Weigel's Courage tosses off two glasses of schnapps. Apart from this extenuating circumstance, she provided no justification for Courage's haggling, scolding and raging throughout the scene.

A detail

There was a kind of by-play between the soldier who gets no schnapps from Courage and the soldier drinking schnapps at the bar. It expressed the hostility between the haves and the have-nots. The drinker grins scornfully and drains his glass with ostentatious enjoyment, the have-not gives him a long hostile stare before turning around in disgust and going defeated to the rear—to wait for a chance to lay hands on the schnapps. Later the drinker will show more sympathy than the thirsty man for the wounded peasant woman.

The contradictions must not disappear

The character of the chaplain is based on a contradiction. He is part scoundrel, part superior intelligence. The actor [Werner] Hinz gave him a wooden, awkward, comical quality, which he retained in his role of good Samaritan. His manner was stiff and cold, as though it were only his clergyman's past that impelled him to turn against his present employer. But something else shone through: his former high position gives him the leadership on the battlefield where he acts in a spirit deriving from the realization that in the last analysis he himself was one of the oppressed. When he helps the injured, it becomes clear that he too is to be pitied.

The scene is dependent on pantomime

The effect of the battlefield scene depends entirely on the meticulous pantomime with which Kattrin shows her mounting anger at her mother's inhumanity. Angelika Hurwicz ran back and forth like an alarmed hen between the wounded peasants and Mother Courage. Up to the point when she began to argue, in gestures, with her mother, she made no attempt to repress the voluptuous curiosity that horror inspires in infantile persons. She carried the baby out of the house like a thief; at the end of the scene she lifts the baby up in the air, prodding it with both hands, as though to make it laugh. If her mother's share in the spoils is the fur coat, hers is the baby.

Kattrin

In the battlefield scene Kattrin threatens to kill her mother because she refuses the wounded peasants her linen. It is necessary to show an intelligent Kattrin from the start. (Her infirmity misleads actors into representing her as dull.) At the beginning she is fresh, gay and even-tempered—Hurwicz gave her a kind of awkward charm even in the conversation with her brother in scene 3. True, the helplessness of her tongue communicates itself to her body; but it is the war that breaks her, not her infirmity; in technical terms, the war must find something that remains to be broken.

The whole point is missed if her love of children is depreciated as mindless animal instinct. Her saving of the city of Halle is an intelligent act. How else would it be possible to bring out what must be brought out, namely, that here the most helpless creature of all is ready to help?

A detail

At the end of the scene Kattrin lifted the baby into the air, while Courage rolled up the fur coat and threw it into the wagon: both women had their share of the spoils.

Music and pauses

Music played an essential part in the fifth (battlefield) scene.
 Victory march: from the start to "Help me, somebody."
 From after "They got my arm" to "I'm not giving anything."
 From after ". . . happy in all this misery" to the end of the scene.

Pauses after:
 "The mayor must have paid him."
 "Where's the linen?"
 "The blood's coming through." [This line spoken by the chaplain is deleted from the final text. It followed "your victory's costing me a pretty penny."]

Scene 6

Prosperity has set in, but Kattrin is disfigured

Mother Courage, grown prosperous, is taking inventory; funeral oration for the fallen field marshal Tilly. Conversation about the duration of the war; the chaplain proves that the war is going to go on for a long time. Kattrin is sent to buy merchandise. Mother Courage declines a proposal of marriage and insists on firewood. Kattrin is permanently disfigured by some soldiers and rejects Yvette's red shoes. Mother Courage curses the war.

Over-all arrangement

Mother Courage, grown prosperous, is taking inventory; funeral oration for the fallen field marshal Tilly. Courage interrupts her counting of merchandise to serve brandy to some soldiers who are playing hooky from the funeral. She virtuously reproves them, declaring that she feels sorry for generals because the common people don't give their grandiose plans proper support. Meanwhile she is looking for worms in a tin box. The regimental clerk listens in vain, hoping to catch her in a subversive utterance.

Conversation about the duration of the war; the chaplain proves that the war will go on for a long time. The right section of the stage is the private part. To the left are the bar and the guest table at which the clerk and the chaplain are sitting. There is by-play between right and left when the drinking soldier sings for Kattrin and she smiles at him, while Courage, with a bundle of belt buckles which she is counting, comes over to the table to ask the chaplain-bartender how long he thinks the war will go on. All through his cynical comments she stands deep in thought: Should she lay in new supplies?

Kattrin is sent to buy merchandise. When the chaplain-bartender says the war will go on for a long time, Kattrin runs angrily behind the wagon. Courage laughs, brings her back and sends

her to the camp with a big basket to buy merchandise. "Don't let them take anything away from you, think of your dowry."

Mother Courage declines a proposal of marriage and insists on firewood. Courage has sat down on a stool beside her wagon; she fills a pipe and tells the bartender to chop some firewood. He chops clumsily, complaining that his talents are lying fallow, and, probably with a view to avoiding physical labor, asks her to marry him. She hints that she doesn't want to take anybody into her business, and leads him gently back to the chopping block.

Kattrin is permanently disfigured by some soldiers and rejects Yvette's red shoes. Kattrin staggers in with a basket full of merchandise. She collapses at the entrance to the tent and Courage has to drag her over to her stool and dress her wound. Kattrin rejects the red shoes that her mother brings out to comfort her; they are now useless. With silent reproach she crawls into the wagon.

Mother Courage curses the war. Slowly Courage brings forward the new supplies, which Kattrin has defended at such cost, and gets down on her knees to look them over in the place where she was taking inventory at the beginning of the scene. She recognizes that war is a miserable source of income and for the first and last time curses the war.

Inventory

Again Courage has changed. Increasing prosperity has made her softer and more human. Both qualities attract the chaplain and he proposes to her. For the first time we see her sitting briefly at rest, not working.

Funeral oration for Tilly

In the course of many performances it was found that Courage's funeral oration for the field marshal is more effective if during the pause, when all are looking to the rear and the funeral march has grown loud and solemn, the clerk, who is slightly tipsy, rises from his chair and watches Courage closely, suspecting that in this oration she is ridiculing the field marshal. He sits down again in disappointment, because Courage has not said anything demonstrably incriminating.

(The pause during the funeral march must be long; otherwise the funeral scene will not produce the right effect.)

A detail

In the funeral oration for field marshal Tilly ("I feel sorry when a general or an emperor passes away like this") Weigel added—after "he doesn't know any better"—"Jesus Christ, the worms have got into my biscuits." While saying this she laughed. Here Mother Courage releases the merriment which, with the clerk looking on, she was unable to express in her evasively subversive speech.

Pantomime

The chaplain's remarks on the longevity of the war must not take on an independent existence. They are the answer to Courage's anxious question as to whether she can risk taking in new merchandise. While the chaplain was talking, Weigel mimed Courage's anxiety and calculations.

A detail

The drunken soldier addresses his song to Kattrin. She smiles at him. For the last time before she is disfigured the spectator is reminded that she is capable of love.

A point to consider

Violent occupations lead actors to shout. The actor playing the chaplain shouted occasionally while chopping wood. The scene suffered.

[. . .]

Kattrin

Again sitting huddled on the chest as during the drunken soldier's song, the injured girl merely touches her forehead

gingerly once or twice to make sure where the wound is; otherwise, except for the willingness with which she lets herself be bandaged, she gives no indication of knowing what the scar will mean to her. Protest is expressed by her lack of interest in Yvette's red shoes and by the way she crawls into the wagon: she blames her mother for what has happened to her.

Contradiction

Courage has cursed the war while gathering up the supplies in defence of which her daughter has been disfigured.

Resuming the inventory begun at the start of the scene, she now counts the new articles.

Scene 7

Mother Courage at the height of her business career

Mother Courage has corrected her opinion of the war and sings its praises as a good provider.

Over-all arrangement

Mother Courage has corrected her opinion of the war and sings its praises as a good provider. Pulled by Kattrin and the chaplain-bartender, the wagon comes in from the rear and rolls along the footlights. Courage walks beside them, arguing with them; then, while singing, she turns to the audience. Pause.

Signs of prosperity

After some forty performances it seemed to us that in scene 6, where she takes inventory, Courage should have rings on her fingers and a chain of silver talers round her neck as a sign of

the relative prosperity she had achieved. But after a few more performances one of us discovered that this weakened her speech about the courage of the poor, and we decided to put the signs of prosperity in scene 7. Here, where she retracts her condemnation of war, her recently acquired signs of prosperity show her up for what she is: bribed.

In this short scene Weigel showed Courage in the full possession of her vitality, as previously only in scene 5 (the battlefield scene); in scene 5, however, she was gloomy; here she was cheerful.

[. . .]

Scene 8

Peace threatens to ruin Mother Courage's business. Her brave son performs one heroic deed too many and dies an ignominious death

Courage and the chaplain hear a rumor that peace has broken out. The cook reappears. The fight for the feedbag. An old friend who has made a good thing of the war; Pete the Pipe is unmasked. The downfall of Eilif, Mother Courage's brave son; he is executed for one of the misdeeds that had brought him rewards during the war. The peace comes to an end; Courage leaves the chaplain and goes on with the cook in the wake of the Swedish army.

Over-all arrangement

Courage and the chaplain hear a rumor that peace has broken out. On the right stand an old woman and her son who have come from the city with all sorts of household goods to sell. It is early in the morning, and Courage, still half asleep, answers sulkily from the wagon left. Then bells are heard from the right, the chaplain crawls out from under the wagon where he has been

sleeping and Courage sticks her head out of the wagon. The bells seem to have made the old woman happy—not Mother Courage.

The cook reappears. The bells of peace bring all sorts of visitors. First comes—from the right like the rest—the cook, ragged, with all his possessions in a bundle. The chaplain is not pleased to see him, but Courage, who is braiding her hair, runs out to meet him and shakes his hand heartily. She invites him over to a wooden bench in front of the wagon, while the chaplain goes behind the wagon to put on his clericals. Amid the ringing of the bells they sit there almost like lovers, telling each other about the bankruptcy that peace has brought them.

The fight for the feedbag. When the chaplain comes back—he stands in the middle of the stage like a last incisor in a toothless mouth—the cook begins to demolish him. Courage climbs into her wagon to get her pack ready; she is going to sell the merchandise she bought when the chaplain promised her a long war. The cook starts unwrapping his feet because he means to stay, and the chaplain is obliged to beg him humbly not to drive him out. The cook merely shrugs his shoulders.

An old friend who has made a good thing of the war; Pete the Pipe is unmasked. Another visitor. Fat and asthmatic, walking with the help of a cane, the Countess Starhemberg, the former camp whore, enters, clothed in black silk and followed by a servant. She has dismounted from her carriage to call on Mother Courage. She catches sight of the cook, known to her as Pete the Pipe, and angrily denounces him to Courage, who has difficulty in preventing her from attacking him with her cane.

The downfall of Eilif, Mother Courage's brave son; he is executed for one of the misdeeds that brought him rewards during the war. When the women have left, the cook gloomily puts his foot bindings on again and the chaplain relishes his triumph. Their conversation turns to melancholy recollections of the good old war days. Blown in by the bells of peace, soldiers with arquebuses bring in a richly dressed lieutenant—Eilif. His courage deserts him when he hears that his mother is not there. The chaplain gives him a swallow of brandy and, a clergyman once again, accompanies him to the place of execution.

The peace comes to an end; Courage goes on with the cook, in the wake of the Swedish army. The cook tries to get Kattrin to come out of the wagon so he can beg some bread from her. Courage comes running in, overjoyed. The peace is over. The cook does not mention Eilif's death. With the cook's help she packs her belongings into the wagon and they go on without the chaplain.

Advance preparation

In her conversation with the chaplain in scene 6 Weigel very carefully laid the groundwork for her conversation with the cook in scene 8. She said "He was a nice man" a little more warmly and thoughtfully than required by her good-natured rebuff of the chaplain. Consequently in scene 8 she had an audience who knew what was what. This enabled her to take a dry, matter-of-fact tone with the cook. Knowing what it knew, the audience could be touched as well as amused that the subject of their love dialogue should be the fact that they were both ruined.

The dignity of misery

In the cockfight between the chaplain and the cook, Hinz as the chaplain obtained a powerful and natural effect when, suddenly throwing all arrogance to the winds, he begged the cook not to squeeze him out of his place with Courage because, having become a better man, he could no longer practice the clergyman's profession. His fear of losing his job lent him a new dignity.

Humiliations

The cook too is capable of enduring humiliations. At the end of the dialogue in which he triumphs over the chaplain, he removes his shoes and foot wrappings like a man who has come to the end and goal of a long peregrination. Yvette finds him barefooted, which embarrasses the aging Don Juan. After he has been unmasked and the chaplain has lectured him, he sorrow-

fully puts his footwear back on. The episode in which he begs Kattrin for food was played brilliantly by Bildt. His bundle slung over his shoulder, ready to hit the road, he first tapped his stick nonchalantly on the drum hanging from the wagon. Talking into the wagon, he uttered the words "ham" and "bread" in the tone of a gourmet and connoisseur: the starving cook.

Good business

Yvette Pottier is the only character in the play who strikes it rich; she has sold herself for a good price. She has been as badly disfigured by good food as Kattrin by her scar; she is so fat one has the impression that eating has become her only passion. She speaks with the accent of the Austrian aristocracy. [. . .]

War the provider

Courage comes back from the village exhausted from running but overjoyed that the war has started up again. In high spirits she lets the cook relieve her of her pack. The prospect of good business will enable her to take the cook in. She speaks lightheartedly of the possibility of seeing her son again. "Now there's war again, everything will work out all right" [not in the final text]. She is going to ride over his grave.

A detail

While they are packing, Kattrin appears. She sees the cook staring at her scar, covers it with her hand and turns away. She has come to fear the light.

Again in scene 11, when the soldiers drag her out of the wagon, she holds her hand over her eye.

Scene 9

Times are hard, the war is going badly. Because of her daughter, she refuses the offer of a home

The cook has inherited a tavern in Utrecht. Kattrin hears the cook refuse to take her along to Utrecht. The "Song of the Temptations of the Great." Kattrin decides to spare her mother the need to make a decision, packs her bundle and leaves a message. Mother Courage stops Kattrin from running away and goes on alone with her. The cook goes to Utrecht.

Over-all arrangement

Times are hard. The cook has inherited a tavern in Utrecht. In the early dawn of a stormy winter day Courage and the cook, both in rags, bring the wagon to a stop outside a presbytery. The cook morosely unharnesses himself and admits to Courage that he means to go to Utrecht where he has inherited a tavern. He asks her to go with him. Sitting shivering on the shaft, Courage complains of the bad business situation: the war is no longer finding much to feed on.

Kattrin hears the cook refuse to take her along to Utrecht. The cook interrupts the conversation between mother and daughter about the peaceful life in Utrecht, and motions Courage to step to one side with him (to the right, in front of the presbytery). Hidden beside the wagon, Kattrin hears the cook refuse to take her along.

The cook and Courage sing the "Song of the Temptations of the Great." While they sing their begging song, Courage desperately thinks over the cook's offer, presumably her last hope of settling down.

Kattrin decides to spare her mother the need to make a decision, packs her bundle and leaves a message. By the end of the begging song, Courage has made up her mind to decline the offer. She still goes into the presbytery with the cook for the sake of the soup.

Kattrin comes in with a bundle and deposits her mother's skirt with the cook's trousers over it on the wagon shaft.

Mother Courage stops Kattrin from running away and goes on alone with her. Courage catches Kattrin just as she is about to steal away. She has brought a dish of soup. Feeding her as one would a child, she assures her that it has never occurred to her to desert the wagon. She throws the cook's bundle and trousers out of the wagon, puts herself and Kattrin in harness and starts off with her (behind the house, to the right).

The cook goes to Utrecht. The cook sees that the women and wagon are gone. He silently picks up his bundle and starts on his way, right rear, to settle down in Utrecht.

The cook

In this scene the cook must not under any circumstances be represented as brutal. The tavern he has inherited is too small to keep three people, and the customers cannot be expected to put up with the sight of the disfigured Kattrin. That's all there is to it. Courage does not find his arguments unreasonable. Weigel showed plainly that Courage thought the proposition over—she thinks every proposition over. This she did by looking over toward the wagon during the first stanza of the begging song with an expression compounded of indecision, fear and pity.
[. . .]

A detail

In this scene, in which her arguments are rather thin, Courage spoke to her daughter as one speaks to a person who is hard of hearing. Her loud, slow delivery also gives the impression that she is speaking in the name of the cook as well, and in this does not feel at all sure of herself.

Kattrin's demonstration

In laying out the trousers and skirt Kattrin tries to leave her mother a message explaining why she has gone away. But Hur-

wicz also indicated a note of resentment by glancing at the presbytery where her mother and the cook were presumably eating soup, then looking at her composition and stifling an uncanny, malignant giggle by raising her hand to her mouth before sneaking away.

A detail

While saying the words "Don't go thinking I've given him the gate on your account," Courage put a spoonful of soup into Kattrin's mouth.

[. . .]

The cook starts for Utrecht

Scenes of this kind must be fully acted out: Courage and Kattrin harness themselves to the wagon, push it back a few feet so as to be able to circle the presbytery, and then move off to the right. The cook comes out, still chewing on a piece of bread, sees his belongings, picks them up and goes off to the rear with long steps. We see him disappear. Thus the parting of the ways is made visible.

Scene 10

Still on the road

Mother and daughter hear someone in a peasant house singing the "Song of Home."

The song in the Munich production

A fine variation used in the Munich production: the song was sung with unfeeling, provocative self-assurance. The arrogant pride of possession expressed in the singing turned the listeners on the road into damned souls.

Expression not wanted

The two women enter, pulling the wagon. They hear the voice from the peasant house, stop, listen, and start off again. What goes on in their minds should not be shown; the audience can imagine.

A detail

In one of the later performances Weigel, when starting off again, tossed her head and shook it like a tired draft horse getting back to work. It is doubtful whether this gesture can be imitated.

Scene 11

Mute Kattrin saves the city of Halle

A surprise attack is planned on the city of Halle; soldiers force a young peasant to show them the way. The peasant and his wife tell Kattrin to join them in praying for the city. Kattrin climbs up on the barn roof and beats the drum to awaken the city. Neither the offer to spare her mother in the city nor the threat to smash the wagon can make her stop drumming. Kattrin's death.

Over-all arrangement

A surprise attack is planned on the city of Halle; soldiers force a young peasant to show them the way. A lieutenant and two soldiers come to a farm at night. They drag the peasants, still half asleep, out of the house and Kattrin out of her wagon. By threatening to kill the peasants' only ox they force the young peasant to serve as their guide. (They lead him to the rear; the party go out right.)

The peasant and his wife tell Kattrin to join them in praying for the city. The peasant moves a ladder over to the barn (right), climbs up and sees that the woods are swarming with armed men. He

omes down, he and his wife talk it over and decide not to ndanger themselves by trying to warn the city. The peasant voman goes over to Kattrin (right front) and tells her to pray God to help the city. The three of them kneel down and pray.

Kattrin climbs up on the barn roof and beats the drum to awaken the ity. From the peasant woman's prayer Kattrin learns that the children in Halle are in danger. Stealthily she takes the drum from the wagon, the same drum she had brought back when she was disfigured. With it she climbs up on the barn roof. She starts drumming. The peasants try in vain to make her stop.

Neither the offer to spare her mother in the city nor the threat to smash the wagon can make her stop drumming. At the sound of the drum the lieutenant and the soldiers come back with the young peasant. The soldiers take up a position by the wagon and the lieutenant threatens the peasants with his sword. First one of the soldiers, then the lieutenant moves to the center to make promises to Kattrin. The peasant goes over to a log (left front) and chops at it with an ax to drown out the sound of the drum. Kattrin is victorious in the noise contest, the lieutenant starts to go into the house to set it on fire, the peasant woman indicates the wagon. One of the soldiers kicks the young peasant and forces him to batter the wagon with a plank, the other soldier is sent off for a musket. He sets up the musket, the lieutenant orders him to fire.

Kattrin's death. Kattrin falls forward, the drumsticks in her drooping hands stike one full beat followed by a feeble beat; for a moment the lieutenant is triumphant, then the cannon of Halle respond, taking up the rhythm of Kattrin's drumbeats.

Bad comedians always laugh
Bad tragedians always weep

In sad scenes just as much as in comic ones precision must be combined with ease; the hand that guides the arrangement must be both firm and relaxed. The actors take their positions and form their groups in very much the same way as the marbles tossed into a wooden bowl in certain roulette-like children's games fall into hollows, with the difference that in the games

it is not decided in advance which marbles will fall into which hollows, whereas in theatrical arrangements there only seems to be no advance decision. And indeed the reason for the stiffness or heaviness that is so characteristic of sad scenes in the German theater is that in tragedy the human body is unjustifiably neglected and so seems to be afflicted with muscular cramp. Which is deplorable.

Kattrin's two fears

Kattrin's muteness does not save her. The war gives her a drum. With this unsold drum she must climb up on the barn roof, and save the children of Halle.

Conventional heroism must be avoided. Kattrin is ridden by two fears: her fear for the city of Halle and her fear for herself.

"The dramatic scene"

Audiences were especially stirred by the drum scene. Some explained this by saying that it is the most dramatic scene in the play and that the public likes its theater dramatic rather than epic. In reality the epic theater, while capable of portraying other things than stirring incidents, clashes, conspiracies, psychological torments and so on, is also capable of portraying these. Spectators may identify themselves with Kattrin in this scene; empathy may give them the happy feeling that they too possess such strength. But they are not likely to have experienced such empathy throughout the play—in the first scenes, for example.

Alienation

If the scene is to be saved from a wild excitement amid which everything worth noticing is lost, close attention must be given to alienation.

For example: if the conversation of the peasants is swallowed up by a general hubbub, the audience will be in danger of being

"carried away"; then they will fail to take note how the peasants justify their failure to act, how they fortify each other in the belief that there is nothing they can do, so that the only remaining possibility of "action" becomes prayer.

In view of this, the actors in rehearsal were made to add "said the man" or "said the woman" after each speech. For example:

" 'The sentry will see them in time,' said the woman."
" 'They must have killed the sentry,' said the man."
" 'If there were more of us,' said the woman."
" 'All by ourselves up here with a cripple,' said the man."
" 'We can't do a thing. Do you think . . .' said the woman."
" 'Not a thing,' said the man," and so on.

Kattrin's drumming

Kattrin keeps watching what is going on down below. Consequently her drumming breaks off after the following sentences.

"Jesus, what's she doing?"
"I'll cut you to pieces."
"We've got a friendly proposition."
"No wonder with your mug!"
"We'll have to set the house on fire."

Detail in tempestuous scenes

Such scenes as the one where the peasant tries to drown the noise of Kattrin's drumming by chopping wood must be fully acted out. As she drums, Kattrin must look down at the peasant and accept the challenge. In tempestuous scenes the director needs a certain amount of stubbornnesss to make miming of this sort last long enough.

A detail

Hurwicz showed increasing exhaustion while drumming.

The ritual character of despair

The lamentations of the peasant woman, whose son the soldiers have taken away and whose farm they threaten when Kattrin starts her drumming to wake the townspeople, must have a certain routine quality about it; it must suggest a "set behavior pattern." The war has been going on too long. Begging, lamenting, and informing have frozen into fixed forms: those are the things you do when the soldiery arrive.

It is worth foregoing the "immediate impression" of a particular, seemingly unique episode of horror so as to penetrate a deeper stratum of horror and to show how repeated, constantly recurring misfortune has driven people to ritualize their gestures of self-defense—though of course these ritual gestures can never free them from the reality of fear, which on the stage must permeate the ritual.

[. . .]

Scene 12

Mother Courage moves on

The peasants have to convince Courage that Kattrin is dead. The lullaby for Kattrin. Mother Courage pays for Kattrin's burial and receives the condolences of the peasants. Alone, Mother Courage harnesses herself to the empty wagon; still hoping to get back into business, she follows the ragged army.

Over-all arrangement

The peasants have to convince Courage that Kattrin is dead. The wagon is standing on the empty stage. Mother Courage is sitting with the dead Kattrin's head in her lap. The peasants are standing in a hostile knot at the dead girl's feet. Courage speaks as if her daughter were only sleeping, deliberately disregarding

the reproaches of the peasants who are saying that she is to blame for Kattrin's death.

The lullaby for Kattrin. The mother's face is bent low over her daughter's face. Her song fails to pacify the peasants.

Mother Courage pays for Kattrin's burial and receives the condolences of the peasants. When she realizes that her last child is dead, she rises painfully to her feet and hobbles around the corpse (on the right) and along the footlights to behind the wagon. She comes back with a sheet of canvas. The peasants ask her if she has no one else; she answers over her shoulder: "Yes, there's one of them left. Eilif." And with her back to the audience she lays the canvas over the body. Then at the head end of the body she pulls it up over the face and stands behind the body, facing the audience. The peasant and his son give her their hands and bow ceremoniously before carrying the body away (to the right). The woman also gives Courage her hand, goes to the right and stops again in indecision. The women exchange a few words, then the peasant woman goes away.

Alone, Mother Courage harnesses herself to her empty wagon; still hoping to get back into business, she follows the ragged army. Slowly the old woman goes to the wagon, unrolls the cord which Kattrin had until then been pulling, takes a stick, examines it, pulls the loop of the second cord through, wedges the stick under her arm and moves off. The last stanza of the "Mother Courage Song" has begun when she was bending down over the shaft. The revolving stage begins to turn and Mother Courage circles the stage once. The curtain falls as she turns right rear for the second time.

The peasants

The peasants' attitude toward Courage is hostile. She has caused them great difficulties and they will have her on their hands if she cannot catch up with the departing army. As they see it, she is to blame for what has happened. Besides, she is an unsedentary element, and now in wartime belongs with the incendiaries, cutthroats and looters who follow in the wake of armies. In condoling with her by giving her their hands, they are only doing what is customary.

The bow

During the whole scene Weigel showed an almost bestial stupor. All the more beautiful was her deep bow when the body was carried away.

The lullaby

The lullaby must be sung without any sentimentality or desire to provoke sentimentality. Otherwise its significance is lost. The idea underlying this song is murderous: this mother's child must fare better than other children of other mothers. By slight emphasis on the "you," Weigel portrayed Courage's treacherous hope of bringing her child, and perhaps hers alone, through the war. To this child who had lacked even the most ordinary things, she promised the most extraordinary.

Paying for the burial

Even in paying for the burial, Weigel gave one last hint of Courage's character. She fished a few coins out of her leather bag, put one back and gave the peasants the rest. This did not in the least detract from the overpowering effect of desolation.

The last stanza

The last stanza of the "Mother Courage Song" was struck up by the musicians in the box while Courage was slowly harnessing herself to the wagon. It gives powerful expression to her still unshattered hope of getting her cut from the war. It gains in power if the illusion that the song is being sung by marching armies in the distance is dropped.
[. . .]

Timing

At the end as at the beginning the wagon must be seen rolling along. Of course the audience would understand if it were simply pulled away. When it goes on rolling there is a moment of

irritation ("this has been going on long enough"). But when it goes on still longer, a deeper understanding sets in.

The pulling of the wagon in the last scene

For scene 12 the peasants' house and the barn with roof (from scene 11) were removed from the stage; only the wagon and Kattrin's body remained. The word "Saxony" in big letters is hoisted into the flies when the music starts. Thus the wagon is hauled off a completely empty stage recalling scene 1. Mother Courage described a complete circle with it on the revolving stage, passing the footlights for the last time. As usual, the stage was brightly lit.

Realistic discoveries

In giving the peasants the money for Kattrin's burial, Weigel quite mechanically puts back one of the coins she has taken out of her purse. What does this gesture accomplish? It shows that in all her grief the business woman has not wholly forgotten how to reckon—money is hard to come by. This little gesture has the power and suddenness of a discovery—a discovery concerning human nature, which is molded by conditions. To dig out the truth from the rubble of the self-evident, to link the particular strikingly with the universal, to capture the particular that characterizes a general process, that is the art of the realist.

A change in the text

After "I'll manage, there isn't much in it," Courage added, first in the Munich, then in the Berlin production: "I've got to get back into business."

Mother Courage learns nothing

In the last scene Weigel's Courage seemed to be eighty years old. And she understands nothing. She reacts only to remarks connected with the war, such as that she mustn't be left behind, and takes no notice when the peasants brutally accuse her of being to blame for Kattrin's death.

In 1938, when the play was written, Courage's inability to learn from the unprofitable character of the war was a prophecy. At the time of the 1948 Berlin production the wish was expressed that at least in the play Courage would understand.

In order that the realism of this play should benefit the spectator, that is, in order that the spectator should learn something, the theater must work out a way of playing it which does not lead to audience identification with the principal character (heroine).

To judge by press reviews and statements of spectators, the original production in Zurich, for example, though artistically on a high level, merely pictured war as a natural catastrophe and ineluctable fate, confirming the belief of the petit-bourgeois members of the audience in their own indestructibility and power to survive. But even for the equally petit-bourgeois Mother Courage the decision whether or not to join in was left open throughout the play. It follows that the production must have represented Courage's business activity, her desire to get her cut and her willingness to take risks, as perfectly natural and "eternally human" phenomena, so that there was no way out. Today the petit bourgeois can no longer in fact keep out of the war, as Courage could have done. And probably no performance of the play can give a petit bourgeois anything more than a real horror of war and a certain insight into the fact that the big business deals that constitute war are not made by the little people. A play is more instructive than reality, because in it the war situation is set up experimentally for the purpose of giving insight; that is, the spectator assumes the attitude of a student—provided the production is right. The proletarians in the audience, the members of a class which really can take action against war and eliminate it, must be given an insight—

which of course is possible only if the play is performed in the right way—into the connection between war and commerce: the proletarian as a class can do away with war by doing away with capitalism. Here, of course, a good deal depends on the growth of self-awareness among the proletariat, a process that is going on both inside and outside the theater.

The epic element

As for the epic element in the Deutsches Theater production, indications of it could be seen in the arrangement, in the delineation of the characters, in the accurate execution of detail, and in the spirited rhythm of the entire performance. Moreover, the contradictions that pervade the play were not taken over ready-made, but worked out, and the parts, visible as such, fitted well into the whole. Nonetheless, the central aim of the epic theater was not achieved. Much was shown, but the element of showing was absent. Only in a few rehearsals devoted to recasting was it brought out clearly. Here the actors "demonstrated," that is, they showed the new members of the cast certain positions and tones, and the whole took on the wonderfully relaxed, effortless, and unobtrusive quality that stimulates the spectator to think and feel for himself.

No one missed this fundamental epic element; and that is probably why the actors did not dare to provide it.

Concerning these notes

It is to be hoped that the present notes, indicating a few of the ideas and devices of various kinds that are necessary for the performance of a play, will not make an impression of misplaced seriousness. It is difficult in writing about these things to convey the carefree lightness that is essential to the theater. Even in their instructive aspect, the arts belong to the realm of entertainment.

[From *Mutter Courage und ihre Kinder. Text/Aufführung/ Anmerkungen.* Henschel-Verlag, East Berlin, 1956.]

Two Ways of Playing Mother Courage

When the title role is played in the usual way, so as to communicate empathy, the spectator (according to numerous witnesses) experiences an extraordinary pleasure: the indestructible vitality of this woman beset by the hardships of war leaves him with a sense of triumph. Mother Courage's active participation in the war is not taken seriously; the war is a source, perhaps her only source, of livelihood. Apart from this element of participation, in spite of it, the effect is very much as in *Schweyk*, where—in a comic perspective, to be sure—the audience triumphs with Schweyk over the plans of the belligerent powers to sacrifice him. But in the case of Mother Courage such an effect has far less social value, precisely because her participation, however indirect it may seem, is not taken into consideration. The effect is indeed negative. Courage is represented chiefly as a mother, and like Niobe she is unable to protect her children against fate —in this case, war. At most, her merchant's trade and the way she plies it give her a "realistic, un-ideal" quality; they do not prevent the war from being seen as fate. It remains, of course, wholly evil, but after all she comes through it alive, though deformed. By contrast Weigel, employing a technique which prevents complete empathy, treated the merchant's trade not as a natural but as a historical one—that is, belonging to a historical, *transient* period—and war as the best time for it. Here too the war was a self-evident source of livelihood, but this spring from which Mother Courage drank death was a polluted one. The merchant-mother became a great living contradiction, and it was this contradiction which utterly disfigured and deformed her. In the battlefield scene, which is cut in most productions, she was really a hyena; she parted with the shirts because she saw her daughter's hatred and feared violence; she cursed at the soldier with the coat and pounced on him like a tigress. When her daughter was disfigured, she cursed the war with the same profound sincerity that characterized her praise of it in the scene immediately following. Thus she played the contra-

dictions in all their irreconcilable sharpness. Her daughter's rebellion against her (when the city of Halle is saved) stunned her completely and taught her nothing. The tragedy of Mother Courage and of her life, which the audience was made to feel deeply, lay in a terrible contradiction which destroyed a human being, a contradiction which has been transcended, but only by society itself in long and terrible struggles. What made this way of playing the part morally superior was that human beings— even the strongest of them—were shown to be destructible.

> [Written 1951. From GW *Schriften zum Theater*, p. 895. First published in *Theaterarbeit*, 1952.]

[Misfortune in itself is a poor teacher]

The audience gave off the acrid smell of clothing that had not been properly cleaned, but this did not detract from the festive atmosphere. Those who had come to see the play had come from ruins and would be going back to ruins. There was more light on the stage than on any square or in any house.

The wise old stage manager from the days of Max Reinhardt had received me like a king, but what gave the production its hard realism was a bitter experience shared by all. The dressmakers in the workshops realized that the costumes had to be richer at the beginning of the play than at the end. The stage hands knew how the canvas over Mother Courage's wagon had to be: white and new at the beginning, then dirty and patched, then somewhat cleaner, but never again really white, and at the end a rag.

Weigel's way of playing Mother Courage was hard and angry; that is, her Mother Courage was not angry; she herself, the actress, was angry. She showed a merchant, a strong crafty woman who loses her children to the war one after another and still goes on believing in the profit to be derived from war.

A number of people remarked at the time that Mother Courage learns nothing from her misery, that even at the end she

does not *understand.* Few realized that just this was the bitterest and most meaningful lesson of the play.

Undoubtedly the play was a great success; that is, it made a big impression. People pointed out Weigel on the street and said: "Mother Courage!" But I do not believe, and I did not believe at the time, that the people of Berlin—or of any other city where the play was shown—understood the play. They were all convinced that they had learned something from the war; what they failed to grasp was that, in the playwright's view, Mother Courage was to have learned nothing from her war. They did not see what the playwright was driving at: that war teaches people nothing.

Misfortune in itself is a poor teacher. Its pupils learn hunger and thirst, but seldom hunger for truth or thirst for knowledge. Suffering does not transform a sick man into a physician. Neither what he sees from a distance nor what he sees face to face is enough to turn an eyewitness into an expert.

The audiences of 1949 and the ensuing years did not see Mother Courage's crimes, her participation, her desire to share in the profits of the war business; they saw only her failure, her sufferings. And that was their view of Hitler's war in which they had participated: it had been a bad war and now they were suffering. In short, it was exactly as the playwright had prophesied. The war would bring them suffering, and the inability to learn from it.

The production of *Mother Courage and Her Children* is now in its sixth year. It is certainly a brilliant production, with great actors. Undoubtedly something has changed. The play is no longer a play that came too late, that is, *after* a war. Today a new war is threatening with all its horrors. No one speaks of it, but everyone knows. The masses are not in favor of war. But life is so full of hardships. Mightn't war do away with these? Didn't people make a very good living in the last war, at any rate till just before the end? And aren't there such things as successful wars?

I am curious to know how many of those who see *Mother Courage and Her Children* today understand its warning.

[Written 1954. From GW *Schriften zum Theater*, p. 1147.]

Notes on *Mother Courage and Her Children*

Mother Courage and Her Children was first performed in Zurich during the Second World War, with the extraordinary Therese Giehse in the title role. Despite the antifascist and pacifist orientation of the Zurich Schauspielhaus company, which at that time consisted largely of German refugees, the production made it possible for the bourgeois press to speak of the "Niobe tragedy" and of the "heart-rending vitality of this mother animal." Warned, the author made a few changes for the Berlin production. The original text follows.

Scene 1, p. 142

MOTHER COURAGE . . . Be careful, all of you, you'll need to be. And now we'll climb up and drive on.

THE SERGEANT I'm not feeling so good.

THE RECRUITER Maybe you caught cold when you took your helmet off in the wind.
  (*The sergeant grabs the helmet*)

MOTHER COURAGE And now give me back my papers. Somebody else might ask for them, and there I'd be without any papers. (*She puts them away in the tin box*)

THE RECRUITER (*to Eilif*) At least you could take a look at the boots. And then we'll have a drink, just you and me. I'll show you I've got the money, come behind the wagon.
  (*They go behind the wagon*)

THE SERGEANT I don't get it. I always stay in the rear. There's no safer place for a sergeant. You can send the men up forward to win glory. You've spoiled my dinner. It won't go down, I know it. Not a bite.

MOTHER COURAGE (*going toward him*) Don't take it to heart. Don't let it spoil your appetite. Just keep behind the lines. Here, take a drink of schnapps, man. And no hard feelings.
  (*She reaches into the wagon and hands him a drink*)

THE RECRUITER (*has taken Eilif's arm and is pulling him away toward the rear*) One way or another, you're sunk. You've pulled a cross, so what? A bonus of ten guilders, and you'll

be a brave man and you'll fight for the king, and the women will tear each other's hair out over you. And you can clout me one on the kisser for insulting you. (*Both go out*)

(*Mute Kattrin has seen the abduction and emits raucous sounds*)

MOTHER COURAGE Just a minute, Kattrin, just a minute. The sergeant's not feeling so good, he's superstitious. I hadn't thought of that. And now we'll be going. Where's Eilif got to?

SWISS CHEESE He must have gone with the recruiter. He was talking with him the whole time.

Scene 5, p. 174

MOTHER COURAGE (*to the others*) What's that? You can't pay? No money, no schnapps. Plenty of victory marches for the Lord, but no pay for the men.

THE SOLDIER (*threatening*) I want schnapps. I came too late for the looting. They only gave us permission to loot the city for an hour. The general says he's not a monster. The mayor must have paid him, that's what I hear.

THE CHAPLAIN (*staggers in*) There's still some wounded in the house. The peasant and his family. Help me, somebody. I need linen.

(*The second soldier goes out with him*)

MOTHER COURAGE I haven't got any. The Regiment's bought up all my bandages. You think I'm going to rip up my officers' shirts for the likes of them?

THE CHAPLAIN (*calling back*) I need linen, I tell you.

MOTHER COURAGE (*rummaging around in her wagon*) Nothing doing. They won't pay, they got nothing to pay with.

THE CHAPLAIN (*bending over a woman whom he has carried out*) Why did you stay here in all that gunfire?

THE PEASANT WOMAN (*feebly*) Farm.

MOTHER COURAGE You won't catch them leaving their property. My beautiful shirts. Tomorrow the officers will be coming over, and I won't have a thing. (*She throws down one, which Kattrin takes to the peasant woman*) Why should I part with my belongings? I didn't start the war.

THE FIRST SOLDIER They're Protestants. Why do they have to be Protestants?

MOTHER COURAGE   Who cares about their religion? They've lost their farm.

THE SECOND SOLDIER   They're no Protestants. They're Catholics like us.

THE FIRST SOLDIER   How do we know who we're shooting at?

A PEASANT (*whom the chaplain brings in*)   My arm is broken. (*The anguished cry of a baby is heard from the house*)

THE CHAPLAIN   Don't move.

MOTHER COURAGE   Bring the baby out.

(*Kattrin runs into the house*)

MOTHER COURAGE (*ripping up shirts*)   Half a guilder apiece. I'm ruined. Don't move her when you dress the wound. Maybe it's her back. (*To Kattrin, who emerges from the ruins with a baby and goes about cradling it in her arms*) Oh, so you've found another baby to carry around? Give that baby back to its mother this minute, or it'll take me all day to get it away from you. Do you hear me? (*Kattrin pays no attention to her*) Your victory's costing me a pretty penny. There, that's enough, chaplain. Don't run hog-wild with my linen. I won't stand for it.

THE CHAPLAIN   I need more, the blood's coming through.

MOTHER COURAGE (*looking down at Kattrin*)   There she sits, happy in all this misery; give it back this minute, the mother's coming to. (*While Kattrin at last reluctantly brings the baby to the peasant woman, she rips up another shirt*) I'm not giving anything, you can't make me, I've got to think of myself. (*To the second soldier*) Don't stand there gaping, go back and tell them to stop that music, I can see right here that they've won a victory. Take a drink of schnapps, chaplain, don't argue, I've got trouble enough. (*She has to come down from the wagon to snatch her daughter away from the first soldier, who is drunk*) You beast, haven't you had enough victories for today? Stop. You're not running out on me, you've got to pay first. (*To the peasant*) Your baby's all right. Put (*Pointing to the woman*) something under her. (*To the first soldier*) Then leave your coat here, it's stolen anyway. (*The first soldier totters away. Mother Courage goes on ripping up shirts*)

THE CHAPLAIN   There's still somebody in there.

MOTHER COURAGE   Don't worry, I'll rip them all up.

Scene 7, p. 185
Highway. The chaplain, Mother Courage and Kattrin are pulling the
wagon. It is dirty and bedraggled, but new wares are hanging on it.
MOTHER COURAGE (*sings*)

Some people think they'd like to ride out
The war, leave danger to the brave
And dig themselves a cozy hideout—
They'll dig themselves an early grave.
I've seen them running from the thunder
To find a refuge from the war—
But once they're resting six feet under
They wonder what they hurried for.

(*She plays the refrain "The Spring is Come" on her Jew's harp*)

Scene 12, p. 209
PEASANTS   You'll have to be going, woman. There's only one
more regiment to come. You can't go alone.
MOTHER COURAGE   She's still breathing. Maybe I can get her
to sleep.

The revolutionary impetus of the Reformation had been destroyed by the Peasant Wars, the greatest disaster in German
history. What remained was business and cynicism. Like her
friends and customers and almost everyone else, Mother Courage—I say this as a help to producers of the play—is aware of
the purely mercantile character of war, and that is precisely
what attracts her. She believes in the war to the very end. It
doesn't so much as dawn on her that only the powerful can hope
to benefit by war. Those who suppose that the victims of catas-
trophes will learn a lesson from them are mistaken. As long as
the masses are the *object* of politics, they cannot look upon what
happens to them as an experiment, but only as a fate; they learn
no more from a catastrophe than a guinea pig learns about
biology. It is not the playwright's business to make Mother

Courage see clearly in the end—she sees certain things toward the middle of the play, at the end of scene 6, and then loses sight of them—what matters to the playwright is that the audience should see.

[From GW *Stücke*, pp. 1439 ff.]

Editorial Note

The first typescript of *Mother Courage*, in Brecht's own typing with its characteristic absence of capital letters, was made in 1939, though there is also what may be a slightly earlier draft of the first few pages in verse. Amended by Brecht and by his collaborator Margarete Steffin, who died in 1941, it was then duplicated for the Zurich production and again in 1946 by the Kurt Reiss agency in Basel. This seems to have been the text which Brecht circulated to some of his friends, and of which one scene was accordingly published in the Moscow *Internationale Literatur* before the première, while a copy served as the basis for H.R. Hays's first American translation. Brecht made a few further additions and alterations to the 1946 version, which was once again duplicated for the Deutsches Theater production of 1949. Brecht's own copies of this Deutsches Theater script bear yet more notes and small amendments, as well as cuts which were disregarded in the published version. This appeared as *Versuche 9* in 1949, continuing the gray paperbound series of Brecht's writings which had been interrupted in 1933.

The main shifts of emphasis in the play were indicated by Brecht in his own notes which followed the first publication of the play in the *Versuche* (1949) and have been reprinted in subsequent editions (pp. 390–394 above). The final versions of these passages, with the exception of the last (which concludes the play) are to be found in the additions to the Deutsches Theater typescript. In the case of the last scene, the major change took place subsequently, between the *Versuche* edition of 1949 and the reprint of 1950. It consisted in the insertion of the stage directions showing Mother Courage first covering her daughter's body, then handing over money to the peasants who carry it away, and of the last sentence "I've got to get back in business."

In previous versions, too, she was made to join in the refrain of the final song. Now, presumably, she was too old and exhausted to do more than pull her wagon.

These changes were, as Brecht said, calculated to bring out Courage's short-sighted concentration on business and alienate the audience's sympathies. Thus in scene 1 she now became distracted by the chance of selling a belt buckle; in scene 5 she no longer helped the others to make bandages of her expensive shirts; while in scene 7 she was shown prospering (her lines up to "The stay-at-homes are the first to get it" were new, while the scene title "Mother Courage at the height of her business career" and the silver necklace of the stage direction were added after the 1949 edition). Besides these, however, Brecht made earlier alterations to two of the main characters—the cook and the camp prostitute Yvette—and to virtually all the songs, whose independent role in the play became considerably strengthened as a result. Scene 8 seems to have called for repeated amendment, thanks partly to Brecht's uncertainty about the Yvette–cook relationship, which in turn depended on the choice of song for scene 3, where it is first expressed. Another confusion which has perhaps left its mark on the final text concerns religion: the first typescript gave the chaplain the Catholic title of "Kaplan" throughout, putting Courage initially in the Catholic camp, which the Lutherans then overran in scene 3. Though Brecht corrected this on the script, to conform with the rest of the story, the religious antagonism emerges none too clearly even in the final version.

Brecht's first typescript also numbered the scenes rather differently, so as to run from 1 to 11, omitting the present scenes 7 and 10. He altered this to make 9 scenes, a division which he retained in the 1946 script, writing the original scene titles, to correspond with it, very nearly in their present form. "The Story" (pp. 331 ff. above) refers to this numbering, as also does a note attached to the typescript:

The minor parts can easily be divided among a small number of actors. For instance the sergeant in scene 1 can also play the wounded peasant in scene 5 and the young man in scene 7 [8]; the general in scene 2 can be the clerk in scene 4 and the old peasant in scene 9 [11], and so on. Moreover the soldier in

scene 3, the young soldier in scene 4 and the lieutenant in scene 9 [II] can be performed by the same actor without alteration of makeup.

Settings and costumes

High road with a Swedish city in the background/Inside the general's tent/Camp/Outside an officer's tent/In a bombarded village/In a canteen tent during rain/In the woods outside a city/Outside a rectory in the winter/Near a thatched peasant dwelling.

The chief item of scenery consists in Courage's wagon, from which one must be able to deduce her current financial situation. The brief scenes on the high road which are appended to scenes 6 and 8 [now scenes 7 and 10] can be played in front of the curtain.

So far as the costumes are concerned, care must be taken to avoid the brand-new elegance common in historical plays. They must show the poverty involved in a long war.

The following scene-by-scene résumé of the changes follows the same numbering, the present scene numbers being given in square brackets.

1. [*1*]

In Brecht's first typescript the family arrive to the sound of a piano-accordion, not a Jew's harp, and there are some minor differences in the Mother Courage song.

2. [2]

The cook's original name "Feilinger" is amended to "Lamb" on the first typescript. The general's reference to the king and Eilif's reply were added to this; the general's following "You're something like him already" was an afterthought added on the Deutsches Theater script (according to Manfred Wekwerth it was meant to refer to the enthusiasm with which Eilif drank). Eilif's *"doing a war dance with his sabre"* was penned by Brecht on the 1946 script.

The song itself is taken over from Brecht's first collection of

poems, *Die Hauspostille* (1927), and derives originally from the
verse at the end of Kipling's short story *Love o' Women*.

3. [*3*]

The three sub-scenes (divided by the passage of time) are numbered 3, 3a and 3b, of which only the first has a title. Yvette
originally was Jessie Potter, amended on the first typescript to
Jeannette Pottier; she had become Yvette by 1946. The scene
started with Mother Courage's remark to Swiss Cheese "Here's
your underdrawers," everything to do with the ordnance officer
being added to the first typescript (p. 151).

Instead of the "Song of Fraternization," Jessie *"sings the song
of Surabaya-Johnny"* (from *Happy End*), immediately after the
words "Then I'll talk about it, because it makes me feel better,"
Courage having just said "Just don't start in on your Johnny."
The text of this song is not reproduced in the typescript, but a
first version of Johnny's description is inserted, with Jeannette
"growing up on Batavia" and the man being a "ship's cook,
blond, a Swede, but skinny." In pen, Batavia is changed to
Flanders, ship's cook to army cook and Swede to Dutchman. A
"Song of Pipe-and-Drum Henny" is added, which is a slightly
adapted version of "Surabaya-Johnny" in three verses (the refrain appears only in the 1946 script). In the text of this song,
which still fits the Weill music, Burma is amended to Utrecht
and the fish market (in "You were something to do with the fish
market / And nothing to do with the army") to a tulip market.
Besides the beginning ("When I was only sixteen") the second
quatrain of the second verse was absorbed in the "Song of
Fraternization," which is substituted in Brecht's amended copy
of the 1946 script. This also adds that the Cook was called "Pipe-
Henny" because he never took his pipe out of his mouth when
he was doing it.

Some light on the camp prostitute's varying ages is cast by her
ensuing remark about her failure to run him to earth. In the first
typescript it happened "twenty years ago," in the 1946 and
Deutsches Theater scripts "ten years ago," before being reduced to the present "five" some time between 1949 and 1953.

The chaplain's "Song of the Hours" occurs for the first time in the Deutsches Theater script, where it consists of seven verses only and is sung before the curtain to introduce sub-scene 3b. In Mother Courage's subsequent speech on corruptibility (p. 168) there is a section which was cut in this script but is of interest for its anticipation of *The Caucasian Chalk Circle:*

> I used to know a judge in Franconia who was so out for money, even small sums from poor people, that he was universally regarded as a good man right up into Saxony, and that's some way. People talked about him as if he were a saint, he'd listen to everybody, he was tough about the amount— wouldn't let anyone say they were penniless if they had anything—widow or profiteer, he treated them all alike, all of them had to give.

4. [*4*]

The young soldier was originally complaining about the delay in getting his base pay. Brecht's amendments to his typescript introduced the idea of a special reward, as well as giving Mother Courage more to say. The song was called "The Song of Waiting" in this typescript and was amended at every stage, first and foremost by adding the (spoken) parentheses.

5. [*5*]

See p. 391 above. The cry "Pshagreff!"—Polish Psia Krew (blood of a dog)—near the end was simply "Stop!" until after the 1949 edition.

6. [*6*]

This scene appeared in the Moscow monthly *Internationale Literatur* (then edited by J. R. Becher), No. 12, 1940. Courage's speech beginning "Money first!" was very much longer there, as also in the first two scripts. The drunken soldier and his song were additions to the first typescript; Courage's suggestion that he may have been responsible for the attack on Kattrin being

an addition to the 1946 script. In *Internationale Literatur* and prior to the Deutsches Theater version Kattrin accepts the red shoes at the end of the scene and "sets about her work; she has calmed down."

6a. [7]

See p. 393 above.

7. [8]

This scene (Eilif's death) is the most heavily amended, partly in order to get the confrontation of the cook and Yvette straight. Originally, on the first typescript, she denounces him as "That's Surabaya-Johnny," which prompts Courage to hum the refrain of the song. Courage previously has a song of her own, following the chaplain's "Off war, you mean. Aha!" (p. 190), which she introduces by the lines:

> If the Emperor's on top now, what with the King of Sweden being dead, all it'll mean is that the taxes go to the Emperor. Ever seen a water wheel? Mills have them. I'm going to sing you a song about one of those water wheels, a parable featuring the great. (*She sings the Song of the Water Wheel*)

—a song to Eisler's music which is to be found in Brecht's *The Roundheads and Peakheads*. It was omitted from the 1946 script.

8. [9]

The fourth (St. Martin) verse of the "Solomon Song" (itself of course partly taken over from the *Threepenny Opera*) made its appearance in the 1946 script. The cook's tavern was originally in Uppsala, amended when he became a Dutchman.

8a. [10]

The scene was originally un-numbered. The title was added between the 1949 and 1953 *Versuche* editions.

9. [*11*]

The date of the title was at first March 1635 and the threatened town Havelberg. The only change of any substance took place after the peasant's "We could get one [pine tree] and knock her down . . . ," where in all three scripts the soldiers proceeded to fetch one and actually tried to dislodge Kattrin with it. This was deleted on Brecht's Deutsches Theater script, which incidentally bears marks showing exactly where the drumbeats should fall.

9a. [*12*]

See p. 393, 395. On the first typescript lines 5–7 of the song originally read

> He gets his uniform and rations
> The regiment gives him his pay.
> The rest defeats our comprehension
> Tomorrow is another day.

before Brecht amended them to read as now.

APPENDIX

Galileo
BY BERTOLT BRECHT
Translated by Charles Laughton

It is my opinion that the earth is very noble and admirable
by reason of so many and so different alterations and generations which are incessantly made therein.
—GALILEO GALILEI

CHARACTERS

There are two wordless roles: The DOGE *in Scene Two and* PRINCE COSMO DI MEDICI *in Scene Four. The ballad of Scene Nine is filled out by a pantomime: among the individuals in the pantomimic crowd are three extras (including the "*KING OF HUNGARY*"),* COBBLER'S BOY, THREE CHILDREN, PEASANT WOMAN, MONK, RICH COUPLE, DWARF, BEGGAR, *and* GIRL.

Scene One

In the year sixteen hundred and nine
Science' light began to shine.
At Padua City, in a modest house
Galileo Galilei set out to prove
The sun is still, the earth is on the move.

Galileo's scantily furnished study. Morning. Galileo is washing himself.
A bare-footed boy, Andrea, son of his housekeeper, Mrs. Sarti, enters
with a big astronomical model.

GALILEO   Where did you get that thing?

ANDREA   The coachman brought it.

GALILEO   Who sent it?

ANDREA   It said "From the Court of Naples" on the box.

GALILEO   I don't want their stupid presents. Illuminated manuscripts, a statue of Hercules the size of an elephant—they
never send money.

ANDREA   But isn't this an astronomical instrument, Mr. Galilei?

GALILEO   That is an antique too. An expensive toy.

ANDREA   What's it for?

GALILEO   It's a map of the sky according to the wise men of
ancient Greece. Bosh! We'll try and sell it to the university.
They still teach it there.

ANDREA   How does it work, Mr. Galilei?

GALILEO   It's complicated.

ANDREA   I think I could understand it.

GALILEO (*interested*)   Maybe. Let's begin at the beginning. Description!

ANDREA   There are metal rings, a lot of them.

GALILEO   How many?

ANDREA   Eight.

GALILEO   Correct. And?

ANDREA   There are words painted on the bands.

GALILEO   What words?

ANDREA   The names of stars.

GALILEO   Such as?

ANDREA   Here is a band with the sun on it and on the inside band is the moon.

GALILEO   Those metal bands represent crystal globes, eight of them.

ANDREA   Crystal?

GALILEO   Like huge soap bubbles one inside the other and the stars are supposed to be tacked on to them. Spin the band with the sun on it. (*Andrea does*) You see the fixed ball in the middle?

ANDREA   Yes.

GALILEO   That's the earth. For two thousand years man has chosen to believe that the sun and all the host of stars revolve about him. Well. The Pope, the Cardinals, the princes, the scholars, captains, merchants, housewives, have pictured themselves squatting in the middle of an affair like that.

ANDREA   Locked up inside?

GALILEO (*triumphant*)   Ah!

ANDREA   It's like a cage.

GALILEO   So you sensed that. (*Against the model*) I like to think the ships began it.

ANDREA   Why?

GALILEO   They used to hug the coasts and then all of a sudden they left the coasts and spread over the oceans. A new age was coming. I was on to it years ago. I was a young man, in Siena. There was a group of masons arguing. They had to raise a block of granite. It was hot. To help matters, one of them wanted to try a new arrangement of ropes. After five minutes' discussion, out went a method which had been employed for

a thousand years. The millenium of faith is ended, said I, this is the millenium of doubt. And we are pulling out of that contraption. The sayings of the wise men won't wash anymore. Everybody, at last, is getting nosey. I predict that in our time astronomy will become the gossip of the market place and the sons of fishwives will pack the schools.

ANDREA   You're off again, Mr. Galilei. Give me the towel. (*He wipes some soap from Galileo's back*)

GALILEO   By that time, with any luck, they will be learning that the earth rolls round the sun, and that their mothers, the captains, the scholars, the princes and the Pope are rolling with it.

ANDREA   That turning-round-business is no good. I can see with my own eyes that the sun comes up in one place in the morning and goes down in a different place in the evening. It doesn't stand still, I can see it move.

GALILEO   You see nothing, all you do is gawk. Gawking is not seeing. (*He puts the iron washstand in the middle of the room*) Now: that's the sun. Sit down. (*Andrea sits on a chair. Galileo stands behind him*) Where is the sun, on your right or on your left?

ANDREA   Left.

GALILEO   And how will it get to the right?

ANDREA   By your putting it there, of course.

GALILEO   Of course? (*He picks Andrea up, chair and all, and carries him round to the other side of the washstand*) Now where is the sun?

ANDREA   On the right.

GALILEO   And did it move?

ANDREA   I did.

GALILEO   Wrong. Stupid! The chair moved.

ANDREA   But I was on it.

GALILEO   Of course. The chair is the earth, and you're sitting on it.

(*Mrs. Sarti, who has come in with a glass of milk and a roll, has been watching*)

MRS. SARTI   What are you doing with my son, Mr. Galilei?

ANDREA   Now, mother, you don't understand.

MRS. SARTI   You understand, don't you? Last night he tried to tell me that the earth goes round the sun. You'll soon have

him saying that two times two is five.

GALILEO (*eating his breakfast*)   Apparently we are on the threshold of a new era, Mrs. Sarti.

MRS. SARTI   Well, I hope we can pay the milkman in this new era. A young gentleman is here to take private lessons and he is well-dressed and don't you frighten him away like you did the others. Wasting your time with Andrea! (*To Andrea*) How many times have I told you not to wheedle free lessons out of Mr. Galilei? (*Mrs. Sarti goes*)

GALILEO   So you thought enough of the turning-round-business to tell your mother about it.

ANDREA   Just to surprise her.

GALILEO   Andrea, I wouldn't talk about our ideas outside.

ANDREA   Why not?

GALILEO   Certain of the authorities won't like it.

ANDREA   Why not, if it's the truth?

GALILEO (*laughs*)   Because we are like the worms who are little and have dim eyes and can hardly see the stars at all, and the new astronomy is a framework of guesses or very little more —yet.

(*Mrs. Sarti shows in Ludovico Marsili, a presentable young man*)

GALILEO   This house is like a marketplace. (*Pointing to the model*) Move that out of the way! Put it down there!

(*Ludovico does*)

LUDOVICO   Good morning, sir. My name is Ludovico Marsili.

GALILEO (*reading a letter of recommendation he has brought*)   You came by way of Holland and your family lives in the Campagna? Private lessons, thirty scudi a month.

LUDOVICO   That's all right, of course, sir.

GALILEO   What is your subject?

LUDOVICO   Horses.

GALILEO   Aha.

LUDOVICO   I don't understand science, sir.

GALILEO   Aha.

LUDOVICO   They showed me an instrument like that in Amsterdam. You'll pardon me, sir, but it didn't make sense to me at all.

GALILEO   It's out of date now.

(*Andrea goes*)

LUDOVICO   You'll have to be patient with me, sir. Nothing in science makes sense to me.

GALILEO   Aha.

LUDOVICO   I saw a brand new instrument in Amsterdam. A tube affair. "See things five times as large as life!" It had two lenses, one at each end, one lens bulged and the other was like that. (*Gesture*) Any normal person would think that different lenses cancel each other out. They didn't! I just stood and looked a fool.

GALILEO   I don't quite follow you. What does one see enlarged?

LUDOVICO   Church steeples, pigeons, boats. Anything at a distance.

GALILEO   Did you yourself—see things enlarged?

LUDOVICO   Yes, sir.

GALILEO   And the tube had two lenses? Was it like this? (*He has been making a sketch*)
(*Ludovico nods*)

GALILEO   A recent invention?

LUDOVICO   It must be. They only started peddling it on the streets a few days before I left Holland.

GALILEO (*starts to scribble calculations on the sketch; almost friendly*)   Why do you bother your head with science? Why don't you just breed horses?
(*Enter Mrs. Sarti. Galileo doesn't see her. She listens to the following*)

LUDOVICO   My mother is set on the idea that science is necessary nowadays for conversation.

GALILEO   Aha. You'll find Latin or philosophy easier. (*Mrs. Sarti catches his eye*) I'll see you on Tuesday afternoon.

LUDOVICO   I shall look forward to it, sir.

GALILEO   Good morning. (*He goes to the window and shouts into the street*) Andrea! Hey, Redhead, Redhead!

MRS. SARTI   The curator of the museum is here to see you.

GALILEO   Don't look at me like that. I took him, didn't I?

MRS. SARTI   I caught your eye in time.

GALILEO   Show the curator in.
(*She goes. He scribbles something on a new sheet of paper. The Curator comes in*)

CURATOR   Good morning, Mr. Galilei.

GALILEO   Lend me a scudo. (*He takes it and goes to the window, wrapping the coin in the paper on which he has been scribbling*) Redhead, run to the spectacle-maker and bring me two lenses; here are the measurements. (*He throws the paper out of the window. During the following scene Galileo studies his sketch of the lenses*)

CURATOR   Mr. Galilei, I have come to return your petition for an honorarium. Unfortunately I am unable to recommend your request.

GALILEO   My good sir, how can I make ends meet on five hundred scudi?

CURATOR   What about your private students?

GALILEO   If I spend all my time with students, when am I to study? My particular science is on the threshold of important discoveries. (*He throws a manuscript on the table*) Here are my findings on the laws of falling bodies. That should be worth 200 scudi.

CURATOR   I am sure that any paper of yours is of infinite worth, Mr. Galilei. . . .

GALILEO   I was limiting it to 200 scudi.

CURATOR (*cool*)   Mr. Galilei, if you want money and leisure, go to Florence. I have no doubt Prince Cosmo de Medici will be glad to subsidize you, but eventually you will be forbidden to think—in the name of the Inquisition. (*Galileo says nothing*) Now let us not make a mountain out of a molehill. You are happy here in the Republic of Venice but you need money. Well, that's human, Mr. Galilei, may I suggest a simple solution? You remember that chart you made for the army to extract cube roots without any knowledge of mathematics? Now that was practical!

GALILEO   Bosh!

CURATOR   Don't say bosh about something that astounded the Chamber of Commerce. Our city elders are businessmen. Why don't you invent something useful that will bring them a little profit?

GALILEO (*playing with the sketch of the lenses; suddenly*)   I see. Mr. Priuli, I may have something for you.

CURATOR   You don't say so.

GALILEO   It's not quite there yet, but . . .

CURATOR   You've never let me down yet, Galilei.

GALILEO   You are always an inspiration to me, Priuli.

CURATOR   You are a great man: a discontented man, but I've always said you are a great man.

GALILEO (*tartly*)   My discontent, Priuli, is for the most part with myself. I am forty-six years of age and have achieved nothing which satisfies me.

CURATOR   I won't disturb you any further.

GALILEO   Thank you. Good morning.

CURATOR   Good morning. And thank you.

(*He goes. Galileo sighs. Andrea returns, bringing lenses*)

ANDREA   One scudo was not enough. I had to leave my cap with him before he'd let me take them away.

GALILEO   We'll get it back some day. Give them to me. (*He takes the lenses over to the window, holding them in the relation they would have in a telescope*)

ANDREA   What are those for?

GALILEO   Something for the senate. With any luck, they will rake in 200 scudi. Take a look!

ANDREA   My, things look close! I can read the copper letters on the bell in the Campanile. And the washerwomen by the river, I can see their washboards!

GALILEO   Get out of the way. (*Looking through the lenses himself*) Aha!

Scene Two

No one's virtue is complete:
Great Galileo liked to eat.
You will not resent, we hope,
The truth about his telescope.

The great arsenal of Venice, overlooking the harbor full of ships. Senators and Officials on one side, Galileo, his daughter Virginia and his friend Sagredo, on the other side. They are dressed in formal, festive clothes. Virginia is fourteen and charming. She carries a velvet cushion on which lies a brand new telescope. Behind Galileo are some Artisans from the arsenal. There are onlookers, Ludovico amongst them.

CURATOR (*announcing*)   Senators, Artisans of the Great Arsenal of Venice; Mr. Galileo Galilei, professor of mathematics at your University of Padua.
(*Galileo steps forward and starts to speak*)

GALILEO   Members of the High Senate! Gentlemen: I have great pleasure, as director of this institute, in presenting for your approval and acceptance an entirely new instrument originating from this our great arsenal of the Republic of Venice. As professor of mathematics at your University of Padua, your obedient servant has always counted it his privilege to offer you such discoveries and inventions as might prove lucrative to the manufacturers and merchants of our Venetian Republic. Thus, in all humility, I tender you this, my optical tube, or telescope, constructed, I assure you, on the most scientific and Christian principles, the product of seventeen years patient research at your University of Padua.
(*Galileo steps back. The senators applaud*)

SAGREDO (*aside to Galileo*)   Now you will be able to pay your bills.

GALILEO   Yes. It will make money for them. But you realize that it is more than a money-making gadget? — I turned it on the moon last night . . .

CURATOR (*in his best chamber-of-commerce manner*) Gentlemen: Our Republic is to be congratulated not only because this new acquisition will be one more feather in the cap of Venetian culture . . . (*Polite applause*) . . . not only because our own Mr. Galilei has generously handed this fresh product of his teeming brain entirely over to you, allowing you to manufacture as many of these highly saleable articles as you please. . . . (*Considerable applause*) But Gentlemen of the Senate, has it occurred to you that—with the help of this remarkable new instrument—the battlefleet of the enemy will be visible to us a full two hours before we are visible to him? (*Tremendous applause*)

GALILEO (*aside to Sagredo*) We have been held up three generations for lack of a thing like this. I want to go home.

SAGREDO What about the moon?

GALILEO Well, for one thing, it doesn't give off its own light.

CURATOR (*continuing his oration*) And now, Your Excellency, and Members of the Senate, Mr. Galilei entreats you to accept the instrument from the hands of his charming daughter Virginia.

(*Polite applause. He beckons to Virginia who steps forward and presents the telescope to the Doge*)

CURATOR (*during this*) Mr. Galilei gives his invention entirely into your hands, Gentlemen, enjoining you to construct as many of these instruments as you may please.

(*More applause. The Senators gather round the telescope, examining it, and looking through it*)

GALILEO (*aside to Sagredo*) Do you know what the Milky Way is made of?

SAGREDO No.

GALILEO I do.

CURATOR (*interrupting*) Congratulations, Mr. Galilei. Your extra five hundred scudi a year are safe.

GALILEO Pardon? What? Of course, the five hundred scudi! Yes!

(*A prosperous man is standing beside the Curator*)

CURATOR Mr. Galilei, Mr. Matti of Florence.

MATTI You're opening new fields, Mr. Galilei. We could do with you at Florence.

CURATOR Now, Mr. Matti, leave something to us poor Venetians.

MATTI   It is a pity that a great republic has to seek an excuse to pay its great men their right and proper dues.

CURATOR   Even a great man has to have an incentive. (*He joins the Senators at the telescope*)

MATTI   I am an iron founder.

GALILEO   Iron founder!

MATTI   With factories at Pisa and Florence. I wanted to talk to you about a machine you designed for a friend of mine in Padua.

GALILEO   I'll put you on to someone to copy it for you, I am not going to have the time.—How are things in Florence? (*They wander away*)

FIRST SENATOR (*peering*)   Extraordinary! They're having their lunch on that frigate. Lobsters! I'm hungry! (*Laughter*)

SECOND SENATOR   Oh, good heavens, look at her! I must tell my wife to stop bathing on the roof. When can I buy one of these things?

(*Laughter. Virginia has spotted Ludovico among the onlookers and drags him to Galileo*)

VIRGINIA (*to Ludovico*)   Did I do it nicely?

LUDOVICO   I thought so.

VIRGINIA   Here's Ludovico to congratulate you, father.

LUDOVICO (*embarrassed*)   Congratulations, sir.

GALILEO   I improved it.

LUDOVICO   Yes, sir. I am beginning to understand science.

(*Galileo is surrounded*)

VIRGINIA   Isn't father a great man?

LUDOVICO   Yes.

VIRGINIA   Isn't that new thing father made pretty?

LUDOVICO   Yes, a pretty red. Where I saw it first it was covered in green.

VIRGINIA   What was?

LUDOVICO   Never mind. (*A short pause*) Have you ever been to Holland?

(*They go. All Venice is congratulating Galileo, who wants to go home*)

Scene Three

January ten, sixteen ten:
Galileo Galilei abolishes heaven.

Galileo's study at Padua. It is night. Galileo and Sagredo at a telescope.

SAGREDO (*softly*) The edge of the crescent is jagged. All along the dark part, near the shiny crescent, bright particles of light keep coming up, one after the other and growing larger and merging with the bright crescent.

GALILEO How do you explain those spots of light?

SAGREDO It can't be true . . .

GALILEO It *is* true: they are high mountains.

SAGREDO On a star?

GALILEO Yes. The shining particles are mountain peaks catching the first rays of the rising sun while the slopes of the mountains are still dark, and what you see is the sunlight moving down from the peaks into the valleys.

SAGREDO But this gives the lie to all the astronomy that's been taught for the last two thousand years.

GALILEO Yes. What you are seeing now has been seen by no other man beside myself.

SAGREDO But the moon can't be an earth with mountains and valleys like our own any more than the earth can be a star.

GALILEO The moon *is* an earth with mountains and valleys,— and the earth *is* a star. As the moon appears to us, so we appear to the moon. From the moon, the earth looks something like a crescent, sometimes like a half-globe, sometimes a full-globe, and sometimes it is not visible at all.

SAGREDO Galileo, this is frightening.

(*An urgent knocking on the door*)

GALILEO I've discovered something else, something even more astonishing.

(*More knocking. Galileo opens the door and the Curator comes in*)

CURATOR There it is—your "miraculous optical tube." Do you

know that this invention he so picturesquely termed "the fruit of seventeen years research" will be on sale tomorrow for two scudi apiece at every street corner in Venice? A shipload of them has just arrived from Holland.

SAGREDO   Oh, dear!

(*Galileo turns his back and adjusts the telescope*)

CURATOR   When I think of the poor gentlemen of the senate who believed they were getting an invention they could monopolize for their own profit. . . . Why, when they took their first look through the glass, it was only by the merest chance that they didn't see a peddler, seven times enlarged, selling tubes exactly like it at the corner of the street.

SAGREDO   Mr. Priuli, with the help of this instrument, Mr. Galilei has made discoveries that will revolutionize our concept of the universe.

CURATOR   Mr. Galilei provided the city with a first rate water pump and the irrigation works he designed function splendidly. How was I to expect this?

GALILEO (*still at the telescope*)   Not so fast, Priuli. I may be on the track of a very large gadget. Certain of the stars appear to have regular movements. If there were a clock in the sky, it could be seen from anywhere. That might be useful for your shipowners.

CURATOR   I won't listen to you. I listened to you before, and as a reward for my friendship you have made me the laughing-stock of the town. You can laugh—you got your money. But let me tell you this: you've destroyed my faith in a lot of things, Mr. Galilei. I'm disgusted with the world. That's all I have to say. (*He storms out*)

GALILEO (*embarrassed*)   Businessmen bore me, they suffer so. Did you see the frightened look in his eyes when he caught sight of a world not created solely for the purpose of doing business?

SAGREDO   Did you know that telescopes had been made in Holland?

GALILEO   I'd heard about it. But the one I made for the Senators was twice as good as any Dutchman's. Besides, I needed the money. How can I work, with the tax collector on the door-step? And my poor daughter will never acquire a husband

unless she has a dowry, she's not too bright. And I like to buy books—all kinds of books. Why not? And what about my appetite? I don't think well unless I eat well. Can I help it if I get my best ideas over a good meal and a bottle of wine? They don't pay me as much as they pay the butcher's boy. If only I could have five years to do nothing but research! Come on. I am going to show you something else.

SAGREDO   I don't know that I want to look again.

GALILEO   This is one of the brighter nebulae of the Milky Way. What do you see?

SAGREDO   But it's made up of stars—countless stars.

GALILEO   Countless worlds.

SAGREDO   (*hesitating*)   What about the theory that the earth revolves round the sun? Have you run across anything about that?

GALILEO   No. But I noticed something on Tuesday that might prove a step towards even that. Where's Jupiter? There are four lesser stars near Jupiter. I happened on them on Monday but didn't take any particular note of their position. On Tuesday I looked again. I could have sworn they had moved. They have changed again. Tell me what you see.

SAGREDO   I only see three.

GALILEO   Where's the fourth? Let's get the charts and settle down to work.

(*They work and the lights dim. The lights go up again. It is near dawn*)

GALILEO   The only place the fourth can be is round at the back of the larger star where we cannot see it. This means there are small stars revolving around a big star. Where are the crystal shells now that the stars are supposed to be fixed to?

SAGREDO   Jupiter can't be attached to anything: there are other stars revolving round it.

GALILEO   There is no support in the heavens. (*Sagredo laughs awkwardly*) Don't stand there looking at me as if it weren't true.

SAGREDO   I suppose it is true. I'm afraid.

GALILEO   Why?

SAGREDO   What do you think is going to happen to you for saying that there is another sun around which other earths

revolve? And that there are only stars and no difference between earth and heaven? Where is God then?

GALILEO   What do you mean?

SAGREDO   God? Where is God?

GALILEO (*angrily*)   Not there! Any more than he'd be here—if creatures from the moon came down to look for him!

SAGREDO   Then where is He?

GALILEO   I'm not a theologian: I'm a mathematician.

SAGREDO   You are a human being! (*Almost shouting*) Where is God in your system of the universe?

GALILEO   Within ourselves. Or—nowhere.

SAGREDO   Ten years ago a man was burned at the stake for saying that.

GALILEO   Giordano Bruno was an idiot: he spoke too soon. He would never have been condemned if he could have backed up what he said with proof.

SAGREDO (*incredulously*)   Do you really believe proof will make any difference?

GALILEO   I believe in the human race. The only people that can't be reasoned with are the dead. Human beings are intelligent.

SAGREDO   Intelligent—or merely shrewd?

GALILEO   I know they call a donkey a horse when they want to sell it, and a horse a donkey when they want to buy it. But is that the whole story? Aren't they susceptible to truth as well? (*He fishes a small pebble out of his pocket*) If anybody were to drop a stone . . . (*Drops the pebble*) . . . and tell them that it didn't fall, do you think they would keep quiet? The evidence of your own eyes is a very seductive thing. Sooner or later everybody must succumb to it.

SAGREDO   Galileo, I am helpless when you talk.
(*A church bell has been ringing for some time, calling people to mass. Enter Virginia, muffled up for mass, carrying a candle, protected from the wind by a globe*)

VIRGINIA   Oh, father, you promised to go to bed tonight, and it's five o'clock again.

GALILEO   Why are you up at this hour?

VIRGINIA   I'm going to mass with Mrs. Sarti. Ludovico is going too. How was the night, father?

GALILEO   Bright.

VIRGINIA   What did you find through the tube?

GALILEO   Only some little specks by the side of a star. I must draw attention to them somehow. I think I'll name them after the Prince of Florence. Why not call them the Medicean planets? By the way, we may move to Florence. I've written to His Highness, asking if he can use me as Court Mathematician.

VIRGINIA   Oh, father, we'll be at the court!

SAGREDO (*amazed*)   Galileo!

GALILEO   My dear Sagredo, I must have leisure. My only worry is that His Highness after all may not take me. I'm not accustomed to writing formal letters to great personages. Here, do you think this is the right sort of thing?

SAGREDO (*reads and quotes*)   "Whose sole desire is to reside in Your Highness' presence—the rising sun of our great age." Cosmo di Medici is a boy of nine.

GALILEO   The only way a man like me can land a good job is by crawling on his stomach. Your father, my dear, is going to take his share of the pleasures of life in exchange for all his hard work, and about time too. I have no patience, Sagredo, with a man who doesn't use his brains to fill his belly. Run along to mass now.

(*Virginia goes*)

SAGREDO   Galileo, do not go to Florence.

GALILEO   Why not?

SAGREDO   The monks are in power there.

GALILEO   Going to mass is a small price to pay for a full belly. And there are many famous scholars at the court of Florence.

SAGREDO   Court monkeys.

GALILEO   I shall enjoy taking them by the scruff of the neck and making them look through the telescope.

SAGREDO   Galileo, you are traveling the road to disaster. You are suspicious and skeptical in science, but in politics you are as naive as your daughter! How can people in power leave a man at large who tells the truth, even if it be the truth about the distant stars? Can you see the Pope scribbling a note in his diary: "10th of January, 1610, Heaven abolished?" A moment ago, when you were at the telescope, I saw you tied to

the stake, and when you said you believed in proof, I smelt burning flesh!

GALILEO   I am going to Florence.

(*Before the next scene a curtain with the following legend on it is lowered*)

By setting the name of Medici in the sky, I am bestowing immortality upon the stars. I commend myself to you as your most faithful and devoted servant, whose sole desire is to reside in Your Highness' presence, the rising sun of our great age.

—GALILEO GALILEI

Scene Four

Galileo's house at Florence. Well-appointed. Galileo is demonstrating his telescope to Prince Cosmo di Medici, a boy of nine, accompanied by his Lord Chamberlain, Ladies and Gentlemen of the Court and an assortment of university Professors. With Galileo are Andrea and Federzoni, the new assistant (an old man). Mrs. Sarti stands by. Before the scene opens the voice of the Philosopher can be heard.

VOICE OF THE PHILOSOPHER   Quaedam miracula universi. Orbes mystice canorae, arcus crystallini, circulatio corporum coelestium. Cyclorum epicyclorumque intoxicatio, integritas tabulae chordarum et architectura elata globorum coelestium.

GALILEO   Shall we speak in everyday language? My colleague Mr. Federzoni does not understand Latin.

PHILOSOPHER   Is it necessary that he should?

GALILEO   Yes.

PHILOSOPHER   Forgive me. I thought he was your mechanic.

ANDREA   Mr. Federzoni is a mechanic and a scholar.

PHILOSOPHER   Thank you, young man. If Mr. Federzoni insists . . .

GALILEO   I insist.

PHILOSOPHER   It will not be as clear, but it's your house. Your Highness . . . (*The Prince is ineffectually trying to establish contact with Andrea*) I was about to recall to Mr. Galilei some of the wonders of the universe as they are set down for us in the Divine Classics. (*The Ladies "ah"*) Remind him of the "mystically musical spheres, the crystal arches, the circulation of the heavenly bodies—"

ELDERLY LADY   Perfect poise!

PHILOSOPHER   "—the intoxication of the cycles and epicycles, the integrity of the tables of chords and the enraptured architecture of the celestial globes."

ELDERLY LADY   What diction!

PHILOSOPHER   May I pose the question: Why should we go out of our way to look for things that can only strike a discord in this ineffable harmony?

(*The Ladies applaud*)

FEDERZONI   Take a look through here—you'll be interested.

ANDREA   Sit down here, please.

(*The Professors laugh*)

MATHEMATICIAN   Mr. Galilei, nobody doubts that your brain child—or is it your adopted brain child?—is brilliantly contrived.

GALILEO   Your Highness, one can see the four stars as large as life, you know.

(*The Prince looks to the Elderly Lady for guidance*)

MATHEMATICIAN   Ah. But has it occurred to you that an eyeglass through which one sees such phenomena might not be a too reliable eyeglass?

GALILEO   How is that?

MATHEMATICIAN   If one could be sure you would keep your temper, Mr. Galilei, I could suggest that what one sees in the eyeglass and what is in the heavens are two entirely different things.

GALILEO (*quietly*)   You are suggesting fraud?

MATHEMATICIAN   No! How could I, in the presence of His Highness?

ELDERLY LADY   The gentlemen are just wondering if Your Highness' stars are really, really there!

(*Pause*)

YOUNG LADY (*trying to be helpful*)   Can one see the claws on the Great Bear?

GALILEO   And everything on Taurus the Bull.

FEDERZONI   Are you going to look through it or not?

MATHEMATICIAN   With the greatest of pleasure.

(*Pause. Nobody goes near the telescope. All of a sudden the boy Andrea turns and marches pale and erect past them through the whole length of the room. The Guests follow with their eyes*)

MRS. SARTI (*as he passes her*)   What is the matter with you?

ANDREA (*shocked*)   They are wicked.

PHILOSOPHER   Your Highness, it is a delicate matter and I had no intention of bringing it up, but Mr. Galilei was about to demonstrate the impossible. His new stars would have broken the outer crystal sphere—which we know of on the authority of Aristotle. I am sorry.

MATHEMATICIAN   The last word.

FEDERZONI   He had no telescope.

MATHEMATICIAN   Quite.

GALILEO (*keeping his temper*)   "Truth is the daughter of Time, not of Authority." Gentlemen, the sum of our knowledge is pitiful. It has been my singular good fortune to find a new instrument which brings a small patch of the universe a little bit closer. It is at your disposal.

PHILOSOPHER   Where is all this leading?

GALILEO   Are we, as scholars, concerned with where the truth might lead us?

PHILOSOPHER   Mr. Galilei, the truth might lead us anywhere!

GALILEO   I can only beg you to look through my eyeglass.

MATHEMATICIAN (*wild*)   If I understand Mr. Galilei correctly, he is asking us to discard the teachings of two thousand years.

GALILEO   For two thousand years we have been looking at the sky and didn't see the four moons of Jupiter, and there they were all the time. Why defend shaken teachings? You should be doing the shaking. (*The Prince is sleepy*) Your Highness! My work in the Great Arsenal of Venice brought me in daily contact with sailors, carpenters, and so on. These men are unread. They depend on the evidence of their senses. But they taught me many new ways of doing things. The question is whether these gentlemen here want to be found out as fools

by men who might not have had the advantages of a classical education but who are not afraid to use their eyes. I tell you that our dockyards are stirring with that same high curiosity which was the true glory of Ancient Greece.
(*Pause*)

PHILOSOPHER I have no doubt Mr. Galilei's theories will arouse the enthusiasm of the dockyards.

CHAMBERLAIN Your Highness, I find to my amazement that this highly informative discussion has exceeded the time we had allowed for it. May I remind Your Highness that the State Ball begins in three-quarters of an hour?
(*The Court bows low*)

ELDERLY LADY We would really have liked to look through your eyeglass, Mr. Galilei, wouldn't we, Your Highness?
(*The Prince bows politely and is led to the door. Galileo follows the Prince, Chamberlain and Ladies towards the exit. The Professors remain at the telescope*)

GALILEO (*almost servile*) All anybody has to do is look through the telescope, Your Highness.
(*Mrs. Sarti takes a plate with candies to the Prince as he is walking out*)

MRS SARTI A piece of homemade candy, Your Highness?

ELDERLY LADY Not now. Thank you. It is too soon before His Highness' supper.

PHILOSOPHER Wouldn't I like to take that thing to pieces.

MATHEMATICIAN Ingenious contraption. It must be quite difficult to keep clean. (*He rubs the lens with his handkerchief and looks at the handkerchief*)

FEDERZONI We did not paint the Medicean stars on the lens.

ELDERLY LADY (*to the Prince, who has whispered something to her*) No, no, no, there is nothing the matter with your stars!

CHAMBERLAIN (*across the stage to Galileo*) His Highness will of course seek the opinion of the greatest living authority: Christopher Clavius, Chief Astronomer to the Papal College in Rome.

Scene Five

Things take indeed a wondrous turn
When learned men do stoop to learn.
Clavius, we are pleased to say,
Upheld Galileo Galilei.

A burst of laughter is heard and the curtains reveal a hall in the Collegium Romanum. High Churchmen, monks and Scholars standing about talking and laughing. Galileo by himself in a corner.

FAT PRELATE (*shaking with laughter*) Hopeless! Hopeless! Hopeless! Will you tell me something people won't believe?

A SCHOLAR Yes, that you don't love your stomach!

FAT PRELATE They'd believe that. They only do not believe what's good for them. They doubt the devil, but fill them up with some fiddle-de-dee about the earth rolling like a marble in the gutter and they swallow it hook, line, and sinker. Sancta simplicitas!
(*He laughs until the tears run down his cheeks. The others laugh with him. A group has formed whose members boisterously begin to pretend they are standing on a rolling globe*)

A MONK It's rolling fast, I'm dizzy. May I hold on to you, Professor? (*He sways dizzily and clings to one of the scholars for support*)

THE SCHOLAR Old Mother Earth's been at the bottle again. Whoa!

MONK Hey! Hey! We're slipping off! Help!

SECOND SCHOLAR Look! There's Venus! Hold me, lads. Whee!

SECOND MONK Don't, don't hurl us off on to the moon. There are nasty sharp mountain peaks on the moon, brethren!

VARIOUSLY Hold tight! Hold tight! Don't look down! Hold tight! It'll make you giddy!

FAT PRELATE And we cannot have giddy people in Holy Rome.
(*They rock with laughter. An infuriated Monk comes out from a large*

door at the rear holding a Bible in his hand and pointing out a page with his finger)

INFURIATED MONK   What does the Bible say—"Sun, stand thou still on Gideon and thou, moon, in the valley of Ajalon." Can the sun come to a standstill if it doesn't ever move? Does the Bible lie?

FAT PRELATE   How did Christopher Clavius, the greatest astronomer we have, get mixed up in an investigation of this kind?

INFURIATED MONK   He's in there with his eye glued to that diabolical instrument.

FAT PRELATE (*to Galileo, who has been playing with his pebble and has dropped it*)   Mr. Galilei, something dropped down.

GALILEO   Monsignor, are you sure it didn't drop up?

INFURIATED MONK   As astronomers we are aware that there are phenomena which are beyond us, but man can't expect to understand everything!

(*Enter a very old Cardinal leaning on a Monk for support. Others move aside*)

OLD CARDINAL   Aren't they out yet? Can't they reach a decision on that paltry matter? Christopher Clavius ought to know his astronomy after all these years. I am informed that Mr. Galilei transfers mankind from the center of the universe to somewhere on the outskirts. Mr. Galilei is therefore an enemy of mankind and must be dealt with as such. Is it conceivable that God would trust this most precious fruit of His labor to a minor frolicking star? Would He have sent His Son to such a place? How can there be people with such twisted minds that they believe what they're told by the slave of a multiplication table?

FAT PRELATE (*quietly to Cardinal*)   The gentleman is over there.

OLD CARDINAL   So you are the man. You know my eyes are not what they were, but I can see you bear a striking resemblance to the man we burned. What was his name?

MONK   Your Eminence must avoid excitement, the doctor said . . .

OLD CARDINAL (*disregarding him*)   So you have degraded the earth despite the fact that you live by her and receive everything from her. I won't have it! I won't have it! I won't be a nobody

on an inconsequential star briefly twirling hither and thither.
I tread the earth, and the earth is firm beneath my feet, and
there is no motion to the earth, and the earth is the center of
all things, and I am the center of the earth, and the eye of the
creator is upon me. About me revolve, affixed to their crystal
shells, the lesser lights of the stars and the great light of the
sun, created to give light upon me that God might see me—
Man, God's greatest effort, the center of creation. "In the
image of God created He him." Immortal . . . (*His strength fails
him and he catches for the Monk for support*)

MONK   You mustn't overtax your strength, Your Eminence.
(*At this moment the door at the rear opens and Christopher Clavius
enters followed by his Astronomers. He strides hastily across the hall,
looking neither to right nor left. As he goes by we hear him say—*)

CLAVIUS   He is right.
(*Deadly silence. All turn to Galileo*)

OLD CARDINAL   What is it? Have they reached a decision?
(*No one speaks*)

MONK   It is time that Your Eminence went home.
(*The hall is emptying fast. One little Monk who had entered with
Clavius speaks to Galileo*)

LITTLE MONK   Mr. Galilei, I heard Father Clavius say: "Now it's
for the theologians to set the heavens right again." You have
won.

(*Before the next scene a curtain with the following legend on it is
lowered*)
. . . . . . As these new astronomical charts enable us to
determine longitudes at sea and so make it possible to
reach the new continents by the shortest routes, we would
beseech Your Excellency to aid us in reaching Mr. Galilei,
mathematician to the Court of Florence, who is now in
Rome . . . . . .

> —From a letter written by a member
> of the Genoa Chamber of Commerce
> and Navigation to the Papal Legation.

Scene Six

When Galileo was in Rome
A Cardinal asked him to his home
He wined and dined him as his guest
And only made one small request.

Cardinal Bellarmin's house in Rome. Music is heard and the chatter of many guests. Two Secretaries are at the rear of the stage at a desk. Galileo, his daughter Virginia, now 21, and Ludovico Marsili, who has become her fiancé, are just arriving. A few Guests, standing near the entrance with masks in their hands, nudge each other and are suddenly silent. Galileo looks at them. They applaud him politely and bow.

VIRGINIA   O father! I'm so happy. I won't dance with anyone but you, Ludovico.

GALILEO (*to a Secretary*)   I was to wait here for His Eminence.

FIRST SECRETARY   His Eminence will be with you in a few minutes.

VIRGINIA   Do I look proper?

LUDOVICO   You are showing some lace.

(*Galileo puts his arms around their shoulders*)

GALILEO (*quoting mischievously*)
Fret not, daughter, if perchance
You attract a wanton glance.
The eyes that catch a trembling lace
Will guess the heartbeat's quickened pace.
Lovely woman still may be
Careless with felicity.

VIRGINIA (*to Galileo*)   Feel my heart.

GALILEO (*to Ludovico*)   It's thumping.

VIRGINIA   I hope I always say the right thing.

LUDOVICO   She's afraid she's going to let us down.

VIRGINIA   Oh, I want to look beautiful.

GALILEO You'd better. If you don't they'll start saying all over again that the earth doesn't turn.

LUDOVICO (*laughing*) It *doesn't* turn, sir.

(*Galileo laughs*)

GALILEO Go and enjoy yourselves. (*He speaks to one of the Secretaries*) A large fête?

FIRST SECRETARY Two hundred and fifty guests, Mr. Galilei. We have represented here this evening most of the great families of Italy, the Orsinis, the Villanis, the Nuccolis, the Soldanieris, the Canes, the Lecchis, the Estensis, the Colombinis, the . . .

(*Virginia comes running back*)

VIRGINIA Oh father, I didn't tell you: you're famous.

GALILEO Why?

VIRGINIA The hairdresser in the Via Vittorio kept four other ladies waiting and took me first. (*Exit*)

GALILEO (*at the stairway, leaning over the well*) Rome!

(*Enter Cardinal Bellarmin, wearing the mask of a lamb, and Cardinal Barberini, wearing the mask of a dove*)

SECRETARIES Their Eminences, Cardinals Bellarmin and Barberini.

(*The Cardinals lower their masks*)

GALILEO (*to Bellarmin*) Your Eminence.

BELLARMIN Mr. Galilei, Cardinal Barberini.

GALILEO Your Eminence.

BARBERINI So you are the father of that lovely child!

BELLARMIN Who is inordinately proud of being her father's daughter.

(*They laugh*)

BARBERINI (*points his finger at Galileo*) "The sun riseth and setteth and returneth to its place," saith the Bible. What saith Galilei?

GALILEO Appearances are notoriously deceptive, Your Eminence. Once when I was so high, I was standing on a ship that was pulling away from the shore and I shouted, "The shore is moving!" I know now that it was the ship which was moving.

BARBERINI (*laughs*) You can't catch that man. I tell you, Bellarmin, his moons around Jupiter are hard nuts to crack. Unfor-

tunately for me I happened to glance at a few papers on astronomy once. It is harder to get rid of than the itch.

BELLARMIN.   Let's move with the times. If it makes navigation easier for sailors to use new charts based on a new hypothesis let them have them. We only have to scotch doctrines that contradict Holy Writ.

(*He leans over the balustrade of the well and acknowledges various Guests*)

BARBERINI   But Bellarmin, you haven't caught on to this fellow. The scriptures don't satisfy him. Copernicus does.

GALILEO   Copernicus? "He that withholdeth corn the people shall curse him." Book of Proverbs.

BARBERINI   "A prudent man concealeth knowledge." Also Book of Proverbs.

GALILEO   "Where no oxen are, the stable is clean, but much increase is by the strength of the ox."

BARBERINI   "He that ruleth his spirit is better than he that taketh a city."

GALILEO   "But a broken spirit drieth up the bones." (*Pause*) "Doth not wisdom cry?"

BARBERINI   "Can one walk on hot coals and his feet not be scorched?" — Welcome to Rome, Friend Galileo. You recall the legend of our city's origin? Two small boys found sustenance and refuge with a she-wolf and from that day we have paid the price for the she-wolf's milk. But the place is not bad. We have everything for your pleasure—from a scholarly dispute with Bellarmin to ladies of high degree. Look at that woman flaunting herself. No? He wants a weighty discussion! All right! (*To Galileo*) You people speak in terms of circles and ellipses and regular velocities—simple movements that the human mind can grasp—very convenient—but suppose Almighty God had taken it into his head to make the stars move like that . . . (*He describes an irregular motion with his fingers through the air*) . . . then where would you be?

GALILEO   My good man—the Almighty would have endowed us with brains like that . . . (*Repeats the movement*) . . . so that we could grasp the movements . . . (*Repeats the movement*) . . . like that. I believe in the brain.

BARBERINI   I consider the brain inadequate. He doesn't answer.

He is too polite to tell me he considers *my* brain inadequate. What is one to do with him? Butter wouldn't melt in his mouth. All he wants to do is to prove that God made a few boners in astronomy. God didn't study his astronomy hard enough before he composed Holy Writ. (*To the Secretaries*) Don't take anything down. This is a scientific discussion among friends.

BELLARMIN (*to Galileo*)   Does it not appear more probable—even to you—that the Creator knows more about his work than the created?

GALILEO   In his blindness man is liable to misread not only the sky but also the Bible.

BELLARMIN   The interpretation of the Bible is a matter for the ministers of God. (*Galileo remains silent*) At last you are quiet. (*He gestures to the Secretaries. They start writing*) Tonight the Holy Office has decided that the theory according to which the earth goes around the sun is foolish, absurd, and a heresy. I am charged, Mr. Galilei, with cautioning you to abandon these teachings. (*To the First Secretary*) Would you repeat that?

FIRST SECRETARY (*reading*)   "His Eminence, Cardinal Bellarmin, to the aforesaid Galilei: The Holy Office has resolved that the theory according to which the earth goes around the sun is foolish, absurd, and a heresy. I am charged, Mr. Galilei, with cautioning you to abandon these teachings."

GALILEO (*rocking on his base*)   But the facts!

BARBERINI (*consoling*)   Your findings have been ratified by the Papal Observatory, Galilei. That should be most flattering to you . . .

BELLARMIN (*cutting in*)   The Holy Office formulated the decree without going into details.

GALILEO (*to Barberini*)   Do you realize, the future of all scientific research is . . .

BELLARMIN (*cutting in*)   Completely assured, Mr. Galilei. It is not given to man to know the truth: it is granted to him to seek after the truth. Science is the legitimate and beloved daughter of the Church. She must have confidence in the Church.

GALILEO (*infuriated*)   I would not try confidence by whistling her too often.

BARBERINI (*quickly*) Be careful what you're doing—you'll be throwing out the baby with the bath water, friend Galilei. (*Serious*) We need you more than you need us.

BELLARMIN Well, it is time we introduced our distinguished friend to our guests. The whole country talks of him!

BARBERINI Let us replace our masks, Bellarmin. Poor Galilei hasn't got one.

(*He laughs. They take Galileo out*)

FIRST SECRETARY Did you get his last sentence?

SECOND SECRETARY Yes. Do you have what he said about believing in the brain?

(*Another cardinal—the Inquisitor—enters*)

INQUISITOR Did the conference take place?

(*The First Secretary hands him the papers and the Inquisitor dismisses the Secretaries. They go. The Inquisitor sits down and starts to read the transcription. Two or three Young Ladies skitter across the stage; they see the Inquisitor and curtsy as they go*)

YOUNG GIRL Who was that?

HER FRIEND The Cardinal Inquisitor.

(*They giggle and go. Enter Virginia. She curtsies as she goes. The Inquisitor stops her*)

INQUISITOR Good evening, my child. Beautiful night. May I congratulate you on your betrothal? Your young man comes from a fine family. Are you staying with us here in Rome?

VIRGINIA Not now, Your Eminence. I must go home to prepare for the wedding.

INQUISITOR Ah. You are accompanying your father to Florence. That should please him. Science must be cold comfort in a home. Your youth and warmth will keep him down to earth. It is easy to get lost up there. (*He gestures to the sky*)

VIRGINIA He doesn't talk to me about the stars, Your Eminence.

INQUISITOR No. (*He laughs*) They don't eat fish in the fisherman's house. I can tell you something about astronomy. My child, it seems that God has blessed our modern astronomers with imaginations. It is quite alarming! Do you know that the earth—which we old fogies supposed to be so large—has shrunk to something no bigger than a walnut, and the new universe has grown so vast that prelates—and even cardinals

—look like ants. Why, God Almighty might lose sight of a Pope! I wonder if I know your Father Confessor.

VIRGINIA Father Christopherus, from Saint Ursula's at Florence, Your Eminence.

INQUISITOR My dear child, you father will need you. Not so much now perhaps, but one of these days. You are pure, and there is strength in purity. Greatness is sometimes, indeed often, too heavy a burden for those to whom God has granted it. What man is so great that he has no place in a prayer? But I am keeping you, my dear. Your fiancé will be jealous of me, and I am afraid your father will never forgive me for holding forth on astronomy. Go to your dancing and remember me to Father Christopherus.

(*Virginia kisses his ring and runs off. The Inquisitor resumes his reading*)

Scene Seven

> *Galileo, feeling grim,*
> *A young monk came to visit him.*
> *The monk was born of common folk.*
> *It was of science that they spoke.*

Garden of the Florentine Ambassador in Rome. Distant hum of a great city. Galileo and the Little Monk of Scene Five are talking.

GALILEO Let's hear it. That robe you're wearing gives you the right to say whatever you want to say. Let's hear it.

LITTLE MONK I have studied physics, Mr. Galilei.

GALILEO That might help us if it enabled you to admit that two and two are four.

LITTLE MONK Mr. Galilei, I have spent four sleepless nights trying to reconcile the decree that I have read with the moons of Jupiter that I have seen. This morning I decided to come to see you after I had said Mass.

GALILEO   To tell me that Jupiter has no moons?

LITTLE MONK   No, I found out that I think the decree a wise decree. It has shocked me into realizing that free research has its dangers. I have had to decide to give up astronomy. However, I felt the impulse to confide in you some of the motives which have impelled even a passionate physicist to abandon his work.

GALILEO   Your motives are familiar to me.

LITTLE MONK   You mean, of course, the special powers invested in certain commissions of the Holy Office? But there is something else. I would like to talk to you about my family. I do not come from the great city. My parents are peasants in the Campagna, who know about the cultivation of the olive tree, and not much about anything else. Too often these days when I am trying to concentrate on tracking down the moons of Jupiter, I see my parents. I see them sitting by the fire with my sister, eating their curded cheese. I see the beams of the ceiling above them, which the smoke of centuries has blackened, and I can see the veins stand out on their toil-worn hands, and the little spoons in their hands. They scrape a living, and underlying their poverty there is a sort of order. There are routines. The routine of scrubbing the floors, the routine of the seasons in the olive orchard, the routine of paying taxes. The troubles that come to them are recurrent troubles. My father did not get his poor bent back all at once, but little by little, year by year, in the olive orchard; just as year after year, with unfailing regularity, childbirth has made my mother more and more sexless. They draw the strength they need to sweat with their loaded baskets up the stony paths, to bear children, even to eat, from the sight of the trees greening each year anew, from the reproachful face of the soil, which is never satisfied, and from the little church and Bible texts they hear there on Sunday. They have been told that God relies upon them and that the pageant of the world has been written around them that they may be tested in the important or unimportant parts handed out to them. How could they take it, were I to tell them that they are on a lump of stone ceaselessly spinning in empty space, circling around a second-rate star? What, then, would be the use of their

patience, their acceptance of misery? What comfort, then, the
Holy Scriptures, which have mercifully explained their cru-
cifixion? The Holy Scriptures would then be proved full of
mistakes. No, I see them begin to look frightened. I see them
slowly put their spoons down on the table. They would feel
cheated. "There is no eye watching over us, after all," they
would say. "We have to start out on our own, at our time of
life. Nobody has planned a part for us beyond this wretched
one on a worthless star. There is no meaning in our misery.
Hunger is just not having eaten. It is no test of strength.
Effort is just stooping and carrying. It is not a virtue." Can
you understand that I read into the decree of the Holy Office
a noble motherly pity and a great goodness of the soul?

GALILEO (*embarrassed*)   Hm, well at least you have found out that
it is not a question of the satellites of Jupiter, but of the
peasants of the Campagna! And don't try to break me down
by the halo of beauty that radiates from old age. How does a
pearl develop in an oyster? A jagged grain of sand makes its
way into the oyster's shell and makes its life unbearable. The
oyster exudes slime to cover the grain of sand and the slime
eventually hardens into a pearl. The oyster nearly dies in the
process. To hell with the pearl, give me the healthy oyster!
And virtues are not exclusive to misery. If your parents were
prosperous and happy, they might develop the virtues of
happiness and prosperity. Today the virtues of exhaustion
are caused by the exhausted land. For that my new water
pumps could work more wonders than their ridiculous superhuman efforts. Be fruitful and multiply: for war will cut
down the population, and our fields are barren! (*A pause*) Shall
I lie to your people?

LITTLE MONK   We must be silent from the highest of motives:
the inward peace of less fortunate souls.

GALILEO   My dear man, as a bonus for not meddling with your
parents' peace, the authorities are tendering me, on a silver
platter, persecution-free, my share of the fat sweated from
your parents, who, as you know, were made in God's image.
Should I condone this decree, my motives might not be disinterested: easy life, no persecution and so on.

LITTLE MONK   Mr. Galilei, I am a priest.

GALILEO   You are also a physicist. How can new machinery be evolved to domesticate the river water if we physicists are forbidden to study, discuss, and pool our findings about the greatest machinery of all, the machinery of the heavenly bodies? Can I reconcile my findings on the paths of falling bodies with the current belief in the tracks of witches on broom sticks? (*A pause*) I am sorry—I shouldn't have said that.

LITTLE MONK   You don't think that the truth, if it is the truth, would make its way without us?

GALILEO   No! No! No! As much of the truth gets through as we push through. You talk about the Campagna peasants as if they were the moss on their huts. Naturally, if they don't get a move on and learn to think for themselves, the most efficient of irrigation systems cannot help them. I can see their divine patience, but where is their divine fury?

LITTLE MONK (*helpless*)   They are old!

(*Galileo stands for a moment, beaten; he cannot meet the little monk's eyes. He takes a manuscript from the table and throws it violently on the ground*)

LITTLE MONK   What is that?

GALILEO   Here is writ what draws the ocean when it ebbs and flows. Let it lie there. Thou shalt not read. (*Little Monk has picked up the manuscript*) Already! An apple of the tree of knowledge, he can't wait, he wolfs it down. He will rot in hell for all eternity. Look at him, where are his manners?—Sometimes I think I would let them imprison me in a place a thousand feet beneath the earth where no light could reach me, if in exchange I could find out what stuff that is: "Light." The bad thing is that, when I find something, I have to boast about it like a lover or a drunkard or a traitor. That is a hopeless vice and leads to the abyss. I wonder how long I shall be content to discuss it with my dog!

LITTLE MONK (*immersed in the manuscript*)   I don't understand this sentence.

GALILEO   I'll explain it to you, I'll explain it to you.

(*They are sitting on the floor*)

Scene Eight

Eight long years with tongue in cheek
Of what he knew he did not speak.
Then temptation grew too great
And Galileo challenged fate.

Galileo's house in Florence again. Galileo is supervising his Assistants Andrea, Federzoni, and the Little Monk who are about to prepare an experiment. Mrs. Sarti and Virginia are at a long table sewing bridal linen. There is a new telescope, larger than the old one. At the moment it is covered with a cloth.

ANDREA (*looking up a schedule*) Thursday. Afternoon. Floating bodies again. Ice, bowl of water, scales, and it says here an iron needle. Aristotle.

VIRGINIA Ludovico likes to entertain. We must take care to be neat. His mother notices every stitch. She doesn't approve of father's books.

MRS. SARTI That's all a thing of the past. He hasn't published a book for years.

VIRGINIA That's true. Oh Sarti, it's fun sewing a trousseau.

MRS. SARTI Virginia, I want to talk to you. You are very young, and you have no mother, and your father is putting those pieces of ice in water, and marriage is too serious a business to go into blind. Now you should go to see a real astronomer from the university and have him cast your horoscope so you know where you stand. (*Virginia giggles*) What's the matter?

VIRGINIA I've been already.

MRS. SARTI Tell Sarti.

VIRGINIA I have to be careful for three months now because the sun is in Capricorn, but after that I get a favorable ascendant, and I can undertake a journey if I am careful of Uranus, as I'm a Scorpion.

MRS. SARTI What about Ludovico?

VIRGINIA He's a Leo, the astronomer said. Leos are sensual. (*Giggles*)

(*There is a knock at the door, it opens. Enter the Rector of the University, the philosopher of Scene Four, bringing a book*)

RECTOR (*to Virginia*) This is about the burning issue of the moment. He may want to glance over it. My faculty would appreciate his comments. No, don't disturb him now, my dear. Every minute one takes of your father's time is stolen from Italy. (*He goes*)

VIRGINIA Federzoni! The rector of the university brought this. (*Federzoni takes it*)

GALILEO What's it about?

FEDERZONI (*spelling*) De maculis in sole.

ANDREA Oh, it's on the sun spots!

(*Andrea comes one side, and the Little Monk the other, to look at the book*)

ANDREA A new one!

(*Federzoni resentfully puts the book into their hands and continues with the preparation of the experiment*)

ANDREA Listen to this dedication. (*Quotes*) "To the greatest living authority on physics, Galileo Galilei."—I read Fabricius' paper the other day. Fabricius says the spots are clusters of planets between us and the sun.

LITTLE MONK Doubtful.

GALILEO (*noncommittal*) Yes?

ANDREA Paris and Prague hold that they are vapors from the sun. Federzoni doubts that.

FERDERZONI Me? You leave me out. I said "hm," that was all. And don't discuss new things before me. I can't read the material, it's in Latin. (*He drops the scales and stands trembling with fury*) Tell me, can I doubt anything?

(*Galileo walks over and picks up the scales silently. Pause*)

LITTLE MONK There is happiness in doubting, I wonder why.

ANDREA Aren't we going to take this up?

GALILEO At the moment we are investigating floating bodies.

ANDREA Mother has baskets full of letters from all over Europe asking his opinion.

FEDERZONI The question is whether you can afford to remain silent.

GALILEO I cannot afford to be smoked on a wood fire like a ham.

ANDREA (*surprised*) Ah. You think the sun spots may have some-

thing to do with that again? (*Galileo does not answer*)

ANDREA   Well, we stick to fiddling about with bits of ice in water. They can't hurt you.

GALILEO   Correct.—Our thesis!

ANDREA   All things that are lighter than water float, and all things that are heavier sink.

GALILEO   Aristotle says—

LITTLE MONK   (*reading out of a book, translating*) "A broad and flat disk of ice, although heavier than water, still floats, because it is unable to divide the water."

GALILEO   Well, now I push the ice below the surface. I take away the pressure of my hands. What happens?
(*Pause*)

LITTLE MONK   It rises to the surface.

GALILEO   Correct. It seems to be able to divide the water as it's coming up, doesn't it?

LITTLE MONK   Could it be lighter than water after all?

GALILEO   Aha!

ANDREA   Then all things that are lighter than water float, and all things that are heavier sink. Q. e. d.

GALILEO   Not at all. Hand me that iron needle. Heavier than water? (*They all nod*) A piece of paper. (*He places the needle on a piece of paper and floats it on the surface of the water. Pause*) Do not be hasty with your conclusion. (*Pause*) What happens?

FEDERZONI   The paper has sunk, the needle is floating.

VIRGINIA   What's the matter?

MRS. SARTI   Every time I hear them laugh it sends shivers down my spine.
(*There is a knocking at the outer door*)

MRS. SARTI   Who's that at the door?
(*Enter Ludovico. Virginia runs to him. They embrace. Ludovico is followed by a servant with baggage*)

MRS. SARTI   Well!

VIRGINIA   Oh! Why didn't you write that you were coming?

LUDOVICO   I decided on the spur of the moment. I was over inspecting our vineyards at Bucciole. I couldn't keep away.

GALILEO   Who's that?

LITTLE MONK   Miss Virginia's intended. What's the matter with your eyes?

GALILEO (*blinking*)   Oh yes, it's Ludovico, so it is. Well! Sarti, get

a jug of that Sicilian wine, the old kind. We celebrate.
(*Everybody sits down. Mrs. Sarti has left, followed by Ludovico's Servant.*)

GALILEO Well, Ludovico, old man. How are the horses?

LUDOVICO The horses are fine.

GALILEO Fine.

LUDOVICO But those vineyards need a firm hand. (*To Virginia*) You look pale. Country life will suit you. Mother's planning on September.

VIRGINIA I suppose I oughtn't, but stay here, I've got something to show you.

LUDOVICO What?

VIRGINIA Never mind. I won't be ten minutes. (*She runs out*)

LUDOVICO How's life these days, sir?

GALILEO Dull.—How was the journey?

LUDOVICO Dull.—Before I forget, mother sends her congratulations on your admirable tact over the latest rumblings of science.

GALILEO Thank her from me.

LUDOVICO Christopher Clavius had all Rome on its ears. He said he was afraid that the turning around business might crop up again on account of these spots on the sun.

ANDREA Clavius is on the same track! (*To Ludovico*) My mother's baskets are full of letters from all over Europe asking Mr. Galilei's opinion.

GALILEO I am engaged in investigating the habits of floating bodies. Any harm in that?
(*Mrs. Sarti re-enters, followed by the Servant. They bring wine and glasses on a tray*)

GALILEO (*hands out the wine*) What news from the Holy City, apart from the prospect of my sins?

LUDOVICO The Holy Father is on his death bed. Hadn't you heard?

LITTLE MONK My goodness! What about the succession?

LUDOVICO All the talk is of Barberini.

GALILEO Barberini?

ANDREA Mr. Galilei knows Barberini.

LITTLE MONK Cardinal Barberini is a mathematician.

FEDERZONI A scientist in the chair of Peter!
(*Pause*)

GALILEO (*cheering up enormously*)   This means change. We might live to see the day, Federzoni, when we don't have to whisper that two and two are four. (*To Ludovico*) I like this wine. Don't you, Ludovico?

LUDOVICO   I like it.

GALILEO   I know the hill where it is grown. The slope is steep and stony, the grape almost blue. I am fond of this wine.

LUDOVICO   Yes, sir.

GALILEO   There are shadows in this wine. It is almost sweet but just stops short.—Andrea, clear that stuff away, ice, bowl and needle.—I cherish the consolations of the flesh. I have no patience with cowards who call them weaknesses. I say there is a certain achievement in enjoying things.

(*The Pupils get up and go to the experiment table*)

LITTLE MONK   What are we to do?

FEDERZONI   He is starting on the sun.

(*They begin with clearing up*)

ANDREA (*singing in a low voice*)
    The Bible proves the earth stands still,
    The Pope, he swears with tears:
    The earth stands still. To prove it so
    He takes it by the ears.

LUDOVICO   What's the excitement?

MRS. SARTI   You're not going to start those hellish goings-on again, Mr. Galilei?

ANDREA
    And gentlefolk, they say so too.
    Each learned doctor proves,
    (If you grease his palm): The earth stands still.
    And yet—and yet it moves.

GALILEO   Barberini is in the ascendant, so your mother is uneasy, and you're sent to investigate me. Correct me if I am wrong, Ludovico. Clavius is right: these spots on the sun interest me.

ANDREA   We might find out that the sun also revolves. How would you like that, Ludovico?

GALILEO   Do you like my wine, Ludovico?

LUDOVICO   I told you I did, sir.

GALILEO   You really like it?

LUDOVICO   I like it.

GALILEO   Tell me, Ludovico, would you consider going so far as to accept a man's wine or his daughter without insisting that he drop his profession? I have no wish to intrude, but have the moons of Jupiter affected Virginia's bottom?

MRS. SARTI   That isn't funny, it's just vulgar. I am going for Virginia.

LUDOVICO (*keeps her back*)   Marriages in families such as mine are not arranged on a basis of sexual attraction alone.

GALILEO   Did they keep you back from marrying my daughter for eight years because I was on probation?

LUDOVICO   My future wife must take her place in the family pew.

GALILEO   You mean, if the daughter of a bad man sat in your family pew, your peasants might stop paying the rent?

LUDOVICO   In a sort of way.

GALILEO   When I was your age, the only person I allowed to rap me on the knuckles was my girl.

LUDOVICO   My mother was assured that you had undertaken not to get mixed up in this turning around business again, sir.

GALILEO   We had a conservative Pope then.

MRS. SARTI   Had! His Holiness is not dead yet!

GALILEO (*with relish*)   Pretty nearly.

MRS. SARTI   That man will weigh a chip of ice fifty times, but when it comes to something that's convenient, he believes it blindly. "Is His Holiness dead?" — "Pretty nearly!"

LUDOVICO   You will find, sir, if His Holiness passes away, the new Pope, whoever he turns out to be, will respect the convictions held by the solid families of the country.

GALILEO (*to Andrea*)   That remains to be seen. — Andrea, get out the screen. We'll throw the image of the sun on our screen to save our eyes.

LITTLE MONK   I thought you'd been working at it. Do you know when I guessed it? When you didn't recognize Mr. Marsili.

MRS. SARTI   If my son has to go to hell for sticking to you, that's my affair, but you have no right to trample on your daughter's happiness.

LUDOVICO (*to his Servant*)   Giuseppe, take my baggage back to the coach, will you?

MRS. SARTI   This will kill her. (*She runs out, still clutching the jug*)

LUDOVICO (*politely*)   Mr. Galilei, if we Marsilis were to countenance teachings frowned on by the church, it would unsettle
our peasants. Bear in mind: these poor people in their brute
state get everything upside down. They are nothing but animals. They will never comprehend the finer points of astronomy. Why, two months ago a rumor went around, an
apple had been found on a pear tree, and they left their work
in the fields to discuss it.

GALILEO (*interested*)   Did they?

LUDOVICO   I have seen the day when my poor mother has had
to have a dog whipped before their eyes to remind them to
keep their place. Oh, you may have seen the waving corn
from the window of your comfortable coach. You have, no
doubt, nibbled our olives, and absentmindedly eaten our
cheese, but you can have no idea how much responsibility
that sort of thing entails.

GALILEO   Young man, I do not eat my cheese absentmindedly.
(*To Andrea*) Are we ready?

ANDREA   Yes, sir.

GALILEO (*leaves Ludovico and adjusts the mirror*)   You would not
confine your whippings to dogs to remind your peasants to
keep their places, would you, Marsili?

LUDOVICO (*after a pause*)   Mr. Galilei, you have a wonderful
brain, it's a pity.

LITTLE MONK (*astonished*)   He threatened you.

GALILEO   Yes. And he threatened you too. We might unsettle
his peasants. Your sister, Fulganzio, who works the lever of
the olive press, might laugh out loud if she heard the sun is
not a gilded coat of arms but a lever too. The earth turns
because the sun turns it.

ANDREA   That could interest his steward too and even his
money lender—and the seaport towns. . . .

FEDERZONI   None of them speak Latin.

GALILEO   I might write in plain language. The work we do is
exacting. Who would go through the strain for less than the
population at large!

LUDOVICO   I see you have made your decision. It was inevitable.
You will always be a slave of your passions. Excuse me to
Virginia, I think it's as well I don't see her now.

GALILEO   The dowry is at your disposal at any time.

LUDOVICO   Good afternoon. (*He goes followed by the Servant*)

ANDREA   Exit Ludovico. To hell with all Marsilis, Villanis, Orsinis, Canes, Nuccolis, Soldanieris. . . .

FEDERZONI   . . . who ordered the earth stand still because their castles might be shaken loose if it revolves . . .

LITTLE MONK   . . . and who only kiss the Pope's feet as long as he uses them to trample on the people. God made the physical world, God made the human brain. God will allow physics.

ANDREA   They will try to stop us.

GALILEO   Thus we enter the observation of these spots on the sun in which we are interested, at our own risk, not counting on protection from a problematical new Pope . . .

ANDREA   . . . but with great likelihood of dispelling Fabricius' vapors, and the shadows of Paris and Prague, and of establishing the rotation of the sun . . .

GALILEO   . . . and with *some* likelihood of establishing the rotation of the sun. My intention is not to prove that I was right but to find out *whether* I was right. "Abandon hope all ye who enter—an observation." Before assuming these phenomena are spots, which would suit us, let us first set about proving that they are not—fried fish. We crawl by inches. What we find today we will wipe from the blackboard tomorrow and reject it—unless it shows up again the day after tomorrow. And if we find anything which would suit us, that thing we will eye with particular distrust. In fact, we will approach this observing of the sun with the implacable determination to prove that the earth stands still and only if hopelessly defeated in this pious undertaking can we allow ourselves to wonder if we may not have been right all the time: the earth revolves. Take the cloth off the telescope and turn it on the sun.

(*Quietly they start work. When the corruscating image of the sun is focused on the screen, Virginia enters hurriedly, her wedding dress on, her hair disheveled, Mrs. Sarti with her, carrying her wedding veil. The two women realize what has happened. Virginia faints. Andrea, Little Monk and Galileo rush to her. Federzoni continues working*)

Scene Nine

On April Fool's Day, thirty two,
Of science there was much ado.
People had learned from Galilei:
They used his teaching in their way.

*Around the corner from the market place a Street Singer and his Wife,
who is costumed to represent the earth in a skeleton globe made of thin
bands of brass, are holding the attention of a sprinkling of representative
citizens, some in masquerade who were on their way to see the carnival
procession. From the market place the noise of an impatient crowd.*

BALLAD SINGER (*accompanied by his Wife on the guitar*)
When the Almighty made the universe
He made the earth and then he made the sun.
Then round the earth he bade the sun to turn—
That's in the Bible, Genesis, Chapter One.
And from that time all beings here below
Were in obedient circles meant to go:
    Around the pope the cardinals
    Around the cardinals the bishops
    Around the bishops the secretaries
    Around the secretaries the aldermen
    Around the aldermen the craftsmen
    Around the craftsmen the servants
    Around the servants the dogs, the chickens, and the beg-
      gars.
(*A conspicuous reveller—henceforth called the Spinner—has slowly
caught on and is exhibiting his idea of spinning around. He does not
lose dignity, he faints with mock grace*)

BALLAD SINGER
Up stood the learned Galileo
Glanced briefly at the sun
And said: "Almighty God was wrong

In Genesis, Chapter One!"
    Now that was rash, my friends, it is no matter small
For heresy will spread today like foul diseases.
    Change Holy Writ, forsooth? What will be left at all?
    Why: each of us would say and do just what he pleases!
(*Three wretched Extras, employed by the chamber of commerce, enter. Two of them, in ragged costumes, moodily bear a litter with a mock throne. The third sits on the throne. He wears sacking, a false beard, a prop crown, he carries a prop orb and sceptre, and around his chest the inscription "The King of Hungary." The litter has a card with "No. 4" written on it. The litter bearers dump him down and listen to the Ballad Singer*)

BALLAD SINGER

Good people, what will come to pass
If Galileo's teachings spread?
No altar boy will serve the mass
No servant girl will make the bed.
    Now that is grave, my friends, it is no matter small:
    For independent spirit spreads like foul diseases!
    (Yet life is sweet and man is weak and after all—
    How nice it is, for a little change, to do just as one pleases!)
(*The Ballad Singer takes over the guitar. His Wife dances around him, illustrating the motion of the earth. A Cobbler's Boy with a pair of resplendent lacquered boots hung over his shoulder has been jumping up and down in mock excitement. There are three more children, dressed as grownups among the spectators, two together and a single one with mother. The Cobbler's Boy takes the three Children in hand, forms a chain and leads it, moving to the music, in and out among the spectators, "whipping" the chain so that the last child bumps into people. On the way past a Peasant Woman, he steals an egg from her basket. She gestures to him to return it. As he passes her again he quietly breaks the egg over her head. The King of Hungary ceremoniously hands his orb to one of his bearers, marches down with mock dignity, and chastises the Cobbler's Boy. The parents remove the three Children. The unseemliness subsides*)

BALLAD SINGER

The carpenters take wood and build
Their houses—not the church's pews.
And members of the cobblers' guild

Now boldly walk the streets—in shoes.
The tenant kicks the noble lord
Quite off the land he owned—like that!
The milk his wife once gave the priest
Now makes (at last!) her children fat.

    Ts, ts, ts, ts, my friends, this is no matter small
    For independent spirit spreads like foul diseases
    People must keep their place, some down and some on top!
    (Though it is nice, for a little change, to do just as one
    pleases!)

(*The Cobbler's Boy has put on the lacquered boots he was carrying.
He struts off. The Ballad Singer takes over the guitar again. His Wife
dances around him in increased tempo. A Monk has been standing
near a rich Couple, who are in subdued costly clothes, without masks:
shocked at the song, he now leaves. A Dwarf in the costume of an
astronomer turns his telescope on the departing Monk, thus drawing
attention to the rich Couple. In imitation of the Cobbler's Boy, the
Spinner forms a chain of grownups. They move to the music, in and
out, and between the rich Couple. The Spinner changes the Gentleman's bonnet for the ragged hat of a Beggar. The Gentleman decides
to take this in good part, and a Girl is emboldened to take his dagger.
The Gentleman is miffed, throws the Beggar's hat back. The Beggar
discards the Gentleman's bonnet and drops it on the ground. The King
of Hungary has walked from his throne, taken an egg from the
Peasant Woman, and paid for it. He now ceremoniously breaks it
over the Gentleman's head as he is bending down to pick up his bonnet.
The Gentleman conducts the Lady away from the scene. The King of
Hungary, about to resume his throne, finds one of the Children sitting
on it. The Gentleman returns to retrieve his dagger. Merriment. The
Ballad Singer wanders off. This is part of his routine. His Wife sings
to the Spinner*)

WIFE
Now speaking for myself I feel
That I could also do with a change.
You know, for me . . . (*Turning to a reveller*) . . . you have appeal
Maybe tonight we could arrange . . .
(*The Dwarf-Astronomer has been amusing the people by focusing his
telescope on her legs. The Ballad Singer has returned*)

BALLAD SINGER

No, no, no, no, no, stop, Galileo, stop!
For independent spirit spreads like foul diseases
People must keep their place, some down and some on top!
(Though it is nice, for a little change, to do just as one pleases!)
(*The Spectators stand embarrassed. A Girl laughs loudly*)

BALLAD SINGER AND HIS WIFE

Good people who have trouble here below
In serving cruel lords and gentle Jesus
Who bids you turn the other cheek just so . . . (*With mimicry*)
While they prepare to strike the second blow:
Obedience will never cure your woe
So each of you wake up and do just as he pleases!
(*The Ballad Singer and his Wife hurriedly start to try to sell pamphlets to the spectators*)

BALLAD SINGER   Read all about the earth going round the sun, two centesimi only. As proved by the great Galileo. Two centesimi only. Written by a local scholar. Understandable to one and all. Buy one for your friends, your children and your aunty Rosa, two centesimi only. Abbreviated but complete. Fully illustrated with pictures of the planets, including Venus, two centesimi only.

(*During the speech of the Ballad Singer we hear the carnival procession approaching followed by laughter. A Reveller rushes in*)

REVELLER   The procession!

(*The litter bearers speedily joggle out the King of Hungary. The Spectators turn and look at the first float of the procession, which now makes its appearance. It bears a gigantic figure of Galileo, holding in one hand an open Bible with the pages crossed out. The other hand points to the Bible, and the head mechanically turns from side to side as if to say "No! No!"*)

A LOUD VOICE   Galileo, the Bible killer!

(*The laughter from the market place becomes uproarious. The Monk comes flying from the market place followed by delighted Children*)

Scene Ten

The depths are hot, the heights are chill
The streets are loud, the court is still.

Ante-Chamber and staircase in the Medicean palace in Florence. Galileo, with a book under his arm, waits with his Daughter to be admitted to the presence of the Prince.

VIRGINIA They are a long time.

GALILEO Yes.

VIRGINIA Who is that funny looking man? (*She indicates the Informer who has entered casually and seated himself in the background, taking no apparent notice of Galileo*)

GALILEO I don't know.

VIRGINIA It's not the first time I have seen him around. He gives me the creeps.

GALILEO Nonsense. We're in Florence, not among robbers in the mountains of Corsica.

VIRGINIA Here comes the Rector.

(*The Rector comes down the stairs*)

GALILEO Gaffone is a bore. He attaches himself to you.

(*The Rector passes, scarcely nodding*)

GALILEO My eyes are bad today. Did he acknowledge us?

VIRGINIA Barely. (*Pause*) What's in your book? Will they say it's heretical?

GALILEO You hang around church too much. And getting up at dawn and scurrying to mass is ruining your skin. You pray for me, don't you?

(*A Man comes down the stairs*)

VIRGINIA Here's Mr. Matti. You designed a machine for his Iron Foundries.

MATTI How were the squabs, Mr. Galilei? (*Low*) My brother and I had a good laugh the other day. He picked up a racy pamphlet against the Bible somewhere. It quoted you.

GALILEO   The squabs, Matti, were wonderful, thank you again. Pamphlets I know nothing about. The Bible and Homer are my favorite reading.

MATTI   No necessity to be cautious with me, Mr. Galilei. I am on your side. I am not a man who knows about the motions of the stars, but you have championed the freedom to teach new things. Take that mechanical cultivator they have in Germany which you described to me. I can tell you, it will never be used in this country. The same circles that are hampering you now will forbid the physicians at Bologna to cut up corpses for research. Do you know, they have such things as money markets in Amsterdam and in London? Schools for business, too. Regular papers with news. Here we are not even free to make money. I have a stake in your career. They are against iron foundries because they say the gathering of so many workers in one place fosters immorality! If they ever try anything, Mr. Galilei, remember you have friends in all walks of life including an iron founder. Good luck to you. (*He goes*)

GALILEO   Good man, but need he be so affectionate in public? His voice carries. They will always claim me as their spiritual leader particularly in places where it doesn't help me at all. I have written a book about the mechanics of the firmament, that is all. What they do or don't do with it is not my concern.

VIRGINIA (*loud*)   If people only knew how you disagreed with those goings-on all over the country last All Fools day.

GALILEO   Yes. Offer honey to a bear, and lose your arm if the beast is hungry.

VIRGINIA (*low*)   Did the prince ask you to come here today?

GALILEO   I sent word I was coming. He will want the book, he has paid for it. My health hasn't been any too good lately. I may accept Sagredo's invitation to stay with him in Padua for a few weeks.

VIRGINIA   You couldn't manage without your books.

GALILEO   Sagredo has an excellent library.

VIRGINIA   We haven't had this month's salary yet—

GALILEO   Yes. (*The Cardinal Inquisitor passes down the staircase. He bows deeply in answer to Galileo's bow*) What is he doing in Florence? If they try to do anything to me, the new Pope will

meet them with an iron NO. And the Prince is my pupil, he would never have me extradited.

VIRGINIA   Psst. The Lord Chamberlain.

(*The Lord Chamberlain comes down the stairs*)

LORD CHAMBERLAIN   His Highness had hoped to find time for you, Mr. Galilei. Unfortunately, he has to leave immediately to judge the parade at the Riding Academy. On what business did you wish to see His Highness?

GALILEO   I wanted to present my book to His Highness.

LORD CHAMBERLAIN   How are your eyes today?

GALILEO   So, so. With His Highness' permission, I am dedicating the book . . .

LORD CHAMBERLAIN   Your eyes are a matter of great concern to His Highness. Could it be that you have been looking too long and too often through your marvelous tube? (*He leaves without accepting the book*)

VIRGINIA   (*greatly agitated*)   Father, I am afraid.

GALILEO   He didn't take the book, did he? (*Low and resolute*) Keep a straight face. We are not going home, but to the house of the lens-grinder. There is a coach and horses in his backyard. Keep your eyes to the front, don't look back at that man. (*They start. The Lord Chamberlain comes back*)

LORD CHAMBERLAIN   Oh, Mr. Galilei, His Highness has just charged me to inform you that the Florentine Court is no longer in a position to oppose the request of the Holy Inquisition to interrogate you in Rome.

Scene Eleven

The Pope

A chamber in the Vatican. The Pope, Urban VIII—formerly Cardinal Barberini—is giving audience to the Cardinal Inquisitor. The trampling and shuffling of many feet is heard throughout the scene from the adjoining corridors. During the scene the Pope is being robed for the

conclave he is about to attend: at the beginning of the scene he is plainly Barberini, but as the scene proceeds he is more and more obscured by grandiose vestments.

POPE No! No! No!

INQUISITOR (*referring to the owners of the shuffling feet*) Doctors of all chairs from the universities, representatives of the special orders of the Church, representatives of the clergy as a whole who have come believing with child-like faith in the word of God as set forth in the Scriptures, who have come to hear Your Holiness confirm their faith: and Your Holiness is really going to tell them that the Bible can no longer be regarded as the alphabet of truth?

POPE I will not set myself up against the multiplication table. No!

INQUISITOR Ah, that is what these people say, that it is the multiplication table. Their cry is, "The figures compel us," but where do these figures come from? Plainly they come from doubt. These men doubt everything. Can society stand on doubt and not on faith? "Thou art my master, but I doubt whether it is for the best." "This is my neighbor's house and my neighbor's wife, but why shouldn't they belong to me?" After the plague, after the new war, after the unparalleled disaster of the Reformation, your dwindling flock look to their shepherd, and now the mathematicians turn their tubes on the sky and announce to the world that you have not the best advice about the heavens either—up to now your only uncontested sphere of influence. This Galilei started meddling in machines at an early age. Now that men in ships are venturing on the great oceans—I am not against that of course—they are putting their faith in a brass bowl they call a compass and not in Almighty God.

POPE This man is the greatest physicist of our time. He is the light of Italy, and not just any muddle-head.

INQUISITOR Would we have had to arrest him otherwise? This bad man knows what he is doing, not writing his books in Latin, but in the jargon of the market place.

POPE (*occupied with the shuffling feet*) That was not in the best of taste. (*A pause*) These shuffling feet are making me nervous.

INQUISITOR   May they be more telling than my words, Your Holiness. Shall all these go from you with doubt in their hearts?

POPE   This man has friends. What about Versailles? What about the Viennese court? They will call Holy Church a cesspool for defunct ideas. Keep your hands off him.

INQUISITOR   In practice it will never get far. He is a man of the flesh. He would soften at once.

POPE   He has more enjoyment in him than any man I ever saw. He loves eating and drinking and thinking. To excess. He indulges in thinking-bouts! He cannot say no to an old wine or a new thought. (*Furious*) I do not want a condemnation of physical facts. I do not want to hear battle cries: Church, church, church! Reason, reason, reason! (*Pause*) These shuffling feet are intolerable. Has the whole world come to my door?

INQUISITOR   Not the whole world, Your Holiness. A select gathering of the faithful.

(*Pause*)

POPE (*exhausted*)   It is clearly understood: he is not to be tortured. (*Pause*) At the very most, he may be shown the instruments.

INQUISITOR   That will be adequate, Your Holiness. Mr. Galilei understands machinery.

(*The eyes of Barberini look helplessly at the Cardinal Inquisitor from under the completely assembled panoply of Pope Urban VIII*)

Scene Twelve

June twenty second, sixteen thirty three,
A momentous date for you and me.
Of all the days that was the one
An age of reason could have begun.

Again the garden of the Florentine Ambassador at Rome, where Galileo's assistants wait the news of the trial. The Little Monk and Federzoni are attempting to concentrate on a game of chess. Virginia kneels in a corner, praying and counting her beads.

LITTLE MONK   The Pope didn't even grant him an audience.

FEDERZONI   No more scientific discussions.

ANDREA   The "Discorsi" will never be finished. The sum of his findings. They will kill him.

FEDERZONI (*stealing a glance at him*)   Do you really think so?

ANDREA   He will never recant.
   (*Silence*)

LITTLE MONK   You know when you lie awake at night how your mind fastens on to something irrelevant. Last night I kept thinking: if only they would let him take his little stone in with him, the appeal-to-reason-pebble that he always carried in his pocket.

FEDERZONI   In the room *they'll* take him to, he won't have a pocket.

ANDREA   But he will not recant.

LITTLE MONK   How can they beat the truth out of a man who gave his sight in order to see?

FEDERZONI   Maybe they can't.
   (*Silence*)

ANDREA (*speaking about Virginia*)   She is praying that he will recant.

FEDERZONI   Leave her alone. She doesn't know whether she's on her head or on her heels since they got hold of her. They brought her Father Confessor from Florence.

(*The Informer of Scene Ten enters*)

INFORMER   Mr. Galilei will be here soon. He may need a bed.

FEDERZONI   Have they let him out?

INFORMER   Mr. Galilei is expected to recant at five o'clock. The big bell of Saint Marcus will be rung and the complete text of his recantation publicly announced.

ANDREA   I don't believe it.

INFORMER   Mr. Galilei will be brought to the garden gate at the back of the house, to avoid the crowds collecting in the streets. (*He goes*)

(*Silence*)

ANDREA   The moon is an earth because the light of the moon is not her own. Jupiter is a fixed star, and four moons turn around Jupiter, therefore we are not shut in by crystal shells. The sun is the pivot of our world, therefore the earth is not the center. The earth moves, spinning about the sun. And he showed us. You can't make a man unsee what he has seen.

(*Silence*)

FEDERZONI   Five o'clock is one minute.

(*Virginia prays louder*)

ANDREA   Listen all of you, they are murdering the truth.

(*He stops up his ears with his fingers. The two other pupils do the same. Federzoni goes over the Little Monk, and all of them stand absolutely still in cramped positions. Nothing happens. No bell sounds. After a silence, filled with the murmur of Virginia's prayers, Federzoni runs to the wall to look at the clock. He turns around, his expression changed. He shakes his head. They drop their hands*)

FEDERZONI   No. No bell. It is three minutes after.

LITTLE MONK   He hasn't.

ANDREA   He held true. It is all right, it is all right.

LITTLE MONK   He did not recant.

FEDERZONI   No.

(*They embrace each other, they are delirious with joy*)

ANDREA   So force cannot accomplish everything. What has been seen can't be unseen. Man is constant in the face of death.

FEDERZONI   June 22, 1633: dawn of the age of reason. I wouldn't have wanted to go on living if he had recanted.

LITTLE MONK   I didn't say anything, but I was in agony. Oh, ye of little faith!

ANDREA   I was sure.

FEDERZONI   It would have turned our morning to night.

ANDREA   It would have been as if the mountain had turned to water.

LITTLE MONK (*kneeling down, crying*)   Oh God, I thank Thee.

ANDREA   Beaten humanity can lift its head. A man has stood up and said "no."

(*At this moment the bell of Saint Marcus begins to toll. They stand like statues. Virginia stands up*)

VIRGINIA   The bell of Saint Marcus. He is not damned.

(*From the street one hears the Town Crier reading Galileo's recantation*)

TOWN CRIER   I, Galileo Galilei, Teacher of Mathematics and Physics, do hereby publicly renounce my teaching that the earth moves. I foreswear this teaching with a sincere heart and unfeigned faith and detest and curse this and all other errors and heresies repugnant to the Holy Scriptures.

(*The lights dim; when they come up again the bell of Saint Marcus is petering out. Virginia has gone but the Scholars are still there waiting*)

ANDREA (*loud*)   The mountain did turn to water.

(*Galileo has entered quietly and unnoticed. He is changed, almost unrecognizable. He has heard Andrea. He waits some seconds by the door for somebody to greet him. Nobody does. They retreat from him. He goes slowly and, because of his bad sight, uncertainly, to the front of the stage where he finds a chair, and sits down*)

ANDREA   I can't look at him. Tell him to go away.

FEDERZONI   Steady.

ANDREA (*hysterically*)   He saved his big gut.

FEDERZONI   Get him a glass of water.

(*The Little Monk fetches a glass of water for Andrea. Nobody acknowledges the presence of Galileo, who sits silently on his chair listening to the voice of the Town Crier, now in another street*)

ANDREA   I can walk. Just help me a bit.

(*They help him to the door*)

ANDREA (*in the door*)   "Unhappy is the land that breeds no hero."
GALILEO   No, Andrea: "Unhappy is the land that needs a hero."

(*Before the next scene a curtain with the following legend on it is lowered*)

You can plainly see that if a horse were to fall from a height of three or four feet, it could break its bones, whereas a dog would not suffer injury. The same applies to a cat from a height of as much as eight or ten feet, to a grasshopper from the top of a tower, and to an ant falling down from the moon. Nature could not allow a horse to become as big as twenty horses nor a giant as big as ten men, unless she were to change the proportions of all its members, particularly the bones. Thus the common assumption that great and small structures are equally tough is obviously wrong.

—From the "Discorsi"

Scene Thirteen

1633–1642.
Galileo Galilei remains a prisoner
of the Inquisition until his death.

A country house near Florence. A large room simply furnished. There is a huge table, a leather chair, a globe of the world on a stand, and a narrow bed. A portion of the adjoining anteroom is visible, and the front door which opens into it. An Official of the Inquisition sits on guard in the anteroom. In the large room, Galileo is quietly experimenting with a bent wooden rail and a small ball of wood. He is still vigorous but almost blind. After a while there is a knocking at the outside door. The Official opens it to a peasant who brings a plucked goose. Virginia comes from the kitchen. She is past forty.

PEASANT (*handing the goose to Virginia*) I was told to deliver this here.

VIRGINIA I didn't order a goose.

PEASANT I was told to say it's from someone who was passing through.

(*Virginia takes the goose, surprised. The Official takes it from her and examines it suspiciously. Then, reassured, he hands it back to her. The Peasant goes. Virginia brings the goose in to Galileo*)

VIRGINIA Somebody who was passing through sent you something.

GALILEO What is it?

VIRGINIA Can't you see it?

GALILEO No. (*He walks over*) A goose. Any name?

VIRGINIA No.

GALILEO (*weighing the goose*) Solid.

VIRGINIA (*cautiously*) Will you eat the liver, if I have it cooked with a little apple?

GALILEO   I had my dinner. Are you under orders to finish me
off with food?

VIRGINIA   It's not rich. And what is wrong with your eyes
again? You should be able to see it.

GALILEO   You were standing in the light.

VIRGINIA   I was not.—You haven't been writing again?

GALILEO (*sneering*)   What do you think?

(*Virginia takes the goose out into the anteroom and speaks to the
Official*)

VIRGINIA   You had better ask Monsignor Carpula to send the
doctor. Father couldn't see this goose across the room.—
Don't look at me like that. He has not been writing. He
dictates everything to me, as you know.

OFFICIAL   Yes?

VIRGINIA   He abides by the rules. My father's repentance is
sincere. I keep an eye on him. (*She hands him the goose*) Tell the
cook to fry the liver with an apple and an onion. (*She goes back
into the large room*) And you have no business to be doing that
with those eyes of yours, father.

GALILEO   You may read me some Horace.

VIRGINIA   We should go on with your weekly letter to the Archbishop. Monsignor Carpula to whom we owe so much was all
smiles the other day because the Archbishop had expressed
his pleasure at your collaboration.

GALILEO   Where were we?

VIRGINIA (*sits down to take his dictation*)   Paragraph four.

GALILEO   Read what you have.

VIRGINIA   "The position of the Church in the matter of the
unrest at Genoa. I agree with Cardinal Spoletti in the matter
of the unrest among the Venetian ropemakers . . ."

GALILEO   Yes. (*Dictates*) I agree with Cardinal Spoletti in the
matter of the unrest among the Venetian ropemakers: it is
better to distribute good nourishing food in the name of charity than to pay them more for their bellropes. It being surely
better to strengthen their faith than to encourage their ac-
quisitiveness. St. Paul says: Charity never faileth. — How is
that?

VIRGINIA   It's beautiful, father.

GALILEO   It couldn't be taken as irony?

VIRGINIA   No. The Archbishop will like it. It's so practical.

GALILEO   I trust your judgment. Read it over slowly.

VIRGINIA   "The position of the Church in the matter of the unrest . . ."

(*There is a knocking at the outside door. Virginia goes into the anteroom. The Official opens the door. It is Andrea*)

ANDREA   Good evening. I am sorry to call so late, I'm on my way to Holland. I was asked to look him up. Can I go in?

VIRGINIA   I don't know whether he will see you. You never came.

ANDREA   Ask him.

(*Galileo recognizes the voice. He sits motionless. Virginia comes in to Galileo*)

GALILEO   Is that Andrea?

VIRGINIA   Yes. (*Pause*) I will send him away.

GALILEO   Show him in.

(*Virginia shows Andrea in. Virginia sits, Andrea remains standing*)

ANDREA (*cool*)   Have you been keeping well, Mr. Galilei?

GALILEO   Sit down. What are you doing these days? What are you working on? I heard it was something about hydraulics in Milan.

ANDREA   As he knew I was passing through, Fabricius of Amsterdam asked me to visit you and inquire about your health. (*Pause*)

GALILEO   I am very well.

ANDREA (*formally*)   I am glad I can report you are in good health.

GALILEO   Fabricius will be glad to hear it. And you might inform him that, on account of the depth of my repentance, I live in comparative comfort.

ANDREA   Yes, we understand that the church is more than pleased with you. Your complete acceptance has had its effect. Not one paper expounding a new thesis has made its appearance in Italy since your submission. (*Pause*)

GALILEO   Unfortunately there are countries not under the wing of the church. Would you not say the erroneous condemned theories are still taught—there?

ANDREA (*relentless*)   Things are almost at a standstill.

GALILEO   Are they? (*Pause*) Nothing from Descartes in Paris?

ANDREA   Yes. On receiving the news of your recantation, he shelved his treatise on the nature of light.

GALILEO   I sometimes worry about my assistants whom I led into error. Have they benefited by my example?

ANDREA   In order to work I have to go to Holland.

GALILEO   Yes.

ANDREA   Federzoni is grinding lenses again, back in some shop.

GALILEO   He can't read the books.

ANDREA   Fulganzio, our little monk, has abandoned research and is resting in peace in the church.

GALILEO   So. (*Pause*) My superiors are looking forward to my spiritual recovery. I am progressing as well as can be expected.

VIRGINIA   You are doing well, father.

GALILEO   Virginia, leave the room.

(*Virginia rises uncertainly and goes out*)

VIRGINIA   (*to the Official*) He was his pupil, so now he is his enemy.—Help me in the kitchen.

(*She leaves the anteroom with the Official*)

ANDREA   May I go now, sir?

GALILEO   I do not know why you came, Sarti. To unsettle me? I have to be prudent.

ANDREA   I'll be on my way.

GALILEO   As it is, I have relapses. I completed the "Discorsi."

ANDREA   You completed what?

GALILEO   My "Discorsi."

ANDREA   How?

GALILEO   I am allowed pen and paper. My superiors are intelligent men. They know the habits of a lifetime cannot be broken abruptly. But they protect me from any unpleasant consequences: they lock my pages away as I dictate them. And I should know better than to risk my comfort. I wrote the "Discorsi" out again during the night. The manuscript is in the globe. My vanity has up to now prevented me from destroying it. If you consider taking it, you will shoulder the entire risk. You will say it was pirated from the original in the hands of the Holy Office.

(*Andrea, as in a trance, has gone to the globe. He lifts the upper half*

and gets the book. He turns the pages as if wanting to devour them.
In the background the opening sentences of the "Discorsi" appear:
MY PURPOSE IS TO SET FORTH A VERY NEW SCIENCE DEALING WITH
A VERY ANCIENT SUBJECT—MOTION. . . . AND I HAVE DISCOVERED
BY EXPERIMENT SOME PROPERTIES OF IT WHICH ARE WORTH KNOW-
ING. . . .)

GALILEO   I had to employ my time somehow.

(*The text disappears*)

ANDREA   Two new sciences! This will be the foundation stone
of a new physics.

GALILEO   Yes. Put it under your coat.

ANDREA   And we thought you had deserted. (*In a low voice*) Mr.
Galilei, how can I begin to express my shame. Mine has been
the loudest voice against you.

GALILEO   That would seem to have been proper. I taught you
science and I decried the truth.

ANDREA   Did you? I think not. Everything is changed!

GALILEO   What is changed?

ANDREA   You shielded the truth from the oppressor. Now I see!
In your dealings with the Inquisition you used the same superb common sense you brought to physics.

GALILEO   Oh!

ANDREA   We lost our heads. With the crowd at the street cor-
ners we said: "He will die, he will never surrender!" You
came back: "I surrendered but I am alive." We cried: "Your
hands are stained!" You say: "Better stained than empty."

GALILEO   "Better stained than empty."—It sounds realistic.
Sounds like me.

ANDREA   And I of all people should have known. I was twelve
when you sold another man's telescope to the Venetian Senate, and saw you put it to immortal use. Your friends were
baffled when you bowed to the Prince of Florence: Science
gained a wider audience. You always laughed at heroics.
"People who suffer bore me," you said. "Misfortunes are due
mainly to miscalculations." And: "If there are obstacles, the
shortest line between two points may be the crooked line."

GALILEO   It makes a picture.

ANDREA   And when you stooped to recant in 1633, I should have
understood that you were again about your business.

GALILEO   My business being?

ANDREA   Science. The study of the properties of motion, mother of the machines which will themselves change the ugly face of the earth.

GALILEO   Aha!

ANDREA   You gained time to write a book that only you could write. Had you burned at the stake in a blaze of glory they would have won.

GALILEO   They have won. And there is no such thing as a scientific work that only one man can write.

ANDREA   Then why did you recant, tell me that!

GALILEO   I recanted because I was afraid of physical pain.

ANDREA   No!

GALILEO   They showed me the instruments.

ANDREA   It was not a plan?

GALILEO   It was not.

(*Pause*)

ANDREA   But you have contributed. Science has only one commandment: contribution. And you have contributed more than any man for a hundred years.

GALILEO   Have I? Then welcome to my gutter, dear colleague in science and brother in treason: I sold out, you are a buyer. The first sight of the book! His mouth watered and his scoldings were drowned. Blessed be our bargaining, whitewashing, deathfearing community!

ANDREA   The fear of death is human.

GALILEO   Even the church will teach you that to be weak is not human. It is just evil.

ANDREA   The church, yes! But science is not concerned with our weaknesses.

GALILEO   No? My dear Sarti, in spite of my present convictions, I may be able to give you a few pointers as to the concerns of your chosen profession.

(*Enter Virginia with a platter*)

In my spare time, I happen to have gone over this case. I have spare time.—Even a man who sells wool, however good he is at buying wool cheap and selling it dear, must be concerned with the standing of the wool trade. The practice of science

would seem to call for valor. She trades in knowledge, which is the product of doubt. And this new art of doubt has enchanted the public. The plight of the multitude is old as the rocks, and is believed to be basic as the rocks. But now they have learned to doubt. They snatched the telescopes out of our hands and had them trained on their tormentors: prince, official, public moralist. The mechanism of the heavens was clearer, the mechanism of their courts was still murky. The battle to measure the heavens is won by doubt; by credulity the Roman housewife's battle for milk will always be lost. Word is passed down that this is of no concern to the scientist who is told he will only release such of his findings as do not disturb the peace, that is, the peace of mind of the well-to-do. Threats and bribes fill the air. Can the scientist hold out on the numbers?—For what reason do you labor? I take it the intent of science is to ease human existence. If you give way to coercion, science can be crippled, and your new machines may simply suggest new drudgeries. Should you then, in time, discover all there is to be discovered, your progress must then become a progress away from the bulk of humanity. The gulf might even grow so wide that the sound of your cheering at some new achievement would be echoed by a universal howl of horror.—As a scientist I had an almost unique opportunity. In my day astronomy emerged into the market place. At that particular time, had one man put up a fight, it could have had wide repercussions. I have come to believe that I was never in real danger; for some years I was as strong as the authorities, and I surrendered my knowledge to the powers that be, to use it, no, not *use* it, *abuse* it, as it suits their ends. I have betrayed my profession. Any man who does what I have done must not be tolerated in the ranks of science.

(*Virginia, who has stood motionless, puts the platter on the table*)

VIRGINIA   You are accepted in the ranks of the faithful, father.

GALILEO (*sees her*)   Correct. (*He goes over to the table*) I have to eat now.

VIRGINIA   We lock up at eight.

ANDREA   I am glad I came. (*He extends his hand. Galileo ignores it and goes over to his meal*)

GALILEO (*examining the plate; to Andrea*) Somebody who knows me sent me a goose. I still enjoy eating.

ANDREA And your opinion is now that the "new age" was an illusion?

GALILEO Well.—This age of ours turned out to be a whore, spattered with blood. Maybe, new ages look like blood-spattered whores. Take care of yourself.

ANDREA Yes. (*Unable to go*) With reference to your evaluation of the author in question—I do not know the answer. But I cannot think that your savage analysis is the last word.

GALILEO Thank you, sir.

(*Official knocks at the door*)

VIRGINIA (*showing Andrea out*) I don't like visitors from the past, they excite him.

(*She lets him out. The Official closes the iron door. Virginia returns*)

GALILEO (*eating*) Did you try and think who sent the goose?

VIRGINIA Not Andrea.

GALILEO Maybe not. I gave Redhead his first lesson; when he held out his hand, I had to remind myself he is teaching now. —How is the sky tonight?

VIRGINIA (*at the window*) Bright.

(*Galileo continues eating*)

Scene Fourteen

The great book o'er the border went
And, good folk, that was the end.
But we hope you'll keep in mind
You and I were left behind.

Before a little Italian customs house early in the morning. Andrea sits upon one of his traveling trunks at the barrier and reads Galileo's book. The window of a small house is still lit, and a big grotesque shadow, like an old witch and her cauldron, falls upon the house wall beyond. Barefoot children in rags see it and point to the little house.

CHILDREN (*singing*)
    One, two, three, four, five, six,
    Old Marina is a witch.
    At night, on a broomstick she sits
    And on the church steeple she spits.

CUSTOMS OFFICER (*to Andrea*)   Why are you making this journey?

ANDREA   I am a scholar.

CUSTOMS OFFICER (*to his Clerk*)   Put down under "reason for leaving the country": Scholar. (*He points to the baggage*) Books! Anything dangerous in these books?

ANDREA   What is dangerous?

CUSTOMS OFFICER   Religion. Politics.

ANDREA   These are nothing but mathematical formulas.

CUSTOMS OFFICER   What's that?

ANDREA   Figures.

CUSTOMS OFFICER   Oh, figures. No harm in figures. Just wait a minute, sir, we will soon have your papers stamped. (*He exits with Clerk*)

   (*Meanwhile, a little council of war among the Children has taken place. Andrea quietly watches. One of the Boys, pushed forward by the others, creeps up to the little house from which the shadow comes, and takes the jug of milk on the doorstep*)

ANDREA (*quietly*)   What are you doing with that milk?

BOY (*stopping in mid-movement*)   She is a witch.
  (*The other Children run away behind the Custom House. One of them shouts*) "Run, Paolo!"

ANDREA   Hmm!—And because she is a witch she mustn't have milk. Is that the idea?

BOY   Yes.

ANDREA   And how do you know she is a witch?

BOY (*points to shadow on house wall*)   Look!

ANDREA   Oh! I see.

BOY   And she rides on a broomstick at night—and she be-witches the coachman's horses. My cousin Luigi looked through the hole in the stable roof, that the snow storm made, and heard the horses coughing something terrible.

ANDREA   Oh!—How big was the hole in the stable roof?

BOY   Luigi didn't tell. Why?

ANDREA   I was asking because maybe the horses got sick be-cause it was cold in the stable. You had better ask Luigi how big that hole is.

BOY   You are not going to say Old Marina isn't a witch, because you can't.

ANDREA   No, I can't say she isn't a witch. I haven't looked into it. A man can't know about a thing he hasn't looked into, or can he?

BOY   No!—But THAT! (*He points to the shadow*) She is stirring hell-broth.

ANDREA   Let's see. Do you want to take a look? I can lift you up.

BOY   You lift me to the window, mister! (*He takes a sling shot out of his pocket*) I can really bash her from there.

ANDREA   Hadn't we better make sure she is a witch before we shoot? I'll hold that.
  (*The Boy puts the milk jug down and follows him reluctantly to the window. Andrea lifts the boy up so that he can look in*)

ANDREA   What do you see?

BOY (*slowly*)   Just an old girl cooking porridge.

ANDREA   Oh! Nothing to it then. Now look at her shadow, Paolo.

(*The Boy looks over his shoulder and back and compares the reality and the shadow*)

BOY   The big thing is a soup ladle.

ANDREA   Ah! A ladle! You see, I would have taken it for a broomstick, but I haven't looked into the matter as you have, Paolo. Here is your sling.

CUSTOMS OFFICER (*returning with the Clerk and handing Andrea his papers*)   All present and correct. Good luck, sir.

(*Andrea goes, reading Galileo's book. The Clerk starts to bring his baggage after him. The barrier rises. Andrea passes through, still reading the book. The Boy kicks over the milk jug*)

BOY (*shouting after Andrea*)   She *is* a witch! She *is* a witch!

ANDREA   You saw with your own eyes: think it over!

(*The Boy joins the others. They sing*)

One, two, three, four, five, six,
Old Marina is a witch.
At night, on a broomstick she sits
And on the church steeple she spits.

(*The Customs Officers laugh. Andrea goes*)

VINTAGE BIOGRAPHY AND AUTOBIOGRAPHY

VINTAGE POLITICAL SCIENCE
AND SOCIAL CRITICISM

VINTAGE CRITICISM,
LITERATURE, MUSIC, AND ART

VINTAGE WORKS OF SCIENCE
AND PSYCHOLOGY

VINTAGE HISTORY—AMERICAN